AMERICA'S WILDERNESS

The Complete Guide to More Than 600 National Wilderness Areas

BY BUCK TILTON

ISBN 0-935701-47-8

Copyright © 1996
by Buck Tilton

America's Wilderness
The Complete Guide to More Than 600 National Wilderness Areas

All rights reserved. This book may not be reproduced in full or in part without the written permission of the publisher, except for use by a reviewer in the context of a review. Inquiries and excerpt requests should be addressed to:

> Publishing Manager
> Foghorn Press
> 555 DeHaro Street, Suite 220
> San Francisco, CA 94107

To order individual books, please call Foghorn Press: 1-800-FOGHORN (364-4676) or (415) 241-9550. Foghorn Press titles are distributed to the book trade by Publishers Group West, Emeryville, California. To contact your local sales representative, call 1-800-788-3123.

No liability is assumed with respect to the information or content of this book. No one should participate in any of the activities described in this book unless they recognize and personally assume the associated risks.

Library of Congress ISSN Data:
June 1996
America's Wilderness
The Complete Guide to More Than 600 National Wilderness Areas
First Edition
ISSN 1088-3266

The Color of Commitment

Foghorn Press has always been committed to printing on recycled paper, but up to now, we hadn't taken the final plunge to use 100 percent recycled paper because we were unconvinced of its quality. And until now, those concerns were valid. But the good news is that quality recycled paper is now available. We are thrilled to announce that Foghorn Press books are printed with Soya-based inks on 100 percent recycled paper, which has a 50 percent post-consumer waste content. The only way you'd know we made this change is by looking at the hue of the paper—a small price to pay for environmental integrity. You may even like the color better. We do. And we know the earth does, too.

Printed in the United States of America

This book is lovingly dedicated to Zachary Gray Tilton, my treasured son, born January 11, 1995, during a pause in the work of writing.

Preface

Shortly before my sixteenth birthday, in 1964, Congress passed the Wilderness Act, establishing the National Wilderness Preservation System (NWPS), the first steps ever taken by a nation to preserve wild land in its natural condition. Since then, I have been fascinated by wild places, and I have spent much of my life exploring them. As the number of areas added to the NWPS has grown, ballooning from the original 54 to more than 640, I have dreamed of writing a book that introduces each of these precious lands to the people who share in their ownership, the American people. I was surprised that no one had ever written such a book . . . but Foghorn Press offered to publish it and I got down to the actual research.

The job was monumental. After almost three years of pestering government offices, I found that precious little information existed about many of the well-hidden and seldom seen areas. Although it has added immeasurably to the complexity of my task, I'm overjoyed to report that more areas are designated as Wilderness every few years. On October 31, 1994, just as I began to see the light at the end of the research tunnel, Congress passed the California Desert Protection Act, increasing the size of the NWPS by about 7.66 million acres and the number of areas by 70. The NWPS now preserves approximately 4.7 percent of the land that we call America.

I hope this book increases your appreciation of the lands we have already protected, and will kindle (or rekindle) your desire and willingness to become involved in Wilderness preservation. With this book you will be able to plan trips into America's wild lands, and plan you should, in order to maintain your personal safety and the survival of the Wilderness itself. I hope that you visit, and when you visit, that you Leave No Trace of your stay. So pack up and head out, hike and camp, paddle and climb, fish and hunt. Watch moonrises and moose feeding knee-deep in placid waters, and scan the skies for the easy flight of great blue herons.

More than anything, my hope is that Wilderness will mean as much to you as it does to me. May your spirit soar! —*Buck Tilton*

Acknowledgments

No book reaches this stage without the help of numerous people. *America's Wilderness* would not have been possible without the efforts of a vast army of human beings. Hundreds of employees of the Bureau of Land Management, the National Park Service, the U.S. Forest Service, and the U.S. Fish and Wildlife Service graciously offered information in answer to my letters and phone calls. Many of America's Wilderness areas are difficult to access, without definite boundaries, and cloaked at least partly in mystery, even to some of the people in the offices who manage them. Dozens of those people went miles out of their way to help me find facts vital to this book. Many private citizens generously donated their time providing more information. Mike Francis and Pam Miller of the Wilderness Society were wonderfully helpful in fact-gathering. Vicki Morgan, Howard Rabinowitz, and especially Judith Pynn of Foghorn Press were unfailingly supportive and enthusiastic about the project. The editorial assistance of Brian ("BT") Thomas was crucial to getting the job done on time. Melissa Gray patiently changed uncountable diapers on our son and gently quieted his hunger while I pounded the keyboard of our computer. Thank you all so very much.

Credits

Publishing Manager	Rebecca Poole Forée
Senior Editor	Howard Rabinowitz
Associate Editor	Karin Mullen
Project Editors	Mona Behan, Lisa Zuniga Carlsen, Barbara Tannenbaum
Production Manager	Michele Thomas
Editorial Assistant	Aimee Larsen
Production Assistant	Alexander Lyon
Proofreader	Mary Anne Moore
Acquisitions Editor	Judith Pynn
Cover Design	Stuart L. Silberman, Michele Thomas
Cover Photo	Teton Range, Wyoming, by James W. Kay/West Stock

TABLE OF CONTENTS

How to Use This Book 7
Introduction 9

Alabama	33	Nevada	357
Alaska	36	New Hampshire	367
Arizona	75	New Jersey	371
Arkansas	138	New Mexico	373
California	147	New York	392
Colorado	238	North Carolina	393
Florida	267	North Dakota	403
Georgia	280	Ohio	406
Hawaii	291	Oklahoma	407
Idaho	294	Oregon	410
Illinois	301	Pennsylvania	441
Indiana	307	South Carolina	443
Kentucky	309	South Dakota	449
Louisiana	311	Tennessee	451
Maine	313	Texas	460
Massachusetts	316	Utah	465
Michigan	317	Vermont	478
Minnesota	328	Virginia	483
Mississippi	331	Washington	495
Missouri	334	West Virginia	521
Montana	341	Wisconsin	525
Nebraska	355	Wyoming	530

Author's Choice: Buck's Top Ten 544
Wilderness Areas At-A-Glance 547
Wilderness Resources 559
Index 560

HOW TO USE THIS BOOK

America's Wilderness begins with an introduction that includes a brief history of Wilderness designation in America as well as guidelines on how you can tour these wildlands without leaving a trace of your visit. The subsequent 44 chapters feature every state in the nation that holds a designated Wilderness; six states do not have designated Wilderness areas. Within these 44 chapters you'll find each Wilderness area listed in alphabetical order.

Every Wilderness area begins with a brief introductory description that will give you a sense of what the region is like, but it's certainly far from exhaustive. I very strongly urge you to research a Wilderness area prior to your visit by contacting the sources provided. I also recommend reading an entire chapter before selecting a place to visit; information in one Wilderness area sometimes pertains to several other areas in the same state. In order to avoid redundancy, at times I gave certain information in one area's description, but left it out of another. For example, several North Carolina Wildernesses contain *pocosins*, a term I defined only once.

Total Wilderness areas: An area wholly within a state counts as one Wilderness in this book. When two or more agencies share the management of an area, I have still counted it as one Wilderness. For example, a portion of Colorado's Powderhorn Wilderness is managed by the U.S. Forest Service (USFS) and a portion is managed by the Bureau of Land Management (BLM), but I have considered it as a whole. When an area extends across state lines I have treated each state's portion as a distinct area.

Total Wilderness acreage: Acreages in this book are based on research from Congressional Records. Exact surveys have not been completed on all areas, and measurements of acreages are often estimates.

Wilderness Essentials: In the shaded box after each listing, you'll find the following information:

(1) Size: Acreages are based on Congressional Records and may vary if and when actual surveys are performed.

(2) Year Designated: Dates listed in this book are from Congressional Records.

(3) Location: The general region of the state where a Wilderness lies is given (and illustrated) to help you locate the area on a map.

(4) Easiest Access: I have given directions to each area from the nearest major city or a fairly prominent locale. These directions are based on either my personal experience or information supplied by locals. There may be other (perhaps even easier) routes to the area.

(5) Season: I have subjectively chosen the seasons that I believe are best for a visit.

(6) Wilderness Fees/Permits: Required fees and/or permits are noted in this section.

HOW TO USE THIS BOOK

(7) Maps: I have provided information on sources for specific maps, particularly Wilderness maps, whenever I was able to locate them. Also listed are United States Geological Survey (USGS) topographic maps that cover specific areas. Two topographic map scales are most useful for Wilderness travelers: (1) Large Scale (1:250,000), on which 1 inch equals 3.9 miles, and (2) Standard Quadrangles, either 7.5 minute (usually 1:25,000) or 15 minute (usually 1:63,360), on which 1 inch equals approximately 1 mile. In the Alaska chapter, I often provided the names of large-scale maps due to the sheer immensity of the area covered. In the Lower 48, I listed 7.5-minute or 15-minute maps.

USGS topographic maps can be obtained from many sources. The three most common are:

(a) By mail from the USGS.

> For a free index (providing map locations, local dealers, and prices) covering all of the United States, write to: USGS Map Distribution, Box 25286, Building 810, Federal Center, Denver, CO 80225.
>
> Alaska maps can also be ordered from: USGS Earth Science Information Center, 101 Twelfth Avenue, Box 12, Fairbanks, AK 99701.

(b) Over the counter from USGS offices:
- USGS, Room 101, 4230 University Drive, Anchorage, AK.
- USGS, New Federal Building, Room 126, 101 Twelfth Avenue, Fairbanks, AK.
- USGS, Building 3, Room 3128, 345 Middlefield Road, Menlo Park, CA.
- USGS, Federal Center, Building 810, Lakewood, CO.
- USGS, Main Interior Building, Room 2650, 1849 C Street NW, Washington, DC.
- USGS, 1400 Independence, Rolla, MO.
- USGS, Building 3101, Stennis Space Center, MS.
- USGS, Federal Building, Room 8105, 125 South State Street, Salt Lake City, UT.
- USGS National Center, Room 1C402, 12201 Sunrise Valley Drive, Reston, VA.
- USGS, U.S. Post Office Building, Room 135, 904 W. Riverside Ave., Spokane, WA.

(c) Over the counter or by mail from commercial dealers.

> Refer to the Yellow Pages in your local phone book or contact the USGS to order a free listing of more than 2,800 commercial dealers.
>
> Excellent maps are also available from USFS and BLM offices and from commercial publishers including:

- DeLorme Mapping, P.O. Box 298, Freeport, ME 04032; (207) 865-4171.
- Trails Illustrated, P.O. Box 3610, Evergreen, CO 80439; (800) 962-1643.

(8) Management: Here you'll find the name, address, and phone number of the managing agency or agencies responsible for a Wilderness. The staff at these offices usually can give you detailed information, often for free.

Note: Wilderness remains because the "wild" has not been removed from it. As such, venturing into a Wilderness area often involves some risk. You alone are responsible for caring for yourself when you enter a wildland. Changes may occur in roads, trails, fees, permits, phone numbers, and other information. Distances and altitudes, when included, are often based on estimates. You are strongly encouraged to contact the area's managing agency before entering a specific Wilderness.

> "This we know: All things are connected. Whatever befalls the earth befalls the sons of the earth. Man did not weave the web of life; he is merely a strand in it. Whatever he does to the web, he does to himself."
>
> —Chief Seattle

INTRODUCTION

The first humans saw no special distinction between themselves and the landscape around them, nothing to distinguish wilderness from non-wilderness. They knew themselves simply as part of all that was. As human cultures formed and flowed, they most often developed with appreciation, awe, and reverence for the wild land. Human relationships with the earth were pragmatic and spiritual, functional and worshipful, severe and sublime. No mental walls separated person and place.

Walls were built, nevertheless, a fact that often causes me to sigh with a great sense of loss. When were they built? That remains a source of debate. Perhaps early construction of these mental boundaries can be traced to the Judeo-Christian tradition; certainly most Jewish and Christian mystics drew a bold line separating Human from Nature. But other cultures made this distinction without nudging from Judeo-Christian teachings, including ancient China and Rome. In the first century B.C., for example, Romans complained that too much of the earth remained, in the words of the poet Lucretius, "greedily possessed by mountains and the forests of wild beasts."

This tradition also persisted on our fair shores. In what is now known as the American Southwest, long before the first white settlers ventured across the ocean, a vast Anasazi civilization apparently clear-cut themselves out of a place to live about 800 years ago. After Columbus dropped anchor, and for hundreds of years afterward, "wilderness" and "America" were synonymous, but the association did not encourage preservation of the New World's prodigious natural resources. Cotton Mather, circa 1690,

INTRODUCTION

bemoaned leaving England for "the sorrows of a wilderness" in the colonies. Samuel Johnson's 1755 *Dictionary* defined wilderness as "a tract of solitude and savageness." To the American pioneer, wilderness was an obstacle to be overcome, an enemy to be defeated. Alexis de Tocqueville's 1831 visit to the Territory of Michigan produced this comment on the American attitude toward the land: "They are insensible to the wonders of inanimate nature and they may be said not to perceive the mighty forests that surround them till they fall beneath the hatchet."

As alienation between humans and wildland became manifest in the expanding United States, it did not, I am grateful to report, go unnoticed nor unheralded. As early as 1818, Estwick Evans wrote: "There is something in the very name of wilderness, which charms the ear, and soothes the spirit of man. There is religion in it." Abandoning the city for the shore of Walden Pond in 1845, Henry David Thoreau penned: "I wish to speak a word for Nature, for absolute freedom and wildness, as contrasted with a freedom and culture merely civil—to regard man as an inhabitant, or a part and parcel of Nature, rather than a member of society. . . ." Ralph Waldo Emerson, who died in 1882, celebrated in his essays things untamed by mankind. "Nature is loved," he wrote, "by what is best in us." And perhaps wilderness found its most active and respected advocate in John Muir, who wrote in 1901 that "wildness is a necessity; and that the mountain parks and reservations are useful not only as fountains of lumber and irrigating rivers, but as fountains of life."

World wars preoccupied the United States during the first half of the 1900s, but then came 1945, bringing relative peace and a rapid increase in leisure time. Backpack purchases ran into the millions, and the eyes of America looked further and further away from roads and civilized outposts. A passion for wilderness blossomed, and the nation split crudely into two camps: those who wished to develop wildlands, and those who wished to conserve and preserve. Although the arguments continue, often with enormous fervor, the National Wilderness Preservation System (NWPS) was established in 1964 to designate and protect wilderness lands. These protected pieces of America, so revered by "what is best in us," are the subject of this book.

Wilderness Preservation: A Brief History

Though government involvement in wilderness began in earnest on March 1, 1872, when President Ulysses S. Grant signed the Yellowstone National Park Act, preservation was low on the list of federal priorities for the park's two million acres. The act stated Yellowstone was to be a "pleasuring ground for the benefit and enjoyment of the people," and hotels, restaurants, and roads were developed to enhance that goal with little regard to preserving the natural riches that prompted the formation of the park in the first place.

Worried about such cavalier attitudes toward the country's wild places—particularly in his beloved California—John Muir founded the Sierra Club in 1892. For more than 100 years, the Sierra Club has been active in efforts to save the environment and preserve as much land as possible in pristine condition.

Within the federal government itself, pleas arose on behalf of wilderness preservation. As early as 1917, United States Forest Service (USFS) landscape architect Frank Waugh said that wilderness was "enticing" and had a "direct human value" that should be considered along with the economic development of a forest. In 1919, Arthur Carhart, another agency landscape architect, was called upon to develop a plan for roads and summer cabins around Trappers Lake in Colorado's White River National Forest. After falling in love with the unspoiled beauty of the area, Carhart suggested the best plan would be to leave it alone. Never before had someone within the government officially recommended that a specific piece of land be left wild. Carhart resigned in 1922, reportedly frustrated over the lack of interest in wilderness preservation, but his influence had produced a surprising decision by the Denver office of the USFS to allow Trappers Lake to remain undeveloped.

Quietly eloquent and persistent, yet another USFS employee, Aldo Leopold, spent many years working to preserve wild western regions. In

INTRODUCTION

1924, his efforts were rewarded with the creation of the first Roadless area protected by the agency: 574,000 acres of Gila National Forest in New Mexico. With Leopold's vision, the U.S. Forest Service in 1929 developed guidelines for regulating the use of Gila and later-designated "Primitive areas." These regulations, providing for compatible and prohibited uses of forests, marked the first step toward bona fide wilderness management, as opposed to simply setting aside a tract of land.

Leopold and co-worker Bob Marshall founded the Wilderness Society in January 1935. They were joined by six other dedicated men, including Benton MacKaye and Ernest Oberholtzer, who shared a common vision of systematic protection of America's most revered wild places. The society would eventually lead the fight for government preservation of wilderness.

While he directed the U.S. Forest Service's Division of Recreation and Lands, Bob Marshall was instrumental in firming up the protection of lands designated as Primitive. Under Marshall, what became known as the "U" regulations were formulated, classifying protected national forestland as either a Wilderness area (100,000-plus acres), a Wild area (less than 100,000 acres), or a Roadless area (to be managed primarily for recreational use). The regulations prohibited mechanized vehicles and timber harvesting in areas designated as Primitive. After a brief lifetime filled with vigorous wilderness advocacy, Marshall died suddenly in 1939. Without his attention, the Forest Service began to ease off on protection and encourage development.

In the 1950s and early 1960s, under the leadership of Howard Zahniser, the Wilderness Society took command of the struggle for congressional legislation to designate and protect wilderness. Zahniser brought together the Wilderness Society, the Sierra Club (under the direction of David Brower), and the National Wildlife Federation, as well as gaining the support of Senator Hubert Humphrey and Representative John Saylor. Humphrey and Saylor were responsible for submitting the first wilderness bills into the Senate and House in 1956. Opposition was great from the U.S. Forest Service, the

INTRODUCTION

National Park Service, the timber industry, the mining industry, and not a few ranchers. After more than eight grueling years of predictable and heated debate, involving 18 hearings, thousands of pages of documentation, and 66 drafts, the Wilderness Act was signed by President Lyndon B. Johnson on September 3, 1964.

The Wilderness Act of 1964

With the passage of the Wilderness Act, the United States set out on a trail untraveled by any other nation in history: the path to preservation of wildlands in their natural condition. In some of the most fluent words ever to come out of Congress, the Wilderness Act defined both the overriding goal of the National Wilderness Preservation System and the very concept of *wilderness*:

"Sec. 2. (a) In order to assure that an increasing population, accompanied by expanding settlement and growing mechanization, does not occupy and modify all areas within the United States and its possessions, leaving no lands designated for preservation and protection in their natural condition, it is hereby declared to be the policy of the Congress to secure for the American people of present and future generations the benefits of an enduring resource of wilderness. For this purpose there is hereby established a National Wilderness Preservation System. . . .

"(c) A wilderness, in contrast with those areas where man and his own works dominate the landscape, is hereby recognized as an area where the earth and its community of life are untrammeled by man, where man himself is a visitor who does not remain. An area of wilderness is further defined to mean in this Act an area of undeveloped Federal land retaining its primeval character and influence, without permanent improvements or human habitation, which is protected and managed so as to preserve its natural conditions and which (1) generally appears to have been affected primarily by the forces of nature, with the imprint of man's work substantially unnoticeable; (2) has outstanding opportunities for solitude or a primitive and unconfined type of recreation; (3) has at least 5,000 acres of land

INTRODUCTION

or is of sufficient size as to make practicable its preservation and use in an unimpaired condition; and (4) may also contain ecological, geological, or other features of scientific, educational, scenic, or historical value."

Much of the articulate wording of the Wilderness Act came from the mind and heart of Howard Zahniser. He chose the word "untrammeled" to describe his feelings about wilderness preservation, and a fine choice it was—according to the Merriam Webster dictionary, "untrammeled" means that nothing has been done to "prevent or impede the free play of."

Zahniser died in his sleep four months before the historical sweep of President Johnson's pen. Although the 54 areas within national forestland already termed Wilderness, Wild area, or Canoe area were designated under the act, Zahniser would have been disappointed with the meager allotment of only 9.1 million acres of Wilderness out of the 191 million acres within the National Forest System, and with the absence of lands from the National Park System and the National Wildlife Refuge System.

The U.S. Forest Service, an agency of the Department of Agriculture, was directed to consider and present Wilderness recommendations concerning the 34 remaining Primitive areas that had yet to be designated as a Wilderness area or a Wild area. They were given 10 years to mull it over. The Secretary of the Interior was told to have his agencies review, also within a decade, every Roadless area of 5,000 contiguous acres or more on national parkland or other units of the National Park System (managed by the National Park Service), as well as on national wildlife refuges and game ranges (managed by the U.S. Fish and Wildlife Service).

The process of Wilderness designation, as addressed by the act, was composed of three stages:

(1) An agency reviews its holdings and recommends an area for Wilderness designation to that agency's head, who then presents the recommendation to the president of the United States.

(2) The president transmits the recommendation, which must include maps and a definition of boundaries, to Congress.

The Original Wilderness Areas of the National Wilderness Preservation System (1964)

1. Sierra Ancha, Arizona
2. Galiuro, Arizona
3. Chiricahua, Arizona
4. Superstition, Arizona
5. Mazatzal, Arizona
6. Cucamonga, California
7. Thousand Lakes, California
8. Caribou, California
9. San Jacinto, California
10. Hoover, California
11. San Gorgonio, California
12. South Warner, California
13. Domeland, California
14. Mokelumne, California
15. Yolla Bolly–Middle Eel, California
16. Ansel Adams, California
17. Marble Mountain, California
18. John Muir, California
19. Rawah, Colorado
20. La Garita, Colorado
21. Mount Zirkel, Colorado
22. West Elk, Colorado
23. Maroon Bells–Snowmass, Colorado
24. Selway-Bitterroot, Idaho/Montana
25. Boundary Waters, Minnesota
26. Gates of the Mountains, Montana
27. Cabinet Mountains, Montana
28. Anaconda-Pintlar, Montana
29. Bob Marshall, Montana
30. Jarbidge, Nevada
31. Great Gulf, New Hampshire
32. Wheeler Peak, New Mexico
33. San Pedro Parks, New Mexico
34. White Mountain, New Mexico
35. Pecos, New Mexico
36. Gila, New Mexico
37. Linville Gorge, North Carolina
38. Shining Rock, North Carolina
39. Gearhart Mountain, Oregon
40. Mountain Lakes, Oregon
41. Mount Hood, Oregon
42. Diamond Peak, Oregon
43. Mount Washington, Oregon
44. Strawberry Mountain, Oregon
45. Kalmiopsis, Oregon
46. Three Sisters, Oregon
47. Eagle Cap, Oregon
48. Mount Adams, Washington
49. Goat Rocks, Washington
50. Glacier Peak, Washington
51. North Absaroka, Wyoming
52. Bridger, Wyoming
53. Teton, Wyoming
54. Washakie, Wyoming

INTRODUCTION

(3) Congress may follow the recommendation, reject the recommendation, or alter it. If the land is designated Wilderness, an act of Congress is required.

The National Wilderness Preservation System

Two pivotal events occurred in 1968, one when Congress considered a bill that would add a non-Primitive area (Montana's Lincoln-Scapegoat) to the NWPS. Almost immediately, conservation groups began to make Wilderness proposals directly to Congress, bypassing the process as laid out in the Wilderness Act. The USFS, possibly to stall citizen-sponsored considerations for Wilderness, went beyond their original requirement and inventoried all potential Wilderness areas on national forestland. They came up with approximately 56 million acres in 1,449 areas and a plan to study the areas. (Scapegoat Wilderness was designated in 1972 despite strenuous USFS objection.)

The second pivotal event involved the first addition to the original NWPS, San Rafael Wilderness in California. A parcel of 4,700 acres was not included by the USFS in their approximately 150,000-acre proposal. They claimed it had obvious human interference. The Sierra Club championed the area, claiming it was irreplaceable condor habitat. A bruising debate ended with the 4,700 acres remaining unprotected, but the stage was set for environmental groups to play an ever-increasing role in Wilderness designation.

In the early 1970s, the U.S. Forest Service undertook the Roadless Area Review and Evaluation (RARE), their study of the 1,449 possible Wilderness areas to determine which ones should be studied further. RARE designated only 274 areas on 12.3 million acres as Wilderness Study Areas (WSAs). Criticism soared. The study had taken only eight months! The study had considered only recreational and economic factors and no ecological factors! The study had virtually ignored the eastern United States! The Sierra Club sued. Although the case was dismissed, public trust in the RARE process was destroyed.

INTRODUCTION

In the second half of the 1970s, three new acts significantly increased the extent of the NWPS. First, the Eastern Wilderness Act of 1974 made the criteria for Wilderness designation more liberal by designating areas with previous human use that had grown wild for a significant amount of time, and it considered areas smaller than 5,000 acres. This resulted in the earmarking of 16 new areas in 13 states for a total of 207,000 acres. Second, the Federal Land Policy and Management Act of 1976 (FLPMA) mandated the Bureau of Land Management (BLM) to review areas without roads under its management, select Wilderness Study Areas, and make recommendations to Congress by 1991. (The BLM, the largest land manager in the United States, had been left out of the original Wilderness Act.) Finally, the Endangered American Wilderness Act of 1978, signed by President Jimmy Carter, designated 1.3 million acres in 17 new areas. Since many of the new areas were outside the RARE lands, Congress had chosen to act independently of agency recommendations. By the end of 1978, the total acreage of the NWPS had approximately doubled.

In 1977, prompted by pressures put on the Carter Administration by the timber industry and other opponents of Wilderness, the U.S. Forest Service initiated RARE II. The second RARE process included more eastern land, incorporated evaluation of noneconomic values, and inventoried 2,919 areas without roads on 62 million acres. The final RARE II Environmental Impact Statement (EIS), made public in 1979, recommended 624 areas on 15 million acres for Wilderness designation. The EIS further released 1,981 areas on 36 million acres from Wilderness study, and proposed more study for 314 areas on 10.7 million acres. The Secretary of Resources for the State of California, Huey Johnson, sued the USFS in order to protect a select list of California areas that had been opened for development. The Federal District Court found for Johnson in 1980 and ordered that Wilderness could not be developed without a detailed environmental impact statement for each area. Designation of national forestland came to a standstill.

As the 1990s approached, the question of how to designate potential Wilderness land was largely answered by the passage of more and more

INTRODUCTION

individual state Wilderness bills. Statewide bills, approved by Congress, proved a much handier system of Wilderness designation than huge nationwide bills. In 1980 Congress passed state bills designating Wilderness in Colorado, Louisiana, New Mexico, Missouri, and South Carolina.

Despite glacial progress within the U.S. Forest Service, 1980 also saw the total acreage of the NWPS skyrocket to approximately 80 million acres when about 56 million acres of Alaskan lands were designated by President Carter's signature on the Alaska National Interest Lands Conservation Act (ANILCA). Most of these lands were under management of the National Park Service and the U.S. Fish and Wildlife Service.

In 1984 alone, 21 state bills designating 8.6 million acres as new Wilderness were passed. In 1988, Washington got more than 1.7 million acres of Wilderness in Olympia, North Cascades, and Rainier National Parks. Nevada received designation for 733,000 acres of national forestland in 1989, and the Tongass Reform Act of 1990 added 1.2 million acres within six new Wilderness areas of Alaska.

By 1990, the NWPS contained 42 units of the National Park System comprising approximately 39 million acres (33 million of which lay within eight Alaskan parks), and 75 units of the National Wildlife Refuge System consisting of approximately 20 million acres.

The BLM, responsible for managing approximately one-eighth of the United States, made recommendations of which lands should be designated Wilderness Study Areas to the president in 1991. One-quarter of a million BLM acres had already been designated Wilderness in 1984, and passage of the Arizona Desert Wilderness Act in 1990 added 1.1 million acres of BLM land, plus 1.3 million acres of other Arizona Wilderness, almost all of it on national wildlife refuges. By the end of 1993, designated Wilderness within the BLM included more than 1.6 million acres in 68 units.

In 1991, California had more than a half million acres designated as new Wilderness. Colorado got an additional 612,000 acres in 1993. As of September 3, 1994, the 30th anniversary of the Wilderness Act, about 63

INTRODUCTION

percent of the NWPS was set in Alaska, more than 30 percent stood in 11 western states, and roughly 5 percent was in the eastern half of the United States (with about half of the eastern Wilderness land lying in two areas: Minnesota's Boundary Waters and Florida's Everglades).

On October 31, 1994, President Bill Clinton signed the California Desert Protection Act, a bill that had been hanging in political limbo for nearly nine years, the biggest public-lands bill in the history of the Lower 48 and the largest addition to the NWPS outside of ANILCA. Approximately 7.7 million acres of arid Southern California desertland was designated Wilderness: (1) On BLM land, 66 new Wilderness areas were created, three of them shared with the USFS, and additions were made to three existing areas for a grand total of about 3.6 million acres. (2) BLM land was given to the National Park System in two new Wilderness areas (Mojave Wilderness and Death Valley Wilderness) and additional land was added to Joshua Tree Wilderness for a total of almost four million acres. (3) About 9,000 acres of Wilderness were designated on two wildlife refuges (Havasu Wilderness and Imperial Wilderness).

Today, the NWPS includes approximately 4.7 percent of America. At least one of America's designated Wildernesses, administered by one or more federal agencies in 44 of the 50 states, lies less than a half day's drive from almost every citizen of the United States.

The National Wilderness Preservation System consists of:
(1) National Park Service, 45 units, 43 million acres, 41 percent of total acreage of NWPS.
(2) U.S. Forest Service, 400 units, 35 million acres, 34 percent of total acreage of NWPS.
(3) U.S. Fish and Wildlife Service, 77 units, 20.7 million acres, 20 percent of total acreage of NWPS.
(4) Bureau of Land Management, 137 units, 5.3 million acres, 5 percent of total acreage of NWPS.
Total: 659 units, 104 million acres.

INTRODUCTION

(Note: If you add the total Wilderness areas in this book for each state, you will find the sum is 642. This is because numerous units of the NWPS are managed by more than one agency and I have counted each management-shared unit as one.)

Wilderness Land Management Agencies

"The Congress shall have the Power to dispose of and make all needful Rules and Regulations respecting the Territory or other Property belonging to the United States." Thus, one simple sentence of the U.S. Constitution gave birth to a great complexity of land-management issues that includes, but is far from limited to, the National Wilderness Preservation System. Government agencies currently administer approximately 727 million acres, roughly 32 percent of the 2.2 billion acres that make up the total landmass of the United States. Seven hundred million of those 727 million acres are managed by four agencies: the U.S. Forest Service in the Department of Agriculture, and, in the Department of the Interior, the National Park Service, the Bureau of Land Management, and the U.S. Fish and Wildlife Service.

The United States Forest Service was established in 1905 and shoulders responsibility for the management of America's national forests and grasslands. One hundred fifty-six national forests make up almost 98 percent of this agency's land. Eighteen national grasslands and a few other units comprise the rest of the 191 million acres ruled by the USFS. All national forests are used for multiple purposes, including outdoor recreation, grazing (by special permit), timber, watershed, wildlife preservation, and fishing. Prior to the Wilderness Act, the Multiple-Use Sustained-Yield Act of 1960 established that wildlands were consistent with the purposes of outdoor recreation. The National Forest Management Act of 1976 also stipulated that all forest plans must include coordination of Wilderness with other uses.

The National Park Service, established in 1916, today is responsible for almost 80 million acres of national parks, national monuments, and other related units, such as battlefields, lakeshores, seashores, historic sites,

INTRODUCTION

memorials, and rivers. The NPS currently manages 367 units of a staggering variety—from more than 7 million acres in Gates of the Arctic National Park in Alaska to the 0.02-acre Thaddeus Kosciuszko National Memorial in Pennsylvania. The NPS protects the resources under its management with allowances for recreation. In addition to the Wilderness Act, Congress has frequently mandated additional Wilderness studies in legislation establishing new park-system units.

The Bureau of Land Management was established in 1946 and bears responsibility for all national public lands, all the land not privately owned, state owned, or under the management of another agency. BLM land totals over 342 million acres, almost all of it in the 11 contiguous western states and Alaska. Operating under a multiple-use mission, the BLM works primarily with renewable resources (mostly grazing), mineral development, and surveying of federal lands. The Federal Land Policy and Management Act (FLPMA) requires the BLM to manage Wilderness Study Areas within its domain "so as not to impair the suitability of such areas for preservation as wilderness." This requirement is to assure the areas are not damaged until Congress determines whether or not these areas should be added to the National Wilderness Preservation System. FLPMA also requires the BLM to manage designated Wilderness under the same principles that guide the U.S. Forest Service.

The United States Fish and Wildlife Service (USF&WS) was established in 1956 and given responsibility for the National Wildlife Refuge System, a total landmass of more than 90 million acres. USF&WS priorities include protecting migratory birds, endangered species, marine mammals, and freshwater and anadromous fish. Approximately 700 field units in 49 states, Puerto Rico, the Pacific Islands, and the Virgin Islands make up the National Wildlife Refuge System. The USF&WS evaluates land for Wilderness designation under the Wilderness Act.

Why manage Wilderness? Because We the People steadily impact and influence wildlands unless—and even if—some government agency is responsible for the management of an area. Wilderness management does

INTRODUCTION

not mean management of natural resources per se, but management of human use of those resources. Does designation ensure preservation? No. The best chance for preserving the Wilderness qualities of an area remains in the hands of sound management. Careful management principles include:

(1) managing a Wilderness area as a distinct resource with inseparable parts to protect the interconnected web of life;
(2) attaining the highest level of purity in Wilderness character within legal constraints in order to keep an area as wild and natural as possible;
(3) managing the use of other resources and activities within a Wilderness in a manner compatible with the Wilderness;
(4) allowing natural processes to operate freely;
(5) preserving air and water quality;
(6) producing benefits to humans while preserving Wilderness character;
(7) preserving outstanding opportunities for solitude or a primitive and unconfined recreation experience;
(8) controlling and reducing the adverse physical and social impacts of human visitation through education or minimum regulation;
(9) favoring Wilderness-dependent activities;
(10) excluding the sight, sound, and other tangible evidence of motorized equipment or mechanical transport whenever possible;
(11) removing existing structures and terminating uses and activities not essential to Wilderness management or not provided for by law;
(12) accomplishing necessary Wilderness management work with the minimum tools;
(13) establishing specific management objectives with public involvement in a plan for each Wilderness;
(14) harmonizing Wilderness and adjacent land-management activities;
(15) managing Wilderness with interdisciplinary scientific skills;

(16) managing special exceptions provided for by Wilderness legislation with minimum impact on the area. Congress allows management agencies to permit certain uses to continue within designated Wildernesses if those uses existed prior to designation. These activities include:

(a) hunting, fishing, and trapping under state and federal laws, which require a valid license in most areas;

(b) outfitting and guiding services under special-use permits that are deemed proper and necessary for meeting Wilderness purposes;

(c) measures to control fire, insects, and diseases;

(d) aircraft or motorboat use;

(e) access to private- and state-owned lands within Wilderness;

(f) collection of information about resources in a manner compatible with the preservation of Wilderness;

(g) developing valid and existing mineral rights;

(h) livestock grazing.

Of Wilderness and Waterways

Thousands of miles of water in hundreds of waterways flow through the designated Wilderness areas of America, and the legislative trend has been to protect water, as well as land, within the National Wilderness Preservation System. Yet a loophole exists in the Wilderness Act allowing the president of the United States to approve water development in Wilderness areas. For this reason, passage of the Wild and Scenic Rivers Act of 1968, signed by President Johnson, provided a precious addition to Wilderness preservation, and many rivers within designated Wilderness areas have been further protected through Wild and Scenic designation. I have attempted to note all the Wild and Scenic Rivers in Wilderness areas.

Wilderness Preservation: The Future

When it comes to preservation of our country's wild places, much already exists that may be regarded with gratitude, the fruit of the efforts of many

INTRODUCTION

people both dead and living. But gratitude is not enough. Preservation of wildlands for future generations is an idea with many powerful opponents. Many people, including members of Congress, think that preserving wilderness means merely protecting nice views, and have failed to grasp the importance of preserving entire ecosystems. They don't understand that wilderness preservation is a biological imperative as well as a source of aesthetic enjoyment and spiritual renewal. Even though the NWPS today encompasses roughly 4.7 percent of America, at least twice that much land stands worthy and in need of preservation. Tens of millions of precious acres should be added to the National Wilderness Preservation System: life-sustaining national forestland, watersheds, desertland, and wetland.

Expanding the NWPS should not pose financial difficulties. President Johnson also signed the Land and Water Conservation Act, which established a fund for recreational land purchases, and approximately $900 million a year has accumulated in that fund. As of the end of 1994, Congress had appropriated only about 25 percent of the fund for land purchases; the rest was borrowed for other government purposes. Most of the unappropriated money will never be recovered, but America should demand that, from now on, the fund be used for its intended purpose: land purchase and preservation.

Another problem is the fact that the agencies responsible for implementing the Wilderness Act have failed to follow all of its directives, including recommending new areas for preservation by the specified deadlines. The USFS must continue to consider roadless lands still eligible for Wilderness status, and designated wild forestland should be managed as directed by the Wilderness Act. Special permits, for instance, have been inappropriately issued, allowing exploratory helicopters from oil and gas companies to land in Alaska Wildernesses under the management of the U.S. Forest Service.

To date, millions of acres of national parkland in almost two dozen parks and monuments in the Lower 48 have been proposed as Wilderness

INTRODUCTION

and await the disposition of Congress. Another 6.2 million acres in 17 parks, monuments, and national recreation areas have been recommended but have not been sent by the president to Congress. ANILCA mandated the further study of national parkland in Alaska that resulted in the recommendation of 16 million acres in 13 park units for designation. The Secretary of the Interior was given until 1987 to forward the Alaska recommendations to the president; he has ignored the deadline.

Millions of acres of BLM land have been recommended and await the disposition of Congress. Attempts in Utah to reclaim a Civil War–era law allowing construction of roads where footpaths currently exist threaten irreplaceable wild red-rock country under BLM management.

Almost two million acres on 22 national wildlife refuges in the Lower 48 have been recommended for Wilderness designation, proposals upon which Congress has yet to act. In Alaska, 52.6 million acres in 15 refuge system units were found suitable as Wilderness, but administrative policies have undermined designation. To complicate matters, the National Wildlife Refuge Administrative Act of 1966 may permit development of refuges (for oil, gas, mineral, timber, farming) if it is deemed compatible with the primary purpose of the refuge (i.e., to protect fish and wildlife habitat). Wilderness designation precludes those developmental activities. The coastal plain of the Arctic National Wildlife Refuge, perhaps the last place on Earth where Arctic ecosystems remain intact, may be destroyed by oil and gas development.

Your Involvement in Wilderness Preservation

Here's where you can enter this story: know what you have. Wilderness belongs to all citizens of the United States. Explore your natural legacy in books, newspapers, and magazines, through television programs and on-line computer services. Explore on foot, by paddle, or on horseback, and become familiar with rivers and mountains, deserts and canyons, flora and fauna, the sound and feel of the wild. And Leave No Trace of your exploration (see page 26).

INTRODUCTION

Stay informed. Many big issues make national news, but many special issues never command a large public audience. Join a watchdog organization, either a national group (such as the Wilderness Society, the Sierra Club, or the National Wildlife Federation) or a regional organization (such as the Wyoming Outdoor Council, the Southern Utah Wilderness Association, or the Alaska Center for the Environment). Newsletters and action alerts from such groups will keep you up to date on important issues.

Take action by writing letters. The National Environmental Policy Act (NEPA) of 1969 provides the legal basis for public involvement in decisions made by your government concerning your environment. Convey your main point clearly and politely in the first sentence of your letter. Be concise about the issue, and name the specific land-management unit and the specific legislation or action that concerns you. If you've had personal experiences in a particular Wilderness, mention them. Address your letters to specific public officials. Include your return address to allow the public official a chance to answer. Take time to offer your constructive criticism and your support.

Take action by volunteering. As Edward Abbey wrote: "Wilderness needs no defense, only more defenders." Federal agencies that manage Wildernesses need volunteers for patrols, visitor contacts, trail maintenance, Study Area monitoring, and other activities.

The Wilderness Experience: Leave No Trace

As a visitor to Wilderness, you will pass through and you will not remain. You will enter a primitive environment where you will be self-sufficient. Almost without exception, you will find no established shelters, no developed campgrounds, no safe drinking water, no rest rooms, and no detailed trail signs. You will travel by foot or canoe or horseback because, except under special conditions, no motorized or mechanized vehicles, including bicycles and hang gliders, are allowed. You may leave established trails to seek wonder, solitude, and challenge, but you travel with the responsibility to walk with care. Once humans spoke of wilderness survival as their

INTRODUCTION

ability to survive the impact of wildland. Now wilderness survival has come to mean the wildland's ability to survive your impact.

In 1991, the National Outdoor Leadership School (NOLS) in Lander, Wyoming, entered into an agreement with the United States Forest Service, the National Park Service, and the Bureau of Land Management to help develop curricula and training for a program called Leave No Trace. This program is designed to promote the skills and ethics visitors need to protect both the wildland and the user. In the words of Paul Petzoldt, founder of NOLS: "We know we cannot conserve our wilderness areas adequately, even with all the restrictions, without educating the user." Leave No Trace, take only pictures, kill only time!

Here briefly are the guidelines of the Leave No Trace program:

(1) Plan Ahead and Prepare.
- Repackage your food into resealable plastic bags, leaving glass, cans, and aluminum at home.

- Choose your equipment with care. Avoid packing brightly colored clothing (except blaze orange during hunting season) or equipment to reduce the visual impact of your visit. Carry equipment that allows you to reduce your physical impact, such as lightweight stoves, freestanding tents, and collapsible water containers.

- Know the area and what to expect. Gather information. Match your intended trip to your expectations and outdoor skill level. Choose areas not overused by other humans. Do not travel alone, but select your companions wisely. Know your physical limitations and pace yourself accordingly. Inform someone responsible of your route and your intended time of return. Know whom to contact if you must leave the Wilderness for help.

(2) Travel and Camp on Durable Surfaces.
- Stay on trails whenever possible and avoid cutting across switchbacks. Your shortcuts will destroy soil structure and vegetation, and accelerate erosion.

INTRODUCTION

- Camp in places where you will be invisible to other travelers: well away from main trails, at least 200 feet away from water sources.
- If you have a choice between an obviously well used campsite and a nearby pristine spot, you'll do far less damage settling where the damage has already been done. A campsite used more than 10 times does not significantly deteriorate with further use. But leave it in as good condition as you found it.
- If you have a choice between a slightly used campsite and a pristine spot, choose the pristine spot. Most of a site's damage occurs the first couple of times it is used improperly. Allow the slightly used spot to restore itself.
- When choosing a pristine spot, the ideal campsites are without vegetation or even soil: rocks, sand, gravel, snow. Second-best sites are soil-based and without vegetation. Your camp will compact the soil, but recovery will be rapid.
- If your campsite choice is between dense vegetation and sparse vegetation, choose dense. Sparse plant life, low shrubs, and saplings take a long time to recover from abuse.
- If your campsite choice is between dry and wet, choose dry. Marshy ground recovers slowly from compaction. Wet grass and dewy flowers die easily when trampled.
- Do not dig trenches around your tent.
- Stay as few nights as possible in one place, especially in areas that are easily damaged.
- Large parties (i.e., groups of more than four or five) should break into smaller camping groups to reduce their impact.
- If you must move a rock or a log for camping convenience, put it back exactly where you found it.
- Wear soft-soled shoes around camp to reduce your impact.

INTRODUCTION

- When walking between your tent, your cooking area, and your water source, follow a variety of paths to avoid creating a trail.

(3) Pack It In, Pack It Out.
- Do not bury anything you packed in. Trash that burns completely may be burned where allowed, but it is better for the Wilderness if you pack out everything you packed in.

(4) Properly Dispose of What You Can't Pack Out.
- Human waste products have a high potential for spreading disease and spoiling another human's Wilderness experience. Bury each individual mass of human waste six to eight inches deep in soil and at least 200 feet from a water source and campsite. Fill in the hole you dug and hide all evidence of its existence. This is called the cat-hole technique. In low-use areas with direct sunlight, decomposition can be maximized by spreading human waste thinly on the surface. This is called the smear technique.
- Do not wash your clothes, dirty dishes, or yourself directly in a natural water source. Minimize or avoid use of soap. Carry water at least 200 feet away from water sources to do your washing. Discard all wash water at least 200 feet away from a natural water source.

(5) Leave What You Find.
- Avoid digging up plants, picking wildflowers, or breaking limbs from trees. Wilderness areas, especially in high-use regions, can be denuded with surprising rapidity.
- Do not take anything out of the Wilderness. Objects of antiquity (arrowheads, pottery shards, etc.) and prehistoric habitations are protected by federal law. Look, photograph, delight—but don't touch.

(6) Minimize Use and Impact of Fires.
- Cook on a small gas stove.
- If campfires are permitted and necessary, keep yours small. Use only dead and down wood. Do not build a fire ring or fires on rocks. Build

INTRODUCTION

fires in shallow pits or on sand. Let the wood burn to fine ash. Drown and scatter the ash widely before you leave. Fill in the pit when you're finished, and hide all signs of its existence.

Ten Additional Guidelines

(1) If you enjoy packing with animals, your attention to Leave No Trace must be even more careful. Make sure stock (horses, llamas, goats) is allowed in the Wilderness of your choice. Keep groups small, and use lightweight equipment to reduce the number of animals needed and the impact of your camp. Make sure there is adequate natural feed at your campsite so your stock doesn't remove feed needed by wildlife. Some Wildernesses allow no grazing. If you pack in hay, pack out the extra. Do not leave partially eaten hay or manure piled up around where you camp. Water your stock where the stream bank is substantial enough to withstand the impact. Use hobbles if you need to constrain your stock. Place hitchlines where the ground is rocky and protect the trees you hitch your stock to by using straps. If you use pickets, use metal pickets and move them every few hours.

(2) Maintain a safe distance from and do not disturb wildlife.

(3) In bear country, avoid bear confrontations by (a) traveling in groups; (b) camping in spots with no evidence of bear usage: scat, tracks, and claw marks on trees; (c) hanging food, trash, and all aromatic items (such as toothpaste and soap) 10 to 12 feet off the ground and 10 to 12 feet from the trunk of a tree; (d) sleeping well away from where you cook; (e) sleeping in clothes other than the clothes you wore while cooking.

(4) Hunting is allowed in most areas. Know when hunting seasons are open and either wear blaze orange or choose another area.

(5) Pets are usually allowed, but you must have them under control at all times. In some Wilderness areas, pets must be kept on a leash. Check with the managing agency.

INTRODUCTION

(6) Know wilderness medicine and carry a first-aid kit. Learn how to treat and prevent hypothermia, heat illness, sprained or broken ankles and sprained knees, small wounds, and gastrointestinal distress. Be able to recognize and treat serious and life-threatening injuries, and know whom to contact for rescue assistance.

(7) Carry a map and review the terrain you'll be traveling. Carry a compass and know how to use it.

(8) Pack for the worst possible weather conditions you might encounter. Layers of clothing, which can be removed as you warm up and added as you cool down, provide the best protection and versatility. Rainwear is essential yearlong to ward off wet, cold, and wind. Protect feet and ankles by wearing sturdy boots while hiking, but slip on light shoes around camp to reduce your impact on the terrain. Extra socks are a necessity.

(9) Do not drink water directly from natural sources. Carry the means to disinfect all drinking water. Anything that can make you sick dies in water that has been brought to the point of boiling (there's no need for a prolonged boil). Some water filters remove all harmful protozoa, bacteria, and viruses—read the label to see how much protection your particular filter affords. Chemical disinfectants (such as iodine and chlorine) kill most harmful waterborne organisms if they are used correctly. Some protozoa are not killed by chemical disinfectants. Follow directions carefully.

(10) Avoid disease by washing your hands after bowel movements and before food preparation. Pour food from containers instead of reaching in for handfuls. Avoid the temptation to share water bottles, cups, spoons, and uneaten food.

Leave No Trace materials (both in general and specific to certain geographic areas) and information on training programs are available from the NOLS Leave No Trace Office, 288 Main Street, Lander, WY 82520; (800) 332-4100.

INTRODUCTION

Preserve Wilderness—And Enjoy It

It seems an unrealistic, yet infinitely appealing, goal for one person to visit all the designated Wilderness areas in America. Over my lifetime, I have visited many, some before they were designated; most of my journeys have been noted briefly in this book. My greatest personal experiences of Wilderness have tended to be transitory: early morning light, a sudden fiery sunset, the crisp gold of aspen in fall, the highlights of fresh snow, thunder and lightning resounding in the bottom of a canyon, the track of a rising full moon on placid water, rounding a corner on a trail to find a breathtaking view. Rendered to their essence, these wonders each become the ultimate experience, a perfect moment.

Designated Wilderness, for as long as it lasts, will assure that the essence of these sublime experiences will be preserved for our future enjoyment, as well as those who come after. A great diversity of plant and animal life will be maintained. Medical and scientific research will have an irreplaceable living laboratory. Evidence of early human activity will be preserved for coming generations. Places for human solitude, for replenishment and growth of the human spirit, will survive.

However you define it, Wilderness benefits from individuals who care enough to act to preserve and protect what remains.

Wallace Stegner summed it up with typical poignancy: "Something will have gone out of us as a people if we ever let the remaining wilderness be destroyed." But Edward Abbey offered perhaps the best advice of all: "Do not burn yourselves out. Be as I am—a reluctant enthusiast . . . a part-time crusader, a half-hearted fanatic. Save the other half of yourselves and your lives for pleasure and adventure. It is not enough to fight for the land; it is more important to enjoy it. While you can. While it is still here. So get out there and hunt and fish and mess around with your friends, ramble out yonder and explore forests, encounter the grizz, climb the mountains, bag the peaks, run the rivers, breathe deep the yet sweet and lucid air, sit quietly for a while and contemplate the precious stillness, that lovely, mysterious and awesome space."

> "Wilderness...a beautiful piece of the world, a place where you can be serene, that will let you contemplate and connect two consecutive thoughts, or that if need be can stir you up as you were made to be stirred up, until you blend with the wind and water and earth you almost forgot you came from."
>
> —David Brower

ALABAMA

Total Wilderness areas: 2
Total Wilderness acreage: 33,396

Early pioneers in Alabama found that a large part of the state was covered in a forestland so thick and rich that sunlight never touched vast stretches of the ground. Creek and Chickasaw Indians called this forest home, as did wildlife so abundant it was thought to be numberless. Today only two small areas set within two of Alabama's four national forests have qualified for Wilderness designation. They preserve small stands of virgin woodland and other timbered country that has remained virtually undisturbed for many years.

Cheaha Wilderness

From the stone tower on the summit of Cheaha Mountain, Alabama's highest point at 2,407 feet, a dense second-growth woodland stretches south across Cheaha State Park and into Cheaha Wilderness. For a scenic peek over the area, an asphalt road leads to the top of the mountain, off State Route 49.

Best known for its elevated terrain and overlooks with panoramic views, the Wilderness attracts hikers to the Cheaha section of the Pinhoti Trail, Alabama's longest walking path. This stretch of the trail runs from northeast to southwest across the entire Wilderness, a distance of about 10 miles. Primarily following a ridge system through Talladega National Forest, the Pinhoti crosses the top of Cheaha Mountain. To the Creeks *pinhoti* means "turkey's home." Indeed, wild turkeys are common trail companions (as are white-tailed deer), and the path is marked with a blaze that looks like a turkey track. From the white-sand beach of Lake Chinnabee, the Chinnabee Silent Trail leads into the Wilderness, just east of the lake, and joins with three established trails at about 6.5 miles: Chinnabee Silent, Pinhoti, and Odom. A shelter is located

ALABAMA

approximately midway to the trail juncture. The Odom Trail runs almost due south from the juncture, covering approximately eight miles of the area. Wilderness camping and campfires are allowed. Fishing and hunting are also permitted; during hunting season hikers are wise to wear bright orange on their outer garments.

Near the edge of the Wilderness, you'll find picnic areas, campsites with hookups for a fee, a motel, and rental cabins.

Cheaha Essentials

Size: 7,490 acres.
Year Designated: 1983; expanded in 1988.
Location: Eastern central Alabama.
Easiest Access: From Talladega, take State Highway 21 northeast for seven miles. Turn east on County Road 96 and drive 12 miles to Forest Service Road 646, which leads two miles to Lake Chinnabee Recreation Area. The road goes into Cheaha State Park and nears the Wilderness boundary.
Season: Fall and spring offer the most appealing weather.
Wilderness Fees/Permits: None. Free primitive camping is allowed anywhere in the forest, except during hunting season, when it is restricted for safety reasons.
Maps: A Cheaha Wilderness Map and a Pinhoti Trail Map are available for $3 each from ANF Interpretive Association, 2946 Chestnut Street, Montgomery, AL 36107. USGS topographic maps are available from the district ranger.
Management: Talladega Ranger District, Talladega National Forest, 1001 North Street, Talladega, AL 35160; (205) 362-2909.

Sipsey Wilderness

Wild-flowing creeks in northwestern Alabama converge to become the Sipsey River, 61 miles of which has been designated Wild and Scenic. Running below sandstone bluffs that rise 30 to 100 feet above the water, through a forest of often imposing second-growth trees and occasional small stands of virgin timber (some of the last virgin timber in the state), the Sipsey and its tributaries slice neatly through the Wilderness. Sinkholes, small caves, and scenic overlooks are plentiful. Less plentiful is the rare flattened musk turtle, an inhabitant of the Sipsey.

Six established trails, all rated easy to moderate, crisscross the area. Several depart from the Sipsey River Recreation Site on the southern boundary, which has sanitary facilities, drinkable water, no developed campsites, and no fee. From here, Trail 209 follows the river north and joins Trail 206 after about eight miles, ending after about 2.5 more miles at a parking lot on the northern boundary. Trail 200 runs north along Borden Creek to meet an old wagon road that gives access to the heart of Sipsey Wilderness; it, too, ends at a parking lot on the northern boundary. A 13-mile loop is possible by taking Trail 204 from the old wagon road and following Trail 209 for the return to the recreation site. Sipsey trails receive moderate to heavy human use year-round. Wilderness camping, building campfires, hunting, and fishing are permitted. Horsepackers are allowed on designated trails.

ALABAMA

Sipsey Essentials

Size: 25,906 acres.
Year Designated: 1975; expanded in 1988.
Location: Northwestern Alabama.
Easiest Access: From Haleyville, take State Highway 195 northeast for 8.5 miles. Turn north on County Road 23 (Kinlock Road) and drive 1.5 miles, then turn east on Cranal Road and continue six miles to the Sipsey River Recreation Site. The Wilderness starts a few feet north of the recreation site.

Season: Fall and spring offer the best weather, and crowds are usually smaller than in summer.
Wilderness Fees/Permits: None.
Maps: A free Wilderness map, with little detail, can be acquired from the district ranger. USGS topographic maps are Bee Branch, Grayson, Kinlock Springs, and Landersville.
Management: Bankhead Ranger District, Bankhead National Forest, P.O. Box 278, Double Springs, AL 35553; (205) 489-5111.

> "If you are old, go by all means; but if you are young, stay away until you've grown older. The scenery of Alaska is so much grander than anything else of the kind in the world that, once beheld, all other scenery becomes flat and insipid. It is not well to dull one's capacity for such enjoyment by seeing the finest first."
>
> —Henry Gannett

ALASKA

Total Wilderness areas: 48
Total Wilderness acreage: 56,770,766

After nine years of research, planning, evaluation, and reevaluation, Congress passed the Alaska National Interest Lands Conservation Act (ANILCA) on December 2, 1980. With one sweep of President Jimmy Carter's pen, 10 new units of the National Park System were established, 3 units were expanded, 10 National Preserves were established, and the size of the park system in America was more than doubled. In Alaska alone, more than 51 million acres are national parkland. Alaska now has 15 units of the National Park System, seven containing designated Wilderness areas. ANILCA expanded seven wildlife refuges and created nine new refuges, more than doubling the size of the National Wildlife Refuge System. The refuge system in Alaska contains more than 77 million acres. Of Alaska's 16 wildlife refuges, 10 contain Wilderness areas. Both of the two largest national forests in America stand within Alaska: approximately 5.6 million acres of the Chugach stretch south and east of Anchorage and almost 17 million acres (larger than the state of West Virginia) of the Tongass cover the southeast portion of the state. Scattered throughout the Tongass are 19 designated Wilderness areas, some established by ANILCA and some by the Tongass Timber Reform Act of 1990. ANILCA added to the few designated Wildernesses already existing within the state of Alaska, and more than doubled the size of the National Wilderness Preservation System (NWPS). Even after the passage of the California Desert Protection Act in 1994, more than half of the NWPS lies in Alaska.

ALASKA

Aleutian Islands Wilderness

A people known as the Aleuts originally settled on these islands. Living off a land poor in sunlight but rich in food, they built seacoast villages and gave Alaska its name: "the Great Land." At their peak population, they numbered somewhere between 15,000 and 25,000. When the Russians invaded in 1745, the peace-loving Aleuts were decimated first by violent attacks and enslavement, and later by disease. By 1831 fewer than 1,000 Aleuts survived, and today their villages exist only on several of the islands.

Actually the peaks of a submarine mountain range, the Aleutian Islands National Wildlife Refuge was set aside in 1980 as a 3.3-million-acre unit of the 4.9-million-acre Alaska Maritime National Wildlife Refuge (AMNWR). (The entire AMNWR contains approximately 3,000 islands, headlands, rocks, islets, spires, and reefs off the Alaskan coast.) The Aleutian Islands Unit consists of 200-plus dots of splendid and forbidding land extending more than 1,100 miles across the sea from the extreme southwestern tip of Alaska. It is a mountainous expanse with numerous lakes, ponds, streams, and 57 volcanoes, of which many are rated as active.

On most of these islands you'll find lush green tundra dotted with summer wildflowers and carpeted with grasses, sedges, mosses, lichens, and heath. Sea otters, which were almost exterminated by first Russian and later U.S. traders, have returned in great numbers and now live in abundance along the kelp-rich shoreline with sea lions and harbor seals. The principal marine fish are halibut, cod, perch, sablefish, yellowfin sole, pollack, sand lance, herring, and salmon. Most of the land mammals, including foxes, reindeer, and caribou, have been introduced by humans.

But the Aleutians are best known for their birds. More than 10 million nest on the islands. Puffins, auklets, gulls, storm petrels, cormorants, terns, kittiwakes, murres, pigeon guillemots, and murrelets are among the most abundant species. The largest known colony of northern fulmars in America—topping one-half million—nest on Chagulak Island. Half of the world's emperor geese spend their winters in the Aleutians. Once Aleutian Canada geese nested across these islands, but now they are rare and may be found only on remote Chagulak and Buldir Islands. Nowhere else in North America can you find whooper swans, tufted ducks, Siberian rubythroats, wood sandpipers, far eastern curlews, and black-headed gulls.

Japan invaded the Aleutians in World War II, and you'll discover many abandoned military installations and war refuse among the islands. The invasion, which claimed the lives of more than 2,500 U.S. military personnel, brought Alaska "closer to home" and was instrumental in the Great Land becoming a state. Active military bases, but no civilian communities, remain on the islands of Adak, Shemya, and Attu. A visitors center is maintained on Adak Island.

The Aleutian Islands Unit is divided into seven island groups: Near Islands, Rat Islands, Delarof Islands, Andreanof Islands, Islands of Four Mountains, Fox Islands, and Krenitzin Islands. Over 57 percent is designated Wilderness.

The major Wilderness islands include all or part of the Near Islands of Attu, Agattu, Alaid, Nizki; all or part of the Rat Islands of Buldir, Kiska, Sobaka Rock, Little Kiska, Tanadak, Segula, Khvostof, Pyramid, Davidof, Rat, Little Sitkin, Amchitka, Bird Rock, Semisopochnoi; all or part of the Delarof Islands of Amatignak, Tanadak, Ulak, Unalga, Dinkum Rocks, Kavalga, Gareloi, Ogliuga, Skagul, Tag, Ilak, Gramp Rock; all or part of the Andreanof Islands of Tanaga, Kanaga, Bobrof, Ringgold, Staten, Argonne, Dora, North,

ALASKA

South, Green, Ina, Crone, Elf, the island north of Elf, Adak including all offshore islands, Kagalaska, Little Tanaga, Chisak, Umak, Aziak, Tanaklak, Asuksak, Kanu, Tagadak, Great Sitkin, Igitkin, Anagaksik, Ulak, Chugul, Tagalak, Ikiginak, Oglodak, Kasatochi, Salt, Atka, Amlia, Sagagik, Tanadak, Agligadak, Seguam; all or part of the Islands of Four Mountains of Amukta, Chugulak, Yunaska, Herbert, Carlisle, Chuginadak, Uliaga, Kagamil; all or part of the Fox Islands of Vsevidof, Kigul, Ogchul, Pustoi, Emerald, Buck, Ogangen, Egg; all or part of the Krenitzin Islands of Avatanak, Kaligagan, Ugamak, Amak, and Sealion Rocks.

Geographically near the Aleutians but administratively a part of the Alaska Peninsula Unit of the AMNWR lie the Sanak Islands. Of these islands several were listed as designated Wilderness in the August 1988 AMNWR Comprehensive Conservation Plan and Wilderness Review: Long, Rabbit, Wanda, Elma, Inikla, Umla, Caton, and other islets and rocks. They do not appear on the current map of U.S. Fish and Wildlife Service Wildernesses in Alaska. I could not determine, after tremendous effort, if these islands are truly designated Wilderness, and I wasn't sure where to list them or even if I should list them. But here they are for your consideration.

In the Aleutians you'll find the foggiest, rainiest, windiest weather in the United States. Sea kayaking is popular but often dangerous due to violent storms and magnificently rocky shorelines. Many of the larger islands offer open country for backpacking including Agattu, Kiska, Semisopochnoi, Tanaga, Kanaga, Adak, Kagalaska, Great Sitkin, Atka, Amlia, Seguam, Umnak, Unalaska, and Unimak. Storm often arrives on the tail of storm, but visiting the islands, for the persistent, may well rate among the wilderness experiences of a lifetime.

Aleutian Islands Essentials

Size: 1,300,000 acres.
Year Designated: 1980.
Location: Off the coast of southwestern Alaska.
Easiest Access: No truly easy access exists for the Aleutians. Regularly scheduled flights from Anchorage serve Adak, Dutch Harbor, and Shemya. Check with the refuge manager.
Season: Summers average about 50 degrees Fahrenheit, and most visitors come between June and August.
Wilderness Fees/Permits: Permission from the appropriate military command is required to land on Adak (U.S. Navy) and Shemya (U.S. Air Force). Some islands are off-limits. Contact the refuge manager.
Maps: USGS 1:250,000 topographic maps are (east to west) Cold Bay, False Pass, Unimak, Unalaska, Umnak, Samalga Island, Amukta, Seguam, Atka, Adak, Garelol Island, Rat Islands, Kiska, and Attu.
Management: Aleutian Islands Unit, Alaska Maritime National Wildlife Refuge, PSC 486, Box 5251, FPO-AP Adak, AK 96506-5251; (907) 592-2406.

Andreafsky Wilderness

The expansive 1.3 million acres of the Andreafsky Wilderness cover only slightly more than 5 percent of the monstrously vast 20-million-acre Yukon Delta National Wildlife Refuge, America's largest unit of the National Wildlife Refuge System. Most of the delta is wetland tundra and marsh, and about one-third of it lies underwater. Here you'll find moose, foxes, beavers, martens, minks, wolves, wolverines, caribou, large populations of black and brown bears, and millions of salmon.

ALASKA

The Andreafsky River and its East Fork, in the northern section, flow southwest along parallel paths and drain into the Yukon River. Forests of white spruce and balsam poplar grow along the riverbanks through the Wilderness. Near the headwaters the forests give way to alpine tundra, and a relatively flat, treeless delta. Fishing is excellent, and the bears know it. Both rivers are scenic, but the East Fork has more trees and runs closer to the mountains. One hundred twenty-five miles of the Andreafsky and 137 miles of the East Fork are designated National Wild and Scenic Rivers, attracting river runners and anglers.

Summers are cool and gentle by Alaskan standards, with days of fog. Winters are cold, dry, and severe. Planes, motorboats, and snowmobiles are allowed in this trailless Wilderness.

Andreafsky Essentials

Size: 1,300,000 acres.
Year Designated: 1980.
Location: Southwestern Alaska.
Easiest Access: Jets fly regularly from Anchorage to the village of Saint Mary's. The village stands 1.25 miles below the confluence of the Andreafsky and its East Fork. From Saint Mary's visitors can arrange to head upriver via a powerboat or a small airplane charter. For more information contact the refuge office in Bethel.
Season: Ice may clog the rivers until early June. August and September usually have fewer insects and enough water to float the rivers.
Wilderness Fees/Permits: None. Use of a helicopter, other than in emergencies, requires a special-use permit. Check with the refuge manager.
Maps: USGS 1:250,000 topographic maps are Holy Cross, Kwiguk, Saint Michael, and Unalakleet. USGS maps showing the rivers in more detail are available. Contact the USGS-Fairbanks at (907) 456-0244.
Management: Yukon Delta National Wildlife Refuge, P.O. Box 346, Bethel, AK 99559; (907) 543-3151.

Arctic Wilderness

No other region of America has seen less human impact than the northeastern corner of Alaska. Here the Brooks Range bulges up near the Arctic Ocean to create a unique combination of habitats, including arctic, subarctic, and alpine ecosystems. Approximately 200 miles by 200 miles, the Arctic National Wildlife Refuge stretches down both sides of the Brooks Range here, occupying almost 20 million acres—the size of South Carolina. Peaks reaching 9,000 feet, the highest in the Brooks, look northward across rolling tundra cut by serpentine rivers and dotted with clusters of freshwater lakes. Farther north lie the barrier islands and saltwater lagoons of the Arctic Ocean. Southward the terrain drops from treeless mountains into broad conifer- and hardwood-covered valleys.

By Arctic standards, the refuge's mammal population is abundant: brown bears, moose, wolves, wolverines, and red foxes everywhere; Dall sheep and marmots in the high mountains; black bears, coyotes, lynx, porcupines, and beavers in the forestland; musk oxen and arctic foxes on the north slopes; polar bears on the ice pack; and the 110,000-member Porcupine caribou herd in winter in the southern portion. Beluga and bowhead whales migrate along the coast with ringed and bearded seals. Migratory birds flock here, some traveling all the way from Antarctica.

ALASKA

About 40 percent of the refuge has been designated Wilderness, including much of the eastern half on both sides of the Brooks Range. Within the refuge flows 155 miles of the Wild and Scenic Sheenjek River and 98 miles of the Wild and Scenic Wind River. River runners travel the waterways, and the backpacking rates as excellent along streams and in the forests. Camping is unrestricted, but visitors must use stoves because firewood is scarce. (In a century a tree may only reach knee-high on a caribou.) Expect cool summers often shrouded in fog, and severe winters. Winds vary from moderate to strong, and a layer of ice remains 1.5 feet underground year-round. Water usually melts by mid- to late June, when mosquitoes hatch. In June and early July, 24 hours of daylight can push temperatures into the 80s, but it usually freezes at night. There's often enough water in the rivers in August to make paddling a canoe—the traditional mode of travel in the refuge—an option, but by September winter has returned.

Arctic Essentials

Size: 8,000,000 acres.
Year Designated: 1980.
Location: Northeastern Alaska.
Easiest Access: Small chartered airplanes fly into the totally roadless refuge from Arctic Village, Fort Yukon, Kaktovik, and Prudhoe Bay.
Season: Mid-June through August.
Wilderness Fees/Permits: None, however permits are required for commercial trips. Check with the refuge manager.
Maps: USGS 1:250,000 topographic maps are Arctic, Barter Island, Black River, Chandalar, Christian, Coleen, Demarcation Point, Flaxman Island, Mount Michelson, Philip Smith Mountains, Sagavanirktok, and Table Mountain.
Management: Arctic National Wildlife Refuge, Room 266, Federal Building and Courthouse, 101 Twelfth Avenue, Box 20, Fairbanks, AK 99701; (907) 456-0250.

Becharof Wilderness

Set where the state begins to slim down into the Alaska Peninsula, 35-mile-by-15-mile Becharof Lake is Alaska's second largest body of inland water (only Lake Iliamna is larger). Becharof Wilderness, about one-third of the Becharof National Wildlife Refuge, extends from the lake's northeastern shore south to the Pacific Ocean. Becharof Lake is also the world's second largest salmon nursery. When the salmon spawn, brown bears cluster here in greater numbers than anywhere else. Some actually den on islands in the lake, a behavior noted nowhere else on Earth. On the coast, Puale Bay provides haul-out beaches for thousands of Stellar sea lions and other sea mammals. Multitudes of seabirds come and go along a coastline cut deeply by misty fjords (steep cliffs falling into narrow saltwater bays). Wolves, moose, and members of a caribou herd numbering 15,000 are commonly sighted.

Becharof shows the scars of recent volcanic activity. Mount Peulik (4,835 feet) leaks gasses from rocks at its foot near the southern shore of Becharof Lake. In 1977, violent eruptions formed the shallow, broad, low-rimmed craters of Ukinrek Maars, also near the lake.

Hunters score an unusually high success rate with bears and caribou. Wildlife observers and photographers are common human visitors. Motorboats, snowmobiles, and small airplanes are allowed, and camping is unrestricted, although bear precautions are in order. Summer temperatures may rise into the 70s. Rainfall has reached 160 inches per year on the Pacific side of the Alaska Peninsula.

ALASKA

Becharof Essentials

Size: 400,000 acres.
Year Designated: 1980.
Location: Southwestern Alaska.
Easiest Access: Fly in by small chartered aircraft from King Salmon.
Season: Fog, drizzle, and ceaseless winds are common all summer and fall, which is when most people visit.

Wilderness Fees/Permits: None, although hunting and fishing are regulated. Check with the refuge manager.
Maps: USGS 1:250,000 topographic maps are Karluk, Mount Katmai, Naknek, and Ugashik.
Management: Becharof National Wildlife Refuge, P.O. Box 277, King Salmon, AK 99613; (907) 246-3339.

Bering Sea Wilderness

The 170,000-acre Bering Sea Unit of the Alaska Maritime National Wildlife Refuge includes about 25 islands and headlands in the Norton Sound, the seabird and seal rookeries on the Pribilof Islands, Hagemeister Island near the coast west of Dillingham, and other smaller islands in the Bering Sea. The Saint Matthew Island Group, consisting of Saint Matthew and small nearby Hall and Pinnacle Islands, has been designated Wilderness. One of the largest seabird concentrations in the North Pacific (3.5 million birds) can be found here in summer, dominated by auklets, common eiders, old-squaws, gulls, murres, and puffins.

Geographically, this Wilderness is the most isolated in all of America, a beautiful land formed by volcanic activity, rising more than 1,500 feet above the sea with sheer cliffs and waterfalls dropping dramatically into icy water. The annual average for visiting ships is fewer than one. On Saint Matthew you'll find one of the few colonies of northern fulmars on Earth, and almost the entire world's population of McKay's buntings nest here. Northern sea lions and seals haul out at several places, and walruses climb ashore at one spot on Saint Matthew. Reindeer, once introduced here, have disappeared. Arctic foxes den here, and polar bears, practically wiped out by hunting, wander over from the mainland occasionally on the winter ice pack. Gray whales are often seen offshore, and sometimes an endangered bowhead whale swims by in winter.

Bering Sea Essentials

Size: 81,340 acres.
Year Designated: 1970.
Location: One hundred twenty miles off the coast of western Alaska.
Easiest Access: The Wilderness islands are extremely rugged and inaccessible. Ocean swells, raging tides, high winds, and rocky shorelines with poor anchorages make visitation difficult. Private charter vessels are available. Contact the refuge manager.
Season: Summer.

Wilderness Fees/Permits: Usually none. Visitation may be restricted due to fragile nesting bird colonies, especially in spring when most of the birds lay their eggs. Check with the refuge manager.
Maps: Nautical charts of the Bering Sea. USGS 1:250,000 topographic map is Saint Matthew.
Management: Bering Sea Unit, Alaska Maritime National Wildlife Refuge, 2355 Kachemak Bay Drive, Suite 101, Homer, AK 99603; (907) 235-6546.

ALASKA

Bogoslof Island Wilderness

Aleuts believed that they heard the "voice of God" (*bogoslof*) as a fiery eruption lifted Bogoslof Island from the cold Bering Sea around 1796. Bogoslof and little Fire Island (about five acres) became Wilderness in 1970 and a subunit of the Aleutian Islands Unit of the Alaska Maritime National Wildlife Refuge in 1980. An active volcanic island, Bogoslof has undergone change as recently as 1993. A single rugged spire, Castle Rock, stands above the island's rocky beaches and black lava. Vegetation on this domed and treeless isle is typical of the Aleutians: grasses, sedges, heath. As many as 90,000 murres, kittiwakes, puffins, and gulls nest here. A rookery of fur seals has grown in size, while a sea lion rookery that peaked with about 5,000 individuals has shrunk.

North of Unalaska Island, Bogoslof is difficult to access and rarely seen except over the gunwales of passing fishing boats. Winds blow almost constantly during cool foggy summers and mild foggy winters. Although the Bering Sea does not freeze here, storms come often and remain long, violently hurling wind and waves against the barren shoreline. The few boats that do arrive find no anchorages, coming only at risk and with special permission of the refuge manager for scientific or educational purposes.

Bogoslof Island Essentials

Size: 175 acres.
Year Designated: 1970.
Location: Off the coast of southwestern Alaska.
Easiest Access: Unalaska is the nearest accessible village, about 800 air miles from Anchorage.
Season: June and July.

Wilderness Fees/Permits: A special-use permit is required. Check with the refuge manager.
Maps: Nautical charts of the Bering Sea. USGS 1:250,000 topographic map is Umnak.
Management: Bogoslof Island Unit, Alaska Maritime National Wildlife Refuge, 2355 Kachemak Bay Drive, Suite 101, Homer, AK 99603; (907) 235-6546.

Chamisso Island Wilderness

Northernmost of five units of the Alaska Maritime National Wildlife Refuge, the Chukchi Sea Unit contains about 200,000 acres on and off of 500 miles of Alaska's northwestern coast. A small subunit of the Chukchi Sea Unit, Chamisso Island and nearby Puffin Island, were combined as a wildlife refuge in 1912, designated Wilderness in 1975, and added to the AMNWR in 1980.

Chamisso has one large sand spit and a low beach zone surrounding a covering of tundra with a few marshy bogs. Although Chamisso Island is much larger, Puffin Island houses many more nesting birds, especially horned puffins, black-legged kittiwakes, and thick-billed murres who build their nests on the steep-walled cliffs that fall into Spafarief Bay. An unusual sight is horned puffins digging burrows in which to lay their eggs, much like tufted puffins do. Eskimos still cross from the mainland to gather eggs, primarily from kittiwakes and murres.

Nothing lives on the islands except for birds and the occasional fox that wanders over on the frozen sea in winter. Walruses, seals, and whales often may be seen in Spafarief Bay. Boating is dangerous due to frequent storms that blow in during cool summers and frigid winters. Daylight never leaves in mid-June and appears briefly as twilight in mid-December.

Chamisso Island Essentials
Size: 455 acres.
Year Designated: 1975.
Location: In Kotzebue Sound off the coast of northwestern Alaska.
Easiest Access: Via a dangerous boat ride from the nearest village, Kotzebue, on the mainland.
Season: June to September.
Wilderness Fees/Permits: Some activities may require a special-use permit. Humans, for instance, are only allowed with a special permit during spring nesting season. Check with the refuge manager.
Maps: USGS 1:63,360 topographic maps are Selawik A-6 and Selawik B-6.
Management: Chukchi Sea Unit, Alaska Maritime National Wildlife Refuge, 2355 Kachemak Bay Drive, Suite 101, Homer, AK 99603; (907) 235-6546.

Chuck River Wilderness

You will find few better examples of the old-growth rain forest that once extended gloriously from California to Alaska than here in Chuck River Wilderness on the mainland coast of southeast Alaska. The U.S. Forest Service describes this area as "one of the last northern mainland stands of riparian spruce forest along a major river not entered with roads or logging activity." The Chuck River flows out of the heart of the area northward to empty into lovely Windham Bay where the Chuck Mining Camp once operated. Windham Bay opens off Stephens Passage and is a relatively popular destination for recreational boaters and small tour boat operators. An eight-mile trail from the bay follows the river valley up to its end. A second trail, approximately 10 miles long, leaves the bay to end at Placer Lakes near the Wilderness's eastern boundary, which abuts Tracy Arm–Fords Terror Wilderness (see below). Elevations range from sea level to about 5,000 feet on the eastern boundary. The region is a major producer of salmon, especially pink salmon, which are commercially harvested here in great numbers. Black bears and mountain goats are known to live in the forested mountains.

Chuck River Essentials
Size: 72,503 acres.
Year Designated: 1990.
Location: Southeastern Alaska.
Easiest Access: From Juneau or Petersburg, take a boat south or north, respectively, to Windham Bay.
Season: Summer.
Wilderness Fees/Permits: None.
Maps: USGS 1:250,000 topographic map is Sumdum.
Management: Chatham Area, Tongass National Forest, 204 Siginaka Way, Sitka, AK 99835; (907) 747-6671.

ALASKA

Coronation Island Wilderness

Rising to almost 2,000 forested feet above the sea, Coronation Island stands off the west coast of Prince of Wales Island, south of Kuiu Island and north of Noyes Island. Stands of tall Sitka spruce and western hemlock dominate the island and extend to the shoreline, which in places falls away at sheer cliffs. Understory vegetation is lush and varied.

Known for its seabird populations that nest or just stop to rest here, Coronation's inhabitants also include wolves and Sitka black-tailed deer, black bears, and bald eagles. Sea otters, sea lions, seals, and seasonal humpback whales are common off the shore.

Strong prevailing winds from the open sea and a ragged coastline make the windward side of the island virtually inaccessible. On the leeward side you'll find some protected coves and beaches guarded by rocky shoals that make all approaches risky. Wilderness camping is unrestricted, but bring along your own firewood—under a constant canopy of foggy skies, the wood here never dries out. Fishing and hunting are allowed.

Coronation Island Essentials

Size: 19,232 acres.
Year Designated: 1980.
Location: Southeastern Alaska.
Easiest Access: Coronation is 110 air miles from Ketchikan. Charter floatplanes are available in Ketchikan, but landing may be impossible. Catching a boat from Craig is a better idea, but sea travel around the island is usually hazardous.
Season: A temperate maritime climate makes the weather relatively mild year-round. However, summers are definitely warmer and offer a greater chance for sunshine as well as calmer seas.
Wilderness Fees/Permits: None.
Maps: Nautical charts of southeastern Alaska. A tide table is a must for boaters. USGS 1:63,360 topographic maps are Craig D-7 and Craig D-8.
Management: Thorne Bay Ranger District, Tongass National Forest, P.O. Box 1, Thorne Bay, AK 99919; (907) 828-3304.

Denali Wilderness

Native Athabascans have always referred to Mount McKinley as *Denali*, or "The High One." The mammoth mountain is the centerpiece of Denali National Park Wilderness, which comprises about one-third of Denali National Park and Preserve. Formerly known as Mount McKinley National Park, it was established first as a wildlife refuge in 1917, then designated Wilderness in 1980 at the same time the size of the park was tripled and the name was changed. At six million acres, the entire unit is now bigger than the state of Massachusetts.

The Wilderness encompasses the high heart of the Alaska Range, including Mount McKinley. At 20,320 feet, McKinley is the highest point in North America and the tallest mountain on Earth when measured from base to summit. I have reached this unspeakably magnificent summit twice on three expeditions. My two short but infinitely worthwhile visits to the top were both via

ALASKA

the West Buttress, by far the most popular route up the mountain. A long ascent of the Kahiltna Glacier is followed by the steepest section of the route, the headwall from 14,000 feet to 16,000 feet. Then travel proceeds along a thin-topped ridge to a plateau at 17,000 feet; from here, it is a relatively steep climb to Denali Pass. The route continues at a much less severe angle from the pass to finish in a push up the last dome-like rise to the summit. At least two weeks of high-altitude walking is required for most climbs. While climbing on the West Buttress is not technically demanding, it is as cold as you can imagine and then some.

Mountaineers have long been irresistibly drawn to this fabulous land of perpetual snow and danger. The upthrust of the range creates its own weather, usually frigid and windy, with clouds that hide the mountains as much as 75 percent of the time. On the northern slopes of the Alaska Range, the Wilderness drops to tundra, a world of dwarf shrubs and miniature wildflowers adapted to the short growing season. Tundra gives way to *taiga*, a Russian word for "land of little sticks," and here scant tree growth lines many miles of river.

Tundra and taiga provide homes for 37 recorded species of mammals, including Dall sheep, caribou, grizzly bears, and moose. Smaller mammals include foxes, weasels, lynx, martens, marmots, pikas, voles, and lemmings. Flowering plants number more than 430 species, and 159 species of birds have been sighted, including the ptarmigan, which changes from brown to snow-white. Denali remains a subarctic Wilderness of unparalleled proportions.

Denali Essentials

Size: 1,900,000 acres.
Year Designated: 1980.
Location: Southern central Alaska.
Easiest Access: The park entrance lies 240 miles north of Anchorage and 120 miles south of Fairbanks on a road that stays open all year.
Season: Summers are cool, wet, and windy with a chance of snow. The rest of the year gets mostly wintry weather.
Wilderness Fees/Permits: A $3 fee is charged to everyone entering the park. Special permits must be purchased by those who want to climb Mount McKinley and Mount Foraker. Climbers must contact the Talkeetna Ranger Station, Box 588, Talkeetna, AK 99676; (907) 733-2231. The climbing fee is currently $150 per person.
Maps: USGS 1:63,360 topographic maps may be purchased from the park rangers for $2.50 each. USGS 1:250,000 topographic maps are Healy, Kantishna River, Mount McKinley, and Talkeetna. An excellent climber's map is available for $12.50.
Management: Denali National Park and Preserve, P.O. Box 9, Denali Park, AK 99755; (907) 683-2686.

Endicott River Wilderness

Between Glacier Bay and Lynn Canal, the Endicott River is born in the broad brush-covered flats within the Chilkat Mountains of Tongass National Forest. The river flows easterly, down a deep glacier-carved canyon to the salt water of Lynn Canal. At 5,280 feet, Mount Young stands above the rest of this Wilderness in the northwestern portion near the 40-mile boundary it shares with Glacier Bay National Park. Above timberline is the high country, a region of active glaciers extending south and west that drops into short alpine trees and thick brush in the upper drainage of the river. Along the river you'll find mighty coastal trees, a dense rain forest of spruce and hemlock interspersed with boggy muskegs typical of southeastern Alaska, deluged by an average rainfall of 92 inches each year.

Brown and black bears, mountain goats, and a few moose live here. Black-tailed deer are present, but heavy snowfall limits their numbers. Within the river, chum, coho, and pink salmon abound during the spawning season, drawing bald eagles in profusion. I have counted 100 eagles from the seat of a Boston whaler anchored just offshore in the canal near the mouth of the Endicott River, their clumps of dark feathers fluffed against the drizzling rain.

There are no trails, but sturdy backpacking will take you up along the waterway and over a low pass into Glacier Bay National Park. You will probably see no other humans. Avalanche danger runs high in winter. Camping is unrestricted, but building campfires is difficult work due to persistent rain. Firearms are permitted.

Endicott River Essentials

Size: 98,729 acres.
Year Designated: 1980.
Location: Southeastern Alaska.
Easiest Access: From Haines, take a boat to the confluence of the Endicott River and Lynn Canal. Storms can often make the boating treacherous and difficult for visitors. Travel about 2.5 miles by foot along the river to the eastern edge of the Wilderness. Small planes are sometimes able to land on a bar near the river's mouth.
Season: May through September, with fall being especially wet.
Wilderness Fees/Permits: None.
Maps: USGS 1:250,000 topo map is Juneau.
Management: Chatham Area, Tongass National Forest, 204 Siginaka Way, Sitka, AK 99835; (907) 747-6671.

Forrester Island Wilderness

During the day you'll ask yourself how more than one million birds of 13 species could be nesting here. But at night vast populations of Leach's storm petrels, fork-tailed petrels, Cassin's auklets, and rhinoceros auklets leave their underground burrows to feed in the ocean around the isolated islands of Forrester, Lowrie, and Petrel. An estimated 780,000 storm petrels nest on Petrel Island alone. These islands and numerous nearby rocks were established as a wildlife refuge in 1912, and were designated Wilderness in 1970. In 1980 they were added as a subunit of the 475,000-acre Gulf of Alaska Unit of the Alaska Maritime National Wildlife Refuge, at the southeastern end of the state.

Forrester Island itself lies under a heavy forest of spruce and hemlock with a few lodgepole pine and red cedar bordering open muskegs. In small ravines and in areas of windfall on this mountainous piece of land the thick scrub, a web of berry bushes and devil's club, discourages travel. The shoreline has many sheer cliffs and few beaches, as does the shoreline of Petrel Island, which is also heavily forested. The nearby Lowrie Islands lie essentially flat.

To schedule your visit for the best time, avoid the spring nesting season. Almost all the available soil contains lengthy burrows, and one false step could end many of the lives developing within buried eggs.

ALASKA

Forrester Island Essentials

Size: 2,832 acres.
Year Designated: 1970.
Location: Southeastern Alaska.
Easiest Access: With no maintained anchorages or airstrips, these islands are only accessible by boat, usually coming from Craig.
Season: May through September.

Wilderness Fees/Permits: Restrictions may apply. Contact the refuge manager.
Maps: USGS 1:63,360 topographic map is Dixon Entrance D-5.
Management: Gulf of Alaska Unit, Alaska Maritime National Wildlife Refuge, 2355 Kachemak Bay Drive, Suite 101, Homer, AK 99603; (907) 235-6546.

Gates of the Arctic Wilderness

When Bob Marshall explored this region in the early 1930s, two looming peaks near the head of the North Fork of the Koyukuk River (Boreal Mountain and Frigid Crags) left a lasting impression on him. He dubbed them "The Gates of the Arctic." Straddling the central Brooks Range and looming entirely above the Arctic Circle, the 8.5-million-acre Gates of the Arctic National Park and Preserve protects a mass of land four times larger than Yellowstone National Park. The park is managed primarily as Wilderness.

On the south slopes visitors will find a sampling of thin boreal forest. The ragged, majestic peaks of the Brooks Range invite exploration and give way northward to rolling tundra, too far north for many trees to grow, where barren-ground caribou travel in huge herds and grizzly bears roam away their solitary lives. Moose, wolves, Dall sheep, black bears, and smaller mammals share the park. Eagles and hawks soar overhead. On the extreme northern verge the land is polar desert, one of the driest places on Earth.

Remote glacier-carved valleys split the range, drained by clear rivers and dotted with alpine lakes. Anglers head here for the grayling, char, and chum salmon often found in abundance in the rivers. Although no established trails exist, backpacking is becoming increasingly popular in Gates of the Arctic. Many hikers carry a firearm for protection from bears, but attacks are uncommon. Climbers are attracted to the Arrigetch Peaks and Mount Igikpak. Sport hunting and trapping is allowed on the preserve section. Although camping is unrestricted, wood is scarce and campfires are discouraged.

Waterways suitable for floating or paddling are seemingly endless and include all or part of six Wild and Scenic Rivers: all 83 miles of the Alatna River, which roars out of the Arrigetch Peaks; all 52 miles of the crystalline John River; all 110 miles of the Kobuk River, with its sweeping vistas of the Brooks Range; all 102 miles of the North Fork of the Koyukuk River, running through a glacier-carved valley; part of the 330 miles of the Noatak River, the longest member of the Wild and Scenic family in America; and all 44 miles of the remote and seldom visited Tinayguk River.

Gates of the Arctic Essentials

Size: 7,052,000 acres.
Year Designated: 1980.
Location: Northern central Alaska.
Easiest Access: Most visitors are dropped off by floatplane from Bettles or Anaktuvuk Pass. Ranger stations are maintained in both villages. Guide services are available.
Season: August usually brings rain, and June and July are thick with mosquitoes. Temperatures may drop to freezing at any time.

Wilderness Fees/Permits: None. An Alaska State license is required for fishing, which is true for most of the state.
Maps: USGS 1:250,000 topographic maps are Ambler River, Chandalar, Chandler Lake, Hughes, Killik River, Philip Smith Mountains, Survey Pass, and Wiseman.
Management: Gates of the Arctic National Park and Preserve, P.O. Box 74680, Fairbanks, AK 99707; (907) 456-0281.

Glacier Bay Wilderness

In 1794, when Captain George Vancouver sailed through Icy Strait west of present-day Juneau, Alaska, the entrance to today's Glacier Bay was a wall of ice that extended more than 100 miles northward. By 1916, the ice had retreated 65 to 70 miles and the bay was formed. The glaciers continue to retreat on the bay's eastern and southeastern sides, but they have begun to grow on the western side. Some of the world's greatest tidewater glaciers exist in Glacier Bay, at least 12 of them still calving (breaking off) into salt water. The park section of 3.28-million-acre Glacier Bay National Park and Preserve has been designated Wilderness.

Surrounded by a spectacular, glaciated horseshoe rim of mountains, the bay is sheltered by the Fairweather Range to the west and the Saint Elias Mountains on the north. The highest peaks, topped by Mount Fairweather at 15,300 feet, stand almost three miles above the sea and attract intrepid mountaineers. No trails exist, but backpacking is growing increasingly popular, often along numerous icy streams sometimes welcoming and sometimes choked with brush. Brown and black bears are numerous on shore. Firearms are not permitted in the park section.

Most visitors see the Wilderness by boat, and the sea kayaking ranks among the best in the world. The main bay divides into East and West Arms, which are split into many inlets. The water is dotted with islands, and the paddling goes on and on in eye-aching splendor. Beardslee Islands are noted especially for their excellent beach camping. Marble Islands have the most seabird colonies and are closed to human traffic from the first of May until the first of September. Whales, seals, sea lions, and porpoises are usually seen in the cold plankton-rich sea. Expect rain and strong wind interspersed with cool temperatures under cloudy skies.

ALASKA

Glacier Bay Essentials

Size: 2,770,000 acres.
Year Designated: 1980.
Location: Southeastern Alaska.
Easiest Access: Flights and boats from Juneau arrive in Gustavus, where bus service is available to park headquarters at Bartlett Cove. Tour-guides and kayak rentals are available.
Season: Mid-May through mid-September with spring and early summer offering the best weather. Midsummer is ideal for whale watching.
Wilderness Fees/Permits: Visitors are required to obtain a free permit to enter the park. When you register for backcountry use, you will be issued a bear-proof food canister, which you must carry at all times.
Maps: Nautical charts of Glacier Bay and USGS topographic maps are available from the Alaska National History Association in Gustavus; call (907) 697-2230. Sixteen USGS topographic maps (1:63,360 scale) are required to cover the entire shoreline ($2.50 each). USGS 1:250,000 topographic maps are Juneau, Mount Fairweather, Skagway, and Yakutat.
Management: Glacier Bay National Park and Preserve, Gustavus, AK 99826; (907) 697-2231.

Hazy Islands Wilderness

The former Hazy Islands National Wildlife Refuge, established in 1912, was designated Wilderness in 1970 and incorporated as a subunit into the Alaska Maritime National Wildlife Refuge, Gulf of Alaska Unit, in 1980. Far offshore, beaten by wind and wave, Big Hazy Island and her four smaller sisters stick out of the frigid sea, providing predator-free nesting areas for large populations of common murres, pigeon guillemots, glaucous-winged gulls, horned puffins, and tufted puffins. Brandt's cormorants nest here, one of only two islands they inhabit in Alaska.

Remote, without anchorages or campsites, beaten by frequent storms under high winds, the rocks called Hazy Islands are seldom seen and human visitation is discouraged to protect the birds and the humans. This is Alaska's smallest Wilderness area.

Hazy Islands Essentials

Size: 32 acres.
Year Designated: 1970.
Location: Southeastern Alaska.
Easiest Access: About 10 miles west of Coronation Island, Hazy Islands can be seen from the air by a small plane departing from Sitka, Ketchikan, Petersburg, or Wrangell. Visitors can also approach carefully by boat.
Season: May through September.
Wilderness Fees/Permits: Regulations restrict visitation during spring nesting season. Contact the refuge manager.
Maps: USGS 1:250,000 topographic map is Craig.
Management: Gulf of Alaska Unit, Alaska Maritime National Wildlife Refuge, 2355 Kachemak Bay Drive, Suite 101, Homer, AK 99603; (907) 235-6546.

ALASKA

Innoko Wilderness

Along the eastern bank of the Yukon River, bordered on the north by the Khotol Hills and the south and east by the Kuskokwim Mountains, Innoko National Wildlife Refuge is split into two huge halves that together contain 3.85 million acres. The southeastern portion of the refuge, roughly one-third of the total area, has been designated Wilderness. A transition zone between the boreal forestland of interior Alaska and the open tundra of western Alaska, Innoko stands well over half in wetlands of muskeg and marsh, lakes, meandering rivers, and streams dotted with islands of black spruce and an understory of mosses, lichens, and shrubs.

Paper birch and white spruce cover hills rolling up from the Yukon and Innoko Rivers, and along the rivers you'll find numerous privately owned subsistence camps used periodically for hunting and fishing by Native Alaskans. The rivers, bound with willows and alder, run rich with salmon, whitefish, sheefish, grayling, and northern pike. All the lakes have northern pike except the shallow bodies of water that freeze to the bottom in winter.

More than 20,000 beavers live in these wetlands, the densest population in the state, along with moose and caribou, black and brown bears, red foxes, coyotes, lynx, otters, wolves, and wolverines. An estimated 65,000 white-fronted and lesser Canada geese spend their summers here with more than 380,000 other waterfowl and shorebirds, including pintails, scaups, shovelers, scoters, widgeons, red-necked grebes, lesser yellowlegs, and Hudsonian godwits. Hungry mosquitoes cloud the summer landscape.

Of the few human visitors, moose hunters are the most common. They find no trails, no facilities, and no immediate aid from the refuge staff of seven permanent employees who live 70 air miles away. Camping is unrestricted, except on private inholdings. Campfires are permitted, and firewood is abundant.

You could get rained on anytime in spring, summer, or fall, and temperatures could drop to freezing any night of the year. Winter temperatures sometimes reach 60 degrees below zero Fahrenheit. From May through July light is almost constant, and the sun never sets in mid-June. In mid-December the sun never rises. If you come, bring rubber boots for walking. You'll need binoculars for observing all the wildlife—except the mosquitoes, of course, which are inescapable.

Innoko Essentials

Size: 1,240,000 acres.
Year Designated: 1980.
Location: Southwestern central Alaska.
Easiest Access: Chartered aircraft arrive regularly from Anchorage, Bethel, and Galena, but most often from McGrath.
Season: June through September for foot and boat traffic within the refuge. September is the time to come for moose hunting.
Wilderness Fees/Permits: None for backcountry visitation. Permits are required for hunting or fishing. Contact the Innoko refuge manager for more details.
Maps: USGS 1:250,000 topographic maps are Holy Cross, Iditarod, Nulato, Ophir, and Unalakleet.
Management: Innoko National Wildlife Refuge, Box 69, McGrath, AK 99627; (907) 524-3251.

ALASKA

Izembek Wilderness

On the tip of the Alaska Peninsula, 320,893-acre Izembek National Wildlife Refuge sees a quarter-million migratory birds land every fall, including the entire world's population of black brants and thousands of Canada and emperor geese, ducks, and shorebirds. Izembek Lagoon (5 by 30 miles) contains one of the largest eelgrass beds in the world, providing food and shelter for migratory birds. Tundra swans live on the refuge year-round. Gray, minke, and killer whales migrate along the coast by the thousands. Sea otters are the most common inhabitants of the lagoon. Hundreds of thousands of salmon begin and end their life cycles on the refuge. The brown bear habitat is unparalleled, and caribou wander through in herds. Smoking volcanoes and glaciated mountains tower over lakes and meandering rivers that drain into lagoons opening on the Bering Sea. The castlelike Aghileen Pinnacles form a portion of the boundary between Izembek and the Alaska Peninsula National Wildlife Refuge.

Hunting and fishing draw many visitors. No maintained trails exist, and the terrain can be rugged. All of the refuge has been designated Wilderness, except the land along a gravel road system and several private inholdings.

Izembek Essentials

Size: 300,000 acres.
Year Designated: 1980.
Location: At the tip of southwestern Alaska.
Easiest Access: Flights from Anchorage land regularly in Cold Bay. Forty miles of gravel road from Cold Bay enter the refuge.
Season: September and October are spectacular times to visit, but the refuge is famous for weather dominated by wind, rain, and fog.
Wilderness Fees/Permits: None for backcountry visitation. Hunting and fishing are strictly regulated. Check with the Izembek refuge manager for more details.
Maps: USGS 1:250,000 topographic map is Cold Bay.
Management: Izembek National Wildlife Refuge, P.O. Box 127, Cold Bay, AK 99571; (907) 532-2445.

Karta River Wilderness

Karta Bay, one of the western extensions off the head of Kasaan Bay, forms the eastern border of Karta River Wilderness on east-central Prince of Wales Island. The area includes the drainage of the Karta River system (which empties into the southwest corner of Karta Bay) and two major lakes, Salmon and Karta. Fire burned the area around the turn of the century, but second-growth spruce and hemlock stand an average of 60 feet tall. One of Alaska's most recent additions to the National Wilderness Preservation System, Karta River Wilderness is best known for large salmon runs and the scenic quality of the large river drainage system. Wildlife fills the area, including black bears, black-tailed deer, beavers, otters, minks, martens, and weasels. Trumpeter swams are commonly seen on the river. Native Americans, particularly the Haida, historically lived around the bay and utilized the rich food sources of this area.

51

ALASKA

Karta River Essentials

Size: 38,046 acres.
Year Designated: 1990.
Location: Southeastern Alaska.
Easiest Access: Approximately 42 air miles northwest of Ketchikan. Most visitors come by floatplane or boat.
Season: Cloud and drizzle are common year-round. August promises more sun and less rain.

Wilderness Fees/Permits: None.
Maps: Detailed maps of the Prince of Wales Island are available from the district ranger for $3. USGS 1:250,000 topographic map is Craig.
Management: Ketchikan Ranger District, Tongass National Forest, 3031 Tongass Avenue, Ketchikan, AK 99901; (907) 225-2148.

Katmai Wilderness

In June of 1912, a week of severe earthquakes preceded the dramatic eruption of Novarupta Volcano. Hot pumice and ash were ejected in such quantities that a haze darkened the sky over most of the Northern Hemisphere. Trees were carbonized by blasts of superheated wind and gas. When Novarupta quieted, more than 40 square miles of lush green Alaska lay buried under ash as deep as 700 feet. The eruption was at least 10 times more violent than that of Mount Saint Helens in 1980. No one was killed because no one was anywhere nearby. Innumerable small holes and cracks appeared in the Novarupta ash, and gas and steam rose into the air. When Robert Griggs explored the region in 1916 on behalf of the National Geographic Society, he called it "The Valley of 10,000 Smokes."

Today 15 active volcanoes line Shelikof Strait, which separates Katmai National Park and Preserve from Kodiak Island. Katmai protects this volcanic "laboratory" and, equally important, large numbers of brown bears. (Although brown and grizzly bears are considered the same species, grizzlies live at least 100 miles from shore and don't grow to be as huge, due to a more limited diet.) Salmon spawn in Katmai in vast numbers, attracting the bears. Here you'll find huge lakes whose edges provide nesting spots for swans, ducks, loons, and grebes. The area is shared by moose and caribou and numerous smaller mammals. A campground exists inside the park, and preregistration is required. The campground has water, pit toilets, food-storage caches, fire pits (but firewood is limited), and picnic tables. Meals are available at nearby Brooks Lodge. Most of Katmai National Park has been designated Wilderness, and very little of it is ever seen by human eyes.

Katmai Essentials

Size: 3,473,000 acres.
Year Designated: 1980.
Location: Southwestern Alaska.
Easiest Access: Flights from Anchorage, 290 air miles away, serve the village of King Salmon, which lies about six miles from the park's western side. Charter flights from King Salmon.
Season: Visitors and mosquitoes are thickest in summer, when the sun typically shines about one day in five.

Wilderness Fees/Permits: A free backcountry permit must be picked up from the park ranger.
Maps: USGS 1:250,000 topographic maps are Afognak, Iliamna, Karluk, Mount Katmai, and Naknek.
Management: Katmai National Park and Preserve, P.O. Box 7, King Salmon, AK 99613; (907) 246-3305.

ALASKA

Kenai Wilderness

For almost 100 years, the Kenai Peninsula has attracted hunters of moose, Dall sheep, and other wild game. In 1941 President Roosevelt designated more than 1.7 million acres as the Kenai National Moose Range. In 1980 the Moose Range was expanded to almost two million acres, renamed the Kenai National Wildlife Refuge, and well over half of it was designated Wilderness. The area comprises the western slopes of the Kenai Mountains with their ancient glaciers rising to 6,612 feet, nine river systems (many originating from the expansive Harding Ice Field), and the spruce-birch lowland forest that extends to the shores of Cook Inlet.

Unlike most of Alaska's wildlands, Kenai lies near Anchorage and draws scores of human visitors to its scenic grandeur (only 17 wildlife refuges in the entire United States receive more visitors). More than 200 miles of established trails give access to much of the backcountry. Driving south from Anchorage on the Sterling Highway, at milepost 56.9, you'll find the scenic Fuller Lakes Trail, 5.5 miles round-trip with a high point of 1,690 feet. From Fuller Lakes you can bushwhack into wildlife-rich lands. Hundreds of splendid small lakes are accessible through a system of canoe trails, including the popular Swanson River Canoe Trail. Fishing brings many people to the area, including fly-ins to more remote lakes. Motorized boats are allowed on the larger lakes but not on the canoe trails. Kenai produces an abundant crop of wild berries. I went primarily to walk on the fascinating Harding Ice Field, a trip requiring an ice ax, crampons, and the ability to catch your breath when exposed to breathtaking views. The Harding is a barren, broken expanse of ice, not for the unprepared and inexperienced. Brown bears are relatively scarce here except in the less-visited places. Many species of mammals and birds call Kenai home. The howling of wolves often breaks the night stillness. Be prepared for insects.

Kenai Essentials

Size: 1,350,000 acres.
Year Designated: 1980.
Location: Southern central Alaska.
Easiest Access: The northern Wilderness boundary is only 20 air miles from Anchorage, but most people drive the 110 miles along State Highway 1 to the visitors center near Soldotna.
Season: The ice breaks up on the low lakes in May and on the high lakes in July. Snow covers the ground by November. Late summer and fall are the wettest seasons.

Wilderness Fees/Permits: Certain activities may require a special-use permit. Check with the refuge manager.
Maps: A free map without much detail is available from the refuge manager. USGS 1:250,000 topographic maps are Kenai, Seldovia, and Seward.
Management: Kenai National Wildlife Refuge, P.O. Box 2139, Soldotna, AK 99669; (907) 262-7021.

ALASKA

Kobuk Valley Wilderness

Here in 1.7-million-acre Kobuk Valley National Park, 26 miles north of the Arctic Circle and enclosed by the Baird and Waring Mountains, the climate has changed little (or not at all) since the late Pleistocene era. Remnant flora grow as reminders of the vast Arctic steppe tundra that once bridged present-day Alaska and Asia. At the western end of the Brooks Range, where the mountains descend gently toward the Chukchi Sea, the park contains a transition zone between boreal forestland and open tundra. Strangely out of place, 25 square miles of the crescent-shaped Great Kobuk Sand Dunes shift in Arctic winds. Summer temperatures may rise above 100 degrees Fahrenheit.

The park lies along the valley of the central Kobuk River which, along with all of the 70 miles of the Wild and Scenic Salmon River, attracts canoeists and kayakers in search of easy scenic paddling. The banks of the Salmon are lined with colorful gravel and surrounded by strikingly scenic terrain, while the clear waters are teeming with its namesake fish. A boreal forest lines most of the valley. Great herds of caribou still migrate across the park in summer and winter. Archaeological sites dating back 12,000 years give evidence of long human occupation, and Onion Portage on the Kobuk River, with 30 layers of artifacts, is considered one of the most significant sites in America.

The ancients who inhabited this region were hunter-gatherers, and today's Eskimos harvest caribou, moose, bears, fish, waterfowl, and many edible and medicinal plants from this far northern Wilderness. Lacking road and trail, Kobuk allows fishing but no sport hunting. Camping is unrestricted except on archaeological sites and the many private inholdings that dot the land, especially along the river. Motorized boats and small aircraft are allowed in the park.

Kobuk Valley Essentials

Size: 190,000 acres.
Year Designated: 1980.
Location: Northwestern Alaska.
Easiest Access: Regular flights from Anchorage and Fairbanks land in Kotzebue. Local air and boat service is available to park visitors.
Season: June through September for foot and boat traffic.
Wilderness Fees/Permits: None.
Maps: USGS 1:250,000 topographic maps are Ambler River, Baird Mountains, Selawik, and Shungnak.
Management: Kobuk Valley National Park, P.O. Box 1029, Kotzebue, AK 99752; (907) 442-3890.

Kootznoowoo (Admiralty Island) Wilderness

Native Tlingit know Admiralty Island by the name *Kootznoowoo*, or "Fortress of Bears," and for thousands of years Native Americans have prospered among its rich natural resources. Sheer remoteness and dense coastal forests of Sitka spruce, Sitka alder, and western hemlock have created the "fortress," and even today massive Alaskan brown bears outnumber the human inhabitants of Admiralty. Sitka black-tailed deer abound, and bald eagles (the greatest concentration in the world) nest in trees along the rockbound shoreline, with the densest population usually found in

ALASKA

Seymour Canal on the eastern side of the island. According to estimates, there are two bald eagles for every one brown bear. The British named the island Admiralty, but the Russians called it *Ostrov Kutsnoi* ("Fear Island"). Seals, sea lions, and whales play offshore year-round, visited periodically by swans and other migratory waterfowl. The forest floor rolls gently and lays thickly covered with undergrowth, and muskegs occasionally open the tall forest canopy. Rocky spires break through along the island's high crest with peaks at about 2,000 feet. Protected as Admiralty Island National Monument in 1978, all but the northern end of the island has been designated Wilderness.

A 26-mile cross-island canoe and kayak trail, including seven miles of portages, is open all year, connecting a complex of lakes and streams between Mole Harbor and Mitchell Bay. Sea kayaking along the coastline of the island provides views of excellent scenery and endless wildlife. About 25 miles of marked foot trails join the eight major lakes in this region of the island. Seven trail cabins and 12 remote recreational cabins are available for rent on Admiralty Island. Human visitors often legally carry a firearm because it makes them feel better about the prospect of running into bears. I carried a firearm here, and I felt safer, although the only bear I spotted eyed me suspiciously and left me alone.

The land still sustains around 450 Tlingit who live in the village of Angoon on the island's western side at the mouth of Mitchell Bay. Visitors must respect the personal and cultural privacy of the Tlingit as well the natural and fragile wonder of Kootznoowoo.

Kootznoowoo (Admiralty Island) Essentials

Size: 945,569 acres.
Year Designated: 1980.
Location: Southeastern Alaska.
Easiest Access: Angoon, the only village on the island, can be reached by airplane, boat, or ferry from Juneau.
Season: The area is damp most of the year, with summer bringing the most visitors and the warmest temperatures.
Wilderness Fees/Permits: None, unless cabin rental is desired. Cabins require advance registration and cost $25 per night. Contact the Forest Service at (907) 586-8751.
Maps: A canoe and kayak route map is available for $3 from the monument office. USGS 1:250,000 topographic maps are Juneau, Sitka, and Sumdum.
Management: Admiralty Island National Monument, Tongass National Forest, 8461 Old Dairy Road, Juneau, AK 99801; (907) 586-8790.

Koyukuk Wilderness

Think of 3.5-million-acre Koyukuk National Wildlife Refuge, and water comes to mind: there are 14 rivers, hundreds of meandering creeks, more than 15,000 lakes, all forming the floodplain of the Koyukuk River. Surrounding the village of Huslia, the lands of the refuge are still of utmost importance to the native Alaskans who live here. There are no roads and no maintained trails, but the lower Koyukuk River provides a "highway" through the heart of the refuge. Moose are everywhere, as dense a population as any in the state, and hunters record excellent success rates. Brown and black bears wade into the rivers in nightless summer to escape swarms of mosquitoes and other biting insects. Lynx, coyotes, red foxes, wolves, and wolverines are common. Beavers abound, and numerous migratory waterfowl build their nests in the river basin.

West of Huslia, a portion of the refuge is protected as Wilderness, primarily preserving the startling Nogahabara Sand Dunes, which were formed by winds swirling pulverized rock.

Although camping and campfires are permitted, the villagers do not encourage tourism, and there are many private inholdings within the refuge. Fishing and some hunting are allowed although they are subject to restrictions; moose hunting predominates. Motorboats, snowmobiles, and small airplanes are also permitted at the refuge.

Koyukuk Essentials

Size: 400,000 acres.
Year Designated: 1980.
Location: Western central Alaska.
Easiest Access: By air or by boat, from Galena it's approximately 20 miles to the Wilderness's eastern edge.
Season: June through September for foot and boat traffic.
Wilderness Fees/Permits: None for backcountry visitation, but hunting and fishing are strictly regulated. Contact the refuge manager.
Maps: USGS 1:250,000 topographic maps are Hughes, Kateel River, Melozitna, Nulato, and Shungnak to cover the entire refuge.
Management: Koyukuk National Wildlife Refuge, P.O. Box 287, Galena, AK 99741; (907) 656-1231.

Kuiu Wilderness

Bordered on the east by Sumner Strait and on the west by Chatham Strait, Kuiu Wilderness, near the southern end of Kuiu Island, shares a boundary on the north with Tebenkof Bay Wilderness (see below). Three major bays (Port Malmesbury, Port Beauclerc, and Affleck Canal) indent an extensive coastline of smaller bays, coves, and canals that offers many safe anchorages. Several small offshore islands are included in this Wilderness of forest and muskeg. Peaks rise to over 2,000 feet. A portage trail from Affleck Canal crosses the spruce- and hemlock-forested Wilderness to Petrof Bay in Tebenkof. Black bears, wolves, smaller furbearers, and marine mammals share this temperate, wet maritime area with numerous sea, shore, and land birds. Fishery values are high, and fishing boats are common sights in the bays of Kuiu. Recreational use is relatively heavy, with hiking, fishing, and boating attracting the most visitors.

Kuiu Essentials

Size: 60,576 acres.
Year Designated: 1990.
Location: Southeastern Alaska.
Easiest Access: Thirty-five miles south of the community of Kake. Most visitors arrive by boat.
Season: Summer tends to be the driest time to visit.
Wilderness Fees/Permits: None.
Maps: A Kuiu Island map showing canoe and kayak routes is available for $3 from the Forest Service Information Center, Centennial Hall, 101 Egan Drive, Juneau, AK 99801. USGS 1:250,000 topographic maps are Petersburg and Port Alexander.
Management: Stikine Area, Tongass National Forest, P.O. Box 309, Petersburg, AK 99833; (907) 772-3841.

ALASKA

Lake Clark Wilderness

If I could only see one Alaskan Wilderness again, I would probably choose to return to magnificent Lake Clark. I flew down from Anchorage to Port Alsworth in 1983 in a small fixed-wing plane and hiked into the base of Mount Iliamna with dreams of climbing it, but a change in weather kept me low. It was a minor disappointment, barely thought of now among the memories of distant snowcapped peaks, lush forest trails, and hushed expanses of clear water.

Here the Aleutian Range meets the Alaska Range in the Chigmit Mountains, an area known as Alaska's Alps. The mighty rain forest along Cook Inlet rises to alpine tundra and sparkling lakes sheltered by mountain fastnesses. Drainages plunge thunderously down hundreds of waterfalls. Vast numbers of moose, brown and black bears, wolves, wolverines, red foxes, Dall sheep, and caribou make their home here. Slender and 50 miles long, Lake Clark itself reflects tall ragged spires of rock, and salmon and trout run in great numbers. Originally a national monument, Lake Clark's status was changed to National Park and Preserve in 1980, and about two-thirds was designated Wilderness.

Three Wild and Scenic Rivers offer excellent opportunities for travel in the area: 11 miles of the gorgeous Chilikadrotna River with sections of wild white water; 22 miles of the shallow Mulchatna River flowing out of a jewel called Turquoise Lake; and 51 miles of the unsung Tlikakila River, which runs through one of the most fabulous glacial valleys in America. Tlikakila's waters eventually shed into Lake Iliamna, just outside the Wilderness boundary, the only place in the United States where inland seals live.

Two active volcanoes dominate the landscape, visible from the Kenai Peninsula across Cook Inlet: Mount Iliamna (10,016 feet) and Mount Redoubt (10,197 feet). In 1966 Redoubt erupted, spewing ash across Anchorage.

One ranger station exists on Lake Clark itself in the settlement of Port Alsworth, but you'll find no facilities or trails within the Wilderness. Once just a trickle, the number of backpackers has been increasing. Visitors will find few experiences to parallel Lake Clark.

Lake Clark Essentials

Size: 2,470,000 acres.
Year Designated: 1980.
Location: Southwestern Alaska.
Easiest Access: Air charter flights are available from Anchorage, Homer, Kenai, and Iliamna.
Season: June through September.
Wilderness Fees/Permits: None.
Maps: USGS 1:250,000 topographic maps are Iliamna, Kenai, Lake Clark, Lime Hills, Seldovia, and Tyonek.
Management: Lake Clark National Park and Preserve, 4230 University Drive, Suite 311, Anchorage, AK 99508; (907) 271-3751.

ALASKA

Maurelle Islands Wilderness

Maurelle Islands, a group of nearly 30 dots of land rising less than 400 feet above the waves at their highest point, are best known for the abundance of marine mammals that populate their waters: humpback whales, sea otters, sea lions, and seals. Windswept beaches occasionally break the rocky shoreline. Tall stands of Sitka spruce and western hemlock, often tortured by the wind, thickly cover most of the islands. Numerous rocky shoals make boating around the Maurelles potentially dangerous, but the sea kayaking can be worth the risk. Black bears, black-tailed deer, and wolves inhabit the larger islands in limited numbers. Seabirds and bald eagles are commonly seen.

Motorized boats and small floatplanes are permitted to land, and camping is unrestricted. Strong winds and rain can delay pickups for those who have been dropped off, and make campfires difficult to start and maintain.

Maurelle Islands Essentials

Size: 4,937 acres.
Year Designated: 1980.
Location: Off the coast of Southeastern Alaska.
Easiest Access: The Wilderness is situated 73 air miles west of Ketchikan. Flights and ferries are available to the villages of Craig and Klawock on Prince of Wales Island. Boats depart from the villages westward to the Maurelles.
Season: April through August offer the best weather.
Wilderness Fees/Permits: None.
Maps: USGS 1:63,360 topographic maps are Craig C-5 and Craig C-6.
Management: Thorne Bay Ranger District, Tongass National Forest, P.O. Box 1, Thorne Bay, AK 99919; (907) 225-3101.

Misty Fiords Wilderness

Of 2,294,343-acre Misty Fiords National Monument on the southern tip of the Alaska Panhandle, all but about 156,000 acres near the middle have been designated Wilderness. Part of the vast coastal rain forest, the cloud-shrouded monument can get showered with 160 inches of rain annually. The region is marked by deep valleys with steep slopes and sharp intervalley ridges formed by volcanism and carved by glaciation. From the sea the slopes appear to be an unbroken carpet of spruce and hemlock, but the forest floor stands open at numerous muskegs dominated by sphagnum moss. Ridges rise above timberline to alpine heaths and grasses. Numerous steep-walled inlets of the sea called fjords (spelled "fiords" by the U.S. Forest Service) offer excellent sea-kayaking opportunities, although 25-foot changes in tides and sudden storms make all boat use potentially dangerous. "Ideal" beach camps may be underwater two hours after pitching a tent. Behm Canal, the longest waterway into the Wilderness, runs for over 100 miles, extraordinary in length and depth. Old lava flows and extensive glaciers add to the wonder.

Tongass National Forest maintains 15 recreational cabins, 12 on inland freshwater lakes and 3 on saltwater. Advance cabin registrations are required. About 15 miles of wet trails punch into the interior. Winter skiing continues to become

ALASKA

increasingly popular, but the avalanche danger often rates as high.

Both brown and black bears, mountain goats, and black-tailed deer are common sights. Moose, martens, wolves, wolverines, and river otters may be found in abundance. All five species of salmon share the waters with sea lions, harbor seals, killer whales, and porpoises. Migratory birds, from hummingbirds to trumpeter swans, fill the skies.

Misty Fiords Essentials

Size: 2,142,243 acres.
Year Designated: 1980.
Location: Southeastern Alaska.
Easiest Access: With no roads, access is limited to charter flights, charter boats, and private boats from Ketchikan, the nearest full-service community.
Season: June and July are the "driest" months in Misty Fiords.
Wilderness Fees/Permits: None. Cabin rental is $25 per night.
Maps: A map is available for $3 from the monument ranger. USGS 1:250,000 topographic maps are Bradfield Canal, Ketchikan, and Prince Rupert.
Management: Misty Fiords National Monument, Tongass National Forest, 3031 Tongass Avenue, Ketchikan, AK 99901; (907) 225-2148.

Noatak Wilderness

Together with neighboring Gates of the Arctic Wilderness (see above), Noatak National Preserve (more than 6.5 million acres) protects almost the entirety of the largest untouched river basin in America, that of the Noatak River. All the preserve, except for about 700,000 acres around the village of Noatak, has been designated Wilderness.

From glacial melt on Mount Igikpak in the Brooks Range (in Gates of the Arctic National Park), the mostly gentle Noatak River flows westward 425 miles through the heart of the preserve to Kotzebue Sound, patiently carving the scenic Grand Canyon of the Noatak along its course. From its source to its confluence with the Kelly River, 330 miles have been designated Wild and Scenic, making it the longest river in the Wild and Scenic System. More and more visitors each year come to canoe and kayak on the Noatak, and almost the entire river may be paddled easily. Those who fish can try to catch Arctic char, grayling, whitefish, or salmon.

Here in the land of the summer midnight sun, above the Arctic Circle, the huge Western Arctic caribou herd roams, 200,000-plus strong. Backpacking in the foothills, among the bears, wolves, lynx, and Dall sheep, has been increasing in popularity, and backcountry travelers must move with care, as this land is fragile. Bird life abounds in the migratory seasons.

Camping is unrestricted, but you should avoid the numerous private lands on the lower Noatak River. Firewood is scarce. Campsites are best on river sandbars and high, dry tundra knobs. Plan on encountering swarms of ravenous mosquitoes during summer. Motorboats, small airplanes, and snowmobiles are permitted. Hunting and fishing are allowed.

ALASKA

Noatak Essentials

Size: 5,800,000 acres.
Year Designated: 1980.
Location: Northwestern Alaska.
Easiest Access: Go by air from Fairbanks or Anchorage to Bettles or Kotzebue. Charter flights are available from both villages. Charter boats upriver are available in Kotzebue.
Season: Short, warm, buggy summers are followed by long, cold winters. August is best.
Wilderness Fees/Permits: None.
Maps: USGS 1:250,000 topographic maps are Ambler River, Baird Mountains, Delong Mountains, Howard Pass, Killik River, Misheguk Mountains, and Noatak.
Management: Noatak National Preserve, P.O. Box 287, Kotzebue, AK 99752; (907) 442-3890.

Nunivak Island Wilderness

Off the coast of the delta formed by the Yukon and Kuskokwim Rivers lies 1.1-million-acre Nunivak Island, managed as part of the 20-million-acre Yukon Delta National Wildlife Refuge. Nunivak's southern half has been designated Wilderness.

Lava flows and craters found in the interior of the island, some of which hold deep lakes, attest to its volcanic origin. An extensive upland plateau stands 500 to 800 feet above sea level and supports a large herd of reindeer. Introduced in 1920, the herd now numbers over 4,000 individuals. The Eskimos of the village of Mekoryuk, the only community on the island, own and manage the reindeer. More than 40 rivers combine to drain the upland. Tundra, which dominates the landscape, gives way to rocky shores and saltwater lagoons filled with eelgrass (feed for migratory waterfowl) and backed by sand dunes. Isolated low mountains and buttes break the tundra. Vast seabird colonies nest on cliffs along the shoreline, and a large variety of migratory birds flock here in season. Sea mammals frequent the coastal region.

Nunivak Island is probably best known for its herd of great shaggy musk oxen. While the Alaskan musk ox became extinct around 1865, these were introduced here from Greenland in 1935. The herd flourished, growing to more than 750 members, and some were shipped to other regions of Alaska. Each year, a lottery determines which hunters will get to shoot a few of the musk oxen, the chance of a lifetime for many. In 1980 the state transferred ownership of the herd to the Eskimos of the village of Mekoryuk, who subsist on musk ox and reindeer.

Nunivak Island Essentials

Size: 600,000 acres.
Year Designated: 1980.
Location: Off the coast of western Alaska.
Easiest Access: Year-round, there are daily flights from Bethel to Mekoryuk.
Season: Summer insects are horrendous. A better bet is to visit in winter and use a snowmobile to see musk oxen.
Wilderness Fees/Permits: None for backcountry visitation, but hunting and fishing are regulated. Check with the refuge manager.
Maps: USGS 1:250,000 topographic maps are Cape Mendenhall and Nunivak Island.
Management: Yukon Delta National Wildlife Area, P.O. Box 346, Bethel, AK 99559; (907) 543-3151.

ALASKA

Petersburg Creek–Duncan Salt Chuck Wilderness

Petersburg Creek spills down a typical U-shaped glacier-cut valley with vertical granite outcroppings along the way. Mountain peaks overlooking the valley reach their highest point at 3,577 feet and slope down to sea-level muskeg flats. The Duncan Salt Chuck, a large, tidally influenced salt marsh, has rocky rapids constricting its opening on the sea, making slack high-tide periods the safest time to approach. Streams within the Wilderness, primarily Petersburg Creek and Salt Chuck Creek, support runs of steelhead trout and pink, sockeye, chum, and coho salmon. Moose and deer, eagles and ospreys, wolves and wolverines, and other furbearers and migratory birds have been identified as full-time or part-time residents. Black bear populations are especially dense. Typical of southeastern Alaska, spruce and hemlock fill most of the forest. Thick undergrowth includes the awesome devil's club, whose spikes are known to rip the clothes off careless hikers. (I bear witness that devil's club is also capable of ripping off human skin, having left patches of myself on several plants.) Wind and rain are common in summer, and wind and snow in winter, with snow accumulations reaching 200 inches on the area's mountaintops.

A 14-inch-wide plank walkway covers part of the 6.5-mile Petersburg Lake National Recreation Trail (often boggy) from the saltwater Wilderness boundary up Petersburg Creek to a USFS cabin on Petersburg Lake. A more primitive trail runs from Petersburg Lake to a cabin in the Duncan Salt Chuck. Cabin use requires reservations and a fee, obtainable from and payable to the Forest Service. Wilderness camping is unrestricted.

The area lies on northeastern Kupreanof Island, near the small village of Kupreanof, just across the Wrangell Narrows from the town of Petersburg. Easy access means a lot of people visit to fish, hunt, picnic, hike, and camp.

Petersburg Creek–Duncan Salt Chuck Essentials

Size: 46,777 acres.
Year Designated: 1980.
Location: Southeastern Alaska.
Easiest Access: The Wilderness area is only four sea miles from the town of Petersburg across the Wrangell Narrows. Floatplanes land on Petersburg Lake.
Season: June and July are the driest months. September to November are wettest.
Wilderness Fees/Permits: None.
Maps: USGS 1:63,360 maps are Petersburg D-3, Petersburg D-4, and Petersburg D-5.
Management: Petersburg Ranger District, Tongass National Forest, P.O. Box 1328, Petersburg, AK 99833; (907) 772-3871.

Pleasant/Lemusurier/Inian Islands Wilderness

In the frigid waters of Icy Strait these scenic islands break the ocean's surface near the entrance to Glacier Bay. Pleasant Island, the easternmost, lays fairly flat and forested with muskegs; its highest point, The Knob, is at approximately 600 feet. At least two of the island's lakes and three of its streams hold fresh water. Alaskans hunt deer and gather other foods with success here, only about two miles from Gustavus across Icy Passage and easily accessible by boat. Of the islands, only Pleasant was left unaffected by the glacial advances that occurred less than two centuries ago; today it provides a valuable area for comparative research in Glacier Bay.

Lemusurier Island, the next island west, reaches 2,180 feet above the sea, stands covered in trees and muskegs, contains streams and small lakes, and is home to deer, which are hunted on a regular basis. It's a longer boat ride to Lemusurier, but good anchorage awaits in Willoughby Cove on the southeastern shoreline.

Several dots of land make up the Inian Islands, westernmost of the Wilderness. A short distance north of the Inian Peninsula of Chichagof Island and picturesque Elfin Cove, the Inians rise to about 1,000 feet on the largest island. Substantial tree cover provides habitat for deer. Recreational use of this Wilderness is on the rise, especially sea kayaking and hunting. Go prepared for wet weather and wet ground. I found rubber boots a must for hiking and a waterproof ground cloth necessary for a semidry camp.

Pleasant/Lemusurier/Inian Islands Essentials

Size: 23,140 acres.
Year Designated: 1990.
Location: Southeastern Alaska.
Easiest Access: By boat from Gustavus, Hoonah, or Elfin Cove.
Season: Late spring through early fall.
Wilderness Fees/Permits: None.
Maps: USGS 1:250,000 topographic maps are Juneau and Mount Fairweather.
Management: Chatham Area, Tongass National Forest, 204 Siginaka Way, Sitka, AK 99835; (907) 747-6671.

Russell Fiord Wilderness

From Disenchantment Bay, at the upper end of Yakutat Bay, heavily glaciated Russell Fiord penetrates about 35 miles inland, but the advance of Hubbard Glacier is slowly squeezing it off from the sea. Russell Fiord and narrow, 15-mile Nunatak Fiord are the most dramatic features of the ice-carved shoreline of this Wilderness. Within the area, which lies between the Fairweather and Brabazon Ranges, you'll find forested river valleys rising to alpine meadows and snowcapped peaks. The headwaters of the Situk River, once considered for Wild and Scenic designation, are here.

Wolves, mountain goats, and large numbers of smaller furbearing animals roam the Wilderness. You'll also encounter brown and black bears, including some of the rare black bears of "blue" coloring who live near glaciers. Harbor seals and sea lions swim up the major rivers and fjords. Birds are plentiful, especially seabirds, and all five species of salmon are known to spawn in the waters. The wealth of natural-food sources has made the area a harvesting ground for the Yakutat Tlingit for many, many years.

One trail, about seven miles long, departs from Forest Service Road 10 west of the town of Yakutat and leads to a U.S. Forest Service cabin on the shores of Situk Lake. From there, you can scramble to Mountain Lake about 1.5 miles away. Most of the interior is rugged and seldom visited. Wilderness camping is unrestricted. Powerboats, snowmobiles, and airplanes are permitted.

Russell Fiord Essentials

Size: 348,701 acres.
Year Designated: 1980.
Location: Southeastern Alaska.
Easiest Access: Floatplanes fly in from Juneau, 200 miles away, and boats and planes arrive from Yakutat, 12 miles west.
Season: May through September.
Wilderness Fees/Permits: None.
Maps: USGS 1:250,000 topo map is Yakutat.
Management: Chatham Area, Tongass National Forest, 204 Siginaka Way, Sitka, AK 99835; (907) 747-6671.

Saint Lazaria Island Wilderness

Rising no more than 160 feet above the surging ocean at the entrance to Sitka Sound, Saint Lazaria Island was established as a refuge for seabirds in 1909, became a Wilderness in 1970, and was added as a subunit to the Alaska Maritime National Wildlife Refuge in 1980. Saint Lazaria has two low summits, forested with old-growth Sitka spruce, which are connected by a bare saddle that is washed by waves at high tide. Cliffs topped with lush grasses fall to the sea.

Among the tangled tree roots, emerging only at night to feed, are the burrows of petrels, tufted puffins, and rhinoceros auklets. Pigeon guillemots build their nests in rocky crevices near common murres, glaucous-winged gulls, and pelagic cormorants. Well over half a million birds lay their eggs on Saint Lazaria, under frequently overcast skies that drizzle rain throughout much of the year and winds that blow moderate to strong.

Humans are asked to not land on the island, and especially not to walk around. Burrows are easily destroyed, and most of the birds will leave their nests when disturbed, allowing the bolder gulls to swoop in and feed on eggs and chicks.

Saint Lazaria Island Essentials

Size: 65 acres.
Year Designated: 1970.
Location: Southeastern Alaska.
Easiest Access: Take a boat from Sitka, the fifth largest city in Alaska, which lies about 15 sea miles east of Saint Lazaria Island.
Season: Late spring into early fall.
Wilderness Fees/Permits: Special permits, free of charge, are required for those who wish to visit the island. Contact the refuge manager.
Maps: USGS 1:250,000 map is Port Alexander.
Management: Gulf of Alaska Unit, Alaska Maritime National Wildlife Refuge, 2355 Kachemak Bay Drive, Suite 101, Homer, AK 99603; (907) 235-6546.

Selawik Wilderness

The 2,150,000-acre Selawik National Wildlife Refuge begins at the east end of Kotzebue Bay where the Bering Land Bridge once connected North America to Asia. Here, on land that once felt the tread of the woolly mammoth, you'll find evidence of the migrations of people, wildlife, and plants that once crossed freely between the landmasses. An estimated 400,000 caribou winter here now, the Western Arctic herd feeding on the lichen-covered foothills. Moose, bears, and smaller furbearing animals are plentiful.

Selawik's most prominent feature is an extensive system of tundra wetlands lying between the Waring Mountains and the Selawik Hills, nesting ground for hundreds of thousands of waterfowl, including birds from six continents. Asiatic whooper swans nest in Selawik and nowhere else in North America. Eskimo curlews, now considered extinct, once flew here and, perhaps, still hide in the great open distances. Yes, this is a bird-watcher's paradise.

Straddling the Arctic Circle, the refuge holds thousands of lakes, ponds, rivers (including the Kobuk and Selawik Rivers), river deltas, streams, and estuaries. Rafters regularly float all 168 miles of the Wild and Scenic (but gentle) Selawik

ALASKA

River, which runs from the Purcell Mountains in the far eastern portion of the refuge to broad, shallow Selawik Lake. The refuge manager can provide a list of guide services for Selawik. Winds may be fierce on the lake. Fishermen can try for tons of fish (sheefish, char, grayling, pike, burbot) in the rivers. Although camping is generally unrestricted, approximately 2,000 native Alaskans reside on inholdings in the refuge, living primarily a subsistence lifestyle. Dry campsites are few and far between.

A "small" strip of land in the northeastern section of the refuge has been designated Wilderness. You'll find no trails, no roads, no assistance if you need help, millions of mosquitoes in summer, and severe cold in winter.

Selawik Essentials

Size: 240,000 acres.
Year Designated: 1980.
Location: Northwestern Alaska.
Easiest Access: Flights from Anchorage land in Kotzebue several times a day. From Kotzebue, Selawik is accessible by boat, plane, snowmobile, ski, and dogsled.
Season: Late June to early October for river trips.
Wilderness Fees/Permits: None for backcountry visitation. Certain activities, especially hunting and fishing, require a special permit. Check with the refuge manager.
Maps: USGS 1:250,000 topographic maps for the refuge, including the Wilderness, are Selawik and Shungnak.
Management: Selawik National Wildlife Refuge, Box 270, Kotzebue, AK 99752; (907) 442-3799.

Semidi Islands Wilderness

Nine major treeless and ragged rock islands, some sided with precipitous cliffs, were combined with many small rocks and islets to form Semidi Islands National Wildlife Refuge in 1932. In 1980 these lands became a subunit of the 715,000-acre Alaska Peninsula Unit of the Alaska Maritime National Wildlife Refuge and a Wilderness area. More than 2.4 million birds, almost half the breeding seabirds of the Alaska Peninsula Unit, nest on the Semidis. Aghiluk Island alone, the largest of the Semidis, is home to more than half a million birds. About 370,000 horned puffins nest in the Semidis along with almost all of the unit's northern fulmars and jaegers, and one million-plus murres. Ancient murrelets and parakeet auklets are among the other species found here. Seabird populations would be even higher, but fox farmers in the 1880s released their animals on some of the larger Semidis, and their descendants consume many eggs and birds annually.

Semidi Islands Wilderness Area is not great in land mass but includes approximately one-quarter million acres of surrounding seabed, providing at least temporary homes for sea otters, sea lions, seals, porpoises, and whales. Exposed to the stormy Gulf of Alaska, drenched by frequent rains, remote and difficult to reach, lying in poorly charted waters, this region is seen by few humans. The dangerous crossing of an unpredictable stretch of sea is simply too great a risk for most.

ALASKA

Semidi Islands Essentials

Size: 250,000 acres.
Year Designated: 1980.
Location: Off the coast of southwestern Alaska, south of the Alaska Peninsula.
Easiest Access: Boats may be chartered out of Kodiak or Sand Point.
Season: May through August.

Wilderness Fees/Permits: Visitation is often not permitted when birds are nesting.
Maps: USGS 1:63,360 topographic map is Sutwik Island A-3.
Management: Alaska Peninsula Unit, Alaska Maritime National Wildlife Refuge, 2355 Kachemak Bay Drive, Suite 101, Homer, AK 99603; (907) 235-6546.

Simeonof Island Wilderness

One of 30 named islands in the Shumagin Group, Simeonof Island was established as a refuge for sea otters in 1958. It became a Wilderness in 1976 and a subunit of the Alaska Peninsula Unit of the Alaska Maritime National Wildlife Refuge in 1980. Refuge "lands" include the water, shoals, and kelp beds within a mile of the island where at least 17 species of whales have been identified (minke whales are the most common), but where surprisingly few sea otters still live. With shores that slope easily to the sea and wide beaches, Simeonof attracts relatively few seabirds. Three streams support salmon.

Cattle and fox ranchers used the island between 1890 and 1930, but they eventually abandoned their ranches. Cattle were returned to the island in 1960, and a herd that was often too large for the island to support scared off the few terns and other birds that nested here. In 1985 the last cow was removed, and a resurgence of bird life is expected.

With a well-protected harbor offering safe anchorage, Simeonof Island lies 58 miles from the mainland and is difficult to reach. Rain, fog, strong winds, and cool temperatures descend on the island, which receives few human visitors. Those who do visit come primarily to see a truly wild piece of earth, and perhaps a few whales. All are asked to leave the wildlife strictly untouched.

Simeonof Island Essentials

Size: 25,855 acres.
Year Designated: 1976.
Location: Off the coast of southwestern Alaska, south of the Alaska Peninsula.
Easiest Access: Take a boat 58 miles from Sand Point.
Season: May through September.

Wilderness Fees/Permits: Restrictions often apply when the birds are nesting in spring.
Maps: USGS 1:250,000 topographic map is Simeonof Island.
Management: Alaska Peninsula Unit, Alaska Maritime National Wildlife Refuge, 2355 Kachemak Bay Drive, Suite 101, Homer, AK 99603; (907) 235-6546.

South Baranof Wilderness

When I was last on the coast near the southern end of Baranof Island, just after it was designated Wilderness, a brown bear of massive proportions approached my campfire. (Of course, all brown bears approaching campfires appear quite massive.) Shouting, banging pots together, and firing my rifle into the air had absolutely no effect on the bear. I backed down the beach and watched him devour everything edible, and several things I had considered inedible, in camp. He strolled off casually, leaving me nervous, hungry, and forever attached to South Baranof Wilderness.

Alexander Baranof, the first governor of Russian America, built his headquarters in nearby Sitka and left his name on this large island. Most of the southern extremity of the island has been designated Wilderness. Bounded on the west by the Gulf of Alaska and on the east by Chatham Strait, here rugged mountains rise to a high point on Mount Ada at 4,528 feet, less than three miles from the neighboring sea. Permanent snowfields and active glaciers blanket the high country above 2,000 feet, giving way to almost impenetrably dense undergrowth in a coastal forest of spruce and hemlock. Many of the mountain valleys end in deep fjords opening onto the wild North Pacific. High lakes spill over waterfalls near the coastline.

Parts of this area receive as much as 400 inches of rain per year, the heaviest precipitation in the state. Hiking here on several trips, I always wore rubber boots. I wore rubber boots while sea kayaking as well, and found the coastline enormously appealing, with numerous beach campsites and extraordinary scenery. Wildlife abounds and, in addition to brown bears, you'll find Sitka black-tailed deer, mink, marten, and otters. Seals, sea lions, whales, and a large population of sea otters are often seen offshore, and crab, shrimp, herring, and halibut are harvested from the sea. Bald eagles, shorebirds, and seabirds flock in great numbers. The streams are rich with salmon and trout.

Within the Wilderness, five U.S. Forest Service cabins can be rented at Avoss Lake, Davidof Lake, Gar Lake, North Plotnikof Lake, and Rezanof Lake. About six miles of maintained trail provide access to the cabins. Fly-ins to the cabins are allowed. Along the coast, boaters will find ample opportunities to anchor in relatively sheltered coves.

South Baranof Essentials

Size: 319,568 acres.
Year Designated: 1980.
Location: Southeastern Alaska.
Easiest Access: The Wilderness lies about 20 miles south of Sitka and is accessible by boat.
Season: May through September. October through December often brings fierce storms.
Wilderness Fees/Permits: None.
Maps: USGS 1:250,000 topographic map is Port Alexander.
Management: Chatham Area, Tongass National Forest, 204 Siginaka Way, Sitka, AK 99835; (907) 747-6671.

South Etolin Island Wilderness

From a spruce and hemlock forest at sea level, the South Etolin Island Wilderness rises above the tree line to a height of over 3,700 feet on Mount Etolin. In the northern portion you'll find steep terrain with rocky peaks and high mountain lakes. The southern section of the Wilderness is gentle forested land, which receives an average of 90 inches of rain per year. Several smaller islands abut South Etolin's eastern, western, and southern shorelines. Twenty-eight streams have been identified as habitat for trout and salmon.

Black bears, Sitka black-tailed deer, and moose are relatively numerous, while brown bears are rare. In 1987, 50 elk were introduced, an unusual move because these large deer are not indigenous. The herd is apparently doing well, but the exact number of elk currently on the island is not known. Waterfowl and shorebirds are plentiful in spring and fall, and harbor seals haul out on the beaches. Bald eagles nest along many inlets. The main shoreline and areas surrounding the smaller islands provide excellent opportunities for sea kayakers, but many submerged rocks make it dangerous for motorized boats. No established trails exist. Despite its nearness to Ketchikan, Wrangell, Meyers Chuck, and other villages, this area receives little visitation.

South Etolin Island Essentials

Size: 83,642 acres.
Year Designated: 1980.
Location: Southeastern Alaska.
Easiest Access: Take a boat from Ketchikan, Wrangell, or Meyers Chuck. Floatplanes may be able to land on some of the larger lakes.
Season: June and July are typically driest.
Wilderness Fees/Permits: None.
Maps: USGS 1:250,000 topographic map is Petersburg.
Management: Wrangell Ranger District, Tongass National Forest, P.O. Box 51, Wrangell, AK 99929; (907) 874-2323.

South Prince of Wales Wilderness

The southwestern corner of Prince of Wales Island, a complex network of bays and inlets, and a cluster of islands known as the Barrier Islands make up this Wilderness. On Prince of Wales Island the topography of the southern portion of the area undulates gently around numerous streams, lakes, and wetlands. In the northern portion the terrain rises abruptly to over 2,400 feet. Precipitation in excess of 100 inches per year has created a lush forest of Sitka spruce, western hemlock, Alaska cedar, and western red cedar with a ground cover of shrubs and grasses. Many of the streams are major salmon runs. Black bears, wolves, and black-tailed deer are common. No trails and no facilities exist.

The Barrier Islands are composed of approximately 75 small islands, ranging from a few acres to over 500 acres, and many smaller rocks. Frequent and fierce storms of the vast North Pacific buffet these islands. Among these attractive little bits of land tidal surges can be sudden and powerful. Humpback whales, Stellar sea lions, and seals are often sighted, and sea otters are especially plentiful. Here you'll find an exemplary southeastern Alaska Wilderness, remote and seldom visited by humans.

ALASKA

South Prince of Wales Essentials

Size: 90,996 acres.
Year Designated: 1980.
Location: Southeastern Alaska.
Easiest Access: Catch a boat or floatplane from Craig or Ketchikan.
Season: Summer, when storms are less frequent and less fierce.

Wilderness Fees/Permits: None.
Maps: USGS 1:63,360 topographic maps are Craig A-1 and Craig A-2, Dixon Entrance D-1, Dixon Entrance D-2, and Dixon Entrance D-3.
Management: Craig Ranger District, Tongass National Forest, P.O. Box 500, Craig, AK 99921; (907) 826-3271.

Stikine-LeConte Wilderness

From permanent ice fields along the Canadian border, this mainland Wilderness drops to the ocean. The Stikine River (*stikine* means "great" in Tlingit), dotted with many islands, divides the area. Confined to a narrow gorge, the Stikine may be paddled for 158 miles from Telegraph Creek, British Columbia, to the ocean. North of the river the LeConte, Shakes, and Popof Glaciers slope seaward, with the LeConte actively calving icebergs into LeConte Bay. Below the glaciers and north of the river the terrain is predominantly glacier-worn rock above the tree line descending to steep slopes and deep valleys. Dense stands of spruce and hemlock and undergrowth make hiking difficult. South of the river you'll find steep, sparsely vegetated mountains with many hanging glaciers toward the eastern boundary and typical spruce and hemlock forest toward the coast. Along the river grow stands of willow and cottonwood, unusual for this region. Many lakes are set at higher elevations and drain through streams to lower elevations. The weather is typical of southeastern Alaska: wet, with about 90 inches of rain annually.

Moose live along the Stikine and its drainages, while mountain goats dwell in the high country. Black and brown bears roam the forests with many smaller furbearing animals. Harbor seals are plentiful in LeConte Bay. The Stikine River tideflats are a major resting and feeding area for migratory waterfowl.

Chief Shakes Hot Springs, which has an enclosed bathhouse, is accessible to many from Petersburg and Wrangell up the easily navigated river. It has become a popular site for alcohol consumption, fistfights, and the discharge of firearms. The U.S. Forest Service receives more and more complaints each year about "irresponsible and dangerous operation of powerboats." Away from the river the Wilderness quietly invites those who desire solitude. There are 13 U.S. Forest Service cabins accessible via several short trails.

Stikine-LeConte Essentials

Size: 448,841 acres.
Year Designated: 1980.
Location: Southeastern Alaska.
Easiest Access: Primary access is up the Stikine River by boat or floatplane north from Wrangell.
Season: April to September are when the most visitors come.

Wilderness Fees/Permits: None.
Maps: A Stikine River map is available for $3 from the Forest Service Information Center, Centennial Hall, 101 Egan Drive, Juneau, AK 99801. USGS 1:250,000 topographic maps are Bradfield Canal, Petersburg, and Sumdum.
Management: Wrangell Ranger District, Tongass National Forest, P.O. Box 51, Wrangell, AK 99929; (907) 874-2323.

ALASKA

Tebenkof Bay Wilderness

A complex system of bays with many small islands, islets, and coves is the prominent feature of Tebenkof Bay Wilderness on Kuiu Island. The southern boundary of this Wilderness marks the northern boundary of Kuiu Wilderness (see above), and the two are managed practically as one. Muskeg bogs, small lakes, and many small creeks (the entire watershed of the bay) are scattered throughout the area. Coastal spruce and hemlock rise from sea level to alpine plant communities above 2,000 feet. Sea, shore, and land birds (including beautiful trumpeter swans) inhabit and migrate through the area. Black bears, wolves, and smaller furbearing animals are common in the interior, and marine mammals are often seen from shore. Trout and salmon fill the streams, and fishing vessels come for Dungeness and Tanner crabs, shrimp, herring, and halibut in the waters offshore. Once this area was occupied by Tlingit Indians and signs of their use still may be seen.

Beware of swift tidal currents when approaching by boat. Rain keeps the area wet year-round. You'll find no trails or facilities of any kind, but camping is unrestricted and human visitors are few.

Tebenkof Bay Essentials
Size: 66,839 acres.
Year Designated: 1980.
Location: Southeastern Alaska.
Easiest Access: From Kake, travel approximately 60 miles south by boat.
Season: June and July are typically the driest months.
Wilderness Fees/Permits: None.
Maps: A Kuiu Island map is available for $3 from the Forest Service Information Center, Centennial Hall, 101 Egan Drive, Juneau, AK 99801. USGS 1:63,360 topographic maps are Petersburg B-6 and C-6, and Port Alexander B-1 and C-1.
Management: Stikine Area, Tongass National Forest, P.O. Box 309, Petersburg, AK 99833; (907) 772-3841.

Togiak Wilderness

At 4.2 million acres, Togiak National Wildlife Refuge covers about the same amount of land as Connecticut and Rhode Island combined, a region important to Eskimo and Native American hunter-gatherers for more than 5,000 years. Over half of the refuge, the northern section, has been designated Wilderness. To the north of Togiak Wilderness stretches the vast Yukon Delta National Wildlife Refuge. Three major river systems, comprising over 1,500 miles of water, lie within Togiak Refuge (Togiak, Kanektok, and Goodnews). More than one million salmon return to these waters each year to spawn. Fishing draws many visitors to Togiak, both humans and brown bears. Floaters often run the rivers, fishing along the way for salmon, trout, char, grayling, and pike. The Togiak River flows wide and easily. The Kanektok and Goodnews are faster, more twisted rivers with a greater variety of fish. None of the rivers contain white water.

ALASKA

The Ahklun Mountains encompass about 80 percent of Togiak National Wildlife Refuge and give way to tundra and coastal plains at lower elevations. The mountains of the Wilderness hide many large lakes. Sea cliffs provide nesting places for approximately one million marine birds, including murres, puffins, auklets, kittiwakes, and cormorants. Beaches provide haul-outs for walrus, sea lions, and harbor seals. Seven species of whales have been identified cruising the coastline during migratory seasons.

You'll find no trails, just millions of mosquitoes in summer, severe winters, few trees, and fewer fellow humans.

Togiak Essentials

Size: 2,270,000 acres.
Year Designated: 1980.
Location: Southwestern Alaska.
Easiest Access: Charter air service is available from Dillingham and Bethel.
Season: June through September.
Wilderness Fees/Permits: Certain activities may require a special-use permit.
Maps: USGS 1:250,000 topographic maps covering the refuge are Bethel, Dillingham, Goodnews Bay, Hagemeister Island, and Nushagak Bay.
Management: Togiak National Wildlife Refuge, P.O. Box 270, Dillingham, AK 99576; (907) 842-1063.

Tracy Arm–Fords Terror Wilderness

Bounded by Canada on the east, this Wilderness is highlighted by two sheer-walled fjords, Tracy Arm and Endicott Arm, both narrow and deep and over 30 miles long. At the head of both fjords tidewater glaciers calve regularly into the sea, making a boat approach to their faces dangerous. Floating chunks of ice, some the size of a three-story building, according to the U.S. Forest Service, often block access to the upper fjords, especially in summer. Permanent ice, in fact, covers about one-fifth of the Wilderness.

In 1899, a naval crewman named Ford paddled into a narrow waterway connected to Endicott Arm and was trapped for six terrible hours in the ripping tidal surge . . . . Hence the name Fords Terror.

Rugged mountains dominate the landmass of the area with steep valleys sparkling with high waterfalls. A typical Alaska rain forest of spruce and hemlock grows to an elevation of about 1,500 feet. Wildlife in the upper forest includes brown and black bears, mountain goats, wolverines, a few Sitka black-tailed deer, and many smaller furbearing animals. Harbor seals rear their young on ice floating in the fjords, and whales and sea lions are often seen in the water. Bald eagles and shorebirds are common near the coastline.

Some of the unnamed peaks attract adventurous mountaineers, but you'll find no trails, no camping restrictions, cool summers, Arctic winters, wet firewood, and infinite solitude.

ALASKA

Tracy Arm–Fords Terror Essentials

Size: 653,179 acres.
Year Designated: 1980.
Location: Southeastern Alaska.
Easiest Access: Air taxis and charter boats depart from Juneau, which lies about 50 miles northwest of the Wilderness.
Season: June through October.

Wilderness Fees/Permits: None.
Maps: USGS 1:250,000 topographic maps are Sumdum and Taku River.
Management: Chatham Area, Tongass National Forest, 204 Siginaka Way, Sitka, AK 99835; (907) 747-6671.

Tuxedni Islands Wilderness

In 1909 two islands at the mouth of Tuxedni Bay off of Cook Inlet—Chisik and Duck—were established as a refuge for seabirds, bald eagles, and peregrine falcons. In 1970 they were designated Wilderness and in 1980 became a subunit of the Gulf of Alaska Unit of the Alaska Maritime National Wildlife Refuge. Most of the refuge lies on Chisik Island (tiny, six-acre Duck Island is a rocky dot with almost no vegetation). Chisik slopes upward out of Cook Inlet from sandy beaches on the southern end to 400-foot cliffs on the northern end. A cannery located on the southern end occupies a small non-Wilderness area of the island.

An understory of salmonberry, alder, and other brushy growth forms an impenetrable, wet jungle over much of Chisik, filling the few openings in the spruce-hemlock forest. The higher elevations are alpine tundra from which the volcanoes of Mounts Redoubt and Iliamna in Lake Clark Wilderness (see above) often can be seen.

Chisik Island has no trails and one U.S. Forest Service cabin for rent. Rangers report the use as light. Camping is unrestricted. Hunting is not allowed, but fishing is permitted, with salmon being sought most often. Small planes and boats land here, but sudden winds and rough waters make access risky.

Tuxedni Islands Essentials

Size: 5,566 acres.
Year Designated: 1970.
Location: Southern Alaska, in Cook Inlet.
Easiest Access: Chartered planes or boats depart from Homer, Kenai, or Soldotna.
Season: May through September.

Wilderness Fees/Permits: Some restrictions may apply. Contact the refuge manager.
Maps: USGS 1:63,360 topographic maps are Kenai A-7 and Kenai A-8.
Management: Gulf of Alaska Unit, Alaska Maritime National Wildlife Refuge, 2355 Kachemak Bay Drive, Homer, AK 99603; (907) 235-6546.

Unimak Island Wilderness

At almost one million acres, huge Unimak Island extends west from the tip of the Alaska Peninsula. Only a relatively thin strip of sea separates Unimak from Izembek National Wildlife Refuge, and Unimak Island may someday transfer from being a subunit of the Aleutian Islands Unit of the Alaska Maritime National Wildlife Refuge to being a part of Izembek. About 93 percent of Unimak Island has been designated Wilderness.

Here you'll see the nearly perfect cone of Shishaldin Volcano, the highest cone in the Aleutians. At 9,372 feet, it served as a navigational aid first for Aleuts and later for Russian seafarers. Shishaldin and two other Unimak volcanoes are active, surrounded by extensive lava flows and fields of bare ash. On the highest peaks of the island lie perpetual snowfields, some covering glaciers. Fisher Caldera has gone dormant and is now filled with icy water.

The coastline features steep bluffs with many offshore sea stacks where seabirds and marine mammals may be seen frequently. Near the shoreline, wetlands provide nesting, feeding, and resting habitat for waterfowl and shorebirds, including whistling swans, geese (Canada, emperor, and black brant), sea ducks, mallards, pintails, gadwalls, green-winged and common teal, common goldeneyes, and greater scaup. Brown bears have migrated to Unimak, swimming from the mainland and living near caribou, wolves, and wolverines.

The coast of Unimak offers sea kayaking possibilities, and the interior, although typically wet and virtually without trail, provides an opportunity to hike across rolling tundra and treeless grasslands, a wild and lonesome land. Carry a stove and plenty of fuel; firewood is scarce away from the driftwood-littered shore.

Unimak Island Essentials

Size: 910,000 acres.
Year Designated: 1980.
Location: Southwestern Alaska.
Easiest Access: Chartered boats and small planes depart from Unalaska.
Season: June through September.
Wilderness Fees/Permits: None for backcountry visitation. Some activities, such as hunting and fishing, require a special permit. Contact the refuge manager.
Maps: USGS 1:250,000 topographic maps are False Pass and Unimak.
Management: Aleutian Islands Unit, Alaska Maritime National Wildlife Refuge, 2355 Kachemak Bay Drive, Homer, AK 99603; (907) 235-6546.

Warren Island Wilderness

Warren Peak rises dramatically from the sea to 2,329 feet above Warren Island, off the northwestern coast of Prince of Wales Island, about 75 air miles from Ketchikan. Covered in typically dense coastal spruce-hemlock rain forest, the area usually gets battered by extremely strong, wet winds that have twisted many of the trees near the shoreline.

A few small, protected coves and beaches dent the leeward side of the island, but the rest of the shoreline is rock and windswept cliffs protected by dangerous shoals. Lack of boat anchorages and floatplane landing sites, combined with exposure to the open sea, makes access difficult, and Warren Island is, in fact, inaccessible much of the year.

ALASKA

Sea lions, seals, whales, and sea otters may be seen along the shoreline, and Sitka black-tailed deer, black bears, and wolves have been spotted inland. Bald eagles live here, but Warren Island is best known for its seabirds.

You'll find no trails, no chance to get wet firewood started most of the year, no facilities of any kind, and little chance of help if trouble arises. Here lies an opportunity for a totally unspoiled Wilderness experience.

Warren Island Essentials

Size: 11,181 acres.
Year Designated: 1980.
Location: Southeastern Alaska.
Easiest Access: Boats may be chartered from the nearest villages, Craig and Klawock. Air services fly from Ketchikan, Sitka, Petersburg, and Wrangell.
Season: The best chances for a safe landing are from April through August.
Wilderness Fees/Permits: None.
Maps: USGS 1:63,360 topographic map is Craig D-6.
Management: Craig Ranger District, Tongass National Forest, P.O. Box 500, Craig, AK 99921; (907) 826-3271.

West Chichagof-Yakobi Wilderness

When I was a resident of Sitka, I spent many days sea kayaking near Chichagof and Yakobi Islands, wary of the tidal surges, thrilled by the wildlife, startled by the "blow" of a humpback whale less than 30 feet off my bow, filled by the fish that took my bait, soaked by rain, blown by wind, and awed by the majestic trees that rise suddenly to great heights near the shore.

Chichagof Island and, just to the north, smaller Yakobi Island, were named for a Russian admiral and a general, respectively. Their mountainous western portions, including numerous storm-battered smaller islands, have been designated Wilderness, a land one-third of which stands thickly covered in Sitka spruce and western hemlock and the rest with alpine tundra, muskegs, and an intricate and delightful complex of bays, coves, lagoons, reefs, promontories, narrow passages, tidal meadows, estuaries, and windswept scrub forestland. Along the coast and on some of the small islands great grassy glades spread out beneath open spruce cover.

The western shore opens on the Pacific Ocean, but many sheltered bays dent the coast and offer safe harbor.

The diminutive Sitka black-tailed deer is common here. Brown bears are frequently sighted, along with an abundance of smaller furbearing animals. Migratory waterfowl frequent West Chichagof-Yakobi in remarkable numbers, and marine mammals are everywhere: sea otters at Surge and Khaz Bays; sea lion rookeries at White Sister Islands, Cape Cross, and Cape Bingham; seals hauling out on every other rock.

Long before the Russians came, Tlingit Indians began utilizing this area for its rich natural resources. The village of Pelican lies only a short distance from the Wilderness boundary. Mined for its gold, Chichagof produced almost a million ounces of the yellow metal. Some evidence of old operations persist to this day.

The U.S. Forest Service maintains three rental cabins on Chichagof: two heavily used at White Sulphur Hot Springs and Goulding Lake, and one considerably less used at Suloia Lake. One cabin stands on Yakobi at Greentop Harbor. You'll find about 11 miles of marked trail, and Wilderness camping is unrestricted.

ALASKA

West Chichagof-Yakobi Essentials

Size: 264,747 acres.
Year Designated: 1980.
Location: Southeastern Alaska.
Easiest Access: Boats and floatplanes can be chartered in Sitka. It is possible to paddle the 20 miles from Sitka to the islands.
Season: May through October.

Wilderness Fees/Permits: None.
Maps: USGS 1:63,360 topographic maps are Mount Fairweather A-2 and Sitka B-5, B-6, C-5, C-6, C-7, D-6, D-7, and D-8.
Management: Chatham Area, Tongass National Forest, 204 Siginaka Way, Sitka, AK 99835; (907) 747-6671.

Wrangell-Saint Elias Wilderness

Vitus Bering saw a mountain rising far above anything else around and recorded the sighting on July 16, 1741, the first Russian written report of land in Alaska. Bering named Cape Saint Elias four days later, on Elias' saint day, and the name was later given as well to the 18,008-foot mountain (the second highest peak in the United States) that dominates what is now Wrangell-Saint Elias National Park and Preserve, the largest unit of the National Park System. Here you'll find 12,400,000 acres of national parkland, the most extensive glaciated country of Alaska (with more than 100 glaciers), a vastly rugged land that holds nine of North America's 16 highest peaks (many over 16,000 feet), the 90-mile-long and 4,000-foot-thick Bagley Ice Field (North America's largest subpolar ice field), and the unsurpassed Malaspina Glacier, which spreads 50 percent larger than the state of Delaware.

It is a land of remote valleys, wild rivers, and a fabulous wildlife population that includes the world's finest Dall sheep, grizzly bears, black bears, caribou, moose, bison, mountain goats, wolves, wolverines, beavers, coyotes, foxes, and marmots. In the north the glaciated peaks drop to tundra and boreal forested uplands. In the south massive glaciers spread from the mountains almost to the Gulf of Alaska. Several trails provide foot or horse access, but large braided rivers will often stop your progress. Mosquitoes are thick in the low country during the summer, and enough snow accumulates in the high country to make avalanches a year-round danger. The bold and the prepared, however, will discover Wilderness travel (by boot, ski, boat, or horse) at its unparalleled grandest.

Within the park, 8,700,000 acres have been designated Wilderness, the largest in the National Wilderness Preservation System. On the Canadian side of the border lies Kluane National Park, and together these two areas house this continent's most spectacular mountain kingdom.

Wrangell-Saint Elias Essentials

Size: 8,700,000 acres.
Year Designated: 1980.
Location: Southeastern Alaska.
Easiest Access: From Chitina, take the road to McCarthy (four-wheel-drive or high-clearance-vehicle required). You can also arrange a fly-in from Glennallen, Gulkana, or Yakutat.
Season: May through September.

Wilderness Fees/Permits: None.
Maps: USGS 1:250,000 topographic maps are Bering Glacier, Cordova, Gulkana, Icy Bay, McCarthy, Mount Saint Elias, Nabesna, Valdez, and Yakutat.
Management: Wrangell-Saint Elias National Park and Preserve, P.O. Box 29, Glennallen, AK 99588; (909) 822-5235.

> "Stepping into wilderness and looking past ourselves, we see the vivid space of great forests, mountains, rivers, and deserts. You might say the wilderness experience gives us a standard by which to measure our sanity . . . [It] calls out the wilderness inside ourselves, and we're always surprised by its sane and gentle nature."
>
> —Albert Saijo

ARIZONA

Total Wilderness areas: 90
Total Wilderness acreage: 4,470,948

Ask people what Arizona looks like, and they will usually describe a vast expanse of hot, dry desertland. That's because almost half of the state, the southern and western sections, lies on either the Sonoran, Mojave, or Great Basin Deserts. But in these deserts are mountains that are high enough to trap moisture and support forest. And two-fifths of northern Arizona is part of the immense Colorado Plateau, a fantasy world of colorful and sculpted canyons that includes the incomparable Grand Canyon. The world's largest forest of ponderosa pine grows on the Colorado Plateau here. Two hundred miles of the Mogollon Rim mark the end of the plateau with a steep plunge of 2,000 feet on average to the desert floor.

About 45 percent of Arizona is federally owned, and the state claims the second most Wilderness areas in the country. The Bureau of Land Management (BLM) administers approximately 12.5 million acres, mostly desert, upon which 47 Wildernesses have been designated. Six national forests manage about 11.2 million acres and 36 Wilderness areas. One of these areas is managed jointly by the BLM and the U.S. Forest Service. Four Wildernesses are managed by the National Park Service, and four are on wildlife refuges, including the state's two largest pieces of the National Wilderness Preservation System.

Apache Creek Wilderness

Small, remote, and relatively rugged, Apache Creek Wilderness offers rolling hills of juniper and piñon pine interspersed with outcroppings of granite. Time and wind and water have smoothed the rock, providing excellent habitat for mountain lions and numerous bird species. Three natural springs feed several important riparian ecosystems, including Apache Creek itself. Elevations range from 5,200 feet to 7,200 feet.

You'll find no maintained trails, and there are currently no public access points, but hiking and camping are unrestricted. U.S. Forest Service roads encircle the area. Bring maps and a compass.

Apache Creek Essentials

Size: 5,420 acres.
Year Designated: 1984.
Location: Central Arizona.
Easiest Access: From Chino Valley, take State Highway 89 south for two miles. Turn west on the Outer Loop and go five miles to a stop sign. Turn north on County Road 5 and drive about 20 miles to the Walnut Creek Work Station. You can hike up Apache Creek into the Wilderness.
Season: Fall to spring.
Wilderness Fees/Permits: None.
Maps: Topographic maps are available for $3 each from the U.S. Forest Service, Public Affairs Office, 517 Gold Avenue SW, Albuquerque, NM 87102; (505) 842-3292.
Management: Chino Valley Ranger District, Prescott National Forest, P.O. Box 485, Chino Valley, AZ 86323; (520) 636-2302.

Aravaipa Canyon Wilderness

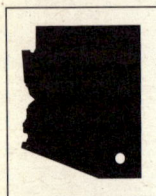

As a prime example of the Southwest's desert country, narrow and twisting Aravaipa Canyon has few if any equals. It is a stretch of incredible scenic wonder, filled with biological treasures that have attracted enough human traffic to make overuse a problem since the 1960s. Aravaipa Creek, shaded by cottonwoods, has cut a trough up to 1,000 feet deep in the Galiuro Mountains, and the canyon walls are wondrously carved and painted in subtle sandy colors. The creek runs year-round from springs, seeps, and tributary streams, and along the water grows one of the lushest riparian habitats in southern Arizona. The main canyon's length is about 11 miles, and the Wilderness extends well beyond it to include surrounding tablelands and nine side canyons. Seven species of native desert trout may be found here, along with desert bighorn sheep, an extensive variety of large and small mammals and reptiles, and at least 238 species of birds. Caves and ledges provide habitat for 12 known species of bats.

Solitude may be difficult to find in Aravaipa, and without an advance reservation you may not find yourself here at all. The attention is well deserved since you'll find few places in the state where canyon hiking is as spectacular. Although no trails are marked, a route follows a well-used path along the canyon, crossing through the creek several times. Most people rate the hiking as easy. The canyon grows so narrow in places that wading in the creek is the only option. Be prepared to encounter lightning storms, flash floods, and poisonous snakes, insects, and plants. Even though the high walls and water keep the canyon floor more humid than the surrounding desert, the summer heat can be extreme.

ARIZONA

Aravaipa Canyon Essentials

Size: 19,700 acres.
Year Designated: 1984; expanded in 1990.
Location: Southeastern Arizona.
Easiest Access: From Safford, take U.S. 70 northwest for approximately 15 miles. Turn west on Klondyke Road and drive approximately 45 miles to a parking lot and trailhead at the east entrance. Klondyke Road is passable for all vehicles except during the occasional July and August rainstorm. Before heading out during these months, call the BLM to check road conditions.
Season: Late fall to early spring are best if you want to avoid the heat.
Wilderness Fees/Permits: Permits are required. Groups are limited to 50 people per day. Maximum stay is three days and two nights. The fee is $1.50 per person per day payable at self-service fee stations at the trailheads.
Maps: USGS topographic maps are Booger Canyon, Brandenburg Mountain, Holy Joe Peak, and Oak Grove Canyon.
Management: BLM Gila Resource Area, 425 East Fourth Street, Safford, AZ 85546; (520) 428-4040.

Arrastra Mountain Wilderness

Wild and remote, difficult to access, this sprawling Wilderness preserves imposing landscapes and vividly colorful geologic features. The Poachie Range runs northwest-southeast through the north-central portion of the area and rises to almost 5,000 feet. Southern slopes descend gradually and are interspersed with isolated volcanic plugs and numerous drainages, several of which have been incised deeply into bright orange mudstone. The western and southern portions of the Wilderness encompass more than 20 miles of the ephemeral Big Sandy and Santa Maria Rivers. On the west side of the Big Sandy stands Artillery Peak, a 1,200-foot volcanic plug dominating the Artillery Mountains. In the eastern portion of the area, you'll find pristine Peoples Canyon where several springs support two miles of interconnected pools shaded by hundreds of sycamores, willows, and cottonwoods. These pearls of water attract birds, which in turn lure bird-watchers.

Lacking both trails and road access, Arrastra Mountain gets tramped on by only a few backpackers. All travel here is a challenge of the highest desert Wilderness order.

Arrastra Mountain Essentials

Size: 126,760 acres.
Year Designated: 1990.
Location: Western Arizona.
Easiest Access: From Interstate 40, drive south on U.S. 93, which runs roughly parallel to, but three to six miles away from, the Wilderness's northeast boundary. After 59 miles, where northbound State Highway 97 branches off from U.S. 93, turn south on a very difficult jeep road (four-wheel drive required) that leads four miles to Peoples Canyon and a trailhead where you can leave your vehicle.
Season: Fall to spring.
Wilderness Fees/Permits: None.
Maps: USGS topographic maps are Arrastra Mountain, Arrastra Mountain NE, Arrastra Mountain SE, Artillery Peak NE, Artillery Peak SE, Malpais Mesa SW, and Palmerita Ranch.
Management: BLM Kingman Resource Area, 2475 Beverly Avenue, Kingman, AZ 86401; (520) 757-3161.

ARIZONA

Aubrey Peak Wilderness

A large cliff-encircled mesa, Aubrey Peak dominates the middle of the eastern half of this Wilderness. It is a land of stark geologic formations eroded by wind and water into brightly colored volcanic sculptures, a world of natural windows, tufa caves, spires, slickrock terraces, and tinajas (deep, water-filled pockets). You'll find numerous other mesas, buttes, volcanic plugs, and serpentine canyons. The Wilderness is set in a transition zone between the Mojave and Sonoran Deserts. Stands of imposing saguaro, paloverde, ironwood, and smoke trees, typical of the Sonoran Desert, merge with Joshua trees and other species found in the Mojave to create a patchwork quilt of vegetation. Available water makes this area a desert bird-watcher's paradise. Keep your eyes peeled for verdins, crissal thrashers, black-throated sparrows, Abert's towhees, and black-tailed gnatcatchers, to name but a few. If you're lucky, you may catch a glimpse of a herd of desert bighorn sheep. Discovered here recently, this species is unusual for this region.

There are no established trails, but the hiking is easy. Just follow the washes and orient yourself using the distinctive rock formations. Occasional old jeep roads lead to some long-abandoned mines.

Aubrey Peak Essentials

Size: 15,900 acres.
Year Designated: 1990.
Location: Western Arizona.
Easiest Access: From Kingman, take Interstate 40 west and south to Yucca. Take the Alamo Road for 50 miles to where a powerline with double wood posts crosses the road. The Wilderness boundary intersects Alamo Road at this point. Head west into the Wilderness from there.
Season: Fall to spring.
Wilderness Fees/Permits: None.
Maps: USGS topographic maps are Planet 2 NE and Planet SE.
Management: BLM Kingman Resource Area, 2475 Beverly Avenue, Kingman, AZ 86401; (520) 757-3161.

Baboquivari Peak Wilderness

On Arizona's smallest designated Wilderness, Baboquivari Peak rises sharply to dominate the scenic desert terrain of the east side of the Baboquivari Range, near the Mexican border. On the western side of the range lies the Papago Indian Reservation; visitors must buy a permit to enter the reservation. Baboquivari, near the southern end of the area, rates as the only major peak in the state requiring technical climbing ability to reach the summit, a popular attraction for rock climbers. Elevations range from 7,730 feet on the summit to 4,500 feet on the desert floor. Vegetation in the higher country includes oak, walnut, and piñon; saguaro, paloverde, and chaparral grace the lower elevations.

You can hike along animal tracks that human feet have pounded into informal trails. The Nature Conservancy maintains a public-access route to the edge of the Wilderness from Humphrey Ranch in Thomas Canyon. The hiking is strenuous, but your rewards are solitude and splendid vistas. Always carry plenty of water.

ARIZONA

Baboquivari Peak Essentials

Size: 2,065 acres.
Year Designated: 1990.
Location: Southern Arizona.
Easiest Access: From Tucson, take State Highway 86 west about 22 miles. Turn south on State Highway 286 and drive about 30 miles to the entrance to Thomas Canyon.
Season: Fall to spring.
Wilderness Fees/Permits: None.
Maps: USGS topographic map is Baboquivari Peak.
Management: BLM Tucson Resource Area, 12661 East Broadway, Tucson, AZ 85748; (520) 722-4289.

Bear Wallow Wilderness

Some of the largest acreage of virgin ponderosa pine in the Southwest stands on Bear Wallow Wilderness, venerable reminders of a once extensive forest of these giants. Down the length of the area, through a blanket of pine, fir, and spruce, beautiful Bear Wallow Creek flows year-round, shaded by green riparian hardwoods. The creek provides a habitat for the endangered Apache trout; anglers can try for other species in the creek and its north and south forks. Early explorers were impressed by the large number of well-used wallows, which revealed how plentiful the area's population of black bears was. Black bears still abound, and you may see elk, deer, squirrels, and a diverse community of smaller mammals, birds, and reptiles. Wildflowers bloom in profusion, especially during the summer rains. Poison ivy grows tall and dangerously abundant.

Five trails offer foot and horse access to Bear Wallow. The Reno Trail (1.9 miles) and the Gobbler Point Trail (2.7 miles) drop into the canyon of the creek from easily accessible trailheads on Forest Service roads. The Bear Wallow Trail follows the rocky stream bed 7.6 miles to the boundary of the San Carlos Apache Indian Reservation. The Schell Trail (2.8 miles) connects the Bear Wallow Trail and the canyon floor to the Rose Spring Trail (5.4 miles), which skirts the southern boundary along the precipitous Mogollon Rim, the southern edge of the vast Colorado Plateau. From atop the Mogollon Rim the views are tremendous. Visitors to the San Carlos Reservation must have an advance permit. For information and permits, contact the San Carlos Tribal Office, Box O, San Carlos, AZ 85550. Human use of Bear Wallow is light.

Bear Wallow Essentials

Size: 11,080 acres.
Year Designated: 1984.
Location: Eastern Arizona.
Easiest Access: From Alpine, take U.S. 191/666 south for 30 miles. Turn west on Forest Service Road 54 and go about six miles to a fork in the road. Take the north fork until the road ends at a parking area and the Rose Spring Trailhead, which is below the road at a signed gate in the fence.
Season: Fall to spring.
Wilderness Fees/Permits: None.
Maps: USGS topographic map is Baldy Bill.
Management: Alpine Ranger District, Apache-Sitgreaves National Forest, P.O. Box 469, Alpine, AZ 85920; (520) 339-4384.

ARIZONA

Beaver Dam Mountains Wilderness

The jagged mountains and gently sloping alluvial plain of Beaver Dam Mountains Wilderness straddle the Arizona-Utah border. Management of the Wilderness is shared by the BLM in both states (see Utah, Beaver Dam Mountains Wilderness). It is further divided into northeastern and southwestern units by Cedar Pockets Road. South of Beaver Dam lies Paiute Wilderness, which is separated by the corridor of Interstate 15.

Joshua trees, desert shrubs, and scattered grasses are the primary vegetation. Several rare plant species have also been identified here. Notable wildlife include desert bighorn sheep, the endangered desert tortoise, and large numbers of raptors. The woundfin minnow, another species threatened with extinction, lives in the Virgin River, which flows through the eastern section of the area for 13 miles. River rafters and kayakers have been increasingly attracted to the Virgin River, but water levels can be too low for this form of travel in the fall and winter. Backpacking in the Wilderness has seen a substantial increase in recent years. The Virgin River Campground is open year-round, providing 115 campsites and a campground host for $4 a site per night.

There are no trails, so hone your cross-country skills before heading out.

Beaver Dam Mountains Essentials

Size: 17,003 acres in Arizona (19,600 total).
Year Designated: 1984.
Location: Northwestern Arizona.
Easiest Access: From Saint George, Utah, take Interstate 15 south for approximately 15 miles toward Mesquite. Take the first Arizona exit (18), which leads to the Cedar Pockets Rest Area and the Virgin River Campground.
Season: Fall to spring.
Wilderness Fees/Permits: None.
Maps: USGS topographic maps are Castle Cliff, Jarvis Peak, Littlefield, and Mountain Sheep Spring.
Management: BLM Interagency Offices, 345 East Riverside Drive, Saint George, UT 84970; (801) 628-4491.

Big Horn Mountains Wilderness

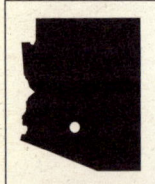

Big Horn Peak towers 1,800 feet above a desert plain near the middle of this Wilderness. Neighboring escarpments add to this area's exceptional scenic value. Nine miles of the jumbled ridgeline of the Big Horn Mountains cross the Wilderness, surrounded by small hills, fissures, chimneys, and slim canyons. Here you'll find desert bighorn sheep as well as Gila monsters, kit foxes, and desert tortoise. Other permanent residents include golden eagles, prairie falcons, barn owls, and great horned owls, all of whom nest on the walls of the canyons. Just to the north of this area, separated only by a thin jeep road, lies Hummingbird Springs Wilderness (see below).

Although there are no trails, hikers can access the area via unmaintained dirt roads from the northern, eastern, and western boundaries. In addition to backpackers, the area draws expert rock climbers to its tall cracked walls. There are plenty of primitive campsites.

ARIZONA

Big Horn Mountains Essentials

Size: 20,600 acres.
Year Designated: 1990.
Location: Western central Arizona.
Easiest Access: From Phoenix, take Interstate 10 west about 58 miles to the Salome Road exit. Drive about one mile north on Salome Road. Turn north on the unmaintained dirt road and continue for approximately four miles to the western boundary. Four-wheel-drive vehicles are recommended.
Season: Fall to spring.
Wilderness Fees/Permits: None.
Maps: USGS topographic maps are Big Horn Peak, Burnt Mountain, and Little Horn Peak.
Management: BLM Lower Gila Resource Area, 2015 West Deer Valley Road, Phoenix, AZ 85027; (602) 780-8090.

Cabeza Prieta Wilderness

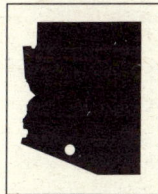

You may have a hard time enjoying a peaceful wildland experience at Cabeza Prieta, despite the fact that it's Arizona's largest Wilderness. Part of Cabeza Prieta National Wildlife Refuge, the majority of the Wilderness lies within the Barry M. Goldwater Air Force Range. That means low-flying aircraft, bound for the gunnery area just north of the refuge, often fill the desert skies. When the bombs are dropping, all entry into the region is banned, but you might stumble upon unexploded ordinance any day.

Cabeza Prieta shares 56 miles of border with Mexico, and across the refuge runs the remains of El Camino del Diablo (The Devil's Highway), a trail first blazed in 1540. Connecting Mexico to California, it was named for the many travelers who died along the way. Rugged mountains and broad desert valleys dotted with sand dunes and lava flows dominate the region.

Established in 1939 to preserve a Sonoran Desert ecosystem, the refuge has primarily protected the desert bighorn sheep, but the endangered Sonoran pronghorn has also benefited greatly. You may see mule deer, rabbits, kangaroo rats, and pocket gophers living among the creosote bushes, mesquite, ocotillo, chollas, and even the occasional massive elephant tree. Hot and dry, conditions at the refuge are ideal for reptiles such as side-blotched lizards, desert horned lizards, Great Basin whiptails, and six species of rattlesnakes. Among these are sidewinders, Mojave rattlers, and western diamondback rattlers.

Hikers will find no maintained trails. You must bring your own water, you cannot build campfires, and the area is not patrolled (handy to know in case you encounter trouble). Hiking may be hazardous to your health, but you'll find exemplary desert backpacking here. Bring a compass. Organ Pipe Cactus National Monument shares the eastern border.

ARIZONA

Cabeza Prieta Essentials

Size: 803,418 acres.
Year Designated: 1990.
Location: Southern Arizona.
Easiest Access: From Yuma, take Interstate 8 east approximately 107 miles to Gila Bend. Take State Highway 85 south about 46 miles to the refuge office in Ajo.
Season: The heat only lets up in winter and in the evening.
Wilderness Fees/Permits: An advance permit must be acquired from the refuge and a Military Hold-Harmless Agreement must be signed.
Maps: A free map is available from the refuge manager.
Management: Cabeza Prieta National Wildlife Refuge, 1611 North Second Avenue, Ajo, AZ 85321; (520) 387-6483.

Castle Creek Wilderness

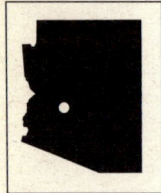

On the stark eastern slopes of the Bradshaw Mountains, Castle Creek Wilderness stands between Phoenix and Flagstaff, easily accessible from both. Extremely rugged topography rises to granite peaks that top off at 7,000 feet on Juniper Ridge, offering overlooks of the Agua Fria River. In the Wilderness' southeastern corner the elevation drops to 2,800 feet. Saguaro cactus, paloverde, mesquite, jojoba, catclaw, and grasslands dominate the lower elevations. Up higher you'll find chaparral communities of scrubby live oak, mountain mahogany, and manzanita with piñon and juniper on southern slopes. Dense populations of mule deer and javelina inhabit this area, along with a few mountain lions, bobcats, black bears, elk, coyotes, rabbits, foxes, skunks, and badgers. Snakes and lizards live here, and numerous birds soar overhead, including doves, quail, hawks, owls, ravens, jays, and many smaller species.

You'll find limited water, despite the name, and raging summer temperatures. Nine maintained trails offer a total of 23 miles of hiking through the area. The Algonquin Trail (five miles) runs north-south with trailheads on Forest Service Roads 52 and 259. Twin Peaks Trail (7.75 miles) snakes through the Wilderness from Horsethief Recreation Area to end at a junction with the Castle Creek Trail. When joined to Trail 239, the major east-west pathway, the Castle Creek Trail forms a 5.7-mile loop.

Castle Creek Essentials

Size: 26,030 acres.
Year Designated: 1984.
Location: Central Arizona.
Easiest Access: From Mayer, southeast of Prescott, take Main Street through town and continue a short distance to Antelope Creek Road. Turn southeast and drive approximately nine miles to Cordes. Turn south on Forest Service Road 259 and drive about 20 miles to Crown King. Turn south on Forest Service Road 259A and drive a half mile to Forest Service Road 52, then turn southeast and drive 2.2 miles to the Algonquin Trail turnoff. The trailhead is 100 yards north of the turnoff.
Season: Late fall to early spring.
Wilderness Fees/Permits: None.
Maps: Topographic maps are available for $3 each from the U.S. Forest Service, Public Affairs Office, 517 Gold Avenue SW, Albuquerque, NM 87102; (505) 842-3292.
Management: Bradshaw Ranger District, Prescott National Forest, 2230 East Highway 69, Prescott, AZ 86301; (520) 445-7253.

ARIZONA

Cedar Bench Wilderness

Cedar Bench falls along a broad northwest-southeast trending ridge or "bench," and from this elevated perch visitors can glimpse stunning views of the desert's vivid colors. The Wilderness occupies the dividing line between the Verde River and the Agua Fria River drainages, with the Wild and Scenic Verde River forming a portion of its eastern boundary. The Verde is a dangerous and difficult waterway, seldom run except during peak flow, that supports at least 21 species of animals and fish that are endangered or of special interest to biologists. Elevations in the area range between 4,500 feet and 6,700 feet with a primary vegetative cover of chaparral and lesser amounts of piñon pine and Utah juniper. There are two trails from Brown's Spring, one heading west across the Wilderness for 4.4 miles and the other heading south for 6 miles. If you enjoy solitude and wildlife observation, your efforts will be well rewarded.

Cedar Bench Essentials

Size: 14,950 acres.
Year Designated: 1984.
Location: Central Arizona.
Easiest Access: From Camp Verde, head about 15 miles south on Salt Mine Road (Forest Service Road 574) to the Brown's Spring Trailhead.
Season: Fall to spring.
Wilderness Fees/Permits: None.
Maps: Topographic maps are available for $3 each from the U.S. Forest Service, Public Affairs Office, 517 Gold Avenue SW, Albuquerque, NM 87102; (505) 842-3292.
Management: Verde Ranger District, Prescott National Forest, P.O. Box 670, Camp Verde, AZ 86322-0670; (520) 567-4121.

Chiricahua National Monument Wilderness

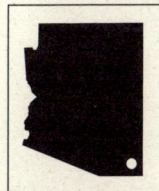

About 27 million years ago, give or take a few millennia, Turkey Creek Caldera spewed forth white-hot ash that settled, cooled, and fused into a 2,000-foot-thick layer of dark volcanic rock, forming the Chiricahua Mountains. Then nature's sculptors (wind, water, ice) began whittling away at the rock to eventually create craggy grottoes, towering rock spires, massive stone columns, and balanced rocks weighing hundreds of tons. Known to the Apache Indians as "Land of the Standing-Up Rocks," this 11,985-acre wonderland of stone was renamed Chiricahua National Monument by the National Park Service.

The Wilderness encompasses most of the monument. Here you will find a relatively moist, cool "island" standing above and distinctly separate from the surrounding Sonoran and Chihuahuan Deserts, an island where snow falls in winter and temperatures in the summer hover "mildly" in the 90s. The rare birds that congregate here—such as sulphur-bellied flycatchers, Mexican chickadees, and Elegant trogons—make this a bird-watcher's paradise. Among the mammals you might see are Apache fox squirrels, coatimundis, and peccaries. Trees include the Chihuahua pine and the Apache pine. Cacti in the lowlands give way to oaks, alligator juniper, and Arizona cypress in the canyons, chaparral on the ridges, and fir and aspen on the highest slopes.

ARIZONA

A one-way scenic drive crosses the monument and about 20 miles of trails give access to the Wilderness: the 2.4-mile Natural Bridge Trail, which leads to, naturally, a bridge, and the one-mile Faraday Meadows Trail in the north; the 1.5-mile Rhyolite Canyon Trail in the south, which leads to the Heart of Rocks. (A gathering of spectacular rock formations, Heart of Rocks is probably the most wonderful spot in the Wilderness.) The Rhyolite Canyon Trail splits off on the 1.6-mile Echo Canyon Loop Trail, which in turn forks onto the short Hallstone Trail (less than one mile long). No overnight camping is allowed in the Wilderness. A campground with 26 sites is available on a first-come, first-served basis. No services exist in the monument other than an informative visitors center. Stock up on supplies in Willcox.

Chiricahua National Monument Essentials

Size: 10,290 acres.
Year Designated: 1976; expanded in 1984.
Location: Southeastern Arizona.
Easiest Access: From Interstate 10 in Willcox, go south on State Highway 186 and follow the signs approximately 40 miles to the monument.
Season: Open all year, but most visitors come in March, April, and May.
Wilderness Fees/Permits: The entrance fee to the monument is $4.
Maps: A free map is available from the monument ranger.
Management: Chiricahua National Monument, Dos Cabezas Route, Box 6500, Willcox, AZ 85643; (520) 824-3560.

Chiricahua Wilderness

More than a century ago the great chiefs Cochise and Geronimo took the Chiricahua Mountains as their hunting grounds. From here the Apache defended their homeland by launching surprise attacks on U.S. Army troops and pioneer settlements, and here the Chiricahua Apache Indian Reservation stood for a short time. Today, the Wilderness adjoins Chiricahua National Monument. Home to some of the most starkly spectacular geology of the southwestern United States, this mountainous realm rises to a climax on Chiricahua Peak at 9,797 feet.

Many of the unusual birds that live here are most often seen in Mexico. The terrain supports diverse plant life, such as cactus and fine stands of ponderosa pine, Mexican white pine, Apache pine, Chiricahua pine, Douglas fir, Engelmann spruce, white fir, aspen, juniper, piñon, madrona, and oak. Wildlife includes peccaries, coatimundies, and a plentiful supply of hungry black bears.

Due to dense brush and timber growth, steep elevations, precipitous canyon walls, an undependable water supply, and the threat of flash floods, few humans venture from the 13 established pathways in the well-developed trail system. Trailheads at Pole Bridge and Morse Canyon give easy access to the Wilderness, and the Morse Canyon Trail rewards hikers for their efforts with excellent views over some of the roughest country in southeastern Arizona.

ARIZONA

Chiricahua Essentials

Size: 87,700 acres.
Year Designated: 1964; expanded in 1984.
Location: Southeastern Arizona.
Easiest Access: From Interstate 10 in Willcox, drive about 40 miles south on State Highway 186. From Chiricahua National Monument, go south on State Highway 181 for about 11 miles to Turkey Creek Road (Forest Service Road 41). On Turkey Creek Road, drive east about 9.8 miles to the Pole Bridge Trailhead or 11 miles to the Morse Canyon Trailhead.
Season: Summers are only moderately hot for Arizona, and winters are usually cold.
Wilderness Fees/Permits: None for the Wilderness; there is a fee to visit the monument.
Maps: USGS topographic maps are Chiricahua Peak, Fife Peak, Portal, Portal Peak, Rustler Park, Stanford Canyon, and Swede Peak.
Management: Douglas Ranger District, Coronado National Forest, RR 1, Box 228-R, Douglas, AZ 85607; (520) 364-3468.

Cottonwood Point Wilderness

On the map, this piñon-, juniper-, and sagebrush-covered Wilderness looks like two small "peninsulas" divided by Cottonwood Canyon. Extending south from the Arizona-Utah border, the land rises to 6,322 feet on Cottonwood Point itself at the lower end of the western peninsula. Craggy pinnacles and 1,000-foot cliffs of multicolored Navajo sandstone cap this irregular plateau. Between the crags lie deep and narrow canyons, the wetter ones filled with willow and cottonwood. Mule deer, bobcat, and mountain lions hide in this area, and coyotes lift their voices to splendid moonlit nights. Immediately to the north lies Utah's Canaan Mountain Wilderness Study Area.

The BLM describes this convoluted, rugged country as "reminiscent of the landscapes of Zion National Park." Without trails and difficult to access, Cottonwood Point receives few human visitors. It's a prime opportunity for quiet canyon backpacking and horsepacking.

Cottonwood Point Essentials

Size: 6,500 acres.
Year Designated: 1984.
Location: Northern Arizona.
Easiest Access: From Colorado City, drive between about three miles south on State Highway 389. Turn east on Road 237 and drive one mile to an unmarked dirt road. Turn north and drive a short distance until you're near the Wilderness' western boundary. Access is tricky; contact the BLM before heading out.
Season: Fall to spring.
Wilderness Fees/Permits: None.
Maps: USGS topographic maps are Colorado City and Moccasin.
Management: BLM Interagency Offices, 345 East Riverside Drive, Saint George, UT 84970; (801) 628-4491.

ARIZONA

Coyote Mountains Wilderness

With their steep, rugged peaks, massive rounded bluffs, sheer cliff faces, and large open canyons, the Coyote Mountains might well remind you of a desert Yosemite. The second smallest Wilderness in Arizona, this area offers a fine opportunity to have a challenging backcountry experience. Part of the challenge is getting permission to cross the private and Native American reservation lands that completely surround the area. No legal access exists; consult the BLM about getting into the area.

Once within the Wilderness boundaries, you'll find a highly scenic area rising to a high point of 6,529 feet. Rich in wildlife, it is home to deer and bighorn sheep. Vegetation includes paloverde, saguaro, chaparral, and woodlands of oak. Several miles of old trails wander through the Wilderness. Artists come to paint, hunters to track, amateur geologists to examine the rocks, while hikers occasionally wander through, seeking solitude.

Coyote Mountains Essentials

Size: 5,080 acres.
Year Designated: 1990.
Location: Southern Arizona.
Easiest Access: From Tucson, follow State Highway 86 west to Three Points. Continue 16 miles west on State Highway 86, then turn south on Indian Reservation Route 39 and drive about four miles to Pan Tak Pass. Hike due east into the mountains and you'll cross the Wilderness boundary within two-tenths of a mile.
Season: Fall to spring.
Wilderness Fees/Permits: Permission to park and access the area must be obtained from private landholders or by calling the Tohono O'odham Indians at (520) 746-1222.
Maps: USGS topographic maps are Kitt Peak, Palo Alto Ranch, Pan Tak, and San Pedro.
Management: BLM Tucson Resource Area, 12661 East Broadway, Tucson, AZ 85748; (520) 722-4289.

Dos Cabezas Mountains Wilderness

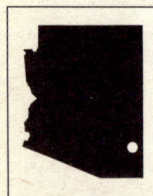

Sculpted with steep slopes and granite outcroppings, the rugged and remote Dos Cabezas Mountains rise in elevation from 4,080 feet to 7,587 feet on Government Peak in the southeast corner. Seasonal waterfalls tumble down boulder-strewn Government Peak, creating pools that invite a dip. Two other peaks rise above 7,000 feet. From the high elevations, you'll be rewarded with outstanding views of Sulphur Springs and San Simon Valleys and the faint outlines of numerous mountain ranges in the distance. Several springs attract an abundance of wildlife, including white-tailed deer, mule deer, mountain lions, golden eagles, and bald eagles. The endangered peregrine falcon migrates through the area. In Buckeye Canyon the beautiful collared lizard suns itself on desert-hot rocks. Mountain shrub, desert shrub, and riparian vegetation cover the Wilderness.

The Bureau of Land Management maintains a picnic area in Happy Camp Canyon, near the eastern boundary amid tall sycamores. From Happy Camp, an abandoned road leads up Howell Canyon, past remnants of turn-of-the-century mining operations.

ARIZONA

Dos Cabezas Mountains Essentials

Size: 11,998 acres.
Year Designated: 1990.
Location: Southeastern Arizona.
Easiest Access: From Interstate 10 in Bowie, travel south on Apache Pass Road toward Fort Bowie and continue for about five miles. Continue past the end of the pavement. Look for an old windmill near a road heading southwest; turn onto this road and drive about 2.5 miles, bearing right when the road forks. Just past the fork, turn south on an unmarked dirt road and continue one-quarter mile to Happy Camp Canyon.
Season: Fall to spring.
Wilderness Fees/Permits: None.
Maps: USGS topographic maps are Bowie Mountain North, Dos Cabezas, and Luzena.
Management: BLM San Simon Resource Area, 425 East Fourth Street, Safford, AZ 85546; (520) 428-4040.

Eagletail Mountains Wilderness

Fifteen miles of the Eagletail Mountains' rough ridgeline run through the northern section of this Wilderness, including 3,300-foot Eagletail Peak. Cemetery Ridge lies along the southern border. Geology buffs can examine several distinct rock strata throughout these mountains, and everyone can marvel at such geologic wonders as natural arches, high spires and monoliths, jagged sawtooth ridges, and numerous washes between six and eight miles long. Courthouse Rock, a huge granite monolith, stands over 1,000 feet above the desert floor near the northern border and attracts technical rock climbers. Between the two main ridges stretches a vast desert plain of ocotillo, cholla, creosote, ironwood, saguaro cactus, barrel cactus, Mormon tea, mesquite, and sand. Summer temperatures rage and send up thermals upon which raptors ride as they scan the landscape for a desert rodent snack. The great horned owl and the coyote live here, but they keep themselves well hidden from backpackers, campers, and horseback riders.

Eagletail Mountains Essentials

Size: 89,000 acres.
Year Designated: 1990.
Location: Western Arizona.
Easiest Access: From Phoenix, take Interstate 10 west for approximately 58 miles to Exit 81. Drive five miles south on Harquahala Road, then turn west on Courthouse Rock Road and continue for five miles. A four-wheel-drive vehicle will be necessary to reach the Wilderness boundary, which lies about one mile past the end of the maintained road.
Season: Late fall to early spring.
Wilderness Fees/Permits: None.
Maps: USGS topographic maps are Eagletail Mountains, Hope, and Little Horn Mountains.
Management: BLM Yuma Resource Area, 3150 Winsor Avenue, Yuma, AZ 85365; (520) 726-6300.

ARIZONA

East Cactus Plain Wilderness

An immense desert with an intricate crescent-dune topography, the Cactus Plain is a land of shifting sands interspersed with more stable structures. This Wilderness encompasses the eastern third of the plain. Dense dune-shrub vegetation grows here, and some of the plants—such as woolly heads, sand flat milk vetch, Death Valley Mormon tea, and linearleaf sand spurge—are seldom, if ever, found elsewhere in Arizona. The elf owl, flat-tailed horned lizard, and the Mojave Desert fringe-toed lizard roam this land, often beyond human purview. Desert quiet reigns on Cactus Plain, and the early morning and late afternoon sunlight slants eerily across a barren and pinkish land. You'll find no trails. Carry plenty of water, and be sure to bring a map and compass.

East Cactus Plain Essentials

Size: 14,630 acres.
Year Designated: 1990.
Location: Western Arizona.
Easiest Access: From Phoenix, take Interstate 10 west to the Vicksburg exit (45) and go north about 10 miles to Vicksburg. Turn northwest on State Highway 72 and continue about 18 miles to Bouse, then turn north on the Swansea Road. Continue for eight miles, at which point Swansea Road forms the southeast boundary of the Wilderness.
Season: Late fall to early spring.
Wilderness Fees/Permits: None.
Maps: USGS topographic map is Buckskin Mountain West SW.
Management: BLM Havasu Resource Area, 3189 Sweetwater Avenue, Lake Havasu City, AZ 86403; (520) 855-8017.

Escudilla Wilderness

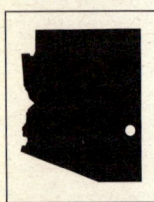

You can see towering Escudilla Mountain from just about anywhere in the neighborhood (the neighborhood of eastern Arizona, that is). The third highest mountain in Arizona (10,912 feet), Escudilla sits on the third smallest Wilderness in the state, home to 500 acres of mountain meadows. The Wilderness encompasses the upper reaches of the mountain, and aspen cover about 40 percent of the area, regrowth from a terrible fire in 1953. It was here that Aldo Leopold arrived at the side of a wounded wolf "in time to watch a fierce green fire dying in her eyes," an experience that changed his life. The last known grizzly bear in Arizona was killed here, and Leopold wrote: "Somehow it seems that the spirit of the bear is still there, prowling the huge meadows, lurking in the thick stands of aspen and spruce, wandering the steep slopes that looking down from is like looking out of the window of an airplane."

Two trails give access to Escudilla Wilderness, one maintained and the other not. The six-mile, maintained Escudilla National Recreation Trail, approaches the summit from the Terry Flat Loop Road and once led to a lookout tower. The Government Trail starts at the base of the mountain and also climbs to the summit. Although the Government Trail is popular among hikers, the U.S. Forest Service discourages travel there. You will find little water, only views that reach to Flagstaff 100 miles away.

ARIZONA

Escudilla Essentials

Size: 5,200 acres.
Year Designated: 1984.
Location: Eastern Arizona.
Easiest Access: From Springerville, near the New Mexico border, take U.S. 191/666 south for approximately 22 miles. Turn east on Forest Service Road 56 and drive about 4.5 miles to a parking lot and the maintained trailhead.

Season: Fall, when the aspen turn gold.
Wilderness Fees/Permits: None.
Maps: Topographic maps are available for $3 each from the U.S. Forest Service, Public Affairs Office, 517 Gold Avenue SW, Albuquerque, NM 87102; (505) 842-3292.
Management: Alpine Ranger District, Apache-Sitgreaves National Forest, P.O. Box 469, Alpine, AZ 85920; (520) 339-4384.

Fishhooks Wilderness

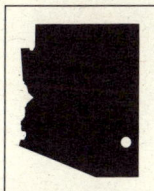

Sharing a long northeastern border with San Carlos Indian Reservation, Fishhooks Wilderness is a haven of solitude in an isolated and seldom visited region of Arizona. Ruggedly beautiful with grand vistas, the area contains Upper, Middle, and Lower Fishhooks, and Sam, Steer Springs, and Dutch Pasture Canyons, all of which offer pleasant hiking among shady riparian vegetation. Wells, springs, and tanks supply the area's water. Set in the Gila Mountains, Gila Peak, on the southern side of the Wilderness, rises to 6,629 feet and supports a border piñon pine forest found only in southeastern Arizona. On lower benches and slopes you'll roam through grasslands and chaparral. Be forewarned: if you want to wander into the reservation you'll need a special permit.

Fishhooks Essentials

Size: 10,833 acres.
Year Designated: 1990.
Location: Southeastern Arizona.
Easiest Access: From Phoenix, take U.S. 60 about 93 miles east to Globe. Continue 47 miles east on U.S. 70 to Geronimo. Take the rough Diamond Bar Road north about 15 miles to Diamond Bar Spring and the western boundary.

Season: Fall to spring.
Wilderness Fees/Permits: None.
Maps: USGS topographic maps are Ash Creek Ranch, Gila Peak, and San Carlos NE.
Management: BLM Gila Resource Area, 425 East Fourth Street, Safford, AZ 85546; (520) 428-4040.

Fossil Springs Wilderness

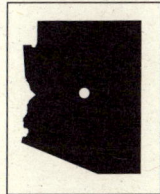

"Where there is water, there is life," the saying goes, and Fossil Springs proves it's true every day of the year. At the bottom of a steep and wide canyon, at the edge of the Colorado Plateau just south of the Mogollon Rim, a group of springs pump water to the surface at the rate of about 20,000 gallons per minute. That endless water supply supports one of the most diverse riparian ecosystems in the state—more than 30 species of trees set among native desert shrub. It also creates a haven for abundant wildlife: elk and deer higher up; javelina, coyote, skunk, ring-tailed cat, fox, and smaller

ARIZONA

mammals lower down; and more than 100 species of birds.

The canyon of Fossil Springs extends northeast for about 12 miles and splits into Sandrock Canyon and Calf Pen Canyon, as well as several other sheer-walled side canyons. You'll discover an area that has retained much of its natural integrity, a clean and pristine place to visit. Traces of early Native American civilization may be found here. The Mail Trail (3.1 miles), once used by horseback mail deliverers, the Fossil Springs Trail (2 miles), and the Flume Road Trail (3.5 miles) provide access to the Wilderness, but few humans ever venture beyond the springs region. You should plan on several days of backpacking to explore the hidden parts of the Wilderness.

Fossil Springs Essentials

Size: 11,550 acres.
Year Designated: 1984.
Location: Central Arizona.
Easiest Access: From Strawberry, drive 4.5 miles west on Forest Service Road 708 to the Fossil Springs Trail parking area.
Season: Fall and spring.
Wilderness Fees/Permits: None.
Maps: Topographic maps are available for $3 each from the U.S. Forest Service, Public Affairs Office, 517 Gold Avenue SW, Albuquerque, NM 87012; (505) 842-3292.
Management: Beaver Creek Ranger District, Coconino National Forest, HC 64, Box 240, Rimrock, AZ 86335; (520) 567-4501.

Four Peaks Wilderness

Rising from desert foothills near the center of the Wilderness, a major mountain with four peaks can be seen from great distances in all directions. From the craggy summits the land drops down a complex series of ridges and drainages to bluffs and deep gorges. Elevations vary from around 1,600 feet to 7,657 feet on Brown's Peak, the highest of the four peaks.

Ponderosa pine and some Douglas fir grow in the highlands. A few aspen stand on the north side of Brown's Peak. Intermediate elevations have produced impenetrable thickets of manzanita, Gambel oak, and piñon pine. Below 4,000 feet, grasslands blend into the Upper Sonoran Desert and impressively huge saguaro cacti thrive. The narrow canyons are pleasingly shaded with cottonwoods and sycamores.

One of the densest black bear populations in Arizona lives in this Wilderness. Other mammals include ring-tailed cats, skunks, coyotes, deer, javelinas, and mountain lions. Keep your eyes open for rattlesnakes, scorpions, black widow spiders, centipedes, and millipedes.

If you climb the mountain be prepared for temperatures noticeably cooler than down below. Lightning storms occur regularly during "desert monsoon season" (July and August) and flash floods are common. Snow accumulates here in winter.

A 40-mile trail network offers ample hiking opportunities. Some trails, such as Brown's Trail (two miles) and Pigeon Trail (two miles), are in excellent shape, while others are in poor condition, among them the Cane Spring Trail (2.3 miles) and the Oak Flat Trail (1.8 miles). Most of the trails receive little human use. The notable exceptions are Brown's Trail and the Four Peaks Trail, a 10-miler that traverses the northern and eastern flanks of Four Peaks. Springs and streams are seasonal, and water is often impossible to find.

ARIZONA

Four Peaks Essentials
Size: 53,500 acres.
Year Designated: 1984.
Location: Central Arizona.
Easiest Access: From Mesa, take State Highway 87 north to about 11 miles past the Verde River Bridge. Turn east onto Four Peaks Road 143 and drive 18.8 miles to Forest Service Road 648. Turn south and continue 1.3 miles to the trailhead for the Brown's, Pigeon, and Four Peaks Trails.
Season: Fall and spring.
Wilderness Fees/Permits: None, but group size is limited to 15.
Maps: Topographic maps are available for $3 each from the U.S. Forest Service, Public Affairs Office, 517 Gold Avenue SW, Albuquerque, NM 87102; (505) 842-3292.
Management: Mesa Ranger District, Tonto National Forest, P.O. Box 5800, Mesa, AZ 85211-5800; (602) 835-1161.

Galiuro Wilderness

The precipitous, rocky, and brushy Galiuro Mountains rise abruptly in blocklike uplifts from the almost flat desert plains. Nineteen miles in length and six miles in width (on average), they are almost all designated Wilderness. Erosion has done its work here, creating many rugged cliffs with brightly colored rocks and exposed soils. Bisected by two main canyons, Redfield and Rattlesnake, the mountains support vegetation varying from semidesert grasslands through piñon, juniper, oak, and brush to mixed conifers and even aspens in the higher elevations. From about 4,000 feet the ground rises to 7,671 feet on Bassett Peak.

You'll find no perennial streams but riparian areas appear throughout the Wilderness. Several springs supply water almost year-round: Power's Garden, Mud Spring, Corral Spring, Juniper Spring, South Field Spring, Kielberg Dam, Walnut Spring, Cedar Spring, and Holdout Spring. The plentiful wildlife includes black bears, mountain lions, javelinas, coyotes, bighorn sheep, and pronghorn antelope, as well as many smaller mammals and birds. Near the summit of Bassett Peak you may come across the wreckage of a World War II B-24 bomber. The plane crashed there on a training run in January of 1943, killing all 11 men on board. A plaque mounted on one of the wings commemorates their final resting place.

While there are a number of hiking trails, they are poorly marked and infrequently maintained. Maps and a compass are recommended. Off the trails the topography makes walking extremely difficult. Human use of this area is light.

Galiuro Essentials
Size: 76,317 acres.
Year Designated: 1964; expanded in 1984.
Location: Southeastern Arizona.
Easiest Access: From State Highway 266 in Bonita, take Aravaipa Road north for 19 miles. Turn west on Forest Service Road 253 and drive 8.5 miles to Deer Creek and the trailheads.
Season: Fall to spring.
Wilderness Fees/Permits: None.
Maps: USGS topographic maps are Bassett Peak, Cherry Spring Peak, Harrison Canyon, Kennedy Peak, Rhodes Peak, and Winchester Mountains.
Management: Safford Ranger District, Coronado National Forest, P.O. Box 709, Safford, AZ 85548; (520) 428-4150.

ARIZONA

Gibralter Mountain Wilderness

On the western edge of the Buckskin Mountains where they flatten toward the lower Colorado River, Gibralter Mountain rises only 1,568 feet above sea level, a raggedy mass of volcanic rock cut by many deep, sandy washes and rocky canyons. Among the eroded volcanic tuff beds you'll find numerous fascinating alcoves and caves, and along the heights are rewarding vistas in all directions. Every year several hundred people come on foot and on horseback to see the sights and to photograph the colorful panoramas dotted with creosote bush, cholla, barrel cactus, and paloverde. Patient and observant wildlife watchers catch glimpses of desert bighorn sheep. A few rock climbers have discovered this area. The winding washes make fine pathways of travel. While some see it only as a barren land, others have found Gibralter Mountain a serene and beautiful desert refuge.

Gibralter Mountain Essentials

Size: 18,805 acres.
Year Designated: 1990.
Location: Western Arizona.
Easiest Access: From Phoenix, drive west on Interstate 10 to the Quartzite exit, about 20 miles from the California border. Take State Highway 95 north for 23 miles, then turn west on State Highway 72. Two miles south of Parker turn east on paved Shea Road and continue five miles. Turn north on Cienega Springs Road, which leads along the western boundary. Four-wheel-drive vehicles are recommended once you leave the pavement.
Season: Fall to spring.
Wilderness Fees/Permits: None.
Maps: USGS topographic maps are Black Peak NE, Black Peak SE, Black Peak SW, Cross Roads, and Monkeys Head.
Management: BLM Havasu Resource Area, 3189 Sweetwater Avenue, Lake Havasu City, AZ 86403; (520) 855-8017.

Grand Wash Cliffs Wilderness

You won't find the Colorado River, the force of nature that eons ago carved the Grand Wash Cliffs of Arizona, anywhere near the cliffs themselves. Today the Colorado flows about 20 miles to the south, sculpting the Grand Canyon. But this Wilderness, marking the transition zone between the Colorado Plateau and Basin and Range Provinces, preserves the river's intricate handiwork—rugged canyons, scenic escarpments, and colorful sandstone buttes. Most remarkable are the 12 miles of towering cliffs themselves, which are cut into two giant steps, the first about 2,000 feet high, and the second a 1,000-foot leap to the Shivwits Plateau. Between the two steps lies a shelf that stretches one to three miles wide. Several canyons cut deeply into the sculpted cliffs and provide opportunities for tough scrambling to the top where a piñon-juniper woodland overlooks a plain of Mojave desert shrubs below. Roads lead to the northern portion where the walking is relatively easy.

There are no maintained trails in this sparse land, but you will find an opportunity for extraordinary canyon hiking, if you don't mind the effort. Gila monsters, desert tortoises, and desert bighorn sheep live here in solitude. Access is difficult, but seekers of solitude will find it well worth the effort.

ARIZONA

Grand Wash Cliffs Essentials

Size: 36,300 acres.
Year Designated: 1984.
Location: Northwestern Arizona.
Easiest Access: From the Utah/Arizona border, drive two miles south on Interstate 15 to Exit 27. Take the unmarked dirt roads east and north for approximately five miles to Mount Trumbell Loop, then drive south for about 37 miles to Mount Dellenbaugh Road. Head 18 miles southwest to Hidden Wash and follow an unmarked dirt road nine miles west to the boundary. A four-wheel-drive vehicle is recommended.
Season: Fall to spring.
Wilderness Fees/Permits: None.
Maps: USGS topographic maps are Cane Springs SE, Grand Gulch Bench, Last Chance Canyon, Mustang Point, Olaf Knolls, and Saint George Canyon.
Management: BLM Interagency Offices, 345 East Riverside Drive, Saint George, UT 84970; (801) 628-4491.

Granite Mountain Wilderness

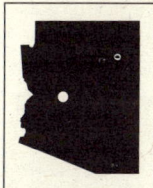

Ragged boulders, some as big as a house, stack on top of each other to an elevation of 7,626 feet in Granite Mountain Wilderness, an area about eight miles away from Prescott. From the summit of Granite Mountain itself you can look across the entire city of Prescott, as well as the towns of Chino Valley and Skull Valley. On southern slopes chaparral (a community of plants including shrub live oak, mountain mahogany, manzanita, and squaw bush) dominates with scattered stands of piñon and juniper. On northern slopes you'll also find piñon, juniper, and some pine and oak higher up. Mule deer and javelina inhabit the area, along with an occasional mountain lion, bobcat, badger, fox, skunk, coyote, rabbit, and smaller rodents.

On the southwest side of the mountain a vertical cliff attracts many technical rock climbers. Hikers, horseback riders, and hunters may be found here in abundance, primarily on two main trails. Trail 261 is a "highway" easily accessible from a parking lot at Granite Basin Recreation Area that leads 3.5 miles to eye-stretching vistas. Trail 308 crosses two miles of the northern section of the area and draws more horse riders than foot traffic. Well off the trails, over the mountain from Prescott, you may still have a chance to find Arizona solitude, but travel over the rocky outcroppings is difficult.

Granite Mountain Essentials

Size: 9,800 acres.
Year Designated: 1984.
Location: Central Arizona.
Easiest Access: From Prescott, take the Granite Basin Road north to Granite Basin Recreation Area, a distance of less than 10 miles.
Season: Fall to spring.
Wilderness Fees/Permits: None.
Maps: A Wilderness map is available for $4 from the U.S. Forest Service, Public Affairs Office, 517 Gold Avenue SW, Albuquerque, NM 87102; (505) 842-3292.
Management: Bradshaw Ranger District, Prescott National Forest, 2230 East Highway 69, Prescott, AZ 86301; (520) 445-7253.

ARIZONA

Harcuvar Mountains Wilderness

This desert encompasses over 10 miles of the Harcuvar Mountains' ridgeline, from an elevation of 2,400 feet on the bajadas to more than 5,100 feet on the mountainous crest. Plant and animal communities thrive on diverse landforms, including a 3,500-acre "island" of interior chaparral habitat on the northern ridgeline that hides a few species of wildlife cut off from their parent populations: rosy boas, Gilbert's skinks, and desert night lizards. Desert bighorn sheep live alongside mountain lions, desert tortoises, golden eagles, and several species of hawks. Isolated from the rest of the world, the Harcuvar Mountains offer splendid and lonely backpacking in the canyons and on the ridges.

Harcuvar Mountains Essentials

Size: 25,287 acres.
Year Designated: 1990.
Location: Western Arizona.
Easiest Access: From Wickenburg, take U.S. 60 approximately 50 miles west to Wenden. Head about eight miles north on the Alamo Dam Access Road. From here, jeep trails lead east about four miles to the western boundary. Four-wheel-drive vehicles are recommended.

Season: Fall to spring.
Wilderness Fees/Permits: None.
Maps: USGS topographic maps are Alamo Dam SE, Cunningham Pass, E.C.P. Peak, and Webber Canyon.
Management: BLM Havasu Resource Area, 3189 Sweetwater Avenue, Lake Havasu City, AZ 86403; (520) 855-8017.

Harquahala Mountains Wilderness

Harquahala means "running water high up" in the language of one early native tribe. This elevated region, set on one of western Arizona's largest desert ranges, was so named for its numerous perennial seeps and springs. The Harquahalas reach a high point on the western side on Harquahala Peak at 5,691 feet, the uppermost elevation in the southwestern part of the state. From the summit of the peak the panorama includes surrounding desert and mountains up to 100 miles away. Natural mountain springs support a rare habitat among Sonoran Desert mountains, a screened interior canyon system with exceptional natural diversity. Rare cacti live here among relict "islands" of chaparral and desert grasslands. Here you'll find high peaks and foothills, deep rocky canyons and valleys, and ridges dropping to bajadas. Sunset Canyon falls 1,600 feet from the steep east rim of the mountains. Brown's Canyon, which stretches for nine miles across the northeastern portion, houses the endangered desert tortoise and is seldom visited. This area also sustains the largest mule deer herd in western Arizona, a sizable raptor population, and one of the few increasing desert bighorn sheep herds.

In the 1920s the Smithsonian Institute built an observatory on Harquahala Peak and a rough trail for mules to carry up supplies. The obscure Harquahala Peak Trail runs about 5.4 miles one-way to the ruins of the observatory; rock cairns mark the way. The rest of the Wilderness offers some of Arizona's most appealing desert solitude . . . but not in summer, when the heat sends the mercury to the top of the thermometer.

ARIZONA

Harquahala Mountains Essentials

Size: 22,865 acres.
Year Designated: 1990.
Location: Western Arizona.
Easiest Access: Drive between 12 and 17 miles west on U.S. 60 from Wickenburg. Before Wenden, turn south on one of several unmarked jeep trails leading five miles to the northern boundary. Four-wheel-drive is required.

Season: Fall to spring.
Wilderness Fees/Permits: None.
Maps: USGS topographic maps are Harquahala Mountain and Socorro Peak.
Management: BLM Lower Gila Resource Area, 2015 West Deer Valley Road, Phoenix, AZ 85027; (602) 863-4464.

Hassayampa River Canyon Wilderness

The Hassayampa River flows freely for several miles along the southern and eastern portions of this Wilderness, supporting a riparian habitat. The area reaches a high point on Sam Powell Peak at 4,015 feet in the western portion, where you'll also discover a striking geological monolith called The Needle. Side canyons and uplands are covered in chaparral, paloverde, and saguaro.

Visitors come to backpack or horsepack and to photograph the landscape. A piece of private land exists within the Wilderness boundary and should not be crossed without prior permission. The easiest access also crosses private land and permission should be obtained prior to your visit.

Hassayampa River Canyon Essentials

Size: 11,840 acres.
Year Designated: 1990.
Location: Western central Arizona.
Easiest Access: From Phoenix, take U.S. 60 north approximately 50 miles to Wickenburg. Follow Constellation Road northeast for 17 miles to the Williams Ranch. The Wilderness lies immediately to the northwest.

Season: Fall to spring.
Wilderness Fees/Permits: Permission must be obtained to cross private land. For details, contact the BLM.
Maps: USGS topographic maps are Morgan Butte, Sam Powell Peak, Wagoner, and Yarnell.
Management: BLM Phoenix Resource Area, 2015 West Deer Valley Road, Phoenix, AZ 85027; (602) 780-8090.

Havasu (Needles) Wilderness

Extending for 24 miles and 44,371 acres along the lower Colorado River, partly in Arizona and partly in California, Havasu National Wildlife Refuge was established in 1941 to provide habitat and protect wildlife, including quail, geese, ducks, grebes, cranes, rails, herons, egrets, falcons, eagles, bighorn sheep, coyotes, porcupines, foxes, and bobcats. Here you may see the endangered desert tortoise and the poisonous Gila monster. The refuge is divided into four distinct areas: (1) the popular boating, canoeing, and fishing section of Topock Marsh in the north; (2) the narrow and scenic boating

ARIZONA

destination of 18-mile-long Topock Gorge near the central and south-central refuge; (3) the Havasu Wilderness Area, which is entirely in California (see California, Havasu Wilderness); and (4) the Needles Wilderness Area on the Arizona side.

The blue-green waters of the Colorado River flow gently through Topock Gorge (*havasu* means "clear blue-green waters"), forming the eastern boundary of Needles Wilderness. Through the gorge, reddish orange cliffs overhang the river. In the north, towering Fremont cottonwoods dominate the marshland. High rocky desert rises to mesas and the Needles Peaks themselves. Exemplary desert hiking through creosote, ocotillo, blue-green paloverde, and pockets of saguaro promises solitude, but camping is allowed only along the Arizona shoreline below the buoy designating the south entrance to Topock Gorge. Fires are not permitted in the Wilderness. June through September see average temperatures of 115 degrees Fahrenheit.

Havasu (Needles) Essentials

Size: 14,606 acres in Arizona (17,801 total).
Year Designated: 1990.
Location: Western Arizona.
Easiest Access: From Lake Havasu City, enter Lake Havasu and travel by boat north to Topock Gorge.
Season: Late fall to early spring.
Wilderness Fees/Permits: None.
Maps: A free map is available from the refuge manager.
Management: Havasu National Wildlife Refuge, Box 3009, Needles, CA 92763; (619) 326-3853.

Hells Canyon Wilderness

A scenic portion of the Hieroglyphic Mountain Range, this area is home to numerous peaks, mostly over 3,000 feet, encircling and isolating Burro Flats from the rest of the world. Hells Canyon is further isolated by private land on its southern, eastern, and northern sides. The most prominent of the peaks are Garfias Mountain at 3,381 feet and Hellgate Mountain at 3,339 feet. Several cliffs on the mountains attract climbers, and the canyons make for relatively easy hiking. Most of this Wilderness is covered by Sonoran Desert vegetation: saguaro, paloverde, barrel cactus, ocotillo, and desert grasses. Easily accessible, primitive camping sites are plentiful.

Hells Canyon Essentials

Size: 9,200 acres.
Year Designated: 1990.
Location: Central Arizona.
Easiest Access: From Morristown, on U.S. 60 west of Phoenix, take State Highway 74 east for approximately three miles. Turn north on Castle Hot Springs Road and continue for approximately 20 miles, then turn south on Cedar Basin Road. Cedar Basin forms the western boundary, and you can park at the head of several washes and hike east into the Wilderness. A four-wheel-drive vehicle is strongly recommended. Private land lies along the eastern, northern, and southern boundaries.
Season: Fall to spring.
Wilderness Fees/Permits: None.
Maps: USGS topographic maps are Garfias Mountain and Governors Peak.
Management: BLM Phoenix Resource Area, 2015 West Deer Valley Road, Phoenix, AZ 85027; (602) 780-8090.

ARIZONA

Hellsgate Wilderness

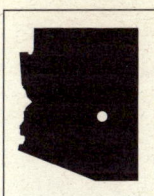

Lying at the base of the Mogollon Rim, upper Tonto Creek has incised a 1,000-foot-deep canyon that runs entirely through the center of this Wilderness. A perennial waterway, Tonto Creek creates deep emerald pools sometimes separated by impassable falls. The area also contains Haigler Creek with its impressive rock formations. Elevations range from 6,440 feet atop Horse Mountain in the northeast corner to 2,960 feet where Tonto Creek leaves the area in the southwest. Trout, catfish, and smallmouth bass inhabit both creeks, popular destinations with anglers. Abundant water helps support an abundance of wildlife: black bears, mountain lions, mule deer, coyotes, gray foxes, javelinas, beavers, and many small mammals and birds.

You will find exceptionally rough and broken terrain with moderate to very steep slopes on long rocky ridges. Archaeology buffs will encounter evidence of prehistoric use. Six trailheads give access to the Wilderness, but human use is relatively light, especially off-trail, and the U.S. Forest Service reports that foot travel can be very difficult. If you follow either creek you'll have to swim at some point. Snowfall may be substantial in winter.

Hellsgate Essentials

Size: 36,780 acres.
Year Designated: 1984.
Location: Central Arizona.
Easiest Access: From Payson, take State Highway 260 east for 11.4 miles to Forest Service Road 405A. Drive one-half mile south and turn west on Forest Service Road 893, which immediately places you at Hellsgate Ridge.
Season: Fall or spring.
Wilderness Fees/Permits: None.
Maps: Topographic maps are available for $3 each from the U.S. Forest Service, Public Affairs Office, 517 Gold Avenue SW, Albuquerque, NM 87102; (505) 842-3292.
Management: Payson Ranger District, Tonto National Forest, 1009 East Highway 260, Payson, AZ 85541; (520) 474-2269.

Hummingbird Springs Wilderness

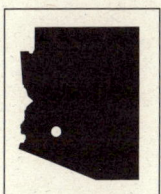

Northeast of Hummingbird Springs, which sits near the middle of this Wilderness, a colorful escarpment, Sugarloaf Mountain, climbs steeply from the Tonopah Desert to 3,418 feet and lends this area remarkable scenic value. Over eight miles of the Big Horn Mountains are included in this Wilderness. Here you'll find hills and washes and bajadas abounding with saguaro, ocotillo, cholla, paloverde, and mesquite, habitat for desert bighorn sheep, mule deer, and desert tortoise. Kit foxes and Gila monsters race along the ground while Cooper's hawks, prairie falcons, and golden eagles rule the skies.

Without maintained trails, the area can be backpacked easily, and primitive campsites abound. The water from Hummingbird Springs runs into a catchment accessible via a non-Wilderness jeep trail slicing into the area from the southern boundary. This jeep trail is all that separates Hummingbird Springs Wilderness from Big Horn Mountains Wilderness to the south.

ARIZONA

Hummingbird Springs Essentials

Size: 30,170 acres.
Year Designated: 1990.
Location: Western central Arizona.
Easiest Access: From Phoenix, take Interstate 10 west about 45 miles to the Tonopah exit. From here, take an unmaintained dirt road north approximately 12 miles to the water catchment. Four-wheel-drive vehicles are recommended.

Season: Fall to spring.
Wilderness Fees/Permits: None.
Maps: USGS topographic maps are Big Horn Peak, Burnt Mountain, Hummingbird Springs, and Little Horn Peak.
Management: BLM Lower Gila Resource Area, 2015 West Deer Valley Road, Phoenix, AZ 85027; (602) 863-4464.

Imperial Wilderness

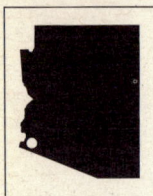

You might be surprised to find a lush river ecosystem in the midst of the Sonoran Desert, the hottest and driest in the United States, a land of prickly cacti and specially adapted plants and animals. But thanks to Imperial Dam, that's exactly what you get in this Wilderness. The dam, an irrigation diversion structure, raised the level of the lower Colorado River, the boundary between California and Arizona, and in the process formed many backwater lakes varying in size from one-half acre to 700 acres. Here, in 1941, the Imperial National Wildlife Refuge was established to preserve all forms of life found in the lower Colorado River region. The 25,765 acres of the refuge stretch along 30 miles on both sides of the river in Arizona and California. A portion of the refuge in Arizona was designated Wilderness in 1994, followed by a piece of the California side (see California, Imperial Wilderness).

When enough rain falls the desert bursts into stunning bloom: yellow paloverde, lavender smoke trees and ironwood, pink beavertails, red prickly pears, and purple and gold bellyflowers (so named because you must lie on your belly to appreciate these small blossoms). Mule deer come to drink from the river beside great blue herons while desert bighorn sheep watch from multihued hills nearby. Gambel's quail are ubiquitous, and feral burros and wild Appaloosa horses can be seen from time to time. Resident and migratory birds are abundant. Beavers inhabit the waters, which may contain a few of the endangered Colorado squawfish—sometimes known to reach five feet in length.

Backwater lakes attract anglers who fish, typically with great success, for largemouth and striped bass. With a canoe you can put in at the upper boundary for easy paddling down to Martinez Lake Marina at the lower end. Because no overnight camping is allowed on the refuge, you'll have to camp at Picacho State Recreation Area on the California side. They have developed campgrounds as well as boat-in sites. For reservations, phone (619) 765-0755. Hikers who wander into the Wilderness must carry plenty of water, a map, and a compass; each year, a few careless visitors get into jams that result in costly search-and-rescue operations.

ARIZONA

Imperial Essentials
Size: 9,220 acres in Arizona (15,056 total).
Year Designated: 1990.
Location: Western Arizona.
Easiest Access: From Yuma, take U.S. 95 north approximately 25 miles. Go west on Martinez Lake Road and follow the signs 12 miles to the refuge.
Season: Mid-October to May.
Wilderness Fees/Permits: None.
Maps: A free map is available from the refuge manager.
Management: Imperial National Wildlife Refuge, P.O. Box 72217, Martinez Lake, AZ 85365; (520) 783-3371.

Juniper Mesa Wilderness

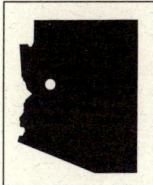

Flat-topped Juniper Mesa, running east-west, dominates this Wilderness on the southern end of the Juniper Mountains. The mesa is broken by steep canyons that open onto rolling hills with elevations ranging from 7,050 feet down to 5,650 feet. Southern slopes are vegetated primarily with piñon pines and Utah junipers, northern slopes with ponderosa pines and alligator junipers. Although there are no perennial streams and unreliable springs (especially during long periods of dry weather), wildlife is relatively abundant, including black bears, mule deer, bobcats, and Abert's squirrels. There are trails into the area, but human use is light. Hunters are the most frequent visitors.

Juniper Mesa Essentials
Size: 7,600 acres.
Year Designated: 1984.
Location: Central Arizona.
Easiest Access: From Seligman on Interstate 40, take County Route 5 south for 29 miles to the Walnut Creek Work Station. From there, take Forest Service Road 95F north for 1.5 miles to the southern boundary.
Season: Fall to spring.
Wilderness Fees/Permits: None.
Maps: Topographic maps are available for $3 each from the U.S. Forest Service, Public Affairs Office, 517 Gold Avenue SW, Albuquerque, NM 87102; (505) 842-3292.
Management: Chino Valley Ranger District, Prescott National Forest, P.O. Box 485, Chino Valley, AZ 86323; (520) 636-2302.

Kachina Peaks Wilderness

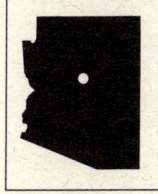

Rising to truly majestic summits, Kachina Peaks Wilderness area boasts 12,643-foot Humphrey's Peak, the highest point in Arizona. The Wilderness is part of a large and heavily vegetated composite volcano, which bears signs of a rich geologic past that included violent eruptions and lava flows. Arizona's best examples of Ice Age glaciation can be found here in lateral and medial moraines and abandoned stream beds. Erosion and frost have helped shape this area. The only arctic-alpine vegetation in the state grows up here in a fragile two-square-mile zone.

Because of this delicate ecosystem, hikers must stay on designated trails, and no camping or campfires are allowed above the tree line or

ARIZONA

within the Inner Basin. The climb to the top of Humphrey's Peak is a nontechnical five-mile walk up the sometimes steep Humphrey's Trail. Here and nowhere else on Earth grows the fragile San Francisco Peaks groudsel. Groups are limited to a maximum of 10 people.

In addition to some of the best and highest views in Arizona, this area gives visitors a chance to climb in the snow and ice and to set up a winter campsite. Some people come for the cross-country skiing in the winter, while summer sees an influx of backpackers.

These peaks are sacred to tribes including the Havasupai, Hopi, Navajo, and Zuni. Several religious shrines have been identified in the Wilderness, some of which are currently in use. Please respect ongoing religious rites and do not disturb any artifacts you may find in the area.

Kachina Peaks Essentials

Size: 18,200 acres.
Year Designated: 1984.
Location: Central Arizona.
Easiest Access: From Flagstaff, take U.S. 180 north for eight miles. Turn northeast on Forest Service Road 516 and follow it up the mountain for 6.5 miles to the Snowbowl Ski Area. The Humphrey's Trail heads northward from the parking lot.
Season: Year-round. May and June are driest. Thunderstorms often occur in July and August.
Wilderness Fees/Permits: None.
Maps: Topographic maps are available for $3 each from the U.S. Forest Service, Public Affairs Office, 517 Gold Avenue SW, Albuquerque, NM 87102; (505) 842-3292.
Management: Peaks Ranger District, Coconino National Forest, 5075 North Highway 89, Flagstaff, AZ 86004; (520) 526-0866.

Kanab Creek Wilderness

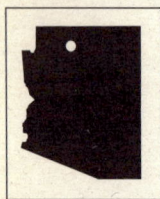

One of the major tributaries of the Colorado River, Kanab Creek is the largest tributary canyon system on the north side of the Grand Canyon. From its origin about 50 miles north in southern Utah, Kanab Creek and its feeder streams have cut a network of gorges with vertical walls deep into the Kanab and Kaibab Plateaus. Above the canyon rims the land is arid and the vegetation sparse, consisting mostly of desert shrub blackbush and sagebrush. In the creek bottom you'll find a dreamlike canyonland: richly colorful walls sculpted by wind and water into a maze of fins, knobs, and potholes, surrounded by lush riparian vegetation. Elevations range from 2,000 feet at the river to about 6,000 feet on the rim, and snow often falls in winter. Most of the slopes are angled in excess of 40 degrees. The upper reaches provide winter range for large Kaibab mule deer, and desert bighorn sheep dwell on the canyon cliffs. Almost all of Arizona's chukar partridges live here along with many smaller mammals, toads, frogs, lizards, and snakes.

Some of the most fascinating ancient rock art in the Southwest can be found in this Wilderness. Several trails lead into the area, but you should think twice before lacing up those hiking boots: the access is arduous, the hiking strenuous, and the environment "hostile" (with summer temperatures peaking at up to 120 degrees Fahrenheit). In addition, there are only a "few year-round" springs and the trails are poorly maintained. Lightning strikes the ridge tops, and storms upstream may result in flash floods miles downstream.

ARIZONA

Kanab Creek Essentials

Size: 77,100 acres (68,250 acres USFS; 8,850 acres BLM).
Year Designated: 1984.
Location: Northern Arizona.
Easiest Access: From Fredonia, follow U.S. 89A south approximately 32 miles to Jacob Lake. Head west on Forest Service Road 461 for six miles to the start of Kanab Creek in Snake Gulch.
Season: September through early May, depending on the snowfall.
Wilderness Fees/Permits: None.
Maps: The North Kaibab Recreation Map is available for $2 from the district ranger.
Management: North Kaibab Ranger District, Kaibab National Forest, 430 South Main, Fredonia, AZ 86022; (602) 643-7395. BLM Interagency Offices, 345 East Riverside Drive, Saint George, UT 84970; (801) 628-4491.

Kendrick Mountain Wilderness

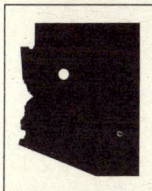

Kendrick Mountain is one of many remnants of the vast San Francisco Mountain volcanic field of central Arizona. With an elevation of 10,418 feet, Kendrick Peak stands cloaked to the very summit with ponderosa pine, Douglas fir, white fir, corkbark fir, Engelmann spruce, oak, and aspen. On some of the steeper slopes you'll find old-growth forest, valuable habitat for spotted owls, black bears, and goshawks. On north and west slopes stretch large mountain meadows where elk and mule deer graze. From the mountain you'll have fabulous views of the Grand Canyon to the north and the distant red rocks of Oak Creek and Sycamore Canyons to the south.

Well-maintained trails offer access to Kendrick Mountain. The Kendrick Mountain Trail is one of the highest in the northern half of the state, gently climbing four miles through the forest to the top of the peak from the east. You'll see an old cabin near the summit. The Pumpkin Trail runs 5.5 miles from a parking lot on the northwestern corner through forest and meadow to the summit on the west; it is steep in places. Two other trails access northern portions of the Wilderness, and both join the Kendrick Mountain or Pumpkin Trails to lead to Kendrick Peak. Water sources are unreliable, so pack in plenty.

Kendrick Mountain Essentials

Size: 6,510 acres.
Year Designated: 1984.
Location: Northern central Arizona.
Easiest Access: From Williams, take Interstate 40 east to the Parks exit. Turn left back across the overpass and left at the intersection. Turn north on Forest Service Road 141 and drive eight miles. Continue north on Forest Service Road 194 for about 4.5 miles, then turn east on Forest Service Road 171. Drive two miles, then turn north on Forest Service Road 190, which leads to the parking lot for the Kendrick Mountain Trail.
Season: Late spring to early fall.
Wilderness Fees/Permits: None.
Maps: USGS topographic maps are Kendrick and Moritz Ridge.
Management: Chalender Ranger District, Kaibab National Forest, 501 West Bill Williams Avenue, Williams, AZ 86046; (602) 635-2676. Peaks Ranger District, Coconino National Forest, 5075 North Highway 89, Flagstaff, AZ 86004; (520) 526-0866.

ARIZONA

Kofa Wilderness

In the early part of the 1900s the King of Arizona (KOFA) Mine scoured this land for precious mineral deposits. Today, in a twist of fate, the 660,000-acre Kofa National Wildlife Refuge protects the region's precious plant and animal life, including: 1,000 desert bighorn sheep, a species nearly hunted to extinction prior to Kofa's establishment in 1939; less than 100 California palm trees, remnants of wetter days; and the rare Kofa Mountain barberry, found only in southwest Arizona. About five-sixths of the refuge has been designated Wilderness, making this Arizona's second largest. In the north lie the Kofa Mountains, to the south the Castle Dome Mountains. Both are magnificently jagged peaks looming thousands of feet above the pristine desert floor of King Valley, which separates them.

Kofa offers opportunities for unparalleled desert hiking. More than 300 miles of abandoned roads and trails provide access year-round, but summer temperatures are usually searingly hot, keeping all but the most intrepid hikers at bay. Explore Kofa Queen Canyon in the daylight for a peek at a desert bighorn; bring binoculars and sit patiently and quietly to better your chances of a sighting. Backpacking and camping are allowed anywhere except on a few private inholdings, but camps must be set more than one-quarter of a mile from any water source. Stays are limited to 14 days. Campfires are permitted, but they must be small and fueled by deadwood only. At night, shy desert mammals may scurry close to the edge of the light cast by your campfire. Beware of rattlesnakes when gathering firewood. Limited hunting is permitted, and rockhounding is allowed only in the Crystal Hill region in the northern portion.

Kofa Essentials

Size: 516,200 acres.
Year Designated: 1990.
Location: Western Arizona.
Easiest Access: From Yuma, take U.S. 95 north for 53 miles to King Road, one of four well-marked refuge entrances.
Season: Fall to spring.

Wilderness Fees/Permits: None.
Maps: A free map is available from the refuge manager.
Management: Kofa National Wildlife Refuge, P.O. Box 6290, Yuma, AZ 85366-6290; (520) 783-7861.

Mazatzal Wilderness

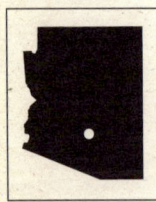

In the language of the Aztecs *mazatzal* means "an area inhabited by deer," but just how the word reached Arizona, or what significance it holds, remains somewhat of a mystery. Yes, deer inhabit the area. Yes, evidence shows that humans, among them the Yavapai and Tonto Apache, have exerted their influence here for at least 5,000 years. But there is no indication that the Aztecs themselves ever journeyed to this rough desert region.

Established as a Primitive area in 1938, Mazatzal became pre–Wilderness Act "wilderness" in 1940 and one of the original Wilderness areas in 1964. Narrow, vertical, difficult-to-access canyons fill the central and eastern portions, while the Verde River rolls through the western portion. The rolling riparian terrain along both sides of the Verde constitutes Arizona's only Wild River area.

ARIZONA

Given how close Mazatzal is to Mesa, a major population center, this is a remarkably remote and beautiful area. Elevations range from 2,100 feet at Sheep Bridge in the southwest to 7,903 feet on Mazatzal Peak. Sonoran Desert shrubland in the west rises to semidesert grasslands, then mountain shrubs such as manzanita and turbinella oak. The higher elevations support scattered piñon-juniper woodlands and a few ponderosa pines and Douglas fir.

With about 240 miles of excellent to poor trails and other hikeable tracks, backpackers should find plenty of routes to trek. The Verde River Trail follows the river for about 28 miles and invites horsepackers. The Mazatzal Divide Trail, the prime north-south route, runs about 29 miles and stays in excellent condition. The scenic Barnhardt Trail, 6.2 miles long, attracts many hikers but is not recommended for horses. Off the trails, you may find hiking impossible. Group size is limited to 15, but smaller groups are encouraged. Length of stay is limited to 14 days. Summer temperatures often reach 110 degrees Fahrenheit, and there is precious little shade to provide relief. Lightning storms are common in July and August.

Mazatzal Essentials

Size: 251,912 acres.
Year Designated: 1964; expanded in 1984.
Location: Central Arizona.
Easiest Access: From Mesa, take the Beeline Highway (State Route 87) north to the junction with State Highway 188. Continue on State Route 87 for four more miles to Forest Service Road 419, then head west 4.7 miles to the Barnhardt Trailhead. Four-wheel-drive vehicles are recommended.
Season: Fall to spring.
Wilderness Fees/Permits: None.
Maps: A Wilderness map is available for $3 from the U.S. Forest Service, Public Affairs Office, 517 Gold Avenue SW, Albuquerque, NM 87102; (505) 842-3292.
Management: Cave Creek Ranger District, Tonto National Forest, P.O. Box 5068, Carefree, AZ 85377; (602) 488-3441. Payson Ranger District, Tonto National Forest, 1009 East Highway 260, Payson, AZ 85541; (520) 474-2269.

Miller Peak Wilderness

In 1540–41 the Coronado Expedition skirted this area on a quest for riches, opening a southern doorway through which later Europeans entered the New World. Miller Peak Wilderness, one of the most rugged, wildlife-filled areas in southern Arizona, lies between the city of Sierra Vista and the Mexican border in the southern half of the Huachuca Mountains. It is near the southern terminus of the proposed 750 miles of the north-south Arizona Trail.

More than 170 species of birds have been spotted here, including 14 kinds of hummingbirds, as well as more than 60 species of reptiles and 78 species of mammals. Elevations range from 5,200 feet to 9,466 feet atop Miller Peak, the highest and southernmost peak in the United States. Once cloaked in pine and fir, this land was devastated by forest fires and has been predominantly converted to oak and grass vegetation. Many sheer cliffs rise hundreds of feet above the canyon floors. At least 21 trails, many well maintained, lead through the Wilderness from its eastern, western, and southern boundaries. The Crest Trail (11.5 miles) reaches the top of Miller Peak. Throughout the area visitors may encounter evidence of the region's bygone mining and ranching days.

ARIZONA

Miller Peak Essentials

Size: 20,190 acres.
Year Designated: 1984.
Location: Southern Arizona.
Easiest Access: From Sierra Vista, take U.S. 92 south for 14 miles. Turn south on Forest Service Road 61 (Coronado Road) and drive six miles to Coronado National Memorial, where the Crest Trail begins.
Season: Fall to spring.

Wilderness Fees/Permits: None.
Maps: Topographic maps are available for $3 each from the U.S. Forest Service, Public Affairs Office, 517 Gold Avenue SW, Albuquerque, NM 87102; (505) 842-3292.
Management: Sierra Vista Ranger District, Coronado National Forest, 5990 South Highway 92, Hereford, AZ 85615; (520) 378-0311.

Mount Baldy Wilderness

Captain George Wheeler, who surveyed much of the American Southwest in the 1870s, wrote that the view from Mount Baldy was "the most magnificent and effective of any among the large number that have come under my observation." In other words, he liked it . . . he really liked it. So do the scores of day hikers who visit Mount Baldy Wilderness today, making it one of the most popular hiking areas in Arizona.

An extinct volcano rising to 11,403 feet, Mount Baldy stands within the Fort Apache Indian Reservation; the Wilderness occupies its eastern slope. Most of the forest covering the mountain is mixed conifers with ponderosa pine in the lower elevations and fir and spruce higher up. Large meadows break open the forest, carpeted in summer with wildflowers such as Indian paintbrush, columbine, penstemon, iris, and lupine. Until winter cloaks the area in snow, elk and deer are commonly seen. Beavers, mountain lions, coyotes, bobcats, and black bears live here with a variety of smaller mammals. Bald eagles, falcons, and hawks circle beneath the sun. Summer thunderstorms are frequent, as are lightning strikes on the mountain.

Two major trails crisscross the Wilderness. The popular West Baldy Trail (Sheep's Crossing) follows the West Fork of the Little Colorado River for seven miles. The East Baldy Trail (Phelp's Cabin) follows the East Fork of the Little Colorado for seven miles and receives much less foot traffic. The trails join near the reservation boundary to form a 14-mile loop. The last half mile to the top of mountain, on Apache land, is closed.

Mount Baldy Essentials

Size: 7,079 acres.
Year Designated: 1970.
Location: Eastern Arizona.
Easiest Access: From Eagar, take State Highway 260 west for 21 miles. Turn south on U.S. 273; both trailheads are within eight miles, just off this road.
Season: May and June are the driest months, July and August the rainiest. After Labor Day the human traffic subsides.

Wilderness Fees/Permits: None, but overnight groups may not exceed six people.
Maps: A Wilderness map is available for $4 from the U.S. Forest Service, Public Affairs Office, 517 Gold Avenue SW, Albuquerque, NM 87102; (505) 842-3292.
Management: Springerville Ranger District, Apache-Sitgreaves National Forest, P.O. Box 640, Springerville, AZ 85938; (520) 333-4372.

ARIZONA

Mount Logan Wilderness

Geologically speaking, Mount Logan was an active volcanic area until only recently. Today, this spot is sort of a local secret, not appearing on many maps. Just south of Mount Trumbull Wilderness and north of the Grand Canyon, this mountain region features basalt ledges breaking ponderosa pine forests (with some virgin growth) on the upper climbs, with piñon and juniper on the lower, steeper rocky slopes. In the northern portion of the area, Mount Logan rises to 7,966 feet. A large, natural, and colorful amphitheater known as Hells Hole occupies Logan's western side. Below Hells Hole lies Hells Hollow, suggesting someone had a devilish time naming the landmarks in this scenic country.

Mount Logan is not quite as steep as nearby Mount Trumbull. Many small rodents inhabit the area, sharing their turf with mule deer, mountain lions, wild turkeys, coyotes, bobcats, spotted skunks, porcupines, and Kaibab squirrels. Backpackers and hunters are among the few, infrequent human visitors to explore Mount Logan Wilderness.

Mount Logan Essentials

Size: 14,600 acres.
Year Designated: 1984.
Location: Northern Arizona.
Easiest Access: From Fredonia, take Highway 389 west for nine miles. Drive about 46 miles south on County Road 109 (Mount Trumbull Road). Bear right on County Road 5 and turn onto BLM Road 1044; the Wilderness lies to the southwest.
Season: Fall to spring.
Wilderness Fees/Permits: None.
Maps: USGS topographic maps are Cold Spring and Mount Logan.
Management: BLM Interagency Offices, 345 East Riverside Drive, Saint George, UT 84970; (801) 628-4491.

Mount Nutt Wilderness

At 5,216 feet, Mount Nutt presides over a colorful and wild terrain encompassing eight miles of the central and highest portion of the Black Mountains. Along the main ridgeline you'll find prominent mesas that have been cut into a series of steep canyon mazes. The outlying area is ringed by volcanic plugs.

More than 100 desert bighorn sheep are known to make their home in the Wilderness. Numerous springs in the area sustain small oases of large cottonwoods, willows, and oaks. A parcel of privately held land exists in the western portion. Human visitors come to backpack, hunt, scramble on the rocks, and take photographs in the morning and evening when the sun casts a delightful glow on the carved volcanic landforms.

ARIZONA

Mount Nutt Essentials

Size: 27,530 acres.
Year Designated: 1990.
Location: Western Arizona.
Easiest Access: From Kingman, take Interstate 40 southwest for three miles to the Oatman Road exit. Travel 10 miles west on Oatman Road; continue west on Navaho Road, which runs about two miles east of the boundary. Four-wheel-drive vehicles are recommended for the jeep trails leading to the boundary.
Season: Fall to spring.
Wilderness Fees/Permits: None.
Maps: USGS topographic maps are Mount Nutt, Oatman, Secret Pass, and Union Pass.
Management: BLM Kingman Resource Area, 2475 Beverly Avenue, Kingman, AZ 86401; (520) 757-3161.

Mount Tipton Wilderness

This Wilderness contains the entire northern half of the imposing Cerbat Mountains. Although 7,148-foot Mount Tipton dominates the area, the real eye-catching attraction, the true centerpiece of the Wilderness, is located north of and below Tipton: the Pinnacles, immense tusklike rows of maroon-colored spires towering above open, yellow desert valleys. If you make the physically challenging climb up Mount Tipton, you'll discover a stand of large ponderosa pines on the northeast side and tremendous views in all directions, including the Pinnacles. Deep washes divided by descending ridges, small valleys, and bowls are found throughout the area. Unlike the nearby Black Mountains, the Cerbats are highly vegetated on their upper slopes with piñon pine, shrub live oak, manzanita, bear grass, and desert ceanothus. Large granite outcroppings break the ridgelines, the gray and red rock contrasting with the green vegetation. You'll probably encounter mule deer and raptors, and perhaps catch a glimpse of a kit fox, bobcat, and a Gambel's quail or two. The BLM maintains two waterless campgrounds on Big Wash Road on the southern boundary. Backcountry explorers should pack plenty of water in with them.

Mount Tipton Essentials

Size: 31,070 acres.
Year Designated: 1990.
Location: Northwestern Arizona.
Easiest Access: From Kingman, take U.S. 93 north to 1.5 miles past the Chloride turnoff. Take Big Wash Road east five miles to the Wilderness, which lies immediately north of the road for the next two miles.
Season: Fall to spring.
Wilderness Fees/Permits: None.
Maps: USGS topographic maps are Chloride, Grasshopper Junction, Mount Tipton, and Mount Tipton 3 SE.
Management: BLM Kingman Resource Area, 2475 Beverly Avenue, Kingman, AZ 86401; (520) 757-3161.

ARIZONA

Mount Trumbull Wilderness

Just north of the Grand Canyon and Mount Logan Wilderness Area, located at the southern end of the Uinkaret Plateau, Mount Trumbull is a large, basalt-capped mesa rising to 8,028 feet. Steep south and west slopes are dominated by piñon and juniper with cliff rose, manzanita, silktassel, and shrub live oak. You may see groves of aspen and Gambel oak with big sage, agave, and cactus lower down. On top of this plateau is a pristine forest of ponderosa pine that has never felt the logger's saw.

Mule deer, Kaibab squirrels, coyotes, bobcats, mountain lions, jackrabbits, skunks, porcupines, big brown bats, and other smaller mammals inhabit the area. Wild turkeys, hawks, owls, and other birds are abundant. Close to the ground many lizards, skinks, and snakes slither and scamper, among them the western diamondback rattler.

The Mount Trumbull Trail climbs about five miles round-trip to the summit. The trail fades out as you near the top, so bring a map and compass. Not far from the base of the mountain the BLM maintains a campground at Nixon Spring, where water is available.

Mount Trumbull Essentials

Size: 7,900 acres.
Year Designated: 1984.
Location: Northern Arizona.
Easiest Access: From Fredonia, take State Highway 389 west for approximately nine miles. Turn south on County Road 109 (Mount Trumbull Road) and drive about 46 miles. Bear right on County Road 5 and head about six miles to Nixon Flat. Mount Trumbull rises to the north.
Season: Fall and spring.
Wilderness Fees/Permits: None.
Maps: USGS topographic maps are Mount Trumbull NE, Mount Trumbull NW, and Mount Trumbull SE.
Management: BLM Interagency Offices, 345 East Riverside Drive, Saint George, UT 84970; (801) 628-4491.

Mount Wilson Wilderness

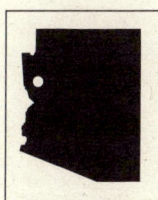

Only 30 miles from Las Vegas, Nevada, Mount Wilson Wilderness encompasses eight miles of Wilson Ridge with its summit on Mount Wilson at 5,445 feet in the northwest corner. Approaching this area from U.S. 93, you'll see a stark and forbidding landscape, a harsh and seemingly waterless countryside. Looks, however, can be deceiving, as the area hides several dependable year-round springs that support wildlife, including more than 100 desert bighorn sheep. The high country along Wilson Ridge rises in places to more than 3,000 feet above the desert floor, providing eye-stretching views over Lake Mead and the colored cliffs, badlands, mountains, and deserts in the distance. The Wilderness is almost completely surrounded by Lake Mead National Recreation Area, which is administered by the National Park Service. Backpackers will find many primitive campsites.

ARIZONA

Mount Wilson Essentials

Size: 23,600 acres.
Year Designated: 1990.
Location: Northwestern Arizona.
Easiest Access: From Kingman, take U.S. 93 north for about 50 miles. Turn northeast on paved Temple Bar Road and head eight miles, then turn northwest on a jeep trail that runs three miles to the eastern boundary.

Season: Fall to spring.
Wilderness Fees/Permits: None.
Maps: USGS topographic maps are Nelson 1 NE and Petroglyph Wash.
Management: BLM Kingman Resource Area, 2475 Beverly Avenue, Kingman, AZ 86401; (520) 757-3161.

Mount Wrightson Wilderness

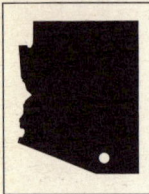

Rising a magnificent 7,000 feet from the desert floor, 9,452-foot-high Mount Wrightson is visible from great distances. At the core of the Santa Rita Mountains, this Wilderness has rough hillsides, deep canyons, and lofty ridges and peaks surrounded on all sides by semiarid hills and sloping grasslands. Ponderosa pine and Douglas fir dominate the upper elevations. The stream-fed canyons support an abundance of plant and animal life, including many montane Mexican plants that grow nowhere else north of the border. Bird-watchers will find many species seen few other places in the United States.

At the foot of Madera Canyon on the edge of the Wilderness, a developed recreation area serves as a popular jumping-off point for backpackers. Camping on the peak of Mount Wrightson makes for a rare nighttime treat: vast, quiet solitude with the shimmering backdrop of Tucson a mere 35 miles in the distance.

Mount Wrightson Essentials

Size: 25,260 acres.
Year Designated: 1984.
Location: Southern Arizona.
Easiest Access: From Tucson, take Interstate 19 south to Exit 63. Follow Continental/White House Canyon Road east for eight miles. Turn south on Madera Canyon Road and drive six miles to Madera Canyon and the Wilderness border.

Season: Fall to spring.
Wilderness Fees/Permits: None.
Maps: Topographic maps are available for $3 each from the U.S. Forest Service, Public Affairs Office, 517 Gold Avenue SW, Albuquerque, NM 87102; (505) 842-3292.
Management: Nogales Ranger District, Coronado National Forest, 2251 North Grand Avenue, Nogales, AZ 85621; (520) 281-2296.

ARIZONA

Muggins Mountains Wilderness

Just south of Yuma Military Proving Ground stands a cluster of rugged peaks at the western extreme of the Muggins Mountains, a region of colorful geologic strata and scenic landforms situated close to the California border. The most prominent summits are Muggins Peak at 1,424 feet, Klothos Temple at 1,193 feet, and Long Mountain at 914 feet. Deeply cut drainages, such as Twin Tanks Wash and Long Mountain Wash, dissect the area. A few hardy day hikers, backpackers, and rock climbers make the trek here, but there is an excellent chance you'll have this dry area to yourself. When crossing the military ground, visitors are required to stay on the main road.

Muggins Mountains Essentials

Size: 8,855 acres.
Year Designated: 1990.
Location: Southwestern Arizona.
Easiest Access: From Yuma, take Interstate 8 east to the Ligurta exit (21). Head east through Ligurta for one mile, then turn north on Dome Valley Road and drive about four miles. From the point at which the road begins to bend west, you can hike east for about a mile into Twin Tanks Wash.
Season: Fall to spring.
Wilderness Fees/Permits: None.
Maps: USGS topographic maps are Dome, Ligurta, Red Bluff Mountain, and Wellton.
Management: BLM Yuma Resource Area, 3150 Winsor Avenue, Yuma, AZ 85365; (520) 726-6300.

Munds Mountain Wilderness

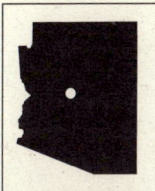

Arizona is well known for its red-rock formations, conjuring up images of magnificent crimson outcroppings set against azure skies. Munds Mountain Wilderness is home to many of these ruggedly beautiful specimens, along with several traditional high mesas common to central Arizona. Elevations on the mountain itself range from 3,600 feet to 6,825 feet, and moderate to steep slopes climb all along the Mogollon Rim. Cliff faces are marked with extensive outcroppings of Coconino and Supai sandstone, and ramp basalt flows everywhere.

Among the area's most picturesque landmarks are Courthouse Butte and magical Bell Rock. Along Horse Mesa are Jacks Canyon and Wood Canyon, both of which have outstanding riparian habitats. Desert sagebrush, desert grass and short grass plains, oak brush, chaparral, oak woodlands, and piñon-juniper woodlands fill the terrain. Visitors will encounter pools of water to dip in, rocks to climb, birds to track in the skies, some fine desert backpacking, and a slew of fantastic photo opportunities.

Relatively easily accessed from Flagstaff, the Wilderness's trails attract many recreationists. Two of them, the Hot Loop Trail and the Jacks Canyon Trail, veer away from crowded areas and lead to spectacular sights. Hot Loop climbs six miles to the top of Horse Mesa, while Jacks Canyon ventures 4.3 miles to a narrow saddle, where it joins the Munds Mountain Trail.

ARIZONA

Munds Mountain Essentials

Size: 18,150 acres.
Year Designated: 1984.
Location: Central Arizona.
Easiest Access: From Flagstaff, take U.S. 89A south. At Sedona, take State Highway 179 south for seven miles. Turn east on Forest Service Road 793 and drive two miles to the Hot Loop Trailhead.
Season: Fall to spring.
Wilderness Fees/Permits: None.
Maps: Topographic maps are available for $3 each from the U.S. Forest Service, Public Affairs Office, 517 Gold Avenue SW, Albuquerque, NM 87102; (505) 842-3292.
Management: Sedona Ranger District, Coconino National Forest, P.O. Box 300, Sedona, AZ 86336; (520) 282-4119.

Needle's Eye Wilderness

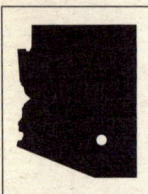

The Mescal Mountains cut across the middle of this Wilderness, their southwestern flank forming a spectacular striped slope of Paleozoic limestone that looms more than 2,500 feet high. The Gila River flows through this country and forms the Wilderness's southern border. The river threads through a marvelous section of steep-walled canyon so narrow it's earned the name Needle's Eye. Several small slickrock side canyons wind down to the Gila, bisecting the area. The narrow river channel lies tangled in dense riparian growth, often making travel difficult. The San Carlos Apache Indian Reservation occupies the territory to the north and south, and private land surrounds the rest of this Wilderness, eliminating open public access; you must obtain permission to enter here. If you enjoy hardy adventures, you'll discover a great deal of solitude in Needle's Eye.

Needle's Eye Essentials

Size: 9,201 acres.
Year Designated: 1990.
Location: Southern central Arizona.
Easiest Access: From Phoenix, take U.S. 60 to Globe and continue for nine miles along U.S. 70. At Cutter, turn south on either Coolidge Dam Road or Ranch Creek Road and drive about 17 miles south to the boundary.
Season: Fall to spring.
Wilderness Fees/Permits: You must obtain a recreation permit from the San Carlos Apache Tribe or ask permission to cross State Trust lands and private lands in advance. Contact the BLM for details.
Maps: USGS topographic maps are Christmas, Coolidge Dam, and Mescal Warm Springs.
Management: BLM Phoenix Resource Area, 2015 West Deer Valley Road, Phoenix, AZ 85027; (602) 780-8090.

ARIZONA

New Water Mountains Wilderness

Despite its name, this land of colorful craggy spires, sharp ridges, sheer rock outcrops, natural arches, and slickrock canyons receives less than five inches of rainfall annually, so you should pack in your own water. Bordered on the south by Kofa Wilderness (see above) and on the north by Interstate 10, New Water Mountains offers great backpacking. About 20 old roads are closed to car traffic and can be easily followed on foot.

Black Mesa, a large volcanic butte, stands in the northwest corner 1,200 feet above the Ranegras Plain and 3,639 feet above sea level, the highest point in the Wilderness. Vegetation is sparse. Saguaro, creosote, ocotillo, and cholla dot the hills, and paloverde and ironwood line the washes. New Water and Dripping Springs are prime lambing areas for desert bighorn sheep. Hunters track sheep and mule deer here.

New Water Mountains Essentials

Size: 21,680 acres.
Year Designated: 1990.
Location: Western Arizona.
Easiest Access: Take Exit 26 (Gold Nugget Road) on Interstate 10 and travel south for about seven miles to the northern boundary.
Season: Late fall to early spring.
Wilderness Fees/Permits: None.
Maps: USGS topographic maps are Crystal Hill, New Water Mountains, and New Water Well.
Management: BLM Yuma Resource Area, 3150 Winsor Avenue, Yuma, AZ 85365; (520) 726-6300.

North Maricopa Mountains Wilderness

Ranging from about 1,000 feet to 2,813 feet, the North Maricopa Mountains are a jumble of isolated summits and long ridges separated by washes and bajadas (desert slopes). As you would expect, they're not far north of South Maricopa Mountains Wilderness. About 10 miles of the North Maricopas stand in the Wilderness surrounded by vast desert plains that support saguaro, cholla, ocotillo, and other typical Sonoran plant species. You may sight a desert bighorn sheep, desert tortoise, coyote, bobcat, fox, and deer here, or see a Gambel's quail dart away at your approach while a raptor soars overhead. The old Butterfield Stage Road forms a portion of the southern boundary, and beyond the road backpackers and horsepackers find an ample supply of solitude.

North Maricopa Mountains Essentials

Size: 63,600 acres.
Year Designated: 1990.
Location: Southern Arizona.
Easiest Access: From Interstate 8 at Gila Bend, take State Highway 238 northeast for 15 miles; turn north on one of several unmarked dirt roads, which lead to the southern boundary for the next seven miles. Four-wheel-drive vehicles are recommended.
Season: Fall to spring.
Wilderness Fees/Permits: None.
Maps: USGS topographic maps are Butterfield Pass, Cotton Center, Cotton Center NW, Cotton Center SE, Margies Peak, and Mobile NW.
Management: BLM Lower Gila Resource Area, 2015 West Deer Valley Road, Phoenix, AZ 85027; (602) 863-4464.

North Santa Teresa Wilderness

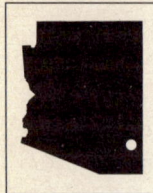

Just south of and sharing a border with the San Carlos Indian Reservation, North Santa Teresa preserves Black Rock, a geologic landmark of special spiritual significance to many Indians. Rising nearly 1,000 feet from its base, towering darkly over the desert floor, Black Rock possesses an undeniably mystical aura. Unfortunately, the rock has been abused by vandals in the past, which has made the San Carlos Apaches protective of the area. The remainder of the mile-long rhyolitic plug of which it is a part stands encircled by steep cliffs of several hundred feet. In the southeast portion of the Wilderness Jackson Mountain rises to 5,890 feet and is dissected by numerous canyons and washes. This boulder-strewn area supports dense desert and mountain shrub, grassland, and riparian vegetation.

Surrounded by reservation and private land, North Santa Teresa Wilderness offers no open public access. To obtain permission to enter, contact the San Carlos Apaches or private landowners prior to your visit.

North Santa Teresa Essentials

Size: 6,590 acres.
Year Designated: 1990.
Location: Southeastern Arizona.
Easiest Access: From Phoenix, take U.S. 60 east approximately 93 miles to Globe. Continue about 52 miles east on U.S. 70 to Fort Thomas. Turn south on Black Rock Road and travel southwest for about 16 miles to the northern Wilderness boundary.
Season: Fall to spring.
Wilderness Fees/Permits: Recreation permits are available from the San Carlos Apache Indian Tribe. Permission may be granted by adjacent private landowners. For details, contact the BLM.
Maps: USGS topographic map is Jackson Mountain.
Management: BLM Gila Resource Area, 425 East Fourth Street, Safford, AZ 85546; (520) 428-4040.

Organ Pipe Cactus Wilderness

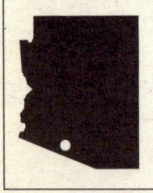

Almost in the heart of the vast Sonoran Desert, 329,199-acre Organ Pipe Cactus National Monument hugs the Mexican border and celebrates a desert full of life: 550 species of vascular plants, 53 species of mammals, 43 species of reptiles, and more than 278 species of birds. The monument is especially a testament to the life of the organ pipe, a large multispined cactus rare in the United States. In May, June, and July, the organ pipe blooms at night, its lavender-white flowers opening after the sun goes down, when the desert awakens to elf owls, kangaroo rats, javelinas, coyotes, jackrabbits, and many snakes. Bighorn sheep and lizards roam during the day.

From Mount Ajo at 4,024 feet, atop the Ajo Range on the eastern border, the land falls away to broad alluvial desert plains studded with cacti and creosote bushes, isolated canyons, dry arroyos, and stark desert mountains. Summer temperatures have been known to reach an unbelievably scorching 175 degrees Fahrenheit, but winter brings daytime temperatures in the 60s and 70s and chilly nights. About 95 percent of the monument has been designated Wilderness, making this Arizona's third largest Wilderness.

ARIZONA

No reliable water sources exist in Organ Pipe Cactus except at the 208-site campground near the visitors center. The camp is open year-round on a first-come, first-served basis for a fee. The National Park Service maintains few trails, but cross-country backpacking is allowed throughout the monument, except in a few historically sensitive areas. This open country offers some of the best desert hiking in America, but check in with the ranger first for your own safety.

Organ Pipe Cactus Essentials

Size: 312,600 acres.
Year Designated: 1978.
Location: Southern Arizona.
Easiest Access: From Ajo, take State Highway 85 south to the visitors center, five miles north of the Mexico border.
Season: February and March are the most popular months.
Wilderness Fees/Permits: A $4 entrance fee is charged. Free backcountry permits are required; they are issued on a limited basis, based on the number of people visiting a particular region.
Maps: A free map is available from the ranger.
Management: Organ Pipe Cactus National Monument, Route 1, Box 100, Ajo, AZ 85321; (520) 387-6849.

Paiute Wilderness

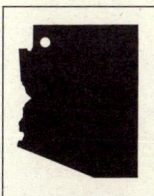

The Virgin Mountains are aptly named, as they have remained virtually unblemished by human intrusion. These mountains form the backbone of Paiute Wilderness, a geological amalgam of granite, gneiss, and limestone. Tucked deep within secret canyons are beautiful pools of water, well worth the effort it takes to find them. Sullivan Canyon in the north is strewn with boulders, exceptionally lovely, and fire-hot in summer. From atop Mount Bangs, the Paiute's highest point at 8,012 feet (over 5,600 feet above the desert floor), you'll get a panoramic view of the whole area and the Mojave Desert to the west. Up on Bangs you'll find ponderosa pine growing higher than piñon pine, shrub oak, and sagebrush, interspersed with Joshua trees, yucca, and barrel cactus. More than 250 animal species have been identified in this area, including mule deer, mountain lions, desert bighorn sheep, desert tortoises, and Gila monsters. Only the corridor of Interstate 15 separates Paiute from Beaver Dam Mountains Wilderness to the north.

Along the eight-mile Virgin Ridge Loop Trail you can climb with great physical effort to a high, pine-clad ridge or, after three miles, drop down to Atkin Spring. From here, a short hike through a natural opening leads to beautiful Sullivan Canyon. Finding a level camping spot may prove difficult. The Paiute is a magnificent 55-square-mile Wilderness that is slowly being discovered.

113

ARIZONA

Paiute Essentials

Size: 84,700 acres.
Year Designated: 1984.
Location: Northwestern Arizona.
Easiest Access: From the Utah/Arizona border, take Interstate 15 southwest two miles to Black Rock Junction (Exit 27). Turn south on BLM Road 1009 and drive about 20 miles; the boundary lies just west of the junction of BLM Roads 1009 and 1004. Follow BLM Road 1004 (Elbow Canyon) to Cougar Spring and a parking lot below Virgin Ridge.
Season: Fall to spring. Winter can get cold.
Wilderness Fees/Permits: None.
Maps: USGS topographic maps are Cane Springs, Elbow Canyon, Jacobs Well, Littlefield, Mount Bangs, Mountain Sheep Spring, Mustang Knoll, Purgatory Canyon, and Wolf Hole Mountain West. The BLM's Arizona Strip District Visitor Map shows the Wilderness.
Management: BLM Interagency Offices, 345 East Riverside Drive, Saint George, UT 84770; (801) 628-4491.

Pajarita Wilderness

Botany lovers, listen up: you should not miss this little Wilderness. More than 660 species of plants have been identified within its borders, 17 of them found nowhere else on Earth. Botanists have called Pajarita one of the most intriguing small areas in the United States. Its wildflowers alone attract photographers from around the world. Hugging the border of Mexico, Pajarita is dominated by the narrow and twisting, steep-walled Sycamore Canyon. While a seasonal stream doesn't flow through Sycamore, it does have year-round pools of water and serves as a major migration corridor for wildlife. Rolling hills and oak woodlands lie outside several canyons. Elevations range from 3,800 feet to 4,800 feet.

A popular day-hiking destination, the seven-mile Sycamore Canyon Trail starts at Hank and Yank Spring and traverses the length of the canyon. It intersects the Border Trail four miles into the Wilderness.

Pajarita Essentials

Size: 7,420 acres.
Year Designated: 1984.
Location: Southern Arizona.
Easiest Access: From seven miles north of Nogales, on Interstate 15, take the Ruby Road exit (State Route 289) west for about 15 miles to Sycamore Canyon.
Season: Fall to spring.
Wilderness Fees/Permits: None.
Maps: Topographic maps are available for $3 each from the U.S. Forest Service, Public Affairs Office, 517 Gold Avenue SW, Albuquerque, NM 87102; (505) 842-3292.
Management: Nogales Ranger District, Coronado National Forest, 2251 North Grand Avenue, Nogales, AZ 85621; (520) 281-2296.

ARIZONA

Paria Canyon–Vermilion Cliffs Wilderness

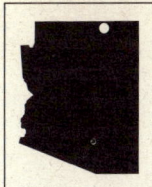

Have you ever dreamt of glimpsing the heart of the earth? It is laid bare in Paria Canyon, where towering walls streaked with desert varnish soar above serpentine canyons so narrow in places the sky is reduced to a ribbon of faded blue. You can wander among vast red-rock amphitheaters, sandstone arches, intricate eroded sculptures, woodland terraces, and hanging gardens of ferns and orchids. This fantastic Wilderness snakes from southern Utah (see Utah, Paria Canyon-Vermilion Cliffs Wilderness) south along extravagant Paria Canyon. West of the canyon, the massive and multicolored Vermilion Cliffs rise as much as 3,000 feet, an escarpment dominating the rest of the Wilderness with its thick Navajo sandstone face, boulder-bound slopes, and rugged arroyos.

The trek through Paria Canyon ranks among the best backpacking adventures in the world. From White House to Lee's Ferry, the main canyon stretches over 38 miles, all of it involving moderately strenuous hiking. In early spring, the most popular season, your feet will get wet often in ankle- to knee-deep water. Numerous side canyons beg to be explored. The first 23 miles from the ranger station are fairly open and obstacle-free; after that the going gets more rugged, requiring travel on terraces above the Paria River. The first seven miles may be waterless, especially in May and June. When you cross into the Narrows, about four miles from White House, you enter a five-mile section that offers no escape from flash floods (common from July through September). From White House you'll hike approximately 7.5 miles in Utah before entering Arizona. Plan to spend a full week here; carry a weather forecast.

Almost all hikers travel down canyon from the north. Entering Lee's Ferry in the south is not recommended; it places you too far from an accurate weather forecast by the time you reach the potentially dangerous Narrows. No campfires are allowed in Paria. Group size is limited to 10 people, but smaller groups are recommended. You must pack out everything you pack in.

Paria Canyon-Vermilion Cliffs Essentials

Size: 90,046 acres in Arizona (110,000 total).
Year Designated: 1984.
Location: Northern Arizona.
Easiest Access: From Page, take U.S. 89 north into Utah for approximately 30 miles. Turn south at the sign to the Paria Information Station. Continue on this dirt road two miles to the White House Trailhead. You must hike 2.5 miles into the canyon before entering the Wilderness.
Season: Fall to spring; early spring is the most popular time.
Wilderness Fees/Permits: Visitors are required to register at the ranger station.
Maps: USGS topographic maps are Bitter Springs, Coyote Buttes, Emmett Wash, Ferry Swale, House Rock Emmett Hill, House Rock Spring, Lee's Ferry, Navajo Bridge, One Toe Ridge, Poverty Flat, The Big Knoll, Water Pockets, and Wrather Arch. Ask the BLM about their *Hiker's Guide to Paria Canyon* ($8, $2 postage).
Management: BLM Interagency Offices, 345 East Riverside Drive, Saint George, UT 84970; (801) 628-4491.

ARIZONA

Peloncillo Mountains Wilderness

Ragged and rugged, the Peloncillo Mountains stretch north from Mexico to the Gila River, and New Mexico is just across the border from this Wilderness. The historic Butterfield Stage Route forms the southern boundary, but within the area you won't find many history buffs—in fact, you'll find few signs of human activity at all. Violent volcanic upheaval pushed these mountains into a veritable maze of canyons extending in all directions. Little Doubtful Canyon on the eastern side is extraordinarily scenic with an extensive Emory and Arizona white oak forest on the bottom, but access gates at its mouth are often locked by landowners. Other canyons worth exploring include Ward, Indian Springs, Midway, Old Horseshoe, Millsite, and West Doubtful. Elevations range from about 4,000 feet to 6,401 feet, and the views are worth the climb to higher ground. Among the vegetation in this high, dry land is mesquite, snakeweed, burroweed, turpentine bush, creosote, catclaw, whitethorn, agave, prickly pear, and juniper. Desert bighorn sheep have been reintroduced, and peregrine falcons soar in the bright skies. A large deer population attracts a few hunters.

Peloncillo Mountains Essentials

Size: 19,650 acres.
Year Designated: 1990.
Location: Southeastern Arizona.
Easiest Access: From Interstate 10 at San Simon, go north on Indian Springs Road for 10 miles to the western border of the Wilderness and Ward Canyon.
Season: Fall to spring.
Wilderness Fees/Permits: None.
Maps: USGS topographic maps are Doubtful Canyon, Engine Mountain, Orange Butte, and San Simon.
Management: BLM San Simon Resource Area, 425 East Fourth Street, Safford, AZ 85546; (520) 428-4040.

Petrified Forest Wilderness

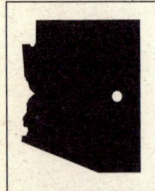

About 225 million years ago this area was a vast floodplain crossed by many streams. Tall, stately, pinelike trees grew here, sheltering a myriad of reptiles. When the trees fell, they washed into the water to be buried under silt, mud, and volcanic ash. Groundwater seeped through the logs, bearing silica that later crystallized into quartz, which ultimately petrified the wood. After centuries of burial and upheaval, the land became the high, dry Arizona tableland seen today. While the forces of erosion sculpted the Painted Desert, they also brought the petrified wood slowly to the surface.

In 1906, the United States established Petrified Forest National Monument. By 1962, the area had been expanded and its name was changed to Petrified Forest National Park. Over half of the park has been designated Wilderness.

Interstate 40 cuts through the park. North of the highway lies the protected portion of the Painted Desert, most of it preserved as Wilderness. A large piece of the southern portion of the park, primarily along Puerco Ridge, has also been designated. In addition to the petrified wood logs, visitors can observe remnants of petroglyphs and stone houses built by early human settlers to this region, dating back approximately 2,000 years. Wilderness backpack camping is allowed in the National Park.

ARIZONA

Petrified Forest Essentials

Size: 50,260 acres.
Year Designated: 1970.
Location: Northeastern Arizona.
Easiest Access: From Flagstaff, take Interstate 40 east for approximately 113 miles to the park entrance at Exit 311.
Season: Open all year. Summers are hot.

Wilderness Fees/Permits: The park entrance fee is $5 per vehicle or $3 per person. A free backpacking permit is required.
Maps: A map is available from the park ranger.
Management: Ranger, Petrified Forest National Park, AZ 86028; (520) 524-6228.

Pine Mountain Wilderness

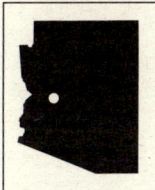

At 6,814 feet, Pine Mountain is the highest point on the Verde River Rim, which slashes across this area from northeast to southwest. Steep and rocky southeastern slopes fall toward the Verde, Arizona's only Wild and Scenic River. On the rim you'll find an "island" of tall ponderosa pine and Douglas fir surrounded by desert mountains and hot dry mesas covered in piñon and juniper, cut by rugged canyons. The rim overlooks the Verde River with fine views out across the desert. Despite scant water, wildlife abounds here on forested slopes and in the canyons, especially game animals. Hunters report ample opportunities for mule deer, white-tailed deer, black bears, and mountain lions. Javelina hunters are particularly successful.

Pine Mountain Wilderness straddles the boundary between Prescott and Tonto National Forests. Not far to the north lies Cedar Bench Wilderness (see above). Backpackers will find well-maintained trails, but plenty of water must be carried. Horseback riders should pack along supplemental feed. The Nelson Trail enters from the northern boundary to cross 8.2 miles of chaparral vegetation and join the scenic Verde Rim Trail (5.3 miles), which leads into Cedar Bench. From the Nelson Trail, hikers can also access the Pine Mountain Trail, which leads 1.2 miles to the mountain summit.

Pine Mountain Essentials

Size: 20,061 acres.
Year Designated: 1972.
Location: Central Arizona.
Easiest Access: Exit Interstate 17 at the Dugas Interchange (Exit 268). From Exit 268, take Dugas Road 12 miles east to Dugas, then take Forest Service Road 68 southeast for 12 miles to the Nelson Trailhead.
Season: Fall to spring.

Wilderness Fees/Permits: None.
Maps: Topographic maps are available for $3 each from the U.S. Forest Service, Public Affairs Office, 517 Gold Avenue SW, Albuquerque, NM 87102; (505) 842-3292.
Management: Verde Ranger District, Prescott National Forest, P.O. Box 670, Camp Verde, AZ 86322-0670; (602) 567-4121. Tonto National Forest, P.O. Box 5348, Phoenix, AZ 85010; (602) 225-5200.

ARIZONA

Pusch Ridge Wilderness

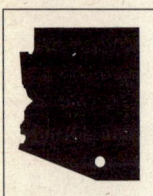

Pusch Ridge rises from the desert floor to over 9,000 feet above sea level, affording a clear view over the sprawling metropolis of Tucson. Unfortunately, more and more people are climbing Pusch Ridge to take in that view and revel in the cool shade of pine, fir, aspen, and maple. No Wilderness in Coronado National Forest is more heavily visited than Pusch Ridge, and slowly but surely its Wilderness qualities are being trampled to death by boot and shoe. In the process, wildlife species have been increasingly disturbed and threatened.

It's no secret what attracts people to the region. Here in the essentially dry Santa Catalina Mountains several streams originate in the high country. Scorching summer temperatures may be 30 degrees cooler than in the nearby city. An extensive trail system provides access to Pusch Ridge; trailheads near Tucson are easy to reach, as are those at higher elevations along General Hitchcock Highway, which ascends Mount Lemmon. Hikers crossing this extremely steep terrain find themselves among rocky bluffs and towering peaks. It's a scenic spot, but one that is being palpably ruined by overvisitation. It is recommended that you seek a Wilderness experience elsewhere.

Pusch Ridge Essentials

Size: 56,933 acres.
Year Designated: 1978.
Location: Southern Arizona.
Easiest Access: From Tucson, take the Mount Lemmon/General Hitchcock Highway north. The Wilderness lies all along the highway to the west and is accessible from numerous parking lots and pullouts for the next 24 miles to the top of Mount Lemmon.
Season: Year-round.
Wilderness Fees/Permits: None.
Maps: A Wilderness map is available for $4 from the U.S. Forest Service, Public Affairs Office, 517 Gold Avenue SW, Albuquerque, NM 87102; (505) 842-3292.
Management: Santa Catalina Ranger District, Coronado National Forest, 5700 N Sabino Canyon Road, Tucson, AZ 85715; (520) 749-8700.

Rawhide Mountains Wilderness

Just beyond Alamo Dam, the Bill Williams River cuts through this Wilderness, dividing two mountain ranges, the Rawhides to the north and the Buckskins to the south. For more than five miles the river traverses the colorful 600-foot-deep Bill Williams Gorge, a stretch of white water that attracts many river runners. Several small rocky side canyons join the river, their waters feeding into the main flow over low falls. The riparian habitat supports cottonwood and willow, and provides habitat for beavers, several species of raptors, amphibians, and reptiles. At least one pair of bald eagles nest here.

The Rawhide Mountains are low, with elevations from 700 feet to 2,430 feet. Numerous outcroppings break the skyline, and several washes and canyons cut through the Rawhides. Mississippi Wash is probably the most notable, a winding canyon with several waterfalls. The Buckskin Mountains are higher and more scenically appealing, with elevations from 1,700 feet to 3,927 feet on Ives Peak, but they are less easily accessed. Blessed with year-round water, the area makes a fine choice for extended backpacking trips.

ARIZONA

Rawhide Mountains Essentials
Size: 41,600 acres.
Year Designated: 1990.
Location: Western Arizona.
Easiest Access: From Wenden on U.S. 60, take Alamo Dam Road north for about 34 miles to Alamo Lake State Park. The Bill Williams River, which runs through the wilderness, is easily accessible from here.
Season: Fall to spring.
Wilderness Fees/Permits: None, but the gorge may be closed in late winter and early spring when the eagles nest.
Maps: USGS topographic maps are Artillery Peak SE, Artillery Peak SW, Buckskin Mountains East NE, Buckskin Mountains East NW, Buckskin Mountains West NE, and Plant 2 SE.
Management: BLM Havasu Resource Area, 3189 Sweetwater Avenue, Lake Havasu City, AZ 86403; (520) 855-8017.

Red Rock–Secret Mountain Wilderness

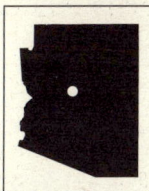

Tan, buff, and predominantly red-rock cliffs mark the edge of the Colorado Plateau across this Wilderness, just east of Sycamore Canyon Wilderness (see below). Here the high mesas of Secret Mountain and Wilson Mountain jut out into the lower country, and outstanding canyons as deep as 1,500 feet drain into beautiful Oak Creek and the Verde River. The high rims are rather cool and moist compared with the lower desertland, and a wide variety of vegetation supports plentiful wildlife, including elk, mule deer, white-tailed deer, javelinas, coyotes, rabbits, mountain lions, and black bears. A close look at the canyon walls may reveal ancient rock art and long-abandoned cliff dwellings.

Although this is one of Arizona's most accessible Wildernesses, you can still find solitude here, largely due to the deep canyons, the many hidden grottoes, and the dense riparian vegetation. The rough terrain prevents trails from crossing the entire area. The Secret Canyon Trail meanders delightfully for 4.2 miles along Secret Canyon as it climbs Secret Mountain. The Devil's Bridge Trail leads nine-tenths of a mile to a natural red sandstone bridge.

Red Rock–Secret Mountain Essentials
Size: 43,950 acres.
Year Designated: 1984.
Location: Central Arizona.
Easiest Access: From Flagstaff, take U.S. 89A south to West Sedona. Turn north on Dry Creek Road and drive two miles, then turn north on Forest Service Road 152 and continue 1.5 miles to Devil's Bridge Trailhead. The road can be impassable when wet.
Season: Fall to spring.
Wilderness Fees/Permits: None.
Maps: Topographic maps are available for $3 each from the U.S. Forest Service, Public Affairs Office, 517 Gold Avenue SW, Albuquerque, NM 87102; (505) 842-3292.
Management: Peaks Ranger District, Coconino National Forest, 5075 North Highway 89, Flagstaff, AZ 86004; (520) 526-0866. Sedona Ranger District, Coconino National Forest, P.O. Box 300, Sedona, AZ 886336; (520) 282-4119.

ARIZONA

Redfield Canyon Wilderness

A narrow red-walled chasm, boulder-strewn Redfield Canyon lies bound by tall cliffs pocked with eroded caves. With a bit of exploration you may find cascades and deep refreshing pools hidden in side canyons. Some small canyons in the area contain perennial streams. In the eastern portion of the Wilderness, Galiuro Escarpment rises impressively, an example of the fault-block development for which the Basin and Range Province is known.

You'll find no established trails here, but the canyons are suitable for hiking. Over the years photographers have been drawn to the scenic, water-rich side canyons of Redfield. A substantial portion of the western half of the area is privately owned; you must obtain permission before crossing it.

Redfield Canyon Essentials

Size: 6,600 acres.
Year Designated: 1990.
Location: Southeastern Arizona.
Easiest Access: From Tucson, take Interstate 10 east to Benson. Turn north on Pomerene Road and drive about 45 miles to Redington; just beyond the bridge, turn east. From here you'll need permission to continue across State Trust Lands and private land into the Wilderness.
Season: Spring and fall.
Wilderness Fees/Permits: Obtain access permission from the State Land Department and private landowners. Contact the BLM for more information.
Maps: USGS topographic maps are Cherry Spring Peak and The Mesas.
Management: BLM Tucson Resource Area, 12661 East Broadway, Tucson, AZ 85748; (520) 722-4289.

Rincon Mountain Wilderness

Wrapping around three sides of Saguaro National Monument just east of Tucson, this sharply rising, mountainous Wilderness serves to further protect and preserve the monument's odd and sometimes all-too-human-shaped cacti, the monarchs of the Sonoran Desert. Elevations range from 3,600 feet to 7,700 feet. The lower elevations are rolling and rocky with desert grasses while the upper elevations are dramatic rock outcroppings and steep hillsides of piñon, juniper, and oak above deep canyons.

Several trails provide access to the Wilderness's solitude-rich canyon bottoms and the high ridgelines of the Rincons, but reaching the trailheads themselves can be difficult, except via a well-developed trail system that originates in Saguaro National Monument. At times vehicles can access the eastern boundary on Forest Service Road 35 up Happy Valley. Off the trails, especially at higher elevations, the terrain makes foot travel difficult and horse travel virtually impossible.

ARIZONA

Rincon Mountain Essentials
Size: 38,590 acres.
Year Designated: 1984.
Location: Southern Arizona.
Easiest Access: Saguaro National Monument headquarters are in the Rincon Mountain Unit on Old Spanish Trail at Freeman Road, two miles east of Tucson.
Season: Fall to spring.
Wilderness Fees/Permits: A $4 entrance fee per vehicle is charged for the monument's Rincon Mountain Unit, and a permit is required to enter the Wilderness through the monument.
Maps: Topographic maps are available for $3 each from the U.S. Forest Service, Public Affairs Office, 517 Gold Avenue SW, Albuquerque, NM 87102; (505) 842-3292.
Management: Santa Catalina Ranger District, Coronado National Forest, 5700 North Sabino Canyon Road, Tucson, AZ 85715; (520) 749-8700.

Saddle Mountain Wilderness

Straddling the eastern edge of the Kaibab Plateau this Wilderness is a rugged land of narrow drainage bottoms set beside steep and very steep scarps (a line of cliffs produced by faulting or erosion). The gentle slopes on the main ridge of the area drop dramatically to form the Nankoweap Rim on the south. Elevations range from about 6,000 feet on Marble Canyon Rim to 8,000 feet on Saddle Mountain itself, a prominent ridge with a profile that resembles a saddle, horn and all. Utah juniper and piñon pine in the lowlands give way to mixed conifers in the highlands.

In 1960 a raging fire destroyed approximately 8,000 acres of trees, but the vegetation in the area has rebounded, creating exceptional mule deer habitat. Regrowth vegetation includes a dense mass of locust, oak, aspen, elderberry, and young coniferous trees. A perennial stream flows in the North Canyon of the Wilderness, spawning ground for the endangered Apache trout. Four year-round springs, three in North Canyon and one in South Canyon, provide water. Pronghorn antelope and a small herd of buffalo can be seen in House Rock Valley in the north. Grouse and turkeys live in the timber, and other mammals, birds, and reptiles are permanent residents, including rattlesnakes.

The Saddle Mountain Trail parallels the main ridge for approximately four miles and rewards hikers with spectacular views of the Grand Canyon, Marble Canyon Gorge, Cocks Comb, House Rock Valley, and the Vermilion Cliffs. Trails trace the bottom of both the North and South Canyons, seven and four miles long, respectively. This area receives relatively heavy human use (backpackers, hunters, cross-country skiers, photographers), but in winter and early spring snow often makes access difficult.

ARIZONA

Saddle Mountain Essentials

Size: 40,600 acres.
Year Designated: 1984.
Location: Northern Arizona.
Easiest Access: From Fredonia, take U.S. 89A east until you are approximately 19 miles past Jacob Lake. Turn south on Forest Service Road 445 (or Forest Service Road 1049, which joins 445) and drive approximately 18 miles. Turn west onto Forest Service Road 631, which dead-ends in about five miles at the North Canyon Trailhead. To reach the South Canyon Trailhead, stay on Forest Service Road 445 for six more miles and turn west on Forest Service Road 211, which leads to the trailhead in about six miles.
Season: Spring to fall.
Wilderness Fees/Permits: None.
Maps: The North Kaibab Recreation Map is available for $3 from the district ranger.
Management: North Kaibab Ranger District, Kaibab National Forest, P.O. Box 248, Fredonia, AZ 86022; (520) 643-7395.

Saguaro Wilderness

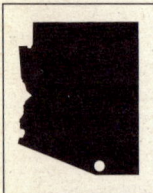

Sprouting in the shade of another desert plant, the saguaro cactus grows only a few inches in its first five years of life and a few feet in its first 30 years. At age 75 the cactus stands 15 to 20 feet tall and begins developing its first branches as it absorbs water through an extensive root system. A mature cactus can live up to 170 years, often measuring in at over 30 feet tall, weighing 6 to 10 tons, and holding one ton of water. The saguaro is truly king of the Sonoran Desert.

Saguaro National Monument was established in 1933 and given national parkland status in 1994. The area contains 84,000 saguaro-preserving acres. Divided into two units by Tucson, the western Tucson Mountain Unit includes just over 21,000 relatively flat acres and the eastern Rincon Mountain Unit almost 63,000 acres, rising steeply in places from 2,800 feet to 8,666 feet on Mica Mountain. Most of the park has been designated Wilderness.

Traversed by well-maintained dirt roads, the Tucson Mountain Unit receives mostly day-use visitors. Although it offers a visitors center, the Rincon Mountain Unit is primarily roadless, mostly attracting backpackers who enter almost exclusively via the Douglas Spring Trail. Rincon's trail system contains about 77 miles of maintained pathways, but overnight camping is limited to six sites. Water is usually available.

Under the cover of night this desert's wildlife begins to stir, with deer, javelinas, rabbits, coyotes, and squirrels roaming the terrain. Birds are abundant in season. When occasional and gentle winter rains dampen the area, the land bursts into wild and colorful bloom, including the saguaro's white blossom, Arizona's state flower.

ARIZONA

Saguaro Essentials

Size: 71,400 acres.
Year Designated: 1976.
Location: Southern Arizona.
Easiest Access: From Tucson, take the Old Spanish Trail about five miles east of the city limits to the Rincon Mountain Unit.
Season: February through May for a chance to see the desert in full bloom.

Wilderness Fees/Permits: A fee of $4 per vehicle or $2 per person is charged for the Rincon Mountain Unit; a camping permit is required. Entry to the Tucson Mountain Unit is free.
Maps: Three maps cover the entire area. They are available from the ranger for $4 each.
Management: Saguaro National Park, 3693 South Old Spanish Trail, Tucson, AZ 85730; (602) 733-5100.

Salome Wilderness

If you hike rough and lonesome Salome Canyon, the major canyon that runs almost the entire length of this Wilderness, you probably won't encounter another human being. However, you may see remnants of the Salado Indians, who lived here until vanishing about 700 years ago. As you work your way north the land becomes increasingly rugged with many bedrock outcroppings. It culminates in Hell's Hole, a region of precipitous bluffs and impenetrably dense brush. The upper reaches of Salome Creek and Workman Creek, two small perennial streams, snake through the bottom of this scenic canyon and fill small, delightful pools almost all year long. Water is sometimes available from several small springs. Elevations range from 2,600 feet at lower Salome Creek to 6,500 feet on Hopkins Mountain. Semidesert grasslands and chaparral dominate the vegetation. Winters usually freeze, and summer temperatures often exceed 100 degrees Fahrenheit. Mountain lions are prevalent, along with hawks, ravens, deer, and many smaller animals.

Several trails provide access to the area. From the Reynolds Trailhead, hikers can follow the Hell's Hole Trail, which descends steeply for 5.3 miles and dead-ends in Hell's Hole.

Salome Essentials

Size: 18,950 acres.
Year Designated: 1984.
Location: Central Arizona.
Easiest Access: From Claypool, just west of Globe, take State Highway 88 northwest for about 15 miles. Turn north on State Highway 288 and drive about 27 miles to the Reynolds Trailhead on the west side of the road, near the Reynolds Creek Group Site.

Season: Fall to spring.
Wilderness Fees/Permits: None.
Maps: Topographic maps are available for $3 each from the U.S. Forest Service, Public Affairs Office, 517 Gold Avenue SW, Albuquerque, NM 87102; (505) 842-3292.
Management: Pleasant Valley Ranger District, Tonto National Forest, P.O. Box 450, Young, AZ 85554; (520) 462-3311.

ARIZONA

Salt River Canyon Wilderness

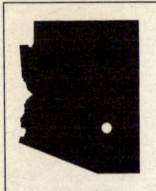

Many describe the vista where U.S. 60 crosses the Salt River Canyon, between the Fort Apache and San Carlos Indian Reservations, as the most dramatic in Arizona. Here the highway descends 2,000 feet of steep switchbacks, crosses a bridge, and ascends the opposite side of the canyon. About 25 miles below the bridge the river enters Tonto National Forest and the spectacular steep-walled canyon bisects Salt River Canyon Wilderness. Although this 22-mile stretch of river was once considered for Wild and Scenic designation, it was denied thanks to the machinations of powerful water-development interests. Within the area elevations range from 2,200 feet at the canyon's lower end to 4,200 feet on White Ledge Mountain. More than 200 species of wildlife have been identified along the river. Access to this area is very difficult, and there are no maintained trails. About half of the area's human visitors are skilled white-water navigators, who venture down the Salt River during the short and dangerous river-running season from March 1 to May 15.

Salt River Canyon Essentials

Size: 32,800 acres.
Year Designated: 1984.
Location: Eastern Arizona.
Easiest Access: From Phoenix, take U.S. 60 west to Salt River Canyon, just three miles north of Seneca.
Season: Fall to spring.
Wilderness Fees/Permits: None.

Maps: Topographic maps are available for $3 each from the U.S. Forest Service, Public Affairs Office, 517 Gold Avenue SW, Albuquerque, NM 87102; (505) 842-3292.
Management: Pleasant Valley Ranger District, Tonto National Forest, P.O. Box 450, Young, AZ 85554; (520) 462-3311.

Santa Teresa Wilderness

Looking for an extraordinary desert mountain Wilderness experience? Then head to the Santa Teresa Mountains, but be forewarned: the going's not easy. Between Aravaipa Canyon Wilderness (see above) and the San Carlos Apache Indian Reservation, adjoining the BLM's North Santa Teresa Wilderness, access here is difficult. The Santa Teresas are a network of rugged mountains with bald summits, deep canyons, and sprawling mesas. Elevations range from less than 4,000 feet to 7,481 feet on the summit of Cottonwood Peak. Holdout and Mud Spring Mesas dominate the central Wilderness. Extremely rugged Holdout Canyon typifies the Santa Teresas: abundant caves and alcoves hollow into eroded cliffs with picturesque formations. Thick chaparral vegetation covers the terrain with stands of ponderosa pine and Douglas fir on the north flanks and the crest of Cottonwood Peak. Black bears live here among coatimundi, javelina, and mountain lions. Peregrine falcons soar overhead, hunting for prey. Several foot trails give access to the more interesting spots in the Wilderness; some are maintained by cowboys driving their stock, but they are difficult to follow. Human use of the area is very light. Water flows year-round from a few springs.

ARIZONA

Santa Teresa Essentials

Size: 26,780 acres.
Year Designated: 1984.
Location: Southeastern Arizona.
Easiest Access: From Tucson, take Interstate 10 east until you are 12 miles past Willcox. Turn north on U.S. 191 and drive 17 miles, then turn west on State Highway 266 (which becomes the Bonita-Klondike Road) and continue 24 miles. Turn northeast on Klondyke Road and head six miles, then turn north on Forest Service Road 677 and drive four miles to the northwestern boundary.
Season: Fall to spring.
Wilderness Fees/Permits: None.
Maps: USGS topographic maps are Buford Hill, Cobre Grande Mountain, Jackson Mountain, and Klondyke.
Management: Safford Ranger District, Coronado National Forest, P.O. Box 709, Safford, AZ 85548-0709; (520) 428-4150.

Sierra Ancha Wilderness

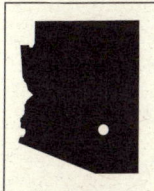

Centuries ago the Salado Indians built and lived in cliff dwellings in this region, and the ruins of many of them still stand today. An "original" Arizona Wilderness, Sierra Ancha was established as a Primitive area in 1933 and as a Wilderness in 1964. Uranium exploration carved a few roads into this area in the 1950s, roads now being reclaimed by natural processes. Exceptionally rough, scenic, and often inaccessible, Sierra Ancha consists of precipitous box canyons, towering vertical cliffs, and pine-covered mesas. Elevations range from 4,000 feet near Cherry Creek to more than 7,400 feet on several high peaks, with the highest point on Aztec Peak at 7,733 feet. Chaparral covers lower elevations with turbinella oak, manzanita, and mountain mahogany. Some piñon and juniper cloak the east side of the Wilderness, dropping to semidesert brush and grassland below. Snow falls in the highland in winter, and summers tend to be outrageously hot. Several springs usually offer water year-round, but there is no guarantee.

Thirteen trailheads give access to a well-maintained network of foot and horse pathways. The Center Mountain Trail climbs 2.5 miles for some excellent views of the surrounding area.

Sierra Ancha Essentials

Size: 20,850 acres.
Year Designated: 1964.
Location: Central Arizona.
Easiest Access: From the junction of U.S. 60 and State Highway 88, travel northwest on State Highway 88 for about 15 miles. Turn north on State Highway 288 and go 27.6 miles to Forest Service Road 410. Turn east on Forest Service Road 410 and drive 2.5 miles to Forest Service Road 235. Turn north and continue 2.5 miles to the Billy Lawrence Trailhead and Center Mountain Trail. Four-wheel-drive vehicles are recommended.
Season: Fall to spring.
Wilderness Fees/Permits: None.
Maps: Topographic maps are available for $3 each from the U.S. Forest Service, Public Affairs Office, 517 Gold Avenue SW, Albuquerque, NM 87102; (505) 842-3292.
Management: Pleasant Valley Ranger District, Tonto National Forest, P.O. Box 450, Young, AZ 85554; (520) 462-3311.

ARIZONA

Sierra Estrella Wilderness

Bordered entirely on the north and east by the Gila Indian Reservation, Sierra Estrella Wilderness contains knife-edged ridgelines, steep slopes, and rocky canyons, one of the most rugged mountainous areas of Arizona. In the northeast corner Butterfly Mountain rises 2,600 feet above the desert plain to an elevation of 4,119 feet in only two miles, a challenge for backpackers and climbers. These extreme elevation changes have produced diverse plant communities: saguaro, cholla, ocotillo, paloverde, and elephant bush lower down, shrub live oak and a few junipers higher up. A remnant herd of desert bighorn sheep roams these mountains. Other permanent residents include the Gila monster, giant spotted whiptail lizard, desert tortoise, mountain lion, mule deer, coyote, javelina, golden eagle, prairie falcon, and Cooper's hawk.

Though Sierra Estrella is not far from Phoenix, few humans venture into this Wilderness. If you wander through, you may stumble across evidence of old mining activity. A four-wheel-drive vehicle is required to reach the two public-access points; along the way you'll cross some extremely sandy, deep washes.

Sierra Estrella Essentials

Size: 14,500 acres.
Year Designated: 1990.
Location: Southern central Arizona.
Easiest Access: From Phoenix, take Interstate 10 south to Exit 162. Turn south on State Route 347 (Maricopa Road) and drive 17 miles to State Route 238. Head west for 13 miles to Mobile, then travel north 12 miles on unimproved dirt roads to the base of the mountains and the southern Wilderness boundary.
Season: Fall to spring.
Wilderness Fees/Permits: None.
Maps: USGS topographic maps are Mobile NE and Montezuma Peak.
Management: BLM Lower Gila Resource Area, 2015 West Deer Valley Road, Phoenix, AZ 85027; (602) 863-4464.

Signal Mountain Wilderness

A thin four-wheel-drive road is all that separates Signal Mountain Wilderness from Woolsey Peak Wilderness (see below) to the south. Signal Mountain itself, rising just north of the center of the area, reaches a summit at 2,182 feet (1,200 feet above the surrounding desert floor). Here you'll find sharp volcanic peaks, steep-walled canyons, ragged ridgelines, arroyos (slim, usually dry riverways), and plains spreading out from the washes. Paloverde, saguaro, and creosote bushes are scattered throughout the bajadas and upland regions. Washes are lined with mesquite, ironwood, acacia, and more paloverde. Wildlife watchers may see desert bighorn sheep, desert tortoises, and several species of raptors. A large number of quail live here, and quail and mule deer hunters are frequent visitors. Rock climbers are beginning to flock to the valleys and canyons around Signal Mountain, where bold cracked faces offer a multitude of routes of varying difficulty.

ARIZONA

Signal Mountain Essentials
Size: 15,250 acres.
Year Designated: 1990.
Location: Southwestern Arizona.
Easiest Access: From Phoenix, head west on Interstate 10 for 10 miles to State Route 85 (Oglesby Road). Head south 5.5 miles to Elliot Road, then go west for six miles to Old Highway 80. Drive southwest for eight miles to Agua Caliente Road, then head west for about nine miles to the Wilderness boundary. Four-wheel-drive vehicles are recommended.
Wilderness Fees/Permits: None.
Maps: USGS topographic maps are Quail Springs Wash and Woolsey Peak.
Management: BLM Lower Gila Resource Area, 2015 West Deer Valley Road, Phoenix, AZ 85027; (602) 863-4464.

South Maricopa Mountains Wilderness

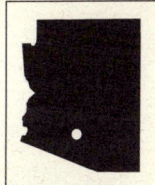

A low-elevation Sonoran mountain range, the Maricopas stretch for 13 miles across this Wilderness of extensive desert plains. The eastern portion of the area contains an isolated and screened interior formed by long ridges and lone peaks separated by washes and plains. The western portion is primarily flat desert. Vegetation consists of cholla, saguaro, ocotillo, paloverde, and mesquite. Desert bighorn sheep, coyotes, bobcats, foxes, deer, Gambel's quail, various raptors, desert tortoises, and numerous reptiles live here. An area of varied landforms and vast untamed wildness, South Maricopa is difficult to access, even though the corridor of Interstate 8 forms the southern boundary.

South Maricopa Mountains Essentials
Size: 60,800 acres.
Year Designated: 1990.
Location: Southern Arizona.
Easiest Access: From Interstate 8 at Gila Bend, take State Highway 238 northeast. After 12 miles, turn south on one of several primitive roads; access may be blocked by active railroad tracks and rights-of-way. Four-wheel-drive vehicles are strongly recommended.
Season: Fall to spring.
Wilderness Fees/Permits: None.
Maps: USGS topographic maps are Big Horn, Blue Plateau, Bosque, Conely Well, Estrella, Gila Bend, and Lost Horse Peak.
Management: BLM Lower Gila Resource Area, 2015 West Deer Valley Road, Phoenix, AZ 85027; (602) 863-4464.

Strawberry Crater Wilderness

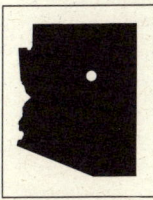

Part of the huge San Francisco volcanic field, Strawberry Crater is one of its roughly 600 craters and cones, all 50,000 to 100,000 years old. The crater once sent lava flowing across the northwestern corner of this Wilderness, and low cinder cones dominate the southern end. Here are gently rolling hills covered in piñon and juniper, cinder-strewn terrain ranging in elevation from 5,500 feet to 6,000 feet. From the tops of many of the cinder cones you can see the Painted Desert, Hopi Buttes,

ARIZONA

and mesas of the valley of the Little Colorado River. Game animals and smaller mammals may be seen throughout the area. At dawn and dusk the area's fascinating geology and twisted junipers offer excellent subjects for photographers. Solitude awaits amid limitless horizons. The region has an eerie sense of timelessness. In summer, temperatures soar; pack in plenty of water.

Strawberry Crater Essentials

Size: 10,140 acres.
Year Designated: 1984.
Location: Northern central Arizona.
Easiest Access: From Flagstaff, take U.S. 89 north for 15 miles; exit at Sunset Crater National Monument and follow the paved loop road north for about 11 miles toward Wupatki National Monument. Strawberry Crater lies between Sunset and Wupatki.
Season: Late fall to early spring.
Wilderness Fees/Permits: None.
Maps: Topographic maps are available for $3 each from the U.S. Forest Service, Public Affairs Office, 517 Gold Avenue SW, Albuquerque, NM 87102; (505) 842-3292.
Management: Peaks Ranger District, Coconino National Forest, 5075 North Highway 89, Flagstaff, AZ 86004; (520) 526-0866.

Superstition Wilderness

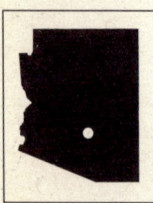

It has been said that strange perils and sudden death lurk among the stark canyons and dangerous trails of the Superstition Mountains. The Lost Dutchman came in search of fabled riches, and his legend is believed to have lured many to unmarked graves here. Although there is no guarantee that you'll find buried treasure, you are sure to discover miles and miles of desolate and barren mountains, seemingly endless and haunting canyons, raging summer temperatures that can surpass 115 degrees Fahrenheit, and a general dearth of water. Even the area's earliest known inhabitants, the hardy Hohokam and Salados peoples, established only very small villages and cliff dwellings in this harsh and fabulous country between 800 and 1400 A.D. The Superstitions do have certain hidden wonders: lush riparian hideaways that provide cool water and respite from the hot sun.

Legends of riches aside, the Wilderness value of the Superstitions has long been recognized. Established as a Primitive area in 1939, it was named a pre-Wilderness Act "wilderness" in 1940 and became an official Wilderness in 1964. Elevations range from approximately 2,000 feet on the western boundary to 6,265 feet on Mound Mountain. In the western portion rolling land is surrounded by steep, often vertical terrain. Weaver's Needle, a dramatic volcanic plug, rises to 4,553 feet. The central and eastern portions are less topographically severe, but travel is still limited in many places to maintained trails. Vegetation is primarily that of the Sonoran Desert, with semidesert grassland and chaparral higher up. Dense brushland covers hundreds of acres. A few isolated pockets of ponderosa pine may be found at the highest elevations. Lightning storms frequently rage in July and August and flash floods are a constant danger. Light snow may fall in winter. Rattlesnakes, scorpions, centipedes, millipedes, black widow spiders, recluse spiders, and the Walapai tiger kissing bug all live here. There are no perennial streams. Ranchers graze domestic cattle near springs by special permit.

Despite the harsh setting, much of Superstition Wilderness, especially the Peralta and First Water Trails, is overused by humans. These two trailheads receive about 80 percent of the

ARIZONA

annual human traffic, and the U.S. Forest Service calls the 6.3-mile Peralta one of the most heavily used trails in Arizona. Other trails within the Wilderness, in particular the Tule, Upper Horrell, and Miles Ranch Trails, are virtually untrodden. There are about 180 miles of trails, ranging from excellent to poor, as well as other unmaintained tracks. Group size is limited to 15, but management prefers smaller groups. Visitors may not stay longer than 14 days.

Superstition Essentials

Size: 159,757 acres.
Year Designated: 1964; expanded in 1984.
Location: Central Arizona.
Easiest Access: From Apache Junction, take U.S. 60/70 east about 8.5 miles to the Peralta Road 77 turnoff; go eight miles down this road to the Peralta Trailhead. To reach the Tule Trailhead, start from the junction of U.S. 60 and State Highway 88, west of Globe. Follow State Highway 88 north and west for 21.2 miles, then turn west on Forest Road 449 and drive approximately two miles. Turn north on an unmarked road and continue three-quarters of a mile to the trailhead.
Season: Fall to spring.
Wilderness Fees/Permits: None.
Maps: A Wilderness map is available for $4 from the U.S. Forest Service, Public Affairs Office, 517 Gold Avenue SW, Albuquerque, NM 87102; (505) 842-3292.
Management: Mesa Ranger District, Tonto National Forest, P.O. Box 5800, Mesa, AZ 85211-5800; (602) 835-1161.

Swansea Wilderness

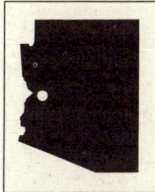

A six-mile stretch of the Bill Williams River, rarely seen by humans, cuts a deep gorge through the center of Swansea Wilderness. The river flows into the south end of nearby Lake Havasu on Havasu National Wildlife Refuge, creating a riparian habitat. In the northern portion of the Wilderness you'll find eroded volcanic dikes and plugs with precipitous cliffs, an extension of Black Mesa. The Buckskin Mountains form much of the western portion, and here the topography is subtle, rounded desert with a complex drainage system leading to the river. There are no trails, but you can hike along the water and up some of the side canyons. Rock climbing and horseback riding draw a few human visitors.

Swansea Essentials

Size: 15,755 acres.
Year Designated: 1990.
Location: Western Arizona.
Easiest Access: On Interstate 10, take the Vicksburg exit (45). Head north, then turn northwest on State Route 72 and drive 20 miles to Bouse. Take Swansea Road north through Midway and drive another 14 miles to the ghost town of Swansea. The Wilderness lies to the north. Four-wheel drive is recommended.
Season: Fall to spring.
Wilderness Fees/Permits: None.
Maps: USGS topographic maps are Buckskin Mountains West NE (Advance), Buckskin Mountains West NW (Advance), and Planet SE (Advance).
Management: BLM Havasu Resource Area, 3189 Sweetwater Avenue, Lake Havasu City, AZ 86403; (520) 855-8017.

ARIZONA

Sycamore Canyon Wilderness

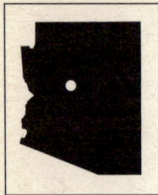

This sprawling Arizona Wilderness encompasses all of Sycamore Canyon, from its pine- and fir-forested rim on the Colorado Plateau down through the Mogollon Rim to its desert mouth in the Verde Valley. The canyon winds for over 20 miles along Sycamore Creek, at places stretching seven miles from rim to rim. Carved walls reveal layers of lovely red sandstone, spectacular white limestone, and rugged brown lava. Pinnacles tower above the high, colorful cliffs, and the water of the creek allows a rich habitat to flourish, including sycamores, walnuts, and cottonwoods. It is one of Arizona's most dramatic and beautiful canyons.

Many ring-tailed cats, wide-eyed cousins of the raccoon, live here, along with black bears, mountain lions, seasonal elk and deer, rattlesnakes, scorpions, and many smaller animals. Canyon wrens and hermit thrushes send their delightful songs along the trail with you.

Although you can choose from several trails, year-round water is limited to the lower reaches of the canyon. Take the 11-mile-long Sycamore Rim Trail Loop for a great look into the canyon. Backpackers should always carry ample water when venturing up the canyon. It's best to avoid the screaming-hot summers. A small portion of the southern end, from a half mile above Parson's Spring, has been closed to overnight camping. The Wilderness lies within three national forests: Coconino, Kaibab, and Prescott.

Sycamore Canyon Essentials

Size: 55,937 acres.
Year Designated: 1972; expanded in 1984.
Location: Central Arizona.
Easiest Access: From Interstate 40, four miles east of Williams, take the Williams Junction exit (167) and go south on Forest Service Road 141 about 12 miles. Turn southeast on Forest Service Road 56 and drive about 1.5 miles to the Sycamore Rim Trailhead, start of the Sycamore Rim Trail Loop.
Season: Fall to spring.
Wilderness Fees/Permits: None.
Maps: Topographic maps are available for $3 each from the U.S. Forest Service, Public Affairs Office, 517 Gold Avenue SW, Albuquerque, NM 87102; (505) 842-3292.
Management: Sedona Ranger District, Coconino National Forest, P.O. Box 300, Sedona, AZ 86336; (520) 282-4119.

Table Top Wilderness

Visible from Phoenix 45 miles to the north, 4,373-foot-high Table Top Mountain rises to a flat 40-acre summit of desert grassland, the highest point in the Wilderness. Below the summit on the southwest side grows a dense forest of saguaro cacti. Surrounding the mountain you'll find flat-topped mesas, narrow ridges descending to bajadas, wide canyons, lava flows, and washes lined with mesquite and ironwood. Vegetation includes abundant cacti, paloverde, and creosote. The giant spotted whiptail lizard and the Ajo Mountain whipsnake share their domain with desert bighorn sheep, desert tortoises, coyotes, quail, and javelina (a gregarious, nocturnal piglike peccary).

The strenuous, four-mile Table Top Trail leads from the southwest corner to the top of the mountain and a splendid panoramic view of distant mountains and desert plains. This area receives light human use, mostly backpackers and horsepackers.

Table Top Essentials

Size: 34,400 acres.
Year Designated: 1990.
Location: Southern Arizona.
Easiest Access: From the junction of Interstate 10 and Interstate 8, take Interstate 8 west for approximately 32 miles to Exit 144. Follow Vekol Road south for 12 miles to the western boundary and the Table Top Trailhead. The road in is maintained but sometimes rough.

Season: Fall to spring.
Wilderness Fees/Permits: None.
Maps: USGS topographic maps are Antelope Peak, Indian Butte, Little Table Top, and Vekol Mountains NE.
Management: BLM Lower Gila Resource Area, 2015 West Deer Valley Road, Phoenix, AZ 85027; (602) 863-4464.

Tres Alamos Wilderness

Columns of colorful stone are the most striking landscape features of Tres Alamos, a Wilderness in the southern Black Mountains. The landscape tops out at Sawyer Peak (4,293 feet), the highest point in the Black Mountains. The eastern portion of the area contains the Blacks' scenic ridgelines, canyons, and washes, while the western side consists of lower desert bajadas (slopes) and plains. On the bajadas and hills you'll find saguaro and paloverde. Joshua trees and creosote bushes dot the plains, and mesquite and acacia line the washes. The Gila monster lives here in seclusion, and prairie falcons and golden eagles rule the skies.

Although there are no established trails, the area is suitable for hiking and camping. Horsepackers sometimes journey through.

Tres Alamos Essentials

Size: 8,700 acres.
Year Designated: 1990.
Location: Western Arizona.
Easiest Access: From Wickenburg, take U.S. 93 north for approximately 21 miles. Follow Tres Alamos Road west for approximately six miles; when the road splits, take the north fork, which leads seven miles to the southern boundary.

Season: Fall to spring.
Wilderness Fees/Permits: None.
Maps: USGS topographic maps are Date Creek Ranch NW, Ives Peak, and Smith Peak NE.
Management: BLM Lower Gila Resource Area, 2015 West Deer Valley Road, Phoenix, AZ 85027; (602) 863-4464.

ARIZONA

Trigo Mountains Wilderness

You're practically in another state in Trigo Mountains Wilderness, the Golden State to be precise. Only a thin strip of Imperial National Wildlife Refuge along the lower Colorado River separates this Wilderness from California. The Yuma Military Proving Ground lies to the east. A road divides the area into northern and southern sections. Here you'll find 14 miles of the Trigo Mountain ridgeline cut by Red Cloud Wash in the south, Chip Wash in the center, and Hart Mine Wash in the north. Numerous washes further dissect the area's sawtoothed ridges. Water often seeps to the surface in several springs. Folks set off on extended horsepacking and backpacking trips along the washes, and rock climbers scale the Trigo Mountains. The Colorado River supports diverse wildlife, including bighorn sheep, mule deer, gray foxes, coyotes, and ringtailed cats.

Trigo Mountains Essentials

Size: 29,095 acres.
Year Designated: 1990.
Location: Southwestern Arizona.
Easiest Access: From Yuma, take U.S. 95 north for 16 miles. Turn west on Martinez Lake Road and drive 11 miles to Imperial National Wildlife Refuge. Take Red Cloud Mine Road 11 miles northwest to Red Cloud Wash and the southern end of the eastern boundary. Four-wheel-drive vehicles are recommended.
Season: Fall to spring.
Wilderness Fees/Permits: None.
Maps: USGS topographic maps are Picacho (Arizona) and Cibola (California).
Management: BLM Yuma Resource Area, 3150 Winsor Avenue, Yuma, AZ 85365; (520) 726-6300.

Upper Burro Creek Wilderness

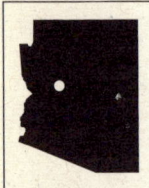

Upper Burro Creek is one of the few perennial streams to flow undammed into the lower desert of Arizona. Thirteen miles of the creek pass through this Wilderness, which is divided into eastern and western sections by a dirt road. Here Burro Creek runs deep through incised bedrock, falling about 1,500 feet in one half-mile stretch. Small waterfalls connect clear pools in which you can take the plunge for a magnificently refreshing desert swim. In some places the creek has backed up into long marshy pools ringed with young trees and thirsty vegetation. Away from the creek the Wilderness preserves rough side canyons and basalt mesas with vertical rock faces, raggedy spires, and desert grassland on their sloping upland surfaces. Negro Ed, a huge butte, dominates part of the area.

Topography has created numerous microhabitats where an abundance of Arizona plant communities intermingle. Bird-watchers are attracted to at least 150 species of avian life, including a great variety of raptors. Among the mammals who inhabit the area are beavers, raccoons, desert cottontails, ring-tailed cats, badgers, skunks (spotted, striped, and hognose), gray foxes, javelinas, bobcats, mountain lions, mule deer, and pronghorn antelope. There are no designated trails, but the stream and side canyons are easy to navigate; along the upper section of the creek the going may be more rigorous. Despite the refreshing presence of water, summers are far too hot for a visit.

ARIZONA

Upper Burro Creek Essentials
Size: 27,900 acres.
Year Designated: 1990.
Location: Western Arizona.
Easiest Access: From Wickenburg, take U.S. 93 north for 44 miles. Turn northeast on State Highway 97 and drive 10 miles to State Highway 96. Follow Highway 96 four miles to Bagdad, then turn west on a long, unmarked road that winds steeply with switchbacks 13 miles up into Upper Burro Creek. A four-wheel-drive vehicle is required.
Season: Fall to spring.
Wilderness Fees/Permits: None.
Maps: USGS topographic maps are Elephant Mountain, Greyback Mountains, Negro Ed, and Pilot Knob.
Management: BLM Kingman Resource Area, 2475 Beverly Avenue, Kingman, AZ 86401; (520) 757-3161.

Wabayuma Peak Wilderness

Located in the Hualapai Mountains, 7,601-foot Wabayuma Peak towers over this Wilderness of massive ridges. Extending out from the peak in a semicircle to the north, south, and west, the ridges plunge almost 5,000 feet in five miles to the desert below. Rocky outcroppings, spires, and crags dominate the canyons between the ridges, and Sonoran and Mojave vegetation dot the desert. Here you'll find the northernmost stands of saguaro cactus. Above the desert chaparral and piñon-juniper woodlands thrive, as do ponderosa pine and Gambel oak above 7,000 feet. Many wildflowers bloom in this area through the summer, and springs provide water.

This is fine country for extended backpacking or horsepacking trips. Summer temperatures have been known to be bearable, even pleasant at times, allowing year-round Wilderness visitation. The moderately difficult Wabayuma Peak Trail climbs about three miles one-way to the summit, partly marked by blazes on ponderosa pines. The Bureau of Land Management maintains Wild Cow Springs Campground, closed in winter, about 13 miles from the trailhead. Despite its name, the campground is usually without water.

Wabayuma Peak Essentials
Size: 38,400 acres.
Year Designated: 1990.
Location: Western Arizona.
Easiest Access: From Kingman, take Hualapai Mountain Road approximately 12 miles south to Hualapai Mountain County Park. From there, take BLM Road 2123 (Hualapai Ridge Road) about 20 miles southwest to the Wabayuma Peak Trailhead.
Season: Year-round.
Wilderness Fees/Permits: None.
Maps: USGS topographic maps are Hualapai Peak, Kingman SE, Wabayuma Peak, and Yucca NE.
Management: BLM Kingman Resource Area, 2475 Beverly Avenue, Kingman, AZ 86401; (520) 757-3161.

ARIZONA

Warm Springs Wilderness

Dominating this immense, pristine desert landscape near the California border is Black Mesa, 10 miles long and 1,000 feet above the surrounding desert, with edges dissected into a maze of winding canyons. Remnants of ancient mesas and isolated hills jut like islands in the sea of vast encircling desert plain. After wet winters, spring brings a profusion of blooms on ocotillos, cacti, and flowering shrubs and annuals.

A historic old trail from Baker Spring (four miles long) and numerous feral burro tracks provide access to the Wilderness. Most people prefer to enter from Warm Springs itself in the south. Warm Springs and other water sources allow for an extended (if carefully planned) backpacking or horsepacking trip. Map and compass skills are required.

Warm Springs Essentials

Size: 90,600 acres.
Year Designated: 1990.
Location: Western Arizona.
Easiest Access: From Kingman, take Interstate 40 southwest for 40 miles to the Franconia exit (13). From there, follow the long jeep trail north about 15 miles to Warm Springs. Four-wheel-drive vehicles are required.
Season: Fall to spring.
Wilderness Fees/Permits: None.
Maps: USGS topo maps are Boundary Cone, Kingman SW, Mount Nutt, Warm Springs, Warm Springs SE, Warm Springs SW, and Yucca NW.
Management: BLM Kingman Resource Area, 2475 Beverly Avenue, Kingman, AZ 86401; (520) 757-3161.

West Clear Creek Wilderness

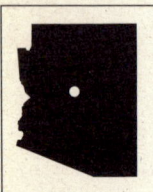

The U.S. Forest Service calls West Clear Creek Wilderness "one of the most rugged, remote canyons in northern Arizona." Clear Creek Canyon, opening on the Verde River on the west, is the longest canyon cutting through the Mogollon Rim along the edge of the Colorado Plateau. The canyon's very steep walls reach as high as 1,000 feet. It extends about 20 miles eastward before splitting into Clover Creek and Willow Valley, which form the headwaters of West Clear Creek. Pine and fir grow higher up, piñon and juniper on the slopes, and along the creek is a riparian habitat dominated by sycamore, alder, and cottonwood.

Despite the fact that the Wilderness is only one-half mile to two miles wide, the canyon offers wonderful opportunities for solitude. As for beauty, serenity, and complexity, the hiking is rarely exceeded in Arizona. Wild, primitive, and trailless, the canyon bottom is narrow and filled with water in places, requiring you to swim or wade if you hike the entire length . . . a challenge to be avoided during storms. A fairly easy trail starts at Bull Pen Ranch, follows the creek six miles, and climbs up the northern slope to the rim. This route is especially popular with anglers, who fish Clear Creek for German brown and rainbow trout. Two more trails, Maxwell (about six-tenths of a mile long) and Tramway (about three-fourths of a mile), also lead to the canyon bottom.

ARIZONA

West Clear Creek Essentials

Size: 13,600 acres.
Year Designated: 1984.
Location: Central Arizona.
Easiest Access: From Camp Verde, take State Highway 260 east for five miles. Turn north on Forest Service Road 618, drive about two miles, then turn east on Forest Service Road 215. From there it is three miles to Bull Pen Ranch.
Season: Fall to spring.
Wilderness Fees/Permits: None.
Maps: Topographic maps are available for $3 each from the U.S. Forest Service, Public Affairs Office, 517 Gold Avenue SW, Albuquerque, NM 87102; (505) 842-3292.
Management: Beaver Creek Ranger District, Coconino National Forest, HC 64, Box 240, Rimrock, AZ 86335; (520) 567-4501. Long Valley Ranger District, Coconino National Forest, HC 31, Box 68, Happy Jack, AZ 86024; (520) 354-2216.

Wet Beaver Wilderness

Winding on a serpentine course through the rim of the Colorado Plateau, Wet Beaver Creek twists through a steep-walled canyon of Supai sandstone and shale. Beyond lovely red cliffs in the lower section, the canyon widens and opens onto the Verde River. It originates about 12 miles east of the Beaver Creek Ranger Station at an elevation of about 6,200 feet and enters the Verde near 3,000 feet. Here you'll find pristine riparian habitat dominated by cottonwoods, sycamores, and alders. Wet Beaver Creek is one of Arizona's finest and rarest natural resources: a perennially flowing desert stream. The year-round waters attract large numbers of wildlife: elk and deer, bears and lions, smaller mammals, reptiles, and birds.

Two major trails, Apache Maid (9.5 miles) and the more popular Bell (10.8 miles), offer easy access to the rim country. Down in the canyon the hiking is fairly easy. Many visitors come to picnic, hike, or fish for trout and bass.

Wet Beaver Essentials

Size: 6,700 acres.
Year Designated: 1984.
Location: Central Arizona.
Easiest Access: From Flagstaff, take Interstate 17 south for 41 miles to Exit 298. Follow Forest Service Road 618 east for about two miles and turn at the sign indicating the Beaver Creek Ranger Station. The Bell Trailhead and the Wilderness boundary are along this road, approximately one mile past the ranger station.
Season: December and January are the wettest months.
Maps: Topographic maps are available for $3 each from the U.S. Forest Service, Public Affairs Office, 517 Gold Avenue SW, Albuquerque, NM 87102; (505) 842-3292.
Management: Beaver Creek Ranger District, Coconino National Forest, HC 64, Box 240, Rimrock, AZ 86336; (520) 567-4501.

ARIZONA

White Canyon Wilderness

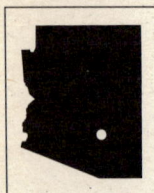

Intricately carved and scenically splendid White Canyon runs north-south through the middle of this Wilderness. Narrow in places, this canyon's walls rise as much as 800 feet above the bottom. Throughout you'll find delicate, eroded formations and numerous side canyons. Sand, slickrock, and willows cover the canyon's bottom. The Rincon, an enormous, amphitheater-like escarpment, stands near the southern boundary. Set in the rugged southeast portion of the Mineral Mountains, this Wilderness features a perennial stream that supports a variety of vegetation from saguaro cacti to chaparral. When rainstorms flood the area, especially during summer "monsoons," waterfalls pour over the rim of White Canyon, or form quiet pools within sculpted terraces. Wildlife includes a myriad of birds, thanks to the steady presence of water, often scarce in other regions. Black bears and mountain lions are permanent residents.

Rock climbers trek here to scale the canyon's vertical faces. Because of its year-round water supply and proximity to Tonto National Forest, this area is a fine choice for extended backpacking trips, despite its relatively small size.

White Canyon Essentials

Size: 5,800 acres.
Year Designated: 1990.
Location: Southern central Arizona.
Easiest Access: From Superior, on U.S. 60, take State Highway 177 south for 8.3 miles. Follow an unmarked dirt road west for approximately two miles to the boundary. Four-wheel drive is strongly recommended.
Season: Late summer to spring.
Wilderness Fees/Permits: None.
Maps: USGS topographic maps are Mineral Mountain and Teapot Mountain.
Management: BLM Phoenix Resource Area, 2015 West Deer Valley Road, Phoenix, AZ 85027; (602) 780-8090.

Woodchute Wilderness

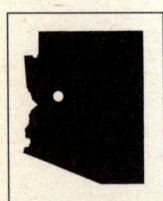

A small, easily accessible Wilderness near the geographic heart of Arizona, Woodchute offers spectacular views of the San Francisco Mountains and panoramic vistas of the central portion of the state. From a low point of 5,500 feet you can climb the Woodchute Trail, the only maintained path inside the area, through dry country of Utah juniper and piñon pine. The trail gradually opens onto higher country dominated by an overstory of second-growth ponderosa pine, finally topping out on the wide, flat mesa at the summit of Woodchute Mountain at 7,800 feet. From trailhead to summit is about 2.75 miles one-way. Along the way you'll see exposed layers of ancient ash from the days of volcanic activity. You'll find no water on the trail but Martin Canyon, which forms the southwestern border, has several tanks just outside of the Wilderness. The Martin Canyon Trail follows the bottom of the canyon for four miles. Years ago, this area was clear-cut to allow for mining operations, but it is slowly being reforested. Woodchute is a heavily visited Wilderness.

ARIZONA

Woodchute Essentials

Size: 5,600 acres.
Year Designated: 1984.
Location: Central Arizona.
Easiest Access: From Flagstaff, take U.S. 89A south approximately five miles past the town of Jerome to the Potato Patch Campground just east of the summit. Turn west on Forest Service Road 106 and drive three-tenths of a mile to the Woodchute Trailhead.
Season: Fall to spring.
Wilderness Fees/Permits: None.
Maps: Topographic maps are available for $3 each from the U.S. Forest Service, Public Affairs Office, 517 Gold Avenue SW, Albuquerque, NM 87102; (505) 842-3292. USGS maps are Hickey Mountain and Munds Draw.
Management: Chino Valley Ranger District, Prescott National Forest, P.O. Box 485, Chino Valley, AZ 86323; (520) 636-2302. Verde Ranger District, Prescott National Forest, P.O. Box 670, Camp Verde, AZ 86322-0670; (520) 567-4121.

Woolsey Peak Wilderness

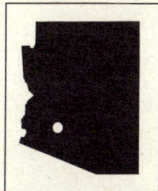

Woolsey Peak stands at 3,270 feet above sea level and approximately 2,500 feet above the Gila River (to the south). It is a geographical landmark visible from much of southwestern Arizona. The Painted Rock Dam blocks the Gila River not far from the southwestern corner of the area. Encompassing a major portion of the Gila Bend Mountains, it is just barely separated from the smaller Signal Mountain Wilderness (see above) to the north. You'll find sloping lava flows, basalt mesas, ragged peaks, and broken ridges dotted with saguaro, cholla, paloverde, creosote, and bursage. Desert mesquite, paloverde, and ironwood grow in the washes thoughout this rugged and expansive desert Wilderness.

The region is especially inviting for its desert backpacking. Desert bighorn sheep, mule deer, bobcats, mountain lions, hawks, and owls might make an appearance while you're tramping through here.

Woolsey Peak Essentials

Size: 61,000 acres.
Year Designated: 1990.
Location: Southwestern Arizona.
Easiest Access: From Interstate 8 approximately 14 miles west of Gila Bend, take the Painted Rock Dam exit (102). Head north for 18 miles to the Painted Rock Dam Spillway. The Wilderness lies due northeast across the riverbed.
Season: Fall to spring.
Wilderness Fees/Permits: None.
Maps: USGS topographic maps are Citrus Valley East, Citrus Valley West, Dendora Valley, Quail Springs Wash, Spring Mountain, and Woolsey Peak.
Management: BLM Lower Gila Resource Area, 2015 West Deer Valley Road, Phoenix, AZ 85027; (602) 863-4464.

> "I charge you to spare, preserve, and cherish some portion of your primitive forests; for when these are cut away I apprehend they will not be easily replaced."
>
> —Horace Greeley

ARKANSAS

Total Wilderness areas: 12
Total Wilderness acreage: 128,362

There's no shortage of natural space in Arkansas. The state contains over 18 million acres of forestland and 3 units of the National Forest System, more than 9,700 miles of waterways and 5 units of the National Park System, some 600,000 acres of lakes and 6 units of the National Wildlife Refuge System, not to mention 47 state parks. Of all these natural places, only 10 relatively small parcels of forestland, 1 section of a wildlife refuge, and 1 slice of national parkland have been deemed worthy of Wilderness designation. Eight of these areas were created by the Arkansas Wilderness Act of 1984.

Big Lake Wilderness

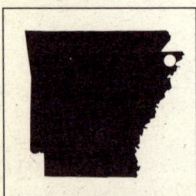

Twenty miles west of the Mississippi River, the 11,038-acre Big Lake National Wildlife Refuge was established in 1915 primarily as a migration habitat for ducks and geese using the Mississippi Flyway. The refuge lies flat, approximately 240 feet above sea level, and consists of 8,138 acres of permanent water interspersed with wooded swampland. During flood periods, 99 percent of the refuge may be submerged in water. The Little River drainage and shallow Big Lake itself (with an average depth of three feet) make up most of the open water, and the lake contains many islands standing barely above water level. Pondweed grows on the water's surface, supplying food for waterfowl. Giant bald cypress, black willow, and buttonbush thrive in swampy areas, while drier ground supports species such as cottonwood, oak, river birch, green ash, and red maple.

Although the U.S. Fish and Wildlife Service originally recommended none of Big Lake Refuge for designation, swampland to the north and east of the lake, the northeastern section of the refuge, has been designated Wilderness. White-tailed deer and many smaller mammals inhabit the area, and in 1993 the first bald eagle eggs hatched in nests just south of the Wilderness. No trails exist. Regulated hunting and fishing are permitted. Big Lake is the state's smallest Wilderness and the only one in eastern Arkansas.

ARKANSAS

Big Lake Essentials

Size: 2,144 acres.
Year Designated: 1976.
Location: Northeastern Arkansas.
Easiest Access: From Blytheville in the extreme northeast of the state, take State Highway 18 west for 15 miles to the refuge.
Season: Generally open to the public March through October, the Wilderness may be open year-round. Check with the refuge manager. Migratory birds flock here in December and January. Baby eagles hatch around April.

Wilderness Fees/Permits: Fishing and frogging are governed by state regulations. Hunting is allowed by special permit only. Check with the refuge manager.
Maps: A free map is available from the refuge manager. Take a map and compass when exploring the swamp.
Management: Big Lake National Wildlife Refuge, P.O. Box 67, Manila, AR 72442; (501) 564-2429.

Black Fork Mountain Wilderness

The Black Fork Mountain Trail, six miles long one-way, passes several pioneer sites dating back to the late 1800s as it winds its way to the top of Black Fork Mountain, over 2,400 feet above sea level. The mountain is actually a 13-mile-long east-west ridge, a geologic uplift that runs well into Oklahoma. The Wilderness boundary also follows the ridge into Oklahoma (see Oklahoma, Black Fork Mountain Wilderness).

Some of the slopes near the top of the ridge on the Oklahoma side are nearly vertical. Rock scree slopes, sometimes called rock "glaciers," flow off in many locations. No maintained trails lead from the Arkansas side of the Wilderness to the Oklahoma side.

In both states the ridge rises to scenic overlooks that offer spectacular vistas of this region. Lower slopes are heavily forested with shortleaf pine, blackjack oaks, and ancient dwarf oaks. Solitude reigns here, as Black Fork Mountain receives few human visitors.

Some of the shrubs and trees in the area are seldom seen anywhere else in this region. Beyond the Ouachita River and Big Creek, which border the Wilderness, the area holds no water except for two small springs on the mountain that flow most of the year. The hiking is considered difficult.

Black Fork Mountain Essentials

Size: 7,568 acres in Arkansas (12,151 acres total).
Year Designated: 1984 in Arkansas.
Location: Western Arkansas.
Easiest Access: From Mena, take U.S. 71 north for six miles. Turn west on U.S. 270 and drive six miles to Forest Service Road 516. Turn north and drive four miles to a small parking lot at the trailhead.
Season: Spring and summer.

Wilderness Fees/Permits: None, but the USFS prefers small groups in order to reduce impact.
Maps: A map is available for $3 from the Ozark Interpretive Association, P.O. Box 1279, Mountain View, AR 72560. USGS topographic maps are Mountain Fork, Page, and Rich Mountain.
Management: Mena Ranger District, Ouachita National Forest, Route 3, Box 220, Highway 71 North, Mena, AR 71953; (501) 394-2382.

ARKANSAS

Buffalo National River Wilderness

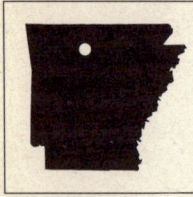

Canoeists paddling the Buffalo find themselves on what may well be the most scenic river in the eastern United States. From its headwaters in the Boston Mountains to its confluence with the White River, the Buffalo's 132 miles are managed by the National Park Service as a National River. Flowing through the Arkansas Ozarks, the river has carved a path out of an ancient seabed, leaving bluffs of sandstone, limestone, and dolomite towering as high as 440 feet above the water. Quiet, languid pools stand between runs of swifter water, often disguising the river's drop of over 2,000 feet during its long journey. You'll see glens that trap noon shadows and hollows hiding curtains of ferns fed by secret waterfalls. While the Buffalo is one of the cleanest rivers in America, you should always purify its water before drinking.

Wildlife watchers frequently spot white-tailed deer, mink, beavers, raccoons, opossums, bobcats, and black bears. On the banks of the upper river, elk are occasionally seen. Eastern elk, exterminated in the 1840s, were replaced with Rocky Mountain elk in 1981, and the herd has been growing slowly ever since.

Buffalo National River Wilderness is divided into three sections (all managed by the National Park Service). The Upper Buffalo Unit adjoins Upper Buffalo Wilderness (managed by Ozark National Forest). Here you'll find the river at its wildest and most primitive. From Ponca to below Kyles Landing, a distance of 11 miles, the Ponca Unit protects the most used section of the river. Watch for storms: the river has been known to rise 25 feet in 24 hours. The Lower Buffalo Unit is the largest, stretching from Buffalo Point Ranger Station to the town of Buffalo City on the White River, a distance of 32 miles. Here the water runs smooth and has few human visitors. The Lower Buffalo Unit adjoins Leatherwood Wilderness (managed by Ozark National Forest). Several trails provide access from the river into the Wilderness areas. From Ponca, the Buffalo River Trail, 26 miles long, offers what is probably the best look at the Wilderness, winding along scenic overlooks and through isolated forestland. Hiking on the upper trail is strenuous. Camping is allowed anywhere in the Wilderness.

Buffalo National River Essentials

Size: 10,529 acres.
Year Designated: 1978.
Location: Northern Arkansas.
Easiest Access: From Harrison, take State Highway 43 south for 26 miles to Ponca.
Season: Backpacking is best in winter when the snakes and ticks are sleeping. The river is heavily visited between late spring and early fall. Go midweek to avoid the crowds.
Wilderness Fees/Permits: None.
Maps: USGS topographic maps are Big Flat, Boxley, Buffalo City, Cozahome, Eula, Fallsville, Hasty, Jasper, Marshall, Maumee, Mount Judea, Osage SW, Ponca, Rea Valley, Snowball, and West Grove. Buffalo River trail and river guidebooks are available from the Eastern National Park and Monument Association at park headquarters in Harrison.
Management: Buffalo National River, Box 1173, Harrison, AR 72602; (501) 741-5443.

ARKANSAS

Caney Creek Wilderness

Located on the southern edge of Ouachita National Forest, Caney Creek Wilderness protects a rugged and lovely portion of the Ouachita Mountains. From heights above 2,000 feet in the east, Short Creek and Caney Creek flow all the way across the area before plunging into the Cossatot River on the western boundary. Along the creeks you'll find beech, large pines, and bottomland hardwoods. Sharp ridges separate the creeks and offer splendid views of the surrounding region. Occasional sandstone outcroppings dot the landscape.

The Caney Creek Trail follows the entire nine-mile length of the creek, crossing it 15 times. As the terrain grows steeper hiking on the path becomes more difficult. Parking lots give access to both ends of the trail. The Buckeye Trail starts at a third parking lot, climbs Buckeye Mountain, and follows a ridge before dropping to join Caney Creek. Traveling a distance of 3.2 miles one-way, the Tall Peak Trail leaves Shady Lake Campground, outside the southeastern Wilderness boundary, and climbs Tall Peak, inside the Wilderness, where a restored lookout tower stands.

Caney Creek Essentials

Size: 14,344 acres.
Year Designated: 1975.
Location: Western Arkansas.
Easiest Access: From Mena, take U.S. 59/71 south for 15 miles. Turn east on State Highway 246 and drive 17 miles. Turn north on Forest Service Road 38 and head nine miles to the lower end of the Caney Creek Trail.
Season: Spring and fall.

Wilderness Fees/Permits: None.
Maps: A map is available for $3 by writing to the Ozark Interpretive Association, P.O. Box 1279, Mountain View, AR 72560. USGS topographic maps are Eagle Mountain and Nichols Mountain.
Management: Mena Ranger District, Ouachita National Forest, Route 3, Box 220, Highway 71 North, Mena, AR 71953; (501) 394-2382.

Dry Creek Wilderness

This little area, the state's second smallest Wilderness, contains numerous high sandstone bluffs and ridges overlooking Dry Creek, a stream that flows only part of the year between Dry Creek Mountain and North Petit Jean Mountain in the Ouachita Range. Rocky outcroppings and steep slopes stand above a dense pine-hardwood forest. Chimney Rock, one of the area's most unique geological features, is a freestanding, chimneylike rock tower that has broken away from a vertical rock wall. Although roads surround the area, an unusually dense black bear population hides here in relative solitude. Ridge tops offer great views of the region. The terrain varies primarily between steep and very steep. The rugged Dry Creek Trail follows the stream for more than five miles, and several branches of the path climb out of the creek bottom to the road on the northern boundary. If the creek isn't running, you should pack along your own water.

ARKANSAS

Dry Creek Essentials

Size: 6,310 acres.
Year Designated: 1984.
Location: Western Arkansas.
Easiest Access: From the junction of State Highways 10 and 23, go east on State Highway 10 for 17 miles. Turn south on County Road 309 and drive five miles to Forest Service Road 18; follow it south for four miles. Turn west on Forest Service Road 3 and continue four miles to a trailhead on the western boundary.
Season: Spring.
Wilderness Fees/Permits: None.
Maps: A free Wilderness map is available from the district ranger.
Management: Cold Springs Ranger District, Ouachita National Forest, P.O. Box 417, Booneville, AR 72927; (501) 675-3233.

East Fork Wilderness

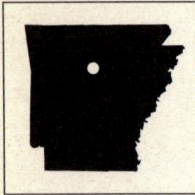

The East Fork of Illinois Bayou, from which this area takes its name, bisects the Wilderness from northeast to southwest, fed by water from Bear Hollow, Mill Creek, and Sycamore Creek. On the southern edge of the Boston Mountains, East Fork is characterized by flat-topped ridges that rise 800 to 1,600 feet above sea level and are separated by steep hollows, some with sheer sandstone walls. Two seasonal ponds are bordered by overcup oak, but the principal trees are white and red oak and hickory with an understory of redbud, dogwood, serviceberry, sassafras, and persimmon.

Unlike a "true" Wilderness area, East Fork bears the scars left by early inhabitants: old homesteads and farms, a cemetery, the remains of old roads. Four parking lots give access to three trails tracing abandoned routes. The East Fork Trail runs the length of the Wilderness, but the most beautiful scenery can be found along the hollows off the trail. Primitive camping is possible throughout the area. Wandering off-trail, you may find evidence of the Osage Indians who lived in this region in the seventeenth and eighteenth centuries. Nature has been given the freedom to reclaim East Fork Wilderness.

East Fork Essentials

Size: 10,777 acres.
Year Designated: 1984.
Location: Northern central Arkansas.
Easiest Access: From Interstate 40 in Atkins, take State Highway 105 north. Highway 105 turns into Scenic Highway 27 and borders part of the western edge of the Wilderness. Follow it to a parking lot/trailhead about 35 miles north of the interstate.
Season: Spring and fall.
Wilderness Fees/Permits: None.
Maps: A colorful Wilderness map is available for $3 by writing to the Ozark Interpretive Association, P.O. Box 1279, Mountain View, AR 72560.
Management: Bayou Ranger District, Ozark-Saint Francis National Forest, Route 1, Box 36, Hector, AR 72843; (501) 284-3150.

ARKANSAS

Flatside Wilderness

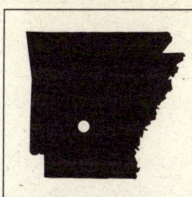

In the extreme eastern Ouachita Mountains is a Wilderness that takes its name from Flatside Pinnacle, a 1,550-foot rock outcropping just outside the northeast boundary. Dominating the skyline are White Oak Mountain, the highest point in the Wilderness at 1,650 feet, and Forked Mountain, at 1,350 feet. From overlooks on the eastern and western sides, the forest below looks like an unbroken canopy of pines and hardwoods. Several small creeks flow through the area. Spanning the entire Ouachita National Forest from east to west, the Ouachita National Recreation Trail starts near Flatside Pinnacle and crosses the Wilderness for 10 miles of rugged hiking to White Oak Mountain. Off-trail hikers will encounter some of the remotest parts of Arkansas.

Flatside Essentials

Size: 10,105 acres.
Year Designated: 1984.
Location: Western central Arkansas.
Easiest Access: From Perryville, take State Highway 9 south for 13.6 miles. Turn west on Forest Service Road 132 and drive 8.3 miles to Forest Service Road 94. Turn north and head three miles to Flatside Pinnacle.
Season: Spring, fall, or winter.
Wilderness Fees/Permits: None.
Maps: A Wilderness map is available for $3 from the Ozark Interpretive Association, P.O. Box 1279, Mountain View, AR 72560.
Management: Winona Ranger District, Ouachita National Forest, 1039 Highway 10 North, Perryville, AR 72126; (501) 889-5176.

Hurricane Creek Wilderness

In the middle of the Boston Mountains, Hurricane Creek tumbles along its boulder-strewn way, sparkling in pool after pool, through the center of this Wilderness. Limestone and sandstone bluffs, some over 100 feet high, loom above the rippling water. Second- and third-growth upland hardwoods, primarily oak and hickory, forest the surrounding lands, growing among narrow, V-shaped valleys. Dogwood, redbud, serviceberry, and witch hazel form the understory. Side drainages into the creek offer rugged traveling. Elevations surpass 2,200 feet on the high ridges.

At the turn of the century, as many as 70 families inhabited Hurricane Creek Valley. While they're long gone, their homes, farms, cemeteries, and roads live on, although nature is gradually reclaiming ground.

The Ozark Highlands Trail (OHT), partly an old pioneer road, crosses the Wilderness in a 19.5-mile, southwest-northeast path, bookended by parking lots. The *Ozark Highlands Trail Guide* rates this section as "one of the most scenic spots in Arkansas." Among the scenery is a huge natural rock bridge that spans Hurricane Creek. A high-water bypass in the OHT allows year-round access but eliminates some of the best scenery. All during the year you'll have to wade across the shallow but slick-bottomed creek, and black bears have been known to raid camps, and some of the land within the boundaries is private . . . none of which should deter you from this pristine slice of Arkansas Wilderness.

ARKANSAS

Hurricane Creek Essentials

Size: 15,177 acres.
Year Designated: 1984.
Location: Northwestern Arkansas.
Easiest Access: From Interstate 40 at Clarksville, take State Highway 123 north about 40 miles to the Big Piney Trailhead, where the OHT enters the Wilderness.
Season: Spring, fall, or winter.

Wilderness Fees/Permits: None.
Maps: Wilderness maps ($3) and guidebooks are available from the Ozark Interpretive Association, P.O. Box 1279, Mountain View, AR 72560.
Management: Buffalo Ranger District, Ozark-Saint Francis National Forest, P.O. Box 427, Jasper, AR 72641; (501) 446-5122.

Leatherwood Wilderness

The Ozarks are known for their ridgetop country, and some of the loveliest specimens can be found in Leatherwood Wilderness. The Wilderness is named for the region's largest drainage, clear-flowing Leatherwood Creek, which runs across the northern portion and into the Buffalo River. The creek, in turn, takes its name from a slow-growing shrub that produces pale yellow flowers in March and April; its extremely flexible wood has been dubbed "leatherwood." Steep V-shaped valleys separate the high ridges, valleys often sided with sheer rock walls or benches that drop in marvelous "stair-steps" to the drainages below. Glades of cedar hide among a forest of oak, gum, and hickory. White-tailed deer, wild turkeys, and black bears are known to live here, though they're seldom seen by the casual human visitor. What you will see are the ruins of old homesteads, farms, and roads that are slowly returning to a natural condition.

Leatherwood Wilderness shares its western border with the Lower Buffalo Wilderness Unit of Buffalo National River Wilderness (see above). On the east lies Forest Service Road 1100 (Push Mountain Road) with several trailheads and one parking lot. From the parking lot, the trail winds up Spencer Hollow to eventually join Leatherwood Creek and trickle down to the Buffalo River. Hunting and fishing are allowed, camping is unrestricted, and horsepackers are allowed on trails in this area, the largest Wilderness in Arkansas.

Leatherwood Essentials

Size: 16,956 acres.
Year Designated: 1984.
Location: Northern Arkansas.
Easiest Access: From Mountain Home, take State Highway 5 about 15 miles south toward Norfolk. Just before Norfolk turn east and south on Forest Service Road 1100 and drive approximately two miles to the parking lot.
Season: Early spring and late fall.

Wilderness Fees/Permits: None.
Maps: A colorful Wilderness map is available for $3 by writing to the Ozark Interpretive Association, P.O. Box 1279, Mountain View, AR 72560.
Management: Sylamore Ranger District, Ozark-Saint Francis National Forest, P.O. Box 1, Highway 14 North, Henderson Building, Mountain View, AR 72560; (501) 269-3228.

ARKANSAS

Poteau Mountain Wilderness

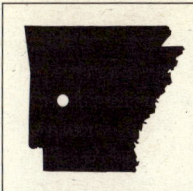

Extensive folding and faulting of the terrain in bygone days created the steep east-west ridges of Poteau Mountain, a subrange of the Ouachita Mountains. Erosion from many streams has carved deep slices out of the ridges. The streams feed a typical Ozark forest of dense pines and hardwoods broken by rocky outcroppings that often provide scenic overlooks. This Wilderness has two distinct sections, east and west, which are separated by a wide strip of land along the mountain upon which car traffic is allowed. Within the Wilderness no maintained trails exist, but hikers may find and follow old, overgrown logging roads. The eastern section is dominated by East Poteau Mountain; the western section rises briskly up two drainages, Rock Creek and Posey Creek, and is accessible from a road on the southern boundary.

Poteau Mountain Essentials

Size: 10,884 acres.
Year Designated: 1984.
Location: Western Arkansas.
Easiest Access: From Waldron, take U.S. 71 north for 5.6 miles, then turn west on Forest Service Road 158 and drive two miles to the southern Wilderness boundary.
Season: Spring and fall.
Wilderness Fees/Permits: None.
Maps: A free Wilderness map is available from the district ranger.
Management: Poteau Ranger District, Ouachita National Forest, P.O. Box 2255, Waldron, AR 72958; (501) 637-4174.

Richland Creek Wilderness

Beautiful Richland Creek traverses this area, cutting its way through a thick forest with abundant wildlife, secluded off-creek hideaways, and ridges that rise to towering vistas. Set within the Boston Mountains (which encompass most of Ozark National Forest), this Wilderness is a land of narrow valleys bordered by steep slopes and vertical limestone and sandstone bluffs rising as much as 100 feet above the drainages. Some of these stone formations contain fossilized remains of now extinct species.

Richland Creek and Long Devil's Fork Creek meet near the very heart of this area on their eastward journey. Within one-quarter mile of these creeks, bluffs more than a mile long loom over Richland Creek. Beyond these bluffs lies land more typical of the Ozarks, an oak-hickory forest with scattered shortleaf pines and an understory of ferns, blueberries, dogwood, and blackhaw.

Long since logged off, the land has no virgin timber, and the "trails" of are often old logging roads. But the scenery is some of the finest in the state, especially the first four miles of the Ozark Highlands Trail (OHT) after it leaves Richland Creek Campground and skirts the southern and eastern boundaries of the Wilderness. Unfortunately, according to the *Ozark Highlands Trail Guide,* the OHT misses "perhaps the most scenic spot in the state." To reach this plum destination, hike up the creek from the campground to Devil's Fork, then bushwhack up that drainage to Twin Falls, a total hike of about three miles. You'll find nothing finer in Arkansas.

ARKANSAS

Richland Creek Essentials

Size: 11,822 acres.
Year Designated: 1984.
Location: Northwestern Arkansas.
Easiest Access: From Interstate 40 at Russellville, drive 36 miles on State Highway 7 to Pelsor. Turn east on State Highway 16 and head approximately 10 miles to Forest Service Road 1205. Turn north and drive about eight miles to Richland Creek Campground on the eastern boundary of the Wilderness.

Season: Spring, fall, and winter.
Wilderness Fees/Permits: None.
Maps: Wilderness maps ($3) and guidebooks are available from the Ozark Interpretive Association, P.O. Box 1279, Mountain View, AR 72560.
Management: Buffalo Ranger District, Ozark-Saint Francis National Forest, P.O. Box 427, Jasper, AR 72641; (501) 446-5122.

Upper Buffalo Wilderness

Here you'll be among the headwaters of the extraordinarily pretty Buffalo National River, which flows down the center of this Wilderness through a rough forested land of steep slopes that descend into deep valleys. People once made their homes down in the valleys, but the last resident moved out in 1948. However, you'll see their old homes, stone fences surrounding pastures, antiquated farm equipment, worn-out roads, and silent cemeteries. The area offers a measure of wildness and solitude not often found in Arkansas. The interior of the Upper Buffalo is so remote the quality of its rich water supply, in runs and runnels and rivulets, is classified as excellent. (No matter how clear the water looks, you would be wise to purify it before drinking.)

Squirrels are everywhere in the Upper Buffalo, and squirrel hunters report their success runs from good to superior, perhaps better than anywhere else in the southern United States. White-tailed deer, wild turkeys, and black bears are the largest resident species, with a fair number of smaller animals including foxes, raccoons, minks, beavers, skunks, opossums, bobcats, and woodchucks.

White oaks, red oaks, and hickory populate the forest. The summer climate is known to be hot and humid. A few people choose to visit the Upper Buffalo in winter when January temperatures may drop below zero. During the cold months, ice encrusts a number of small waterfalls and hangs in frozen drips from overhangs, and a cold peace settles on the land. No matter what the season, you'll have to find your way through the area without the assistance of maintained trails.

Upper Buffalo Essentials

Size: 11,746 acres.
Year Designated: 1975.
Location: Northwestern Arkansas.
Easiest Access: From Interstate 40 at Clarksville, take State Highway 21 north for 27 miles. Turn west on Forest Service Road 1410, which dead-ends approximately two miles later at a track leading to the old Curtis Cemetery near the southeastern Wilderness boundary.

Season: Fall through early spring.
Wilderness Fees/Permits: None.
Maps: A Wilderness map is available for $3 by writing to the Ozark Interpretive Association, P.O. Box 1279, Mountain View, AR 72560.
Management: Buffalo Ranger District, Ozark-Saint Francis National Forest, P.O. Box 427, Jasper, AR 72641; (501) 446-5122.

> "In God's wildness lies the hope of the world—the great, fresh, unblighted, unredeemed wilderness. The galling harness of civilization drops off, and the wounds heal ere we are aware."
>
> —John Muir

CALIFORNIA

Total Wilderness areas: 129
Total Wilderness acreage: 13,987,677

California is a state of extremes. It contains the highest and lowest points in the Lower 48, the largest trees on Earth, America's driest desert and hottest place—as well as one of its wettest. You can ski in the mountains and swim comfortably in the ocean on the same day. California has the largest human population of the 50 states and the most territory in federal ownership (about half the state) with the exception of Alaska. It is a vast land, about 800 miles long with approximately 1,340 miles of sea coast, some 5,000 lakes, and 30,000 miles of rivers and streams. With passage of the California Desert Protection Act of 1994, California now has the second most designated Wilderness land (after Alaska) and the largest number of Wilderness areas of any state. The California Desert Protection Act designated some areas so remote even the land managers are unable to completely document what hides there. California also contains the largest Wilderness area in the Lower 48 and one of the smallest. Due to its population and popularity, California has the most Wilderness restrictions on human use.

CALIFORNIA

Agua Tibia Wilderness

The steep, chaparral-covered mountains of Agua Tibia Wilderness give way to stands of fir, pine, and oak at higher elevations that rise above 4,400 feet on Agua Tibia Mountain and above 5,000 feet on Eagle Crag. Untouched by wildfire for what may be more than a century, some of the dense stands of chaparral have manzanita and red shank reaching higher than 20 feet. Although light snow may fall in winter, summer temperatures often exceed 100 degrees Fahrenheit and water may be hard to find.

The Dripping Springs Trail (about 6.8 miles long), part of approximately 25 miles of pathways, receives light human use and provides the main access to the area. The trail crosses boulder-strewn Arroyo Seco Creek and climbs Agua Tibia Mountain with splendid views of the mountains of southern California. From the crest of the mountain, the Palomar-McGee Trail (about 5.5 miles) enters a forest, descends to Crosley Saddle, and continues south near Eagle Crag before branching off into the Wilderness. No overnight use of pack stock is permitted, and campfires, hibachis, and barbecues are not allowed. Groups are limited to 15 people. The western portion of the Wilderness is dry and seldom seen.

Agua Tibia Essentials

Size: 15,933 acres.
Year Designated: 1975.
Location: Southwestern California.
Easiest Access: From Interstate 15 in Temecula, take State Highway 79 east for approximately 10 miles to Dripping Springs Campground. The Dripping Springs Trail leaves the southern end of the campground.
Season: Winter through early spring.
Wilderness Fees/Permits: A free permit is required to enter the Wilderness. Contact the district ranger.
Maps: USGS topographic maps are Pechanga and Vail Lake.
Management: Palomar Ranger District, Cleveland National Forest, 1634 Black Canyon Road, Ramona, CA 92065; (619) 788-0250.

Ansel Adams Wilderness

Formerly known as Minarets Wilderness, the name of this large and magnificent region was changed in 1984 to honor Ansel Adams, the noted photographer and environmentalist. You'll find rugged country here that includes the dramatic alpine scenery east of the Sierra crest, and the North Fork, Middle Fork, and lower South Fork of the San Joaquin River, with their deep, granite-walled gorges and their plenitude of rainbow, golden, and brook trout. The Minarets Range offers challenges for experienced climbers. Elevations range from about 7,000 feet to 14,000 feet, and some of the lower stretches display scattered benches, small plateaus, and a dense forest cover divided by sparkling streams and lakes. The central portion contains numerous mountain lakes. Rich in wildlife, this area is a summer range for large herds of deer.

Many pathways traverse the area, including the Pacific Crest National Scenic Trail for approximately 12 miles and the John Muir Trail for about 16; human use is heavy. Firewood is scarce

CALIFORNIA

above 10,000 feet, campfires are prohibited in some places, and backpacking stoves are a must. A small piece of Ansel Adams Wilderness (665 acres) extends into the eastern side of Yosemite National Park. The splendor of this region would be well served by less human traffic.

Ansel Adams Essentials

Size: 229,334 acres.
Year Designated: 1964 (USFS), 1984 (NPS).
Location: Eastern central California.
Easiest Access: From U.S. 395 in Mammoth Lakes, take Route 203 for approximately 19 miles to Devil's Postpile National Monument. The Pacific Crest Trail enters the Wilderness four miles northwest of the monument.
Season: Mid-July through August.
Wilderness Fees/Permits: A free permit is required for overnight use. A quota system is in effect from July 1 through Labor Day. Reservations ($3 per person) are advised. Day use requires no permit. Contact a district ranger.
Maps: A Wilderness map is available for $3 from the district rangers.
Management: Pineridge Ranger District, Sierra National Forest, P.O. Box 300, Shaver Lake, CA 93664; (209) 855-5360. Minarets Ranger District, Sierra National Forest, North Fork, CA 93643; (209) 877-2218. Mammoth Ranger District, Inyo National Forest, P.O. Box 148, Mammoth Lakes, CA 93546; (619) 647-2505. Mono Lake Ranger District, Inyo National Forest, P.O. Box 429, Lee Vining, CA 93541; (619) 647-6525. Yosemite National Park, P.O. Box 577, Yosemite, CA 95389; (209) 372-0200.

Argus Range Wilderness

Nestling against the Argus Range, a thin and narrow north-south mountain chain, this Wilderness stretches for 28 miles along the west side of the Panamint Valley, just south and west of Death Valley National Park and just east of the China Lake Naval Weapons Center. (If the Navy decides to install a space-energy laser facility within 15 years after Wilderness designation, a road may be built across the area.) Elevations here vary from about 2,800 feet on the east side to more than 7,500 feet on the west. The Argus Range is comprised of dry desert mountains with steep slopes and highly dissected canyons. Remains of old mining activity and a few prehistoric sites are scattered throughout the Wilderness. You may find several springs supporting a small population of desert bighorn sheep. Vegetation includes creosote scrub communities on the lower slopes, occasional piñon-juniper communities at higher elevations, and virtually nothing on the steep slopes and canyon walls.

Trails are not maintained here, but you should find some relatively easy hiking up several canyons that open on the east side.

CALIFORNIA

Argus Range Essentials
Size: 74,890 acres.
Year Designated: 1994.
Location: Eastern California.
Easiest Access: From State Highway 190 approximately 30 miles south of Stovepipe Wells, turn south on Panamint Valley Road and proceed for approximately eight miles. Turn west on Minietta Road and go about four miles. Turn south on Nadeau Road, and then west on one of at least a dozen old four-wheel-drive tracks that lead to the edge of the Wilderness.
Season: Winter.
Wilderness Fees/Permits: None.
Maps: USGS topographic maps for the area are China Gardens, Darwin, Homewood Canyon, Maturango Peak, Maturango Peak SE, Panamint Springs, Revenue Canyon, and Slate Range Crossing.
Management: BLM Ridgecrest Resource Area, 300 South Richmond Road, Ridgecrest, CA 93555; (619) 384-5400.

Big Maria Mountains Wilderness

Gently sloping *bajadas*, or desert slopes, rise to numerous rough and craggy peaks separated by steep canyons in Big Maria Mountains Wilderness. The Big Marias lie just south of a major drainage called Big Wash and just west of the Colorado River and the Arizona border. The northwest boundary follows a power line south, then turns southeast to trace the contours of the base of the mountains. Foxtail cactus and California barrel cactus dot the dry and desolate landscape, and a small herd of deer depend on the waters of the river for their lives.

There are no trails, but several old jeep tracks, now closed to vehicular traffic, provide foot access into the Wilderness.

Big Maria Mountains Essentials
Size: 47,570 acres.
Year Designated: 1994.
Location: Southeastern California.
Easiest Access: From Blythe, take U.S. 95 north for approximately 11 miles to the vicinity of the Palo Verde Dam. Continue north past the dam on U.S. 95, and turn west on one of several four-wheel-drive tracks that lead to the edge of the Wilderness.
Season: Winter.
Wilderness Fees/Permits: None.
Maps: USGS topographic maps are Big Maria Mountains NE, Big Maria Mountains NW, Big Maria Mountains SE, Big Maria Mountains SW, Blythe NE, and McCoy Wash.
Management: BLM Palm Springs-South Coast Resource Area, 63-500 Garnet Avenue, P.O. Box 2000, North Palm Springs, CA 92258; (619) 251-4800.

CALIFORNIA

Bigelow Cholla Garden Wilderness

Bigelow chollas, also known as jumping chollas, are single-stemmed members of the cactus family that branch out only near the top, and their very dark trunks help to distinguish them from their near relatives. While the cacti don't really jump, I can testify from personal experience that the sharp spines can find their way into your skin when you'd swear you never touched a plant. They will form dense colonies, reproducing almost entirely when sections are knocked off a parent plant. The largest concentration of Bigelow chollas in the California Desert can be found in the aptly named Bigelow Cholla Garden Wilderness. Here at the northern extreme of the dark and volcanic Sacramento Mountains, Interstate 40 forms the northern boundary. Several large tracts of privately owned land stand within the Wilderness.

There are no trails or water, but you'll find it relatively easy to wander in the area, which has very few elevation changes.

Bigelow Cholla Garden Essentials

Size: 10,380 acres.
Year Designated: 1994.
Location: Southeastern California.
Easiest Access: From Needles, take Interstate 40 west for approximately 18 miles, turning southeast on the dirt road at Camino. The Wilderness is immediately south of Interstate 40 and to the east of the dirt road.
Season: Winter.
Wilderness Fees/Permits: None.
Maps: USGS topographic maps are Bannock, Flat Top Mountain, and West of Flat Top Mountain.
Management: BLM Needles Resource Area, 101 West Spikes Road, Needles, CA 92363; (619) 326-3896.

Bighorn Mountains Wilderness

The north-central portion of this Wilderness area holds the rugged Bighorn Mountains and the eastern foothills of the San Bernardino Mountains. It presents a rare transition zone between the yucca- and Joshua tree-covered desert floor and stands of Jeffrey pine in the higher country. The Bighorns lift all the way to 7,500 feet on Granite Peak. Mule deer, mountain lions, and bobcats make their homes here, and golden eagles soar in the bright skies. The creek through Rattlesnake Canyon flows northward and divides the Wilderness into distinct eastern and western sections, and numerous resident and migratory birds alight to drink its waters. A third section lies to the southeast of the two larger sections. The three sections are separated by non-Wilderness corridors. The western portion of the western section reaches into San Bernardino National Forest.

CALIFORNIA

Bighorn Mountains Essentials

Size: 39,185 acres.
Year Designated: 1994.
Location: Central southern California.
Easiest Access: From State Highway 247 (Old Woman Springs Road) approximately 31 miles north of Yucca Valley, and just west of a landing strip on the south side of the road, turn south on the old jeep trail that leads into Rattlesnake Canyon.
Season: Late fall to early spring.
Wilderness Fees/Permits: None.
Maps: USGS topographic maps are Big Bear City, Bighorn Canyon, Onyx Peak, Rattlesnake Canyon, Rimrock, and Yucca Valley North.
Management: BLM Barstow Resource Area, 150 Coolwater Lane, Barstow, CA 92311; (619) 255-8700. San Bernardino National Forest, 144 North Mountain View Avenue, San Bernardino, CA 92408; (714) 383-5588.

Black Mountain Wilderness

Black Mountain stands at 3,941 feet, a mesa rising above an expanse of desolate, ancient lava flows. The mountain lies in the northwest corner of the Wilderness, and from the summit, the area drops in elevation to 2,080 feet. You'll find a deposit of fine-grained sand in the southeast corner, and not much else other than an occasional golden eagle or prairie falcon circling in search of food.

There are no trails, but a spring exists near Opal Mountain not far outside the northwest boundary, across Opal Mountain Road. A significant amount of privately owned acreage exists within the area that should not be used without permission.

Black Mountain Essentials

Size: 13,940 acres.
Year Designated: 1994.
Location: Central southern California.
Easiest Access: From Hinkley, on State Highway 58, take Black Canyon Road north for approximately 13 miles to Black Canyon, with Black Mountain rising on the east side.
Season: January through March.
Wilderness Fees/Permits: None.
Maps: USGS topographic maps are Bird Spring, Lockhart, Opal Mountain, and Water Valley.
Management: BLM Barstow Resource Area, 150 Coolwater Lane, Barstow, CA 92311; (619) 255-8700.

Bright Star Wilderness

Bright Star Canyon encloses Kelso Creek and leaves Sequoia National Forest to cross the southern portion of the BLM's Bright Star Wilderness. In the northwest portion, Cortez Canyon has been carved out of the Kelso Mountains. In the northeast portion, Kelso Peak stands at 5,090 feet with drainages falling off to the north, south, and east. To the west, the Kelso Mountains join the Piute Mountains outside the Wilderness.

The upper slopes are dotted with piñon pine and juniper, while the lower slopes are brushy and broken by large granite outcroppings. The valley below is boulder-strewn and dense with Joshua trees. Here the Mojave Desert meets the

CALIFORNIA

Sierra Nevada, allowing for a wide variety of wildlife. The entire Wilderness lies within the BLM's Jawbone-Butterbredt Area of Critical Environmental Concern.

There are no designated trails for backpackers. Old tracks enter from the north in Cortez Canyon, from the northwest along Piñon Creek, and from the south into Bright Star Canyon.

Bright Star Essentials

Size: 9,520 acres.
Year Designated: 1994.
Location: Central southern California.
Easiest Access: From Lake Isabella, take State Highway 178 east for approximately 14 miles. Turn south on the Kelso Valley Road and go about 16 miles to find the point at which old tracks leave the road heading west into the Wilderness.

Season: Early spring and late fall.
Wilderness Fees/Permits: None.
Maps: USGS topographic maps are Cane Canyon, Claraville, Piñon Mountain, and Woolstalf Creek.
Management: BLM Ridgecrest Resource Area, 300 South Richmond Road, Ridgecrest, CA 93555; (619) 384-5400.

Bristol Mountains Wilderness

Together, a portion of the low, rolling Bristol Mountains and a tilted volcanic plain form Bristol Mountains Wilderness. The lack of water and extreme open distances make for a dry and desolate hunk of land that poses a challenge for the most accomplished desert hiker. The Wilderness shares its eastern border (Budweiser Wash) with Mojave National Preserve and Granite Chief Wilderness (see below). Interstate 40 forms much of the southern boundary, while a pipeline traces the northern. Some parcels of privately owned land (old mining claims) exist within the area. You must obtain permission before crossing them. There are no trails.

Bristol Mountains Essentials

Size: 68,515 acres.
Year Designated: 1994.
Location: Southeastern California.
Easiest Access: From Barstow, take Interstate 40 east for approximately 51 miles. Take the Ludlow exit and follow the dirt road north about two miles, turning east on the old pipeline road. The Wilderness lies to the south of the pipeline. Four-wheel-drive vehicles are recommended.

Season: Early spring and late fall.
Wilderness Fees/Permits: None.
Maps: USGS topographic maps are Ash Hill, Broadwell Lake, Brown Buttes, Budweiser Wash, East of Broadwell Lake, East of Siberia, Glasgow, Kelson Dunes, Ludlow, Siberia, and West of Budweiser Wash.
Management: BLM Barstow Resource Area, 150 Coolwater Lane, Barstow, CA 92311; (619) 255-8700.

CALIFORNIA

Bucks Lake Wilderness

Bordered by Bucks Lake on the south, this relatively small area boasts a broad diversity of vegetation (brush fields, conifers, oaks, pure stands of red fir) and topography (bare rocky slopes, cliffs, quaking bogs, small alpine meadows) with elevations ranging from about 2,000 feet in the Feather River Canyon to 7,017 feet atop Spanish Peak. The higher elevations are separated from the lower by a long escarpment along which the Pacific Crest Trail runs for approximately 13 miles, granting the occasional spectacular view to the east and north. Throughout the area, you'll stumble upon small lakes and ponds, primarily near the base of the escarpment.

You may see cattle grazing around Bucks Lake, a holdover from the pre-Wilderness days. Several trails connect with the Pacific Crest Trail (PCT) from a number of trailheads. This area receives only light human use.

Bucks Lake Essentials

Size: 21,000 acres.
Year Designated: 1984.
Location: Northern California.
Easiest Access: From State Highway 70 in Quincy, go west for approximately 17 miles on Bucks Lakes Road to Bucks Lake. Access the Pacific Crest Trail two miles east of Bucks Lake on Bucks Lake Road.
Season: Spring and fall.
Wilderness Fees/Permits: A permit is required if you want a campfire.
Maps: A Wilderness map is available for $3 from the forest ranger.
Management: Plumas National Forest, P.O. Box 11500, Quincy, CA 95971; (916) 283-2050.

Cadiz Dunes Wilderness

Winds swept the sand from Cadiz Dry Lake to form the low, buff-colored dunes that are the distinctive feature of this Wilderness area. These dunes form a rare habitat for an amazing abundance of flora and fauna. Although the top layer of sand is dry, the underlying layers are moist due to capillary action that coaxes water up from far below. Crickets and other insects live beneath the surface, hunted by the seldom-seen fringe-toed lizard. Blooms of sand verbena, desert lily, and other flowers can be seen. Creosote and burrowood grow here, along with a variety of other perennial shrubs. Seeds from the flowering plants feed kangaroo rats, mice, and other small mammals. Kit foxes, skunks, snakes, owls, and coyotes search for prey at the dunes' edge.

Lacking trails and water, the dunes don't exactly throw out the welcome mat to human visitors, which may be all for the good, since they fare better if they are not trod upon. Compaction of the sand can lead to a disturbance in the region's delicate balance of nature.

CALIFORNIA

Cadiz Dunes Essentials

Size: 39,740 acres.
Year Designated: 1994.
Location: Southeastern California.
Easiest Access: From Twentynine Palms, take State Highway 62 east for 62 miles. Turn north on Cadiz Road and travel about 26 miles. For the next five miles, the road forms the northeastern Wilderness boundary.
Season: Spring and late fall.
Wilderness Fees/Permits: None.
Maps: USGS topographic maps are Cadiz Lake, Cadiz Lake NE, Cadiz Lake NW, and Chubbuck.
Management: BLM Palm Springs-South Coast Resource Area, P.O. Box 2000, 63-500 Garnet Avenue, North Palm Springs, CA 92258; (619) 251-4800.

Caribou Wilderness

Reminders of the volcanic and glacial origin of the Caribou Wilderness can be seen throughout this forested plateau. The forest is composed predominantly of lodgepole pine sprinkled with a mixture of Jeffrey pine, white and red fir, western white pine, and hemlock. Crater peaks, cinder cones, and numerous depressions have filled with water to become splendid timber-fringed lakes. The larger lakes support brook and rainbow trout, and black-tailed deer and black bears grace the Wilderness alongside squirrels, chipmunks, and the protected pine marten. You may see bald eagles and ospreys overhead, and mergansers and grebes on the ponds and lakes. Some of the water, percolating up through the porous volcanic aquifer, forms the head of the Susan River, a major water source for the eastern slope of the Cascade Mountains. On the western border, which is shared by Lassen Volcanic National Park, stands Red Cinder, the area's highest point at 8,375 feet. From this high place, and from the tops of Black Cinder Rock and North and South Caribou Peaks, you'll find terrific views of the towering mountains that surround the Wilderness.

A well-maintained trail system offers access along relatively easy slopes, but off the trails, the land is often rough and broken. Lakes are usually frozen well into June. Summer on the trails brings dashes of wildflower color and thick clusters of water lilies on the ponds—not to mention clouds of devilish mosquitoes. From Silver Lake, just outside the eastern boundary, the Caribou Lake Trail enters the Wilderness for approximately one mile, to split south about six miles to the Hay Meadows Trailhead, and north about four miles to the Cone Lake Trailhead. At Triangle Lake on the north trail, a path travels west about one mile before entering the national park. Receiving moderate human use, this area offers a chance for wondrous solitude.

Caribou Essentials

Size: 20,625 acres.
Year Designated: 1964.
Location: Northern California.
Easiest Access: From Westwood, on State Highway 36, take State Highway A-21 north for about 14 miles. Turn west onto the gravel surface of Silver Lake Road and make your bumpy way approximately 10 miles to Silver Lake.
Season: Late summer through early fall.
Wilderness Fees/Permits: None.
Maps: A Wilderness map is available from the forest supervisor. USGS maps are Bogard Buttes and Red Cinder.
Management: Lassen National Forest, 55 South Sacramento Street, Susanville, CA 96130; (916) 257-2151.

CALIFORNIA

Carrizo Gorge Wilderness

Some of the most expansive views in the entire California Desert—vistas often extending for more than 100 miles—exist in Carrizo Gorge Wilderness. From overlooks, you can see the Chocolate Mountains, the Salton Sea to the northeast, Mount Signal on the Mexican border, and Anza-Borrego Desert State Park, which shares the Wilderness' eastern border. The eastern boundary actually runs near the western edge of Carrizo Gorge itself, where the In-Ko-Pah Mountains rise up from the desert. This Wilderness represents the only ecological transition zone in the NWPS between the low Colorado Desert and the dry California coastal mountains. Peninsular bighorn sheep find this remote, rugged region to their liking, and three herds call the area home. The San Diego coast horned lizard also lives here, eyeing the skies warily for Swainson's hawks, golden eagles, and other birds of prey. California fan palms line the edges of dry washes and narrow canyons, creating oases in the parched terrain.

You will not find much in the way of trails from the west side, though several springs might provide water. From the east side, via Anza-Borrego Desert State Park, you can access Carrizo Gorge on a jeep trail, and the Wilderness on foot.

Carrizo Gorge Essentials

Size: 15,700 acres.
Year Designated: 1994.
Location: Southwestern California.
Easiest Access: From San Diego, take Interstate 8 east about 65 miles. Take the Boulevard/Manzanita exit south and follow State Route 94 east about two miles. Turn north on McCain Valley Road. The Wilderness lies to the east.
Season: Winter.
Wilderness Fees/Permits: None.
Maps: USGS topographic maps are Jacumba, Sombrero Peak, and Sweeney Pass.
Management: BLM El Centro Resource Area, 1661 South Fourth Street, El Centro, CA 92243; (619) 337-4400.

Carson-Iceberg Wilderness

This Wilderness straddles the Sierra Nevada Crest, divided between Toiyabe and Stanislaus National Forests. Here you'll find spectacular high country, with 12 peaks rising above 12,000 feet and numerous other peaks over 9,000 feet, broad river valleys, perennial creeks with small waterfalls, granite-strewn slopes, and several, meadow-filled valleys. Here are the headwaters of the East Fork of the Carson River, the Clark Fork of the Stanislaus, and the Mokelumne River. The Carson River, named for Kit Carson, and a distinctive granite formation called the Iceberg on the southern boundary give this area its name. You'll hike often in a thick forest of pines (Jeffrey, sugar, lodgepole, western white) and firs (red and white). Lakes, fairly common on the eastern side, are few and far between on the western side. Conversely, precipitation averaging 50 inches per year on the western slopes drops to about 15 inches per year on the eastern slopes, with about 80 percent falling as snow. Snowpacks usually linger into June, but the remainder of the summer is

CALIFORNIA

generally dry and mild with periodic afternoon thunderstorms and nighttime temperatures that could drop below freezing any day of the year.

The Pacific Crest Trail runs the length of this area for over 26 miles. The trail up Amot Creek to Wolf Creek Pass (about 15 miles) provides a scenic route to the PCT. About 200 total miles of foot and horse trails give access to this outstanding Wilderness, where human use is light to moderate especially on the eastern (Toiyabe) side.

Carson-Iceberg Essentials

Size: 160,000 acres.
Year Designated: 1984.
Location: Eastern central California.
Easiest Access: From Sonora Junction on U.S. 395, about 18 miles north of Bridgeport, take State Route 108 west. About eight miles west of Sonora Pass, turn north on Tuolumne County Road and proceed for seven miles to Peaceful Pines Campground and the trailhead for Amot Creek. You can access the PCT from Sonora Pass.
Season: June through September.
Wilderness Fees/Permits: Free permits are required for overnight use. You may self-register at trailheads on the eastern side. Reservations are required on the western side.
Maps: A Wilderness map is available for $3 from the district rangers.
Management: Calaveras Ranger District, Stanislaus National Forest, P.O. Box 500, Hathaway Pines, CA 95233; (209) 795-1381. Carson Ranger District, Toiyabe National Forest, 1536 South Carson, Carson City, NV 89701; (702) 882-2766.

Castle Crags Wilderness

Sheer granite cliffs, towering spires reaching up to 7,200 feet, and steep canyons hide five small alpine lakes in Castle Crags Wilderness. Indians held these rock formations in awe, rarely if ever, venturing into the heights, and battling the white miners who attempted to do so; in fact, the 1855 Battle of Castle Crags initiated the Modoc War. Below these rocky outcroppings, granitic intrusions from the Jurassic period, most of the area is covered with fields of brush and a few wet meadows in the heads of several creeks. Mixed conifers (pine, fir, spruce, cedar) grow on the east, west, and north slopes. You will commonly encounter poison oak at lower elevations, where live oaks dominate the landscape. More than 300 species of wildflowers have been identified in the Wilderness, including the Castle Crags harebell, which blooms nowhere else on Earth. Rattlesnakes, black bears, deer, and squirrels abound, as do ticks. The Wilderness shares its southern border with Castle Crags State Park.

You'll find 27.8 miles of maintained trails starting from nine trailheads. The Pacific Crest Trail rambles for 19 miles through the area and offers many splendid views of the Crags. No trails lead to the spires themselves, and although they look inviting to climbers, the granite is crumbly and unsafe. Human use of the area is light.

CALIFORNIA

Castle Crags Essentials

Size: 7,300 acres.
Year Designated: 1984.
Location: Northern California.
Easiest Access: From Redding, take Interstate 5 north for 50 miles to Castle Crags State Park where four trails lead into the Wilderness.
Season: Spring through fall.
Wilderness Fees/Permits: None.
Maps: A Wilderness map that includes Mount Shasta Wilderness is available for $6 from the district ranger.
Management: Mount Shasta Ranger District, Shasta-Trinity National Forest, 204 West Alma Street, Mount Shasta, CA 96067; (916) 926-4511.

Chanchelulla Wilderness

Chanchelulla Peak stands at 6,399 feet, the highest point in Chanchelulla Wilderness, a steeply rugged area with slopes angling as much as 70 degrees. The southern slopes are primarily covered in dense, ankle-twisting chaparral, and the northern slopes are draped in fragrant conifers such as pine, fir, and cedar. Deer find this habitat appealing, and visitors occasionally spot black bears, fishers (a dark-furred member of the marten family), and mountain lions. Birds of prey, owls (including northern spotted owls), and numerous songbirds are residents. It's hot and dry most of the year, devoid of lakes or any accessible streams. You won't find any maintained pathways either, but you might be able to follow a few animal tracks and partially cleared trails leading from Deer Lick Springs in the east and Midas Saddle in the south. Human use is very light, and usually confined to deer hunters. If you're hankering to be alone in a Wilderness area, Chanchelulla should rank high on your list (but don't forget your blaze orange in deer season).

Chanchelulla Essentials

Size: 8,200 acres.
Year Designated: 1984.
Location: Northern California.
Easiest Access: From Red Bluff, take State Highway 36 west for about 52 miles. Turn north on Harrison Gulch Road and go approximately 15 miles. Turn north on Deer Lick Springs Road and travel about three miles to Deer Lick Springs and a trailhead on the eastern side of the Wilderness.
Season: Spring through fall.
Wilderness Fees/Permits: None.
Maps: USGS topographic maps are Chanchelulla Peak West and Dubakella Mountain East.
Management: Hayfork Ranger District, Shasta-Trinity National Forest, P.O. Box 159, Hayfork, CA 96041; (916) 628-5227. Yolla Bolly Ranger District, Shasta-Trinity National Forest, Platina, CA 96076; (916) 352-4211.

CALIFORNIA

Chemehuevi Mountains Wilderness

The Chemehuevi Mountains are a horseshoe-shaped range rising from near the Colorado River, transforming gradually from almost white granite to dark reds and grays in volcanic spires. It's rugged country, requiring rugged boots and rugged clothing. Within the horseshoe, you'll find a large central valley of rolling hills filled with cholla and other species of cactus. Desert tortoises live here, along with bighorn sheep, wild burros, and mule deer.

Chemehuevi Peak rises in the southwestern quadrant to 3,697 feet. You can scramble with nontechnical skills to the summit for great views of Lake Havasu, Topock Gorge, and the central valley. Chemehuevi shares a portion of its eastern border with Havasu Wilderness, a part of the Havasu National Wildlife Refuge (see Havasu Wilderness below). Please remember that no camping is allowed in the refuge.

Hikers most often scoot down 12-mile-long Trampas Wash, which runs west-east across the center of the Wilderness and ends at the Colorado River. Springs in the area are seasonal.

Chemehuevi Mountains Essentials

Size: 64,320 acres.
Year Designated: 1994.
Location: Southeastern California.
Easiest Access: From Needles, take U.S. 95 south for 10 miles, turning east on the old dirt road that follows the pipeline, the northern boundary of the Wilderness. Or continue south on U.S. 95 for two more miles to access the trailhead heading west through Trampas Wash.
Season: Early spring and late fall.
Wilderness Fees/Permits: None.
Maps: USGS topographic maps are Castle Rock, Chemehuevi Peak, Havasu Lake, Monumental Pass, Savahia Peak NE, Snaggletooth, Topock, and Whale Mountain.
Management: BLM Needles Resource Area, 101 West Spikes Road, Needles, CA 92363; (619) 326-2896.

Chimney Peak Wilderness

Here on the eastern slope of the southern Sierra Nevada, you'll find valleys, canyons, alluvial fans, and steep foothills leading up into rugged granite mountains, all encompassed by Chimney Peak Wilderness. Joshua trees, creosote bushes, and desert shrubs dot the valley floors. Higher elevations grow cottonwoods, cactuses, and piñon pine. With Chimney Peak rising in the northeast corner to 2,435 feet, Chimney Creek briskly flows across the eastern boundary, providing a habitat for trout.

The Pacific Crest Trail crosses about eight miles of the area just west and south of the peak's summit. You'll see little evidence of human visitation except for a few traces of the Sacatar Trail, an old wagon road. From Kennedy Meadows outside the northeastern corner, you can hike three miles into the area north of Chimney Peak and join the PCT.

CALIFORNIA

Chimney Peak Essentials

Size: 13,700 acres.
Year Designated: 1994.
Location: Central southern California.
Easiest Access: From Ridgecrest, take U.S. 395 west and then north for approximately 20 miles. Turn west on Nine Mile Canyon Road and go 13 miles to Kennedy Meadows.
Season: Early spring and late fall.

Wilderness Fees/Permits: None.
Maps: USGS topographic maps are Coso Junction, Lamont Peak, Little Lake, Long Canyon, Ninemile Canyon, Pearsonville, Rockhouse Basin, Sacatar Canyon, and White Dome.
Management: BLM Caliente Resource Area, 3801 Pegasus Drive, Bakersfield, CA 93308; (805) 391-6000.

Chuckwalla Mountains Wilderness

Just southeast of Joshua Tree National Park, the Chuckwalla Mountains rise like an island in a sea of sand and stone, a fascinating rock fortress of seemingly endless landforms, geologic textures, and delightful colors. Steep-walled canyons, broad valleys, washes of all sizes, solitary rock outcroppings, and vast expanses of desert combine to create a constantly changing panorama for the traveler. The wildlife and plantlife are as diverse as the topography, characteristic of both the Mojave and Colorado desertlands. Bighorn sheep, deer, wild burros, birds of prey, snakes, foxes, and coyotes make the area their home, and the bajada region in the southwest corner of the Wilderness provides a crucial habitat for the desert tortoise. Ocotillo, cholla, yucca, creosote, barrel cactus, and foxtail cactus cover the landscape in a gardenlike array. A non-Wilderness corridor allows rough-road access to a dense palm oasis, Corn Springs Wash.

This is an excellent area for camping, ridge scrambling, peak bagging, and wash exploring in a desert Wilderness. If it's solitude you crave, the chances are great you'll be alone here.

Chuckwalla Mountains Essentials

Size: 80,770 acres.
Year Designated: 1994.
Location: Southeastern California.
Easiest Access: From Blythe, take Interstate 10 west for approximately 39 miles. Take the Corn Springs exit and travel south for 12 miles through Corn Springs Wash to Corn Springs.
Season: Early spring and late fall.
Wilderness Fees/Permits: None.

Maps: USGS topographic maps are Augustine Pass, Aztec Mines, Chuckwalla Spring, Corn Spring, Desert Center, East of Aztec Mines, Iris Pass, Pilot Mountain, Red Cloud Canyon, and Sidewinder Well.
Management: BLM Palm Springs-South Coast Resource Area, P.O. Box 2000, 63-500 Garnet Avenue, North Palm Springs, CA 92258; (619) 251-4800.

CALIFORNIA

Chumash Wilderness

From Mount Pinos and Mount Abel, which both lie along the northeast boundary and approach 9,000 feet in elevation, the terrain of Chumash Wilderness drops toward the southwest. Small stands of conifers in the heights yield to chaparral—the fire-prone, brushy cover that dominates the mountains of southern California. Bleak ridges stand between steep-walled drainages, and you'll find some of the highest and most rugged terrain in Los Padres National Forest.

A road leads to the summit of Mount Pinos from the town of Frazier Park, and from there, a trail runs five miles west to Mount Abel. From near Mount Abel, a trail descends two miles to Mesa Springs and travels five miles to Nettle Spring Campground. Human use is light.

Chumash Essentials

Size: 38,150 acres.
Year Designated: 1992.
Location: Southwestern California.
Easiest Access: From Ojai, take State Highway 33 north for approximately 35 miles. Head east on Apache Canyon Road for nine miles to the trailhead and camp at Nettle Spring.
Season: Spring and fall.
Wilderness Fees/Permits: Campfire permits are required.
Maps: USGS topographic maps are Apache Canyon, Cuddy Valley, San Guillermo, and Sawmill Mountain.
Management: Mount Pinos Ranger District, Los Padres National Forest, Frazier Park, CA 93225; (805) 245-3731.

Cleghorn Lakes Wilderness

The Cleghorns are dry lakes plunked near the middle of Cleghorn Lakes Wilderness, an area of remarkably different resources. The eastern portion rises into the rugged Bullion Mountains, while the western section stretches out into a vast alluvial desert slope, or bajada. Elevations range from more than 4,100 feet across the four-mile reach of the mountains to 1,400 feet on the desert floor. Bighorn sheep roam the mountains, and the desert tortoise prowls the lowlands. Some of the washes are adorned with gardens of barrel cactuses and smoke trees (almost leafless trees with gray twigs that appear surrounded by a smoky haze from a distance). The lakes will occasionally erupt into spring wildflower bloom. A non-Wilderness road corridor splits off the northwest corner of the Wilderness and leads to the Twentynine Palms Marine Corps Base. You'll find no trails, but old tracks lead into the area: one from the south ending at the abandoned Copper World Mine, a couple that cross the northeast corner.

CALIFORNIA

Cleghorn Lakes Essentials

Size: 33,980 acres.
Year Designated: 1994.
Location: Southeastern California.
Easiest Access: From Twentynine Palms, go north two miles on Adobe Road. Take Amboy Road east for 13 miles, then turn north on Naborly Road and go three miles until you reach the Wilderness boundary. Hike north another two miles to the Copper World Mine.

Season: Early spring and late fall.
Wilderness Fees/Permits: None.
Maps: USGS topographic maps are Bristol Lake SW, Cleghorn Lakes, Dale Lake, East of Valley Mountain, and Lead Mountain SW.
Management: BLM Barstow Resource Area, 150 Coolwater Lane, Barstow, CA 92311; (619) 255-8700.

Clipper Mountains Wilderness

South of the Mojave National Preserve, just across Interstate 40, Clipper Mountains Wilderness encompasses a large mesa standing at approximately 1,000 feet elevation that falls away into surrounding canyons and hills to the southeast beyond Castle Dome. Castle Dome rises to 1,006 feet, a bump near the middle of the area. You may catch glimpses of desert bighorn sheep as you meander through the Wilderness, and you might find water in Chuckwalla Spring near the center of the northern portion or Hummingbird Spring near the eastern boundary. There are no official paths, but you can follow the remains of a World War II trail that climbs easily into the Clippers on the northern side. The Southern California Gas Pipeline and its attendant dirt road form the southern boundary, but parking along the pipeline right-of-way is not permitted.

Clipper Mountains Essentials

Size: 26,000 acres.
Year Designated: 1994.
Location: Southeastern California.
Easiest Access: From Needles, take Interstate 40 west about 50 miles past Essex Road. The Clipper Mountains lie south of Interstate 40 for a 10-mile stretch. With no place to park, you should arrange for someone to drop you off (and, with any luck, pick you up).

Season: Spring and late fall.
Wilderness Fees/Permits: None.
Maps: USGS topographic maps are Blind Hills, Cadiz Summit, Castle Dome, Van Winkle Wash, and West of Blind Hills.
Management: BLM Needles Resource Area, 101 West Spikes Road, Needles, CA 92363; (619) 326-3896.

CALIFORNIA

Cosa Range Wilderness

Encompassing the northern section of the Cosa Range, this Wilderness preserves an area of extensive erosion revealing outstanding displays of volcanic formations and numerous valleys and washes. From high points—primarily Joshua Flat in the east-central portion—you'll discover great views east into the Sierra Nevada and north into Owens Valley. In addition to Joshua Flat, striking Vermillion Canyon runs west from near the middle of the area, offering an especially scenic reason to make the trek. Cactus Flat and McCloud Flat to the south were once active mining regions. You'll see large stands of Joshua trees mixed with low desert shrubs, annuals, cactuses, and creosote bushes. Old tracks lead from the east to Joshua Flat and from the west to Vermillion Canyon. There is ample room to wander without much chance of seeing another human. Carry plenty of water.

Cosa Range Essentials

Size: 50,520 acres.
Year Designated: 1994.
Location: Southeastern central California.
Easiest Access: From Olancha, take U.S. 395 south about one mile. Turn east and travel about seven miles on the old dirt road leading toward Vermillion Canyon. Hike east after you hit the Wilderness boundary.
Season: Early spring and late fall.
Wilderness Fees/Permits: None.
Maps: USGS topographic maps are Centennial Canyon, Haiwee Reservoirs, Upper Centennial Flat, and Vermillion Canyon.
Management: BLM Ridgecrest Resource Area, 300 South Richmond Road, Ridgecrest, CA 93555; (619) 384-5400.

Coyote Mountains Wilderness

The fishhook-shaped Coyote Mountains cover about 40 percent of this austere Wilderness, a desertland of low ridges and washes capped by the forbidding Carrizo Badlands to the north. Carrizo Mountain (734 feet) and the striking Painted Gorge lie in a non-Wilderness intrusion that punches in from the eastern boundary. The entire area falls within the Yuha Desert Recreation Area, and Anza-Borrego Desert State Park lies immediately to the north. You'll find unusual sandstone formations that are estimated to be six million years old, adding a touch of scenic character to the area. On the mountain ridges, you may be privileged to see a barefoot gecko.

What you won't see are any trails in this hot, dry country, though an old track leads up Painted Gorge to the edge of the Wilderness.

CALIFORNIA

Coyote Mountains Essentials

Size: 17,000 acres.
Year Designated: 1994.
Location: Southwestern California.
Easiest Access: From Ocotillo, on Interstate 8, turn northeast on State Route 80 and drive for approximately five miles. Turn north on Painted Gorge Road and follow this about seven miles to the Wilderness boundary.
Season: Winter.
Wilderness Fees/Permits: None.
Maps: USGS topographic maps are Carrizo Mountain and Carrizo Mountain NE.
Management: BLM El Centro Resource Area, 1661 South Fourth Street, El Centro, CA 92243; (619) 337-4400.

Cucamonga Wilderness

Some of the most thickly populated areas of southern California stand under the towering peaks of Cucamonga Wilderness. Rising steeply from the valley floor, the area contains rough terrain, rock cliffs, and sharp, silvered summits with elevations ranging from approximately 5,000 feet to almost 9,000 feet. Here near the San Andreas Fault, you'll see landslides, reminders of earthquake activity. Most of the streams are intermittent, and with characteristic understatement, the USFS reports that water is scarce. Where water does flow in canyon bottoms, the use by humans is typically heavy. Numerous wildlife species do well in the area, including bighorn sheep.

Three trails enter from the west, and two from the east. A trailhead near Mount Baldy leads 3.6 miles to Icehouse Saddle, where a side trail climbs 2.7 miles to Ontario Peak. Cucamonga Peak Trail offers a 2.4-mile vertical side trail to the summit of the peak. All the trails generally follow canyon bottoms or climb ruggedly up steep rocky slopes. You'll see evidence of human activity in much of the area, both on the peaks and in the canyons.

Cucamonga Essentials

Size: 12,981 acres.
Year Designated: 1964; expanded in 1984.
Location: Southwestern California.
Easiest Access: From Interstate 10 near Claremont, take the Mount Baldy Ski Area exit. Go north on Mount Baldy Road about two miles past the town of Mount Baldy. Park at the Icehouse Trailhead on the east side of the road.
Season: Spring through fall.
Wilderness Fees/Permits: A permit is required for day and overnight use. A separate permit may be required for fires and stoves. Contact the district rangers.
Maps: A Wilderness map is available for $3 from district rangers.
Management: Cajon (Lytle Creek) Ranger District, San Bernardino National Forest, Star Route Box 500, Fontana, CA 92336-9704; (714) 887-2576. Mount Baldy (Glendora) Ranger District, Angeles National Forest, 110 North Wabash Avenue, Glendora, CA 91740; (818) 335-1251.

CALIFORNIA

Darwin Falls Wilderness

Carved into numerous shallow depressions and canyons and holding a variety of stark volcanic rock faces, the Darwin Plateau stands guard in the northern portion of this Wilderness. In the south, Darwin Falls spills down spectacular Darwin Canyon. Lined with willows and cottonwoods, the water rises to the surface from a permanent spring outside the northeast Wilderness boundary inside Death Valley National Park. A creosote bush community dominates much of the landscape, giving way to Joshua tree woodlands higher in the hills. Among other desert wildlife, prairie falcons are often spotted. Two springs on the eastern boundary supply additional water.

Darwin Falls Essentials

Size: 8,600 acres.
Year Designated: 1994.
Location: Southeastern central California.
Easiest Access: From Olancha, off U.S. 395, take State Highway 190 east about 44 miles. Turn south on the Old Toll Road just west of Panamint Springs. Go south four miles to Darwin Falls. Check road conditions before leaving the pavement. Hike south up Darwin Canyon for one mile; from there the canyon forms the eastern boundary of the Wilderness.
Season: Early spring and late fall.
Wilderness Fees/Permits: None.
Maps: USGS topographic map is Darwin.
Management: BLM Ridgecrest Resource Area, 300 South Richmond Road, Ridgecrest, CA 93555; (619) 384-5400.

Dead Mountains Wilderness

Running north-south, the Dead Mountains dominate this Wilderness area. The Deads are a jagged, steep, rust-colored range crowned by Mount Manchester (about 4,000 feet). They fall away to sweeping bajadas that slope gradually toward the Colorado River on the east and the Piute Valley on the west. The northeast boundary is the Nevada-California state line. There are no trails, but numerous washes provide easy access into the area. Red Spring, near the middle of the southern portion, may supply water. Numerous parcels of privately owned land lie within the Wilderness.

Dead Mountains Essentials

Size: 48,850 acres.
Year Designated: 1994.
Location: Southeastern California.
Easiest Access: From Needles, take the River Road (Pew Road) north for 16 miles. Turn west at a rock cairn and travel up the wash. The Wilderness lies to the south.
Season: Early spring and late fall.
Wilderness Fees/Permits: None.
Maps: USGS topographic maps are Bannock, East of Homer Mountain, Mount Manchester, and Needles NW.
Management: BLM Needles Resource Area, 101 West Spikes Road, Needles, CA 92363; (619) 326-2896.

CALIFORNIA

Death Valley Wilderness

In 1994, the California Desert Protection Act added 1.3 million acres of BLM land to Death Valley National Monument, bringing its total acreage to approximately 3.3 million acres. The additions extended the monument in all directions except northwest. The monument's status was changed to Death Valley National Park, and most of the land was designated Wilderness, making it by far the largest Wilderness in the Lower 48. The park stretches into Nevada, but that portion remains non-Wilderness.

As the name implies, Death Valley indeed would be an easy place to die. Annual rainfall measures less than half an inch, and for six months each year, heat sears the valley floor, with July temperatures averaging higher than 116 degrees Fahrenheit, making it the driest, hottest spot in North America. During the other six months, the heat is merely miserable.

Yet there is far more to the park than dry heat. Once you've adjusted your mental palette to the area's harsh, subtle beauty, wonders abound. Telescope Peak rises to 11,049 feet, higher than any other point in the park, and, with much of the Panamint Range, stands white under winter snow. (In fact, the climb up to Telescope Peak, where temperatures are cooler, is one of the few hikes considered reasonable in the heat of summer.) Contrast this with nearby Badwater, 15 or so miles to the east as the crow flies, where the earth lies almost 300 feet below sea level, the lowest terrestrial point in the Western Hemisphere. Vast fields of sand dunes shimmer in the sun, and rock outcroppings are carved into shapes of staggering beauty, especially striking at dawn and dusk. Colorful cliffs stand above endless flats of creosote bush. More than 900 species of plants have been identified within the park, and nights come alive to the scurrying of small mammals. Coyotes, gray and kit foxes, bobcats, jackrabbits, and desert tortoises thrive here, as do a plethora of bats, birds, lizards, and snakes. Desert bighorn sheep live in the higher elevations, where you can sometimes tramp through a dry forest of piñon, juniper, mountain mahogany, and a few bristlecone pines. Wildflowers bloom in spectacular variety when enough rain falls during the winter. Ubehebe Crater opens 2,400 feet in diameter, marking where a volcano erupted roughly 1,000 years ago.

You are free to hike the Wilderness, limited only by your courage and ability to carry water, but camping is currently allowed only in designated locations. *Getting Around in the Death Valley Backcountry*, on sale at the Furnace Creek Visitors Center, contains detailed information on hikes.

Death Valley Essentials

Size: 3,158,038 acres.
Year Designated: 1994.
Location: Southeastern California.
Easiest Access: From U.S. 395 in Olancha, take State Highway 190 east for approximately 110 miles to the visitors center.
Season: November to March.
Wilderness Fees/Permits: An entrance fee of $5 per vehicle is charged.
Maps: A map is available from the ranger. DeLorme's *Southern and Central California Atlas and Gazetteer* shows the area in fair detail.
Management: Death Valley National Park, Death Valley, CA 92328; (619) 786-2331.

Desolation Wilderness

Despite the forbidding name, outstanding beauty and accessibility combine in Desolation Wilderness to create one of the most heavily used (and abused) wild areas in the United States. Here on both sides of the Sierra Nevada, averaging 12.5 miles in length and eight miles in width, you'll find elevations ranging from about 6,500 feet to over 10,000 feet, sprinkled with subalpine and alpine trees and other flora. Mostly lacking in dense vegetation, Desolation is a sudden, glacially smoothed expanse west of Lake Tahoe. You'll discover numerous streams and approximately 130 lakes, some reaching 900 acres in size. Snow often blocks the high passes until mid-July. Long recognized for its mountain splendor, Desolation Valley Primitive Area was established in 1931 and then granted Wilderness status in 1969.

The Pacific Crest Trail traverses about 17 miles of the Wilderness north-south, and at one point crosses Dicks Pass (9,380 feet), the highest pass between here and Canada. At least 15 named and numbered trailheads open onto miles of well-maintained and well-trampled pathways. The trailheads at Wrights, Echo, Eagle Falls, and Fallen Leaf receive the heaviest use. The northwest portion of the area is less frequented and requires some map-reading skills to explore.

No campfires are permitted, but you can cook on small stoves. I recommend appreciating what this Wilderness region has to offer, but only by visiting the most isolated sections. Otherwise, head somewhere else.

Desolation Essentials

Size: 63,475 acres.
Year Designated: 1969.
Location: Central eastern California.
Easiest Access: From South Lake Tahoe, take U.S. 50 west for 11 miles to Echo Summit where the Pacific Crest Trail meets the highway. Hike north, and you'll reach the Wilderness boundary in 4.5 miles.
Season: Summer.
Wilderness Fees/Permits: Visitor permits are required year-round. A special permit system allows 700 overnight visitors per day from June 15 to Labor Day. More than half the permits are issued up to 60 days in advance. Contact the forest ranger.
Maps: Wilderness maps are available from the forest ranger on paper or plastic for $3 and $6, respectively.
Management: Eldorado National Forest, 3070 Camino Heights Drive, Camino, CA 95709; (916) 644-6048.

CALIFORNIA

Dick Smith Wilderness

Dick Smith—writer, artist, photographer—was deeply devoted to preservation of the wild and was called by some the "conscience of Santa Barbara." The Wilderness that bears his name is an area of extremely rugged terrain with elevations varying from 3,750 feet along the Cayuma Rim to 6,541 feet atop Madulce Peak to the west. Chaparral dominates the vegetation, but a splendid collection of mixed conifers grows around Madulce Peak. To the east lies the more-open Rancho Nuevo region, with massive sandstone formations and stands of Douglas fir and Great Basin sage. In the higher country, several creeks flow year-round in Indian, Mono, Alamar, Don Victor, Santa Barbara, and other canyons.

Black bears, deer, mountain lions, bobcats, and coyotes reside in the area, and several native species of snakes have been identified (including rattlers—wear your boots). Only a slim road corridor separates Dick Smith from San Rafael Wilderness to the west (see below).

You'll find eight main trails and several side trails totaling about 49 miles; human use is light. Chumash Indians, Spanish soldiers, and early settlers used to cross this area via the Alamar and Puerta Suela Trails. The Bear Canyon Trail provides easy access from the east and crosses into the Wilderness after about two miles.

Dick Smith Essentials

Size: 65,130 acres.
Year Designated: 1984.
Location: Southwestern California.
Easiest Access: From Ventura, take State Highway 33 north for approximately 60 miles. The Bear Canyon Trailhead sits on the west side of the highway, just south of Ozena Forest Service Facility.
Season: Spring through fall.
Wilderness Fees/Permits: A California Campfire Permit is required during fire season.
Maps: A Wilderness map is available for $3 from the district rangers.
Management: Mount Pinos Ranger District, Los Padres National Forest, Frazier Park, CA 93225; (805) 245-3731. Santa Barbara Ranger District, Los Padres National Forest, Los Prietos, Star Route, Santa Barbara, CA 93105; (805) 967-3481.

Dinkey Lakes Wilderness

Here on the western slope of the Sierra Nevada, timbered, rolling terrain dominates most of Dinkey Lakes Wilderness. Almost all of it sits above 8,000 feet, with Three Sisters Peak soaring 10,619 feet near the 16 lakes clustered in the west-central region. Stands of white fir, red fir, and Jeffrey pine are interspersed with large mountain meadows, especially in the north-central region and along Helms Creek. Rocky outcroppings often break the skyline, and snow blankets much of the area from November until June. John Muir Wilderness lies just to the east and north (see below).

Trails are well suited for stock travel, but natural feed is scarce except in the meadows north of First Dinkey Lake and near Nelson Lake. Stock must be camped at least 500 feet from any shoreline. From Courtright Reservoir, the trail up Helms Creek reaches First Dinkey Lake after about 17 miles. Cattle still graze on sections of the area on permits issued prior to designation. Firewood will be very difficult to find near the lakes. Human use is rated as moderate.

CALIFORNIA

Dinkey Lakes Essentials

Size: 30,000 acres.
Year Designated: 1984.
Location: Eastern central California.
Easiest Access: From Fresno, take State Highway 168 north for 45 miles to Shaver Lake. Turn east on Dinkey Creek Road and follow this about 27 miles to Courtright Reservoir. Take the road on the western side of the reservoir for approximately three miles to the trail that leads up Helms Creek.
Season: Mid-June to late October.

Wilderness Fees/Permits: A free permit is required for overnight use. Contact the district rangers.
Maps: A Wilderness map is available for $3.25 from the district rangers.
Management: Kings River Ranger District, Sierra National Forest, 34849 Maxon Road, Sanger, CA 93657; (209) 855-8321 or (209) 841-3404. Pineridge Ranger District, Sierra National Forest, P.O. Box 300, Shaver Lake, CA 93664; (209) 841-3311.

Domeland Wilderness

Extremely rugged country with sparse vegetation, the original Domeland Wilderness was known for its many granite domes and unique geological formations. Additions were made in 1984, primarily on the north side, including a large basin surrounded by rock formations that comprises a more gentle region with mixed conifers and wet meadows. The California Desert Protection Act of 1994 added approximately 36,300 BLM acres on the east (and a little on the south); think piñon-covered mountains, rugged topography, perennial streams, and outstanding opportunities for solitude. Here in Domeland, semiarid mountains dwindle into low desertland. The Wild and Scenic South Fork of the Kern River, one of America's wildest waterways, crosses the Wilderness through deep gorges with bold rock outcroppings and domes interspersed with meadows. The river and its tributaries, which include Fish Creek, attract anglers in search of trout. Although the fishing can be excellent, you often will have to resort to strenuous off-trail hiking.

The Pacific Crest Trail crosses the area north-south and follows the river for about nine miles. Other trails, suitable for foot and horse, give access mostly to the northern section, leaving the south and east seldom explored and difficult to travel. There are about 45 total trail miles.

Domeland Essentials

Size: 130,986 acres.
Year Designated: 1964; expanded in 1984 and 1994.
Location: Southeastern central California.
Easiest Access: From U.S. 395, about eight miles south of Little Lake, turn west on Nine Mile Canyon Road. Take this for about 24 miles to the trailheads (including the PCT) in Kennedy Meadows.
Season: Early summer and late fall.
Wilderness Fees/Permits: None.

Maps: A Wilderness map that, when last checked, does not include the added BLM land is available for $3.25 from the district ranger. USGS topographic maps covering the BLM land are Lamont Peak, Onyx, Rockhouse Basin, Sacatar Canyon, Weldon, and White Dome.
Management: Cannell Meadow Ranger District, Sequoia National Forest, P.O. Box 6, 105 Whitney Road, Kernville, CA 93238; (619) 376-3781. BLM Caliente Resource Area, 3801 Pegasus Drive, Bakersfield, CA 93308; (805) 391-6000.

CALIFORNIA

El Paso Mountains Wilderness

The El Paso Mountains drop into this Wilderness from the southeast, with Black Mountain, at 5,244 feet, serving as the highest point. From the foot of Black Mountain, the terrain sinks into the Black Hills and gives rise to numerous dark volcanic mesas and reddish buttes dissected by narrow canyons—in short, badlands topography. Most human visitors are attracted to an abundance of cultural sites, and the southern portion of the area is included in the Last Chance Archaeological District. Some of the oldest nonmarine fossils ever found in the West were discovered here: ancient camel-like and horse-like animals. Rock hounds also find much to their interest, interrupting their hunt to peer at the occasional desert tortoise, Mojave ground squirrel, or raptor wandering by. Creosote bushes, the most ubiquitous desert plant in the United States, reign supreme over much of the region, while Joshua trees cling to the western side of Black Mountain.

El Paso Mountains Essentials

Size: 23,780 acres.
Year Designated: 1994.
Location: Southeastern central California.
Easiest Access: From Ridgecrest, take State Highway 178 west for 11 miles to Inyokern, turning south on Redrock Inyokern Road. In eight miles, you'll reach the northern point of the Wilderness area. Continue down Redrock Inyokern Road for five miles (along the area's northwestern boundary) and then south on Last Chance Canyon Road (which forms the southwestern boundary).
Season: Early spring and late fall.
Wilderness Fees/Permits: None.
Maps: USGS topographic maps are Freeman Junction, Garlock, Inyokern SE, and Saltdale NW.
Management: BLM Ridgecrest Resource Area, 300 South Richmond Road, Ridgecrest, CA 93555; (619) 384-5400.

Emigrant Wilderness

Sandwiched between Yosemite National Park and Carson-Iceberg Wilderness, Emigrant Wilderness lies on the upper western slope of the central Sierra Nevada. About 25 miles in length and up to 15 miles in width, this scenic region comprises broad expanses of glacier-carved granite, lava-capped peaks, rocky domes, alpine lakes, miles of gushing streams, and deep canyons. The northeastern third of the Wilderness holds most of the volcanic peaks, and the rest of the area consists of sparsely vegetated ridges standing between meadows and lakes (the latter are periodically stocked with trout). Elevations range from around 5,000 feet to 11,570 feet (Leavitt Peak), and heavy winter snows start in October and typically linger well into June. Although summers are generally mild and dry, sudden thunderstorms are common, and any night of the year might bring freezing temperatures. It's no wonder that the few parties who made their way over Emigrant Pass seeking gold in the 1850s found it to be a very difficult route.

The Pacific Crest Trail borders the eastern edge of the Wilderness, part of a 185-mile trail system suitable for foot or horse traffic. The most popular trailheads are Bell Meadow,

Crabtree Camp, Gianelli Cabin, and Kennedy Meadows. From Kennedy Meadows, a trail follows Kennedy Creek for about seven miles to Kennedy Lake and the base of Kennedy Peak. The area is heavily used by humans, especially Emigrant, Deer, Wood, Buck, and Kennedy Lakes.

Emigrant Essentials

Size: 112,191 acres.
Year Designated: 1975; expanded in 1984.
Location: Eastern central California.
Easiest Access: From Modesto, take State Highway 108 east to Sugar Pine. Continue on State Highway 108 for another 44 miles to the Kennedy Meadows exit; go south one mile to the parking lot.
Season: July through September.
Wilderness Fees/Permits: A free visitors permit is required for overnight use. Contact the district ranger.
Maps: A waterproof Wilderness map is available for $6.50 from the district rangers.
Management: Calaveras Ranger District, Stanislaus National Forest, P.O. Box 500, Hathaway Pines, CA 95233; (209) 795-1381. Groveland Ranger District, Stanislaus National Forest, 24545 Highway 120, Groveland, CA 95321; (209) 962-7825. Mi-Wok Ranger District, Stanislaus National Forest, P.O. Box 100, Mi-Wok Village, CA 95346; (209) 586-3234. Summit Ranger District, Stanislaus National Forest, 1 Pinecrest Lake Road, Pinecrest, CA 95364; (209) 965-3434.

Farallon Islands Wilderness

Some of these "little pointed islets in the sea," as they were once fittingly described, were established as the Farallon National Wildlife Refuge in 1909, but the Southeast Farallons were not added until 1969, bringing the total acreage to 211. Southeast Farallon is a main island of about 70 acres (including the only major flat spot on the refuge) and numerous small rocks. Two miles northwest lies Middle Farallon, a single rock 50 yards in diameter. The North Farallons sit four miles farther north, two clusters of precipitous islets and rocks pierced by strong winds and dense fog.

Humans have had devastating and far-reaching effects here—everything from an excessive amount of seabird egg collecting in the 1850s to recent oil spills. The area has been recovering, and sea lions and approximately 400 elephant seals have returned to the Farallons. Estimates place the seabird population at 400,000 including pelicans, cormorants, murres, gulls, auklets, and puffins. Boats that ply the surrounding waters regularly pass near porpoises and sharks, including the great white, as well as gray, humpback, and blue whales in season.

All the islands have received the Wilderness designation except Southeast Farallon, where a lighthouse still warns ships away from its rocky shores. The lighthouse was automated and equipped with solar power in 1994. The Farallons are the smallest California Wilderness, and because of their delicate ecological structure, they remain off-limits to most visitors.

CALIFORNIA

Farallon Islands Essentials

Size: 141 acres.
Year Designated: 1974.
Location: Northern California, about 18 miles off the coast from Point Reyes.
Easiest Access: No public use or visitation is allowed on any of the Farallons, and boats are requested to stay at least 300 feet offshore.
Season: Spring, for animal-viewing by boat.

Wilderness Fees/Permits: Special-use permits are sometimes granted. Contact the refuge manager.
Maps: Nautical charts of the northern California coast.
Management: San Francisco Bay National Wildlife Refuge Complex, P.O. Box 524, Newark, CA 94560; (510) 792-0222.

Fish Creek Mountains Wilderness

From the desert floor, the Fish Creek Mountains resemble a plateau rising as a great wall; only a few dramatic peaks appear from a distance. In truth, the mountains are a rugged land of numerous jagged ridges and peaks standing above twisting canyons and small, hidden valleys—a pristine desert mountainland worthy of a Wilderness adventure. Steep slopes often contain limestone outcroppings that have resisted erosion, and, as a result, rainstorms have created narrow chutes that swirl with runoff. Shielded from intense sunlight and its evaporative powers, pools have formed at the base of these chutes, supplying wildlife with precious water. A portion of the shoreline of ancient Lake Cahuilla, a lake that receded more than 500 years ago, remains visible within the Wilderness. Immediately to the south and west lies Anza-Borrego Desert State Park.

Fish Creek Mountains Essentials

Size: 25,940 acres.
Year Designated: 1994.
Location: Southwestern California.
Easiest Access: From Julian, take State Highway 78 east for approximately 40 miles. Turn south on Split Mountain Road three miles from the San Diego-Imperial county line, and follow the road for about nine miles. Turn west and then south on Gypsum Mine Rail Road, staying on this for another four miles. The Wilderness lies immediately southwest of the railroad, across the wash.
Season: Winter.
Wilderness Fees/Permits: None.
Maps: USGS topographic maps are Borrego Mountain, Carrizo Mountain NE, Harpers Well, and Plaster City NW.
Management: BLM El Centro Resource Area, 1661 South Fourth Street, El Centro, CA 92243; (619) 337-4400.

CALIFORNIA

Funeral Mountains Wilderness

Despite the dreary name, rugged and cheerfully colorful limestone lies in striking bands across Funeral Mountains Wilderness. From the southeast and Nevada, the long alluvial slopes of the Amargosa Desert ascend into the Funeral Mountains, which extend northwest into Death Valley National Park. Elevations range from about 2,200 feet to Bat Mountain's 4,950 feet. Desert bighorn sheep have been spotted in the peaks, but very few humans ever travel into this dry, desolate, and trail-free country.

Funeral Mountains Essentials

Size: 28,110 acres.
Year Designated: 1994.
Location: Southeastern California.
Easiest Access: From Death Valley Junction, take State Highway 190 west for three miles. The Wilderness lies to the north of the road for eight miles before you enter Death Valley National Park.

Season: Winter.
Wilderness Fees/Permits: None.
Maps: USGS topographic maps are Death Valley Junction, East of Echo Canyon, East of Ryan, Echo Canyon, and Franklin Well.
Management: BLM Barstow Resource Area, 150 Coolwater Lane, Barstow, CA 92311; (619) 255-8700.

Garcia Wilderness

Garcia Wilderness preserves the long east-west ridge of Garcia Mountain and separates Santa Lucia and Machesna Mountain Wildernesses (see below). Here you'll find rugged, chaparral-cloaked slopes and oak woodlands highlighted by meadows, grasslands, and lush creekside vegetation. A remarkable diversity of plant and animal life populates the area, and spring reveals a vibrant display of wildflower color.

The Caldwell Mesa Trail offers 11 miles of varied terrain, from quiet meadows to strenuously uphill, rocky slopes. The Sellars Potrero Trail leaves Caldwell Mesa to travel five miles east to the boundary near the Salinas River. The Avenales Trail wanders four miles from Stoney Creek northeast over Garcia Mountain to the Salinas River. Fires are permitted in established fire rings at Balm of Gilead and Buckeye only.

Garcia Essentials

Size: 14,100 acres.
Year Designated: 1992.
Location: Southwestern California.
Easiest Access: From Arroyo Grande, on U.S. 101, take Grand Avenue (Lopez Drive) east and north for three miles. Turn east on Huasna Road and go about 25 miles to Stoney Creek Campground. Park and follow the road to the Caldwell Mesa Trailhead on the right.

Season: Spring through early fall.
Wilderness Fees/Permits: None.
Maps: USGS topographic maps are Caldwell Mesa, La Panza, Los Manchos Hills, and Pozo Summit.
Management: Santa Lucia Ranger District, Los Padres National Forest, 1616 Carlotti Drive, Santa Maria, CA 93454; (805) 925-9538.

CALIFORNIA

Golden Trout Wilderness

The brightly colored California state fish, the golden trout, lives in relative abundance in the waters of Golden Trout Wilderness, and special restrictions apply to anglers. A large drainage basin surrounded by high, jagged peaks dominates the western portion of the Wilderness in Sequoia National Forest. The eastern portion in Inyo National Forest is primarily an extension of the Kern Plateau. Piñon-pine woodlands rise to extensive Jeffrey pine forestland and meadows at middle elevations, and on to red fir, lodgepole pines, and foxtail pines at higher elevations before hitting the timberline.

Two Wild and Scenic Rivers, the North and South Forks of the Kern River, flow across the area. The North Fork rages through stunningly beautiful country and offers one of America's premier multiday white-water adventures, a challenge for the most expert rafter. Summer thunderstorms are common, but water may be scarce away from the rivers during dry spells.

About 150 miles of exceptionally scenic backpacking and horsepacking trails transverse the area, and stock forage is plentiful after the first of July. The Pacific Crest Trail follows parts of the eastern edge of the Wilderness, and the Cottonwood Pass Trail crosses the Wilderness west about 16 miles to Kern Canyon. Human use of Golden Trout is heavy.

Golden Trout Essentials

Size: 303,287 acres.
Year Designated: 1978.
Location: Southern central California.
Easiest Access: From Lone Pine, on U.S. 395, travel west on Whitney Portal Road for four miles. Turn south on Horseshoe Meadows Road and follow it about 20 miles until it ends to access the trails over Cottonwood Pass, Mulkey Pass, and Trail Pass.
Season: June through October.
Wilderness Fees/Permits: A free permit is required for overnight use. Quotas on visitation are in effect for parts of the area during certain times of the year (Cottonwood Lakes, and over Cottonwood Pass into Sequoia-Kings Canyon National Park to the north during the summer). Contact the district rangers.
Maps: A Wilderness map that includes the South Sierra Wilderness is available for $3.25 from the district rangers.
Management: Cannell Meadow Ranger District, Sequoia National Forest, P.O. Box 6, Kernville, CA 93238; (619) 376-3781. Tule River Ranger District, Sequoia National Forest, 32588 Highway 190, Porterville, CA 93257; (209) 539-2607. Mount Whitney Ranger District, Inyo National Forest, P.O. Box 8, Lone Pine, CA 93545; (619) 876-6200.

CALIFORNIA

Golden Valley Wilderness

The Lava Mountains span the northwestern portion of Golden Valley Wilderness, cresting to almost 5,000 feet on Dome Mountain. The Lavas are sliced by several steep-walled canyons arrayed in distinctive bands of multicolored sedimentary rocks. The Almond Mountains reach across the southeastern portion of the area, rising to about 4,500 feet on the broad summit of Almond Mountain. Between these two ranges lies the Golden Valley, a secluded desertland known for its spectacular spring wildflower displays. The arid, rugged terrain of its protective ranges have helped save this valley from human intrusion. The area provides nesting and foraging habitat for raptors and a home for desert tortoises and Mojave ground squirrels. In addition to the numerous flowering annuals, a creosote bush scrub community (creosote bush, cactus, burroweed, brittlebush) dominates the vegetation, and Joshua trees punctuate the mountainsides.

Golden Valley Essentials

Size: 37,700 acres.
Year Designated: 1994.
Location: Southern central California.
Easiest Access: From Ridgecrest, take U.S. 395 south for approximately 17 miles. Turn north and then east on Trona Road one mile north of Red Mountain. Follow this for just under two miles and turn east on Steam Well Road. The Wilderness lies north of the road.
Season: Spring.
Wilderness Fees/Permits: None.
Maps: USGS topographic maps are Cuddeback Lake, Klinker Mountain, Red Mountain, and West of Black Hills.
Management: BLM Ridgecrest Resource Area, 300 South Richmond Road, Ridgecrest, CA 93555; (619) 384-5400.

Granite Chief Wilderness

Here at the headwaters of the American River, Granite Chief Wilderness preserves a scenic area of exposed rock formations, granite cliffs, and glacier-carved valleys, forests, and meadows. The southern section is blanketed with a thick cover of trees: red fir and lodgepole pine higher up, and a mixture of deciduous and evergreen woodlands lower down. Several major streams drain the area. Deers fawn in remarkable numbers, especially in the northwest section, which is part of the French Meadows Game Refuge. Dogs are prohibited there from May 15 through July 15, and humans are discouraged.

A number of trails provide access to the Wilderness. The Pacific Crest Trail crosses the area north-south for about 21 miles along the eastern boundary passing through Five Lakes Basin, where no camping is allowed within 600 feet of the water. The Five Lakes Trail crosses near the middle of the Wilderness, and from the Basin, follows Five Lakes Creek for about nine miles to Hell Hole Reservoir.

Away from Five Lakes, the Wilderness receives light human use, a great attraction for solitude seekers. A precious jewel of a quiet trail drops from the middle of the area down switchbacks into the Picayune Valley, following Picayune Creek about four miles to its confluence with the Middle Fork of the American River.

CALIFORNIA

Granite Chief Essentials

Size: 25,000 acres.
Year Designated: 1984.
Location: Eastern California near Lake Tahoe.
Easiest Access: From State Highway 89, 12 miles south of Truckee, turn west on Alpine Meadows Road and proceed about five miles to the Alpine Meadows Ski Area and the Five Lakes Trail. The Five Lakes Trail will access the PCT after about two miles of hiking toward Five Lakes Basin.
Season: June through September.
Wilderness Fees/Permits: None for entry, but permits are required for the use of campstoves and campfires.
Maps: USGS topographic maps are Granite Chief, Homewood, Tahoe City, and Wentworth Springs.
Management: Foresthill Ranger District, Tahoe National Forest, 22830 Foresthill Road, Foresthill, CA 95631; (916) 367-2224. Truckee Ranger District, Tahoe National Forest, P.O. Box 399, Truckee, CA 95734; (916) 587-3558.

Grass Valley Wilderness

The expansive Grass Valley covers nearly three-fourths of this Wilderness and ranks as its primary topographical feature. The area lies fairly flat, with a series of scattered hills, yellow to reddish brown in color, with elevations from 200 feet to 600 feet above the desert floor to the west.

You'll find a few Joshua trees, but the vegetation is dominated by (you guessed it) a creosote bush scrub community. Raptors forage here, and desert tortoises and Mojave ground squirrels find suitable habitat in this barren area, which is devoid of both water and trails. The non-Wilderness corridor of an old road divides the Wilderness into eastern and western halves, and the China Lake Naval Weapons Center shares the eastern border.

Grass Valley Essentials

Size: 31,695 acres.
Year Designated: 1994.
Location: Southern central California.
Easiest Access: From Ridgecrest, take U.S. 395 south for 17 miles. Turn north and then east on Trona Road about one mile north of Red Mountain; follow this for two miles. Turn east on Steam Wells Road, which becomes Granite Wells Road. Follow this for about 16 miles to where it joins with Twenty Mule Team Road. This junction marks the northernmost point of the area.
Season: Winter.
Wilderness Fees/Permits: None.
Maps: USGS topographic maps are Bird Spring, Blackwater Well, Cuddeback Lake, Fremont Peak, and Slocum Mountain.
Management: BLM Ridgecrest Resource Area, 300 South Richmond Road, Ridgecrest, CA 93555; (619) 384-5400.

Hauser Wilderness

California's southernmost Wilderness on USFS land consists of mountainous terrain with steep slopes dotted by granite boulders and rocky outcroppings. Chaparral and coastal sage rule the vegetation scene, yielding only to upstart woodlands in Salazar and Boneyard Canyons, two north-south slices. Elevations range from 1,600 feet near Barrett Lake (outside the southwest corner) to 3,681 feet on a summit southwest of Bronco Flats in the northeast. Wildlife includes mule deer, owls, golden eagles, San Diego coast horned lizards, and mountain lions, not to mention more than 135 species of birds. Rattlesnakes are often seen basking in the sun, and mosquitoes, ticks, and deerflies are annoyances in the warmer months. You should not expect to find water in the interior except during periods of seasonal runoff.

The Pacific Crest Trail cuts for one mile across the extreme southeast corner of the Wilderness, and the Hauser Creek Trail follows Hauser Canyon for four miles just outside of the southern boundary. No other trails exist, and the rest of area is seldom used by humans. Campfires are not permitted.

Hauser Essentials

Size: 8,000 acres.
Year Designated: 1984.
Location: Southwestern California.
Easiest Access: From Interstate 8, just one mile south and east of Pine Valley, take S1 (Buckman Springs Road) 11 miles south to Morena Village. Turn south on Morena Lake Road and go one mile. Turn left at the airstrip onto Hauser Creek Road, which runs up Hauser Canyon and becomes Hauser Creek Trail after two miles.
Season: Early spring and late fall.
Wilderness Fees/Permits: A free permit is required for overnight use. Contact the district ranger.
Maps: A topographic map that includes Pine Creek Wilderness is available for $3 from the district ranger.
Management: Descanso Ranger District, Cleveland National Forest, 3348 Alpine Boulevard, Alpine, CA 91901; (619) 445-6235.

Havasu Wilderness

Established in 1941, Havasu National Wildlife Refuge stretches along the Colorado River for 24 miles between Needles, and Lake Havasu City, Arizona, with most of the refuge situated in Arizona. Approximately one-third of the refuge—all of it in Arizona—was designated Wilderness in 1990 (see Arizona, Havasu [Needles] Wilderness). California got into the act in 1994, adding almost everything north of Blankenship Bend in the Colorado River, directly across the river from the Needles Wilderness. This area shares its western border with the large, newly designated Chemehuevi Mountains Wilderness (see above).

From the shoreline, the land rises to mesas and high rocky desert, and is endowed with a rich diversity of wildlife despite summer temperatures that are among the highest in the nation. Most human visitors travel the river and see this new California Wilderness only as shoreline. Hiking is permitted, but no camping or campfires are allowed in the area. If you hike, bring a compass and plenty of water.

CALIFORNIA

Havasu Essentials

Size: 3,195 acres in California (17,801 acres total).
Year Designated: 1990 (AZ), 1994 (CA).
Location: Southeastern California.
Easiest Access: From Lake Havasu City, Arizona, travel north on the Colorado River by boat for about 16 miles.

Season: November until March.
Wilderness Fees/Permits: None.
Maps: A free map without much detail is available from the refuge manager.
Management: Havasu National Wildlife Refuge, 1406 Bailey Avenue, Suite B, P.O. Box 3009, Needles, CA 92363; (619) 326-3853.

Hollow Hills Wilderness

Hollow Hills is characterized by a large and gentle bajada that slopes east to west toward Silver Lake, a dry lake that lies just outside the Wilderness' southwest boundary. The bajada is interspersed with washes. Low hills in the east crawl toward the Turquoise Mountains, a gentle range with rounded peaks and smooth-sided ridges. Elevations range from about 300 feet near Silver Lake to a central Wilderness summit of 3,122 feet. The area contains plains, hills, and alluvial fans typical of the California desert. Creosote bush, desert holly, and scale-scrub plant communities dominate the vegetation throughout the area, and desert tortoises and Mojave fringe-toed lizards live here in seclusion. There are no designated hiking trails and no dependable sources of water.

Hollow Hills Essentials

Size: 22,240 acres.
Year Designated: 1994.
Location: Southeastern California.
Easiest Access: From Baker, on Interstate 15, take State Highway 127 north for eight miles. Turn east on Halloran Springs Road. These two roads form the western and northern boundaries of the Wilderness.

Season: Winter and early spring.
Wilderness Fees/Permits: None.
Maps: USGS topographic maps are Baker, Halloran Springs, North of Baker, and Turquoise Mountain.
Management: BLM Barstow Resource Area, 150 Coolwater Lane, Barstow, CA 92311; (619) 255-8700.

Hoover Wilderness

First established as a Primitive area in 1931, then a Wild area in 1957, Hoover Wilderness was one of the original members of the NWPS. Here is an extremely rugged and magnificently scenic area with elevations from around 8,000 feet to more than 12,000 feet, a region of alpine lakes and lovely meadows but little timber. The scarcity of firewood has resulted in a ban on wood fires in the very popular 20 Lakes Basin. Rainbow, brook, and golden trout inhabit the lakes. If you travel with stock, you should pack in all your feed. You may see cattle and sheep grazing, as some permits were issued to ranchers prior to designation. The presence of black bears should encourage you

CALIFORNIA

to hang your food at night. Rain, snow, strong winds, and bitter cold can occur in all seasons. Hoover Wilderness shares its western border with Yosemite National Park and permits are required to hike into the park.

The area, with its well-maintained trail system, receives heavy human use. You'll encounter the least human traffic in the northern portion, but, all things considered, this Wilderness would fare better with less visitation.

Hoover Essentials
Size: 48,601 acres.
Year Designated: 1964.
Location: Eastern central California.
Easiest Access: From Mono Lake, on U.S. 395, take State Highway 120 west for 10 miles. Turn north on Saddlebag Lake Road and go three miles to the lake. Hike north into the Wilderness.
Season: June through September.
Wilderness Fees/Permits: Free permits are required for all overnight use. A quota system is in effect from late June through September 15.

Reservations cost $3 per person, and you are strongly urged to apply via mail three to five weeks in advance. Some permits are issued on day of entry. Day use requires no permit.
Maps: A Wilderness map is available for $3 from the district rangers.
Management: Bridgeport Ranger District, Toyaibe National Forest, P.O. Box 595, Bridgeport, CA 93517-0595; (619) 932-7070. Mono Lake Ranger District, Inyo National Forest, P.O. Box 10, Lee Vining, CA 93541; (619) 647-6525.

Ibex Hills Wilderness

A portion of the Ibex Hills and parts of the Dublin Hills and Black Mountains are preserved in this Wilderness. The Ibex Hills form a craggy, north-south divide between the alluvial slopes of Greenwater Valley on the east and the raggedy Black Mountains on the west. From a low of about 3,000 feet, elevations climb to 4,752 feet on the summit of Ibex Peak on the western boundary. Horizontal rock layers in the mountains are highlighted with distinctive bright red, yellow, and black hues.

The ruins of at least a half-dozen old talc mines are scattered forlornly throughout the area, and a non-Wilderness road corridor extends from the southeast to the major mining region. Visitors have spotted desert bighorn sheep frolicking about, and can occasionally draw water from several springs. Death Valley National Park lies to the west and south.

Ibex Hills Essentials
Size: 26,460 acres.
Year Designated: 1994.
Location: Southeastern California.
Easiest Access: From Baker, on Interstate 15, take State Highway 127 north for 41 miles. Turn west on an old dirt road just one-half mile after Ibex Pass. Drive northwest about three miles to an old mine. The Wilderness lies to the north.

Season: Early spring and late fall.
Wilderness Fees/Permits: None.
Maps: USGS topographic maps are Ibex Pass, Ibex Peak, Salsberry Peak, and Shoshone.
Management: BLM Barstow Resource Area, 150 Coolwater Lane, Barstow, CA 92311; (619) 255-8700.

CALIFORNIA

Imperial Wilderness

Imperial Dam, an irrigation diversion structure, did not form a true reservoir, but it did raise the level of the lower Colorado River, the boundary between California and Arizona, and create many backwater lakes varying in size from one-half acre to 700 acres. In 1941, the Imperial National Wildlife Refuge was established to preserve all forms of life found in the lower Colorado River region. The 25,765 acres of the refuge stretch for 30 miles on both sides of the river. The Arizona portion of the refuge was designated Wilderness in 1990 (see Arizona, Imperial Wilderness); the California portion followed suit in 1994.

The Sonoran Desert, the hottest and driest desert in the United States, with its cactuses and other specially adapted plants and animals, gives way eventually to the lush river ecosystem. When enough rain falls, the desert bursts into stunning bloom: yellow paloverde, lavender smoke trees, ironwood, pink beavertails, red prickly pears, purple and gold bellyflowers (so called because you must lie on your belly to appreciate their small blossoms). Mule deer come to drink from the river beside great blue herons, while desert bighorns stand sentry on multihued hills. Gambel's quails are ubiquitous, and feral burros and wild Appaloosa horses can be seen from time to time. Resident and migratory birds are abundant. Beavers ply the waters, which may contain a few of the endangered Colorado squawfish that have been known to reach up to five feet in length.

Excellent fishing attracts anglers to the backwater lakes for largemouth and striped bass, bluegills, and channel catfish. You can put in a canoe at the upper boundary for easy paddling down to Martinez Lake Marina. You'll have to camp at Picacho State Recreation Area (619-765-0755) on the California side because no overnight camping is allowed on the refuge. This is tricky terrain—search-and-rescue operations must be mounted several times every year to recover hikers who have gotten lost in the Wilderness. Make sure you carry plenty of water, a map, and a compass before setting off.

Imperial Essentials

Size: 5,836 acres in California (15,056 acres total).
Year Designated: 1994.
Location: Southeastern California.
Easiest Access: From Yuma, Arizona, take U.S. 95 north about 25 miles. Turn west on Martinez Lake Road and follow the signs to the refuge.
Season: Mid-October to May.
Wilderness Fees/Permits: None.
Maps: A map is available from the refuge manager.
Management: Imperial National Wildlife Refuge, P.O. Box 72217, Martinez Lake, AZ 85365; (602) 783-3371.

CALIFORNIA

Indian Pass Wilderness

Jagged peaks and spires are incised by mazes of twisting canyons in a distinctive part of the Chocolate Mountains preserved as Indian Pass Wilderness. Desert cloudbursts pour water down the canyons into several tree-lined washes. One of the washes, Julian Wash, dominates the heart of the Wilderness, running east toward the Colorado River and giving this area the local nickname of "Julian Wash Country." The region is crowned by Quartz Peak at 2,200 feet in the western portion.

Proximity to the Colorado River and the Arizona desert contributes to wildlife species not commonly found in California: Colorado River toad, great plains toad, tree lizard. Mule deer scamper over the Wilderness, and the mountains provide ideal homes for desert bighorn sheep. Wild horses and burros sometimes can be seen in the area. Imperial National Wildlife Refuge lies immediately to the east (see Imperial Wilderness above).

Indian Pass Essentials

Size: 33,855 acres.
Year Designated: 1994.
Location: Southeastern California.
Easiest Access: From El Centro, take Interstate 8 east for about 41 miles. Turn north on County Road S-34 (Obilby Road), and then northeast on Indian Pass Road, driving nine miles to the pass. Once over Indian Pass, the road becomes the southern Wilderness boundary.
Season: Early spring and late fall.
Wilderness Fees/Permits: None.
Maps: USGS topographic maps are Buzzards Peak, Picacho NW, Picacho SW, and Quartz Peak.
Management: BLM El Centro Resource Area, 1661 South Fourth Street, El Centro, CA 92243; (619) 337-4400.

Inyo Mountains Wilderness

The north-south Inyo Mountains comprise a high and vast desert range, and the isolated and pristine Wilderness that bears their name encompasses a large portion of this sheerly rugged terrain. The area reaches a high point on Keynot Peak, at about 11,000 feet, and separates the Owens Valley on the west from the Saline Valley on the east. Most of the eastern border is shared with Death Valley National Park. Year-round streams, some cascading over waterfalls, can be found in eight canyons on the rough east side. These steep-walled canyons offer challenges to rock climbers. In addition to Keynot Peak, the prominent summits of New York Butte and Mount Inyo provide tough, nontechnical hikes with splendid views as rewards. Creosote, shadscale scrub, and sagebrush proliferate at lower elevations. You'll find a lush riparian habitat in the moist canyons, and piñon-juniper woodlands on some of the slopes. Bristlecone and limber pine grow in the higher reaches. Inyo Mountains Wilderness lies partly on BLM land and partly within Inyo National Forest.

A rich mining legacy has left a smattering of ruins to explore, and the towers that supported a men-and-salt-bearing tram from the Saline Valley salt mines to Owens Lake can still be seen on Cerro Gordo Peak.

CALIFORNIA

There are 103 miles of unmaintained trails, often difficult to follow, a holdover from historic use. Most of these trails are not shown on maps. From Reward, the old Lonesome Miner Trail (40 miles) will take you south through the highest country to Hunter Canyon. The chance for a solitude-rich Wilderness experience of a high order awaits the adventurous.

Inyo Mountains Essentials

Size: 205,020 acres.
Year Designated: 1994.
Location: Southeastern central California.
Easiest Access: From Lone Pine, take U.S. 395 north about 11 miles. Turn east on Manzanar Reward Road and drive six miles to the trailhead.
Season: Spring and fall.
Wilderness Fees/Permits: None.
Maps: USGS topographic maps are Bee Springs Canyon, Cerro Gordo Peak, Craig Canyon, Dolomite, Mazourka Peak, Nelson Range, New York Butte, Pat Keyes Canyon, Union Wash, Waucoba Canyon, Waucoba Mountain, and Waucoba Springs.
Management: BLM Bishop Resource Area, 785 North Main Street, Suite E, Bishop, CA 93514; (619) 872-4881. Inyo National Forest, 873 North Main Street, Bishop, CA 93514; (619) 873-2400.

Ishi Wilderness

The Yahi Yana Indians lived in this region for over 3,000 years before white settlers arrived around 1850 and promptly exterminated all but the handful who escaped into the harsh and remote canyons of what today is known as Ishi Wilderness. Ishi, whose name is the Yahi word for "man," was the last survivor of the tribe. You may find evidence of the Yahi Yana who lived here, historic pieces of all that remains of these people, and you should leave what you find alone.

Carved by wind and water into basaltic outcroppings, caves, and bizarre pillars of lava, Ishi Wilderness is an up-and-down land of east-west ridges within rugged river canyons. Sun-washed south slopes support chaparral (a mixture of brushes). Pines and oaks grow on the north slopes, where more moisture collects. A lush riparian forest lines the rivers. The two creeks, Deer and Mill, represent the few remaining tributaries of the Sacramento River that still support runs of salmon and steelhead trout. The Tehama deer herd, the largest migratory herd in California, winters in this area, sharing the landscape with wild hogs, black bears, coyotes, mountain lions, bobcats, and rabbits. Several species of raptors nest on the rocky cliffs, and rattlesnakes are commonly seen in the warmer months.

Although many trails rated easy to difficult provide access to this Wilderness—some of which originated as Indian paths—human use is light. Mill Creek Trail follows the creek for 6.5 easy miles, offering magnificent views and many fishing and swimming holes. A small piece of the area (240 acres) is managed by the BLM Ukiah District.

CALIFORNIA

Ishi Essentials

Size: 41,840 acres.
Year Designated: 1984.
Location: Central northern California.
Easiest Access: From Red Bluff, on Interstate 15, take State Highway 36 east for 23 miles. Turn south on Plum Creek Road and drive about 10 miles, turning south again on Ponderosa Way, which roughly follows the eastern boundary and accesses four of the six trailheads. The Mill Creek Trailhead lies about 22 miles down Ponderosa Way.
Season: Year-round.
Wilderness Fees/Permits: A free permit is required for overnight use. Contact the district ranger.
Maps: USGS topographic maps are Butte Meadows NW, Butte Meadows SW, Ishi Caves, and Panther Springs.
Management: Almanor Ranger District, Lassen National Forest, P.O. Box 767, Chester, CA 96020; (916) 258-2141. BLM Ukiah District Office, 555 Leslie Street, Ukiah, CA 95482; (707) 462-3873.

Jacumba Mountains Wilderness

On the eastern flank of California's coastal peninsular ranges, the Jacumba Mountains often appear as a fantastic jumble of granitic rock pushed up by faults in long-gone days. The mountains extend into Mexico, and the southern boundary of the Wilderness is the international border. A broad range, the Jacumbas are really a series of almost parallel ridges separating valleys, with each ridge successively lower than the next, forming a great staircase descending eastward into the Colorado Desert.

Four transitional zones lie within the Wilderness. The western portion, the region near Smugglers Cave, provides homes for mule deer, rare peninsular bighorn sheep, golden eagles, and kangaroo rats. The Myers Valley–Pinto Canyon portion contains small oases of California fan palms. A mountainous ridge separates Myers from Davies Valley, the largest valley in the Wilderness, near the middle of the area, with large stretches of surface cobbles covering the ground. The eastern mountains enclose Skull Valley, a secluded basin with a dry lake.

An eight-mile-long trail, often faint, follows Davies Valley with two opportunities to loop back to the start. Bring a map.

Jacumba Mountains Essentials

Size: 33,670 acres.
Year Designated: 1994.
Location: Southwestern California.
Easiest Access: From El Centro, take Interstate 8 west for 25 miles. Turn south at Ocotillo on State Route S-2 and continue for one mile. Turn east on Route 98 and drive seventenths of a mile to a BLM sign marking the dirt access road to Davies Valley. Four-wheel-drive vehicles are recommended on the dirt road, which will bring you to the boundary in two miles.
Season: Winter.
Wilderness Fees/Permits: None.
Maps: USGS topographic maps are Coyote Wells and In-Ko-Pah Gorge.
Management: BLM El Centro Resource Area, 1661 South Fourth Street, El Centro, CA 92243; (619) 337-4400.

CALIFORNIA

Jennie Lakes Wilderness

Three mountain peaks, including 10,365-foot Mitchell Peak, stand above a lovely and diverse mixture of lakes and streams, meadows and forests in Jennie Lakes Wilderness. Here in the central Sierra Nevada, two major lakes (Jennie Lake, Weaver Lake) and several smaller lakes mingle with many rocky outcroppings. Most of the area lies above 7,000 feet, with red fir, lodgepole pine, and western white pine composing the forests and an abundance of spring wildflowers filling the meadows. Immediately to the east, you'll find Sequoia-Kings Canyon National Park.

Five major trails cross the Wilderness for a total of 26 miles and receive moderate human use. Two of the trails offer loop hikes around the two major lakes, a distance of about 20 miles. These lakes, along with Rowell Meadow, are the primary destinations for backpackers. Trails also provide access from Jennie Lakes Wilderness into the park's backcountry. If you plan to enter the park, you should carry a permit, which is available from the district forest ranger.

Jennie Lakes Essentials

Size: 10,500 acres.
Year Designated: 1984.
Location: Eastern central California.
Easiest Access: From Fresno, take State Highway 180 east for 55 miles. Turn east and then south on the Generals Highway and drive about 12 miles. Turn north and then east on Forest Service Road 14S11, traveling about four miles to the trail leading to Jennie Lake.
Season: Late spring through early fall.
Wilderness Fees/Permits: A permit is required for overnight use. Contact the district ranger.
Maps: A map that includes Monarch Wilderness is available for $3.25 from the district ranger.
Management: Hume Lake Ranger District, Sequoia National Forest, 35860 East Kings Canyon Road, Dunlap, CA 93621; (209) 338-2251.

John Muir Wilderness

Extending for almost 100 miles along the crest of the Sierra Nevada, John Muir Wilderness encompasses typically splendid central California mountain wildland: high peaks (many above 12,000 feet in height), deep canyons, extensive and lovely meadows, hundreds of bright streams, and crystalline lakes. The South and Middle Forks of the San Joaquin River and the North Fork of the Kings River originate in the area. Hey, don't take my word for the beauty of the area; John Muir himself called the Sierra Nevada "the most beautiful of all the mountain chains." Elevations climb from about 4,000 feet to the highest point in the Lower 48, Mount Whitney at 14,495 feet. Mountaineers are attracted to this area for its great diversity of routes and difficulties. Forests in the lower elevations are rich and fragrant, thinning out slowly to bare granite in the highest elevations. Summer thunderstorms are common and dangerous, and snow may fall any day of the year in the higher country.

Hundreds of miles of excellent trails include three of the best-known pathways in America: the Pacific Crest Trail, the John Muir Trail (which

CALIFORNIA

follows almost the same 100-mile path through the Wilderness), and the 10.7-mile Mount Whitney Trail to the summit. Drop-dead gorgeous scenery, yes, but if you're looking for solitude, forget it: the USFS classifies John Muir Wilderness as the most-visited in the state.

John Muir Essentials

Size: 580,675 acres.
Year Designated: 1964; expanded in 1984.
Location: Eastern central California.
Easiest Access: From Mammoth Lakes, on U.S. 395, turn west on State Highway 203 and drive 19 miles to Devil's Postpile National Monument. Head south on the John Muir Trail.
Season: Mid-July through August.
Wilderness Fees/Permits: A free permit is required for overnight use. Quotas determine the number of visitors during high-use seasons. Reservations ($3 per person) are advised. All permits are usually gone before the end of May for that year. Contact the district rangers.
Maps: A Wilderness map that includes Sequoia-Kings Canyon National Park is available for $6 from the district rangers.
Management: Pineridge Ranger District, Sierra National Forest, P.O. Box 300, Shaver Lake, CA 93664; (209) 841-3311. Mammoth Ranger District, Inyo National Forest, P.O. Box 148, Mammoth Lakes, CA 93546; (619) 924-5500. Mount Whitney Ranger District, Inyo National Forest, P.O. Box 8, Lone Pine, CA 93545; (619) 876-6200. White Mountain Ranger District, Inyo National Forest, 798 North Main Street, Bishop, CA 93514; (619) 873-2500.

Joshua Tree Wilderness

The California Desert Protection Act of 1994 transformed Joshua Tree National Monument into a national park and expanded the old designated Wilderness by 131,780 acres. The additions thrust north into the Pinto Mountains, northeast into the Coxcomb Mountains, southeast into the Eagle Mountains, and southwest into the Little San Bernardino Mountains. Most of the park away from road corridors is Wilderness, a fabulous meeting place of two desert ecosystems. The lower, drier Colorado Desert dominates the eastern half of the park, home to abundant creosote bushes, the spidery ocotillo, and the "jumping" cholla cactus. The slightly more cool and moist Mojave Desert covers the western half of the park, serving as a hospitable breeding ground for the undisciplined Joshua tree. You'll find examples of a third ecosystem within the park: five fan-palm oases, where surface or near-surface water gives life to the stately palms. By day, you might spy bighorn sheep on mountainous slopes, numerous lizards lazing in the heat, and eagles soaring in bright sunlight. Still, it's nighttime that truly brings the desert to life, with tarantulas, rattlesnakes, coyotes, jackrabbits, bobcats, kangaroo rats, and burrowing owls responding to the lure of the dry, cool air. You'll witness some of the most fascinating geologic displays to be found in any of Southern California's desertland: twisted rock formations and granite monoliths painted with faded colors into a giant and beautiful mosaic. These rocks are an immense attraction to rock climbers, and I was enticed several years ago to spend four weeks exploring this region.

You won't find a lot of trails, but you will find travel relatively easy in multitudes of arroyos and playas, bajadas, and narrow ravines that require scrambling over skin-scraping boulders. Carry water. It is an intoxicating land, and I look forward to a return visit.

CALIFORNIA

Joshua Tree Essentials
Size: 561,470 acres.
Year Designated: 1976; expanded in 1994.
Location: Southern California.
Easiest Access: The park entrance is near Twentynine Palms, on State Highway 62. Turn south on the Utah Trail, then look for the entrance one mile out of town.
Season: Fall through early summer. From March into early June, the desert wildflowers bloom.
Wilderness Fees/Permits: Park entrance fee is $5. A free backcountry use permit is required, and self-registration is available.
Maps: A free map is available from the park ranger. Trails Illustrated's Map 226 shows the old monument area well.
Management: Joshua Tree National Park, 74485 National Monument Drive, Twentynine Palms, CA 92277; (619) 367-7511.

Kaiser Wilderness

Kaiser Ridge divides this Wilderness into two distinctly different areas. The southern portion rises gradually from near the crowded north shore of Huntington Lake under stands of Jeffrey pine and red fir until it reaches the alpine zone on the ridge. The northern half is much more open, with a steep descent from the ridgeline to 18 small lakes. Most of the lakes require cross-country travel to reach. The northern portion receives heavy human use, but you'll leave the crowds behind if you strike out for the steep, rugged northwest section. Most of Kaiser Ridge is comprised of Kaiser Peak, which lifts to 10,320 feet and provides an excellent view of the central Sierra Nevada from its summit. Snow usually begins to fall in October and refuses to disappear until early June. Immediately to the east lies John Muir Wilderness (see above).

Four trailheads open onto the southern portion. The trail from Upper Billy Creek Campground offers a loop that traverses the ridge for about seven miles to the summit of Kaiser Peak, with an option to drop off into the northern portion. Four trailheads open onto the northern area. The primary point of entry in the north is from Sample Meadow Campground.

Kaiser Essentials
Size: 22,700 acres.
Year Designated: 1976.
Location: Eastern central California.
Easiest Access: From Fresno, take State Highway 168 north for approximately 68 miles to Huntington Lake. Turn west on Huntington Lake Road along the north shore to find four trailheads, including Upper Billy Creek Campground, all leading north into the Wilderness.
Season: June through September.
Wilderness Fees/Permits: A free permit is required for overnight use. A quota system on visitation is in effect from the last Friday in June until mid-September. Contact the district ranger.
Maps: A topographical Wilderness map is available for $3.25 from the district ranger.
Management: Pineridge Ranger District, Sierra National Forest, P.O. Box 300, Shaver Lake, CA 93664; (209) 841-3311.

CALIFORNIA

Kelso Dunes Wilderness

Second tallest of all of California's desert dunes (aced out only by the Eureka Dunes), the Kelso Dunes sweep up 500 to 600 feet, a playground of gleaming white sand blown from the plains of the Devil's Playground to the north and west. Winds are whirled in a circular pattern by mountains to the east, causing the sand to remain fairly stable. The smooth sand provides an excellent surface for tracking the unique movements of the sidewinder rattlesnake, and grasses provide food and water for beetles, crickets, and rodents. In spring, you'll find clusters of gaily colored flowers blooming, and scrambling on the dunes is a popular recreational activity. The dunes section of the Wilderness lies within Mojave National Preserve and is administered by the National Park Service. To the west, the stark and rolling Bristol Mountains perch on the BLM section of this relatively vast Wilderness, a wasteland entered by only the most intrepid desert hikers.

Kelso Dunes Essentials

Size: 129,580 acres.
Year Designated: 1994.
Location: Southeastern California.
Easiest Access: Take the Kelbaker Road exit on Interstate 40 and travel north approximately 14 miles. Look for a dirt road leading three miles west up to Kelso Sand Dunes.
Season: Winter and early spring.
Wilderness Fees/Permits: None.
Maps: USGS topographic maps for the BLM section are Broadwell Lake, Broadwell Mesa, Cowhole Mountain, East of Broadwell Lake, Glasgow, Soda Lake South, West of Broadwell Mesa, West of Budweiser Wash, and West of Glasgow. Maps for the NPS section are Budweiser Wash, Glasgow, Kelso, Kelso Dunes, and West of Glasgow.
Management: BLM Needles Resource Area, 101 West Spikes Road, Needles, CA 92363; (619) 326-3896. Mojave National Preserve, National Park Service, California Desert Information Center, 831 Barstow Road, Barstow, CA 92311; (619) 255-8760.

Kiavah Wilderness

Embracing the eroded hills, canyons, and bajadas of the Scodie Mountains—the southernmost reach of the Sierra Nevada—Kiavah Wilderness lies primarily within Sequoia National Forest but includes a portion on BLM land. Here in the transition zone between the Sierra Nevada and the Mojave Desert, you'll find an unusual mix of plants and animals: creosote bush, Joshua tree, burro bush, and shadscale growing near piñon pine, juniper, canyon oak, and digger pine; yellow-eared pocket mice and lizards watching the skies for raptors.

Trails enter from all sides, often fading into the terrain. The Pacific Crest Trail enters on the northeast from Walker Pass and crosses the area for 16 miles, exiting over Bird Spring Pass to the south. Four-wheel-drive roads forge into the area on non-Wilderness intrusions from the east up Horse Canyon and Cow Heaven Canyon, both accessible from State Highway 14. You should be able to find water in numerous springs.

187

CALIFORNIA

Kiavah Essentials

Size: 88,290 acres.
Year Designated: 1994.
Location: Southern central California.
Easiest Access: From U.S. 395 in Inyokern, travel 16 miles west on State Route 178 to Walker Pass. Hike the PCT southeast into the Wilderness.
Season: Spring and fall.
Wilderness Fees/Permits: None.

Maps: USGS topographic maps are Cane Canyon, Freeman Junction, Horse Canyon, Onyx, Owens Peak, and Walker Pass.
Management: BLM Caliente Resource Area, 3801 Pegasus Drive, Bakersfield, CA 93308; (619) 391-6000. BLM Ridgecrest Resource Area, 300 South Richmond Road, Ridgecrest, CA 93555; (619) 384-5400. Cannell Meadow Ranger District, Sequoia National Forest, 105 Whitney Road, Kernville, CA 93238; (619) 376-3781.

Kingston Range Wilderness

Just north of the Mojave National Preserve, an island of height in a sea of desert lowlands, 17 miles of the Kingston Range form a continuous ridgeline above 6,000 feet, crowned by 7,300-foot Kingston Peak. The southern bajadas of the range slope down into Kingston Wash. More than 500 species of plants, including a small cluster of white fir on the upper slopes of Kingston Peak, make the Wilderness one of the most botanically diverse in all the California desert. Year-round water provides habitat for birds, fish, mammals, and insects. Here you may see the banded gila monster—one of only five places on Earth where this rare reptile has been spotted. An old track along 15 miles of Kingston Wash, easily followed, remains non-Wilderness, and divides the area into southern and northern portions. You can wander aimlessly and alone over great distances in this vast area.

Kingston Range Essentials

Size: 209,608 acres.
Year Designated: 1994.
Location: Southeastern California.
Easiest Access: From Baker, take Interstate 15 east for about 26 miles. Turn north on Kingston Road and go 14 miles to Excelsior Mine Road. Continue north on the Excelsior Mine Road, with the Kingston Range rising to the west. After nine miles, turn southwest along the old track leading through Kingston Wash.
Season: Early spring and late fall.
Wilderness Fees/Permits: None.

Maps: USGS topographic maps are Blackwater Mine, Dumont Dunes, East of Kingston Peak, East of Kingston Spring, Horse Thief Springs, Ibex Pass, Kingston Peak, Kingston Springs, Mesquite Lake, Mesquite Mountains, Pachalka Spring, Silurian Hills, Silurian Lake, Tecopa, Tecopa Pass, Turquoise Mountain, and Valjean Hills.
Management: BLM Barstow Resource Area, 150 Coolwater Lane, Barstow, CA 92311; (619) 255-8700. BLM Needles Resource Area, 101 West Spikes Road, Needles, CA 92363; (619) 326-3896.

Lassen Volcanic Wilderness

In May of 1914, Lassen Peak began a seven-year series of eruptions including a humdinger in 1915 when an enormous mushroom cloud reached seven miles in height. Today, the 106,000-acre Lassen Volcanic National Park serves as a compact laboratory of volcanic phenomena and associated thermal features (mud pots, fumaroles, hot springs, sulfurous vents) with Lassen Peak (10,457 feet) near the center of the park's western half. Lassen Peak and its trail up are non-Wilderness, but almost four-fifths of the park has been designated Wilderness, a land of gorgeous lakes teeming with fish, thick forests of pine and fir, many splendid creeks, and a fascinating hodgepodge of extinct and inactive volcanoes. Best of all, this mountainous country remains relatively uncrowded by California standards. At least 779 plant species and numerous animals have been identified here. The eastern border is shared with Caribou Wilderness (see above), and one trail crosses the boundary.

About 150 miles of trails snake through this Wilderness, almost all with trailheads on State Highway 89, which passes near the middle of the park. A 17-mile-long section of the Pacific Crest Trail crosses from north to south. Open fires and pets are not permitted on the trails. Highway 89 usually closes by late October or early November due to snow. Snow often brings skiers. Some park areas may be closed.

Lassen Volcanic Essentials

Size: 78,982 acres.
Year Designated: 1972.
Location: Northern California.
Easiest Access: From Redding, take State Highway 44 east for 47 miles. Turn south on State Highway 89 for a short drive to the park.
Season: Spring and fall are most delightful. Winter snows are wondrous.
Wilderness Fees/Permits: A vehicle entrance fee of $5 is charged. A free Wilderness permit is required and may be reserved two weeks in advance.
Maps: Trail maps and topographic maps are available either from the park ranger or by mail.
Management: Lassen Volcanic National Park, P.O. Box 500, Mineral, CA 96063-0100; (916) 595-4444.

Lava Beds Wilderness

A million years of volcanic turmoil produced the ragged and seemingly inhospitable landscape of Lava Beds National Monument. But even the youngest cinder cones, hardly more than 1,000 years old, are now covered by vegetation that supports a variety of wildlife. Ground squirrels, deer, marmots, jackrabbits, and rattlesnakes are abundant. In the northern portion, grassland dominates, changing as the ground rises southward to juniper woodlands and, finally, pine in the extreme southern portion. Raptors nest on the cliffs overlooking Tule Lake, which lies just outside the northern boundary within the Tule Lake National Wildlife Refuge; in fact, more wintering bald eagles can be found here than any other place outside Alaska. Thousands of migratory birds pass through in spring and fall. Beneath the surface, at least 200 caves exist, lava tubes formed by flows that cooled on the surface as molten lava still raged below to drain away. These 200 caves, perhaps only a fraction of the miles of caves that have yet to be discovered, lure most human visitors to the area. Elevations range from about 4,000 feet to about 5,700 feet.

The Modoc Indians, abused and murdered by white settlers, made their last stand here, holding off 20 times their number until their final surrender in 1873.

A substantial portion of land has been designated Wilderness on both sides of the road that bisects the monument. Maintained trails give access to the Wilderness, and off the trails, the hiking can be strenuous. Camping is allowed, but not in caves or near their entrances, nor within one-quarter mile of chimneys, overlooks, and trails. Campfires are not allowed. You must carry all your water. Cold weather has been recorded in every month of the year.

Lava Beds Essentials

Size: 28,460 acres.
Year Designated: 1972.
Location: Extreme northern California.
Easiest Access: From Tulelake, take State Highway 139 south for four miles. Turn west at the sign indicating the monument to reach the visitors center.
Season: Fall, for the best bird watching.
Wilderness Fees/Permits: An entrance fee of $4 is charged.
Maps: Maps of the wilderness are available from the visitors center.
Management: Lave Beds National Monument, Box 867, Tulelake, CA 96134; (916) 667-2282.

Little Chuckwalla Mountains Wilderness

Dry, desolate, and rugged, the Little Chuckwalla Mountains, cresting at 2,100 feet, are surrounded by a large, gently sloping bajada incised by a network of washes. In the north part of the Wilderness, a bajada rises gradually to about 400 feet. Here, in portions of the area, you may see desert bighorn sheep, and the southern bajada has been identified as crucial habitat for desert tortoises. Several sensitive plants grow in the Little Chuckwallas, including California snakeweed, Alverson's foxtail cactus, and barrel cactus.

You won't find much in the way of developed trails or water, but you will find an ample supply of solitude.

Little Chuckwalla Mountains Essentials

Size: 29,880 acres.
Year Designated: 1994.
Location: Southeastern California.
Easiest Access: From Interstate 10, 23 miles west of Blythe, take the Ford Dry Lake Exit and travel south on the four-wheel-drive road. For the next 25 miles, this road forms the eastern boundary of the Wilderness.
Season: Early spring and late fall.
Wilderness Fees/Permits: None.
Maps: USGS topographic maps are Chuckwalla Springs, East of Aztec Mines, Hopkins Well, Little Chuckwalla Mountains, and Wiley Well.
Management: BLM Palm Springs-South Coast Resource Area, 63-500 Garnet Avenue, P.O. Box 2000, North Palm Springs, CA 92258; (619) 251-4800.

CALIFORNIA

Little Picacho Peak Wilderness

Within the southern portion of the Chocolate Mountains, with elevations ranging from 200 feet to 1,500 feet, the Little Picacho Peak Wilderness is characterized by dramatic jutting spires and steep ridges. Little Picacho Peak stands in the northern portion amid numerous ravines that gradually descend and broaden into sandy, tree-lined washes. The slopes and plains are covered with the angular cobbles known as desert pavement—a stark contrast to the nearly white bottoms of the washes. A herd of at least 25 desert bighorn sheep live here. The Picacho wild horse herd rambles over a 5,000-acre range in the northwestern corner of the Wilderness. Wild burros roam throughout the area, sharing their abode with desert tortoises and spotted bats.

From a road on the east side, you'll find an old track that runs five miles into the Wilderness near Senator Wash. Most of the area will provide you with extreme solitude.

Little Picacho Peak Essentials

Size: 33,600 acres.
Year Designated: 1994.
Location: Extreme southeastern California.
Easiest Access: From the Arizona state line, take Interstate 8 west. Then take the Fourth Street/Winterhaven exit and go west on Fourth Street approximately eight-tenths of a mile to State Route S-24. Follow S-24 north to Imperial Dam (about 18 miles), turning west at the Imperial Dam sign onto Ferguson Wash Road. The Wilderness lies on the west side of the wash for the next six miles.
Season: Early spring and late fall.
Wilderness Fees/Permits: None.
Maps: USGS topographic maps are Bard, Little Picacho Peak, Picacho, Picacho Peak, and Picacho SW.
Management: BLM El Centro Resource Area, 1661 South Fourth Street, El Centro, CA 92243; (619) 337-4400.

Machesna Mountain Wilderness

From a low point of about 1,600 feet, this Wilderness climbs to the 4,063-foot summit of Machesna Mountain in the southwest section. This is a scenic area, with the scenery getting finer the higher you venture until you can make out the snowcapped Sierra Nevada in the distance. Here in the La Panza mountain range, three-fourths of the area is chaparral brushland, roughly another 10 percent is pine-crowned peaks and majestic rocky crags, and the rest consists of an oak-dotted grassland. A 1,500-acre section has been set aside for the study of a unique strain of Coulter pine. American Canyon is the region's major drainage.

You may see deer, mountain lions, or black bears, but Machesna is best known as critical habitat for the protection of the California condor. Human use is light on the two trails: the American Canyon and the Machesna Mountain, both approximately eight miles long. Primarily national forestland, the Wilderness has about 120 acres that fall under Bureau of Land Management jurisdiction.

191

CALIFORNIA

Machesna Mountain Essentials

Size: 20,000 acres.
Year Designated: 1984.
Location: Southwestern California.
Easiest Access: From San Luis Obispo, take U.S. 101 north for nine miles. Turn east on State Highway 58 (Carrisa Highway) and go three miles. Turn south on the Pozo Road and travel roughly 26 miles to Pozo Summit. From Pozo Summit, a rough jeep trail (Pine Mountain ORV Road) heads south two miles to the boundary.

Season: Spring and fall.
Wilderness Fees/Permits: A free permit must be obtained from the district ranger.
Maps: USGS topographic maps are La Panza, Los Machos Hills, and Pozo Summit.
Management: Santa Lucia Ranger District, Los Padres National Forest, 1616 North Carlotti Drive, Santa Maria, CA 93454; (805) 925-9538. BLM Bakersfield District, 3801 Pegasus Avenue, Bakersfield, CA 93308; (805) 391-6000.

Malpais Mesa Wilderness

The long, north-south oval of Malpais Mesa (2,300 feet) stands dominant in the middle of this Wilderness area perched at the southern end of the Inyo Mountains. Rugged valleys, deep canyons, sheer mountainsides, and smaller mesas can all be found within close proximity. From Death Valley National Park in the east, the bajada rises gradually to the mesa's summit; the terrain drops away much more steeply in the west. Vegetation takes numerous forms: creosote, low desert shrubs, and grasses in the lower elevations; Joshua trees at middle elevations on the eastern side; piñon pines and junipers higher up. Mule deer abound, and golden eagles nest and forage in the area. The remains of the old Santa Rosa Mines lie at the end of a dirt track, part of a non-Wilderness corridor near the foot of the mesa. This is a desolate piece of earth—in Spanish, *malpais* means "bad country."

Malpais Mesa Essentials

Size: 32,360 acres.
Year Designated: 1994.
Location: Southeastern central California.
Easiest Access: From Olancha, take State Highway 190 east for 25 miles. Turn north on Saline Valley Road and drive about six miles. Turn north on Santa Rosa Flat Road, which leads to the Santa Rosa Mines, six miles into the eastern side of the Wilderness.

Season: Early spring and late fall.
Wilderness Fees/Permits: None.
Maps: USGS topographic maps are Centennial Canyon, Cerro Gordo Peak, Keeler, Nelson Range, Santa Rosa Flat, and Talc City Hills.
Management: BLM Ridgecrest Resource Area, 300 South Richmond Road, Ridgecrest, CA 93555; (619) 384-5400.

CALIFORNIA

Manly Peak Wilderness

Quietly isolated, Manly Peak stands at 7,196 feet on the boundary between Death Valley National Park and Manly Peak Wilderness. The Wilderness is comprised entirely of jagged ridges and deep canyons within the Panamint Mountains. Vegetation alters as you gain elevation from around 1,100 feet, where creosote bush scrub dominates, to the higher elevations, where piñon and juniper woodlands reign. The demanding terrain features rapid elevation changes, and the easiest approaches to the summit of Manly Peak are along the ridges to the northeast and east. Streams that flow from springs in the larger canyons feed a riparian habitat of cottonwoods and desert willows, and provide water for wildlife including a herd of desert bighorn sheep. As you explore the area, you'll find some evidence of long-abandoned mining operations.

Manly Peak Essentials

Size: 16,105 acres.
Year Designated: 1994.
Location: Southeastern central California.
Easiest Access: From Ridgecrest, take State Highway 178 north for 45 miles. Turn east on Ballarat Road and proceed 4.5 miles. Turn south on Wingate Wash Road and go another five miles. Turn east on South Park Canyon Road, which leads five miles to the northern Wilderness boundary. These roads require four-wheel-drive vehicles.
Season: Early spring and late fall.
Wilderness Fees/Permits: None.
Maps: USGS topographic maps are Copper Queen Canyon, Manly Fall, Manly Peak, and Sourdough Spring.
Management: BLM Ridgecrest Resource Area, 300 South Richmond Road, Ridgecrest, CA 93555; (619) 384-5400.

Marble Mountain Wilderness

Craggy peaks, abundant meadows, large streams, and a whopping 89 lakes stocked with trout highlight this wild and pleasant area. Adding to the visual interest are many fascinating geological features, including Marble Mountain itself, a stark, red-and-gray marbled peak. Most of the lakes are gems set in rocky settings, and at least one-third of the Wilderness is cloaked in a great variety of trees, dominated by tanbark oak, madrone, and Douglas fir lower down, and whitebark pine, foxtail pine, and mountain hemlock higher up. You will find alpine meadows and bare rock in the highest elevations. Bear, deer, and many other species of wildlife are plentiful. None of the peaks exceed 7,000 feet in height. Long recognized for its wild value, this region became a Primitive area in 1931, a Wilderness in 1953, and a part of the NWPS in 1964.

Numerous trails provide excellent and extensive access to the Wilderness, and human use is rated as moderate except at Sky High, Campbell, Cliff, Summit, Paradise, and Ukonom Lakes, where visitors tend to congregate. The Pacific Crest Trail crosses the entire Wilderness for 32 miles north-south, and accesses many other trails. The Shackleford Creek Trail leads six miles into some of the finest lake country in the Wilderness. Most of the trails offer relatively easy travel for humans and horses, and excellent campsites are to be had along the way.

CALIFORNIA

Marble Mountain Essentials

Size: 241,744 acres.
Year Designated: 1964; expanded in 1984.
Location: Northern California.
Easiest Access: Take the South Yreka/State Route 3 exit on Interstate 5 and go west approximately 20 miles to the Scott River Ranger Station. Turn north on the Scott River Road and go about seven miles. Turn west at the old red schoolhouse; go about four miles, and turn north on Forest Service Road 43N21 (Shackleford Trailhead Road). Look for the trailhead in about six miles.
Season: Spring through fall.

Wilderness Fees/Permits: A campfire permit is required during fire season.
Maps: A map that includes Russian Wilderness is available for $3 from district rangers.
Management: Happy Camp Ranger District, Klamath National Forest, P.O. Box 377, Happy Camp, CA 96038; (916) 493-2243. Salmon River Ranger District, Klamath National Forest, P.O. Box 280, Etna, CA 96027; (916) 467-5757. Scott River Ranger District, Klamath National Forest, 11263 South Highway 3, Fort Jones, CA 96032; (916) 468-5351. Ukonom Ranger District, Klamath National Forest, Drawer 410, Orleans, CA 95556; (916) 627-3291.

Matilija Wilderness

Steep and brushy, overgrown with alder and maple in the canyons with a few stands of conifers in the higher country, the Matilija Wilderness includes the scenic canyons of Matilija Creek, as well as its North Fork. Sixteen miles of the creek have been nominated for Wild and Scenic designation. The creek flows year-round and drains southward, and the elevation climbs steadily and steeply as you hike north. Look for the majestic Matilija poppy, which grows in clumps up to two feet high. You may see black bears, deer, coyotes, bobcats, mountain lions, rattlesnakes, hawks, eagles, and California condors.

Only one trail exists. It follows about eight miles of the North Fork, gaining about 2,000 feet in elevation as it makes its north-south journey, and leaving the Wilderness at a parking lot on Cherry Creek Road. Off-trail, you will probably have an arduous time and see few other humans.

Matilija Essentials

Size: 29,600 acres.
Year Designated: 1992.
Location: Southwestern California.
Easiest Access: From Ojai, take State Highway 33 north for 6.4 miles to Matilija Reservoir. Turn west on Matilija Canyon Road and drive about five miles until you come to a locked gate. Hike the road past the second stream crossing. The Matilija Canyon Trail then heads north into the Wilderness.
Season: Spring through fall.
Wilderness Fees/Permits: None.
Maps: USGS topographic maps are Old Man Mountain and White Ledge Peak.
Management: Ojai Ranger District, Los Padres National Forest, 1190 East Ojai Avenue, Ojai, CA 93023; (805) 646-4348.

CALIFORNIA

Mecca Hills Wilderness

Thanks to the restless San Andreas Fault, the geologic formations of Mecca Hills Wilderness are among the most unusual sites of their kind in the world. Entire regions are exposed layers of eroded rock, some over 600 million years old, and are a source of valuable information to scientists about the effects of tremors on the earth's crust. The area is a badlands labyrinth, a natural maze of small, narrow, steep canyons. Colorful Painted Canyon runs in a general north-south path through the middle of the Wilderness. Sandy washes sprinkled with ironwood, smoke trees, and paloverde divide the area, while ocotillo squat on gentler slopes and the tops of mesas. Bighorn sheep occasionally cross over from the Orocopia Mountains on the east, where they find more water. You may see spotted bats, desert tortoises, and prairie falcons.

The non-Wilderness corridor of Box Canyon Road splits off a small southern section of the area in which you'll find Sheep Hole Oasis and Hidden Springs Canyon (reliable sources for water). If you look closely, you'll discover caves, known locally as grottoes.

Mecca Hills Essentials

Size: 24,200 acres.
Year Designated: 1994.
Location: Southern California.
Easiest Access: From Interstate 10, 27 miles east of Indio, take Highway 195 (Box Canyon Road) south 15 miles to the Coachella Canal. Turn north on Painted Canyon Road and proceed four miles to the center of the Wilderness. Four-wheel-drive vehicles are required.
Season: Early spring and late fall are the optimal times to visit.
Wilderness Fees/Permits: None.
Maps: USGS topographic maps are Cottonwood Basin, Mecca, Mortmar, and Thermal Canyon.
Management: BLM Palm Springs-South Coast Resource Area, 63-500 Garnet Avenue, P.O. Box 2000, North Palm Springs, CA 92258; (619) 251-4800.

Mesquite Mountains Wilderness

Not far from the Nevada state line, the mesalike and lonely Mesquite Mountains, part of the Clark Mountain Range, cover the western and northern portions of this barren Wilderness. The eastern portion of the roughly triangular area is rough and rocky, punctuated by numerous small caves carved out of the porous rock. Creosote grows on the bajadas, and blackbrush and Joshua trees cling to higher ground. Only the Kingston Road separates this Wilderness from North Mesquite Mountains Wilderness (see below). To the east, outside the Wilderness, you'll find the sand dunes of Mesquite Dry Lake, and the Mojave National Preserve lies just to the south.

CALIFORNIA

Mesquite Mountains Essentials

Size: 47,330 acres.
Year Designated: 1994.
Location: Southeastern California.
Easiest Access: From Interstate 15, about 26 miles east of Baker, take the Cima/Kingston Road exit and go north about seven miles on Excelsior Mine/Kingston Road. For the next three miles, the Wilderness lies 500 feet to the northeast. Turn east on Kingston Road to follow the northwest boundary.

Season: Early spring and late fall.
Wilderness Fees/Permits: None.
Maps: USGS topographic maps are Clark Mountain, Ivanpah Lake, Mesquite Lake, Mesquite Mountains, and Pachalka.
Management: BLM Needles Resource Area, 101 West Spikes Road, Needles, CA 92363; (619) 326-3896.

Mojave Wilderness

The East Mojave National Scenic Area was established in 1980. It's a vast piece of land shaped roughly like a wedge of pie, covering most of the ground from the California-Nevada state line west almost to Barstow and between Interstates 15 and 40. In 1994, the California Desert Protection Act altered the status of the area's 1.4 million acres to the Mojave National Preserve and designated slightly less than one half the land as Wilderness.

Here is a meeting place for the Mojave, Sonoran, and Great Basin deserts, where you'll see strange volcanic features: cinder cones and dramatic lava beds, saw-toothed mountains rising in at least seven named ranges, flat-topped mesas, towering sand dunes, dry lake beds, and unique plant communities including the largest Joshua trees in the world. Most of the wildlife sensibly remains hidden during the daylight hours, but you may spot bighorn sheep, mule deer, bobcats, and cougars in the rugged mountains, and rabbits, coyotes, foxes, ground squirrels, pack rats, desert tortoises, lizards, and snakes in the washes and canyons. Raptors soar throughout the park. Much of this area is a desert wonderland, seldom visited by humans, and most of it is amenable to foot travel if you carry maps and plenty of water. You are allowed to hike and camp anywhere.

Mojave Essentials

Size: 695,200 acres.
Year Designated: 1994.
Location: Southeastern California.
Easiest Access: From west of Baker, almost to the Nevada state line, Interstate 15 forms much of the northern Wilderness boundary. From Ludlow, west almost to Needles, Interstate 40 forms much of the southern boundary.
Season: Early spring and late fall.

Wilderness Fees/Permits: None.
Maps: Desert Access Guide Maps 6, 9, and 12 cover the entire area and indicate the Wilderness portions. These maps are available from the California Desert Information Center for $4 each.
Management: Mojave National Preserve, California Desert Information Center, 831 Barstow Road, Barstow, CA 92311; (619) 255-8725.

CALIFORNIA

Mokelumne Wilderness

The Mokelumne River bisects remote mountainous terrain where elevations range from about 4,000 feet near Salt Springs Reservoir outside the southwest corner to over 10,000 feet on Round Top Peak in the north. Shallow valleys lying north of Mokelumne Peak (9,332 feet), in the southern portion of the area, hide many small lakes where the fishing is often worth the hike. The fishing can also be good in the Mokelumne River, but the river canyon is extremely rugged and poison oak grows in profusion along the banks. In general, though, glaciers have smoothed the area, leaving the well-placed trails relatively easy to hike. In spring and summer, several large meadows scattered throughout the wild land bloom with a riot of wildflower color. You'll find stands of timber over much of this Wilderness, but firewood is scarce in the Carson Pass–Round Top portion, and no fires are allowed in many sections, including Frog, Winnemucca, Round Top, Fourth of July, and Emigrant Lakes. The massifs of Raymond Peak hold court in the eastern section, providing some spectacular scenery. By late summer, water often becomes hard to find in the more remote regions.

A prolific trail system that includes 20 miles of the Pacific Crest Trail contributes to moderate to heavy human use. Most feet trample the shores of Fourth of July Lake, the Mokelumne River near Blue Hole, and along Upper Summit City Creek.

Mokelumne Essentials

Size: 104,461 acres.
Year Designated: 1964; expanded in 1984.
Location: Eastern central California.
Easiest Access: From Markleeville, take State Highway 89 south for seven miles to State Highway 4. Head south for 13 miles to Ebbetts Pass and the Pacific Crest Trail.
Season: Spring and early summer.
Wilderness Fees/Permits: Visitor permits are required from May 25 to September 15, and are available by mail or on a walk-in basis from the district rangers. During the summer, they're also available at the Markleeville Guard Station, Markleeville, CA 96120; (916) 694-2911.
Maps: A Wilderness map is available for $3 from the district rangers.
Management: Eldorado National Forest, 3070 Camino Heights Drive, Camino, CA 95709; (916) 644-6048. Calaveras Ranger District, Stanislaus National Forest, Highway 4, Box 500, Hathaway Pines, CA 95233; (209) 795-1381. Carson Ranger District, Toiyabe National Forest, 1536 South Carson, Carson City, NV 59701; (702) 882-2766.

Monarch Wilderness

At the southern end of John Muir Wilderness, on the western border of Sequoia-Kings Canyon National Park, Monarch Wilderness amply lives up to its regal name. Few areas of the United States can boast such an abundance of extravagant mountain scenery. Views from Spanish Mountain may be among the best in the world. Formerly known as the High Sierra Primitive Area, this wildland is steep and rugged, with high ridges standing above deep canyons. Mountain meadows, numerous streams, shallow lakes, and spectacular multicolored rock formations throughout the Wilderness add to the wonder. Elevations range from about 2,000 feet on the banks of the South Fork of the Kings River

197

CALIFORNIA

to 11,077 feet on Hogback Peak. Brush and oak woodlands cover the lower elevations, giving way to pine and red fir, and, finally, giant sequoias in the higher country.

The ragged, brushy terrain in the northwest portion (in Sierra National Forest) has no trails, and travel is extremely difficult. Trails in the rest of the area (in Sequoia National Forest) are mostly steep and strenuous. The Deer Cove Trail from Highway 180 rises 3,000 feet in four miles. Two loop trails provide access into the northern portion, and trails lead from this region into Kings Canyon National Park. Only two trails lead into the southern portion: the Deer Meadow Trail (four miles) and the Kanawyer Trail (seven miles) from Cedar Grove Campground. Sheer ruggedness has kept human use light despite the fact that State Highway 180 splits the area in half.

Monarch Essentials

Size: 45,000 acres.
Year Designated: 1984.
Location: Eastern central California.
Easiest Access: From Fresno, take State Highway 180 east for 55 miles. Turn east and then south on Generals Highway and go about seven miles. Turn north on Big Meadows Road and look for the Deer Meadow Trailhead approximately five miles ahead.
Season: Late spring through early fall.
Wilderness Fees/Permits: A free permit is required for overnight use. Contact the district rangers.
Maps: A Wilderness map that includes the Jennie Lakes Wilderness is available for $3.25 from the district rangers.
Management: Hume Lake Ranger District, Sequoia National Forest, 35860 East Kings Canyon Road, Dunlap, CA 93621; (209) 338-2251. Kings River Ranger District, Sierra National Forest, 34849 Maxon Road, Sanger, CA 93657; (209) 855-8321 or (209) 841-3404.

Mount Shasta Wilderness

Even first-time visitors to the area have no trouble identifying Mount Shasta. Dominating the landscape for several hundred miles in all directions, the mountain looms 14,162 feet, a beautiful snow-cloaked massif, second only to Mount Rainier in height among the famous Cascade Range volcanoes. Although the last documented eruption occurred in 1786, geologists classify Shasta as an active volcano. Most of the Wilderness lies on the upper slopes of the mountain. Below the seven glaciers that drape the mountain's slopes, you'll find a land of scenic wonder: ancient lava flows, a hot sulphur spring, waterfalls tumbling down deep canyons cut through rugged buttes. Stunted and picturesque red and white fir and whitebark pine grow near the tree line (around 8,000 feet). They preside above a forest of pure red fir and mixed conifers that include hemlock, cedar, sugar pine, Jeffrey pine, white fir, and Douglas fir, with an understory of shrubs. On the north side of the mountain, where the lava once flowed, you'll find some aspen, mountain mahogany, and juniper. In July and early August, meadows below timberline explode with wildflower color. Deer and black bears live here with an abundance of ground squirrels and coyotes.

The mountain's outstanding views attract many human visitors armed with crampons and ice axes. No trails lead up Mount Shasta, but trails provide access to the Wilderness and the foot of the mountain. The Avalanche Gulch Route (six miles) is considered the easiest, but the elevation gain is over 7,000 feet, and at least 8 to 12 hours should be alloted for the round-trip. The

CALIFORNIA

glaciers are cracked by crevasses and are more visible in late summer and fall. On the south slopes, rockfall becomes a danger after midsummer. Major storms off the Pacific Ocean can send high winds and snow across the mountain any time of year. Sound preparation is a must.

Mount Shasta Essentials

Size: 37,000 acres.
Year Designated: 1984.
Location: Northern central California.
Easiest Access: From Mount Shasta City, drive east on Alma Street to the first stop sign and turn south. At the next stop sign, turn east, and take the Everitt Memorial Highway for 9.5 miles. Turn north on Lower Sand Flat Road and go eight-tenths of a mile to the junction with Upper Sand Flat Road. Continue straight ahead a short distance; take the right fork and go about a half mile to the Sand Flat Trailhead. This trail leads to Avalanche Gulch.
Season: May through September.
Wilderness Fees/Permits: Permits are required year-round for entry into the Wilderness. Between May 15 and October 15, camping permits are issued by either of the district offices. From October 16 through May 14, permits may be self-issued at the Mount Shasta District office. Day users may self-issue permits year-round.
Maps: A Wilderness map that includes Castle Crags Wilderness is available for $6 from the district rangers.
Management: McCloud Ranger District, Shasta-Trinity National Forest, Drawer 1, McCloud, CA 96057; (916) 964-2184. Mount Shasta Ranger District, Shasta-Trinity National Forest, 204 West Alma Street, Mount Shasta, CA 96067; (916) 926-4511.

Newberry Mountains Wilderness

Rugged and volcanic in origin, the Newberry Mountains rise with relative gentleness toward rather broad and flat tops with elevations ranging from 2,200 feet in the north to 5,100 feet in the south. Deep, mazelike canyons slice through the mountains in all directions. The old Azucar Mine lies just outside the western border, and evidence of past mining activity lies scattershot throughout the area. When the rains cooperate, the western side of the Wilderness erupts into spring wildflower displays. You won't find much in the way of water or trails in the area. You may see a few desert bighorn sheep passing through, or a falcon or eagle hunting from the air.

Newberry Mountains Essentials

Size: 22,900 acres.
Year Designated: 1994.
Location: Southern central California.
Easiest Access: From Barstow, take Interstate 40 east for six miles. Take the Daggett exit and turn south on Camp Rock Road, going four miles to where the road meets, and then runs along, the western Wilderness boundary.
Season: Early spring or late fall.
Wilderness Fees/Permits: None.
Maps: USGS topographic maps are Camp Rock Mine, Minneola, Newberry Springs, and Ord Mountain.
Management: BLM Barstow Resource Area, 150 Coolwater Lane, Barstow, CA 92311; (619) 255-8700.

CALIFORNIA

Nopah Range Wilderness

From the Old Spanish Trail Highway north to the Nevada state line, Nopah Range Wilderness contains a good chunk of the Nopah Range in its eastern portion and a piece of the Resting Spring Range in its west. These ranges embody dramatic geologic landscapes, separated by the north-south Chicago Valley, a flat expanse with numerous winding, light-colored washes. Elevations vary from about 1,800 feet to the 6,395-foot summit of Nopah Peak in the northern section.

Explorers will find a desert symphony of dry mountains, hills, and alluvial fans, badlands, playas, plains, and river washes. Creosote, cactuses, yucca, and other desert shrubs cover the bajadas, adding hints of color and life to the barren mountains that rise above. Wild burros and horses roam the Chicago Valley, and desert bighorn sheep, desert tortoises, golden eagles, and prairie falcons are not uncommon visitors.

Nopah Range Essentials

Size: 110,860 acres.
Year Designated: 1994.
Location: Southeastern California.
Easiest Access: From Shoshone, take State Highway 178 east for two miles. From there, the highway forms the northwest Wilderness boundary ending at the Nevada state line.
Season: Early spring and late fall.
Wilderness Fees/Permits: None.
Maps: USGS topographic maps are Mound Spring, Nopah Peak, North of Tecopa Pass, Resting Spring, Shoshone, Sixmile Spring, Stewart Valley, Tecopa, Twelvemile Spring, and West of Stump Spring.
Management: BLM Barstow Resource Area, 150 Coolwater Lane, Barstow, CA 92311; (619) 255-8700.

North Algodones Dunes Wilderness

Approximately eight miles wide and 40 miles long, the Algodones Sand Dunes system is one of the largest dune complexes in North America. Still, only a relatively small section north of State Highway 78 has been designated Wilderness, while the rest hosts an abundance of outdoor recreational vehicle traffic. The Wilderness lies divided into two distinct zones: the primary dunes on the west side and the secondary dunes on the east. The former are taller and larger, and composed of noticeably coarse sand. The latter are smaller, made up of finer sands that are periodically shifted even farther east by prevailing winds. The secondary dunes are interrupted in places by basins or flats, where you'll find mesquite, smoke tree, ironwood, paloverde, and desert willows. Streams draining from the nearby Chocolate Mountains to the north flow to the edge of the dunes in spring, and form pools where the sand acts like a dam. The area supports the flat-tailed horned lizard, desert tortoises, and the Colorado fringe-toed lizard. In the fine sands of the secondary dunes, you may see the Andrews dune scarab beetle. As you cross the trailless expanse of the dunes, of course carrying plenty of water, you can be assured of an unforgettable desert experience.

CALIFORNIA

North Algodones Dunes Essentials

Size: 32,240 acres.
Year Designated: 1994.
Location: Southern California.
Easiest Access: From Brawley, take State Highway 78 east for 20 miles to the Coachella Canal. The Wilderness lies east of the canal and north of 78 for the next six miles, until you reach the town of Glamis.
Season: Winter and early spring.
Wilderness Fees/Permits: None.
Maps: USGS topographic maps are Acolita, Amos, East of Acolita, Glamis, Glamis NW, and Sombrero Peak.
Management: BLM El Centro Resource Area, 1661 South Fourth Street, El Centro, CA 92243; (619) 337-4400.

North Fork Wilderness

Designated Wild and Scenic, the thin ribbon of the Eel River's North Fork flows through the middle of this Wilderness and through a spectacular gorge lined with mixed conifers in its upper region and an oak forest lower down. Steelhead and salmon live in the river in limited numbers, and fishing is permitted. The steep and rugged Wilderness encompasses the watershed of the North Fork, with streams feeding the river from the east and west. North-facing slopes are timbered in Douglas fir, ponderosa pine, and delightfully fragrant incense cedar. South-facing slopes are generally grassy and overgrown with manzanita and scrub oak. Due to the relatively low elevations, black-tailed deer gather here in substantial numbers, especially when the temperature drops, and attract hunters in the fall who report high success rates.

Remnants of old trails exist, but none are maintained and trail access is invitingly poor. Wilderness access is, in fact, very limited. This is not an area for the novice outdoorsperson. Be handy with map and compass, and be prepared. You'll probably be alone in North Fork Wilderness, except during hunting season.

North Fork Essentials

Size: 8,100 acres.
Year Designated: 1984.
Location: Northwestern California.
Easiest Access: From Mad River, on State Highway 36, take County Road 502 south to Zenia. Turn south on County Road 503 and take this road for about seven miles. Turn east on County Road 520 through Kettenpom Valley and travel five miles to Salt Creek and the western boundary of the Wilderness.
Season: Spring and fall.
Wilderness Fees/Permits: None.
Maps: USGS topographic maps are Long Ridge, Shannon Butte, and Zenia.
Management: Mad River Ranger District, Six Rivers National Forest, Star Route Box 300, Bridgeville, CA 95428; (707) 574-6233.

North Mesquite Mountains Wilderness

Brown and rolling, parched and desolate, North Mesquite Mountains Wilderness primarily encompasses a foothills region with a few steeper mountains thrown in for good measure. A wide, horseshoe-shaped valley lies along the western side, and the higher country of Mesquite Mountains Wilderness (see above) is just across the Kingston Road to the south. You'll find Joshua tree woodlands, yucca, cactuses, blackbrush, and desert grasses growing here, providing habitat for a few species of desert wildlife. Mesquite Valley and Nevada are located not far to the northeast. Rugged and remote, the North Mesquite Mountains feel the tread of few human feet.

North Mesquite Mountains Essentials

Size: 25,540 acres.
Year Designated: 1994.
Location: Southeastern California.
Easiest Access: From Baker, take Interstate 15 about 26 miles east to the Cima Road Exit. Then travel north on the paved Excelsior Mine Road about eight miles until it intersects with the graveled Kingston Road. The Wilderness lies north between these two roads.
Season: Early spring and late fall.
Wilderness Fees/Permits: None.
Maps: USGS topographic maps are Blackwater Mine, East of Kingston Peak, East of Kingston Spring, Mesquite Mountains, Pachalka Spring, Shenandoah Peak, and West of Shenandoah Peak.
Management: BLM Needles Resource Area, 101 West Spikes Road, Needles, CA 92363; (619) 326-3896.

Old Woman Mountains Wilderness

A granite monolith known as the Old Woman Statue inspired the name of these massive mountains, which thrust up from the desert to dominate the Wilderness. From 800 feet at the lowest elevation, the terrain shoots up to more than 5,300 feet on Old Woman Peak, where the view, while not exactly splendid, proves charming and satisfying. Southeast of the peak, near the center of the area, you'll find the Old Woman Statue. Creosote bush scrub covers the Wilderness' lower reaches, mingling with desert scrub at middle elevations and forfeiting to piñon and juniper woodlands on the highest ground. Bighorn sheep, desert tortoises, and raptors inhabit the area. Although the Old Woman Mountains have a long history of use by humans, you won't find much water here even though maps may indicate springs. You may stumble on old tracks from both prehistory and the mining era, though, as well as rough garnets lying on the ground. Carry plenty of water if you decide to hike across the extensive bajadas and up the lengths of long, sandy washes.

Old Woman Mountains Essentials

Size: 146,020 acres.
Year Designated: 1994.
Location: Southeastern California.
Easiest Access: From Essex, on Route 66 (National Trails Highway), take the sand-and-gravel Sunflower Springs Road south for seven miles. From that point, this road traces the northeast Wilderness boundary for 13 miles and requires a four-wheel-drive vehicle.
Season: Early spring and late fall.

Wilderness Fees/Permits: None.
Maps: USGS topographic maps are Cadiz Lake NE, Chubbuck, East of Milligan, Essex, Milligan, Old Woman Statue, Painted Rock Wash, Sheep Camp Spring, Skeleton Pass, and Wilhelm Spring.
Management: BLM Needles Resource Area, 101 West Spikes Road, Needles, CA 92363; (619) 326-3896.

Orocopia Mountains Wilderness

Immediately to the east of Mecca Hills Wilderness (see above), you'll find Orocopia Mountains Wilderness, where the unpredictable forces of nature—primarily the San Andreas Fault—have created a striking landscape of open desert valleys, ridges, and dramatically colored and eroded canyons. The canyons and washes are deep and often extremely long, with exposed walls shaded from bright red to dark black. Despite the harshness of the climate, you should see a wide variety of plants and animals adapted to life in the desert. Bighorn sheep and burro deer live in the mountains, and desert tortoises crawl below. In washes and along stony slopes, you may encounter the spiny-leaved Orocopia sage, Alverson's foxtail cactus, Orcutt's woody aster, and the Mecca aster.

Keep an eye open for evidence of this area's long history—there's everything from the fossilized remains of prehistoric animals resembling horses, camels, and deer to traces of trade routes used by Indians in the not-too-distant past.

Orocopia Mountains Essentials

Size: 40,735 acres.
Year Designated: 1994.
Location: Southern California.
Easiest Access: From Interstate 10, 27 miles east of Indio, take State Highway 195 (Box Canyon Road) south. For the next six miles, numerous old tracks run a short way off of Highway 195 toward the Wilderness to the southeast.

Season: Winter through early spring.
Wilderness Fees/Permits: None.
Maps: USGS topographic maps are East of Red Canyon, Hayfield, Hayfield Spring, Orocopia Canyon, and Red Canyon.
Management: BLM Palm Springs–South Coast Resource Area, 63-500 Garnet Avenue, P.O. Box 2000, North Palm Springs, CA 92258; (619) 251-4800.

Owens Peak Wilderness

Owens Peak, the highest point in the southern Sierra Nevada Mountains at more than 8,400 feet, stands near the center of Owens Peak Wilderness. It presides over mountainous terrain with deep, winding canyons, many with rich riparian vegetation fed by bubbling springs. The Sierra Nevada meets the Great Basin and the Mojave Desert here, creating an unusual ecosystem. You'll find creosote bush scrub communities on the bajadas; scattered yuccas, cactuses, flowering annuals, cottonwoods, and oaks in the canyons and valleys; and juniper and piñon woodlands with sagebrush and digger pines on the upper elevations. Mule deer graze beneath golden eagles and prairie falcons. You may see evidence of active human use of this area dating back to prehistoric times.

The Pacific Crest Trail crosses through the area north-south, entering at Ninemile Canyon on the north and leaving at Walker Pass 22 miles to the south. Other trails leave the PCT to dive off the crest and eventually intersect with roads outside the Wilderness.

Owens Peak Essentials

Size: 74,060 acres.
Year Designated: 1994.
Location: Southern central California.
Easiest Access: From U.S. 395, four miles north of Inyokern, turn west into either Short Canyon, Sand Canyon, or No Name Canyon to reach near the eastern Wilderness boundary. Four-wheel-drive vehicles are required.
Season: Late fall to early spring.
Wilderness Fees/Permits: None.
Maps: USGS topographic maps are Freeman Junction, Lamont Peak, Ninemile Canyon, Owens Peak, and Walker Pass.
Management: BLM Caliente Resource Area, 3801 Pegasus Avenue, Bakersfield, CA 93308; (805) 391-6000. BLM Ridgecrest Resource Area, 300 South Richmond Road, Ridgecrest, CA 93555; (619) 384-5400.

Pahrump Valley Wilderness

The Pahrump Valley in the north, the Mesquite Valley in the southeast, and the California Valley in the west join forces in this desolate, seldom-visited Wilderness. Alluvial slopes in all three valleys ascend gradually southward into the northern Kingston Range, which also lies within the Wilderness. In the mountains, you'll find a rugged piece of earth with many canyons, winding washes, and bajadas. Elevations range from 2,720 feet on a valley floor to 4,569 feet on a mountain summit. The three dry valleys are dotted with desert shrubs and yucca. Wild burros are protected here, and you'll probably see a few of them, along with desert bighorn sheep, desert tortoises, and golden eagles. An old four-wheel-drive track crosses the area from northwest to southeast, and a long waterless way it is. The northeastern border is the Nevada state line.

CALIFORNIA

Pahrump Valley Essentials

Size: 74,800 acres.
Year Designated: 1994.
Location: Southeastern California.
Easiest Access: From Tecopa, take the Old Spanish Trail Highway east about 25 miles through the Nopah Range, where the highway borders the Wilderness on its northwest side.
Season: Early spring and late fall.

Wilderness Fees/Permits: None.
Maps: USGS topographic maps are Blackwater Mine, Green Monster Mine, Horse Thief Springs, West of Shenandoah Peak, and West of Stump Spring.
Management: BLM Barstow Resource Area, 150 Coolwater Lane, Barstow, CA 92311; (619) 255-8700.

Palen-McCoy Wilderness

Within the Palen-McCoy Wilderness lie five distinct desert mountain ranges: the Palen, McCoy, Granite, Little Maria, and Arica. They are separated from each other by broad, sloping bajadas, and don't receive a passel of human visitors. Still, interior valleys and canyons, jagged peaks above dry slopes, and the colorful cobbles of desert pavement present an ever-changing pattern for the rare traveler. An intricate array of washes in the valley between the Palen and McCoy Mountains are heavily draped in ironwood and paloverde trees—in fact, the ironwood forest is the biggest and most lush in the entire California Desert, perhaps in the world. This wood is so heavy that it can sink in water, and Indians once used it extensively for tools and weapons, while eating the seeds as a staple food. The wash woodlands provide habitat for burro deer, bobcats, coyotes, gray foxes, kit foxes, mountain lions, rabbits, mice, kangaroo rats, and numerous species of birds. Old four-wheel-drive tracks crisscross the valley and lead into the mountains, making this Wilderness a vast desert wonderland that is relatively easy to access by foot.

Palen-McCoy Essentials

Size: 270,629 acres.
Year Designated: 1994.
Location: Southeastern California.
Easiest Access: From Blythe, take Interstate 10 west for about 30 miles. Exit at Wileys Well and travel north on the four-wheel-drive road. The McCoys will be immediately to the east, the Palens to the west.
Season: Early spring and late fall.
Wilderness Fees/Permits: None.

Maps: USGS topographic maps are Arica Mountains, Arlington Mine, East of Granite Pass, Ford Dry Lake, Granite Pass, Little Maria Mountains, McCoy Spring, Palen Lake, Palen Mountains, Palen Pass, Sidewinder Well, and West of Palen Pass.
Management: BLM Palm Springs–South Coast Resource Area, 63-500 Garnet Avenue, P.O. Box 2000, North Palm Springs, CA 92258; (619) 251-4800.

CALIFORNIA

Palo Verde Mountains Wilderness

In the heart of the relatively jagged Palo Verde Mountains Wilderness, twin buttes called the Flat Tops stand out prominently. The highest point in the area, Palo Verde Peak, rises to about 1,800 feet in the southern portion. Thumb Peak, with its distinctive shape, stands to the north. A unique palm oasis, Clapp Spring, stands not far east of Thumb Peak and is worth a visit. It's the only permanent water source in the area for wildlife species, such as desert bighorn sheep, desert tortoises, and wild burros. Unlike most desert oases that hide in the shade of deep canyon walls, Clapp Spring bubbles up in the middle of an open landscape. Dry washes divide the slopes of the mountains, where you'll find vegetation such as ironwood, mesquite, and, of course, paloverde. In the southeastern part of the Wilderness, you can find saguaro cactuses, plants rarely seen in California.

Palo Verde Mountains Essentials

Size: 32,310 acres.
Year Designated: 1994.
Location: Southeastern California.
Easiest Access: From Blythe, take State Highway 78 south. Approximately 12 miles south of Palo Verde, turn west on Milpitas Wash Road. The Wilderness lies to the north and east of the road for the next 15 miles.
Season: Winter.
Wilderness Fees/Permits: None.
Maps: USGS topographic maps are Palo Verde Peak, Thumb Peak, West of Palo Verde Peak, and Wiley Well.
Management: BLM El Centro Resource Area, 1661 South Fourth Street, El Centro, CA 92243; (619) 337-4400.

Phillip Burton Wilderness

The Point Reyes Peninsula used to lie a couple hundred miles farther south before the San Andreas Fault decided to shift it to its current location. Unruffled by this forced eviction, the Point Reyes National Seashore presents a serene and sternly beautiful expanse of rock-lined beaches and a forest of fir and pine broken by meadowlands in the south, where roughly one-third of this national parkland has been designated Wilderness. Tall cliffs tower over forested ridges, and chaparral-covered swaths line both sides of a road that splits the Wilderness. More than 40 species of birds and 72 species of mammals have been identified, including seals and other marine animals that often gather along the bays and esteros. From December through April, the far reaches of the peninsula provide a prime spot for catching a glimpse of gray whales as they migrate between their feeding grounds in the Arctic and their breeding grounds in Mexican lagoons.

There are more than 140 miles of trails crisscrossing the area. Most popular is the Bear Valley Trail, running 4.4 miles through forest and meadow to the sea. In numerous small valleys, you'll find the brush dense and highlighted by stinging nettle and poison oak—good reason to stay on the trails. Cliff edges are often crumbly and should be avoided, and their bases are dangerous because of falling rocks. Riptides often make a dip in the ocean dangerous, but if you care to brave the chilly waters, non-Wilderness swimming beaches exist nearby. Overnight camping is allowed only at four hike-in campgrounds: Coast, Sky, Glen, and Wildcat. Weather is often cool and damp with dense fog common in summer. Although it's usually not that difficult to find a spot for solitary contemplation, human use is heavy.

Phillip Burton Essentials

Size: 25,370 acres.
Year Designated: 1976.
Location: Central coastal California.
Easiest Access: From San Francisco, take Highway 1 north to Olema. Turn west on Bear Valley Road and continue for one-half mile to the Bear Valley Visitors Center.
Season: Open year-round, but spring and fall are usually the most appealing. Winter is best for whale watching.
Wilderness Fees/Permits: No fees are charged, but free camping permits are required and advance reservations are strongly recommended (up to 60 days prior to your visit); phone (415) 663-1092.
Maps: Excellent trail maps are available at the visitors center.
Management: Point Reyes National Seashore, Point Reyes Station, CA 94956; (415) 663-8522.

Picacho Peak Wilderness

Dark gray, massive mountains extending southeast from Indian Pass make up the central and western portions of the diminutive Picacho Peak Wilderness. Mica Peak stands near the center of this range, the highest point in the Wilderness at 1,499 feet. South of these mountains, benchland rolls away, dissected by narrow arroyos with vertical walls. The northeastern section of the area makes up a third distinctive region: open basins and large washes overlooked by small peaks. In Gavilan Wash on the north and Carrizo Wash on the east, you'll find the lowest points in the region. Carrizo Wash holds a natural rock tank at the foot of Carrizo Falls that traps the runoff from desert cloudbursts. From above the tank, rainwater cascades 40 feet down a series of rock ledges into a pool lined with cattails, a desert oasis for a variety of wildlife including bighorn sheep.

You may see some wild horses and burros roaming Picacho Peak Wilderness, or a desert tortoise burrowing into the soft volanic soil. You also may discover a couple of old jeep tracks to follow. Picacho Peak itself lies southeast of the Wilderness boundary.

Picacho Peak Essentials

Size: 7,700 acres.
Year Designated: 1994.
Location: Southeastern California.
Easiest Access: From Interstate 8, 13 miles west of Yuma, Arizona, take Ogilby Road (S-34) north for 17 miles. Turn east on Indian Pass Road and travel nine miles. The Wilderness lies south of the road and Gavilan Wash, which is bordered by Indian Pass Road.
Season: Early spring and late fall are the best times to visit.
Wilderness Fees/Permits: None.
Maps: USGS topographic maps are Hedges, Picacho Peak, Picacho SW, and Quartz Peak.
Management: BLM El Centro Resource Area, 1661 South Fourth Street, El Centro, CA 92243; (619) 337-4400.

CALIFORNIA

Pine Creek Wilderness

Gently sloping from about 2,000 feet elevation in the south to 4,000 feet in the north, Pine Creek and its numerous tributaries drain this Wilderness in a north-south direction. With the exception of the creek itself, home to rainbow trout and bass, most of the streams dry up part of the year. Chaparral and scrub oak entirely dominate the vegetation, with some riparian and oak woodlands emerging from the stream bottoms. You may see deer, coyotes, mountain lions (if you're living right), gray foxes, hawks, owls, and several species of reptiles—no wonder a few hunters have discovered this area. You might also encounter small herds of private livestock grazing because their owners were issued permits prior to designation.

Several trails provide access, and receive only light human use. The Horsethief Trail on the west side switchbacks down into Horsethief Canyon and takes you 1.2 miles to the waters of Pine Creek. Only small stoves are permitted; no campfires, barbecues, or hibachis. Groups are limited to 15 people.

Pine Creek Essentials

Size: 13,100 acres.
Year Designated: 1984.
Location: Southwestern California.
Easiest Access: Exit Interstate 8, eight miles east of Alpine, at State Highway 79 (Japatul Road). Travel south 7.5 miles to a trailhead leading to Horsethief Canyon on the east side of the road.
Season: Winter through early spring.
Wilderness Fees/Permits: A free permit is required for entrance into the Wilderness. Contact the district ranger.
Maps: A topographic map that includes Hauser Wilderness is available for $3 from the district ranger.
Management: Descanso Ranger District, Cleveland National Forest, 3348 Alpine Boulevard, Alpine, CA 91901; (619) 445-6235.

Pinnacles Wilderness

More than 23 million years ago, according to the prevailing theory of plate tectonics, the Pacific Plate ground past the North American Plate, wrenching off a piece and creating the San Andreas Rift Zone. Molten lava poured through the rift, and a huge volcanic mountain was formed. Eons of wind and water, heat and frost wore down the mountain and produced the starkly angular crags and spires of today's Pinnacles National Monument. Movement of the Pacific Plate carried the Pinnacles with infinite slowness to their present location, approximately 195 miles north of the place of their birth. A chaparral plant community has grown up on the rugged lower slopes of the area, prime habitat for black-tailed deer, rabbits, gray foxes, raccoons, and bobcats.

High peaks divide the monument into eastern and western portions. Road access is available to both sides, but no roads connect the two. Camping is permitted at a picnic area on the west side all year except on Friday, Saturday, and Sunday nights from February 11 to May 31, and a fee is charged. About 30 miles of foot trails provide access to the Wilderness, but no camping is allowed because of the fragile nature of this relatively small area. Technical rock climbers will find a wealth of routes of varying difficulty, and the sport has been growing in popularity here.

CALIFORNIA

Pinnacles Essentials

Size: 12,952 acres.
Year Designated: 1976.
Location: Western central California.
Easiest Access: From Soledad, on U.S. 101, take State Highway 146 east for 13 miles to the picnic area, where camping is allowed on the west side. The road grows steep and narrow.
Season: Winters are wet, and summers are hot and dry. Spring and fall offer pleasant weather.
Wilderness Fees/Permits: There is an entrance fee of $4 per vehicle.
Maps: A free map is available from the monument ranger.
Management: Pinnacles National Monument, Paicines, CA 95043; (408) 389-4485.

Piper Mountain Wilderness

The Piper, Sylvania, and Inyo Mountains meet in Piper Mountain Wilderness. Alluvial fans cover large portions of the eastern side of the area. Wide, barren plains and dry hills form much of the landscape. The region is divided into three separate sections by non-Wilderness four-wheel-drive roads (along the seven miles of northeast-southwest Horse Thief Canyon, and north-south from Chocolate Mountain to the edge of Death Valley National Park). Sagebrush and piñon-juniper woodlands are the most common vegetation, though conifers grow in some of the higher elevations. Desert bighorn sheep live in at least three locations within this area. At the base of the Inyo Mountains, you'll discover one of the northernmost stands of Joshua trees.

Piper Mountain Essentials

Size: 72,575 acres.
Year Designated: 1994
Location: Central eastern California.
Easiest Access: From Big Pine, take State Highway 168 east and north for 38 miles. Turn south on Eureka Valley Road, which forms the northeast Wilderness boundary for 13 miles.
Season: Early spring and late fall.
Wilderness Fees/Permits: None.
Maps: USGS topographic maps are Chocolate Mountain, Cowhorn Valley, Deep Springs Lake, Horse Thief Canyon, Joshua Flats, Soldier Pass, and Sylvania Canyon.
Management: BLM Ridgecrest Resource Area, 300 South Richmond Road, Ridgecrest, CA 93555; (619) 384-5400.

Piute Mountains Wilderness

Squeezed between a state highway and a pipeline, the small range of the Piute Mountains is preserved by Wilderness designation. These mountains are bisected by an extensive system of connecting washes. A non-Wilderness four-wheel-drive track divides the area into east and west sections. The track leads to a water tank that collects rain from desert storms. At least two springs may supply water.

Little known and little used by humans, these mountains have long been considered sacred by the Mojave Indians.

CALIFORNIA

Piute Mountains Essentials

Size: 36,840 acres.
Year Designated: 1994.
Location: Southeastern California.
Easiest Access: From Needles, take Interstate 40 west. Exit at Mountain Springs Road about 27 miles west of Needles, and take Route 66 (National Trails Highway) south. The southern edge of the highway's right-of-way serves as the northern boundary until the town of Essex.
Season: Early spring and late fall.
Wilderness Fees/Permits: None.
Maps: USGS topographic maps are Essex, Fenner, Fenner Spring, Little Piute Mountains, and West of Flattop Mountain.
Management: BLM Needles Resource Area, 101 West Spikes Road, Needles, CA 92363; (619) 326-3896.

Red Buttes Wilderness

This Wilderness was named for the reddish orange hue that a high content of iron and magnesium lends to its dramatic topographical formations. Split into two pieces by the California-Oregon state line (see Oregon, Red Buttes Wilderness), the bulk of Red Buttes Wilderness lies in California, straddling the stonebound crest of the Siskiyou Mountains from the Red Buttes themselves to Sucker Creek Gap. You'll find meadows, fields of brush, and rocky slopes rising to craggy peaks. Cold streams rush down heavily eroded valleys and through extensive stands of old-growth ponderosa pine, sugar pine, incense cedar, and Douglas fir. White and red fir and mountain hemlock grow on the upper slopes.

Approximately 13 miles long and six miles wide, the area features elevations ranging from about 2,800 feet in Butte Fork Canyon to 6,740 feet on the east summit of the Red Buttes themselves. In the higher elevations, you'll find several small lakes huddled delightfully in scenic basins. Azalea Lake, the largest at 20 acres, sits in the western half of the California portion. Black-tailed deer, black bears, bobcats, all manner of rodents and weasels, and other wildlife are abundant.

Trail 957 crosses the area eight miles in an east-west direction, following the flow of the Applegate River much of the time. It connects to trails leading into Oregon at Azalea Lake. The shores of Azalea Lake, the most popular destination on the California side, have been beat to death by hikers and horsepackers; camping is not allowed near the water.

Red Buttes Essentials

Size: 16,150 acres in CA (19,900 acres total).
Year Designated: 1984.
Location: Northern California.
Easiest Access: From Medford, Oregon, take State Highway 238 about 13 miles west to Ruch. Turn south on the road that follows the Applegate River to Applegate Lake. Keep going about 20 miles to the trailhead for Trail 957, three miles south of the Oregon border.
Season: Spring and fall.
Wilderness Fees/Permits: None.
Maps: A Wilderness map is available for $2 from the district ranger.
Management: Applegate Ranger District, Rogue River National Forest, 6941 Upper Applegate Road, Jacksonville, OR 97530; (503) 899-1812.

CALIFORNIA

Resting Spring Range Wilderness

Between Death Valley National Park and the Nevada state line, the Resting Spring Range sweeps up from vast bajadas across rolling hills to a picturesque north-south spine—a line of extremely coarse and rugged rock formations with jagged summits above deep, hidden canyons. Elevations vary from 2,040 feet to Stewart Peak's 5,264 feet. From subdued browns and tans, the colors of the mountains sometimes run to intense pinks, reds, greens, and black. To the west lies the valley of the Amargosa River, and in the area's northwest corner, the huge spread of Eagle Mountain juts abruptly from the flat expanse of the wide river valley. The colorful sides of Eagle Mountain are a delightful contrast to the dull shades and sparse vegetation of the valley floor. Desert bighorn sheep share the land with wild horses and wild burros. You may see several species of raptors, including golden eagles and prairie falcons, circling overhead. The non-Wilderness corridor of a four-wheel-drive road splits off a southern section of the area leading to the old Baxter Mine. You will not find trails. You *will* find solitude.

Resting Spring Range Essentials

Size: 78,868 acres.
Year Designated: 1994.
Location: Southeastern California.
Easiest Access: From Death Valley Junction, take State Highway 127 for nine miles south to Eagle Mountain. For the next 15 miles, the highway forms the western Wilderness boundary.
Season: Winter.
Wilderness Fees/Permits: None.
Maps: USGS topographic maps are Bole Spring, Eagle Mountain, East of Deadman Pass, Resting Spring, Sixmile Spring, Stewart Valley, and Twelvemile Spring.
Management: BLM Barstow Resource Area, 150 Coolwater Lane, Barstow, CA 92311; (619) 255-8700.

Rice Valley Wilderness

The northwestern tip of the Big Maria Mountains, rising to about 2,000 feet above sea level, gives way to the broad, flat plains of Rice Valley within this Wilderness. Rice Valley is the southern end of a vast sheet of sand extending from Cadiz Valley in the north southward across Ward Valley. Relatively small as far as dunes go, the buff-colored sand of Rice Valley rises 30 to 40 feet above the valley floor and stretches in a long, narrow band along the middle of the region. Beyond the mountains, this is a Wilderness of sand.

CALIFORNIA

Rice Valley Essentials
Size: 40,820 acres.
Year Designated: 1994.
Location: Southeastern California.
Easiest Access: From Blythe, take Lovekin Boulevard north until it becomes Midland Road at the edge of town. Follow Midland Road for 17 miles. Turn north and go about five miles on the four-wheel-drive road to the Eagle Nest Mines, which lie on the southern boundary.
Season: Winter.
Wilderness Fees/Permits: None.
Maps: USGS topographic maps are Big Maria Mountains NW, Grommet, Rice, and Styx.
Management: BLM Palm Springs–South Coast Resource Area, 63-500 Garnet Avenue, P.O. Box 2000, North Palm Springs, CA 92258; (619) 251-4800.

Riverside Mountains Wilderness

With an eastern boundary that runs roughly parallel to the Colorado River, Riverside Mountains Wilderness varies from gently sloping bajadas to a rugged interior with numerous peaks and a craggy skyline. Canyons in the interior emerge from the mountains to open into washes that divide the bajadas. Big Wash crosses the western section and provides easy foot access. The northern section includes artifacts from several old mining operations. Foxtail cactuses and California barrel cactuses, both sensitive plants, dot the landscape. A small herd of burro deer call this Wilderness home.

Riverside Mountains Essentials
Size: 22,380 acres.
Year Designated: 1994.
Location: Southeastern California.
Easiest Access: From Blythe, take U.S. 95 north for 32 miles to past Lost Lake Resort. For the next four miles, several four-wheel-drive tracks go west to the Wilderness boundary.
Season: Winter.
Wilderness Fees/Permits: None.
Maps: USGS topographic maps are Big Maria Mountains NE, Big Maria Mountains NW, Parker SE, and Vidal.
Management: BLM Palm Springs–South Coast Resource Area, 63-500 Garnet Avenue, P.O. Box 2000, North Palm Springs, CA 92258; (619) 251-4800.

Rodman Mountains Wilderness

Colorful escarpments, white mountains splotched with red and black, a maze of canyons, and majestic bajadas come together in Rodman Mountains Wilderness. From northwest to southeast across the middle of the area, a large lava flow forms a long mesa that slices the terrain in two. More than a half-dozen natural tanks lie within the lava. Two of the tanks, named Hidden and Deep, contain thousands of gallons of water. Canyons with nearly vertical walls form deep drainage channels that cascade with water during desert storms. Faults created the valleys and ridges that play over the eastern and western portions of the area. Seven-mile Box Canyon is a non-Wilderness swath through the eastern portion, separating a small, far-eastern section from the rest of the Wilderness. The Rodman Mountains are one of only seven core breeding areas for raptors in the California Desert, and golden eagles and prairie falcons thrive here. Bighorn sheep have not been spotted in these mountains, but they have been seen in Newberry Mountains Wilderness (see above) to the west.

Rodman Mountains Essentials
Size: 27,690 acres.
Year Designated: 1994.
Location: Central southern California.
Easiest Access: From Interstate 40, just east of Daggett, take Camp Rock Road 18 miles south to Troy Road. The Wilderness lies northeast of the junction.
Season: Early spring and late fall.
Wilderness Fees/Permits: None.
Maps: USGS topographic maps are Camp Rock Mine, Newberry Springs, Silver Bell Mine, and Troy Lake.
Management: BLM Barstow Resource Area, 150 Coolwater Lane, Barstow, CA 92311; (619) 255-8700.

Russian Wilderness

Russian Wilderness sits astride a major ridge dividing the Scott River and Salmon River drainages with steep slopes and broad, U-shaped glacial valleys surrounded by granite peaks. You'll find 22 named lakes, most of them set like jewels in cirques high in the valleys and drained by streams. Lakes and streams contain rainbow, brook, and brown trout. A diverse array of plants can be found here, including 17 species of conifers—probably more than anywhere else in the world. The forests are laced with meadows, and rocky pinnacles and bluffs rise in numerous locations. Wildlife species include bountiful populations of deer and bears. Elevations range from 4,800 feet to Russian Peak's 8,200 feet.

An extensive trail system generally crosses steep and rocky ground, difficult going for stock animals. Stock forage is limited in most of the lakeside campsites. The Pacific Crest Trail (PCT) runs the entire length of the area north-south for about 17 miles, but stays high with few campsites and snow until late in the season. Despite its steep three miles, the Paynes Lake Trail to 17-acre, 50-feet-deep Paynes Lake is the most popular of the Wilderness pathways. Overall, human use is light.

Russian Essentials
Size: 12,000 acres.
Year Designated: 1984.
Location: Northern California.
Easiest Access: From Etna, on State Highway 3, travel 10 miles south and west on the Etna-Soames Bar Road to Etna Summit and the Pacific Coast Trail. The northern Wilderness boundary is two miles south.
Season: Spring through fall.
Wilderness Fees/Permits: None, but a campfire permit is required during fire season.
Maps: A Wilderness map that includes Marble Mountain Wilderness is available for $3 from the district rangers.
Management: Salmon River Ranger District, Klamath National Forest, P.O. Box 280, Etna, CA 96027; (916) 467-5757. Scott River Ranger District, Klamath National Forest, 11263 South Highway 3, Fort Jones, CA 96032; (916) 468-5351.

Sacatar Trail Wilderness

The 11-mile-long Sacatar Trail, an old wagon road and one of the few reminders that humans ever traveled regularly through this area, provides relatively easy access into this rugged and pristine Wilderness on the eastern slope of the southern Sierra Nevada Mountains. Valleys, canyons, and alluvial fans rise into steep hills that eventually peak along ridge tops and granite summits with elevations of more than 7,800 feet. Creosote bush, Joshua trees, and desert shrubs in the lower elevations change to scattered piñon and juniper woodlands dotted with cactuses higher up. In several of the canyons, you'll find springs that feed riparian habitats of cottonwoods, willows, and grasses. Mule deer flourish, along with golden eagles, prairie falcons, and other raptors, as well as game birds such as quail and dove. The Pacific Crest Trail passes not far to the west outside the boundary.

Sacatar Trail Essentials

Size: 51,900 acres.
Year Designated: 1994.
Location: Southern central California.
Easiest Access: From Little Lake, on U.S. 395, head north about three miles and turn west on the dirt road that leads up Sacatar Canyon. Go farther north on U.S. 395 to find the dirt roads into either Portuguese Canyon (two miles, four-wheel-drive vehicles only), Lewis Canyon (four miles), or Tunawee Canyon (2.5 miles on the north end). All lead to the eastern boundary.
Season: Spring or fall.
Wilderness Fees/Permits: None.
Maps: USGS topographic maps are Coso Junction, Lamont Peak, Little Lake, Long Canyon, Ninemile Canyon, and Sacatar Canyon.
Management: BLM Caliente Resource Area, 3801 Pegasus Avenue, Bakersfield, CA 93308; (805) 391-6000. BLM Ridgecrest Resource Area, 300 South Richmond Road, Ridgecrest, CA 93555; (619) 384-5400.

Saddle Peak Hills Wilderness

Smallest of the areas designated by the California Desert Protection Act of 1994, this Wilderness includes the northern end of the Saddle Peak Hills and the northwestern portion of the Silurian Valley. The southern and western boundaries are shared with Death Valley National Park. The hills are cut by curvy faults. Elevations range from 500 feet on the floor of the Silurian Valley to about 2,500 feet atop the hills. The terrain is typical of Southern California's desertland and desert mountains.

Saddle Peak Hills Essentials

Size: 1,440 acres.
Year Designated: 1994.
Location: Southeastern California.
Easiest Access: From Baker, take State Highway 127 north for about 38 miles to Ibex Springs Road. The Wilderness lies west of the highway for another three miles.
Season: Early spring and late fall.
Wilderness Fees/Permits: None.
Maps: USGS topographic maps are Ibex Pass and Saddle Peak Hills.
Management: BLM Barstow Resource Area, 150 Coolwater Lane, Barstow, CA 92311; (619) 255-8700.

CALIFORNIA

San Gabriel Wilderness

Extremely rugged and scenic terrain ranging in elevation from about 1,600 feet to 8,200 feet predominates in San Gabriel Wilderness. Dense thickets of chaparral in the low country yield to mixed pine- and fir-covered slopes and ridge tops, which rise in turn to majestic peaks and meadows rich with spring wildflowers. The area lies on the southern slopes of the San Gabriel Mountains, between the Angeles Crest and the West Fork of the San Gabriel River. A variety of wildlife lives in the higher elevations. Fishing will probably be fine in most of the streams.

Several paths lead into the interior of the area, where you can venture off-trail into some regions without too much difficulty. There are three entryways: Bear Creek (11 miles); Mount Waterman (10 miles), with a one-mile-long side trail to Twin Peak Saddle; and Devil's Canyon, which drops four miles into the canyon itself. Wood fires are not permitted because high fire danger threatens year-round. Backpacking stoves are permitted. Human use is moderate.

San Gabriel Essentials

Size: 36,118 acres.
Year Designated: 1968.
Location: Southwestern California.
Easiest Access: From Los Angeles, take State Highway 2 (Angeles Crest Highway) approximately 39 miles north and then east to the Devil's Canyon Trailhead on the east side of the road.
Season: Year-round, but it's hot in the summer.
Wilderness Fees/Permits: None, except a campfire permit is required for stove use.
Maps: The area is shown on the Angeles National Forest Map, available for $3.25 from the district rangers.
Management: Arroyo Seco Ranger District, Angeles National Forest, Oak Grove Park, La Canada, CA 91011; (818) 790-1151. Mount Baldy Ranger District, Angeles National Forest, 110 North Wabash, Glendora, CA 91740; (818) 335-1251.

San Gorgonio Wilderness

High above the crowded cities of Southern California, San Gorgonio Wilderness embraces the summit of the San Bernardino Mountain Range on national forestland and slides down the eastern slope onto 37,980 acres of BLM land added in 1994. An exquisite virgin forest protects meadows and two small lakes, while a forest opens onto massive barren slopes reaching from timberline to the top of San Gorgonio Mountain. At 11,502 feet, this is the highest point in all of Southern California. Unparalleled views of the area and the nearby desert can be seen from San Gorgonio Mountain and other high summits, including San Bernardino Peak (10,624 feet) and East San Bernardino Peak (10,630 feet). The entire area lies rough and rugged, with water often difficult to find. On the BLM land, which can be accessed from State Highway 62 at Morongo Valley, the topography alters rapidly from low hills and canyons to steep mountainsides. You'll find a great diversity of flora and fauna typical of deserts and alpine zones, coastal and mountain environments.

About 100 miles of trails, heavily used by humans, provide access to the area, primarily in the northern section with its lakes and high peaks. The San Bernardino Peak Divide Trail traverses 17.7 miles through some wondrous high country and ends at San Gorgonio Mountain. Wood fires are prohibited except in designated places. Grazing of livestock in meadows is prohibited.

San Gorgonio Essentials

Size: 94,702 acres.
Year Designated: 1964; expanded in 1984 and 1994.
Location: Southwestern California.
Easiest Access: From Redlands, take State Highway 38 east and then north for 21 miles to the Angeles Forest Service Facility and the San Bernardino Peak Divide Trailhead, which lies on the western side of the Wilderness.
Season: Spring through fall.
Wilderness Fees/Permits: Permits are required, and quotas limit the number issued for each trailhead. Contact the district ranger.
Maps: A Wilderness map covering the USFS section is available for $3 from the district ranger. USGS topographic maps covering the BLM section are Catclaw Flat, Morongo Valley, Onyx Peak, Rimrock, and White Water.
Management: San Gorgonio Ranger District, San Bernardino National Forest, Mill Creek Station, 34701 Mill Creek Road, Mentone, CA 92359; (714) 794-1123. BLM Palm Springs-South Coast Resource Area, 63-500 Garnet Avenue, P.O. Box 2000, North Palm Springs, CA 92258; (619) 251-4800.

San Jacinto Wilderness

Unique among designated areas, San Jacinto Wilderness, managed by the USFS, lies split in half by the Mount San Jacinto State Park and Wilderness, which is managed by the California Department of Parks and Recreation. The Boundaries embrace the grand San Jacinto Mountains (elevations from 6,000 feet to 10,000 feet), and the flora and fauna varies from desert to alpine. Steep cliffs and ridges descend dramatically from pine-covered peaks in the northern half of the Wilderness. In the central section, high mountain plateaus shelter lush, stream-splashed meadows surrounded by magnificent forests. In the south, a section known as the Desert Divide lies densely covered with stands of chaparral. On this divide's eastern flank, you'll find several deep, eroded, boulder-strewn desert canyons. Near the center of the Wilderness, two exceptional rock-climbing areas exist: Tahquitz Rock, with sustained routes of up to 1,000 feet, and Suicide Rock, with extremely difficult routes up to 400 feet.

Sixteen named trails provide access to the Wilderness, ranging in difficulty from easy to strenuous. The Pacific Crest Trail crosses the area for approximately 23 miles north-south. Human use is heavy.

CALIFORNIA

San Jacinto Essentials

Size: 32,040 acres.
Year Designated: 1964; expanded in 1984.
Location: Southwestern California.
Easiest Access: From Interstate 10 just eight miles west of Palm Springs, take State Highway 111 southeast for about one mile. Turn southwest on Snow Creek Road and go about two miles to where it joins the Pacific Crest Trail. Hike south into the Wilderness.
Season: June to October.

Wilderness Fees/Permits: A permit is required for day and overnight use. Quotas limit the number of people who can enter via the Devil's Slide Trailhead. Contact the district ranger for more information.
Maps: A Wilderness map is available for $3 from the district ranger.
Management: San Jacinto Ranger District, San Bernardino National Forest, 54270 Pinecrest, P.O. Box 518, Idyllwild, CA 92349; (714) 659-2117.

San Mateo Canyon Wilderness

Mountains covered with chaparral and coastal sage dominate the landscape of San Mateo Canyon Wilderness. Many deep drainages hide a lush growth of vegetation, with oak woodlands thick in the lower elevations. Annual rainfall averages 15 to 20 inches, most of it falling in winter and early spring; flash floods rip through narrow canyons in heavy downpours. Spring brings a wealth of wildflower blooms. Summers tend to be very hot and dry, though you will probably find small pools in San Mateo Canyon most of the year. Keep an eye open for wildlife: 139 bird species, 37 mammal species, 46 reptile and amphibian species, seven species of fish. Lizards, rattlesnakes, coyotes, skunks, and mice are commonly seen; the elusive mountain lion is rarely seen.

The east-west San Mateo Canyon Trail follows the main canyon for 7.5 miles near the center of the Wilderness, and provides access to what is probably the best camping in the area: fields of grass, shady stands of oak and sycamore, the best chances for water. This trail is joined by at least six others, most of them easy to moderate, including the 5.4-mile Tenaja Falls Trail. Tenaja Falls, when spring brings a rush of water, is a dramatic sight. Poison oak grows richly around the falls even when the creek dries up. Campfires are not permitted. This Wilderness receives light human use and can provide a wild and worthy experience, especially in spring.

San Mateo Canyon Essentials

Size: 39,540 acres.
Year Designated: 1984.
Location: Southwestern California.
Easiest Access: From Interstate 15, go southwest on Clinton Keith Road. Turn west on Tenaja Road and drive 9.9 miles. Turn north on Forest Service Road 7S01 and continue another five miles to the Tenaja Falls Trailhead. Four-wheel-drive vehicles are recommended.
Season: Spring and fall.

Wilderness Fees/Permits: A free permit is required to prior to entering the San Mateo Wilderness. Contact the district ranger for more information.
Maps: A free map without much detail is available from the district ranger. Ask about the specific topographic maps.
Management: Trabuco Ranger District, Cleveland National Forest, 1147 East Sixth Street, Corona, CA 91719; (909) 736-1811.

San Rafael Wilderness

After the initial preservation of land under the Wilderness Act of 1964, the original San Rafael Wilderness (1968) was the first Primitive area added to the NWPS's roster (see the introduction to the book). Here in the chaparral-covered San Rafael Mountains, elevations range from 1,166 feet near the confluence of Manzana Creek and the Sisquoc River in the west to over 6,800 feet on Big Pine Mountain near the eastern boundary and Dick Smith Wilderness (see above). Too rocky and shallow to entice river runners, except perhaps in spring high water, all but two of the Sisquoc's 33 Wild and Scenic miles are within the Wilderness, tumbling through pools and oak-shaded grasslands, over waterfalls and past archaeological sites. The region known as Hurricane Deck stretches for 17 miles of steep escarpments, grassy potreros, dry plateaus, and wind-carved sandstone formations. Wildflowers are abundant March through June. The Wilderness contains the Sisquoc Condor Sanctuary, and black bears and mountain lions also live here with numerous smaller animals.

San Rafael Wilderness has over 125 relatively rugged miles of trails that receive moderate human use. A path follows the Sisquoc River east-west for about 26 miles, and campsites abound. Large portions of the Wilderness are closed during fire season (July through mid-November) because of extreme fire danger.

San Rafael Essentials

Size: 197,010 acres.
Year Designated: 1968; expanded in 1984 and 1992.
Location: Southwestern California.
Easiest Access: From Los Olivos, just off U.S. 101, go north on Figueroa Mountain Road for approximately 14 miles to the national forest boundary. Just beyond the boundary, a four-wheel-drive road leads roughly 10 miles north to the Wilderness boundary and turns into a trail to the Sisquoc River.
Season: Spring.

Wilderness Fees/Permits: A California Campfire Permit is required.
Maps: USGS topographic maps are Bald Mountain, Bates Canyon, Big Pine Mountain, Fox Mountain, Hurricane Deck, Little Pine Mountain, Madulce Peak, Salisbury Potrero, and San Rafael Mountain.
Management: Santa Barbara Ranger District, Los Padres National Forest, Los Prietos, Star Route, Santa Barbara, CA 93105; (805) 967-3481. Santa Lucia Ranger District, Los Padres National Forest, 1616 Carlotti Drive, Santa Maria, CA 93454; (805) 925-9538.

Santa Lucia Wilderness

A stream that flows year-long through Lopez Canyon into Lopez Lake, lush streamside vegetation, and chaparral-covered slopes and peaks that rise above the canyon are the prime ingredients in the lightly visited Santa Lucia Wilderness. Elevations range from about 800 feet down in Lopez Canyon to about 3,000 feet near Hi Mountain Lookout at the eastern end.

Hiking the Lopez Canyon Trail along the stream will expose you to a wide assortment of vegetation, including stands of ancient oaks, much of them flourishing where a wildfire raged in 1985.

You can access the 5.3 miles of the Lopez Canyon Trail from East Cuesta Ridge and find pleasant campsites near the stream. Two 2.6-mile trails descend near Little Falls (with its 50-foot waterfall) and Big Falls (with a pair of dramatic waterfalls) into the canyon from the southern boundary. The Wilderness extends onto 1,733 acres of BLM land.

Santa Lucia Essentials

Size: 20,412 acres.
Year Designated: 1978.
Location: Southwestern California.
Easiest Access: Park at the turnout area at East Cuesta Pass, about two miles north of San Luis Obispo, on U.S. 101. Hike east from a locked gate just uphill from the turnout.
Season: Spring and fall.
Wilderness Fees/Permits: A required, free permit may be obtained from the district ranger.
Maps: USGS topographic maps are Lopez Mountain, Pozo Summit, Santa Margarita Lake, and Tar Spring Ridge.
Management: Santa Lucia Ranger District, Los Padres National Forest, 1616 North Carlotti Drive, Santa Maria, CA 93454; (805) 925-9538. BLM Bakersfield District, 3801 Pegasus Avenue, Bakersfield, CA 93308; (805) 391-6000.

Santa Rosa Wilderness

The California Desert Protection Act of 1994 added 64,340 acres of BLM land to Santa Rosa Wilderness, more than quadrupling the original USFS area and stretching it to the north, east, and south. The stark Colorado Desert, with its agave, ocotillo, and creosote, rises up boulder-strewn and eroded canyons to chaparral, juniper-, and pine-covered ridges. Elevations change drastically from just above sea level to over 7,000 feet. Seemingly desolate and inhospitable, the Santa Rosa Mountains are laced with deep washes and shallow drainages. Several riparian streams flow year-round. Blistering summer heat is sometimes relieved by thunderstorms that send torrents of water down the sandy washes. You'll find Bear Creek Oasis, Lost Canyon Oasis, Guadalupe Canyon, Devil Canyon, and Rockhouse Canyon highly scenic and worth the hike. Many of these regions are important lambing sites for bighorn sheep; in fact, the mountains support the largest herd of rare peninsular bighorn sheep in the United States. Coniferous forests high in these mountains provide habitat for mule deer, while the desert below houses numerous reptiles including the desert slender salamander. Great horned owls soar in the night skies, and falcons and eagles nest and forage throughout the Wilderness.

One maintained trail, the 9.5-mile Cactus Spring Trail, crosses the area past sources of water, but you may find it difficult to follow and strenuous. Old Indian trails are still evident in places, fading in and out of this hard country.

CALIFORNIA

Santa Rosa Essentials

Size: 84,500 acres.
Year Designated: 1984; expanded in 1994.
Location: Southwestern California.
Easiest Access: From Palm Springs, take State Highway 74 south for 16 miles to the Piñon Flat Campground turnoff. Turn south and then east on Forest Service Road 7S09. Go one-half mile to the parking lot for the Cactus Spring Trailhead.
Season: Early spring and late fall.
Wilderness Fees/Permits: None.
Maps: A Wilderness map covering the USFS portion is available for $3 from the district ranger. USGS topographic maps covering the BLM portion are Clark Lake NE, Indio, La Quinta, Martinez Mountain, Rabbit Peak, and Valerie.
Management: San Jacinto Ranger District, San Bernardino National Forest, P.O. Box 518, 54270 Pinecrest, Idyllwild, CA 92349; (714) 659-2117. BLM Palm Springs-South Coast Resource Area, 63-500 Garnet Avenue, P.O. Box 2000, North Palm Springs, CA 92258; (619) 251-4800.

Sawtooth Mountains Wilderness

Ridges extend like fingers from the Laguna Mountains east to become Sawtooth Mountains Wilderness, with elevations from 5,600 feet down to 1,400 feet. Valleys between the ridges unfold to become the desert alluvial fans of Vallecito Valley, Inner Pasture, and Canebrake Canyon. Vegetation transforms from dense chaparral at the higher elevations of the Lagunas to low desert creosote brush. More than 200 plant species have been identified here, many of them under consideration for threatened or endangered status. Although peninsular bighorn sheep once lived here, they are now transient visitors. You may see San Diego horned lizards, spotted bats, and willow flycatchers. Golden eagles, prairie falcons, Cooper's hawks, and other raptors spread their wings overhead.

State Route 2 runs near the northern boundary, but private land prevents legal access from that direction. The Pepperwood Height Trail from the south provides five miles of relatively easy foot or horse access. Springs may supply water.

Sawtooth Mountains Essentials

Size: 35,080 acres.
Year Designated: 1994.
Location: Southwestern California.
Easiest Access: About 21 miles east of Pine Valley, leave Interstate 8 at the Manzanita Boulevard exit. Follow State Route 94 (Old Highway 80) east two miles to McCain Valley Road. Continue about 13 miles to Cottonwood Campground and the Pepperwood Height Trailhead.
Season: Early spring and late fall.
Wilderness Fees/Permits: None.
Maps: USGS topographic maps are Agua Caliente Springs, Monument Peak, and Mount Laguna.
Management: BLM Palm Springs-South Coast Resource Area, 63-500 Garnet Avenue, P.O. Box 2000, North Palm Springs, CA 92258; (619) 251-4800.

Sequoia-Kings Canyon Wilderness

Sequoia National Park, America's second oldest park, was eventually joined with Kings Canyon National Park to form an area described only with multiple superlatives, a parkland of which everything off the beaten track has been designated Wilderness. Here in the heart of California wildland, almost surrounded by other designated Wildernesses, you'll find some of the most glorious scenery on Earth, a world of high peaks, deep canyons, lush meadows, bright lakes, rushing rivers, sparkling streams, and big, big trees.

Nothing living in the world grows larger than giant sequoias. They can achieve over 300 feet in height, more than 2.7 million pounds in weight, bases over 40 feet in diameter, bark over 30 inches thick, and more than 3,200 years in age. No wonder John Muir wrote that "one naturally walked softly and awe-stricken among them." In their shadow one gains a sense of being more in a cathedral than a forest.

To the west, the park descends to dry foothills of oak and chaparral toward the San Joaquin Valley. To the south runs the Middle Fork of the Kaweah River, as well as the Wild and Scenic North Fork of the Kern River. Boating is not allowed within the park, but outside, the Kern provides some of the best white water on the planet. To the east stands the crest of the Sierra Nevada and the highest mountain in the Lower 48, Mount Whitney at 14,495 feet, shared with John Muir Wilderness. Across the heart of the area runs Kings Canyon at depths virtually unparalleled, prompting Muir to dub it "a rival to Yosemite." It is cut by the Wild and Scenic South Fork of the Kings River, which flows out of the park to meet with the Wild and Scenic North Fork of the Kings River. Boating, once again, is not allowed on the riverways within the park. But fishing for rainbow, brown, brook, and golden trout can be outstanding in the Kings River, in the forks of the Kaweah, and in high-mountain lakes and streams. Even if the fish aren't biting, the scenery is worth the trip.

The Pacific Crest Trail-John Muir Trail crosses the park for perhaps 65 miles north-south near the eastern boundary. Numerous other trails provide access to much of the wonders of the area. Humans come in hordes.

Sequoia-Kings Canyon Essentials

Size: 736,980 acres.
Year Designated: 1984.
Location: Eastern central California.
Easiest Access: For the western side, take State Highway 180 from Fresno, about 63 miles to Kings Canyon National Park; or take State Highway 198 from Visalia, about 37 miles to Sequoia National Park. The eastern side is only accessible by foot.
Season: Summer.
Wilderness Fees/Permits: A park entrance fee of $5 per vehicle or $3 per person is charged. Visitation is by permit only. Advance registration, at least three weeks prior to your trip, is strongly recommended. For reservation information, call (209) 565-3708, or write to the park, Attn: Wilderness Permits.
Maps: Trails Illustrated's Map 205, *Sequoia-Kings Canyon National Park*, is an excellent resource.
Management: Sequoia-Kings Canyon National Park, Three Rivers, CA 93271; (209) 565-3341.

CALIFORNIA

Sespe Wilderness

Sespe Wilderness provides ample evidence of past violent geological upthrusts. The landscape is bleak and jagged, and if you climb high enough, you'll find pine trees growing at odd angles on boulder-swept hillsides. Sespe Creek, the last remaining undammed river in Southern California, runs for 31.5 Wild and Scenic miles (most of it in the Wilderness), and 10.5 miles of Upper Sespe Creek are under consideration for designation. Sandstone cliffs rise as much as 500 feet above the water in places, and fabulous sandstone formations stand in portions of the area. You may see petroglyphs and other evidence of ancient Indians. The 53,000-acre Sespe Condor Sanctuary is located here, and you might also spot black bears, deer, mountain lions, bobcats, coyotes, rattlesnakes, red-tailed hawks, and golden eagles. The area is a part of the fourth largest roadless region left in the Lower 48, and it's the one closest to a large metropolitan area.

Numerous trails provide access, and human use is heavy. The Gene Marshall-Piedra Blanca National Recreation Trail leads 8.7 miles through impressive white rocks to pleasant campsites nestled in conifers, a boon when much of the area lies without shade. The Sespe River Trail (17.5 miles) leads past cool swimming holes that thin down to shallows in the dry period, and on to Sespe Hot Springs and some of the hottest natural water in America.

Sespe Essentials

Size: 219,700 acres.
Year Designated: 1992.
Location: Southwestern California.
Easiest Access: From Ojai, take State Highway 33 north for 17.5 miles to Beaver Campground. Hike the Middle Sespe Trail eight miles east to where it joins the Sespe River Trail and enters the Wilderness.
Season: Spring and fall.
Wilderness Fees/Permits: Free camping and campfire permits are required.
Maps: USGS topographic maps are Black Mountain, Cobblestone Mountain, Devils Heart Peak, Fillmore, Lockwood Valley, Lion Canyon, McDonald Peak, Ojai, Piru, San Guillermo, Santa Paula Peak, and Topatopa Mountains.
Management: Ojai Ranger District, Los Padres National Forest, 1190 East Ojai Avenue, Ojai, CA 93023; (805) 646-4348. Mount Pinos Ranger District, Los Padres National Forest, Frazier Park, CA 93225; (805) 245-3731.

CALIFORNIA

Sheep Mountain Wilderness

Extremely rugged terrain dominates Sheep Mountain Wilderness, with elevations from about 2,400 feet to 10,064-foot Mount Baldy (also known as Mount San Antonio), the highest point in the San Gabriel Mountains. The East Fork of the San Gabriel River, Prairie Fork, and Upper Lytle Creek drain the area. Chaparral covers the lower slopes, changing to a mountain forest of mixed Southern California evergreens. A rich diversity of wildlife includes Nelson bighorn sheep, deer, coyotes, bears, and mountain lions. Several inholdings of privately owned land occur within the Wilderness borders and deserve special consideration.

The Pacific Crest Trail skirts the northern boundary crossing Mount Baden-Powell at 9,399 feet. Several trails lead into the interior. The Mine Gulch Trail enters from the north to join the East Fork Trail to cross the entire Wilderness from north to south (about 13 miles total). Human use is moderate.

Sheep Mountain Essentials

Size: 43,600 acres.
Year Designated: 1984.
Location: Southwestern California.
Easiest Access: From Wrightwood, north of Los Angeles, drive east on State Highway 2 (Angeles Crest Highway) for 11 miles to the parking lot at Vincent Gap. The Mine Gulch Trail heads south into the Wilderness.
Season: Year-round, but summers are hot.
Wilderness Fees/Permits: A free visitors permit is required. A California Campfire Permit is required even if you only intend to cook on a backpacking stove. Contact the district rangers.
Maps: A Wilderness map is available from the district rangers.
Management: Arroyo Seco Ranger District, Angeles National Forest, Oak Grove Park, Flintridge, CA 91101; (818) 790-1151. Mount Baldy Ranger District, Angeles National Forest, 110 North Wabash, Glendora, CA 91740; (818) 335-1251. Cajon Ranger District, San Bernardino National Forest, 1209 Lytle Creek Road, Lytle Creek, CA 92358; (909) 887-2576.

Sheephole Valley Wilderness

Both the Sheephole and the Calumet Mountains are encompassed by Sheephole Valley Wilderness, which also includes the vast sandy valley between them. Steep and laden with boulders, the Sheephole Mountains are a granitic mass reaching a height of 4,600 feet. The Calumets are similar in appearance but rise only half as high. Sparsely vegetated, the mountains may produce a nice show of wildflowers in the washes after a substantial seasonal rain. Bighorn sheep live in the Sheephole Mountains, and desert tortoises in the valley.

Without springs and without trails, this Wilderness will be a challenge, even for the most experienced desert hiker. Spectacular Joshua Tree National Park lies across State Highway 62 to the south.

CALIFORNIA

Sheephole Valley Essentials

Size: 174,800 acres.
Year Designated: 1994.
Location: Southern California.
Easiest Access: From Twentynine Palms, take State Highway 62 east for approximately 20 miles. The southern Wilderness boundary lies just north of the highway for the next 21 miles.
Season: Early spring and late fall.
Wilderness Fees/Permits: None.
Maps: USGS topographic maps are Bristol Lake NW, Bristol Lake SW, Cadiz Lake, Cadiz Lake NW, Cadiz Valley NW, Cadiz Valley SE, Cadiz Valley SW, Calumet Mine, Calumet Mountains, Clarks Pass, Dale Lake, East of Dale Lake, and New Dale.
Management: BLM Needles Resource Area, 101 West Spikes Road, Needles, CA 92363; (619) 326-3896.

Silver Peak Wilderness

Encompassing the drainages of Willow Creek and Salmon Creek, Silver Peak Wilderness rises sharply from near the shore of the Pacific Ocean, an area of steep terrain that's part of the Santa Lucia Mountains. Silver Peak lifts to 3,590 feet in the northwestern section. Lush vegetation along the creeks, fern-covered canyons, grass and oak-dotted meadows, and heavy timber are some of the area's features. The Wilderness hides the world's southernmost stand of redwoods, an isolated grove of coastal redwoods. Also hidden here is a grove of rare Sargent cypress, gray pines, and Santa Lucia fir. Waterfalls brighten some of the streams in spring. From the higher country, on a clear day, you can see the Big Sur coastline to the north, the Pacific Ocean rolling restlessly to the west, and the Salinas Valley to the east. You may spot deer and squirrels, rabbits and raccoons, and perhaps hear a gobble from a wild turkey.

Trails require moderate to strenuous exercise. The most popular pathway follows Salmon Creek for about 3.5 miles and offers a great view of Salmon Creek Falls. From Salmon Creek, you can take the trail leading to Redwood Creek (two miles) or other trails climbing north across the Wilderness.

Silver Peak Essentials

Size: 14,500 acres.
Year Designated: 1992.
Location: Southwestern central California on the coast.
Easiest Access: From San Simeon, take U.S. 1 north 1.5 miles past the Monterey County line. Look for the Salmon Creek Trailhead on the east side of the highway.
Season: Spring through early fall.
Wilderness Fees/Permits: Campfire permits are required from May through November.
Maps: USGS topographic maps are Alder Peak, Burnett Peak, and Burro Mountain.
Management: Monterey Ranger District, Los Padres National Forest, 406 South Mildred Avenue, King City, CA 93930; (408) 385-5434.

CALIFORNIA

Siskiyou Wilderness

Forested ridges and craggy peaks with lower slopes densely covered with brush generally describes Siskiyou Wilderness. You'll also discover fragile mountain meadows, open glades, shallow lakes, and the Wild and Scenic South Fork of the Smith River, which forms a large portion of the western boundary. Clear Creek and the headwaters of the East Fork of the Illinois River flow perennially through the Wilderness. Summer populations of steelhead attract anglers. The area is noted for its great diversity of plant life, and includes one of the world's largest concentrations of lily species and perhaps as many as 20 species of conifers. Here grows the rare Brewers spruce (the "weeping" spruce). Forage is limited, and stock users are advised to carry feed. Summers are usually very warm, but cold can strike any night of the year and severe storms are common year-round.

The Clear Creek National Recreation Trail crosses 20.5 miles of the northern portion and provides access to some of the more scenic parts of the Wilderness. Human use is light and concentrated on the trails that lead to lakes. Much of the area lacks trails and is difficult to access cross country because of the dense brush. Many authorities on the subject suspect Bigfoot could be hiding out in the untrammeled regions.

Siskiyou Essentials

Size: 153,000 acres.
Year Designated: 1984.
Location: Northwestern California.
Easiest Access: From U.S. 199 in California's extreme northwestern corner, eight miles from the Oregon border, turn south on Forest Service Road 18N07. Follow the road about 12 miles to the Clear Creek Trailhead.
Season: July to mid-October.

Wilderness Fees/Permits: None.
Maps: A free Wilderness map is available from the district rangers. Ask about specific USGS topographic maps.
Management: Happy Camp Ranger District, Klamath National Forest, P.O. Box 377, Happy Camp, CA 96039; (916) 493-2243. Gasquet Ranger District, Six Rivers National Forest, P.O. Box 228, Gasquet, CA 95543; (707) 457-3131.

Snow Mountain Wilderness

Snow Mountain is the southernmost peak in the North Coast Range. In Snow Mountain Wilderness, you'll find the transition zone between the Coast Range and the lower valley foothills. Higher elevations are relatively flat and eroded, with some stands of red fir and large expanses of bare ground with trails that provide vast overlooks. Mid-elevations are covered in red, white, and Douglas fir and ponderosa pine growing on steep to very steep slopes dissected by stream-cut ravines. Chaparral brushlands and oak woodlands dominate the lowest elevations with many opportunities for relatively easy cross-country travel. The Middle Fork of Stony Creek forms the primary drainage, shadowed in many places by rocky bluffs. You'll see some regions recently destroyed by fire. The diversity of wildlife is great: 122 species including deer, bear, mountain lion, eagle, and hawk.

There are about 52 miles of trails suitable for horsepacker or backpacker. If you prefer horseback and less-peopled places, you'll find

225

CALIFORNIA

this area an exceptional choice. The Overlook Loop provides an excellent vantage point from which to survey the Wilderness: 6.5 miles across old burns, up to high vistas, down into Dark Hollow Creek, and back to the Summit Springs Trailhead. Human use is light.

Snow Mountain Essentials

Size: 37,000 acres.
Year Designated: 1984.
Location: Northwestern central California.
Easiest Access: From Stonyford, take Fouts Spring Road (PFS Route M10) west to Fouts Springs. Continue on M10 for another 17 miles to Summit Springs Trailhead, which leads to the Overlook Trail.
Season: Late spring through early fall.

Wilderness Fees/Permits: None.
Maps: A Wilderness map is available for $3 from the district rangers.
Management: Upper Lake Ranger District, Mendocino National Forest, 10025 Elk Mountain Road, Upper Lake, CA 95485; (707) 275-2361. Stonyford Ranger District, Mendocino National Forest, 5080 Lodoga Stonyford Road, Stonyford, CA 95979; (916) 963-3128.

South Nopah Range Wilderness

Easily rolling alluvial slopes (bajadas) from the east and west sweep gently up to the south end of the rugged folds of the Nopah Mountain Range in the South Nopah Range Wilderness. Shaded with soft colors, the Nopah Range is composed of sedimentary rocks capped at about 4,200 feet. The California Valley extends into the eastern Wilderness. Desert bighorn sheep may be seen here, especially in the northern portion, along with wild horses and wild burros. A few prairie falcons have been spotted hunting over the low desert regions. Vegetation is sparse but the environment is known to support the ivory-spined agave plant. You should see evidence of old mining activity in the southern portion. You won't find any trails or much water to drink. Just across the Old Spanish Trail on the north end lies Nopah Range Wilderness (see above).

South Nopah Range Essentials

Size: 16,780 acres.
Year Designated: 1994.
Location: Southeastern California.
Easiest Access: From Tecopa, take the Old Spanish Trail east about three miles. The road forms the northern Wilderness boundary for the next eight miles.
Season: Early spring and late fall.

Wilderness Fees/Permits: None.
Maps: USGS topographic maps are North of Tecopa Pass, Resting Spring, Tecopa, and Tecopa Pass.
Management: BLM Barstow Resource Area, 150 Coolwater Lane, Barstow, CA 92311; (619) 255-8700.

South Sierra Wilderness

With Golden Trout Wilderness on its northern boundary and Domeland Wilderness on its southern (except for the road to Kennedy Meadows), South Sierra Wilderness straddles the crest of the Sierra Nevada at the southern end of the range. Here you'll find fragile meadowland with a great diversity of flora and fauna situated between forested ridges, rolling hills, and craggy peaks. On the western side (in Sequoia National Forest), the terrain is relatively gentle and easy to travel, forested in fir and pine. The crest and eastern portion (in Inyo National Forest) is far more steep and dissected, making for rugged and strenuous travel; it's an arid landscape, spotted by piñon and juniper. Elevations range from 6,100 feet near Kennedy Meadows to 12,123 feet on Olancha Peak. The Wild and Scenic South Fork of the Kern River and a few perennial streams drain the area, all of which lies in the watershed of the Kern. Much of the Wilderness is dry part of the year.

The Pacific Crest Trail (PCT) crosses about 11 miles of the Wilderness in a north-south direction. About 30 miles of trails suitable for both hiker and horse receive light human use.

South Sierra Essentials

Size: 63,000 acres.
Year Designated: 1984.
Location: Southern central California.
Easiest Access: From U.S. 395, seven miles south of Little Lake, turn west on Nine Mile Canyon Road. Take this for 24 miles to Kennedy Meadows and the trailheads heading north (including the Pacific Coast Trail).
Season: Spring and fall.
Wilderness Fees/Permits: Campfire permits are required. Contact the district rangers.
Maps: A Wilderness map is available for $3.25 from the district rangers.
Management: Cannell Meadow Ranger District, Sequoia National Forest, P.O. Box 6, 105 Whitney Road, Kernville, CA 93238; (619) 376-3781. Mount Whitney Ranger District, Inyo National Forest, P.O. Box 8, Lone Pine, CA 93545; (619) 876-6200.

South Warner Wilderness

On an isolated spur of the Cascade Range you'll find the Warner Mountains and the South Warner Wilderness, which stretches about 18 miles long and 8 miles wide. Elevations vary from 5,800 feet at Clear Lake near the southwest boundary to 9,892 feet on Eagle Peak, a conspicuous landmark near the center of the area. Gently rolling topography on the western side, highlighted by mountain meadows and clear streams, forested with mixed pines, firs, and aspen, rises to rugged country dominated by ragged peaks where vegetation is sparse. Wildflowers bloom in abundance. Of seven lakes, Clear, Patterson, and North Emerson provide the best fishing for rainbow, brook, brown, and redband trout. Severe storms have been known to roll in every month of the year.

Eight trailheads provide access to about 79 miles of maintained trails suitable for horse or foot traffic. Horsepackers will find outstanding opportunities for quiet travel in lovely surroundings. Most humans visit Clear and Patterson Lakes, Pine Creek Basin, and the Summit Trail, which rambles 22.5 miles north-south through the heart of the Wilderness. Human use of these trails is light—and it's even lighter on another 23 miles of unmaintained trails.

CALIFORNIA

South Warner Essentials

Size: 70,385 acres.
Year Designated: 1964; expanded in 1984.
Location: Northeastern California.
Easiest Access: From Alturas, take County Road 56 south for one mile. Turn east on Parker Creek Road and travel 21 miles to the Pepperdine Trailhead of the Summit Trail.

Season: July through October.
Wilderness Fees/Permits: None.
Maps: A Wilderness map is available for $3 from the district ranger.
Management: Warner Mountain Ranger District, Modoc National Forest, P.O. Box 220, Cedarville, CA 96104; (916) 279-6116.

Stateline Wilderness

Just as its name implies, Stateline Wilderness lies near the Nevada-California state line, a rocky, mountainous part of the far northern extreme of the Clark Mountains. Small, dry, and desolate, this area sees few humans. Desert bighorn sheep migrate between the Clarks in California and the Spring Mountains of Nevada. In the southern portion, tracks lead to the remains of a couple of old mines. The northeast corner of the Mojave National Preserve is just to the southwest of the Wilderness border.

Stateline Essentials

Size: 7,050 acres.
Year Designated: 1994.
Location: Southeastern California.
Easiest Access: Exit Interstate 15 at the Nevada state line and go north on Stateline Pass Road. After about three miles, the Wilderness lies due west of the road for the next five miles. High-clearance vehicles are recommended.

Season: Early spring and late fall.
Wilderness Fees/Permits: None.
Maps: USGS topographic maps are Ivanpah Lake, Mesquite Lake, and State Line Pass.
Management: BLM Needles Resource Area, 101 West Spikes Road, Needles, CA 92363; (619) 326-3896.

Stepladder Mountains Wilderness

Bleak and uninviting to most humans, the dry Stepladder Mountains extend about 10 miles north and south from the center of the Wilderness that bears their name. The mountains make up about 15 percent of the area, with the rest covered by flat bajadas dotted with creosote bush scrub. About 45 square miles of the northern portion are densely covered with Bigelow cholla, and you may find small stands of crucifixion thorn. Stiff, sturdy, and gray green—and quite rare in the California Desert—the crucifixion thorn grows six to eight feet tall at maturity with branches that resemble the crown of thorns placed on the head of Jesus. The larger washes of the Stepladders and the bajadas are habitat for desert tortoises. Bighorn sheep occasionally cross the area.

Stepladder Mountains Essentials

Size: 81,600 acres.
Year Designated: 1994.
Location: Southeastern California.
Easiest Access: From Needles, take U.S. 95 south about 25 miles. Turn west on Turtle Mountain Road and go approximately two miles. The southern Wilderness boundary lies just to the north of the road for the next 17 miles. High-clearance vehicles are recommended.
Season: Early spring and late fall.
Wilderness Fees/Permits: None.
Maps: USGS topographic maps are Mohawk Spring, Savahia Peak NW, Snaggletooth, Stepladder Mountains, Stepladder Mountains NE, Stepladder Mountains NW, Stepladder Mountains SW, and West of Mohawk Spring.
Management: BLM Needles Resource Area, 101 West Spikes Road, Needles, CA 92363; (619) 326-3896.

Surprise Canyon Wilderness

Surprise Canyon Wilderness shares its entire eastern border with Death Valley National Park. It contains small alluvial slopes that gradually rise from the west into the jagged ridges and steep sides of the Panamint Mountains. Canyons cut deeply into the mountains to form the interior of the Wilderness. Old four-wheel-drive tracks crawl through Jail, Hall, and Surprise Canyons and into the park; these non-Wilderness corridors carve the area into four sections. Elevations climb eagerly from about 1,000 feet in the west to more than 7,000 feet in the east, bestowing extraordinary vistas of the Panamint Valley from mountain summits. Creosote bush scrub and desert holly grow on alluvial fans. Cottonwoods and willows stand tall in the canyons, whose rocky walls sometimes support the rare and endangered Panamint daisy. Forests of piñon and juniper annoint the higher elevations. In addition to the views from on high, the Wilderness is graced by the lush riparian habitats of Jail, Surprise, and Happy Canyons (Happy Canyon forms the southern boundary). If you're wondering what inspired the canyon's jaunty moniker, it stems from the "surprise" travelers experience when they stumble into the unexpected springs bubbling from the steep walls of Surprise Canyon; the springs feed a yearlong flow of water. Most of Surprise Canyon has been designated an Area of Critical Environmental Concern in order to protect wildlife (including desert bighorn sheep and Panamint alligator lizards), vegetation, and historic and cultural resources.

Surprise Canyon Essentials

Size: 29,180 acres.
Year Designated: 1994.
Location: Southeastern California.
Easiest Access: From Ridgecrest, take State Highway 178 east until you are about 27 miles past Trona (where the road is called the Trona-Wildrose Road). Turn south on the four-wheel-drive Indian Ranch Road and continue to Surprise Canyon Road.
Season: Early spring and late fall.
Wilderness Fees/Permits: None.
Maps: USGS topographic maps are Ballarat, Jail Canyon, Maturango Peak NE, Panamint, and Telescope Peak.
Management: BLM Ridgecrest Resource Area, 300 South Richmond Road, Ridgecrest, CA 93555; (619) 384-5400.

CALIFORNIA

Sylvania Mountains Wilderness

The Sylvania Mountains are shared by California and Nevada, and the Wilderness starts on the desert floor and rises eastward over gradually rolling hills to rough and mountainous terrain reaching nearly 8,000 feet in height. Sagebrush scrub dominates the vegetation on the east, and gives way to piñon pine and juniper at the higher elevations. From the higher country, you can look south over the Last Chance Range into Death Valley National Park, north across dry Fish Lake Valley, and west to Piper Mountain—the sheer immensity of the region is a humbling experience. You might see deer, chukar partridge, and bighorn sheep roaming about. You won't see trails or water.

Sylvania Mountains Essentials

Size: 17,820 acres.
Year Designated: 1994.
Location: Eastern California.
Easiest Access: From Big Pine, take State Highway 168 east and north about 32 miles. Turn south on Eureka Valley Road, which forms the western Wilderness boundary south of Sylvania Canyon. You can turn east from Eureka Valley Road in six more miles on a track up Sylvania Canyon, which forms the northern boundary.
Season: Early spring and late fall.
Wilderness Fees/Permits: None.
Maps: USGS topographic maps are Horse Thief Canyon, Last Chance Mountain, Sylvania Canyon, and Sylvania Mountains.
Management: BLM Ridgecrest Resource Area, 300 South Richmond Road, Ridgecrest, CA 93555; (619) 384-5400.

Thousand Lakes Wilderness

There may not be a thousand lakes here, but the exaggeration is understandable given the area's seven major bodies of crystalline water and myriad smaller ponds. They are sprinkled throughout an area of mountainous volcanic and glacial formations, rocky ravines, open meadows, and stands of lodgepole pine and red fir. The highest point in Lassen National Forest at 8,677 feet, Crater Peak presides over this water-blessed Wilderness and serves as a reminder of the glacial erosion that wore down Thousand Lakes Volcano to today's terrain. Near the base of the old volcano, you'll find the area's lowest point at 5,546 feet. Mammal enthusiasts might expect sightings of black-tailed deer, black bear, pine marten, and pika, while bird-watchers train their binoculars on goshawks, spotted owls, pileated woodpeckers, and Clark's nutcrackers.

Four trailheads give access to about 22 miles of maintained trails. This area will serve you well if you wish a short Wilderness trip, especially if you enjoy fishing. Many people already know this, and Thousand Lakes receives heavy human use, with trout anglers forming the biggest contingent. From the Bunchgrass Trailhead, you can cross south to north, a scenic six-mile path through the area with the greatest concentration of lakes, and out to the Cypress Trailhead. Snow usually melts by early June, just as the mosquitoes begin to hatch in thick swarms.

CALIFORNIA

Thousand Lakes Essentials

Size: 16,335 acres.
Year Designated: 1964.
Location: Northern California.
Easiest Access: From Mount Shasta, take State Highway 89 south for 25 miles past Doyles Corner. Turn northwest on Forest Service Road 16 and go about seven miles. Turn east on Road 32N45 and continue two miles. Turn north on Road 32N42Y to the Bunchgrass Trailhead.

Season: Late summer and early fall.
Wilderness Fees/Permits: None.
Maps: A Wilderness map is available from the district ranger. USGS topographic maps are Jacks Backbone and Thousand Lakes Valley.
Management: Hat Creek Ranger District, Lassen National Forest, P.O. Box 220, Fall River Mills, CA 96028; (916) 336-5521.

Trilobite Wilderness

Fossilized remains of trilobites, any of numerous extinct Paleozoic marine arthropods with three longitudinal lobes divided into lateral furrows across their backs, may be found here in Trilobite Wilderness, which encompasses a large portion of the broken and dry Marble Mountains.

Alternating dark and light brown striations have been wrought by geologic upheavals, giving these mountains their distinctive marbled look. Long alluvial fans spread out on both sides of the mountains, and the center is dominated by several prominent sandstone peaks with extensive talus slopes tumbling down their sides. With any luck, you'll see members of one of the largest and fastest-growing desert bighorn sheep herds in the Mojave Desert.

Trilobite Essentials

Size: 31,160 acres.
Year Designated: 1994.
Location: Southeastern California.
Easiest Access: From Barstow, take Interstate 40 east 28 miles past Ludlow. Take the Kelbaker Road exit and travel south one mile to where the road intersects a pipeline. Follow the pipeline road east for one mile. The rough pipeline road forms the northern boundary for 11 miles.

Season: Early spring and late fall.
Wilderness Fees/Permits: None.
Maps: USGS topographic maps are Amboy, Brown Buttes, Cadiz, Cadiz Summit, Castle Dome, and Van Winkle Wash.
Management: BLM Needles Resource Area, 101 West Spikes Road, Needles, CA 92363; (619) 326-3896.

Trinity Alps Wilderness

Formerly known as the Salmon-Trinity Alps Primitive Area, the acreage of this rugged and isolated Wilderness of mountain ridges and deep canyons was almost doubled by the California Wilderness Act of 1984. Drained in the south by the Wild and Scenic Trinity River and in the north by the Wild and Scenic Salmon River, numerous rushing streams feed into the rivers, many of them emerging from the region's 55 lakes. Scattered stands of timber, some of them virgin, are opened by large meadows wild with flowers in July and August, and shadowed by barren rock cliffs and stark peaks with elevations up to about 9,000 feet. Black bears are common (despite the name, they're often colored brown or blond), sharing the area with an abundance of other wildlife species. As much as 12 feet of snow falls on the high country every year. A piece of the Wilderness along the Trinity River (4,623 acres) lies on BLM land, while the rest of this vast area, one of the state's largest, is situated on USFS land.

The Pacific Crest Trail crosses about eight miles of the northern Wilderness, one piece of an extensive and dazzlingly scenic trail system. The 4.6-mile trail to the top of Granite Peak ranks among the most strenuous, but intrepid hikers are rewarded with a magnificent view. If you're not quite up to that vertical challenge, the trail to Stoddard and McDonald Lakes stretches out comfortably in an easy 3.5-mile walk through thick forest and meadows with exquisite scenery all around. Numerous loop hikes requiring three to seven days to complete will tempt you to stay longer in this wildland. There are many regions of the Wilderness where you should be able to find extreme solitude.

Trinity Alps Essentials

Size: 500,000 acres.
Year Designated: 1984.
Location: Northern California.
Easiest Access: From Interstate 5, take the South Yreka/State Highway 3 exit. Go south about 10 miles past Callahan, to where the Pacific Crest Trail crosses the road. Hike southeast into the Wilderness.
Season: Mid-June to mid-October.
Wilderness Fees/Permits: Free permits are required from the district rangers.
Maps: A Wilderness map is available for $3 from the district rangers.
Management: Big Bar Ranger District, Shasta-Trinity National Forest, Star Route 1, Box 10, Big Bar, CA 96010; (916) 623-6106. Weaverville Ranger District, Shasta-Trinity National Forest, P.O. Box 1190, Weaverville, CA 96093; (916) 623-2121. Salmon River Ranger District, Klamath National Forest, P.O. Box 280, Etna, CA 96027; (916) 467-5757. Six Rivers National Forest, 500 Fifth Street, Eureka, CA 95501; (707) 442-9242. BLM Ukiah District Office, 555 Leslie Street, Ukiah, CA 95482; (707) 462-3873.

CALIFORNIA

Turtle Mountains Wilderness

Broad, open bajadas stretch out below eroded volcanic spires, cliffs, and multilayered mesas in Turtle Mountains Wilderness, an area that deserves consideration as one of the brightest pearls of the California Desert. The Turtle Mountains are roughly horseshoe shaped, with a large, flat interior valley cut by numerous shallow washes and opening to the southeast into the Vidal Valley. Spectacular red basalt peaks rise as cones in several places, the remnants of volcanoes that spewed fiery lava across the area a few thousand years ago. Colors that rival the canyonlands of Utah paint the Turtle Mountains, especially the northern portion: deep red, pink, brown, gold, green, tan, gray, and black. In the transition zone between the low Colorado Desert and the high Mojave, you should see the northernmost examples of some plants, including California fan palm and crucifixion thorn. Ironwood, paloverde, and smoke tree are also common in the area, as are bighorn sheep, desert tortoises, and numerous raptors. To the east and west, the mountains are separated from the rest of the world by five to ten miles of desert pavement. Names such as Mopah Spring, Mohawk Spring, Coffin Spring, and Horn Spring will tempt you to think water is more abundant here than it really is; don't count on them to be bubbling away when you hike by. Despite the unreliable water sources, the Turtle Mountains remain a desert hiker's delight.

Turtle Mountains Essentials

Size: 144,500 acres.
Year Designated: 1994.
Location: Southeastern California.
Easiest Access: From Needles, take U.S. 95 south about 25 miles. Turn west on Turtle Mountain Road and go about 10 miles until you reach the fork in the road. Take the south fork for approximately three miles to a place called Brown's Cabin or Carson's Well. Hike south into the Wilderness. Four-wheel-drive vehicles are recommended.
Season: Winter through early spring.
Wilderness Fees/Permits: None.
Maps: USGS topographic maps are Arica Mountains, East of Milligan, Horn Spring, Martins Well, Mohawk Spring, Nopah Peaks, Rice, Sablon, Savahia Peak SW, Vidal NW, West of Mohawk Spring, and Wilhelm Spring.
Management: BLM Needles Resource Area, 101 West Spikes Road, Needles, CA 92363; (619) 326-3896.

Ventana Wilderness

Legend relates that the unique notch at the summit of Ventana Double Cone (4,853 feet) was once connected by a rock bridge forming a window, or *ventana* in Spanish. Established as a Primitive area in 1931 and gaining Wilderness status in 1969, Ventana straddles the Santa Lucia Mountains south of the Monterey Peninsula, an area of ruggedly beautiful coastal mountains. You'll find steep-sided, sharp-crested ridges and craggy peaks falling into V-shaped valleys wondrously hidden from the outside world. Elevations range from 600 feet where the Wild and Scenic Big Sur River leaves the Wilderness to 5,750 feet where the boundary circumvents Junipero Serra Peak in the eastern section (which is separated from the main section by Arroyo Seco Indians Road). Most of the streams fall rapidly through narrow canyons over bedrock or exposed boulders, and waterfalls, deep pools, and thermal springs can be found along the major streams. A great diversity of vegetation is dominated by chaparral, the brushy cover that grows over much of Central and Southern California. Grassy meadows and stands of pine are located throughout the area, and virgin coastal redwood trees stand in the deep canyons of the fast-moving Big Sur and Little Sur Rivers. The largest population of mountain lions in America lives in the Santa Lucia Mountains; wild pigs, wild turkeys, and opossums may be found in abundance. Numerous other mammals and birds share the area.

The area offers approximately 197 miles of trails from at least nine trailheads. The Pine Ridge Trail (24 miles) in the middle of the northern section is the most popular. Trails from Little Sur River in the north and Kirk Creek in the south attract many backpackers, and the trail from Kirk Creek up to Vicente Flat offers a challenging 4.3-mile ascent to higher country with extensive views.

Ventana Essentials

Size: 202,144 acres.
Year Designated: 1969; expanded in 1978 and 1984.
Location: Southwestern central California near the coast.
Easiest Access: From Monterey, take State Highway 1 south for 33 miles to Big Sur State Park and the Pine Ridge Trailhead.
Season: Spring through early fall.
Wilderness Fees/Permits: None except campfire permits from May through November, but some trails may be closed to public entry. Contact the district ranger.
Maps: A Wilderness map is available for $3 from the district ranger.
Management: Monterey Ranger District, Los Padres National Forest, 406 South Mildred, King City, CA 93930; (408) 385-5434.

CALIFORNIA

Whipple Mountains Wilderness

Stretching east-west across the Wilderness, the Whipple Mountains are separated into eastern and western halves by a low angle fault. The volcanic formations of the eastern half are a striking brick red, while the western half appears a pale green. Domed peaks and dramatic, eroded pinnacles tower to more than 4,000 feet above valley floors and steep-walled canyons. From the heights, you'll see the Colorado River flowing placidly to the east. The bajadas that flow westward from the mountains are broken by isolated lava rock masses and red sandstone outcroppings.

Sonoran creosote bush scrub and Sonoran thorns are scattered throughout the area, as are dense clusters of paloverde, ironwood, smoke tree, and cholla. Saguaro, foxtail, and Mojave prickly pear cactuses all grow here. Seasonal rains pour down numerous washes that are typically dry. The Whipples support a variety of desert wildlife.

Whipple Mountains Essentials

Size: 77,520 acres.
Year Designated: 1994.
Location: Southeastern California.
Easiest Access: From Parker, Arizona, cross into California on California Route 62 (Aqueduct Road) for about one mile and take Parker Dam Road north. One mile before the dam, turn west on Black Meadow Landing Road and continue six miles to the dirt road that leads to Havasu Palms. Follow the dirt road 2.1 miles to the powerline road. For the next eight miles, the powerline road forms the eastern Wilderness boundary.
Season: Early spring and late fall.
Wilderness Fees/Permits: None.
Maps: USGS topographic maps are Gene Wash, Havasu Lake, Lake Havasu City South, Parker, Parker NW, Savahia Peak, Whipple Mountain SW, and Whipple Wash.
Management: BLM Needles Resource Area, 101 West Spikes Road, Needles, CA 92363; (619) 326-3896.

Yolla Bolly-Middle Eel Wilderness

Located between the North and South Yolla Bolly Mountains in the as-rugged-as-it-comes headwater country of the Wild and Scenic Middle Fork of the Eel River, Yolla Bolly-Middle Eel Wilderness ranges in elevation from about 2,700 feet to 8,000 feet. The river crashes wildly through the Wilderness in a deep canyon for approximately six miles, and, combined with sections of the 48 miles of river outside the Wilderness, forms what is arguably California's finest long white-water run. Chamise and manzanita in the lower elevations give way to dense arrays of pine and fir cloaking numerous ridges. Vast grasslands open many of the steep hillsides. Summer wildflowers dramatically color large mountain meadows. Bear and deer populate the area in relative abundance, and September's hunting season brings the most human visitors. Water, unlike solitude, may be hard to find after midsummer. Most of the Wilderness stands on national forestland, but a section on the western side (8,500 acres) is situated on BLM land.

An extensive and often strenuous trail system provides access in short loops and extended routes deep into the Wilderness. Light human use and suitable pathways make this an ideal destination for horsepackers. The Ides Cove Loop Trail rambles for over 50 miles through some of the best that Yolla Bolly-Middle Eel has to offer.

Yolla Bolly-Middle Eel Essentials

Size: 153,904 acres.
Year Designated: 1964; expanded in 1984.
Location: Northern California.
Easiest Access: From Corning, on Interstate 5, take Corning Road (Route A9) west for about 33 miles past Paskenta. Turn north on Forest Road M2, and again on Road M22. Drive for about 33 more miles to the Ides Cove Loop Trailhead.
Season: May to October, but June is best.
Wilderness Fees/Permits: None.
Maps: A Wilderness map is available for $3 from the district rangers.

Management: Yolla Bolly Ranger District, Shasta-Trinity National Forest, Platina, CA 96076; (916) 352-4211. Corning Ranger District, Mendocino National Forest, 22000 Corning Road, P.O. Box 1019, Corning, CA 96021; (916) 824-5196. Covelo Ranger District, Mendocino National Forest, 78150 Covelo Raod, Covelo, CA 95428; (707) 983-6118. Six Rivers National Forest, 500 Fifth Street, Eureka, CA 95501; (707) 442-9242. BLM Ukiah District Office, 555 Leslie Street, Ukiah, CA 95482; (707) 462-3873.

Yosemite Wilderness

Established in 1890, Yosemite National Park ranks among the first and the best of the National Park System. Surrounded entirely by national forestland in the heart of the Sierra Nevada, fabulous granite faces, domes, and peaks stand above expansive meadows that sprout a lustrous green in summer and are buried in soft, white snow during winter. Beautiful, glacier-filled lakes spill their water down turbulent, sparkling streams and over spectacular waterfalls, while nearby groves of giant sequoias tower to eye-stretching heights.

Park elevations range from about 2,000 feet to more than 13,000 feet, and the area supports an outstanding variety of plant and animal life. Fifty-four miles of the Wild and Scenic Tuolumne River flow through the park, one of the most exquisite mountain rivers on Earth. Seventy-eight miles of the Wild and Scenic Merced River also run in the park, dropping over some of the most fabulous waterfalls in America, and 22 miles of the Merced's Wild and Scenic South Fork flow through extravagant canyons with precipitous rapids. Although there is no navigable white water within the Wilderness iself, just outside these rivers rush and become some of the best whitewater runs on this planet. Yosemite's landmarks have become synonymous with outdoor splendor: El Capitan, Half Dome, Yosemite Falls, Bridalveil Falls, Tuolumne Meadows. The rock-climbing routes on bold and extraordinarily high faces rank among the most challenging in the entire world.

Sadly, there are flies contaminating the wondrous ointment: the park has more than 1,000 buildings, 1,500-plus summer employees, and more than 30 miles of roads upon which at least one million vehicles drive every year. In short, Yosemite is being loved to death.

Of the 747,956 acres within park boundaries, over 94 percent has been designated Wilderness, most of the land falling in the higher country outside Yosemite Valley. More than 700 miles of trails give access to the Wilderness. Many of the trailheads are in Yosemite Valley.

CALIFORNIA

Yosemite Essentials

Size: 677,600 acres.
Year Designated: 1984.
Location: Eastern central California.
Easiest Access: From Manteca, take State Highway 120 east approximately 100 miles to Yosemite Valley.
Season: All seasons offer attractions.
Wilderness Fees/Permits: The park entrance fee is $5. Wilderness permits are required; they are free and available on a quota system. To obtain one you can either: (1) Order by mail between the first of March and May 31 at the Wilderness office at park headquarters (see below). You must give specific dates and specific trails. (2) Apply in person the rest of the year at the park entrances of Yosemite Valley, Badger Pass (winter only), Tuolumne Meadows (summer only), Big Oak Flat, Hetch Hetchy (spring and fall only), and Wawona.
Maps: Topographic maps and trail guides are available from the Yosemite Bookstore, P.O. Box 230, El Portal, CA 95318; (209) 379-2648.
Management: Yosemite National Park, P.O. Box 577, Yosemite, CA 95389; (209) 372-0200.

> "Climb the mountains and get their good tidings. Nature's peace will flow into you as sunshine flows into trees. The winds will blow their own freshness into you, and the storms their energy, while cares will drop off like autumn leaves."
>
> —John Muir

COLORADO

Total Wilderness areas: 37
Total Wilderness acreage: 3,256,594

When thoughts turn to Colorado, they usually light on mountains. Three-fourths of this nation's land above 10,000 feet lies in this single state. Here the Rocky Mountains exceed 300 miles in length and rise 54 times to more than 14,000 feet, and about 830 times to summits between 11,000 and 14,000 feet. But Colorado has more to offer than its showy peaks. It embraces a variety of habitats: from a low point of 3,350 feet where the Arkansas River enters Kansas, great plains rise toward the mountains and cover about two-fifths of eastern Colorado. The western portion of the state levels out into spectacular canyon country on the Colorado Plateau.

The U.S. Forest Service manages 34 Wildernesses in this state so richly blessed with natural wonders. One of them includes a portion managed by the U.S. Fish and Wildlife Service, and two include sections overseen by the Bureau of Land Management. The National Park Service administers three additional areas.

Black Canyon of the Gunnison Wilderness

Two billion years ago, Precambrian gneiss (a coarse-grained, granitelike metamorphic rock that's extremely strong and resistant to erosion) formed the core of this region. In what's now known as the 53-mile-long Black Canyon, the gneiss was worn away with unimaginable slowness by the Gunnison River, creating the deepest narrow canyon in America, a moody terrain where lack of sunlight shrouds the bottom in almost perpetual shadow. The most scenic 12 miles of the canyon, which has been designated Wilderness from rim to rim, is included in the 20,766-acre

COLORADO

Black Canyon of the Gunnison National Monument. At places, the river throbs wildly 2,400 feet below, while at the Narrows, the canyon is only 1,100 feet wide at the rim and as little as 40 feet wide at the bottom. It lies surrounded by a dryland forest of piñon and juniper.

Only the most determined anglers, a group to which I belong, brave the descent to catch Colorado's largest trout, grown fat and happy because of a lack of fishing pressure and a rich food supply. Expert river runners attempt the Gunnison here, carrying over several difficult portages (most people consider the canyon water unrunnable). No well-maintained trails descend the canyon walls, but rangers can give directions to the easiest descents. I found the going steep but not treacherous. Camping is allowed on the canyon bottom.

Climbers often cling to the precipices, where you'll find some of the most demanding routes in the state. These cliffs are not for beginners or the inexperienced. Rangers will give you advice on routes and their difficulty. Pre-climb and post-climb registration is required.

Black Canyon of the Gunnison Essentials

Size: 11,180 acres.
Year Designated: 1976.
Location: Western central Colorado.
Easiest Access: From Montrose, take U.S. 50 east, turning north at the sign to the visitors center, approximately 12 miles.
Season: The river runs highest in spring. Fishing is usually best in the fall.
Wilderness Fees/Permits: A free backcountry permit is required for descent into the canyon. Climbers are required to register.
Maps: USGS topographic maps are Grizzly Ridge and Red Rock Canyon.
Management: Black Canyon of the Gunnison National Monument, P.O. Box 1648, Montrose, CO 81402; (970) 249-7036.

Buffalo Peaks Wilderness

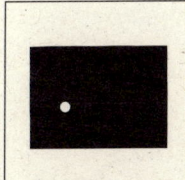

Beaver, elk, mule deer, and one of Colorado's largest herds of bighorn sheep call the Buffalo Peaks Wilderness home, but human visitors are relatively few, preferring the nearby and more glamorous Collegiate Peaks Wilderness (see below). From most of South Park and much of the Arkansas River Valley, the twin Buffalo Peaks—East Buffalo (13,300 feet) and West Buffalo (13,326 feet)—are visible as high, rounded domes. You won't find deep glacial valleys or secluded lakes here. You will find a serene forest of Engelmann spruce, Douglas fir, lodgepole and limber pine, and aspen, as well as several lovely stands of bristlecone pines on some of the south-facing slopes. The forest is laced with large meadows and impressive beaver ponds held in place by elaborate dams. The peace and quiet is seldom broken.

From one of four trailheads, you may ascend from a base covered in piñon and juniper up through a mixed coniferous forest and onto alpine tundra. Buffalo Meadows Trail provides access to the summit of West Buffalo Peak, necessitating a round-trip hike of about 14 miles from the southern end of the trail. Only about 18 miles of trail wind through the area. Off-trail, I found the hiking relatively easy and campsites pleasant and plentiful.

COLORADO

Buffalo Peaks Essentials

Size: 43,410 acres.
Year Designated: 1993.
Location: Central Colorado.
Easiest Access: From Buena Vista, take Forest Service Road 375 (Fourmile Creek Road) about 10 miles north to the Buffalo Meadows Trailhead.
Season: Summers are pleasant. Fall brings splendid color.

Wilderness Fees/Permits: None.
Maps: USGS topographic maps are Harvard Lakes, Jones Hill, Marmot Peak, Mount Sherman, and South Peak.
Management: Leadville Ranger District, San Isabel National Forest, 2015 North Poplar, Leadville, CO 80461; (719) 486-0749. South Park Ranger District, Pike National Forest, P.O. Box 219, Fairplay, CO 80440; (719) 836-2031.

Byers Peak Wilderness

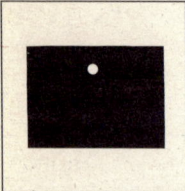

Standing at 12,804 feet, Byers Peak overlooks a Wilderness rendered unique by the fact that about one half of the area consists of alpine tundra, the land above the tree line. Virtually none of the entire Byers Peak Trail, which traverses the area north to south from Bottle Pass to Saint Louis Peak, lies under the shadow of the Engelmann spruce, subalpine fir, or lodgepole pine that cloak the lower elevations. Though Byers Peak Wilderness is small in acreage, only the undeveloped head of Fraser Experimental Forest separates this Wilderness from Vasquez Peak Wilderness (see below), making it a part of a much larger roadless region of Colorado.

Although it lacks the splendor associated with many Colorado Wildernesses, Byers Peak contains several scenic lakes and 23 miles of trails offering panoramic views along some of the finest ridge hiking in the state. Views worth the effort are available from atop the peak itself, accessible via the Byers Peak Trail, a distance of three miles round-trip from the trailhead. Mule deer, elk, ptarmigan, and marmots are common sights, but the main lure of the place is the peace and quiet afforded by one of the Rocky Mountain's most obscure Wildernesses.

Byers Peak Essentials

Size: 8,095 acres.
Year Designated: 1993.
Location: Northern central Colorado.
Easiest Access: From Denver, take Interstate 70 west to U.S. 40 north and go 30 miles to Fraser. Take County Road 73 (St. Louis Creek Road) southwest eight miles to the Byers Peak Trailhead.
Season: Summer and fall.

Wilderness Fees/Permits: None.
Maps: USGS topographic maps are Bottle Pass, Byers Peak, and Ute Peak.
Management: Sulphur Ranger District, Arapaho National Forest, 62429 U.S. Highway 40, Granby, CO 80446; (970) 887-3331. Middle Park Ranger District, Routt National Forest, 210 South Sixth Street, Kremmling, CO 80459; (970) 724-9004.

COLORADO

Cache la Poudre Wilderness

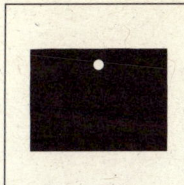

Nine miles of the Little South Fork of the Cache la Poudre River, a part of Colorado's only designated Wild and Scenic River drainage, flow through Cache la Poudre Wilderness. The water has cut a deep and tortured canyon into granitic bedrock, typical of the Front Range of Colorado, to join the Main Fork of the Cache la Poudre River, which forms the northern boundary of the Wilderness. Elevations range from about 6,100 to 8,300 feet, and a dry climate keeps this area snow-free for much of the year, especially on south-facing slopes. Douglas fir and ponderosa and lodgepole pine dominate the forest. Celebrated for their trout, the rivers draw the most human visitors, but lack of trail access and rugged topography make this small Wilderness one of the state's least explored areas.

State Highway 14 along the Main Fork of the Cache la Poudre River sees many campers and even more fly-casting anglers. Trout fishing here is as good as it gets in the state. Once inside the boundary, you'll find the ground marked by only one short maintained path, the Mount McConnel Trail, which runs about three miles in the northern section. Other than this, ill-defined paths created by anglers provide some guidance.

Cache la Poudre Essentials

Size: 9,238 acres.
Year Designated: 1980.
Location: Northern central Colorado.
Easiest Access: From Fort Collins, take State Route 14 north and west about 30 miles to the Mount McConnel Trailhead.
Season: Year-round.
Wilderness Fees/Permits: None.
Maps: USGS topographic maps are Big Narrows and Rustic.
Management: Estes-Poudre Ranger District, Roosevelt National Forest, 1311 South College, Fort Collins, CO 80524; (970) 498-2775.

Collegiate Peaks Wilderness

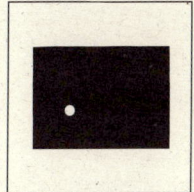

With eight "fourteeners" (peaks exceeding 14,000 feet in elevation), Collegiate Peaks Wilderness probably possesses the highest average elevation of any Wilderness in the Lower 48. You can climb with relative ease Mounts Yale, Oxford, Columbia, and Harvard (the state's third highest point), as well as Huron Peak, Missouri Mountain, Mount Belford, and La Plata Peak (the state's fifth highest point). Another six peaks in the area rise to within 200 feet of 14,000, and a virtually unlimited number of other raw summits offer technical climbing challenges. Not far north of the Collegiate Peaks stands Mount Elbert, the highest point on the Continental Divide. Wide U-shaped valleys open onto utterly breathtaking mountain scenery. Dozens of alpine lakes sparkle at the feet of striking rocky cirques. For startling, glacier-sculpted, high-mountain splendor, this area has few rivals in Colorado.

From Cottonwood Pass, you can ascend the Denny Creek Trail about 1.5 miles, turn east up Delaney Gulch, climb out of the gulch to the ridge, and follow the ridge north to the saddle below Mount Yale. You can tramp the northwest ridge of Mount Yale to the summit along a moderately difficult five-mile route.

COLORADO

As you travel through the area, you might notice unusual and deep indentations in the boundary line. These are a legacy of man's hunt for gold and other valuable metals that are still sought just outside. More than a dozen trailheads create a situation in which no one ever stands more than five miles from a road. About 40 miles of the serpentine Continental Divide snake across the area, and this expansive Wilderness lies in parts of three national forests. The beauty of this place and its ease of access ensure torrents of visitors, especially on weekends.

Collegiate Peaks Essentials

Size: 166,654 acres.
Year Designated: 1980.
Location: Central Colorado.
Easiest Access: From Buena Vista, take Forest Service Road 306 (Cottonwood Pass Road) about eight miles to the Denny Creek Trailhead.
Season: For the most solitude, go midweek during fall.
Wilderness Fees/Permits: None.
Maps: USGS topographic maps are Aspen, Buena Vista, Granite, Hayden Peak, Independence Pass, Italian Creek, Mount Elbert, Mount Harvard, New York Peak, and Pieplant.
Management: Aspen Ranger District, White River National Forest, 806 West Hallum, Aspen, CO 81611; (970) 925-3445. Leadville Ranger District, San Isabel National Forest, 2015 North Poplar, Leadville, CO 80461; (719) 486-0749. Salida Ranger District, San Isabel National Forest, 325 West Rainbow Blvd., Salida, CO 81201; (719) 539-3591. Taylor River Ranger District, Gunnison National Forest, 216 North Colorado, Gunnison, CO 81230; (970) 641-0471.

Comanche Peak Wilderness

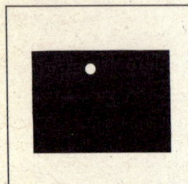

The 70 miles of trails that wind through this attractive Wilderness begin flanked in ponderosa pine and aspen, and then pass through a thick forest of lodgepole and limber pine. From the trails, the Wilderness appears to be nothing but trees until the forest gives way to abundant alpine tundra along the southern boundary near Comanche Peak. Beyond Comanche to the south, lies Rocky Mountain National Park. The Cache la Poudre River tumbles over cascades or runs quietly in pools for over 10 miles to the north and west. The rugged Mummy Range (of which Comanche Peak is a part), combined with the river, forms one of the state's most serpentine Wilderness boundaries. The interior of the area, however, is quite accessible, with few spots more than five miles from a trailhead. For a taste of the area, take the Zimmerman Trail three miles to Sheep Creek, one of the least visited and most rugged sections of the Wilderness.

The Big South Fork of the Cache la Poudre River is largely responsible for draining Comanche Peak, and it joins forces with the Little South Fork to form Colorado's only Wild and Scenic River drainage. Trout fishing can be good on the rivers, as well as in several lakes and streams. A large elk herd roams the area, and lucky visitors might catch a rare glimpse of moose. This Wilderness receives heavy human use.

COLORADO

Comanche Peak Essentials

Size: 66,791 acres.
Year Designated: 1980.
Location: Northern central Colorado.
Easiest Access: From Fort Collins, take State Route 14 north and west approximately 40 miles to the Zimmerman Trail, which leads into the area's most remote region. Prior to the trailhead, turning south on Crown Point Road leads to several other trailheads.

Season: Crowds gather in summer and fall; snow makes access difficult the rest of the year.
Wilderness Fees/Permits: None.
Maps: USGS topographic maps are Boston Peak, Chambers Lake, Comanche Peak, Crystal Mountain, Estes Park, Glen Haven, Kinikinik, and Rustic.
Management: Estes-Poudre Ranger District, Roosevelt National Forest, 1311 South College, Fort Collins, CO 80524; (970) 498-2775.

Eagles Nest Wilderness

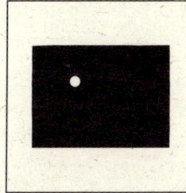

Heavy snow accumulates on the severe heights of Eagles Nest Wilderness in the Gore Range, providing a major contribution to the waters of the Colorado River. Melting snow in spring plunges from the heights to create marshy meadows and sloughs, as well as turbulent thundering creeks when temperatures soar abruptly. This is an area more vertical than horizontal, with sheer rock faces, keen-edged ridges, deep valleys, jagged peaks, and dense forests lower down, and foot travel can be strenuous. Rock climbers have been increasingly drawn to some portions of this Wilderness, especially the southern region around Red Buffalo Pass and Uneva Pass.

Approximately 180 miles of trail provide access to Eagles Nest, most of them dead-ending at a radiant gem of an alpine lake. Two trails, at the northern and southern extremes, cross entirely from one side of the Wilderness to the other side: Cataract Lake to Piney Lake across the north, a distance of 15 miles; and Gore Creek to Red Buffalo Pass to Uneva Pass across the south, a distance of about 19 miles. Off-trail hiking can be difficult, but several informal routes climb the steep passes of the area's craggy core.

Eagles Nest wasn't designated Wilderness without heated controversy. Denver wanted the water. Timber industries wanted the lush spruce forest that covers the lower elevations. Lovers of Wilderness can rejoice that these interests did not prevail, and that one of Colorado's most untamed expanses was preserved.

Eagles Nest Essentials

Size: 133,325 acres.
Year Designated: 1976.
Location: Northern central Colorado.
Easiest Access: From Denver, take Interstate 70 to Vail (about a two-hour drive). Then take Forest Service Road 700 (Red Sandstone Road) five miles north to where the road ends at several trailheads.
Season: Late summer and early fall.

Wilderness Fees/Permits: None.
Maps: USGS topographic maps are Dillon, Frisco, Mount Powell SE, Piney Peak, Squaw Creek, Vail East, Vail Pass, Vail West, and Willow Lakes.
Management: Dillon Ranger District, White River National Forest, 135 Highway 9, Silverthorne, CO 80498; (970) 468-5400.

COLORADO

Flat Tops Wilderness

Arthur Carhart's 1919 visit to Trappers Lake in the verdant embrace of the Flat Tops prompted him to be the first U.S. Forest Service official to initiate a plea for Wilderness preservation (see the book's introduction). No wonder he found the area so entrancing: behind Trappers Lake loom majestic volcanic cliffs, and beyond them a vast subalpine terrain reluctantly yields to alpine tundra (part of the White River Plateau with an average elevation of about 10,000 feet). Approximately 110 trout-laden lakes and ponds, often unnamed, dot the country below numerous flat-topped cliffs. With about half the 100 miles of streams crisscrossing the Wilderness serving as other habitats for trout, this place is an angler's paradise.

The relatively gentle land above the cliffs offers over 160 miles of easy trails. This is ideal country for horse-packers, and, off the trails, the hiking is inviting and limitless. As many as 20,000 summer elk also seem to find the area quite pleasant. A skeletal forest of dead spruce and fir stretches across the higher slopes below the tundra, the eerie legacy of a 1940s budworm epidemic. Here you'll find Colorado's second largest Wilderness, a precious expanse of breathtakingly open land.

Flat Tops Essentials

Size: 235,035 acres.
Year Designated: 1975.
Location: Northwestern central Colorado.
Easiest Access: From two miles north of Meeker, on State Route 13, take County Road 8 east for approximately 40 miles to Forest Service Road 205. This runs east and south about 10 more miles to Trappers Lake. The southern extreme of the Wilderness lies about 20 miles north of Glenwood Springs and Interstate 70.
Season: Summer and fall.
Wilderness Fees/Permits: None.
Maps: USGS topographic maps are Blair Mountain, Buford, Deep Lake, Devil's Causeway, Dome Creek, Dunkley Pass, Lost Park, Meadow Creek Lake, Orno Park, Oyster Lake, Ripple Creek, Sand Point, Sugarloaf Mountain, Sweetwater Lake, and Trappers Lake.
Management: Blanco Ranger District, White River National Forest, 317 East Market, Meeker, CO 81641; (970) 878-4039. Eagle Ranger District, White River National Forest, 125 West Fifth Street, Eagle, CO 81631; (970) 328-6388. Rifle Ranger District, White River National Forest, 0094 County Road 244, Rifle, CO 81650; (970) 625-2371. Yampa Ranger District, Routt National Forest, 300 Roselawn, Yampa, CO 80483; (970) 638-4516.

Fossil Ridge Wilderness

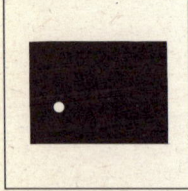

With a trailhead that beckons only 14 miles from my door, Fossil Ridge has seen me many times, most of my visits occurring before the area became one of Colorado's newest Wildernesses in 1993. Here is a small but almost perfect mountain kingdom, with raw granite towering above several beautiful shallow lakes and long valleys carved by ancient glaciers and replete with pine, spruce, fir, and aspen. The limestone ridge rises above 13,000 feet, climbing well beyond the tree line, and contains the fossilized remains of numerous prehistoric sea creatures. Above Lamphier Lake, accessible on a well-developed, three-mile-long trail, a slim cut in the bare rock called

COLORADO

Gunsight Pass (barely shoulder-width!) opens the ridge for foot travel from South Lottis Creek's drainage to Crystal Creek's drainage. Searching for gold, miners dug at several sites still scarred by their efforts, but, to me, these pieces of history somehow seem to enhance the area's overall attractiveness. Square Top Mountain, approximately 12,500 feet high and about an hour's worth of climbing above Lamphier Lake, allows a virtually unparalleled view of almost half of Colorado's fourteeners.

Elk and deer abound, but the truly fortunate catch glimpses of a small group of mountain goats or a larger herd of bighorn sheep. The lakes are stocked with trout. There are about 22 miles of maintained trails.

Fossil Ridge Essentials
Size: 33,060 acres.
Year Designated: 1993.
Location: Central Colorado.
Easiest Access: From Gunnison take U.S. 50 east for 11 miles to Parlin. Turn north on County Road 76 and proceed nine miles to Ohio City. Turn north on Forest Service Road 771 and take this about seven miles to the Lamphier Lake Trailhead.
Season: Winters are long and snowy. Summers and falls are most pleasant.
Wilderness Fees/Permits: None.
Maps: USGS topographic maps are Crystal Creek and Fairview Peak.
Management: Taylor River Ranger District, Gunnison National Forest, 216 North Colorado, Gunnison, CO 81230; (970) 641-0471.

Great Sand Dunes Wilderness

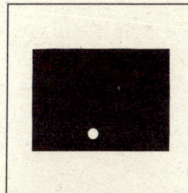

For century after century, the Rio Grande wandered through the San Luis Valley depositing sand along its bed and shores. When the river changed its course, the sand lay exposed to winds that predominantly blow toward the northeast. The winds forced the sand up against the bulwark of the Sangre de Cristo Mountains and created the Great Sand Dunes of Colorado, a piece of territory unique in several ways. Reaching heights of 700 feet, these are the tallest dunes in North America, and the sight of them lying at the very foot of the snow-clad Sangres can be a bit unsettling at first. This is the only Wilderness defined as a saltbush-greasewood ecosystem, with hardy plants that include blowout grass, Indian ricegrass, scurfpea, and prairie sunflower. It's also the only place on Earth where you'll find the Great Sand Dunes tiger beetle and the giant sand treader camel cricket. Kangaroo rats may be seen dancing lightly on the shifting sands, and the night awakens other interesting denizens of the dunes.

Of the 38,659 acres of Great Sand Dunes National Monument, 33,450 (the main sand dunes) have been designated Wilderness. Camping is allowed, but not campfires. You really should stay overnight in order to appreciate the greatest wonder of the dunes: the ever-alternating colors and shadows as the sun moves across the sky and the moon rises.

COLORADO

Great Sand Dunes Essentials

Size: 33,450 acres.
Year Designated: 1976.
Location: Central southern Colorado.
Easiest Access: From Alamosa, take State Route 17 about 15 miles north. Turn east at the sign onto Six Mile Lane. Total distance is 38 road miles.
Season: Winters are blistering cold. Summers are too hot. Go in spring and fall.
Wilderness Fees/Permits: A fee of $4 per vehicle is charged for entrance to the monument. A free permit is required for camping on the dunes.
Maps: USGS topographic maps are Liberty, Sand Camp, and Zapata Ranch, but the free monument map will suffice.
Management: Great Sand Dunes National Monument, Mosca, CO 81146; (719) 378-2312.

Greenhorn Mountain Wilderness

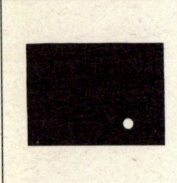

Soaring dramatically from the plains of Colorado, Greenhorn Mountain rises from 7,600 to 12,347 feet in the center of the northern section. Its summit is the highest point in the Wilderness, and nowhere else in the state provides such a vivid and dramatic change from plains to mountains. About two-thirds of the area is forested, and as you hike along, you'll pass quickly from dry oakbrush and ponderosa pine country (or piñon-juniper in some places) through aspen, fir, and spruce, and on to alpine tundra. Most of the east-facing slopes are steep, rocky, and generally bare.

Unusual for Colorado, Greenhorn Mountain Wilderness has no lakes and no towering alpine peaks—and, consequently, few human visitors. Numerous small canyons and sharp ridges are the dominant geological features. A few streams descending from the mountain furnish a habitat for threatened greenback cutthroat trout. With relatively little snow, the area attracts bighorn sheep, elk, and mule deer.

Only 11 miles of trail cross the Wilderness, all in the northern half. The southern half, remote and rugged and waterless, probably has fewer human visitors than any other area of the state. If you're willing to brave the dense woodlands and rough topography, you'll find few places with as much solitude.

Greenhorn Mountain Essentials

Size: 22,040 acres.
Year Designated: 1993.
Location: Southeastern Colorado.
Easiest Access: From Pueblo, take Interstate 25 south for 28 miles. Turn west onto State Route 165 at Colorado City and go eight miles to Rye. Take County Road 250 west about three miles to the Greenhorn Trailhead.
Season: Spring for the most water.
Wilderness Fees/Permits: None.
Maps: USGS topographic maps are Badito Cone, Hayden Butte, Rye, and San Isabel.
Management: San Carlos Ranger District, San Isabel National Forest, 326 Dozier Street, Canon City, CO 81212; (719) 275-4119.

COLORADO

Holy Cross Wilderness

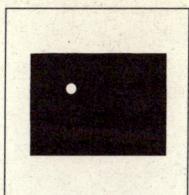

Cascading streams, dozens of emerald green lakes, and wide valleys moistened by melting snow make Holy Cross a watery alpine Wilderness of glistening beauty. Colorado's need for water, in fact, made the fight to defend and designate Holy Cross probably the most hotly debated of all the areas within the state. Dominated by 14,005-foot Mount of the Holy Cross, this Wilderness preserves far more than water: 25 or so peaks rise above 13,000 feet, mighty ridges fling themselves skyward above glacier-carved U-shaped valleys, and numerous aspen groves burn gold in September. Wildlife including deer, elk, black bears, bobcats, and lynx find abundant homes in Holy Cross, and its streams run full of trout.

About 164 miles of trail march into the area, several of them joining to form loops requiring a short shuttle to connect at the trailheads. Hiking the Cross Creek Trail—up the fabulous glacial valley across Fancy Pass past spectacular high lakes and down the valley of the Fall Creek Trail—may be Colorado's most glorious short backpacking trip (about 28 miles). The cross-state Colorado Trail passes through the southeastern corner, where the Continental Divide marks the boundary. Cross-country skiers flock to this area in the winter.

Holy Cross Essentials

Size: 122,037 acres.
Year Designated: 1980.
Location: Central Colorado.
Easiest Access: From Interstate 70, take U.S. 24 south about five miles. Turn west on Forest Service Road 707 and go about one mile to the Cross Creek Trailhead.
Season: In fall, the brilliant gold of the aspen is breathtaking.
Wilderness Fees/Permits: None.
Maps: USGS topographic maps are Fulford, Grouse Mountain, Homestake Reservoir, Minturn, Mount Jackson, Mount of the Holy Cross, and Nast.
Management: Holy Cross Ranger District, White River National Forest, P.O. Box 190, Minturn, CO 81645; (970) 827-5715. Leadville Ranger District, San Isabel National Forest, 2015 North Poplar, Leadville, CO 80461; (719) 486-0749.

Hunter-Fryingpan Wilderness

Snuggled in between the more spectacular Colorado Wildernesses of Holy Cross on the north, Maroon Bells-Snowmass on the west, and Collegiate Peaks on the south, Hunter-Fryingpan lies all but forgotten. It rises to the Continental Divide, sharing its eastern border and the divide with Mount Massive Wilderness (see below). The two are one geographically speaking, and almost became one legislatively. Holding the headwaters of Hunter Creek and the Fryingpan River, many streams in this area provide excellent habitats for large numbers of trout. Here you'll find many of the unnamed and tortured peaks of the Williams Mountains. Forests of aspen in the lower elevations, as well as spruce and fir higher up, are thick and dark, and open on alpine tundra dappled colorfully with summer wildflowers. In the silence of this Wilderness, you'll probably see wildlife that includes elk, mule deer, and secretive smaller, fur-bearing animals. A rich forest of

COLORADO

8,300 acres along Spruce Creek on the northwest side was added to the original Wilderness in 1993.

About 50 miles of trail cross the area, climbing up drainages into the Williams Mountains. The Lost Man Trail up Lost Man Creek crosses South Fork Pass and continues down the South Fork of the Fryingpan River (about 10 miles distance), providing access to the heart of the Wilderness. Many opportunities for solitude exist here.

Hunter-Fryingpan Essentials

Size: 82,580 acres.
Year Designated: 1978; expanded in 1993.
Location: Central Colorado.
Easiest Access: From Aspen, take State Highway 82 east (closed in winter) and go about 15 miles to Lost Man Reservoir and the Lost Man Trailhead.
Season: Winter brings much snow. By midsummer the area is splendid, growing even more so toward fall.
Wilderness Fees/Permits: None.
Maps: USGS topographic maps are Aspen, Independence Pass, Meredith, Mount Champion, Nast, New York Peak, and Thimble Rock.
Management: Aspen Ranger District, White River National Forest, 806 West Hallum, Aspen, CO 81611; (970) 925-3445. Sopris Ranger District, White River National Forest, 620 Main Street, Carbondale, CO 81623; (970) 963-2266.

Indian Peaks Wilderness

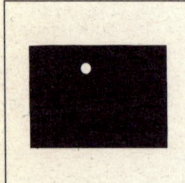

The gray, sharp-toothed outline of the Indian Peaks are visible from Denver, luring many, many human visitors to this Wilderness. Majestic summits, remnant glaciers, 50 or so startlingly blue lakes nestled in cirque basins, and names such as Arapaho, Pawnee, and Lone Eagle lend ambience and beauty to this spectacular mountainous region. The icy remains of the last glacial period that artistically sculpted this rugged terrain may be the southernmost of any glaciers in North America. Approximately 60 percent of the Wilderness stands above the tree line, a fragile region that starts at about 10,700 feet. Chill winds off perpetual snowfields have created an environment below timberline of stunted trees and alpine plants unusual for this part of the state. Early snow dustings in fall accentuate the rocky artistry, while in autumn the gold of aspen and the crimson of willows bathe the lower forest in brilliant color. Fish abound in lakes and streams.

About 110 miles of trails provide access to the area. On the Hessie Trail, you can follow the South Fork of Boulder Creek to King Lake and loop over the High Lonesome Trail to Devils Thumb Pass, down to Jasper Lake, and along the Devils Thumb Trail back to Hessie (a distance of 15 miles). Campfires are not permitted in the eastern portion and around lakes. The Continental Divide runs close to the center of the Wilderness, and pathways lead over several high passes. Rocky Mountain National Park to the north contains 2,922 acres of Indian Peaks Wilderness, where a free park backcountry permit is required for assigned campsites.

COLORADO

Indian Peaks Essentials

Size: 73,296 acres.
Year Designated: 1978; expanded in 1980.
Location: Northern central Colorado.
Easiest Access: From Boulder, take State Route 119 southwest about 16 miles to Nederland. From Nederland, take County Road 130 to the Hessie Trailhead. Total shortest distance from Boulder is about 30 miles.
Season: Fall, for the color and natural artistry.
Wilderness Fees/Permits: A $4 fee is required for overnight camping between June 1 and September 15. Permits are available from the district rangers or at Coast-to-Coast Hardware in Nederland. Rocky Mountain National Park charges $5 per noncommercial vehicle or $3 per person for commercial-vehicle passengers. Contact the park for backcountry permits for their portion of the Wilderness.
Maps: USGS topographic maps are Allenspark, East Portal, Isolation Peak, Monarch Lake, Nederland, Shadow Mountain, and Ward.
Management: Boulder Ranger District, Roosevelt National Forest, 2995 Baseline Road, Boulder, CO 80303; (303) 444-6700. Sulphur Ranger District, Arapaho National Forest, 62429 U.S. Highway 40, Granby, CO 80446; (970) 887-3331. Rocky Mountain National Park, Estes Park, CO 80517; (970) 586-2371.

La Garita Wilderness

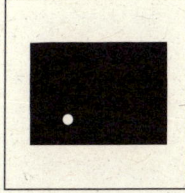

La Garita means "the lookout" in Spanish, and this Wilderness amply deserves the name. From the summit of this Wilderness's single fourteener (14,014-foot San Luis Peak), climbers can gaze across the upper Rio Grande Valley and down the long stretch of the San Luis Valley. About 35 miles of the Continental Divide lie well above a sprawling forestland that provides ideal habitats for huge numbers of elk and mule deer, though the animals may winter on the northern slopes when hard winds scour off the snow cover. On the southern slopes in Wason Park and Silver Park, added in 1993, you'll find a surprising ancient forest of towering spruce and fir. This is a land of rushing streams, broad and gentle alpine meadows, fascinating beaver ponds, long talus slopes, and tremendous mountain beauty.

The Wheeler Geologic Area hides in the southeast corner of the Wilderness. It once claimed to be Colorado's most visited site and is probably the state's most unusual geological formation: fine, light-gray volcanic ash compressed into rock and wildly eroded into a striking series of domes, spires, caves, ledges, pinnacles, ravines, and balanced rocks. The bumpy old road leading to the edge of Wheeler was left out of Wilderness designation, allowing motorized access deep into the area.

Many trailheads open onto approximately 175 miles of pathways, almost all especially well suited for horsepacking. About 27 miles of the Colorado Trail follow the divide through La Garita Wilderness. Traveling to this area often, I have seldom met another human visitor.

COLORADO

La Garita Essentials

Size: 129,626 acres.
Year Designated: 1964; expanded in 1980 and 1993.
Location: Southern central Colorado.
Easiest Access: From Monte Vista, take U.S. 160 west for 31 miles. Turn north on State Route 149 and proceed about 15 miles. Turn north on Forest Service Road 600 and go about 10 miles to the East Bellows Creek Trailhead and the Wheeler Geologic Area.
Season: Midsummer for wildflowers.

Wilderness Fees/Permits: None.
Maps: USGS topographic maps are Bristol Head, Cannibal Plateau, Creede, Mesa Mountain, Mineral Mountain, Pool Table Mountain, and Stewart Peak.
Management: Creede Ranger District, Rio Grande National Forest, Third and Creede Avenue, Creede, CO 81130; (719) 658-2556. Cebolla Ranger District, Gunnison National Forest, 216 North Colorado, Gunnison, CO 81230; (970) 641-0471.

Lizard Head Wilderness

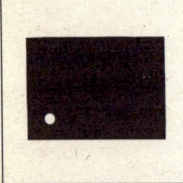

Lizard Head, the peak (13,113 feet), stands spirelike on the eastern side of Lizard Head, the Wilderness, shadowed by both Mount Wilson and Wilson Peak, two of Colorado's fourteeners that incongruously bear the same name. (Got all that?) Not far to the west, you'll find El Diente (or the tooth, in English), the westernmost of the state's 14,000-foot peaks. The province of more experienced climbers, Mount Wilson and El Diente are connected by a famous knife-edged ridge and considered difficult ascents. The summit of Lizard Head, a 400-foot-tall tower of rotten rock, has been voted Colorado's most dangerous and difficult climb by many mountaineers. Ascent is not recommended. Dolores Peak (13,290 feet) stands in the most western portion, just as the San Juan Mountains fade into the dry canyon country of the Colorado Plateau. Here you can stand in snow and look across heat-washed red-rock desertland.

Lizard Head Wilderness is a land of ragged mountain splendor, with lovely cirque lakes, fish living in swift mountain streams that often plunge over dramatic waterfalls, and a spruce-fir forest opened by expanses of alpine vegetation. Magnificent golden aspen blanket the lower slopes in vast unbroken reaches every fall. Human use is light on about 37 miles of strenuous trails.

Lizard Head Essentials

Size: 41,189 acres.
Year Designated: 1980.
Location: Southwestern Colorado.
Easiest Access: From Cortez, take State Route 145 north about 65 miles to Lizard Head Pass. This is where the Lizard Head Trail accesses Lizard Head Peak.
Season: Fall.
Wilderness Fees/Permits: None.

Maps: USGS topographic maps are Dolores Peak, Gray Head, Groundhog Mountain, Little Cone, and Mount Wilson.
Management: Dolores Ranger District, San Juan National Forest, 100 North Sixth Street, Dolores, CO 81323; (970) 882-7296. Norwood Ranger District, Uncompahgre National Forest, 1760 East Grand Avenue, Norwood, CO 81423; (970) 327-4261.

COLORADO

Lost Creek Wilderness

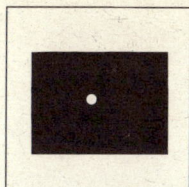

Unlike most of Colorado's jagged Wilderness profiles, Lost Creek is a land of fascinating rounded stone domes and knobs, split boulders, rare granite arches, and tree-lined mountain parks. Its rock formations are among the most amazing in the entire Rocky Mountains. Lost Creek got its name from its habit of disappearing several times into rock piles and reappearing later downhill. In the Tarryall Mountains, toward the southern end of the Wilderness, lives one of Colorado's largest and healthiest bighorn sheep herds. Black bears, deer, elk, and bobcats share the region. The northern section contains most of the Platte River Mountains and the Kenosha Mountains. During the first U.S. Forest Service RARE process (see the book's introduction), Lost Creek received more comments recommending its Wilderness designation than any other Colorado area.

About 100 miles of trails exist. The cross-state Colorado Trail passes through the area. In the southern portion, you can enter the Wilderness via the Goose Creek Trail and hike up the McCurdy Park Trail. Then it's on to the Lake Park Trail and over Hankins Pass to form a loop back to where you started, a total distance of about 23 miles. Although the hike is relatively strenuous, in my opinion this route will take you through the best this area has to offer.

Lost Creek Essentials

Size: 119,790 acres.
Year Designated: 1980; expanded in 1993.
Location: Central Colorado.
Easiest Access: From Denver, take U.S. 285 about 46 miles south and west to Bailey. Turn south on Wellington Lake Road (Forest Service Roads 532 to 543) and go to Wellington Lake (about 12 miles). Then take Forest Service Road 560 another 12 miles to Goose Creek Campground, and go one mile past the campground. Turn on Forest Service Road 558 and travel one more mile to the Goose Creek Trailhead.
Season: Spring, summer, and fall. In winter, snow falls under hard winds.
Wilderness Fees/Permits: None.
Maps: USGS topographic maps are Bailey, Cheeseman, Farnum Peak, Green Mountain, Hackett Mountain, McCurdy Mountain, Mount Logan, Observatory Rock, Shawnee, Tarryall, Topaz Mountain, and Windy Peak.
Management: South Park Ranger District, Pike National Forest, P.O. Box 219, Fairplay, CO 80440; (719) 836-2031.

Maroon Bells-Snowmass Wilderness

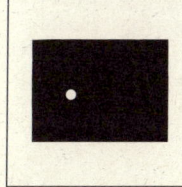

You'll have plenty of human company in Colorado's fourth largest Wilderness. They come because this area may exemplify Rocky Mountain splendor better than any other Wilderness: 100 miles of trail lead over nine passes above 12,000 feet; vast regions lie above the tree line; long glacial valleys point the way to glistening alpine lakes. With six peaks rising above 14,000 feet, this area draws mountaineers by the thousands every year. The awesome, jagged symmetry of the Maroon Bells, reflected in Maroon Lake, is perhaps Colorado's most often photographed mountain scene. A non-Wilderness road punches into the area to Maroon Lake, creating traffic jams in summer.

COLORADO

Climbers come in herds, despite the fact that these peaks are among the most difficult to scale in the state. Caution and skill are advised, but the rewards are stupendous. The Snowmass Creek Trail travels 16 miles to Maroon Lake and provides some of the best views of the Wilderness. Hot springs steam at the head of Conundrum Creek and attract many hikers. In midsummer, the wildflowers are arguably the best anywhere. Although elk and deer still abound in the Elk Mountains, development around Aspen and Snowmass threatens their habitat. The march of people is having a great impact on this area, especially the more accessible northern trails.

Maroon Bells-Snowmass Essentials

Size: 181,138 acres.
Year Designated: 1964; expanded in 1980.
Location: Central Colorado.
Easiest Access: Off State Route 82 just west of Aspen, Forest Service Road 125 (Maroon Creek Road) leads to Maroon Lake, a road only open to tour buses. The Wilderness will be better preserved by turning west on County Road 10 about four miles north of Aspen and driving five miles to the Snowmass Creek Trailhead.
Season: Come after Labor Day to avoid the biggest crowds.
Wilderness Fees/Permits: None.
Maps: USGS topographic maps are Aspen, Basalt, Capitol Peak, Gothic, Hayden Peak, Highland Peak, Marble, Maroon Bells, Mount Sopris, Pearl Pass, Redstone, and Snowmass Mountain.
Management: Aspen Ranger District, White River National Forest, 806 West Hallum, Aspen, CO 81611; (970) 925-3445. Sopris Ranger District, White River National Forest, 620 Main Street, Carbondale, CO 81623; (970) 963-2266. Taylor River Ranger District, Gunnison National Forest, 216 North Colorado, Gunnison, CO 81230; (970) 641-0471.

Mesa Verde Wilderness

About 1,400 years ago, the Anasazi began construction of sandstone dwellings deep within the shady overhangs of Mesa Verde. The Indians flourished for 700 years and then mysteriously disappeared into the mists of time, leaving many fabulous structures well preserved by the dry air and shadowy recesses of the alcoves. More than 52,000 acres of the mesa are protected by Mesa Verde National Park. Within the park, three small and separate sections on the steep north and east boundaries are designated as one Wilderness, serving as buffers to further protect the significant Native American sites. These small areas are exemplary ecosystems of piñon and juniper. Unlike most Wildernesses, here humans are *not* allowed.

You can explore the ruins when they're open, and travel other designated backcountry trails running over about 15 miles of the park. I have, and I loved it. Federal law prohibits harming or removing artifacts. Since hunting is also prohibited, the park has become a haven for deer, elk, black bears, bobcats, and perhaps the largest population of mountain lions in the state.

COLORADO

Mesa Verde Essentials

Size: 8,100 acres.
Year Designated: 1976.
Location: Southwestern Colorado.
Easiest Access: From Durango, take U.S. 160 west for 36 miles to the park entrance.
Season: Full interpretive services begin around mid-June and continue through Labor Day. Come in late spring or early fall to avoid the sometimes dense crowds.
Wilderness Fees/Permits: A fee of $5 per vehicle is charged. Tickets are often required to visit the ruins and must be picked up at the visitors center on the morning of your visit.
Maps: A free map is available from the park ranger.
Management: Mesa Verde National Park, CO 81330; (970) 529-4461.

Mount Evans Wilderness

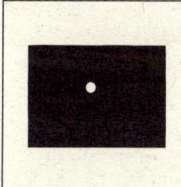

Crawling up into the Wilderness but outside the circuitous boundary, a paved road runs to the top of Mount Evans, the highest paved road in America. The road, two fourteeners (including Evans at 14,264 feet), and the proximity to Denver have created an overcrowded area most of the year. Despite the likelihood of rubbing elbows with other humans, the area offers several unique features I found worthy of a visit. Rare south of the Arctic Circle, the Wilderness contains small regions of arctic tundra. Unlike typical Colorado alpine tundra, which is dry and brittle once the snow recedes, arctic tundra holds numerous small pools of water. You'll find great areas of alpine tundra on the slopes as well. The Mount Goliath Natural Area, on the east side of the road, harbors a stand of 2,000-year-old bristlecone pines. Bighorn sheep and mountain goats are common sights.

About 67 miles of trails provide access to the Wilderness. Abyss Lake, surrounded by fabulous scenery, rests in a rock-rimmed gorge at 12,550 feet in the heart of the Wilderness. You can reach it by hiking seven strenuous miles (one way) up a glacier-carved valley.

Mount Evans Essentials

Size: 74,401 acres.
Year Designated: 1980.
Location: Northern central Colorado.
Easiest Access: From Interstate 70 at Idaho Springs, take State Route 103 south about 10 miles to State Route 5, the Mount Evans Road.
Season: Fall for smaller crowds.
Wilderness Fees/Permits: None, but a road-use fee for the Mount Evans Highway is under consideration.
Maps: USGS topographic maps are Georgetown, Harris Park, Idaho Springs, Mount Evans, Mount Logan, and Shawnee.
Management: Clear Creek Ranger District, Arapaho National Forest, 101 Chicago Creek, Idaho Springs, CO 80452; (970) 567-2901. South Platte Ranger District, Pike National Forest, 19316 Goddard Ranch Court, Morrison, CO 80465; (970) 275-5610.

COLORADO

Mount Massive Wilderness

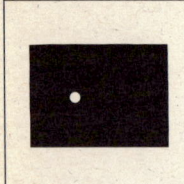

Mount Massive (14,421 feet), Colorado's second highest peak, and other mountains of the Sawatch Range have two distinctive characteristics: great height, and a huge, sloping bulk that makes them relatively easy to climb. Nowhere along the Continental Divide does the ground rise higher than the Sawatch Range, the crest of this continent. Just south of the Wilderness stands Mount Elbert at 14,443 feet, Colorado's highest summit. The divide marks the western boundary of this area, with the Hunter-Fryingpan Wilderness (see above) immediately to the other side. Dry lodgepole pine forests, typical of the eastern slopes of the divide, cover much of the lower elevations and give way to spruce and fir higher up before all trees yield to alpine tundra. Despite the fact that this region was an uplift little touched by glacial activity, a dozen or more lovely glacial lakes lie hidden here.

Approximately 2,500 acres managed by the Leadville National Fish Hatchery comprise part of the Wilderness' eastern section. They are the only designated land within the state managed by the U.S. Fish and Wildlife Service.

The Colorado Trail crosses 10 miles of the eastern region, and only about 10 more miles of trails exist in this Wilderness. Great but rugged regions will tempt you to wander off the trail.

Mount Massive Essentials

Size: 30,540 acres.
Year Designated: 1980.
Location: Central Colorado.
Easiest Access: From Leadville, take U.S. 24 south about three miles. Turn west on State Route 300 and follow this about five miles to the trailhead near the fish hatchery.
Season: Summer and early fall.
Wilderness Fees/Permits: None.
Maps: USGS topographic maps are Homestake Reservoir, Independence Pass, Mount Champion, and Mount Massive.
Management: Leadville Ranger District, San Isabel National Forest, 2015 North Poplar, Leadville, CO 80461; (719) 486-0749. For more information, write: Mountain-Prairie Regional Office, USF&W Service, P.O. Box 25486, Denver Federal Center, Denver, CO 80225.

Mount Sneffels Wilderness

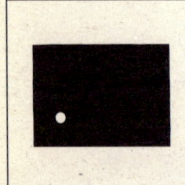

Mount Sneffels, a 14,150-foot intrusion of igneous rock on the eastern verge of this area, stands higher than any other point in the Wilderness. Westward stretches a sheer vertical world of sharp ridges, icy slopes, and ragged peaks. It makes for dangerous climbing typical of the San Juan Mountains, sometimes called America's Switzerland, a land of unsurpassed mountain drama. Technical climbers are still discovering new routes here, but loose volcanic rock often moves the rating from "dangerous" to "very dangerous." In early fall, when light dustings of snow highlight the jagged terrain and the aspens have turned gold, you'll encounter an absolutely indescribable world of wonder. I have considered declaring this Wilderness the most sheerly magnificent in the state.

Fifteen miles of trail, in the eastern and western portions, access some of the finest midsummer wildflower spectacles on the planet, especially in Yankee Boy Basin just outside the eastern boundary, where you'll find the Blue

COLORADO

Lakes Trail leading into the area for about 3.5 miles. The only lakes around, Blue Lakes huddle below the western flank of Mount Sneffels in a deep basin. The forbidding central region of the area is rugged beyond words and relatively seldom explored.

Mount Sneffels Essentials

Size: 16,505 acres.
Year Designated: 1980.
Location: Southwestern Colorado.
Easiest Access: From less than a mile south of Ouray, go about four miles south on Forest Service Road 853 to find Yankee Boy Basin and the Blue Lakes Trailhead on the eastern boundary.
Season: Midsummer to fall.
Wilderness Fees/Permits: None.
Maps: USGS topographic maps are Gray Head, Mount Sneffels, Sams, and Telluride.
Management: Ouray Ranger District, Uncompahgre National Forest, 2505 South Townsend, Montrose, CO 81401; (970) 249-3711. Norwood Ranger District, Uncompahgre National Forest, P.O. Box 388, Norwood, CO 81423; (970) 327-4261.

Mount Zirkel Wilderness

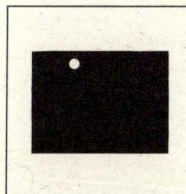

The Continental Divide runs through the heart of Colorado's northernmost Wilderness. At 12,180 feet, Mount Zirkel—named for a petrologist on the 40th Parallel Survey team of 1874—towers over the rest of the area. Mount Zirkel and nearby Big Agnes Mountain form a massif of ragged buttresses and spires that some people claim cannot be matched for beauty in the state.

Just south of the Wyoming border, you'll find that glaciation has left its distinctive mark of high valleys ending in precipitous cirques. Literally hundreds of lakes dot the region, many stocked with trout. Streams flow out of the lakes, providing relatively easy access along 155 combined miles of trails but impeding traffic from lake to lake. The most popular trail, the Slavonia Trail, leads four miles to Gilpin Lake and the heart of the area. Two major rivers in the Wilderness, the Encampment and the Elk, have been proposed for Wild and Scenic designation and offer many miles of lovely valley hiking. On the heights above the rivers, Colorado receives more snow than anywhere else. You'll find a great diversity of ecosystems—from sagebrush meadows to pine forests to alpine tundra—and an opportunity in summer to see many other humans.

Mount Zirkel Essentials

Size: 160,568 acres.
Year Designated: 1964; expanded in 1980 and 1993.
Location: Northern Colorado.
Easiest Access: From Steamboat Springs, take U.S. 40 west one mile. Turn north on County Road 129 and go about 20 miles. Turn east on Forest Service Road 400 and proceed about 10 miles to access the Slavonia Trailhead.
Season: July to October before the snow flies.
Wilderness Fees/Permits: None.
Maps: USGS topographic maps are Boettcher Lake, Buffalo Pass, Davis Peak, Farwell Mountain, Floyd Peak, Mount Ethel, Mount Zirkel, Pitchpine Mountain, Rocky Peak, Teal Lake, and West Fork Lake.
Management: Hahns Peak Ranger District, Routt National Forest, 27 Tenth Street, Steamboat Springs, CO 80487; (303) 879-1870. North Park Ranger District, Routt National Forest, 612 Fifth Street, Walden, CO 80480; (303) 723-8204.

COLORADO

Neota Wilderness

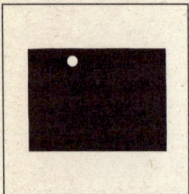

Bordering Rocky Mountain National Park on the south and surrounded by other Wilderness areas, little Neota actually stands in a huge expanse of virtually roadless country. With elevations ranging between 10,000 and 11,896 feet, snow enjoys a long life here. Neota protects flattened ridges of granite atypical of the steep-sided Rockies. Just outside the southwestern boundary, Iron Mountain at 12,265 feet looks down on three main drainages within the area: Trap, Corral, and Neota Creeks. Along the summer-wet valleys of these streams, willows and sedges grow thick and occasionally hide a moose or two. You'll find spruce and fir on the lower slopes, home to deer and elk. You won't find maintained trails or ample opportunities to be alone.

Neota Essentials

Size: 9,924 acres.
Year Designated: 1980.
Location: Northern central Colorado.
Easiest Access: From Fort Collins, take State Route 14 west about 70 miles to Joe Wright Reservoir on the western edge of the Wilderness. From south of the reservoir, a trail leads to Zimmerman Lake sitting in a non-Wilderness dent in the boundary.
Season: Summer or fall.
Wilderness Fees/Permits: None.
Maps: USGS topographic maps are Chambers Lake and Fall River Pass.
Management: Redfeather Ranger District, Roosevelt National Forest, 1311 South College Avenue, Fort Collins, CO 80524; (970) 482-3822.

Never Summer Wilderness

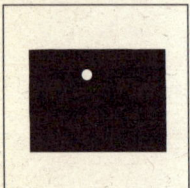

As its name suggests, Never Summer Wilderness gets hit with large amounts of rain and snow that collect on its storm-wracked peaks, which offer relatively gentle terrain and bear names that hint at their cloud-kissed heights: Cirrus, Cumulus, Stratus, and Nimbus. Seventeen summits rise above 12,000 feet, with Howard Mountain towering over all at 12,810 feet. Never Summer supplies water to three main rivers: the Colorado, the North Platte, and the Cache la Poudre. In damp gulches above 10,000 feet trees absorb the abundant moisture and grow old and exceptionally large. Spruce and fir in Bowen Gulch have been measured at four feet in diameter and estimated at 600 years in age, and the Bowen Gulch Trail will take you about five miles into the oldest of the old growth. In the northern section, a series of ponds and bogs provide rare habitats for species seldom seen so far from north-country muskegs: wood frogs, bog bean, pygmy shrew, perhaps even a wolverine or two. Moose have been reintroduced and are faring well. Several lakes and streams shelter trout.

Straddling the Continental Divide, Never Summer has about 20 miles of trails that lead up gulches and cross the divide on two high passes.

COLORADO

Never Summer Essentials
Size: 20,692 acres.
Year Designated: 1980; expanded in 1993.
Location: Northern central Colorado.
Easiest Access: From Interstate 70 take U.S. 40 west about 40 miles to Granby. Turn north on U.S. 34 (closed in winter) and follow this for approximately 20 miles to the Bowen Gulch Trailhead.
Season: Summer, despite the name.
Wilderness Fees/Permits: None.
Maps: USGS topographic maps are Bowen Mountain, Fall River Pass, Grand Lake, and Mount Richthofen.
Management: Sulphur Ranger District, Arapaho National Forest, 62429 Highway 40, Granby, CO 80446; (970) 887-3331.

Platte River Wilderness

The North Platte River enters Routt National Forest four miles south of the Colorado-Wyoming state line and flows through a narrow canyon that is deeply ensconced within forested mountains. The river tumbles into Platte River Wilderness, almost all of which lies in Wyoming (see Wyoming, Platte River Wilderness). On the Colorado side, no Wilderness covers less acreage. The waterway is a popular destination for white-water river enthusiasts.

Platte River Essentials
Size: 770 acres in Colorado (23,000 total).
Year Designated: 1984.
Location: Northern Colorado.
Easiest Access: From U.S. 40 near Granby, take State Highway 125 north for 70 miles. Turn east on Forest Service Road 894 and proceed about two miles to where the road crosses the North Platte River. Hike north.
Season: Late spring through fall.
Wilderness Fees/Permits: None.
Maps: DeLorme's *Colorado Atlas and Gazetteer* will help you navigate this area (as well as many other Wilderness areas in the state).
Management: North Park Ranger District, Routt National Forest, P.O. Box 158, Walden, CO 80480; (970) 723-8204.

Powderhorn Wilderness

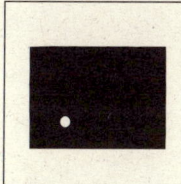

In this Wilderness, the northern verge of the San Juan Mountains reaches out into the Gunnison Basin, a dry land of sagebrush meadows dotted with fish-filled lakes, including Powderhorn Lakes. Scoured by glaciation, the Calf Creek and Cannibal Plateaus are said to be the largest unbroken expanses of alpine tundra in the Lower 48, and I found the feeling of sheer vastness unparalleled in Colorado. You'll discover terrain rolling along at around 12,000 feet with views of even higher mountains in the Elk, Sawatch, and San Juan Ranges, broken only by several escarpments that stand especially lovely in the light of the setting sun. Cannibal Plateau was named for Colorado's famous man-eater, Alferd Packer, who supposedly dined on five friends while lost near here during the winter of 1874. Elk and mule deer roam the plateaus and pass through the stands of aspen, pine, spruce, and fir that blanket the lower elevations.

COLORADO

The southern one-fourth of Powderhorn is managed by Gunnison National Forest, and the northern three-fourths by the Bureau of Land Management. About 45 miles of trails access this seldom-visited area. For an easily accessible hike into the backcountry, take the Devil's Lake Trail for 6.5 miles and find a jewel of water set in a treeless alpine meadow high on the plateau.

Powderhorn Essentials

Size: 60,100 acres.
Year Designated: 1993.
Location: Southwestern Colorado.
Easiest Access: From Gunnison, take U.S. 50 west for nine miles. Turn south on State Route 149 and go about 40 miles to the Devil's Lake Trailhead on the east side of the road.
Season: Summer and fall, for fish and milder temperatures.
Wilderness Fees/Permits: None.
Maps: USGS topographic maps are Cannibal Plateau, Mineral Mountain, Powderhorn Lakes, and Rudolph Hill.
Management: BLM Montrose District Office and Cebolla Ranger District, Gunnison National Forest, both at 216 North Colorado, Gunnison, CO 81230; (970) 641-0471.

Ptarmigan Peak Wilderness

The Williams Fork Mountains leap up and away into Ptarmigan Peak Wilderness from just below the western entrance to the Eisenhower Tunnel on Interstate 70, virtually unnoticed in winter as skiers rush to many nearby developed ski areas. The south slope of the mountains, dominated by Ptarmigan Peak at 12,458 feet, is where you'll find the designated land. A typical lodgepole-pine forest rises to Engelmann spruce and subalpine fir and then on to alpine tundra at the highest elevations. From the boundary along the top of the mountain ridgeline, the terrain drops into the wet, lush, and lovely drainages of the South and Middle Forks of the Williams Fork Rivers. Although these drainages are currently roadless, they remain non-Wilderness because of Denver's growing need for water. But they are certainly worth the hike.

You will not find many miles of trails in this Wilderness. The Ptarmigan Peak Trail just outside Silverthorne crosses Ptarmigan Pass into the drainages to the northeast, a one-way journey of seven miles. The Ute Pass Trail follows the ridgeline boundary from Ptarmigan Pass north to Ute Peak (12,303 feet) and on to Ute Pass, a total distance of about 10 miles.

Ptarmigan Peak Essentials

Size: 13,175 acres.
Year Designated: 1993.
Location: Northern central Colorado.
Easiest Access: The Ptarmigan Peak Trail starts on County Road 2021 just outside Silverthorne. From Highway 9 in Silverthorne, turn north on Tanglewood Drive and proceed one-third mile to a stop sign. Go west on County Road 2021 for eight-tenths of a mile to a parking lot at the trailhead.
Season: Spring and fall.
Wilderness Fees/Permits: None.
Maps: USGS topographic maps are Byers Peak, Dillon, Loveland Pass, and Ute Peak.
Management: Dillon Ranger District, White River National Forest, 135 Highway 9, Silverthorne, CO 80498; (970) 468-5400. Middle Park Ranger District, Routt National Forest, P.O. Box 1210, Kremmling, CO 80459; (970) 724-9004.

COLORADO

Raggeds Wilderness

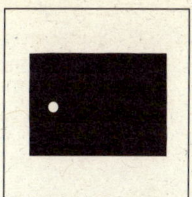

Prominent rocky slopes striking skyward to a serrated ridge give Raggeds Wilderness its well-deserved name. Ragged Mountain in the northern half rises to 12,094 feet, but other wonderfully scenic peaks crest higher. Anthracite Creek has carved the deep Dark Canyon through the heart of a Wilderness that contains numerous other creeks and small lakes. Colorado's most delightfully named Oh-Be-Joyful Pass (11,740 feet), with the long sweep of Oh-Be-Joyful Creek Valley below it, was added to the area in 1993—a most welcome addition that was mightily opposed by developers. A dense coniferous forest covers the creek bottoms. Every fall, you'll see great unbroken expanses of aspens ablaze in shimmering yellow and rock bands of red, gray, and black rising above a patchwork quilt of gold and green, painting a setting glorious enough to soothe any restless spirit. You'll want to shout, as I did, "Oh, be joyful!"

About 50 miles of trail lead into the area. The hiking rates as relatively strenuous, and large portions off the trail are seldom explored. You'll have to ford the Slate River to access the seven miles of the Oh-Be-Joyful Pass Trail, a difficult task during spring runoff.

Raggeds Essentials

Size: 65,019 acres.
Year Designated: 1980; expanded in 1993.
Location: Western central Colorado.
Easiest Access: From Crested Butte, take County Road 317 north about two miles. Turn northwest on Forest Service Road 734 and drive about four miles. Cross Slate Creek on Forest Service Road 754 (no bridge so you'll have to wade or ford in a four-wheel-drive vehicle if the water is low enough) and continue to the Wilderness boundary, a distance of 1.5 miles.
Season: Fall.
Wilderness Fees/Permits: None.
Maps: USGS topographic maps are Chair Mountain, Marble, Marcellina Mountain, Oh-Be-Joyful, and Paonia Reservoir.
Management: Sopris Ranger District, White River National Forest, 620 Main Street, Carbondale, CO 81623; (970) 963-2266. Taylor River Ranger District, Gunnison National Forest, 216 North Colorado, Gunnison, CO 81230; (970) 641-0471.

Rawah Wilderness

Just before the Front Range of the Colorado Rockies fades into Wyoming's Medicine Bow Mountains, the Rawah Wilderness protects a scenic high country of U-shaped glacier-carved valleys and peaks reaching 12,951 feet. To the south and west of the area lies an almost roadless Colorado State Forest, an unofficial extension of the Wilderness. Melting snow fills 26 lakes within the area, lakes enticingly stocked with rainbow, cutthroat, and brook trout. Island Lake and Crater Lake are especially lovely, shadowed by walls that stand approximately 1,000 feet above the water. On the upper forested slopes of the mountains, especially in the southern section, clusters of old-growth spruce and fir abound.

You can expend energy on more than 75 miles of trails. Take the Link Trail in the north for nine miles to join the Rawah Trail. Take the Rawah

Trail across Grassy Pass and continue on down to the West Branch Trail. Take the West Branch Trail up, then turn south on the Blue Lake Trail and continue to the trailhead. You will have accomplished a cross-Wilderness hike of 24 miles that presents a taste of everything this area has to offer. Fall attracts many deer and elk hunters. Bighorn sheep are occasionally spotted, and moose that were reintroduced in the 1970s are now doing well.

Rawah Essentials

Size: 73,020 acres.
Year Designated: 1964; expanded in 1980.
Location: Northern Colorado.
Easiest Access: From Fort Collins, take State Route 14 west about 60 miles to Chambers Lake. Turn north on County Road 103 and go 15 miles. Turn west on County Road 80C, drive two miles to the Link Creek Trailhead.
Season: Summer and fall.
Wilderness Fees/Permits: None.
Maps: USGS topographic maps are Boston Peak, Chambers Lake, Clark Peak, Glendevey, Rawah Lakes, and Shipman Mountain.
Management: Redfeather Ranger District, Roosevelt National Forest, 1311 South College Ave., Fort Collins, CO 80524; (970) 498-1375.

Sangre de Cristo Wilderness

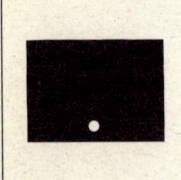

Sangre de Cristo is Spanish for "Blood of Christ," but no one is quite sure why the region was given this name. Was it because of the bloody hues washing the slopes at sunset, or the cry of the dying priest, "sangre de Cristo," as his martyred blood flowed onto the ground near here? Of the long and colorful Spanish influence in these mountains and in the San Luis Valley below there is no doubt. Two four-wheel-drive roads over Medano Pass and Hayden Pass, as well as access to Lily Lake, were slim exclusions from Wilderness designation and split the area into four distinct sections. Unlike most of Colorado's mountains, the high and magnificently rugged Sangres were uplifted suddenly in massive blocks, creating a range of dramatic vertical proportions. Four fourteeners are clumped together in the midsection of the Wilderness, including Crestone Needle (14,197 feet). Many climbers, including me, consider the Needle to be Colorado's most challenging 14,000-foot peak. Three more fourteeners stand together just south of the boundary. Melting snow feeds many creeks and small lakes, and nourishes a forest of oak, aspen, and spruce. Black bears and a few mountain lions live here, along with elk, deer, and bighorn sheep.

Long (about 70 miles) and narrow describes the area, the state's third largest, and the going is rough for the hiker. Most of the 180 miles of trails end at alpine lakes set against virtually unclimbable walls. The Willow Creek Trail pleasantly follows the creek for about five miles to popular fishing lakes at the foot of Kit Carson Peak (14,165 feet). Great Sand Dunes National Monument lies west of the southern boundary.

Sangre de Cristo Essentials

Size: 226,455 acres.
Year Designated: 1993.
Location: Central southern Colorado.
Easiest Access: From Alamosa, take State Route 17 north for 37 miles to Moffat. Turn east on County Road T and proceed about 15 miles to Crestone. The Willow Creek Trailhead lies east of the road in Crestone.
Season: Relatively light snowfall often allows winter access, but summer is more popular.
Wilderness Fees/Permits: None.
Maps: USGS topographic maps are Beck Mountain, Beckwith Mountain, Blanca Peak, Bushnell Peak, Coaldale, Cotopaxi, Crestone, Crestone Peak, Electric Peak, Horn Peak, Howard, Medano Pass, Mosca Pass, Redwing, Rita Alto Peak, Twin Peaks, Valley View Hot Springs, Wellsville, and Zapata Ranch.
Management: Conejos Peak Ranger District, Rio Grande National Forest, 21461 Highway 285, La Jara, CO 81140; (719) 274-5193. Saguache Ranger District, Rio Grande National Forest, 46525 Highway 114, Saguache, CO 81149; (719) 655-2553. Salida Ranger District, San Isabel National Forest, 325 West Rainbow Boulevard, Salida, CO 81201; (719) 539-3591. San Carlos Ranger District, San Isabel National Forest, 326 Dozier Street, Canon City, CO 81212; (719) 275-4119.

Sarvis (Service) Creek Wilderness

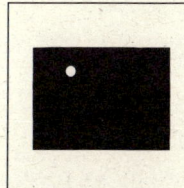

Old-timers sometimes pronounced "service" as "sarvis," and the Sarvis Timber Company once logged near here, lending its name to this Wilderness. Opening occasionally at islands of rock or in meadows of wet mushy ground, the Sarvis Creek Wilderness is foremost an unusually thick forest of lodgepole pine at lower elevations and Engelmann spruce-subalpine fir higher up. Unlike most Colorado Wilderness areas, Sarvis contains no alpine tundra. Service Creek and Silver Creek, the two primary drainages, run westerly through the dense forestland, past small gravel bars and under many dead trees lying across the water, emptying into the Yampa River. At times virtually impenetrable, the tree cover provides homes for large mammals: black bears, mountain lions, elk, and deer.

About 20 miles of trails follow both of the creeks: 11 miles along the Service Creek Trail, and 9 miles along the Silver Creek Trail. If you're willing to undertake a difficult cross-country hike and walk a few miles of road, you can connect the two trails. You'll find many pleasant campsites and few other humans.

Sarvis (Service) Creek Essentials

Size: 47,140 acres.
Year Designated: 1993.
Location: Northern central Colorado.
Easiest Access: From Steamboat Springs, take U.S. 40 east for four miles. Turn south on State Route 131 and continue for approximately five miles. Then take Country Road 18 south about four miles to the Service Creek Trailhead.
Season: Late summer, for fewer insects in the wet areas.
Wilderness Fees/Permits: None.
Maps: USGS topographic maps are Blacktail Mountain, Gore Mountain, Green Ridge, Lake Agnes, Tyler Mountain, and Walton Peak.
Management: Yampa Ranger District, Routt National Forest, 300 Roselawn, Yampa, CO 80483; (970) 638-4516.

COLORADO

South San Juan Wilderness

Ages of volcanic activity followed by the infinitely patient carving of glaciers left the rough, imposing terrain of the remote South San Juan Wilderness, an area typified by steep slopes above broad U-shaped valleys cut sharply deeper by eroding streams. You'll find high peaks and cliffs, as well as jagged pinnacles and ragged ridges, making travel difficult. Elevations rise as high as 13,300 feet. Thirty-two lakes, most of them formed by glacial activity, hold much of the area's moisture and drain into turbulent creeks. The Conejos, San Juan, and Blanco Rivers have their headwaters here, and about 25 miles of the Conejos River has been recommended for Wild and Scenic designation. Erosion of rich volcanic rock in combination with heavy snowfall has produced ideal forestland, certainly among the best in the state. Forest ecosystems rise from the shadowy cover of magnificent lodgepole pine to aspen, then through Engelmann spruce and subalpine fir to alpine tundra. Much of the forestland has a peaceful, parklike quality under the trees where sun-starved undergrowth grows thin and low.

You'll find about 180 miles of trails, and some of the most exemplary backpacking in the state. The Continental Divide crosses the heart of the Wilderness for 42 miles. The South Fork of the Conejos River Trail will lead you to the Conejos Peak Trail, which climbs north to the summit of Conejos Peak and offers a fantastic view into the heart of the area. You can continue down to beautiful Blue Lake and return down the creek to where you started, a total distance of 22 miles. A great bear was killed here in 1979, the last known Colorado grizzly. But rumor, extrapolation, and scientific evidence all join hands to suggest strongly that more grizzlies, if they still live anywhere in Colorado, inhabit the recesses of this rugged Wilderness, which many claim as the wildest left in the state.

South San Juan Essentials

Size: 158,790 acres.
Year Designated: 1980; expanded in 1993.
Location: Southern Colorado.
Easiest Access: From Antonito, take State Highway 17 west for approximately 20 miles. Turn north on Forest Service Road 250 and travel about 12 miles to the South Fork of the Conejos River Trailhead.
Season: Summer, for mild temperatures and no snow.
Wilderness Fees/Permits: None.
Maps: USGS topographic maps are Archuleta Lake, Blackhead Peak, Chromo, Cumbres, Elephant Head Rock, Elwood Pass, Harris Lake, Platoro, Red Mountain, Spectacle Lake, Summit Peak, Summitville, and Victoria Lake.
Management: Conejos Peak Ranger District, Rio Grande National Forest, 21461 Highway 285, La Jara, CO 81140; (719) 274-5193. Pagosa Ranger District, San Juan National Forest, P.O. Box 310, Pagosa Springs, CO 81147; (970) 264-2268.

COLORADO

Uncompahgre Wilderness

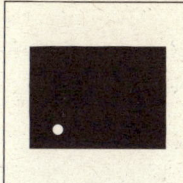

Big Blue Creek flows off Uncompahgre Peak (14,309 feet) in this rough and majestic section of the San Juan Mountains, which was formerly known as Big Blue Wilderness Area. When BLM land was added in 1993, including the rolling gentle tundra of American Flats, the name was changed. Today, the Uncompahgre Wilderness combines USFS land with BLM land on its south side.

Uncompahgre Peak's unusual broad, flat, tilted summit falls away almost vertically on three sides for as much as 1,500 feet, a landmark visible from far away. Its fourth side lies gentle and inviting to many climbers. Below Uncompahgre Peak, the Wilderness is a mountainous land of towering rock castles and sweeping ridges that some claim form the most splendid scenery in the state. Technical climbers find endless routes to challenge their skills. Wetterhorn Peak (14,015 feet) stands not far southwest of Uncompahgre Peak. Water off Wildhorse Peak near the southwest corner combines to create the turbulent and deep Cow Creek Canyon, which is ragged and densely forested enough to prevent any trails being carved in its depths. American Flats lies south of Wildhorse Peak. Numerous forks of the Cimarron River rush out of the central section of this Wilderness, flowing north to eventually become one. You'll find a few small lakes with trout, and many trout in the many streams.

About 110 miles of trails reach up numerous waterways into this beautiful Wilderness. The trail up Matterhorn Creek provides access to Wetterhorn Peak after three miles of hiking. Most climbers approach Uncompahgre Peak on three miles of trail up the Nellie Creek.

Uncompahgre Essentials

Size: 102,525 acres.
Year Designated: 1980; expanded in 1993.
Location: Southwestern Colorado.
Easiest Access: From Lake City, take County Road 20 west up Henson Creek six miles to Nellie Creek, and then 11 miles up to the Matterhorn Creek Trailhead. A four-wheel-drive vehicle is usually required.
Season: Fall.
Wilderness Fees/Permits: None.
Maps: USGS topographic maps are Alpine Plateau, Courthouse Mountain, Dallas, Handies Peak, Lake City, Ouray, Sheep Mountain, Uncompahgre Peak, and Wetterhorn Peak.
Management: BLM Montrose District Office, 216 North Colorado, Gunnison, CO 81230; (970) 641-0471. Ouray Ranger District, Uncompahgre National Forest, 2505 South Townsend, Montrose, CO 81401; (970) 249-3711.

Vasquez Peak Wilderness

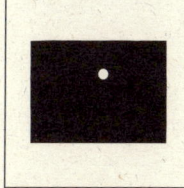

Along the southern boundary of the relatively small Vasquez Peak Wilderness and over Vasquez Peak itself, you'll find that seven miles of the Continental Divide National Scenic Trail offer two distinct and worthy opportunities. First, you'll encounter less crowded conditions than most Colorado Wildernesses, and second, you'll be blessed with extravagant views over a dramatic area, two-thirds of which lie above timberline. Below timberline sits a region of krummholz (or twisted wood), the result of icy temperatures and fierce winds that keep the spruce and fir dwarfed and confined into low-lying mats. Healthy spruce, fir, and pine cloak the lower mountainsides. Vasquez Creek flows heavily off Vasquez Peak to form the main drainage of the area. A deep indentation in the Wilderness boundary from the north maintains Vasquez Creek as non-Wilderness to allow for a collection system that sends much of the water toward Denver.

With much of the 17-mile-long trail system above timberline, sudden summer thunderstorms can make exposure to lightning in the Vasquez Mountains a dangerous risk. Vasquez Pass on the Divide can be reached after three miles of hiking on the Vasquez Peak Trail off Vasquez Creek. You should plan on hiking early and dropping into the trees before afternoon storms break. In winter, avalanches are common.

Vasquez lies near Byers Peak, Ptarmigan Peak, and Eagles Nest Wildernesses (see above) to form a vast, largely roadless region.

Vasquez Peak Essentials

Size: 12,300 acres.
Year Designated: 1993.
Location: Northern central Colorado.
Easiest Access: From Winter Park, take U.S. 40 north about two miles. Turn west and then south on Forest Service Road 148 (Vasquez Road), which leads up Vasquez Creek about five miles to the Vasquez Pass Trailhead.
Season: Spring or fall, for beauty and safety.
Wilderness Fees/Permits: None.
Maps: USGS topographic maps are Berthoud Pass and Byers Peak.
Management: Sulphur Ranger District, Arapaho National Forest, 62429 U.S. Highway 40, Granby, CO 80446; (970) 887-3331.

Weminuche Wilderness

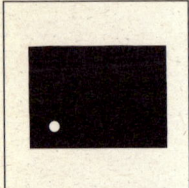

Colorado's largest Wilderness boasts sheer peaks lying about expansive glacial valleys and 63 ice-blue high-country lakes. Along its southern border stands the forest of the Piedra Area, which although non-Wilderness, falls under special state protection prohibiting logging, mining, and motorized vehicles. Together these two areas encompass more than one-half million acres.

This huge Wilderness supports an equally huge elk herd, not to mention sizable numbers of other large mammals. Snowmelt runs downhill in dozens of major waterways. You'll find the headwaters of the Rio Grande and the San Juan Rivers. From the Needle Mountains in the western section, which harbors three fourteeners and the gorge of the Animas River, you can look into the southern section where mesas rise slowly toward the summits of the central and northern sections. In the east, jagged ridges and peaks have been forged by violent volcanic activity.

The Continental Divide Trail runs through the heart of the area for approximately 80 miles. The Colorado Trail crosses 21 miles of the Wilderness from Molas Pass to the Rio Grande, and brings the total trail miles to close to 500. Here is Colorado backpacking at its best—but most crowded. No other Wilderness in the state gets as much traffic or abuse. For the sake of this Wilderness, consider visiting a nearby roadless area—Carson Peak to the north or San Miguel to the northwest—where the beauty is undiminished and, as yet, unspoiled.

COLORADO

Weminuche Essentials

Size: 488,544 acres.
Year Designated: 1975; expanded in 1980 and 1993.
Location: Southwestern Colorado.
Easiest Access: From Silverton, take U.S. 550 south for about eight miles to Molas Pass, where the Colorado Trail enters the Wilderness.
Season: Fall, when you'll encounter fewer people as cold starts to settle in.
Wilderness Fees/Permits: None.
Maps: USGS topographic maps are Cimarron Peak, Columbine Pass, Emerald Lake, Granite Lake, Granite Peak, Howardsville, Lemon Reservoir, Little Squaw Creek, Mountain View Crest, Pagosa Peak, Palomino Mountain, Rio Grande Pyramid, Silverton, Snowdon Peak, Spar City, Storm King Peak, Vallecito Reservoir, Weminuche Pass, Wolf Creek Pass, and Workman Creek.
Management: Animas Ranger District, San Juan National Forest, 110 West 11th Street, Durango, CO 81301; (970) 247-4874. Pine Ranger District, San Juan National Forest, 367 South Pearl Street, Bayfield, CO 81122; (970) 884-2512. Pagosa Ranger District, San Juan National Forest, P.O. Box 310, Pagosa Springs, CO 81147; (970) 264-2268. Creede Ranger District, Rio Grande National Forest, Third and Creede Avenue, Creede, CO 81130; (719) 658-2556. Del Norte Ranger District, Rio Grande National Forest, 13308 West Highway 160, Del Norte, CO 81132; (719) 657-3321.

West Elk Wilderness

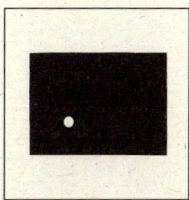

Devoid of fourteeners and sparkling alpine lakes, West Elk's most attractive offering may be a large and untamed area with very few humans. Only during fall hunting season, when numerous bull elks bugle their territorial imperative, do the trails and campsites fill with humans. Elk and deer number in the thousands. But even when orange-clad hunters migrate through, you'll find many mountain passes leading to secluded and seldom-seen valleys filled with beaver ponds and lined with trembling aspen that turn a fantastic and indescribable gold in September—the time I love this area best.

Volcanic activity of 25 million years ago produced long lava flows, sometimes pushing mud before them. Ridges were crumbled and carved by wind and water into fantastic turrets, pinnacles, and crenellated bulwarks. The topography is reflected in many of the area's geographic names: Castle Pass, Castle View, Castle Creek, the Castles.

About two hundred miles of trails, following creeks and ridge tops, offer opportunities for extended loop hikes through the West Elk, the fifth largest Wilderness in Colorado. Most of the trails provide excellent pathways for horse traffic. The Mill Castle Trail travels up to Storm Pass at 12,460 feet, a one-way distance of eight miles, offering extravagant vistas and the best look at the castlelike formations of this area.

COLORADO

West Elk Essentials

Size: 176,092 acres.
Year Designated: 1964; expanded in 1980.
Location: Western central Colorado.
Easiest Access: From Gunnison, take State Route 135 north for four miles. Turn north on County Road 730 and travel about 10 miles. Turn east on County Road 727 and go approximately four miles to the Mill Castle Trailhead.
Season: Early fall, for the golden aspen and bugling elk before the hunters arrive.
Wilderness Fees/Permits: None.

Maps: USGS topographic maps are Anthracite Range, Big Soap Park, Little Soap Park, McIntosh Mountain, Minnesota Pass, Mount Axtell, Mount Guero, Squirrel Creek, West Beckwith Peak, West Elk Peak, and West Elk Peak SW.
Management: Paonia Ranger District, Gunnison National Forest, North Rio Grande Street, Paonia, CO 81428; (970) 527-4131. Taylor River Ranger District, Gunnison National Forest, 216 North Colorado, Gunnison, CO 81230; (970) 641-0471.

> "Treat the earth well . . . it was not given to you by your parents . . . it was lent to you by your children."
>
> —African proverb

FLORIDA

Total Wilderness areas: 17
Total Wilderness acreage: 1,420,335

Lush, subtropical, and rich with wildlife, the Florida Wilderness is like no other in America. The centerpiece is Everglades National Park, Florida's largest contribution to the Wilderness Preservation System. In addition, seven roadless areas protect all that is left of the state's vast pine flatwoods and hardwood swamp ecosystems, with another nine Wildernesses under the jurisdiction of the National Wildlife Refuge System.

Alexander Springs Wilderness

Before reaching Lake Dexter, a bulge in the wide and easy-flowing Saint Johns River, Alexander Springs Creek makes its way through three miles of a subtropical swamp Wilderness. The terrain varies from hardwood swamp to sand pine scrubland—emphasis on the former—with numerous small islands, larger Kimball Island, and several old Indian shell mounds. Keep an eye out for the alligators, deer, and colorful wading birds that make their home here.

There are no trails or old roads in the area, so most visitors explore by boat. The paddling is easy and the view over the gunwale often extraordinary. You can rent a "barge" at Alexander Springs, outside the Wilderness, but haul-backs aren't offered. This, of course, means you must paddle back upstream or haul everything to the put-in. Unfortunately, the Florida Wilderness Act of 1983 allowed motorboats on Alexander Springs Creek.

Alexander Springs Essentials

Size: 7,700 acres.
Year Designated: 1984.
Location: Northern central Florida.
Easiest Access: From Eustis, take State Highway 19 north for eight miles to Altoona. Turn east on County Road 42 and continue for approximately 15 miles. Head north on Forest Service Road 540 for two miles until you reach the boat launch on the creek.
Season: Spring and fall.
Wilderness Fees/Permits: None.
Maps: A forest map that includes Alexander Springs Wilderness is available for $3 from the district ranger.
Management: Seminole Ranger District, Ocala National Forest, Florida State Highway 19N, 1551 Umatilla Road, Eustis, FL 32726; (904) 357-3721.

FLORIDA

Big Gum Swamp Wilderness

This large, nearly level area consists primarily of a poorly drained to very poorly drained freshwater swamp of cypress and gum. The surface is a thick, spongy mat of organic material, sluggishly cut by a few shallow sloughs. Longleaf and slash pine flatwoods with a dense understory of saw palmetto, gallberry, and bay form the perimeter of the swamp. Loggers made off with most of the original timber between 1915 and 1920, and earthen railroad trams, some of which are still visible, penetrated the interior. Over time, all signs of human intrusion into the swamp have greatly subsided.

Boggy terrain, dense vegetation, insects, and warm, humid conditions make travel here extremely challenging—exacerbated by the fact that the trails are not maintained (your best bet is to follow one of the many old logging roads). Deer hunters are the most common visitors. On the northwest side, an old road tunnels through a stand of massive live oaks that tower overhead.

Big Gum Swamp Essentials

Size: 13,600 acres.
Year Designated: 1984.
Location: Northern Florida.
Easiest Access: From Interstate 10 near Lake City, take U.S. 441 north for approximately nine miles. Turn east on Forest Service Road 262 and continue for nine miles, until you reach the western boundary of the Wilderness.
Season: Winter for lower humidity and fewer insects.
Wilderness Fees/Permits: None. Camping may be restricted during hunting season. Contact the district ranger.
Maps: A forest map that includes the Wilderness can be obtained for $3 from the district ranger.
Management: Osceola Ranger District, Osceola National Forest, U.S. Highway 90, P.O. Box 70, Olustee, FL 32072; (904) 752-2577.

Billies Bay Wilderness

Floridians often refer to swamps as "bays," hence the name of this marshy Wilderness. Two-thirds of the area is a hardwood swamp of red maple, bay, loblolly pine, slash pine, sweet gum, and cabbage palm; the other third (the perimeter) is pine flatwoods dominated by longleaf and slash pine. Beneath this lies an understory of palmetto and gallberry. Small stands of scrub oak and sand pine are also interspersed throughout the flatwoods.

The pristine quality of the swamp, a haven for many mammals and birds, made it a prime candidate for Wilderness designation. The swamp contributes to the headwaters of Alexander Springs Creek in the nearby Alexander Springs Wilderness (see above). You won't find any trails or old roads here, but the Florida National Scenic Trail (which provides access to about 1,000 miles of the state) skirts the southwestern corner of the area.

Billies Bay Essentials

Size: 3,120 acres.
Year Designated: 1984.
Location: Northern central Florida.
Easiest Access: From Eustis, take State Highway 19 north for about 11 miles. Turn east on County Road 445 and drive approximately nine miles to the Alexander Springs Campground on the edge of Billies Bay Wilderness.
Season: Spring and fall.
Wilderness Fees/Permits: None. Camping may be restricted during hunting season. Check with the district ranger.
Maps: A forest map that includes the Wilderness is available for $3 from the district ranger.
Management: Seminole Ranger District, Ocala National Forest, Florida State Highway 19N, 1551 Umatilla Road, Eustis, FL 32726; (904) 357-3721.

Bradwell Bay Wilderness

A swamp thick with titi trees, distinguished by their leathery leaves and fragrant white flowers, dominates the second largest Wilderness in Florida. Here, you'll also find a swampland of hardwoods or pine-titi mixtures and small ponds that are either open or covered with aquatic plants.

The climate is subtropical, and rainfall averages 55 inches per year. Summers are hot and sticky with humidity, but temperatures have been known to drop into the teens come winter. With few defined drainages, Bradwell Bay's low areas are generally submerged beneath one to four inches of standing water. The water table lies close to, if not above, ground surface over most of this flat Wilderness. Drier islands of longleaf pine and wire grass border parts of the swamp. White-tailed deer, black bears, and alligators top the food chain.

With sufficient rainfall, canoeists can run the Sopchoppy River, which defines the eastern edge of the area. Hikers can follow old logging roadbeds or take the east-west Florida National Scenic Trail through Bradwell Bay. Truth is, however, that hikers who opt to use the well-marked trail typically end up wading through sections of waist-deep water.

Bradwell Bay Essentials

Size: 24,602 acres.
Year Designated: 1975; expanded in 1984.
Location: Northwestern Florida.
Easiest Access: From Tallahassee, take U.S. 319 south for 20 miles to Medart, where the Florida National Scenic Trail crosses the road. From there, hike west.
Season: Spring and early summer are usually the driest; late summer and fall are wettest.
Wilderness Fees/Permits: None.
Maps: A national forest map that includes the Wilderness is available for $3 from the district ranger.
Management: Wakulla Ranger District, Apalachicola National Forest, U.S. Highway 319, Route 6, Box 7860, Crawfordville, FL 32327; (904) 926-3561.

FLORIDA

Cedar Keys Wilderness

Twelve keys that have been earmarked as protected breeding grounds for colonial birds make up Cedar Keys National Wildlife Refuge. These keys, low islands rising just above the sea, are in fact one of the largest nesting areas in Florida. The four outermost islands have been designated as Wilderness: Seahorse Key, North Key, Snake Key, and Bird Key (also known as Deadman's Key).

A prominent sandy ridge distinguishes Seahorse Key, recalling the island's past life as a huge sand dune (granted this was thousands of years ago). The ridge crests at 52 feet above sea level, making it the highest point on Florida's west coast. The other keys barely make it to 20 feet above the waves. An upland forest of cabbage palm, red bay, live oak, and laurel oak covers the ridge, with an understory of saw palmetto, yaupon, wild olive, prickly pear, eastern red cedar, and Spanish bayonet. Mangrove swamps dominate the lower elevations (about 40 percent of the refuge), with occasional patches of salt marsh.

In the 1960s and 1970s, nesting birds numbered approximately 200,000, but today the yearly average has dwindled to 50,000. The most abundant species are white ibis, common egret, double-crested cormorant, snowy egret, tricolored heron, brown pelican, and great blue heron. Reptiles are common as well, including a dense population of cottonmouth snakes. Due to the shortage of fresh water, however, mammals are scarce.

No camping is allowed, but visitors may come during daylight hours and enjoy shell collecting, picnicking, beachcombing, bird watching, and photography.

Cedar Keys Essentials

Size: 379 acres.
Year Designated: 1972.
Location: Off the coast of western Florida.
Easiest Access: All the keys lie within five boat miles of Cedar Key, but the shallow sand and mudflats surrounding the islands make access difficult except at high tide.
Season: Visitors will see the most birds from March through June.
Wilderness Fees/Permits: The interiors of the islands are closed to public use. Beaches are open year-round except on Seahorse Key, which is closed to visitors March 1 through June 30.
Maps: Nautical charts of the Gulf of Mexico. Contact the refuge manager.
Management: Cedar Keys National Wildlife Refuge, Route 1, Box 1193C, Chiefland, FL 32626; (904) 493-0238.

Chassahowitzka Wilderness

In the language of the Seminole Indians, *Chassahowitzka* means "The Pumpkin Opening Place," although no one seems to remember just how this region earned that moniker. Regardless, Chassahowitzka National Wildlife Refuge encompasses 30,500 acres of mangrove islands, saltwater bays, estuaries, and brackish marshes, fringed with an oak-cypress-cedar hardwood swamp on the eastern side. Except for a northeastern portion, the entire refuge is designated Wilderness. The Homosassa River runs through the northern Wilderness, while the Chassahowitzka River marks the uppermost boundary of the southern Wilderness.

Originally established for the benefit of waterfowl, the area has become increasingly important to endangered West Indian manatees, denizens of the tidal bays, rivers, and creeks of Chassahowitzka. These gentle, waterbound creatures, cousins of the elephant, must eat 10 to 15 percent of their enormous body weight (1,000 pounds or more) every day. They survive, as do some of their fair feathered friends, on musk grass, which grows abundantly here in the shallow bays.

Other resident wildlife species include some 250 birds, more than 40 reptiles and amphibians, and 25 mammals. To see these critters (and to get into the Wilderness at all, for that matter), you will need a boat. Motorists must abide by strict speed restrictions put in place to protect the manatees, but canoeists may go as fast as possible. Conditions on both the Homosassa and Chassahowitzka Rivers are ideal for the latter mode of transportation. Fishing lures anglers year-round. Camping is prohibited.

Chassahowitzka Essentials

Size: 23,580 acres.
Year Designated: 1976.
Location: Western Florida.
Easiest Access: From Saint Petersburg, take U.S. 98 north for approximately 65 miles. Turn west on State Highway 480 and continue driving for about two miles to a boat launch on the Chassahowitzka River.
Season: April through August is the best time to see the manatees.
Wilderness Fees/Permits: Sections of the refuge are closed from October 15 to February 15. Airboat users are required to obtain special permits.
Maps: Maps are available from the refuge manager, but even with one you are likely to get lost among the mangroves.
Management: Chassahowitzka National Wildlife Refuge, 1502 South Kings Bay Drive, Crystal River, FL 32629; (904) 563-2088.

Everglades Wilderness

All life in the Everglades hangs by a wet thread—the fresh water required to sustain the vast and varied species threatened by human intervention. The thread is growing weaker all the time.

This lush but fragile landscape is primarily a marsh of scattered tall grasses. Everglades National Park, which covers about 1.4 million acres, contains only part of the watery expanse known as everglades. Most of the park is a designated Wilderness.

At the heart of the Everglades is a "river of grass," six inches deep and 50 miles wide, a body of water that flows so slowly the movement is imperceptible. From its origin along the shores of Lake Okeechobee, the river drops only 15 feet on the voyage to saltwater Florida Bay.

Don't be fooled by the river's placid nature though, for this is a land of indescribable wonder. Scaly alligators share the marshes with flamingos, roseate spoonbills, egrets and herons, pelicans, cranes, hawks, ibis, storks, frigate birds, kites, skimmers, and hundreds of other colorful birds.

The shallow waters of Florida Bay constitute about one-third of the park. Most of the bay's tiny keys serve as nesting sites for birds, and the salt water teems with fish, porpoises, sea turtles, sharks, and manatees.

You pretty much need a boat to access Florida Bay and the fascinating Wilderness Waterway, a 99-mile marine trail that takes you from Everglades City and the Ten Thousand Islands

FLORIDA

on the north to Flamingo on the south. Along the waterway you'll see virtually every organism that lives in the Caribbean. On one December canoe trip on the Wilderness Waterway, unusually high temperatures gave rise to a choking horde of mosquitoes that kept me boat-bound except for furious tent-erecting sessions each evening. Only on breeze-swept "chickees"—camping platforms perched on stilts above the water—did the cloud of needle-nosed stingers thin. Pests notwithstanding, I was awestruck for the entire journey.

A 38-mile road leads from the park entrance to a visitors center at Flamingo on the southern coast of Florida. From this road, several trails head into the Wilderness, most of them day-hike routes of less than one mile. Four longer trails, ranging in length from four to 13 miles, also can be accessed near Flamingo. When embarking on foot or canoe trails, visitors should carry in all the drinking water they'll need.

Everglades Essentials

Size: 1,296,500 acres.
Year Designated: 1978.
Location: Southern Florida.
Easiest Access: From Miami, take U.S. 1 south for 40 miles to Florida City. Turn east on State Highway 9336 and proceed approximately five miles to the park entrance.
Season: From December to April the warm sun slowly dries out the area. Then the monsoonlike summer rains hit. Mosquitoes range from bad to intolerable.
Wilderness Fees/Permits: Park entrance fees are $5 per vehicle or $3 per person. Backcountry campers are required to obtain a free permit, which is issued up to 24 hours prior to departure. No reservations are taken. Permits must be picked up in person.
Maps: Pick up a park map from the park ranger. A detailed guide to the Wilderness Waterway is also available. Nautical charts covering most of the area's waters are numbers 11351, 11430, 11432, and 11433; charts may be ordered from the Florida Parks and Monuments Association, P.O. Box 279, Homestead, FL 33030; (305) 247-1216.
Management: Everglades National Park, P.O. Box 279, Homestead, FL 33030; (305) 247-6211.

Florida Keys Wilderness

Twenty-two threatened or endangered species live on or around this chain of islands between the Gulf of Mexico and the Atlantic Ocean. Four units of the U.S. Fish and Wildlife Service, known collectively as Florida Keys National Wildlife Refuges (NWR), protect the seemingly endless expanse of sea, sky, and islands draped around Florida's extreme southern coast. These refuges—Key West NWR, Great White Heron NWR, National Key Deer Refuge, and Crocodile Lake NWR—together hold more than 23,000 acres of land and 349,000 acres of open water. Land within Key West, Great White Heron, and National Key Deer has been designated Wilderness.

The sea kayaking here ranks among the best in the country, a distinction that may prove harmful in the long run. Sea kayakers have become the bane of existence for many species, including a remnant sea turtle population. Just as threatening are kayakers who unwittingly displace nesting birds, which often fail to return to their grassy beds.

Although beaches exist on some of the islands, tangles of mangroves make access to many of them difficult. Visitors are permitted only from one hour before sunrise to one hour after sunset, and overnight camping is prohibited. Fishing is a big attraction.

The Wilderness area consists of all the Marquesas Keys; Mooney Harbor Key; all the Gull Keys; Boca Grande Key; Woman Key; Man Key; Little Mullet Key; Big Mullet Key; Cottrell Key; Archer Key; Mule Key; Barracouta Keys; Joe Ingram Key; Crawfish Key; Sand Key; Rock Key; Eastern Dry Rocks; all the keys west of Key West; Crane Key; Little Swash Keys; Upper Harbor Key; Big Spanish Key; Little Spanish Key; Crawl Key; Little Pine Key Mangrove; Water Key Mangroves; Water Key; Little Pine Key; Horseshoe Keys; West Bahia Honda Key; Mayo Key; Annette Key; Howe Key; Water Keys islands in Sections 14, 15, 23, and 26; Cutoe Key islands in Sections 19, 20, and 21; Johnson Keys islands in Sections 19, 29, 30, and 32; and parts of Raccoon Key.

Florida Keys Essentials

Size: 6,197 acres.
Year Designated: 1975; expanded in 1982.
Location: Southern Florida.
Easiest Access: From Miami, take U.S. 1 south toward Key West, a distance of approximately 163 miles. Once you pass Pigeon Key, the Great White Heron NWR will lie north of you all the way to Key West. National Key Deer Refuge overlaps Great White Heron from Bahia Honda Key to Sugarloaf Key. Key West NWR lies past the end of the road from just off Key West to the Marquesas Keys.

Season: Summers are wetter and hotter, but people come here year-round.
Wilderness Fees/Permits: Restrictions often apply, including prohibitions on camping, firearms, metal detectors, and use of watercraft within designated "no entry" zones. Check with the refuge manager.
Maps: Nautical charts covering the coast of southern Florida.
Management: Florida Keys National Wildlife Refuges, P.O. Box 510, Big Pine Key, FL 33043-0510; (305) 872-2239.

Island Bay Wilderness

The tangled masses of roots stemming from mangrove trees often intertwine to form islands, a haven for pelicans, herons, and egrets. The five small mangrove islands here were given protected status in 1908 when they became the Island Bay National Wildlife Refuge, one of the smallest units (totaling a mere 20 acres) in the National Wilderness Preservation System. J. N. "Ding" Darling National Wildlife Refuge now manages the refuge.

No access is provided to these islands, but several shell mounds pay tribute to the Native Americans who once called them home. People who insist on boating out for a visit have been known to dig for artifacts (the last were removed long ago). Such thoughtlessness has caused great harm to this critical bird habitat, a fragile ecology best viewed from a boat anchored at a respectful distance of at least 200 feet.

FLORIDA

Island Bay Essentials

Size: 20 acres.
Year Designated: 1970.
Location: Off the coast of western Florida.
Easiest Access: Island Bay lies about 30 boat miles north of Sanibel Island.
Season: Spring and fall.
Wilderness Fees/Permits: Activities within the wildlife refuge are subject to special restrictions, including prohibitions on picnicking, camping, and the collecting of plants and animals. Check with the refuge manager.
Maps: Consult nautical charts of Florida's west coast.
Management: J. N. "Ding" Darling National Wildlife Refuge, One Wildlife Drive, Sanibel, FL 33957; (813) 472-1100.

J. N. "Ding" Darling Wilderness

Jay Norwood "Ding" Darling, the Pulitzer Prize–winning cartoonist, helped pioneer the conservation movement, serving as head of the U.S. Biological Survey (forerunner of the U.S. Fish and Wildlife Service) and providing strong support for the establishment of the National Wildlife Refuge System. Today, three miles off Sanibel Island, a 12-mile subtropical barrier island of sand and shell bears the name J. N. "Ding" Darling National Wildlife Refuge in honor of this forward-thinking gentleman.

The northern portion of the 5,030-acre refuge is a mass of mangrove islands designated as Wilderness. Scenic Wildlife Drive provides access along the southern edge of the Wilderness, where you can expect summer temperatures in the 90s and winter temperatures in the 70s. Humidity is almost always high, and afternoon rain showers are common.

Mosquitoes are fond of this region, as are alligators. More amiable residents include ospreys, raccoons, brown pelicans, and moorhens. Creatures for whom the refuge was established include migratory songbirds, ducks, herons, and flocks of roseate spoonbills. Motorized boating and sportfishing are allowed.

J. N. "Ding" Darling Essentials

Size: 2,619 acres.
Year Designated: 1976.
Location: Off the coast of western Florida.
Easiest Access: From Fort Myers, take Summerlin Road south across a three-mile causeway to Sanibel Island.
Season: March through May to watch for songbirds and the flights of spoonbills. December through February for the ducks. The critters really come to life at low tide.
Wilderness Fees/Permits: There is an entrance fee of $4 per vehicle or $1 per individual. Wildlife Drive is open from sunrise to sunset, Saturday through Thursday, and is closed every Friday.
Maps: A refuge map is available for free from the refuge manager.
Management: J. N. "Ding" Darling National Wildlife Refuge, One Wildlife Drive, Sanibel, FL 33957; (813) 472-1100.

FLORIDA

Juniper Prairie Wilderness

Not only does this Wilderness cover more ground than any other in Ocala National Forest, it also contains the most diverse ecosystems. An eight-mile stretch of the north-south Florida National Scenic Trail runs through here, providing access to prairies, pine flatwoods, a marsh, even a subtropical jungle of palms, swamp hardwoods, and saw grass near Juniper Springs. Shallow lakes rimmed by oak and pond pine dot the prairies, which in turn are bordered by scrubby sand pine. Remnants of old logging roads likewise delve into the Wilderness.

The Long family, characterized in Marjorie Kinnan Rawlings' book *The Yearling*, settled Pats Island here around 1840. Some of the current residents are much less intriguing: while backpacking near Pats Island in 1984, I spent an hour picking ticks off my partner's body . . . 72 determined little bloodsuckers in all. Most of them had not yet buried their heads, but the experience was memorable nonetheless.

From Juniper Springs Recreation Area Campground, canoeists can enjoy seven miles of easy paddling down a sparkling clear, shallow creek. On the way to a takeout on Highway 19, you might spot alligators, snakes, deer, and numerous wading birds. Canoes are the only craft allowed on Juniper Creek. Rentals are available, and a commercial operator offers haul-backs to the starting point. Cost for canoe and haul-back runs about $20 to $25. Canoe reservations are recommended; phone (904) 625-2808. As with most national forestland, primitive camping is permitted almost everywhere.

Juniper Prairie Essentials

Size: 13,260 acres.
Year Designated: 1984.
Location: Northern central Florida.
Easiest Access: From Ocala, take State Highway 40 east for about 25 miles to Juniper Springs.
Season: Winter, spring, and fall.
Wilderness Fees/Permits: None.
Maps: A forest map that includes the Wilderness is available for $3 from the district ranger.
Management: Lake George Ranger District, Ocala National Forest, Florida State Highway 40E, Route 2, Box 701, Silver Springs, FL 32688; (904) 625-2520.

Lake Woodruff Wilderness

The Native Americans who once lived here harvested the rich food supply and left behind mounds, middens, and artifacts dating back 10,000 years. The native population began to dwindle after the Spanish explorers arrived in the early 1500s. In 1823, Major Joseph Woodruff acquired the DeLeon Springs area (the infamous Fountain of Youth) and gave his name to the nearby lake. In 1964, the same year the Wilderness Act was passed, more than 18,500 acres were set aside as Lake Woodruff National Wildlife Refuge, a migratory bird habitat. About one-fourth of the refuge is timbered swamps.

You'll find very little evidence of human domination in this country of freshwater marshes, lakes, and streams, just plenty of wildlife. Species counted here include at least 200 birds, 42 mammals, 58 reptiles, 33 amphibians, and 68 fish. Ducks account for more than half of the migratory birds. Ospreys likewise abound, and no other refuge echoes more often with the weird cries of the limpkin, a sound that reminds me of an utterly desolate cat in heat. Black bears, armadillos, otters, and unusually long alligators are commonly sighted. In May and June, manatees move into the refuge and nearby Blue Springs. The bulk of the visitors to the refuge come to fish for bass, bream, and crappie.

Approximately 1,000 acres of Wilderness have been established along the western refuge boundary between Honey Creek and the Saint Johns River, and the Alexander Springs Wilderness lies just across the river. With neither road nor trail, the Wilderness receives few human visitors, aside from those who boat along the borders.

Lake Woodruff Essentials

Size: 1,066 acres.
Year Designated: 1976.
Location: Northern central Florida.
Easiest Access: From De Land, take U.S. 17 north for 11 miles to DeLeon Springs, where a sign will direct you to continue one block west on Grand Avenue and then one-half mile south to the refuge office.
Season: Winter, spring, and fall.
Wilderness Fees/Permits: Fishing and hunting are regulated. Some areas may be closed seasonally to protect wildlife. Contact the refuge manager before entering the Wilderness.
Maps: A free map is available from the refuge manager.
Management: Lake Woodruff National Wildlife Refuge, P.O. Box 488, DeLeon Springs, FL 32028; (904) 985-4673.

Little Lake George Wilderness

Neither old roads nor new trails cut through this dense hardwood swampland of cypress, ash, cabbage palm, and red maple, made all the more daunting by insects, reptiles, heat, and humidity. Small representations of poorly drained loblolly-slash-pond pine flatwoods grow on the western side of the Wilderness, while some of the northwest shoreline of Little Lake George forms the eastern boundary.

The Wilderness also stands at the confluence of the Saint Johns and Oklawaha Rivers, both of which provide the primary mode of travel to this remote area. I have found both rivers easy to paddle, with scenery reminiscent of old Tarzan movies, but passing motorboats often shattered my peaceful reveries. Fishing is the main attraction, with various sunfish, bass, and crappie to lure anglers (or vice versa).

Little Lake George Essentials

Size: 2,500 acres.
Year Designated: 1984.
Location: Northern central Florida.
Easiest Access: From Palatka, take State Highway 19 south approximately 15 miles to the Oklawaha River, where you will find a boat ramp on the western edge of the Wilderness.
Season: Winter, spring, and fall.
Wilderness Fees/Permits: None.
Maps: A forest map that includes Little Lake George Wilderness is available for $3 from the district ranger.
Management: Lake George Ranger District, Ocala National Forest, Florida State Highway 40E, Route 2, Box 701, Silver Springs, FL 32688; (904) 625-2520.

Mud Swamp/New River Wilderness

Florida doesn't get any more remote than this: no trails, no old roads, no people. Most of the area is Mud Swamp, a region of very poorly drained clay-rich soil that holds more water than nearby Bradwell Bay Wilderness (see above). Barely peeking above the standing water are many small, isolated islands. Heavy rainfall, especially in summer, combines with heat and humidity to provide the ideal environment for biting insects. In addition to hungry pests, this area houses hungry black bears and hungry alligators. Hiking can be perilous.

The New River, by contrast, is lined with beautiful Atlantic white cedar. It enters from the north and flows through the cypress and gum swamps, relatively thin in understory, that dominate the Wilderness. Most visitors put in canoes at Carr Bridge and paddle down about six miles to old Magnolia Landing (not marked on newer maps). The route, a twisting waterway with numerous channels, is too challenging for novices.

Mud Swamp/New River Essentials
Size: 7,800 acres.
Year Designated: 1984.
Location: Northwestern Florida.
Easiest Access: From Interstate 10 west of Tallahassee, take State Highway 65 south for approximately 30 miles. Turn east on Forest Service Road 13 and proceed about 10 miles to Carr Bridge.
Season: Winter, early spring, and late fall.
Wilderness Fees/Permits: None.
Maps: A forest map that includes the Wilderness is available for $3 from the district ranger.
Management: Apalachicola Ranger District, Apalachicola National Forest, Florida Highway 20, P.O. Box 579, Bristol, FL 32321; (904) 643-2282.

Passage Key Wilderness

A violent hurricane swept through this area in 1920, transforming Passage Key, a mangrove island containing a freshwater lake, into a meandering, slightly vegetated sandbar. A satellite of Chassahowitzka National Wildlife Refuge, one of three refuges known as the Tampa Bay Refuges, Passage Key stands at the mouth of Tampa Bay, where it faces the full force of storms off the Gulf of Mexico. Depending on weather, it ranges in size from 10 acres to well over 30 acres.

This one island represents Tampa Bay's last remaining nesting site for laughing gulls, black skimmers, and royal terns. Easily accessible by boat from the Tampa/Saint Petersburg Metropolitan sprawl, Passage Key has been inundated with humans to the point where the island had to be closed to all visitation. You must observe the key from a distance of at least 200 feet.

FLORIDA

Passage Key Essentials

Size: 36 acres.
Year Designated: 1970.
Location: Off the coast of western Florida.
Easiest Access: From Bradenton, at the southern end of Tampa Bay, drive west on Manatee Avenue (State Route 64) to County Road 789, a distance of about 10 miles. Take County Road 789 north for another 10 miles to the end of the road. You'll be on Bean Point, and Passage Key lies just north of the point.
Season: People who are willing to peer through binoculars from a distance will find abundant birds year-round.
Wilderness Fees/Permits: Closed to human visitation.
Maps: Nautical charts of the coast of western Florida.
Management: Chassahowitzka National Wildlife Refuge, 1502 South Kings Bay Drive, Crystal River, FL 32629; (904) 563-2088.

Pelican Island Wilderness

President Theodore Roosevelt set aside tiny Pelican Island as a bird haven on March 14, 1903, ordering the first federal land dedication to wildlife and thus creating the National Wildlife Refuge System. Pelican Island National Wildlife Refuge is comprised primarily of water in the wide lagoon of the Indian River. Human development near the shoreline currently threatens the fragile but highly productive waters, however, the U.S. Fish and Wildlife Service is trying to acquire an insulating buffer zone along the eastern boundary.

Fifteen threatened and endangered species live here, including manatees. A huge natural supply of fish provide food for wading birds that nest in the area. Other nesting birds crowded onto the island include brown pelicans, common egrets, snowy egrets, reddish egrets, great blue herons, little blue herons, tricolored herons, black-crowned night herons, white ibis, glossy ibis, double-crested cormorants, anhingas, and oyster catchers. Administered by Merritt Island National Wildlife Refuge, this is the smallest unit of the National Wilderness Preservation System.

Pelican Island Essentials

Size: Six acres.
Year Designated: 1970.
Location: Eastern Florida.
Easiest Access: From Melbourne, take U.S. 1 south to Wabasso, a distance of approximately 27 miles. Turn east on State Highway 510 and continue for two miles across the Indian River to the southern extreme of the Wilderness. You'll need a boat to get to Pelican Island.
Season: Birds flock all year. Summer is somewhat hot and humid.
Wilderness Fees/Permits: Setting foot on the island itself is prohibited. You may take a motorboat slowly around or paddle near the island.
Maps: A free map is available from the refuge.
Management: Merritt Island National Wildlife Refuge, P.O. Box 6504, Titusville, FL 32782; (407) 867-0667.

Saint Marks Wilderness

The rare Florida panther is suspected of hiding in Saint Marks National Wildlife Refuge. With 64,000 acres of saltwater and brackish marshes, hardwood swamps, pine flatwoods, and pine-oak uplands, along with some 31,700 acres of water in Apalachee Bay, going undercover ought to be a fairly easy task.

Your chances of spotting panthers are better in the Wilderness, but the refuge is chock-full of wildlife. It not only provides a wintering ground for at least 272 species of waterfowl, including nesting pairs of southern bald eagles, it is home to American alligators, alligator snapping turtles, cottonmouths, rattlesnakes, coral snakes, and many other reptile species. Fifty species of mammals have been identified, including raccoons, white-tailed deer, black bears, foxes, and jaguarundi cats (rare north of Mexico). Feral hogs are commonly sighted. In October, monarch butterflies cluster here by the thousands.

Thirty-five miles of the Florida National Scenic Trail cross the refuge (and the Wilderness) from east to west. Saint Marks NWR stands divided into three units: Panacea, Wakulla, and Saint Marks. The entire designated Wilderness lies within the Saint Marks Unit, from just east of the Saint Marks Lighthouse to the eastern border of the refuge. You'll find here marshland dotted with tree islands and the lower ends of the Pinhook River and the Aucilla River and its swamp. Daylight use only is permitted. Overnight camping is not allowed.

Saint Marks Essentials

Size: 17,350 acres.
Year Designated: 1975.
Location: Northwestern Florida.
Easiest Access: From Tallahassee, take State Highway 363 south for about 20 miles. Turn east on U.S. 98 and continue about three miles to County Road 59, then head south on 59 to the refuge headquarters, about three miles.
Season: Winter for waterfowl. Late spring and early fall for shorebirds.
Wilderness Fees/Permits: Hunting and fishing are regulated by law. Some areas of the refuge may be closed seasonally to boat traffic to reduce the impact on wildlife. Check with the refuge manager.
Maps: A free map is available from the refuge manager.
Management: Saint Marks National Wildlife Refuge, P.O. Box 68, Saint Marks, FL 32355; (904) 925-6121.

> "The more we become separated from that pristine wildness and beauty, the more pleasure does the mind of enlightened man feel in recurring to those scenes."
>
> —George Catlin

GEORGIA

Total Wilderness areas: 14
Total Wilderness acreage: 486,055

Georgia once showcased a significant section of the richest temperate forest in the world, as well as wildlife that included the eastern panther and the eastern elk. But that was 200 years ago. Since then, trees have been cut down, the land mostly plowed under, and the unique animals destroyed, never to return. Except for the Okefenokee, a swamp that comprises three-fourths of Georgia's designated Wilderness, "progress" has trammeled virtually all of the wild country. Two additional pieces of wildlife refuges have been preserved, along with a few remote regions of the southern Appalachians in Chattahoochee National Forest and one piece of national parkland.

Big Frog Wilderness

If you like the notion of crossing state lines on foot, take the steep 6.2-mile Hemp Top Trail from Cohutta Wilderness (see below) in Georgia, near the western boundary of Big Frog, until it dead-ends at Tennessee's Licklog Ridge Trail. If you want to keep hiking, the Licklog Ridge Trail is easy to access.

Only a sliver of Big Frog Wilderness lies in Georgia. The vast majority of this forested mountain Wilderness is actually in Tennessee (see Tennessee, Big Frog Wilderness).

Big Frog Essentials

Size: 83 acres in Georgia (8,055 acres total).
Year Designated: 1984.
Location: Northern Georgia.
Easiest Access: From the intersection of U.S. 411 and State Highway 40 in Tennessee, travel approximately 24 miles on State Highway 40 to Thunder Rock Campground in Tennessee. Take Forest Service Road 45 south for about 2.9 miles, then turn east on Forest Service Road 221 and continue driving until you reach the Licklog Ridge Trailhead, approximately 2.2 miles away.
Season: Spring through fall.
Wilderness Fees/Permits: None.
Maps: USGS topographic map is Hemp Top.
Management: Ocoee Ranger District, Cherokee National Forest, Route 1, Box 348D, Benton, TN 37307; (615) 338-5201.

GEORGIA

Blackbeard Island Wilderness

Edward "Blackbeard" Teach, a notorious pirate feared by many for his murderous, plundering raids, supposedly came here to "bank" some of his ill-gained fortune. Evidence of buried treasure has never been discovered on Blackbeard Island, but there is a wealth of native wildlife and migratory birds.

Preserved as a part of the Bureau of Biological Survey in 1924, these 5,618 acres of maritime forest, salt marsh, freshwater marsh, and beach habitat became Blackbeard Island National Wildlife Refuge in 1940. Interconnected sand dunes, covered thickly with oak and palmetto, separate the numerous ponds and savannas that fill with seasonal rain and provide homes for waterfowl and wading birds on much of the northern portion of the refuge.

Of the land designated as Wilderness on the southern half of the refuge, about 2,470 acres consist of salt marsh, 450 acres of slash pines mixed with live oaks, and 50 acres of white sandy beach. In the thick humidity of summer, the lush beards of Spanish moss hang from the trees, and parrot green manes of resurrection fern grow on the live oaks. Shorebirds, gulls, and terns utilize the refuge year-round, with spring and fall bringing warblers and sandpipers. Many migrant birds winter on Blackbeard, including hermit thrushes, ruby-crowned kinglets, yellow-rumped warblers, black-bellied plovers, and sanderlings.

Both the South Trail and Beach Road offer five-mile loops that begin at refuge headquarters on Blackbeard Creek and take you through the Wilderness area. However, many more people visit the particularly beautiful beach on the non-Wilderness north end of the island. Neither camping nor pets are allowed.

Blackbeard Island Essentials

Size: 3,000 acres.
Year Designated: 1975.
Location: Off the coast of Georgia.
Easiest Access: From Savannah, take U.S. 17 south for about 51 miles. Turn east on Shellman Bluff Road, which terminates at Shellman Bluff after about five miles. There you can launch a boat for a visit.
Season: Although the area is open year-round, winter is the best time to see migratory birds.
Wilderness Fees/Permits: None.
Maps: A free map is available from the refuge manager.
Management: Savannah Coastal Refuges, 1000 Business Center Drive, Parkway Business Center, Suite 10, Savannah, GA 31405; (912) 652-4415.

Blood Mountain Wilderness

Legends tell of the gory battles waged between Creek and Cherokee Indians atop 4,458-foot Blood Mountain, but today the site is famous for being the highest point in this Wilderness. Scenically rugged mountain peaks, rocky outcroppings, waterfalls, and numerous streams (offering 27 miles of trout fishing), all of which lie within the Chestatee Wildlife Management Area, surround the mountain.

The vegetation is primarily second-growth upland and cove hardwoods, a forest that's only about 60 years old. Deer, grouse, wild turkeys, and squirrels live here in abundance, and there are also black bears and raccoons, although in lesser numbers. The Desoto Falls Scenic Area,

GEORGIA

with its high vista points and waterfalls, marks the boundary. Just across U.S. 129 lies Raven Cliffs Wilderness (see below).

Small and big game bring in quite a few hunters, and trout fishing, especially in Dick's Creek and the region north and east of Lake Winfield Scott, attracts their tackle box–toting counterparts. Hikers usually travel the Appalachian Trail (AT), which crosses the area along the crest of the Blue Ridge for 10.75 miles and eventually reaches a rock shelter on Blood Mountain. This trail, according to the USFS, is "the most heavily used portion of the AT in Georgia." Many old logging roads crisscross the area. The Duncan Ridge National Recreation Trail crosses part of the area.

Blood Mountain Essentials

Size: 7,800 acres.
Year Designated: 1991.
Location: Northern Georgia.
Easiest Access: From Atlanta, take U.S. 19 north. Continue north on U.S. 19/129 to the Desoto Falls Scenic Area, a total distance of about 90 miles.
Season: The area is crowded from spring to fall, especially on weekends.
Wilderness Fees/Permits: None.
Maps: A Chattahoochee Visitor Map is available for a $3 fee from the district rangers. USGS topographic maps are Coosa Bald and Neel's Gap.
Management: Brasstown Ranger District, Chattahoochee National Forest, P.O. Box 9, Blairsville, GA 30512; (706) 745-6928. Chestatee Ranger District, Chattahoochee National Forest, 1015 Tipton Drive, Dahlonega, GA 30533; (706) 864-6173.

Brasstown Wilderness

The "capital of the Cherokee" is a steeply rugged Wilderness that drapes across the northern, northeastern, and southwestern flanks of 4,784-foot Brasstown Bald Mountain, the highest point in the state.

Here you'll find boulder fields, rock formations, and streams cascading through narrow gorges, giving way periodically to waterfalls. Second-growth hardwoods dominate this flora-rich region, highlighted in spring and summer by a profusion of wildflowers. Native trout can be found in some of the 14.1 miles of stream. Deer, squirrels, and grouse scurry about the banks, with smaller populations of black bears, woodcocks, and wild turkeys. The threatened or endangered New England cottontail rabbit, southeastern shrew, and pygmy shrew also seek shelter here.

Hikers tend to stick to the only developed trails in the area: the steep 5.5-mile Arkaqua National Recreation Trail, which begins at the Brasstown Bald parking area just outside the Wilderness, and the 4.5-mile Jack's Knob National Recreation Trail, which ties the Appalachian Trail to the same parking lot. During periods of heavy visitation, noise from the Brasstown Bald Visitors Center echoes through the Wilderness.

GEORGIA

Brasstown Essentials

Size: 12,565 acres.
Year Designated: 1986; expanded in 1991.
Location: Northern Georgia.
Easiest Access: From Atlanta, take U.S. 19 north for approximately 80 miles. Turn east on State Highway 180 and continue driving for approximately 10 miles to the Brasstown Bald Visitors Center.
Season: Spring to fall is the most crowded, especially on weekends.
Wilderness Fees/Permits: None.
Maps: USGS topographic maps are Hiawassee and Jack's Gap.
Management: Brasstown Ranger District, Chattahoochee National Forest, P.O. Box 9, Blairsville, GA 30512; (706) 745-6928.

Cohutta Wilderness

Most of mountainous Cohutta, the state's second largest Wilderness, lies in Georgia and within the Cohutta Wildlife Management Area. But a small portion runs over the border into Tennessee (see Tennessee, Cohutta Wilderness). Although loggers worked their way through 70 percent of the forest between 1915 and 1930, oak and pine have all but reclaimed the forest, and a rich growth of hardwoods now fills out the lower elevations: magnolia, maple, buckeye, hornbeam, sassafras, holly, silver bell dogwood, and chestnut, to name but a few.

Spring and summer bring a riot of colorful blooms to many shrubs, vines, and herbaceous plants, ranging from the brilliant orange of flame azalea to the pink and yellow of lady's slippers, the blue cohosh, and the scarlet cardinal flower. But summer also means heat and high humidity, biting insects, and foliage so dense it blocks some views that are truly spectacular in fall and spring.

The Conasauga and Jacks Rivers, two of the state's most prolific trout streams, drop through rocky gorges and flash flood the Wilderness during periods of heavy rain. Anglers can try hooking trout in the many streams, too, while hunters train their sights on white-tailed deer, black bears, and wild boars. More than 100 bird species have been identified in the area (situated along the Appalachian Flyway), along with copperheads, timber rattlesnakes, and other slithering species.

Popular trails follow both the Conasauga and Jacks Rivers, and at least a dozen other footpaths provide access to the Wilderness. Many of the trails require wading through waterways. The 15.7-mile Jacks River Trail, for instance, passes through water no less than 40 times. The colorful blazes that mark most of the trails are easy to follow, even in soggy shoes.

If you're looking for a trail with lighter foot traffic, try the seldom used (except in hunting season) Hickory Creek Trail (8.4 miles), the more strenuous Tearbritches Trail (3.4 miles), or the East Cowpen Trail (seven miles). All three gain a fair amount of elevation and provide excellent views. There's also the 6.2-mile Hemp Top Trail, which connects with the Licklog Ridge Trail on the Tennessee side of the Wilderness. Horses are allowed on many but not all of the trails; contact the district ranger for information.

GEORGIA

Cohutta Essentials

Size: 35,247 acres in Georgia (37,042 total).
Year Designated: 1975.
Location: Northern Georgia.
Easiest Access: From Interstate 75 north of Atlanta, take U.S. 411 north for approximately 45 miles to Eton. Turn west at the one traffic light and drive 18 miles toward Lake Conasauga Recreation Area. The Tearbritches Trailhead will be on your right.

Season: Spring and fall.
Wilderness Fees/Permits: None.
Maps: A Chattahoochee Visitor Map is available for $3 from the district ranger. Detailed trail information is free.
Management: Cohutta Ranger District, Chattahoochee National Forest, 401 Old Ellijay Road, Chatsworth, GA 30705; (706) 695-6736.

Cumberland Island Wilderness

Established in 1972 and managed by the National Park Service, Cumberland Island National Seashore protects sparkling white beaches and sand dunes, freshwater lakes, and saltwater marshes. At 36,545 acres, it is Georgia's largest and southernmost barrier against seaborne storms. The island measures about 16 miles in length and 3 miles at its widest, with approximately 1 mile of water and marshland separating it from the mainland.

A hardwood forest is the centerpiece of the island, providing shade for the deer that attract hunters during four managed seasons. When the hunters appear (usually a few days every month from November through February), visitation and camping are restricted on parts of the island. The first-rate surf fishing attracts another kind of hunter (no license is required).

Attractions include the ruins of Thomas Carnegie's Dungeness Mansion, built in the late 1800s, a short walk from the ferry dock on the southern end of the island. Alligators, loggerhead turtles, and pelicans live on the beaches.

A portion of the northern end of the island has been designated Wilderness, starting approximately four miles north of the ferry dock (you have to take a ferry to get here from the mainland). Camping is allowed only in three locations here: Hickory Hill, Yankee Paradise, and Brickhill Bluff. Trails connecting the dock to the Wilderness campsites are 5.5 miles, 7.4 miles, and 10.6 miles, respectively. Campsites are assigned on a first-come, first-served basis once you reach the island, and a late arrival may mean a long hike before bedtime. A fourth, non-Wilderness campsite is located on the beach. For most of the year, insect repellent is strongly recommended for campers. Bicycles, fires, pets, and indiscriminate dune crossings are not allowed on Cumberland Island, and there are no facilities.

The ferry departs from Saint Marys, Georgia, at 9 A.M. and 11:45 A.M. and runs seven days a week, from March 15 until the end of September. From the first of October to March 15, the ferry operates only from Thursday through Monday. Fares are approximately $10 per adult, lower for children. Advance reservations are strongly recommended; for more information phone (912) 882-4335.

GEORGIA

Cumberland Island Essentials

Size: 8,840 acres.
Year Designated: 1982.
Location: Coastal southeastern Georgia.
Easiest Access: From Jacksonville, take Interstate 95 north for approximately 30 miles. Turn east on State Highway 40 and proceed eight miles to Saint Marys.
Season: Heat and humidity dominate much of the year, subsiding somewhat in winter.

Wilderness Fees/Permits: No fees are charged. Campsite permits are required and must be obtained in advance at the visitors center.
Maps: A free map is available at the visitors center.
Management: Cumberland Island National Seashore, P.O. Box 806, Saint Marys, GA 31558; (912) 882-4335.

Ellicott Rock Wilderness

Rugged terrain, tall peaks, and the Wild and Scenic Chattooga River are the hallmarks of this Wilderness, which is shared by three states (see North Carolina, Ellicott Rock Wilderness; and South Carolina, Ellicott Rock Wilderness). Offering one of the foremost whitewater trips in the eastern United States, the Chattooga floods through the middle of the area, but the wildest water lies below the Wilderness boundary, where boating is not allowed.

The Georgia terrain peaks at 3,672-foot Glade Mountain. Clear perennial trout streams that occasionally drop over small waterfalls scour the numerous steep-walled gorges. Unusual rock formations hover above some of the streams, and several threatened or endangered plants have been identified.

Although logging operations intruded in the early 1900s (as evidence attests), today's forest of hardwoods (upland and cove) is more than 80 years old. Deer, squirrels, grouse, and wild turkeys are common sights in the Georgia portion of the Wilderness, along with the more elusive black bear and raccoon. Wild boars wander in from North Carolina now and then. You may see the remains of the old moonshine stills that once brewed their potions here.

Ellicott Rock Essentials

Size: 2,181 acres in Georgia (9,012 total).
Year Designated: 1975; expanded in 1984.
Location: Northeastern Georgia.
Easiest Access: From Walhalla, South Carolina, take State Highway 28 north for approximately 20 miles. Just west of the Chattooga River (in Georgia), turn northeast on Forest Service Road 646 (Burrell's Ford Road) and continue to the Wilderness boundary.

Season: Spring and fall.
Wilderness Fees/Permits: None.
Maps: A Wilderness map is available for $3 from the USDA Forest Service, 508 Oak Street, Gainesville, GA 30501. USGS topographic maps are Satolah and Tamassee.
Management: Tallulah Ranger District, Chattahoochee National Forest, P.O. Box 438, Clayton, GA 30525; (706) 782-3320.

GEORGIA

Mark Trail Wilderness

The logging roads that once ran along the streams, waterfalls, rocky outcroppings, and high peaks that distinguish the Chattahoochee Wildlife Management Area are rapidly returning to their natural state. The mountains (Horsetrough is the highest at 4,045 feet) are covered in second-growth upland and cove hardwoods in excess of 60 years of age.

Trout fishing is top-notch, with 65 miles of streams chock-full of rainbows, brookies, and browns. Some of the headwaters of the Chattahoochee River flow through here. Deer, squirrels, raccoons, grouse, and wild turkeys dominate among the landlubbing residents, with smaller populations of black bears, woodcocks, and doves.

Most hikers take the Appalachian Trail (AT), which follows the crest of the Blue Ridge through this area for 14 miles. The two shelters on the AT are Low Gap and Blue Mountain. Jack's Knob Trail enters the Wilderness at Henry Knob and travels south before dividing and joining the AT in two places. Less than an hour's hike on a trail on the east side leads to Horsetrough Falls, which plunges year-round. Hunters and anglers are common sights, and hikers appear almost every day from spring through fall. Just across State Highway 75 lies Tray Mountain Wilderness (see below).

Mark Trail Essentials

Size: 16,880 acres.
Year Designated: 1991.
Location: Northern Georgia.
Easiest Access: From Helen, take State Highway 17/75 north for about 13 miles to a parking lot where the Appalachian Trail crosses the road. Hike west.
Season: Spring through fall.
Wilderness Fees/Permits: None.
Maps: USGS topographic maps are Cow Rock, Jack's Gap, and Tray Mountain.
Management: Brasstown Ranger District, Chattahoochee National Forest, P.O. Box 9, Blairsville, GA 30512; (706) 745-6928. Chattooga Ranger District, Chattahoochee National Forest, P.O Box 196, Burton Road, Clarkesville, GA 30523; (706) 754-6221.

Okefenokee Wilderness

The Okefenokee National Wildlife Refuge encompasses some 396,000 acres of the 438,000-acre Okefenokee Swamp, one of the oldest and best-preserved freshwater areas in America. This vast and extravagant bog, measuring about 38 miles long and 25 miles wide, is a huge depression that once lay on the ocean floor. The swamp extends just over the state line into Florida, and its interior (which comprises most of the refuge and lies entirely within Georgia) has been designated the state's largest Wilderness.

Native Americans called the swamp the "land of trembling earth" because the unstable peat deposits that cover much of the swamp floor tremble when stomped on. *Okefenokee* is a corruption of their words. The last tribe to seek sanctuary here, the Seminole, were driven into Florida in 1850 but lived on to become the only Native Americans to refuse to sign a treaty with the U.S. government.

The Suwanee River, tea-colored due to tannic acid, originates in the heart of the swamp and flows in an exquisitely slow fashion on its southwest course toward the Gulf of Mexico. The Saint Marys River flows from the swamp southeast to the Atlantic, forming part of the boundary between Georgia and Florida.

Numerous islands and lakes are found on the flat terrain within the swamp, but dry land seldom stands above the bog. If you visit the Okefenokee you'll probably travel by canoe on one or more of 15 designated canoe trips. You'll paddle through lovely cypress forests and across open "prairies," getting out from time to time to push your canoe over peat blowups and shallow water. You'll probably see herons, egrets, ibis, cranes and bitterns, the endangered red-cockaded woodpecker and wood stork, alligators, and otters (when the alligators are sleeping).

Overnight camping is allowed in designated campsites only, and advance permits are required. The sites often consist of raised wooden platforms where no land exists. After my last trip to Okefenokee a friend drove down for a canoe trip without a permit, went paddling anyway, and was slapped with a substantial fine from the ever-watchful U.S. Fish and Wildlife swamp guardians.

Okefenokee Essentials

Size: 353,981 acres.
Year Designated: 1974.
Location: Southern Georgia.
Easiest Access: From Waycross, take U.S. 1 south for 37 miles to Folkston. Turn southwest on State Highway 121 and continue for eight miles, then head west at the sign marking the east entrance.
Season: There are few to no mosquitoes, cool days, cold nights, and migratory birds from November to March, but you won't see as many alligators. The wading-bird rookeries are most active in April.
Wilderness Fees/Permits: Canoe trails are limited to one party of up to 10 canoes or 20 people maximum per day. An overnight fee of $3 per person per night is charged. Reservations are taken by phone or mail at the refuge office no earlier than two months prior to your trip. Full payment must be made no later than 15 days prior to the start of your trip. Your itinerary must be followed exactly.
Maps: Free maps are available from the refuge manager. Canoe trail maps cost 20 cents.
Management: Okefenokee National Wildlife Refuge, P.O. Box 338, Folkston, GA 31537; (912) 496-3331.

Raven Cliffs Wilderness

Numerous streams and waterfalls, high peaks, and rocky outcroppings combine to create a rugged mountain Wilderness divided between the Chestatee and Chattahoochee Wildlife Management Areas. Elevations range from about 1,800 feet on Boggs Creek to 3,846 feet on Leveland Mountain. A dense forest of hardwoods and scattered pines has recovered from substantial logging operations early in this century—most of the trees have now celebrated their 60th birthday. Approximately 41 miles of trout streams attract many anglers, with Boggs Creek receiving the most use. Deer, squirrels, and grouse tend to steal the spotlight, as black bears, turkeys, and raccoons work behind the scenes. Across U.S. 129 lies Blood Mountain Wilderness (see above).

GEORGIA

The Appalachian Trail follows the crest of the Blue Ridge through this area for 6.6 miles; there's a shelter at Whitley Gap. Another trail, the Raven Cliffs Falls Trail, leads upstream 2.5 miles to the Raven Cliffs Scenic Area, with its high vista points and waterfalls (ravens reportedly nest here, as the name suggests). This Wilderness receives relatively heavy visitor traffic.

Raven Cliffs Essentials

Size: 8,562 acres.
Year Designated: 1986.
Location: Northern Georgia.
Easiest Access: From Atlanta, take U.S. 19 north. Continue north on U.S. 19/129 to Neel's Gap and the Appalachian Trail and hike east. The drive from here to Atlanta takes two hours to cover about 100 miles of road.
Season: Spring to fall is crowded, especially on weekends.
Wilderness Fees/Permits: None.
Maps: USGS topographic maps are Cow Rock and Neel's Gap.
Management: Brasstown Ranger District, Chattahoochee National Forest, P.O. Box 9, Blairsville, GA 30512; (706) 745-6928. Chattooga Ranger District, Chattahoochee National Forest, P.O. Box 196, Burton Road, Clarkesville, GA 30523; (706) 754-6221. Chestatee Ranger District, Chattahoochee National Forest, 1015 Tipton Drive, Dahlonega, GA 30533; (706) 864-6173.

Rich Mountain Wilderness

At 4,050 feet, Rich Mountain anchors an area that includes several threatened and endangered plants and numerous species considered rare in Georgia. About 30 miles of trout streams and waterfalls embellish the rocky outcroppings in this rugged, mountainous terrain. A second-growth hardwood forest provides habitat for deer, squirrels, raccoons, wild turkeys, and grouse, with black bears, quail, and woodcocks making unexpected appearances. The wild hog population has been on the increase.

Small- and big-game hunters are the predominant human users of this Wilderness (which lies within Rich Mountain Wildlife Area). A few hikers and horseback riders occasionally end up here, despite the lack of established trails. Instead, they follow what remains of old logging roads. Private land nearly surrounds the Wilderness.

Rich Mountain Essentials

Size: 9,649 acres.
Year Designated: 1986.
Location: Northern Georgia.
Easiest Access: From Ellijay, take U.S. 76 north for approximately 10 miles. Exit west onto County Road 152 and swing immediately east beneath the overpass and continue 1.8 miles to where the road turns to gravel. Continue approximately four miles on the gravel road to a rough road that turns south and takes you a short distance to the Wilderness boundary, which is marked with a sign.
Season: Spring to fall.
Wilderness Fees/Permits: None.
Maps: USGS topographic maps are Blue Ridge, Cashes Valley, Ellijay, and Tickanetly.
Management: Toccoa Ranger District, Chattahoochee National Forest, East Main Street, Box 1839, Blue Ridge, GA 30513; (706) 632-3031.

GEORGIA

Southern Nantahala Wilderness

After the Cherokee were removed from their "Great Blue Hills of God" (the Blue Ridge Mountains), loggers stripped the trees from the land and shipped them out via the railway. The main line of that railway ran along the Nantahala River, and evidence of it still exists in a Wilderness shared by Georgia and North Carolina (see North Carolina, Southern Nantahala Wilderness).

Steep, rugged, reforested country cut by numerous streams and old drainages characterizes the southern end of the Blue Ridge Mountains. The streams feed the Nantahala, Hiwassee, and Tallulah Rivers, and the wide non-Wilderness right-of-way along the Tallulah neatly divides the Georgia share of the wildland. The eastern section is the northern portion of Georgia's Coleman River Wildlife Management Area. In both sections spruce and fir cover the ridges (opened by grass-heath "balds") and mixed hardwoods grow on the slopes. Elevations here are lower than in Tennessee. Several unique bogs support endangered species such as the bog turtle and rare combinations of other species found nowhere else in the world.

Other than four miles of the Appalachian Trail, which runs north-south through the larger western section, you won't find developed pathways on the Georgia side. However, old roadbeds provide hiking access. Off these old roads and deep in the shade of the many trees, where the walking is difficult, you'll find Georgia at her most unspoiled.

Southern Nantahala Essentials

Size: 12,439 acres in Georgia (23,339 total).
Year Designated: 1984.
Location: Northern Georgia.
Easiest Access: From U.S. 76 in the extreme north of Georgia, turn north on Forest Service Road 70, which follows the Tallulah River and provides access to the eastern and western sections of the Wilderness after about five miles.
Season: Spring and fall.
Wilderness Fees/Permits: None.
Maps: A Wilderness map of Southern Nantahala Wilderness is available for $3.75 from the district ranger.
Management: Tallulah Ranger District, Chattahoochee National Forest, P.O. Box 438, Clayton, GA 30525; (404) 782-3320.

Tray Mountain Wilderness

At 4,430 feet, Tray Mountain dominates the southern portion of this rugged Wilderness, which straddles the crest of the Blue Ridge. From up high, fast-flowing streams tumble down narrow gorges and over many waterfalls. Second-growth hardwoods at least 60 years old are the primary forest cover. Deer, squirrels, grouse, and wild turkeys make common appearances, along with the ever-elusive black bear, raccoons, doves, quail, and woodcocks. About 41 miles of trout streams produce rainbows and browns. You'll see remnants of past logging operations, mostly abandoned roads. Just across State Highway 75 lies Mark Trail Wilderness (see above).

The Appalachian Trail (AT) follows the crest of the Blue Ridge for 16.5 unusually level miles from Unicoi Gap to Dick's Creek Gap, with a shelter at Tray Mountain. The High Shoals Trail leads about 1.5 miles to the High Shoals Scenic Area, where a waterfall drops over dramatic cliffs. Hunters and anglers come often to this area, but the AT attracts the most visitors.

GEORGIA

Tray Mountain Essentials

Size: 9,702 acres.
Year Designated: 1986.
Location: Northern Georgia.
Easiest Access: From Helen, take State Highway 17/75 north for about 13 miles to Unicoi Gap and a parking lot where the Appalachian Trail crosses the road.
Season: Fall, with its rich colors, is the most appealing time to visit.
Wilderness Fees/Permits: None.
Maps: USGS topographic maps are Hightower Bald, Lake Burton, Macedonia, and Tray Mountain.
Management: Brasstown Ranger District, Chattahoochee National Forest, P.O. Box 9, Blairsville, GA 30512; (706) 745-6928. Chattooga Ranger District, Chattahoochee National Forest, P.O. Box 196, Clarkesville, GA 30523; (706) 754-6221. Tallulah Ranger District, Chattahoochee National Forest, P.O. Box 438, Clayton, GA 30525; (706) 782-3320.

Wolf Island Wilderness

Established in 1930 as a sanctuary for migratory birds, Wolf Island National Wildlife Refuge includes Wolf Island (4,519 acres), Egg Island (593 acres), and Little Egg Island (14 acres). All of the refuge has been designated Wilderness. Large expanses of marshes, marshy hammocks, and tidal creeks separate the refuge from the mainland. More than 75 percent of the refuge itself is composed of saltwater marshes where birds hide and feed but do not nest. Scaups, scoters, black ducks, mergansers, and buffleheads are the most commonly seen species. Loggerhead sea turtles and diamondback terrapins have been known to share the wealth.

About 300 acres of Wolf Island is "upland," standing an average of 10 feet above the sea and including a narrow, four-mile strip of oceanfront beach. Sea oats, sandspurs, and other beach-dune perennials grow on the upland. The rest of the island is salt marsh dominated by cordgrass.

Egg Island contains about 200 acres of upland, including 1.5 miles of beach, sporting a dense growth of cedar, greenbrier, and blackberry. Salt marsh dominated by cordgrass covers the remainder of the island. Little Egg Island, a low salt marsh dominated by cordgrass, goes completely underwater at high tide.

Although the saltwater regions of the refuge are open to recreational activities consisting primarily of fishing, the marshes, beaches, and uplands are closed entirely to human visitation.

Wolf Island Essentials

Size: 5,126 acres.
Year Designated: 1975.
Location: Off the coast of Georgia.
Easiest Access: From Savannah, take U.S. 17 south for about 70 miles to Darien, where marinas provide boat access to the refuge, approximately 12 miles east.
Season: Summer and fall for the best fishing, and winter to see more birds.
Wilderness Fees/Permits: The Wilderness lands are closed to the public.
Maps: A free map is available from the refuge manager.
Management: Savannah Coastal Refuges, 1000 Business Center Drive, Parkway Business Center, Suite 10, Savannah, GA 31405; (912) 652-4415.

> "Wilderness.... If we do not preserve it, then we shall be diminished by just that much the unique privilege of being an American."
>
> —Joseph Wood Krutch

HAWAII

Total Wilderness areas: 2
Total Wilderness acreage: 142,370

Cracked like an eggshell, the earth's surface lies broken into a dozen vast, thin, rigid plates that drift slowly, along the lines where they join, over the more plastic mantle below. Deep beneath the sea, near the center of the Pacific Plate, is a "hot spot," a weak area where magma slowly rises toward the surface. Over millennia, this particular hot spot leaked layer after layer of lava, which rose above the salt water and formed an island. The plate shifted, more lava flowed upward, and another island was created. The cycle continued until nature formed the string of islands that we know today as Hawaii.

Life has developed in this unique environment, life that is unique on this earth. In fact, an estimated 90 percent of Hawaii's native species can be found only on these islands. But humans have dug their heels into paradise, bringing with them many mammals that threaten native species with extinction. Creatures that once comprised the magnificent and colorful diversity of Hawaii—the feathered nene, i'iwi, 'amakihi, and 'apapane, the flowered haha and 'ohi'a lehua, the lava cricket, the Kamehameha butterfly, and happyface spider—are now protected within two Wilderness areas that lie on national parkland.

Haleakala Wilderness

The mother of the demigod Maui lodged a complaint with her son: the day was too short to dry her bark cloth. So Maui went to the great mountain and snared the sun's rays and held them fast with ropes. "Give me my life," pleaded the sun. "If you promise to crawl more slowly across the sky," said Maui. And the sun still hangs long in the sky over the island of Maui, whose great mountain is called Haleakala, "the House of the Sun."

Two centuries have passed since the last lava ran from Haleakala Crater. Though dormant, the volcano is not considered extinct and, while no volcanic activity is evident today on Maui, Haleakala may erupt again. The national park that shares its name stretches from 10,023-foot Mount Haleakala north and far eastward to the cascading streams and quiet pools in Kipahulu Valley, which opens onto the sea. Within its borders you'll discover cool lava rocks, cinder cones as high as 600 feet, striking silver plants that bloom only once in their lifetime, and other rare species that grow only in this fragile ecosystem.

No roads or trails connect the Haleakala Crater area to Kipahulu Valley, but both are accessible by paved roads from Kahului.

Across the Wilderness of Haleakala Crater, 36 miles of trails access a land of stark contrasts and sudden weather changes; fog, rain, and chilly breezes are common hiking companions. The eight-mile (round-trip) Sliding Sands Trail descends steeply to the floor of the crater along a loose, cinder surface. The four-mile (one-way) Halemau'u Trail crosses shrub-covered land before dropping via switchbacks to the crater's floor, ending at Holua Cabin. The nine-mile (one-way) Kaupo Trail enters the east end of the crater along rough and rocky ground after crossing private ranchland. All three trails meet at the center of the crater, near the Bottomless Pit.

Camping is limited to three nights per month and restricted to one of three reservation-only cabins and several primitive campgrounds. You must hike on trails only. Pets are not permitted anywhere in the Wilderness. Fires are only allowed in designated fireplaces.

Haleakala Essentials

Size: 19,270 acres.
Year Designated: 1976.
Location: Eastern Maui, Hawaii.
Easiest Access: From Kahului, Maui, take State Highway 37 east to Pakalani. Turn south on State Highway 377 and follow it to State Highway 378. Turn east on State Highway 378 and drive to Haleakala Crater and the park headquarters. The total driving time is approximately three hours round-trip.
Season: Summers are dry and moderately warm. Late afternoon and evening are best for clear skies and spectacular views.
Wilderness Fees/Permits: A park fee of $4 per vehicle is charged at Haleakala Crater, but there is no fee at the coast. Camping in the crater is allowed by permit only. Cabin reservations must be made at least 90 days prior to your visit. Cabin rental costs $5 per person with a minimum charge of $15. Firewood is an additional $4 per night.
Maps: Free park maps are available from the park ranger.
Management: Haleakala National Park, P.O. Box 369, Makawao, HI 96768; (808) 572-9306.

Hawaii Volcanoes Wilderness

I awoke from my first night's sleep in Hawaii to a bird's song so eloquent and so stunningly loud that the memory still thrills me a decade later. On a three-day trip, I hiked in December fog from Lookout Shelter through native rain forest all the way to the cold, snowy summit of Mauna Loa at 13,677 feet. From the peak, breaks in the clouds revealed the result of 70 million years of volcanism: an ever-changing land of indescribable beauty. Mauna Loa ranks as the highest mountain on Earth, more than 30,000 feet when measured from its base at the bottom of the sea. It is a place I would revisit at the drop of a golden mamane petal.

The Big Island of Hawaii is home to Hawaii Volcanoes National Park and its active volcano field. In order to protect humans from hazardous fumes, the areas surrounding erupting vents are closed to travel. You can obtain information on the latest volcanic activity 24 hours a day by phoning (808) 967-7977. The northwestern extension of the park holds Mauna Loa and is designated Wilderness. In the southwestern portion of the park, a large chunk of Wilderness includes several miles of coastline, a small portion southeast of the visitors center, and the 'Ola'a Forest, which is separate from and just north of the park.

More than 150 miles of trail crisscross the park, mostly within Wilderness. The 20-mile Ka'u Desert Trail curls across shadeless lava fields past cinder cones in the park's southwestern section; sturdy shoes and long pants are a must. The Ka'aha Trail, an offshoot of the Ka'u, follows the windswept coast for six miles. The six-mile Napua Trail crosses the Mauna Ulu Lava Shield and the small Wilderness section southeast of Kilauea Caldera. You must remain on trails at all times to protect the fragile environment and to ensure your own safety. Camping is permitted, but open fires, pets, and fishing are not. Two drive-in campgrounds outside the Wilderness are free; both are first come, first served.

Hawaii Volcanoes Essentials

Size: 123,100 acres.
Year Designated: 1978.
Location: Southeastern Hawaii, the main island in Hawaii.
Easiest Access: From Hilo, Hawaii, take State Highway 130 south for eight miles to Kea'au. Turn west on State Highway 11 and drive about 20 miles to the Kilauea Visitors Center.
Season: Summers are drier and warmer. Winters are cool and damp, but offer seclusion.
Wilderness Fees/Permits: Parking is $5 per vehicle. A backcountry permit is required and may be obtained at the Kilauea Visitors Center.
Maps: Obtain a free map from the park ranger.
Management: Hawaii Volcanoes National Park, HI 96718; (808) 967-7311.

> "The earth was created with the assistance of the sun and it should be left as it was. I never said the land was mine to do with as I chose. The only one with that right is the one who made it."
>
> —Chief Joseph

IDAHO

Total Wilderness areas: 6
Total Wilderness acreage: 4,001,617

Mountainous describes the heart of Idaho, a land of steep terrain, restless waterways, and raw beauty. Most of Idaho lies more than one mile above sea level, and great rivers drain the snow-filled high country. Ten national forests cover a large part of the state and protect five Wilderness areas, one of which is shared with the Bureau of Land Management and ranks as the largest unit of the National Wilderness Preservation System in the Lower 48. Idaho is also home to a unique landscape, Craters of the Moon, part of which is managed as Wilderness by the National Park Service.

Craters of the Moon Wilderness

Approximately 2,100 years ago, the last volcanic eruptions spilled lava across central Idaho. When the molten rock cooled, vast lava fields remained, studded with numerous cinder cones and spatter cones, as well as hidden ice caves and lava tubes. Lava sunk into depressions, forming craters that resembled those of the moon—so much so that astronauts once trained here. While the area appears black and totally desolate at first glance, various hardy plants (many that bloom colorfully in spring) and mammals have returned to live in this dry region. An astonishing landscape, about 83 square miles of the region was set aside as Craters of the Moon National Monument in 1924. Well over half the monument, the southern and eastern portions, has been designated Wilderness, and very few humans ever spend a night in this area. Although the national monument offers a designated campground, in the Wilderness few places exist where you can even lie down.

From the visitors center in the northern section, a paved loop road circles some of the major cinder cones and accesses short paths to several large craters; three maintained trails depart from the road to venture into the "moon." One meanders through an area of lava caves, which are tubes that were formed when lava flows cooled more rapidly on the surface than below, leaving a tunnel beneath the upper layer. At least one of the caves contains a perpetual ice sheet that defies the hot Idaho summers. A long trail dead-ends at the Tree Molds area, and a longer one crosses Big Cinder Butte to reach Echo Crater. Trails can be trekked easily on a day hike, the longest being about four miles one way. Wandering off-trail is allowed. The terrain can be rough on footwear, so bring sturdy boots with heavy soles. Primitive camping is allowed, but all water must be packed in. Geological experts predict the lava will flow once again in this region.

Craters of the Moon Essentials

Size: 43,243 acres.
Year Designated: 1970.
Location: Southern central Idaho.
Easiest Access: From Arco, take U.S. 93/20/26 south for 18 miles to the monument.
Season: Spring and fall. The monument campground/loop road closes November to April.
Wilderness Fees/Permits: An entrance fee of $4 per vehicle or $2 per person is charged. A free backcountry permit is required.
Maps: A free map is available from the park ranger. A USGS map of the monument is available for $4 from USGS-Western Distribution Center, Box 25286, Federal Center, Denver, CO 80225; (303) 234-3832.
Management: Craters of the Moon National Monument, P.O. Box 29, Arco, ID 83213; (208) 527-3257.

Frank Church–River of No Return Wilderness

Few places in America, and nowhere outside of Alaska, provide a Wilderness experience to match the sheer magnitude of the Frank Church–River of No Return, the second largest unit of the National Wilderness Preservation System in the Lower 48 (second in size only to California's Death Valley Wilderness). This area combines the old Idaho Primitive Area, the Salmon Breaks Primitive Area, territory on six national forests, and a small swath of land managed by the Bureau of Land Management. Senator Frank Church played a key role in the passage of the Wilderness Act of 1964, and his name was added to the Wilderness in 1984, shortly before his death.

It is a land of clear rivers, deep canyons, and rugged mountains. Two white-water rivers draw many human visitors: the Main Salmon River, which runs west near the northern boundary; and the Middle Fork of the Salmon, which begins near the southern boundary and runs north for about 104 miles until it joins the Main. Reaching 6,300 feet from the river bottom, the canyon carved by the Main Salmon is deeper than most of the earth's canyons—including the Grand Canyon of the Colorado River—and this fast-moving waterway has been dubbed the River of No Return. In the northeastern corner of the Wilderness, the Selway River flows north into the nearby Selway-Bitterroot Wilderness (see below). Trout fishing usually rates from good to excellent, and I've had some of the best fly-fishing trips of my life here. The Middle Fork, the Selway, and a portion of the Main Salmon are Wild and Scenic Rivers. Unlike the sheer walls of the Grand Canyon, these rivers rush below wooded ridges rising steeply toward the sky, beneath eroded bluffs and ragged, solitary crags.

The Salmon River Mountains dominate the interior of the Wilderness. Without a major crest, these mountains splay out in a multitude of minor crests in all directions, and rise gradually to wide summits. East of the Middle Fork, the fabulous Bighorn Crags form a jagged series of summits, at least one topping 10,000 feet. The Bighorns surround 14 strikingly beautiful clearwater lakes. Hiking up from the rivers into the mountains brings sudden elevation changes.

IDAHO

Great forests of Douglas fir and lodgepole pine cover much of the area, with spruce and fir higher up and ponderosa pine at lower altitudes. The forests are broken by grassy meadows and sun-washed, treeless slopes.

A dry country, as little as 15 inches of precipitation falls near the rivers. As much as 50 inches may fall on the mountaintops, but much of it is snow. Despite the dryness, wildlife abounds. As many as 370 species have been identified in a single year, including eight big game animals. A network of 296 maintained trails (approximately 2,616 miles worth) provides access to this seemingly endless area, crossing rivers and streams on 114 bridges. This is a paradise for horsepackers. Thirty-two Forest Service Roads lead to 66 trailheads. Despite the extensive trail system, an amazing 1.5 million acres remains trail-free. Small planes are allowed to land on several primitive airstrips dating back to the days before Wilderness designation. Jet boats are allowed on the Main Salmon. Today 88 outfitters offer float, horsepacking, backpacking, and ski trips. For information, contact the Idaho Outfitters and Guides Association, P.O. Box 95, Boise, ID 83701; (208) 342-1438.

I came to the Frank Church–River of No Return in 1988 and stayed for 62 days, hiking away the long summer and having resupplies flown in by small airplane. My journal records how I saw more than 30 black bears, over 100 rattlesnakes, and only 6 humans, aside from my lone companion. I have, on two other trips, floated the Middle Fork and the Main Salmon in rafts tossed easily by the might of the water, multiday trips that kept me anticipating with keen delight every bend in the canyons. No matter what they call the river, I intend to return.

Frank Church–River of No Return Essentials

Size: 2,361,767 acres of USFS land, plus 802 acres of BLM land.
Year Designated: 1980.
Location: Central Idaho.
Easiest Access: From Salmon, follow the Salmon River north on U.S. 93 for approximately 20 miles. Turn west at North Fork and continue to follow the river for about 40 miles to the Wilderness boundary.
Season: Any time of the year.
Wilderness Fees/Permits: None for off-river use. Permits are required for use of the rivers. For the Middle Fork, contact the Middle Fork Ranger District, Challis National Forest, P.O. Box 337, Challis, ID 83226; (208) 879-5204. For the Main Salmon, contact the North Fork Ranger District, Salmon National Forest, P.O. Box 780, North Fork, ID 83466; (208) 865-2383. A $6 application fee is charged, and there's no guarantee of getting a permit. Apply by January 31.
Maps: All Idaho Forest Service offices sell a two-map set of the Wilderness (south and north) for $3 per map.
Management: Red River Ranger District, Nez Perce National Forest, Elk City, ID 83525; (208) 842-2255. West Fork Ranger District, Bitterroot National Forest, Darby, MT 59829; (406) 821-3269. Big Creek Ranger District/McCall Ranger District, Payette National Forest, P.O. Box 1026, McCall, ID 83638; (208) 634-8151. Cascade Ranger District, Boise National Forest, P.O. Box 696, Cascade, ID 83611; (208) 382-4271. Lowman Ranger District, Boise National Forest, HC 76, Box 3020, Lowman, ID 83637; (208) 259-3361. North Fork Ranger District, Salmon National Forest, P.O. Box 780, North Fork, ID 83466; (208) 865-2383. Cobalt Ranger District, Salmon National Forest, P.O. Box 729, Salmon, ID 83467; (208) 756-2240. Challis Ranger District, Challis National Forest, HC 63, Box 1669, Challis, ID 83226; (208) 879-4321. Middle Fork Ranger District, Challis National Forest, P.O. Box 337, Challis, ID 83226; (208) 879-5204. BLM Coeur D'Alene District Office, 1808 North Third Street, Coeur D'Alene, ID 83814; (208) 769-5000.

Gospel Hump Wilderness

Long before explorers Lewis and Clark first laid eyes on this region in 1805, Nez Perce Indians were hunting the elk, deer, and black bears whose descendants still roam here. Discovery of gold in the 1860s brought a flood of miners into central Idaho that didn't subside until after the turn of the century. Another brief gold rush occurred during the Great Depression, and remnants of gold mining operations are evident.

From Gospel Peak on the west, the area rises to a high point on Buffalo Hump at 8,940 feet. The northern portion contains relatively gentle, heavily forested country that sweeps up the glaciated divide between the South Fork of the Clearwater River and the lower Salmon River, which flows out of the nearby Frank Church–River of No Return Wilderness (see above). From the divide, the terrain becomes the steep and sparsely vegetated Salmon River Breaks. In the waters of Gospel Hump the fishing can be extremely good for resident and anadromous fish. Moose, mountain goats, bighorn sheep, and mountain lions live here.

The area sees extreme variations in weather, with temperatures sometimes soaring to 100 degrees Fahrenheit along the Salmon River while snow whitens the high country. Seasonal roads of fair to poor quality surround the Wilderness, offering access to many miles of maintained and semimaintained trails. Trails that lead from the Breaks into the high country, which many hikers would classify as very challenging, are often impassable due to late snows.

Gospel Hump Essentials

Size: 205,900 acres.
Year Designated: 1978.
Location: Western central Idaho.
Easiest Access: From Grangeville, take State Route 13 east for approximately 10 miles. Turn south and east on State Route 14 along the South Fork of the Clearwater River, the road to Elk City. Drive about 50 miles to seasonal roads leading to the northern and eastern boundaries.
Season: Mid-July to mid-October.
Wilderness Fees/Permits: There are no permits required for backpacking or horsepacking. Permits are required for use of the Salmon River. Contact the North Fork Ranger District, Salmon National Forest, Box 780, North Fork, ID 83466; (208) 865-2383. A $6 application fee is charged, and there's no guarantee of getting a permit. Apply by January 31.
Maps: A free map is available from the district rangers. USGS topographic maps are Buffalo Hump, Burgdorf NE, Burgdorf NW, Dairy Mountain, Florence, Hanover Mountain, Marble Butte, North Pole, Orogrande, Sawyer Ridge, Silverspur Ridge, Sourdough Peak, Warren NE, and Warren NW.
Management: Red River Ranger District, Nez Perce National Forest, Elk City, ID 83525; (208) 842-2255. Slate Creek Ranger District, Nez Perce National Forest, White Bird, ID 83554; (208) 839-2211.

IDAHO

Hells Canyon Wilderness

The view over the edge of Hells Canyon can be deceiving. It just does not seem that deep. But don't be fooled: the gorge, which is cut by the Snake River, reaches a depth of 8,000 feet, making this the deepest canyon in North America.

Managed by the U.S. Forest Service, Hells Canyon National Recreation Area (HCNRA) contains 652,488 acres straddling the border of northeastern Oregon and western Idaho. Split into two distinct halves by the Snake, approximately one-third of HCNRA has been designated Wilderness. About 68 miles of the Snake River is Wild and Scenic, and the prime activity here is white-water rafting. Hells Canyon itself and the Oregon side of the Wilderness are managed by Oregon's Wallowa-Whitman National Forest. A small portion of the Wilderness in Oregon is managed by the BLM (see Oregon, Hells Canyon Wilderness).

The Idaho side of the Wilderness, which lies in parts of Nez Perce and Payette National Forests, is smaller than the Oregon side. On the Idaho side, the Seven Devils Mountain Range dominates the high country, a land of peaks towering 9,000 feet up, rocky slopes, and alpine lakes. The lower elevations are dry, barren, steep slopes that break at the canyon's rim. Idaho-side trailheads stand at Black Lake, Windy Saddle, and Pittsburg Landing. From Pittsburg Landing, the Snake River National Scenic Trail follows 31 miles of the river on the Idaho side.

On the Oregon side, the higher elevations are thinly treed with occasional dense stands of Douglas fir and ponderosa pine. The lower elevations are dominated by grasslands. Clear creeks dissect the isolated Oregon side. A trail from Dug Bar follows the Oregon side of the Snake River and gives access to several other trails. More than 1,500 archaeological sites have been identified here, and federal law requires that visitors leave them undisturbed.

Hells Canyon Essentials

Size: 83,800 acres in Idaho (214,933 acres total).
Year Designated: 1975 in Idaho.
Location: Western Idaho.
Easiest Access: From Riggins, take U.S. 95 north for 27 miles. Just before White Bird turn west at the sign directing you to Pittsburg Landing. Cross the Salmon River within one-half mile, then turn south on Forest Service Road 493 and continue for 17 miles to Pittsburg Landing.
Season: Trails open in June and remain open into October.
Wilderness Fees/Permits: None for backcountry use of the Wilderness. River use requires a permit. Contact Wallowa-Whitman National Forest, P.O. Box 907, Baker, OR 97814; (503) 523-6391. A $6 application fee is charged, and there's no guarantee of getting a permit. Apply by January 31.
Maps: For a free index of Idaho USGS topographic maps, contact the USGS-Western Distribution Branch, P.O. Box 25286, Federal Center, Denver, CO 80225; (303) 234-3832.
Management: Hells Canyon National Recreation Area Headquarters, Wallowa-Whitman National Forest, P.O. Box 490, Enterprise, OR 97828; (503) 426-3151. Hells Canyon National Recreation Area, Payette National Forest, P.O. Box 832, Riggins, ID 83549; (208) 628-3916. Hells Canyon National Recreation Area, Nez Perce National Forest, 3620-B Snake River Avenue, Lewiston, ID 83501; (208) 743-3648.

Sawtooth Wilderness

Named for its jagged mountain skyline, among the most spectacular I've ever seen, the Sawtooth Wilderness also holds deep gorges and lake-filled glacial basins. Comprising the western portion of 754,000-acre Sawtooth National Recreation Area (SNRA), the Wilderness protects the Sawtooth Mountains with approximately 40 peaks reaching 10,000 feet, topped by Thompson Peak at 10,776 feet. Portions of the Wilderness lie within Sawtooth, Challis, and Boise National Forests. Within this area lie the headwaters of the North Fork and Middle Fork of the Boise River, the South Fork of the Payette River, a portion of the Salmon River, and an astonishing 300 lakes. About 85 percent of the water comes from snowmelt. Lakes drain down turbulent streams. Many visitors come for the trout fishing, mountain climbing, hunting, and outstanding camping.

A forest dominated by pine, spruce, and fir provides homes for elk and deer, black bears and mountain goats, and many species of smaller fur-bearing animals. Abundant summer wildflowers blanket the landscape with color. Forty-two Wilderness trails cover about 270 miles. The Redfish Creek/Baron Creek Trail, starting at Redfish Lake, travels for 22 miles and joins other trails to lead into the heart of the Wilderness. Some remarkable regions of the Wilderness are only accessible by off-trail route finding. Open fires are not permitted in some high-use regions, and group size is limited in the area to help stem the tide of human impact. On any given night, temperatures might drop to freezing, and in summer the mosquitoes have been known to provoke visitors.

Sawtooth Essentials

Size: 217,088 acres.
Year Designated: 1972.
Location: Southern central Idaho.
Easiest Access: From Ketchum, the Sawtooth Scenic Route heads north for approximately 65 miles to Redfish Lake and the Redfish Creek/Baron Creek Trailhead.
Season: It may be mid-July before all the trails are open, and snow sometimes closes them by mid-September.
Wilderness Fees/Permits: None for groups of fewer than nine people. Maximum group size is 20 people.
Maps: A Wilderness topographic map is available for $4.25 at SNRA Headquarters. Each of the 31 USGS topographic maps covering the SNRA are also available at the headquarters.
Management: Sawtooth National Recreation Area, Star Route, Ketchum, ID 83340; (208) 726-8291.

Selway–Bitterroot Wilderness

The Bitterroot Mountains form a rugged, glacier-carved border between Idaho and Montana. On both sides of this border is the Selway–Bitterroot Wilderness, the third largest Wilderness in the Lower 48. A much smaller (but still considerable) portion is protected by Montana (see Montana, Selway–Bitterroot Wilderness), and the Idaho side includes the large Moose Creek Ranger District (560,000 roadless acres), the only district in the Forest Service System entirely within a Wilderness. Except for the high crest of the Bitterroots, the area is dominated by ridges broken with raw granite peaks. Below the ridges are deep canyons covered with thick coniferous forest. Hidden low valleys are rich with old-growth cedar,

IDAHO

fir, and larch, and extensive stands of subalpine spruce and fir can be found higher up.

Hundreds of miles of trails, more than 700 in the Moose Creek Ranger District alone, wind through the area, but they are rarely maintained. From Big Fog Saddle a trail suitable for foot and horse traffic marches toward the heart of the area. Along the Selway River, the hiking rates as moderate. Leave the river and you'll find drastic elevation changes, making for difficult going.

Water is plentiful in lakes, bogs, and marshes. The Wild and Scenic Selway River rushes out of the mountains of Idaho to join the Moose Creek drainages and the Middle Fork of the Selway. Many rafters ride the river, and at lower elevations in the Selway River Canyon you'll find the warmest temperatures year-round. But the weather varies like the terrain. Spring and fall bring rain lower down, while it is snowing higher up. Summer days are typically warm and dry with nighttime temperatures low enough to send you burrowing deep into your sleeping bag. You should be prepared for avalanches in winter.

In the high country in summer, mosquitoes and biting flies are frequent campsite companions. Rattlesnakes and black bears are common, and grizzly bears still roam the Selway-Bitterroot, although not in great numbers. Hunters are attracted to elk, deer, mountain lions, and grouse. Hunters may track moose and bighorn sheep with a special permit. Trout fishing can be excellent in well over 100 mountain lakes. By late July, wildflowers bloom at elevations over 5,000 feet, luring many photographers.

Selway–Bitterroot Essentials

Size: 1,089,017 acres in Idaho (1,337,910 acres total).

Year Designated: 1964; expanded in 1980 in Idaho.

Location: Eastern Idaho.

Easiest Access: From U.S. 12 in Lowell, take Forest Road 223, an improved dirt road, and follow the Selway River for approximately 20 miles. Turn north on Forest Road 319, which winds uphill to Big Fog Saddle. Although Forest Road 319 runs only approximately 10 miles, the road is steep and the driving is slow. Three primitive airfields may be used at Moose, Fish Lake, and Shearer, all located in the heart of the Wilderness.

Season: Spring and summer for river rafting; July for wildflowers; fall for hunting; winter for backcountry skiing.

Wilderness Fees/Permits: A permit is needed only for Selway River use. Contact the West Fork Ranger Station, Darby, MT 59829; (406) 821-3269. It costs $6 to apply, and there is no guarantee that a permit will be issued. Apply by January 31.

Maps: A Wilderness map is available for $3 from any local forest ranger.

Management: Forest Supervisor, Clearwater National Forest, U.S. 12 and 126th Street, Orofino, ID 83544; (208) 476-4541. Forest Supervisor, Nez Perce National Forest, 319 East Main, Grangeville, ID 83530; (208) 983-1950. Forest Supervisor, Bitterroot National Forest, 316 North Third Street, Hamilton, MT 59840; (406) 363-3131. Forest Supervisor, Lolo National Forest, Building 24, Fort Missoula, Missoula, MT 59801; (406) 329-3750.

> "I can at best report only from my own wilderness. The important thing is that each man possess such a wilderness, and that he consider what marvels are to be observed there."
>
> —Loren Eisley

ILLINOIS

Total Wilderness areas: 8
Total Wilderness acreage: 30,316

Three hundred million years ago an uplift created mountains thousands of feet high, but natural forces whittled them down to the Shawnee Hills of today's Illinois. Once home to the Shawnee Indians, the area saw an influx of white settlers who began to crowd them out in the early 1800s. Extensive logging and farming operations removed the original forest. When an inventory was made of "natural areas" left in the United States, Illinois ranked 49th out of 50 states. Only Iowa had less untouched land.

In southern Illinois, between the Mississippi and Ohio Rivers and not far above their confluence, stretches nearly 300,000 acres of Shawnee National Forest. Seven small, lovely areas, covering almost 10 percent of the forest, have qualified for Wilderness designation. In the same region, a section of one National Wildlife Refuge rounds out the state's Wilderness holdings.

Bald Knob Wilderness

The largest Wilderness in the state, Bald Knob is located at the farthest extreme of the Ozark Uplift. It would be even bigger if an abandoned dirt road didn't separate it from Clear Springs Wilderness (see below). The old road follows spring-fed Hutchins Creek, which is rated one of the highest-quality waterways in the state. Hutchins Creek has formed a wide, flat valley, unlike most found in the Ozarks. Beyond the creek, the landscape becomes more typical, with high relief, steep slopes (some exceeding 70 degrees), rocky bluffs, and sharp V-shaped creek drainages. If you explore Bald Knob Wilderness, you'll traverse secluded little valleys virtually untouched by humans. Here a mixture of deciduous trees shade the ground on hot summer days and the hiking is easy. Outside of the valleys, the going gets tougher. Hiking and camping are unrestricted.

Bald Knob takes its name from a high rise of ground on the east side that has a large, bold white cross planted on top of it. The cross is visible from many points within the area.

ILLINOIS

Bald Knob Essentials
Size: 5,918 acres.
Year Designated: 1990.
Location: Southern Illinois.
Easiest Access: From Jonesboro, take State Highway 146 east for approximately three miles. Turn north on State Highway 127 and drive approximately nine miles to Bald Knob Road. Turn west on Bald Knob Road, which leads about three miles to the top of Bald Knob.
Season: Spring and fall; avoid the heat and humidity of summer.
Wilderness Fees/Permits: None.
Maps: USGS topographic maps are available for $3 each from the Forest Service office.
Management: Shawnee National Forest, 901 South Commercial Street, Harrisburg, IL 62946. Or call the Jonesboro Ranger District at (618) 833-8576.

Bay Creek Wilderness

Bay Creek runs year-round, creating excellent conditions for woodland species including oak, pine, cedar, and ash, and flowering trees such as dogwood, redbud, wild cherry, and plum. On the north side, Bay Creek Wilderness shares a border with Burden Falls Wilderness (see below). Bluffs colored by bands of iron oxide and unusual limestone and sandstone formations attract human visitors. The rock formations of the Shawnee Hills hold many caves, and one contains primitive wall paintings. Archaeologists believe there are more worthwhile sites yet to be discovered. Hiking and camping are unrestricted. Leave all archaeological sites as you find them, and don't touch "leaves of three"; poison ivy grows here as a vine, a freestanding low plant, and a freestanding high shrub.

Bay Creek Essentials
Size: 2,866 acres.
Year Designated: 1990.
Location: Southern Illinois.
Easiest Access: From Interstate 24 at Vienna, take State Highway 147 east for approximately 10 miles. Continue east on State Highway 145 approximately six miles to Eddyville, then turn north on unpaved County Road 442 and continue about six miles to Bay Creek.
Season: Spring and fall.
Wilderness Fees/Permits: None.
Maps: USGS topographic maps of Bay Creek Wilderness are available for $3 each from the Forest Service office.
Management: Shawnee National Forest, 901 South Commercial Street, Harrisburg, IL 62946. Or call the Vienna Ranger District at (618) 658-2111.

Burden Falls Wilderness

An intermittent stream spills over Burden Falls, a picturesque series of waterfalls that drop a total of about 100 feet, with a greatest single descent of approximately 20 feet. Burden Creek flows northward toward the Little Saline River. The Wilderness shares its southern boundary with Bay Creek Wilderness (see above), and both exemplify the scenic characteristics of the Shawnee Hills: sandstone ledges overlooking bluffs and cliffs on which dry-land communities of red cedar, farkleberry, and blackjack oak grow.

ILLINOIS

At the bottom of the bluffs, greater soil depth supports post oak and, farther from the cliffs, white oak grows in even deeper soil. Several unique species of plant life thrive in the area, including Carolina buckthorn, seldom seen this far north, rock chestnut, prickly pear, royal fern, glade fern, and the cardinal flower. Among the inhabitants of the deciduous forest are white-tailed deer, wild turkeys, gray squirrels, and many other small mammals. The barred owl lives here alongside pileated woodpeckers and eastern bluebirds.

The Burden Falls Trail (3.5 miles) runs above the waterfall. Hunting and fishing are allowed. Hiking and camping in the area are unrestricted. Bird watching and photography (especially when the falls are falling) make this a worthwhile destination.

Burden Falls Essentials

Size: 3,723 acres.
Year Designated: 1990.
Location: Southern Illinois.
Easiest Access: From Harrisburg, take State Highway 145 south for approximately 12 miles. Turn west on graveled Forest Service Road 402 at Delwood and drive about three miles to the Burden Falls Trailhead.
Season: Spring and fall.
Wilderness Fees/Permits: None.
Maps: USGS topographic maps are available for $3 each from the Forest Service office.
Management: Shawnee National Forest, 901 South Commercial Street, Harrisburg, IL 62946. Or call the Vienna Ranger District at (618) 658-2111.

Clear Springs Wilderness

Clear Springs flows heavily into Hutchins Creek, which separates this area from Bald Knob Wilderness to the south (see above). An abandoned farmstead, complete with rusted-over machinery, stands as a reminder of the industry that once supported the economy of this region. Some of the steep slopes lining V-shaped creek drainages are composed of loose chert (flint) fragments, from which even earlier inhabitants formed tools.

On the western boundary you'll discover a spectacular view of the Mississippi and Big Muddy Rivers when you stand on sheer limestone bluffs that rise 400 feet above the valley floor. The deciduous forest, typical of the Ozarks, harbors wild turkeys, deer, and many smaller mammals. You can find threatened (in Illinois) shortleaf pine growing in isolated stands here. Away from the steep valley walls, the hiking rates as easy and pleasant. Many hideaways are ideal spots to set up camp. Hiking and camping are unrestricted.

Clear Springs Essentials

Size: 4,730 acres.
Year Designated: 1990.
Location: Southern Illinois.
Easiest Access: From Jonesboro, take State Highway 146 west for about nine miles. Turn north on Highway 3 and drive approximately three miles. Turn east on Big Muddy River Levee and head to Pine Hills Road, which leads north to the Wilderness in about seven miles.
Season: Spring and fall.
Wilderness Fees/Permits: None.
Maps: USGS topographic maps of Clear Springs Wilderness are available for $3 each from the Forest Service office.
Management: Shawnee National Forest, 901 South Commercial Street, Harrisburg, IL 62946. Or call the Jonesboro Ranger District at (618) 833-8576.

ILLINOIS

Crab Orchard Wilderness

Smack dab in the middle of the Mississippi Flyway, 43,500-acre Crab Orchard National Wildlife Refuge provides a winter feeding and resting area for an average of 120,000 Canada geese each year. Agriculture and logging in the early 1900s so depleted this region of forest, wetland, and grassland that wildlife could barely subsist here. The refuge was formed in 1947 to restore an adequate ground for geese, ducks, wild turkeys, a multitude of white-tailed deer, and small mammals including coyotes, beavers, opossums, and raccoons. Five thousand acres of the refuge are planted each year to feed wildfowl.

Most people visit the refuge to bird-watch, hunt, and fish. Anglers cast a line for bass, bluegill, and crappie on Crab Orchard Lake, Devil's Kitchen Lake, Little Grassy Lake, and many smaller lakes. The Wilderness forms the southern tip of the refuge and encompasses sections of Little Grassy Lake and Devil's Kitchen Lake. Several parking lots and boat launches provide easy access to the water. Within Crab Orchard Wilderness boundaries lie dramatic sandstone outcroppings, wood-lined creeks, and potential seclusion, but there are no maintained trails. Camping is restricted to designated campsites, of which there are none in the Wilderness area (except for preexisting camps for Boy Scouts and Girl Scouts). Fires are not permitted in the Wilderness.

Crab Orchard Essentials

Size: 4,050 acres.
Year Designated: 1976.
Location: Southern Illinois.
Easiest Access: From Marion, take State Route 13 west for approximately eight miles. Turn south on State Route 148 and drive 1.5 miles to the refuge headquarters. Five Wilderness entry points are accessible by road.
Season: Fall, when migrating birds can be seen.

Wilderness Fees/Permits: Entrance fee passes are required for everyone entering the refuge. A 15-day pass costs $3.
Maps: Free refuge maps are available from the manager.
Management: Crab Orchard National Wildlife Refuge, P.O. Box J, Carterville, IL 62918; (618) 997-3344.

Garden of the Gods Wilderness

With heavenly rock formations, canyons, bluffs, and ridges carved over eons by wind and water, it's no secret why Garden of the Gods is the state's most visited landmark. Once home to indigenous peoples, today the area attracts many rock climbers, photographers, and bird-watchers hoping to spy one of the resident raptors. To the north, west, and south the Wilderness bounds the Garden of the Gods Recreation Area. The two areas are connected by six trails, five of which join the Illinois River-to-River Trail, a winding 10-mile trek that crosses the center of the Wilderness in a spacious S-curve.

Views from the summits of massive sandstone formations overlook a thick forest, an especially pleasing sight in fall when the leaves weave a bright tapestry of color. The hiking below the bluffs is easy and quiet through the hardwood trees dotted with moss-covered, sculpted sandstone. Of the many canyons of the Wilderness, Rock Branch Hollow, which runs from the northern boundary south to the middle of the area, probably rates as the most beautiful. Overnight parking is available in the recreation area. Hiking and camping are unrestricted.

Garden of the Gods Essentials

Size: 3,293 acres.
Year Designated: 1990.
Location: Southern Illinois.
Easiest Access: From Harrisburg, take State Highway 145 south for about eight miles. Then turn east on Highway 34, which bends to the south for about nine miles, and head east again onto Karbers Ridge Road and continue for about three miles. Turn north at the well-marked entrance.
Season: Spring and fall.
Wilderness Fees/Permits: None.
Maps: USGS topographic maps are available for $3 each from the Forest Service office.
Management: Elizabethtown Ranger District, Shawnee National Forest, RR 2, Box 4, Elizabethtown, IL 62931; (618) 287-2201.

Lusk Creek Wilderness

Rugged terrain and winding canyons characterize Lusk Creek, unusually diverse topography for Illinois. This Wilderness protects broad, relatively flat ridge tops and terraces overlooking narrow ravines and deep sandstone gulches. Throughout you'll find sheltered caves, sinkholes, and sheer rock walls rising, at some points, 200 feet above the creeks below . . . the stuff of a rock climber's dreams. Lusk Creek itself ranks as one of the state's highest-quality streams. It runs year-round, one of several waterways that do so in the area. Anglers can fish the stream for bass and bluegill. You may find small tracts of virgin timber and spring wildflowers, including wild columbine and French's shooting star.

The Lusk Creek Trail gives access to the Wilderness. From a parking lot on a paved road, a 1.5-mile trek takes you to a precipice called Indian Kitchen, located at a hairpin turn in Lusk Creek Canyon. Evidence reveals that humans used the "Kitchen" in prehistoric times, perhaps as long as 10,000 years ago. The 146-mile River-to-River Trail, completed in 1996, crosses Illinois from Battery Rock on the Ohio River to Devil's Backbone Park on the Mississippi and provides a pathway across Lusk Creek Wilderness. The trail touches all seven Wilderness areas on Shawnee National Forest, and the 18-mile section from Garden of the Gods (see above) across Lusk Creek has been called the least-civilized piece of the Midwest. The hiking may be a little more strenuous than in most of Illinois. Hiking and camping are unrestricted.

Lusk Creek Essentials

Size: 4,796 acres.
Year Designated: 1990.
Location: Southern Illinois.
Easiest Access: From Eddyville, take State Highway 145 north about one mile to the Lusk Creek and River-to-River Trailheads on the east side of the road.
Season: Spring and fall.
Wilderness Fees/Permits: None.
Maps: USGS topographic maps are available for $3 each from the Forest Service office.
Management: Shawnee National Forest, 901 South Commercial Street, Harrisburg, IL 62946. Or call the Vienna Ranger District at (618) 658-2111.

Panther Den Wilderness

The smallest Wilderness in Illinois, Panther Den shares its northern boundary with Crab Orchard Wilderness (see above). Three fingers of Devil's Kitchen Lake extend into the northern section of this area, offering fishing for large and smallmouth bass, crappie, and bluegill. Sandstone bluffs and multilayered rock formations entice canoeists and photographers into the waters of Panther Den. Sheltered overhangs beneath the bluffs provide habitat for the endangered French's shooting star flower. Muskrats, deer, and beavers are common sights. Mink and bobcats (endangered in Illinois) have been seen here, too.

Eons ago a large waterway flowed through this region. Today the valley that it cut is known as Panther Den. Hikers and bird-watchers usually head for this spot, for both the panoramic overlooks and the avian-viewing possibilities found on the 70-foot-high cliffs. Huge blocks have split off from the canyon wall to form narrow crevices that challenge rock climbers. Ancient rock shelters here suggest that people have been using the "Den" for centuries.

Panther Den Essentials

Size: 940 acres.
Year Designated: 1990.
Location: Southern Illinois.
Easiest Access: From Marion, take State Route 13 west for approximately eight miles. Turn south on State Route 148 and drive 1.5 miles to the Crab Orchard National Wildlife Refuge headquarters. Continue past refuge headquarters on State Route 148 about five miles, then turn west on Grassy Road and drive two miles. Turn south on Wolf Creek Road and continue approximately five miles to the Wilderness.
Season: Spring and fall.
Wilderness Fees/Permits: None.
Maps: USGS topographic maps are available for $3 each from the Forest Service office.
Management: Shawnee National Forest, 901 South Commercial Street, Harrisburg, IL 62946. Or call the Jonesboro Ranger District at (618) 833-8576.

> "No friendly roof kept them dry when they mis-guessed whether or not to pitch the tent. No guide showed them which camping spots offered a nightlong breeze, and which a nightlong misery of mosquitoes; which firewood made clean coals, and which only smoke . . . . The wilderness gave them their first taste of those rewards and penalties for wise and foolish acts which every woodsman faces daily, but against which civilization has built a thousand buffers."
>
> —Aldo Leopold

INDIANA

Total Wilderness areas: 1
Total Wilderness acreage: 12,935

The Indiana woods once were thought to be endless. For a long time they stood undisturbed, a barrier holding back a tide of European colonizers and providing a home for indigenous peoples. But the barrier eventually gave way, and the last of the "Indians" were moved from Indiana, against their will, by 1809. Some of the finest hardwood forests in the world fell to the ax and saw. Today one small area represents a slice of the glory the land once knew.

Charles C. Deam Wilderness

Settlers first arrived in Indiana's only Wilderness in 1826. This was one of the last pieces of the state to have its steep hills and narrow ridge tops tamed by humans. As recently as half a century ago, 81 farms dotted the area, every ridge was planted in corn or hay, and 57 miles of roads traversed the higher ground. Although the landscape still shows considerable evidence of human alterations, the Wilderness is slowly returning to its natural wild state. Bird species, including flycatchers, scarlet tanagers, red-eyed vireos, hawks, and woodpeckers, now thrive in the gradually thickening forest. Among the reptiles you'll find are the poisonous timber rattlesnake and the copperhead.

Named for the first Indiana State Forester, the Charles C. Deam Wilderness is bordered on the north by the watery Middle Fork State Wildlife Refuge. The Wilderness stands divided into a northern and smaller southern section by the Tower Ridge Road, and the right-of-way of this road remains non-Wilderness. Old roads can be

INDIANA

followed on foot or horse off of Tower Ridge Road into the Wilderness. Blackwell Campground is maintained at the western end of the road. Chiggers, ticks, and poison ivy thrive in summer months. Horsepacking and hunting are allowed throughout the area.

Charles C. Deam Essentials

Size: 12,935 acres.
Year Designated: 1982.
Location: Southern central Indiana.
Easiest Access: From Bedford, take U.S. 50 east for seven miles. Turn north on Highway 446 and drive until signs begin to identify the Wilderness entry points, a distance of about seven miles.
Season: Temperatures are most pleasant in fall and spring. Leaves turn brilliant colors in fall.
Wilderness Fees/Permits: None.
Maps: A waterproof topographic map is available for $2 from the forest supervisor.
Management: Forest Supervisor, Hoosier National Forest, 811 Constitution Avenue, Bedford, IN 47421; (812) 275-5987.

> "In gaining the lovely and the usable, we have given up the incomparable."
>
> —Wallace Stegner

KENTUCKY

Total Wilderness areas: 2
Total Wilderness acreage: 18,056

When Daniel Boone explored the hills of Kentucky, tree cover was so dense the ground lay dark in perpetual shade. By the time the U.S. Forest Service gained control of more than 670,000 acres of what today is Daniel Boone National Forest (Cumberland National Forest prior to 1966), all the timber had been harvested and forest fires had ravaged almost everything left standing. Under U.S. Forest Service management, a forest of upland hardwoods, cove hardwoods, and yellow pines has returned, but precious little remains worthy of Wilderness designation.

Beaver Creek Wilderness

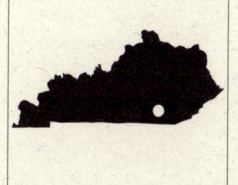

This is a secret spot, a nature lover's paradise almost totally enclosed by towering sandstone cliffs that form an 85-mile, torturously twisting perimeter. Below these high walls, well marked with natural arches and rock houses (sheltering overhangs used by indigenous peoples), lies the Beaver Creek drainage, a mature eastern hardwood forest with dancing streams and rippling waterfalls. Much of the year the forest is alive with flowering trees, shrubs, and low-lying plants. Game and nongame animals make their homes here, including wild turkeys, white-tailed deer, ruffed grouse, red and gray foxes, bobwhite quail, rabbits, muskrats, mink, and raccoons.

Beaver Creek Wilderness is a part of Beaver Creek Wildlife Management Area. Fishing is allowed with a state license, and hunting with a special permit. You may backpack, camp, or ride horseback here. Three maintained trails provide access to the Wilderness: (1) the 5.2-mile Middle Ridge Trail, which rises high for a great view at Three Forks of Beaver Overlook; (2) another, shorter route to the overlook, the half-mile Three Forks of Beaver Trail; and (3) the Three Forks Loop Trail, a pathway of approximately two miles.

KENTUCKY

Beaver Creek Essentials

Size: 4,756 acres.
Year Designated: 1975.
Location: Eastern Kentucky.
Easiest Access: From Somerset, take U.S. 27 south for 18 miles. Turn east on Hammonds Camp Road and drive about three miles. Head right when the road forks and continue a short distance to a parking lot and the Three Forks Trailhead.
Season: Spring and fall are best.
Wilderness Fees/Permits: None. Permits are required for fishing and hunting.
Maps: A special Wilderness map is available for $3 from the district ranger.
Management: Somerset Ranger District, Daniel Boone National Forest, 156 Realty Lane, Somerset, KY 42501; (606) 679-2018 or (606) 679-2010.

Clifty Wilderness

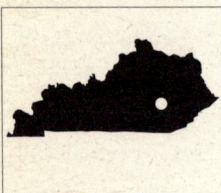

Within the scenic 25,662-acre Red River Gorge Geological Area, magically sculpted by 70 million years of wind and water, Clifty Wilderness is a rugged pocket of cliffs, bluffs, steep canyons, arches, rock shelters, and creeks splashing down boulder-strewn defiles. The Red River divides the Wilderness into northern and southern sections and has been considered for Wild and Scenic designation. Some of the fantastic cliffs stand as high as 200 feet above the bottom, spinelike and with tops so narrow there is barely room to walk on them. This unusual topography has created a greenhouse for a large number of plant species, including more than 750 flowering plants and 170 mosses. At least 15 of the plants here are considered either sensitive, rare, or endangered.

Backpacking, camping, horseback riding, fishing, hunting, and canoeing are allowed at Clifty, but you should be competent at map reading and backcountry navigation before venturing into the heart of the Wilderness. In the southern section, the Swift Camp Creek Trail, the primary access to the Wilderness, follows meandering Swift Camp Creek for 7.2 miles. Along the way it passes huge evergreens, rock shelters, and several small arches as it winds to one of the most remote regions in the Wilderness. The Wildcat Trail follows an abandoned logging road for approximately one mile before descending a drainage for another third of a mile to join the Swift Camp Creek Trail.

Clifty Essentials

Size: 13,300 acres.
Year Designated: 1985.
Location: Eastern Kentucky.
Easiest Access: From the Mountain Parkway southeast of Lexington, exit south at Slade. Take State Highway 11 north for one-tenth of a mile, then turn east on State Highway 15 and drive seven miles. Turn north on State Highway 715 and drive one-third of a mile, then turn east on Rock Bridge Road and continue three miles to the end of the road. Walk the Rock Bridge Nature Trail for one-half mile to the Swift Camp Creek Trailhead.
Season: Spring and fall are the best.
Wilderness Fees/Permits: None for backcountry visitation. Permits are required for fishing and hunting.
Maps: A special Wilderness map is available for $3 from the district ranger.
Management: Stanton Ranger District, Daniel Boone National Forest, 705 West College Avenue, Stanton, KY 40380; (606) 663-2852.

> "The wild places are where we began; when they end, so do we."
> —David Brower

LOUISIANA

Total Wilderness areas: 3
Total Wilderness acreage: 17,046

Virtually unchanged for 100 million years or more, the alligator may be the king of the "jungle" in Louisiana. Most of the southern part of the state is warm, humid, and swampy, the kind of habitat gators prefer, and southern Louisiana has two Wilderness areas managed by the U.S. Fish and Wildlife Service. A third area lies in central Louisiana's Kisatchie National Forest.

Breton Island Wilderness

Located off the delta of the great Mississippi River, Breton Island actually consists of two adjacent islands (north and south) with a combined length of about three miles and a width of less than one mile. Part of a long chain of barrier islands, they comprise only a small section of Breton National Wildlife Refuge. The greater portion of the refuge consists of the Chandeleur Islands, an approximately 20-mile-long crescent of land lying north of Breton. Between Breton and Chandeleur are more islands owned by the state and managed by the refuge. Geologically young, these unstable islands were created in the last 300 years by silt washing down the Mississippi River. On the Gulf of Mexico side of the islands you'll find low sandy beaches tapering into a maze of ponds, inlets, and saltwater marshes.

Hundreds of thousands of seabirds use these islands as nesting and wintering habitat. Endangered brown pelicans have made a dramatic return under careful refuge management. Camping is allowed, but you must remain more than 200 yards from bird colonies. Human visitors are common, sometimes coming for bird watching but primarily for surf fishing. Almost all of the refuge is designated Wilderness.

Breton Island Essentials

Size: 5,000 acres.
Year Designated: 1975.
Location: Off the state's southeastern coast.
Easiest Access: From New Orleans, take State Highway 23 south until you reach the boat launch at the end of the line, Venice. The southern tip of Breton rises above the sea about 12 miles offshore.
Season: Spring, fall, and summer offer excellent fishing and bird watching. In April, May, and June, nesting birds are especially sensitive.
Wilderness Fees/Permits: None.
Maps: Any nautical map of the coast of Louisiana. Contact the refuge manager.
Management: Southeast Louisiana Wildlife Refuges, 1010 Gause Boulevard, Building 936, Slidell, LA 70458; (504) 646-7555.

LOUISIANA

Kisatchie Hills Wilderness

Home to the alligator and the long-legged bird, Bayou Cypre forms the heart of Kisatchie Hills, the state's largest Wilderness. Above the bayou you'll find some of the most unique topography in Louisiana, unusually steep and rugged terrain with flat-topped mesas, sandstone bluffs and outcroppings, and distinct forest ecosystems.

The Backbone Trail follows ridges above the bayou and gives access to three shorter trails. The combined trail system is 10.5 miles. Along the southern border, the Longleaf Vista Recreation Area offers a scenic overlook of the Wilderness. Most of the Wilderness lies within Red Dirt National Wildlife Management Preserve.

Kisatchie Hills Essentials

Size: 8,700 acres.
Year Designated: 1980.
Location: Western central Louisiana.
Easiest Access: From Alexandria, go north and west on Interstate 49 to the Derry exit. Drive south on State Highway 119 for 5.5 miles, then turn west onto Forest Service Road 59 and continue 4.2 miles to the Backbone Trailhead.
Season: Temperatures can dip from December to February. Summers are hot and humid.
Wilderness Fees/Permits: None.
Maps: A topographic map is available for $3 from the district ranger.
Management: Kisatchie National Forest, Southern Region, P.O. Box 5500, Pineville, LA 71360; (318) 473-7160.

Lacassine Wilderness

On the southern end of the Mississippi and Central Flyways, 32,970-acre Lacassine National Wildlife Refuge is primarily a freshwater marsh. Dense growths of maidencane and bull tongue provide migratory habitat and wintering ground for more than 300,000 ducks and 80,000 geese. The refuge supports many other species. The first nesting colony of cattle egrets outside Florida was discovered here. A nesting rookery of roseate spoonbills, unique to Louisiana, can be found in Lacassine Pool. Watch for armadillos, swamp rabbits, minks, otters, and American alligators.

The southern portion of the refuge, south of the pipeline canal and west of Bayou Misere, has been designated Wilderness. Unlike the rest of the refuge, this area has seen relatively little impact from human activity. There are no established trails, and no camping is allowed.

Lacassine Essentials

Size: 3,346 acres.
Year Designated: 1976.
Location: Southwestern Louisiana.
Easiest Access: Traveling west on Interstate 10 from Baton Rouge, take Exit 64 (Jennings) and travel south on State Highway 26 to Highway 14 in Lake Arthur. Take Highway 14 west for seven miles, then turn south on Highway 3056 and drive 4.5 miles to the refuge.
Season: Winter is best for bird watching. Open year-round from one hour before sunrise until one hour after sunset. Boats are allowed from March 15 through October 15.
Wilderness Fees/Permits: None.
Maps: Get a free map from the refuge manager.
Management: Lacassine National Wildlife Refuge, HCR 63, Box 186, Lake Arthur, LA 70549; (318) 774-5923.

> "The clearest way to the universe is through a forest wilderness."
>
> —John Muir

MAINE

Total Wilderness areas: 2
Total Wilderness acreage: 19,392

Although it's as large as the rest of New England put together, Maine has less than one-tenth of the region's population. Most residents are concentrated along the coast between Portsmouth and Bar Harbor. Only 228 linear miles long, the state's convoluted shoreline includes 3,478 miles of rocky bays and inlets and thousands of tiny, fascinating islands. Inland stretches a vast, rolling expanse of second-growth forest dotted with more than 2,500 lakes. Most of this land was purchased by timber companies and private investors during the 1800s. Despite its ample acreage, Maine has remarkably little public land. The state has only two small Wilderness areas, one on a wildlife refuge and the other on a national forest.

Caribou–Speckled Mountain Wilderness

New Hampshire is home to most of White Mountain National Forest, but 49,166 of its acres cross into Maine. Within this expanse lies Caribou–Speckled Mountain Wilderness. Encompassing both Caribou Mountain and Speckled Mountain, it is the state's newest and largest Wilderness, an area of steep terrain along a jumbled mass of ridges opened by numerous ledges and forested with northern hardwoods. Some white pine grows lower down and spruce and fir higher up. Many streams run out of this area, headed for the Androscoggin and Saco Rivers and filling numerous ponds along the way.

Dots or "specks" of hardwoods that color brilliantly in fall cover the flanks of "Old Speck," Maine's third highest peak at 2,906 feet, giving the mountain its name. Speckled Mountain rises near the center of a network of trails that crisscross much of the area. The Bickford Brook Trail climbs 4.3 miles from the west side to the summit of Speckled Mountain. Other trails that reach the summit are the 4.9-mile Cold Brook Trail, which approaches from the south, and the 5.6-mile Red Rock Trail, which begins in the east. Farther north the Caribou Trail provides a path to some of the most attractive ledges in the Wilderness. It climbs 3.5 miles from the west side to the peak of Caribou Mountain, then drops another two miles north away from the area.

MAINE

While the scenery along the trails lacks some of the splendor of the White Mountains, you'll find fewer people, lovely country, and a much greater chance to experience Wilderness. Off-trail bushwhacking is difficult thanks to blueberry, cranberry, and other shrubs that fill the region.

Summer brings the most human visitors and biting insects. In fall the insects are gone, the tapestry of color is extraordinary (and worth a visit), and quiet prevails. Winter snowfall can be heavy, and avalanche danger is high. You'll find numerous campsites with unrestricted camping.

Caribou–Speckled Mountain Essentials

Size: 12,000 acres.
Year Designated: 1990.
Location: Western Maine.
Easiest Access: From Fryeburg, on the Maine/New Hampshire state line, take State Highway 113 north for approximately 20 miles to Cold River Campground. Continue two-tenths of a mile past the turnoff to the campground to the Bickford Brook Trailhead.
Season: Fall is best, especially September and early October.
Wilderness Fees/Permits: None.
Maps: A national forest map highlighted with trails is available from the district ranger for a small fee.
Management: Evans Notch Ranger District, White Mountain National Forest, RFD 2, Box 2270, Bethel, ME 04217; (207) 824-2134.

Moosehorn Wilderness

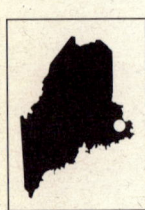

Every year thousands of migratory birds hitch a ride on the Eastern (Atlantic) Flyway, which spans the skies from Maine to Florida. At the northernmost end of the route, many disembark at 23,000-acre Moosehorn National Wildlife Refuge. Although trees in this region have been significantly logged in the past, today a diverse forest stands here, a woodland of aspen, maple, birch, spruce, and fir with scattered stands of white pine. Once scoured heavily by glaciers, the land of the refuge is primarily low, rolling hills dotted with many lakes, bogs, marshes, streams, and rocky outcroppings.

Established in 1937, Moosehorn is the only refuge where people study and manage the American woodcock, a reclusive bird that hides in dense cover of young forests during the day, feeds in clearings at night, and flies an amazing courtship ritual in spring. Bald eagles frequent the refuge, and black bears and white-tailed deer are common. In November, deer hunting is allowed. Despite the name, moose are not as common as you would expect. Ducks, geese, and loons congregate on more than 50 lakes.

The refuge is divided into two units: 16,080 acres of the Baring Unit lie inland, and 6,665 acres of the Edmunds Unit, including tiny Birch and Dog Islands, lie on the rocky Maine coast. Although both units are partially designated Wilderness, sometimes they are considered to be more than one piece of the National Wilderness Preservation System. I have listed them as one.

On the Edmunds Unit, 2,712 acres are Wilderness, approximately the western third of the unit and six acres of Birch and Dog Islands in Cobscook Bay. Porpoises and harbor seals are often seen frolicking from the islands. Along the several miles of coast of the Edmunds Unit, 24-foot tidal fluctuations are normal, but only the island portion of the Wilderness is affected. A loop road passes along the boundary of the inland Wilderness, and several old roads give miles of access to the area. Off the old roads, bushwhacking through heavy brush can be a nightmare.

MAINE

On the larger Baring Unit, the western side and environs of Bearce Lake, the largest body of water on the refuge, contain 4,680 acres of designated Wilderness. Refuge headquarters can be found near the Wilderness boundary, and from there several trails lead to the lake.

Moosehorn Essentials

Size: 7,392 acres.
Year Designated: 1970 (the Edmunds Unit); 1975 (the Baring Unit).
Location: Eastern Maine.
Easiest Access: From Bangor, take State Highway 9 east for approximately 90 miles to Calais. At Calais turn south on U.S. 1 and drive five miles to Charlotte Road. Turn west and head two miles to the sign indicating Moosehorn National Wildlife Refuge headquarters. The Baring Unit lies near the headquarters. The Edmunds Unit is located between Dennysville and Whiting on U.S. 1, approximately 40 miles farther south.
Season: In mid-May the ducks and geese reach peak populations—as do the biting insects.
Wilderness Fees/Permits: None.
Maps: A free map is available from the refuge manager.
Management: Moosehorn National Wildlife Refuge, P.O. Box 1077, Calais, ME 04619; (207) 454-3521.

> *"Even after [Monomoy Island] was designated as wilderness, the human presence lingered here like a migrant bird reluctant to leave."*
>
> —North Cairn

MASSACHUSETTS

Total Wilderness areas: 1
Total Wilderness acreage: 2,420

In what was once a vast hardwood forestland inhabited by bird and beast, there now throbs a throng of humanity called southern New England (Massachusetts, Connecticut, and Rhode Island). Here survive two small specks of land off the southeastern coast of Massachusetts that together form one Wilderness area managed by the U.S. Fish and Wildlife Service.

Monomoy Wilderness

As recently as 1958, this area was an extension of the mainland, the eroding shoreline at the elbow of Cape Cod. Severe winter storms isolated Monomoy Point from the mainland and, 20 years later, separated North Monomoy Island from South Monomoy Island. Ten miles of surf-beaten dunes on the eastern shore of the islands, still-shifting sands that sometimes reach 100 feet in height, give way to salt marsh and then to mudflats on the western shore. The ecosystem is a perfect habitat for migratory birds.

Dubbed a sanctuary for wildlife in 1944, most of 2,710-acre Monomoy National Wildlife Refuge has been designated Wilderness: all of the north island and all but two tracts on the south island. The mainland portion of the refuge remains non-Wilderness. People are known to have lived here from 1711 on, and a lighthouse complex on the south island attests to their presence. Among the migratory birds you may see are grebes, shearwaters, petrels, gannets, bitterns, egrets, herons, swans, geese, ducks, and the endangered piping plover and roseate tern. Hundreds of gray and harbor seals winter along the coastline. Boaters swarm the shores in summer. Camping, fires, and pets are not permitted.

Monomoy Essentials

Size: 2,420 acres.
Year Designated: 1970.
Location: Off the state's southeastern coast.
Easiest Access: From U.S. 6 on Cape Cod, take State Route 137 south for four miles. Turn east on State Route 28 and drive four miles through Chatham to the Chatham Lighthouse. After the lighthouse, follow the signs south a short distance to refuge headquarters. A boat is required for the short trip to the north island.
Season: Spring and fall for thousands of shorebirds, and winter for hundreds of harbor and gray seals.
Wilderness Fees/Permits: None.
Maps: A free map, which is largely devoid of detail, is available from the Monomoy refuge manager.
Management: Great Meadows National Wildlife Refuge Complex, Weir Hill Road, Sudbury, MA 01776; (508) 443-4661.

> "Wilderness [evokes our] capacity for wonder—the power to feel, if not to see, the miracles of life, beauty, and harmony around us."
>
> —William O. Douglas

MICHIGAN

Total Wilderness areas: 14
Total Wilderness acreage: 248,724

Early settlers in Michigan found a towering, majestic forest dominated by white pines that rolled over hills and around deep, clear lakes . . . and they cut the forest down. The Michigan Wilderness Act of 1987 set aside 10 Wilderness areas on three national forests, most of the land covered in second-growth trees, a tiny bit of it in virgin forest, and a piece protecting a unique stretch of sand dunes. Portions of three national wildlife refuges and most of a national park have also been preserved.

Big Island Lake Wilderness

As you might expect, in the middle of Big Island Lake, standing amid placid waters, is—no surprise here—a big island. Twenty-two additional lakes, ranging in size from 5 to 149 acres and joined by short, marked portages, make this Wilderness an excellent waterway for canoeists. The 54 clear-water acres of Twilight Lake are managed for trout. Fishing is popular, but special regulations limit the types of lures you can use and the size of the fish you can keep. Ducks, loons, and great blue herons are often seen feeding on or near the water, and bald eagles are occasional visitors. Sandhill cranes frequent the open upland in the area's northern section.

Logged off between 1890 and the early 1930s, the region has many old stumps scattered among second-growth hardwoods (maple, white birch, beech, and quaking aspen) in the uplands, and hemlock, spruce, and balsam in the low wetlands along streams and bogs. Long-abandoned logging campsites are still evident. Woodland animals include black bears, pine martens, bobcats, raccoons, porcupines, and chipmunks. Although the terrain rolls easily, there are no trails within the forest, and hikers may find the going a challenge.

Between mid-December and mid-March the snowpack averages four feet in depth and attracts snowshoers and cross-country skiers. When the snow melts, 34 inches of annual precipitation keeps the countryside wet. Sadly, traffic sometimes seeps into this Wilderness.

MICHIGAN

Big Island Lake Essentials

Size: 5,500 acres.
Year Designated: 1987.
Location: Northwestern Michigan, on the Upper Peninsula.
Easiest Access: From Marquette, take State Highway 28 east approximately 55 miles to Shingleton. Turn south on State Highway 94 and drive approximately 15 miles to Steuben. The southern Wilderness boundary lies one-half mile northwest of Steuben. To reach the boundary nearest Big Island Lake itself, drive about 1.5 miles west on Road 437, then turn north on Road 445 and drive approximately 5.5 miles.
Season: Spring, when the northern hardwoods display delicate shades of green, and fall, when the leaves become a bright tapestry.
Wilderness Fees/Permits: None.
Maps: A free Wilderness map is available from the district ranger.
Management: Munising Ranger District, Hiawatha National Forest, Munising, MI 49862; (906) 387-2512.

Delirium Wilderness

A few intrepid deer hunters in fall and skiers in winter are just about the only people who visit this Wilderness. A thickly forested swamp with surface water and biting insects, it bears signs of past human influence, such as old logging roads and saw-razed stumps from strip-cutting of cedar trees. Swamp conifers, aspens, and white cedars have returned to the region, with red and jack pines standing in its drier areas. Flat to gently rolling, Delirium Wilderness was smoothed by glaciers, which carved six-acre Delirium Pond. Only 300 feet of elevation separate the area's high point from the low point.

Geographically within the Wilderness, but technically outside its designated boundary, you'll find earthen Sylvester Dam holding back 80-acre Sylvester Pond. The headwaters of the Pine and Waiska Rivers are in the swamp, providing habitat for waterfowl (ducks, loons, herons, and cranes) and small fur-bearing species. Black bears commonly roam the area and rabbits hop through here. There are no established trails, so making your way through these northern wetlands can be physically uncomfortable.

Delirium Essentials

Size: 11,870 acres.
Year Designated: 1987.
Location: Northern Michigan, on the Upper Peninsula.
Easiest Access: From Sault Sainte Marie, take Interstate 75 south approximately 15 miles. Turn west on State Highway M-28 and drive 13 miles, then turn south on Forest Service Road 3352. Follow it three miles to the northern Wilderness boundary. From that point, Forest Service Road 3352 heads west along the boundary, and Forest Service Road 3130 goes east along the boundary.
Season: Late summer through winter. In spring and early summer people are requested to stay away in order to preserve fragile nesting areas.
Wilderness Fees/Permits: None.
Maps: A free Wilderness map is available from the district ranger.
Management: Sault Sainte Marie Ranger District, Hiawatha National Forest, Sault Sainte Marie, MI 49783; (906) 635-5311.

MICHIGAN

Horseshoe Bay Wilderness

Horseshoe Bay dents a slight curve along the northern shore of Lake Huron. This seven-mile-long shoreline is the outstanding feature of Horseshoe Bay Wilderness. Difficult to walk due to rocks and wetness, the 2.5-mile Horseshoe Bay Trail leads from Foley Creek Campground to the shore. The camp offers 54 sites for $4 per night. Sandy beaches cover the southern third of the shoreline, which becomes rocky and marshy in the north.

Hiking off-trail into the Wilderness, you'll find low ridges forested with balsam and cedar separating narrow, shallow swamps. Logging operations of the past have left behind abandoned roads and cedar stumps. Evidence indicates that Native Americans came here to fish the waters of Lake Huron long before loggers ever downed the cedars. A recent budworm infestation killed large numbers of dead trees in some portions of this small Wilderness. Four parcels of private land lie within the Wilderness borders.

Wildlife species are those you would typically find in a wetland: beavers, otters, mink, muskrats, ducks, herons, and gulls. Eagles and ospreys nest in scattered white pines along the shoreline. White-tailed deer, black bears, coyotes, and snowshoe hares may be seen at times. Noise from the heavy traffic on nearby Interstate 75 resounds through the Wilderness.

Horseshoe Bay Essentials

Size: 3,790 acres.
Year Designated: 1987.
Location: Northern Michigan, on the Upper Peninsula.
Easiest Access: From Sault Sainte Marie, take Interstate 75 south 45 miles. Take the Castle Rock exit and drive east one-eighth of a mile. Turn north on the Mackinaw Trail and head six miles to Foley Creek Campground.
Season: Late summer through winter. People are asked to stay away in spring and early summer to avoid intruding on nesting birds.
Wilderness Fees/Permits: None.
Maps: A free Wilderness map is available from the district ranger.
Management: Saint Ignace Ranger District, Hiawatha National Forest, Saint Ignace, MI 49829; (906) 643-7900.

Huron Islands Wilderness

Huron Islands National Wildlife Refuge, a satellite of Seney National Wildlife Refuge, includes eight small islands about three miles from the mainland. Here 200-foot granite walls rise pink and gray above the water of Lake Superior, providing nesting sites for colonies of herring gulls and cormorants. Because of their remote and primitive qualities, these islands have been designated Wilderness.

West Huron Island (also known as Lighthouse Island), the second largest of the eight, still bears signs of human use. The lighthouse, built in 1868, was automated in 1972 and the island was abandoned. Four other buildings still stand, two of them on an 11-acre parcel administered by the U.S. Coast Guard.

On these islands you'll find gnarled red and white pines, white birch and white cedar clinging to the low, glacier-carved terrain. Once home to deer, coyotes, and raccoons, these desolate rocks have been abandoned by most mammals. You may spot a deer mouse or snowshoe hare.

MICHIGAN

Only West Huron Island is open to the public during daylight hours, and access may be difficult due to rough waters and poor anchorage. Camping is prohibited. The other seven islands are closed to human use, except to those with special-use permits.

Huron Islands Essentials

Size: 147 acres.
Year Designated: 1970.
Location: Off the coast of northwestern Michigan in Lake Superior.
Easiest Access: From Marquette, take County Road 550 north approximately 30 miles to Big Bay, where you'll find a suitable launch site for your boat.
Season: Summer is best.
Wilderness Fees/Permits: Visitors are required to register at refuge headquarters prior to arrival.
Maps: Ask the refuge manager about maps.
Management: Seney National Wildlife Refuge, HCR 2, P.O. Box 1, Seney, MI 49883; (906) 586-9851.

Isle Royale Wilderness

French trappers gave 45-mile-long, nine-mile-wide Isle Royale its regal name. Located north of the surging waters of Lake Superior, most of the approximately 134,000 acres of Isle Royale National Park have been designated Wilderness. The largest island in the largest freshwater lake in North America, it is also by far the state's largest Wilderness area.

Created by flowing lava, flattened and smoothed by glaciation and subsequent erosion, the island contains more than 30 lakes; in fact, water covers more of the surface than dry land. In the lakes you may catch northern pike, trout, walleye, and perch without a permit. (Fishing in Lake Superior, however, requires a Michigan license.) Around the lakes and along the shore of the island grows a forest of mixed evergreens and hardwoods. Isle Royale is home to a famously secretive population of timber wolves, which you may hear howling at the moon. Other wildlife includes moose, beavers, red foxes, red squirrels, and snowshoe hares. More than 200 bird species have been spotted.

Human visitors come to hike, camp, fish, and watch wildlife. With miles of splendid coastline indented by numerous protected bays and sheltered coves, this is considered a marvelous destination for sea kayakers. There are 36 established primitive campsites (available on a first-come, first-served basis) set along about 170 miles of trail. The 40-mile Greenstone Ridge Trail traverses the backbone of the island from end to end, climbing three times above 1,300 feet. The most popular trail in the Wilderness, it crosses Mount Desor, at 1,394 feet the highest point on Isle Royale. For more solitude, backpack from Windigo, on the less-visited western end, along the Feldtmann Ridge–Island Mine Trails circuit (24 miles) or the Minong Ridge Trail (28.3 miles). It covers higher ground, offering tougher going and more solitude. Campsites near the shoreline naturally attract boaters.

On the non-Wilderness eastern tip of the island you'll find Rock Harbor Lodge with 60 rooms, 20 cabins, a restaurant, and a store. For reservations contact National Park Concessions at (906) 337-4993 in summer, or (502) 773-2191 in winter. Canoes can be rented at Rock Harbor. There is also a small store at Windigo on the western tip of Isle Royale.

MICHIGAN

Isle Royale Essentials

Size: 131,880 acres.
Year Designated: 1976.
Location: Northwestern Lake Superior.
Easiest Access: Ferry boats run regularly to the island all summer from Houghton and Copper Harbor, and from Grand Portage, Minnesota. Floatplanes fly regularly from Houghton. Cost may run over $150 for a plane ride.
Season: The park is open from April 16 to October 31. August brings the most visitors.
Wilderness Fees/Permits: A free permit is required for camping and boating in the park; it can be picked up on the island.
Maps: Maps and information books are available from the Isle Royale Natural History Association, 87 North Ripley Street, Houghton, MI 49931; (800) 678-6925. Lake Survey Chart 14976 (Isle Royale) is recommended for those who navigate the waters around the park on their own.
Note: Boats less than 20 feet in length are not recommended; conditions can be dangerous due to common and severe storms.
Management: Isle Royale National Park, 800 East Lakeshore Drive, Houghton, MI 49931; (906) 482-0984.

Mackinac Wilderness

By the end of the 1910s, the area that today holds Mackinac Wilderness had been severely logged. But nature's regeneration has allowed second-growth forest to reclaim the land, and some trees have been standing for 60 to 80 years. In the northeastern section you'll find a dense forest of northern hardwoods with stands of birch and aspen growing on low ridges. The rest of the Wilderness consists of large wetlands set between sand ridges, shallow bogs, and marshes with small clumps of trees. Ever-ambitious beavers continually dam drainages, creating seven major ponds. In the northeast, at the edge of the wetlands, seven-acre Spring Lake forms the headwaters of Spring Lake Creek.

Wildlife native to the area include bald eagles, ospreys, sandhill cranes, great blue herons, pileated woodpeckers, ruffed grouse, black bears, raccoons, pine martens, minks, muskrats, red squirrels, and snowshoe hares. White-tailed deer winter here in thick stands of trees.

Most visitors come for Mackinac's most notable feature, the Carp River. Flowing through the heart of the Wilderness, the sandy-bottomed Carp features water-carved riverbanks and numerous oxbows, curves of the river cut off from the main flow as its meanders were straightened over time. Canoeists find the paddling easy with only a few minor rapids near the center of the area. Brook, rainbow, and brown trout spawn in the Carp and its tributaries, luring anglers.

Traveling off the river in Mackinac is a challenge that few humans accept. There are no trails. Although some broken bedrock can cause you to twist your ankle, foot travel in the northern portion rates as fairly easy. The southern portion is mostly tangled with shrubs or wet and mucky. The North Country National Scenic Trail passes close to the northwestern boundary, just outside the Wilderness.

MICHIGAN

Mackinac Essentials

Size: 12,230 acres.
Year Designated: 1987.
Location: Northern Michigan, on the Upper Peninsula.
Easiest Access: From Saint Ignace, take Interstate 75 north approximately seven miles. Turn west on State Highway 123 and drive approximately eight miles. Turn east on Forest Service Road 3450, which immediately forms the southern boundary.
Season: Spring and fall.
Wilderness Fees/Permits: None.
Maps: A free map is available from the ranger.
Management: Saint Ignace Ranger District, Hiawatha National Forest, Saint Ignace, MI 49829; (906) 643-7900.

McCormick Wilderness

Three generations of McCormicks, the descendants of Cyrus McCormick, inventor of the reaping machine, held the deed to this area before Gordon McCormick willed the land to the U.S. Forest Service. McCormick Wilderness has recovered from the logging era that ended in the early 1900s. Today, you'll find a mixture of northern hardwoods and lowland conifers interspersed with small patches of towering white pine, Michigan's state tree. Moose have been reintroduced here and are relatively common sights by Michigan standards. Other forest dwellers include black bears, pine martens, otters, minks, foxes, deer, squirrels, and hares. Birdwatchers enjoy loons and woodpeckers as well as thriving populations of many other feathered species.

Straddling the divide between Lake Superior and Lake Michigan, a region ranging from nearly level terrain to rocky cliffs, McCormick's water is what draws most visitors. The Huron, Dead, Peshekee, and the Wild and Scenic Yellow Dog Rivers all have part of their headwaters here. Many cascading waterfalls on the Yellow Dog make it unnavigable, except by exceptional and perhaps foolhardy river runners. The Yellow Dog is one of few Eastern rivers designated "Wild." Eighteen small lakes add sparkle to the landscape, each surrounded predominantly with swampland and muskegs. Trout, pike, and bass live here, but only in small numbers due to the less-than-fertile waters.

The three-mile White Deer Lake Trail connects County Road 607 to White Deer Lake where the McCormick estate once stood. Remnants of old, unmaintained trails can sometimes be found, but the rest of the Wilderness is fairly rugged, isolated, unspoiled, and relatively difficult to access.

McCormick Essentials

Size: 16,850 acres.
Year Designated: 1987.
Location: Extreme northwestern Michigan, on the Upper Peninsula.
Easiest Access: From Marquette, take U.S. 41 west approximately 23 miles. Turn north at Champion on County Road 607 and drive about 12 miles to the White Deer Lake Trailhead.
Season: Spring and fall.
Wilderness Fees/Permits: None.
Maps: A free map is available from the district ranger.
Management: Kenton Ranger District, Ottawa National Forest, Kenton, MI 49843; (906) 852-3501.

MICHIGAN

Michigan Islands Wilderness

Six small islands in Lake Michigan were established as Michigan Islands National Wildlife Refuge in 1943, and three of these islands have been designated Wilderness: Pismire, Scarecrow, and Shoe. At seven acres, Scarecrow Island is the largest of the three Wilderness isles, which together form one of the smallest units of the National Wilderness Preservation System.

Large submerged limestone shoals located offshore protect a shoreline of rock and cobble. Three colonial bird species—great blue herons, herring gulls, and double-crested cormorants—nest on these islands in substantial numbers. Standing dead green ash trees are the main vegetation, with a lush understory of common elderberry, scattered red-osier dogwood, and an abundance of "weedy" plants. The death of the ash has been blamed on the extensive use by cormorants. In order to protect nesting birds, public visitation is prohibited.

Michigan Islands Essentials

Size: 12 acres.
Year Designated: 1970.
Location: Northeastern Lake Michigan.
Easiest Access: There is no public access.
Season: Not applicable.
Wilderness Fees/Permits: Special-use permits have been issued for educational and research studies only. Contact the refuge manager.
Maps: Contact the refuge manager about maps of the area.
Management: Scarecrow Island is managed by the Shiawassee National Wildlife Refuge, 6975 Mower Road, Saginaw, MI 48601; (517) 777-5930.

Pismire and Shoe Islands are managed by the Seney National Wildlife Refuge, HCR 2, Box 1, Seney, MI 49883; (906) 586-9851.

Nordhouse Dunes Wilderness

Over the past 13,000 years, as the level of Lake Michigan rose and fell, winds swept the exposed sand from the lakebed into a series of rolling dunes, some reaching 140 feet in height. Most of the present dunes date back between 3,500 and 4,000 years.

A wide beach lies between the waves of water and the waves of sand. Unlike the vegetation at most active sand dunes, here you'll find woody patches of juniper, stunted jack pine, some small stands of northern hardwoods, and dune marshes with wetland species such as hemlock and larch. Many of the dunes are lightly covered in dune grass. Set along approximately 7,300 feet of undeveloped shoreline, Nordhouse Dunes is the only designated Wilderness on Michigan's Lower Peninsula.

Many species of waterfowl and songbirds have been identified here, as well as white-tailed deer, coyotes, foxes, raccoons, porcupines, skunks, and squirrels. Visitors come most often during summer and deer-hunting season.

A limited trail system of about 11 miles is minimally marked and sometimes hard to follow. The Nordhouse Dunes Trail (1.4 miles) offers the best peek at the dunes. The trails can be accessed from the nearby Lake Michigan Recreation Area on the northern boundary. All water must be carried. Due to the fragile nature of the dunes, no camping is allowed in the western Open Sand Area, and all other campsites must be chosen with great care to minimize impact.

MICHIGAN

Nordhouse Dunes Essentials

Size: 3,450 acres.
Year Designated: 1987.
Location: Western Michigan.
Easiest Access: From Manistee, take U.S. 31 south approximately 12 miles. Turn west at the sign indicating the Lake Michigan Recreation Area and drive about eight miles to the shore.
Season: Spring and fall.
Wilderness Fees/Permits: None.
Maps: A free map is available from the district ranger.
Management: Manistee Ranger District, Huron-Manistee National Forest, Manistee, MI 49660; (616) 723-2211.

Rock River Canyon Wilderness

From west to east, Rock River and Silver Creek flow through 150-foot-deep canyons that few people have ever roamed. The two canyons are separated by a broad, flat ridge and surrounded by relatively flat uplands. Second-growth northern hardwoods can be seen, alongside stumps from logging operations that denuded the area by the end of the 1930s. In spring, Rock River leaps about 15 feet over Rock River Falls into a pool, pouring into Ginpole Lake, a secluded 13-acre body of water bordered by canyon walls. The waters offer anglers the chance to fish for rainbow trout, brown trout, brook trout, coho salmon, and northern pike. Beyond the lake, Rock River joins Silver Creek and together they flow out of the Wilderness. The wildlife you'll see is typical of a northern hardwood forest, including deer, bears, beavers, mink, muskrats, raccoons, squirrels, hares, woodpeckers, and grouse.

There are no established trails, but old logging roads, skid trails, and two abandoned railroad grades crisscross the area's upland, providing easy routes for foot travel. Within the two canyons are steep walls, densely vegetated with brush and undergrowth, wet on the bottom and almost always unvisited by humans. Along the edge of the canyons, sandstone undercuts form caves up to 40 feet deep, and sometimes in winter ice curtains form when water seeps over the edge and freezes. The fragile sandstone walls support a diversity of unique plants, and climbing is discouraged.

Rock River Canyon Essentials

Size: 4,640 acres.
Year Designated: 1987.
Location: Northern Michigan, on the Upper Peninsula.
Easiest Access: From Marquette, take U.S. 41 south approximately 20 miles. Turn east on State Highway 94 and head approximately 18 miles to Chatham. At the stop sign turn north and drive four miles to Forest Service Road 2276, which forms the eastern and northern boundaries of the Wilderness.
Season: Winter and spring.
Wilderness Fees/Permits: None.
Maps: A free map is available from the district ranger.
Management: Munising Ranger District, Hiawatha National Forest, Munising, MI 49862; (906) 387-2512.

MICHIGAN

Round Island Wilderness

All of Round Island has been designated Wilderness except one acre on the northern tip, a sand and cobblestone spit where a lighthouse stands. More turtle-shaped than round, the island is a small bulge of land above the waters of Lake Huron, and the lighthouse sits on the turtle's nose. Also known by its Native American name Nissawinagong, Round Island preserves several historic and prehistoric sites. Second-growth forest covers the island, home to resident white-tailed deer, raccoons, red squirrels, and foxes.

Gulls, songbirds, and waterfowl come and go. Freshwater fish are often caught in the waters around the island. A limestone cliff stands 76 feet above Lake Huron on the northeastern side, and about two-thirds of a mile of sandy beach extends along the eastern portion of the island. Camping and hiking are unrestricted around this small Wilderness.

The island is well removed from the hustle and bustle of everyday life, but close enough that you can see the mainland in day and the lights of the mainland at night. Heavy boat traffic on Lake Huron can often be heard. What the locals call "heavy seas" make traveling out to Round Island treacherous at times.

Round Island Essentials

Size: 378 acres.
Year Designated: 1987.
Location: Northwestern Lake Huron.
Easiest Access: Take a boat four miles east from Saint Ignace. Round Island lies between Mackinac and Bois Blanc Islands. In winter, you can walk across on a substantial ice pack.
Season: Winter or early spring for solitude.
Wilderness Fees/Permits: None.
Maps: A free map is available from the district ranger.
Management: Saint Ignace Ranger District, Hiawatha National Forest, Saint Ignace, MI 49829; (906) 643-7900.

Seney Wilderness

At first glance, the 95,500 acres of Seney National Wildlife Refuge appear wild, but in fact they are carefully managed to provide habitat for diverse wildlife. But keep looking. About one-third of the refuge, the western portion, has been designated Wilderness. All told, it comprises Michigan's second largest Wilderness area.

Here you may see a bald eagle or a reclusive and endangered eastern timber wolf. The area also harbors moose, black bears, coyotes, deer, foxes, mink, and muskrats. Birds include the black duck, mallard, American widgeon, wood duck, and sharp-tailed grouse.

Once the land of Seney lay beneath an ancient lake. When the lake disappeared, winds swirled sand from its bottom into dunes. Eventually these became covered with trees and brush to form a string of islands in the midst of a vast bogland. Today, most of Seney is "string bogs." The bogs support unusual vegetation such as the carnivorous pitcher plant. Aside from the bogs, the land has many large stumps of white pine that were logged off in the last century. Where the huge, fragrant white pines once stood a forest of aspen and jack pine has sprouted.

Seney Wilderness is open during daylight hours only. No camping is allowed and no established trails exist. Small-game hunting is allowed from September 15 to February 28, and deer hunting is permitted from November 15 to 30.

MICHIGAN

Seney Essentials

Size: 25,150 acres.
Year Designated: 1970.
Location: Northwestern Michigan, on the Upper Peninsula.
Easiest Access: From Marquette, take State Highway 28/94 east approximately 80 miles to Seney. Turn south on State Highway 77 and then drive for about three miles to the refuge headquarters.
Season: Seney is open from August 1 through March 14.
Wilderness Fees/Permits: Registration is required at refuge headquarters.
Maps: A free map is available from the refuge manager.
Management: Seney National Wildlife Refuge, HCR 2, P.O. Box 1, Seney, MI 49883; (906) 586-9851.

Sturgeon River Gorge Wilderness

The Wild and Scenic Sturgeon River rushes out of the northern portion of this Wilderness, over the 20-foot volcanic outcropping of Sturgeon Falls, and through a gorge that reaches 300 feet in depth and a mile in width. It flows all the way to Sturgeon River Campground just outside the southeastern boundary. Throughout this rugged, steep Wilderness, the Sturgeon and Little Silver Rivers and their tributaries have carved falls, rapids, ponds, oxbows, and terraces. Stunning views are possible from the eastern rim of the gorge.

Except for a few naturally bare slopes, most of the land is forested with pine, hemlock, aspen, sugar maple, birch, and basswood. When the leaves of the hardwoods change color in fall, they form a vivid tapestry. On a trek through here you might see deer, bears, mink, otters, beavers, skunks, and foxes. Woodcocks and ruffed grouse are common, and bald eagles and ospreys are seen on occasion. Streams do not produce many trout, and the endangered lake sturgeon finds habitat farther downriver.

There are no established trails in Sturgeon River Gorge Wilderness, and a few overgrown logging roads are hard to find and follow. The North Country National Scenic Trail parallels the northern and eastern boundaries for about eight miles. Sturgeon River Campground offers nine sites on the southeastern boundary for $4 per night. In spring and fall when the water runs highest, kayaking and white-water canoeing are challenging and only recommended for advanced paddlers. If you are an expert, you'll find what is arguably the greatest water in the Midwest.

Sturgeon River Gorge Essentials

Size: 14,500 acres.
Year Designated: 1987.
Location: Extreme northwestern Michigan, on the Upper Peninsula.
Easiest Access: From Sidnaw, on State Highway 28, turn north on Forest Service Road 2200 and drive approximately eight miles to the southeastern boundary of the Wilderness.
Season: Fall is best, and mid- to late September is ideal for color.
Wilderness Fees/Permits: None.
Maps: A free map is available from the district ranger.
Management: Kenton Ranger District, Ottawa National Forest, Kenton, MI 49943; (906) 852-3501.

MICHIGAN

Sylvania Wilderness

Most of Michigan's pristine forestland has been logged off, but here you'll find stands of the rare and treasured trees that once blanketed the state. In 1985 a man named A. D. Johnston purchased 80 acres of this country with the intention of cutting the wood for lumber. After laying eyes on his new property, he fell in love with the land and decided to preserve it. Johnston encouraged friends to buy and save neighboring forestland, and together they formed the Sylvania Club. The U.S. Forest Service eventually gained ownership, and what remains today is an incomparable north country Wilderness, rolling hills covered in virgin trees dating back as much as 400 years, ancient white pines, red pines, hemlocks, yellow birches, basswoods, and sugar maples.

Balanced on the divide between the drainages of Lake Superior and the Mississippi River, Sylvania Wilderness contains 35 deep lakes, almost all of which are landlocked, filled by springs and precipitation. Many of these fabulous lakes are edged with white sand.

Deer, bears, raccoons, skunks, otters, beavers, fishers, porcupines, coyotes, foxes, and squirrels thrive in the forest along with a variety of woodland and water-related birds. Special fishing regulations protect this unusual lake habitat. Only artificial lures may be used, and all bass, some of which reach impressive proportions, must be released.

Unlike most designated Wildernesses, fragile Sylvania has 84 established campsites in 29 locations bordering lakes; they must be reserved in advance. A well-maintained trail system that wanders through the giant trees provides access. Every campsite has an outdoor toilet, tent pads, and fire grills.

On the northern border of the Wilderness, Sylvania Recreation Area offers a major trailhead, 48 drive-in campsites, potable water, flush toilets, and an information center where visitors can register and learn Wilderness ethics. Come here for some of the loveliest backpacking in the Midwest. It's an ideal spot for recreationists to canoe and swim in summer, or ski in winter. No matter when you visit or what you do, plan to Leave No Trace (see page 26 in this book's introduction).

Sylvania Essentials

Size: 18,327 acres.
Year Designated: 1987.
Location: Extreme northwestern Michigan, on the Upper Peninsula.
Easiest Access: From Ironwood, take U.S. 2 east for approximately 35 miles. Before Watersmeet, take County Road 535 south for approximately four miles to Sylvania Recreation Area, which lies along the Wilderness border.
Season: Sylvania is attractive all year.

Wilderness Fees/Permits: Heavy human use has led to the creation of a reservation-only system for overnight camping. Reservations must be made through the Watersmeet Visitors Center; call (906) 358-4724. The cost is $5.
Maps: A map is available for 25 cents from the district ranger.
Management: Watersmeet Ranger District, Ottawa National Forest, Watersmeet, MI 49969; (906) 358-4551.

> "Wilderness to the people of America is a spiritual necessity, an antidote to the high pressure of modern life, a means of regaining serenity and equilibrium."
>
> —Sigurd F. Olson

MINNESOTA

Total Wilderness areas: 3
Total Wilderness acreage: 804,489

Minnesota beckons water lovers. In the northern half of the Land of 10,000 Lakes, a sparsely settled region as wild as anywhere in the west, the canoeing and fishing are on a par with the world's finest. For those who really want to escape, Superior National Forest represents the third largest roadless area in America. Wildlife refuges preserve two other Wildernesses.

Agassiz Wilderness

"Flat" best describes Agassiz, where the terrain elevation rarely varies more than a foot per mile. The Wilderness sinks as low as 1,140 feet above sea level, then "soars" to 1,149 feet. But the unvaried turf does support Minnesota's westernmost stand of black spruce-tamarack forest, along with two boggy bodies of water—Kuriko and Whiskey Lakes—that are both empty of fish. The Whiskey Lake Trail leads about two miles to Whiskey Lake, which is within the Wilderness, but camping is not allowed. If you want to pitch a tent, head for one of the two primitive campgrounds adjacent to Agassiz.

Agassiz Wilderness lies within the 61,449-acre Agassiz National Wildlife Refuge, an area primarily protected for waterfowl production and maintenance. Water covers almost one-sixth of the property (hence its original name, Mud Lake Refuge), with cattail dominating more than 40,000 acres of the wetland. Ducks abound only in migratory seasons, but all kinds of wildlife stick it out year-round. Species spotted within the refuge include 49 mammals, 12 amphibians, and 9 reptiles. Wildlife lovers can hope to catch a glimpse of the resident pack of eastern gray wolves or the nesting pair of bald eagles (who share the skies with close to 300 bird species). Moose and white-tailed deer attract hunters. Temperatures range from minus 47 degrees Fahrenheit to 108 degrees Fahrenheit.

MINNESOTA

Agassiz Essentials

Size: 4,000 acres.
Year Designated: 1976.
Location: Northwestern Minnesota.
Easiest Access: From Thief River Falls, where food and lodging are available, take State Highway 32 north for 12 miles to Holt. To reach the refuge, turn east onto County Road 7 and drive 11 more miles.
Season: Spring and fall are the best times to observe the wildlife.
Wilderness Fees/Permits: Free permits are required for photographers who might reproduce or sell their snapshots. Management recommends getting one regardless of your intentions.
Maps: A free map is available from the refuge manager.
Management: Agassiz National Wildlife Refuge, RR 1, Box 74, Middle River, MN 56737; (218) 449-4115 (rings in Holt).

Boundary Waters Canoe Area Wilderness

Boating, hiking, and camping are the main attractions at Boundary Waters Canoe Area (BWCA), which encompasses more than one million acres. Voyageurs National Park serves as its western boundary, and Canada's Quetico Provincial Park borders the north. The area is more Wilderness than not, with at least 1,200 canoe-trail miles of portage-linked lakes and streams. Further embellishments include 18 hiking trails and nearly 2,200 designated campsites (complete with box latrines and steel fire grates).

Statistics indicate that more people visit this Wilderness than any other in America. In hopes of reducing human impact, regulations prohibit cans and bottles, limit groups to nine people with no more than four boats, permit motorized watercraft only on specific lakes, and confine camping to designated sites (except in the most remote regions of the Wilderness). While some regions draw hikers—and skiers and dogsledders in winter—at least 75 percent of the visitors come with a hankering to paddle. You can get to most of the 80-plus entry points near Crane Lake, Ely, Grand Marais, and Tofte, Minnesota, but only some offer parking lots.

A scenic multiday introduction to BWCA is the relatively easy Seagull Lake-to-Saranaga Lake loop through Alpine and Red Rock Lakes. The portages are gentle, and you'll see numerous islands and cliffs, especially in Seagull Lake.

Boundary Waters Canoe Area Essentials

Size: 798,309 acres.
Year Designated: 1964; expanded in 1978.
Location: Northeastern Minnesota.
Easiest Access: From Grand Marais, take the Gunflint Trail (Route 12) north for approximately 50 miles to Seagull Lake.
Season: Hordes of voracious mosquitoes hatch in summer. By fall, when the forest flames with color and the night frost makes its first appearance, canoeing is at its finest.
Wilderness Fees/Permits: Permits are required year-round. Contact: BWCAW Reservation Service, P.O. Box 450, Cumberland, MD 21501. Phone (800) 745-3399 after February 1. The cost of the permit is $9.
Maps: Outfitters in communities near the Wilderness offer detailed canoe route maps; or, contact the W. A. Fisher Company, P.O. Box 1107, Virginia, MN 55792; (218) 741-9544.
Management: Superior National Forest, P.O. Box 338, Duluth, MN 55801; (218) 720-5324.

Tamarac Wilderness

To the Chippewa Indians, and the Dakotas before them, this dark forest with 21 lakes was a mecca for hunting, fishing, and ricing. Now, many years later, the land serves as a refuge for waterfowl production and a migration habitat. The riches, so to speak, have gone to the birds (although Indians still harvest wild rice when the crop grows heavy), with more than 240 species on the refuge's formal list. Estimated fall duck populations exceed 40,000 birds, and priorities include the reestablishment of trumpeter swans.

The Wilderness consists of four sections of the 42,724-acre Tamarac National Wildlife Refuge: three islands in Tamarac Lake (totaling about 65 acres in the southwest section) and the 2,000-plus-acre northwest corner. White and red pine, once the pride of the Minnesota Territory, are limited now to small stands within the Wilderness, secluded spots that draw bald eagles and ospreys.

Critters seen roaming this expanse range from the harmless white-tailed deer, otter, porcupine, fox, and beaver to the potentially threatening black bear, coyote, and, on rare occasions, timber wolf. The Wilderness doesn't have established hiking trails, and overnight camping is prohibited, but anglers can while away the hours trying to lure northern pike, walleye, largemouth bass, black crappie, bluegill, and yellow perch to the surface.

Tamarac Essentials

Size: 2,180 acres.
Year Designated: 1976.
Location: Northwestern Minnesota.
Easiest Access: From Fargo, North Dakota, take U.S. 10 east for 45 miles to Detroit Lakes, Minnesota. Next, turn east on State Highway 34 and continue for eight miles, then head north on County Road 29 for 10 miles to the refuge.
Season: Migratory birds fly thickest in fall.
Wilderness Fees/Permits: None. Visiting hours are limited to between 5 A.M. and 10 P.M.
Maps: A free map is available from the refuge manager.
Management: Tamarac National Wildlife Refuge, HC 10, Box 145, Rochert, MN 56578; (218) 847-2641.

> "Man always kills the thing he loves, and so we the pioneers have killed our wilderness."
>
> —Aldo Leopold

MISSISSIPPI

Total Wilderness areas: 3
Total Wilderness acreage: 7,300

Of Mississippi's six national forests, the DeSoto covers the most ground, with more than 500,000 acres of what locals call "piney woods"—a forest of longleaf, slash, and loblolly. Three ranger districts manage these pines: Chickasawhay, Biloxi, and Black Creek. But within the entire Mississippi woodland, only two small areas of the Black Creek District have qualified as Wilderness. Mississippi's third Wilderness is a small island managed by the National Park Service.

Black Creek Wilderness

Here is southern Mississippi, "almost the way it used-to-was." Most of this Wilderness, the state's largest, lies in the broad valley of Black Creek, stained a deep caramel color by the tannic acid of decaying vegetation. The creek is Mississippi's only designated Wild and Scenic River (for 21 miles) with the emphasis exclusively on scenic. It bisects the Wilderness, creating a hardwood floodplain of oxbow lakes and thick stands of sweet gum, sweet bay, red maple, oak, pine, and bald cypress. The 5- to 20-foot banks offer plenty of white sandbars suitable for camping or a picnic. You may want to join the many canoeists leisurely paddling the meandering creek. If the water level is running low, keep an eye out for logs.

The Black Creek National Recreation Trail (open only to foot traffic) runs about 41 miles along the drainage of Black Creek, with about 10 miles within the Wilderness. Here you'll be on a part of the Lower Coastal Plain: piney woods growing over low rolling hills with a few moderate ridges. The relatively flat terrain rises 100 feet on Black Creek itself to only 270 feet on nearby uplands.

Although open year-round, this area gets hit with floods (usually starting in late spring) and, perhaps worse, billions of insects that thrive on the summer heat and humidity. Bass and panfish attract anglers, and hunters come in their season, mostly for deer. On many days you'll see no evidence that a human has ever stepped foot in the Wilderness or dipped a canoe paddle into Black Creek.

MISSISSIPPI

Black Creek Essentials

Size: 4,560 acres.
Year Designated: 1984.
Location: Southeastern Mississippi.
Easiest Access: Take State Highway 29 about 18 miles south from New Augusta, or 10 miles north from Wiggins, to a parking lot where the Black Creek Trail crosses the road.
Season: Fall, winter, and early spring.
Wilderness Fees/Permits: None.
Maps: A trail map on waterproof paper is available for $5 from the district ranger. You can purchase a forest map for $3.
Management: Black Creek Ranger District, DeSoto National Forest, 1436 West Border and Frontage Road, Box 248, Wiggins, MS 39577; (601) 928-4422.

Gulf Islands Wilderness

Built through the centuries as sand washed down from the north, these fragile barrier islands are held together by vegetation. Developers have discovered most of this island chain that extends from Texas to Florida, but part of the coastline and some of the islands are protected by the Gulf Islands National Seashore, which measures 150 miles from West Ship Island in Mississippi to Santa Rosa Island in Florida.

Two Mississippi islands have maintained their pristine state: 1,500-acre Petit Bois (pronounced Petty Boy by the locals) and 3,665-acre Horn Island, which includes 28 miles of white sandy beach. Ground cover on the islands ranges from white sand and sea oats to forests of hardwood and slash pine, and parts of both have been designated Wilderness. A section of Horn remains under private ownership, but the park service hopes to eventually claim the entire island.

The surf fishing here is first-rate, definitely among the best in the Gulf, with plenty of pompano, ling cod, mackerel, and sea trout. No license is required for saltwater fishing. Camping is permitted on the islands. If you don't mind carrying in your gear, you can snorkel and watch a rich bird population that includes ospreys and other feathered fish eaters.

Gulf Islands Essentials

Size: 1,800 acres.
Year Designated: 1978.
Location: Off Mississippi's southeastern coast.
Easiest Access: From the bridge on the east side of Biloxi, take U.S. 90 about five miles east. When you reach Park Road, turn south and continue two miles to the Davis Bayou Visitors Center. Bring a boat to get to the islands, which are 10 to 12 miles offshore, or call the visitors center for information on charter boats, available from April to October.
Season: People who can't tolerate the heat appreciate the islands most in the late fall and winter, but storms can make the crossing treacherous then.
Wilderness Fees/Permits: A fee of $4 per vehicle is charged at the visitors center.
Maps: Free maps and brochures are available from the park ranger.
Management: Mississippi Ranger District, Gulf Islands National Seashore, 3500 Park Road, Ocean Springs, MS 39564; (601) 875-9057.

Leaf Wilderness

The tiny Leaf Wilderness lies almost entirely on the floodplain of the east-flowing Leaf River, just north of Black Creek Wilderness. Except for a little western upland, the entire Wilderness consists of meandering sloughs, oxbow lakes, and level terrain of spruce-pine forest or oak-gum-cypress river bottom. Loblolly and shortleaf pines shade the upland, with a dense understory of dogwood, redbud, persimmon, blueberries, and honeysuckle. The only threatening shrub is poison oak, which always seems to find a way to make contact with exposed skin.

The 4.5-mile Leaf Trail, one of two main attractions in the area, crosses the Wilderness and three bridges and a boardwalk to access this piece of Mississippi, where camping is unrestricted. What's the other attraction? White-tailed deer and wild turkeys, which bring in hunters during the fall months.

Leaf Essentials

Size: 940 acres.
Year Designated: 1984.
Location: Southeastern Mississippi.
Easiest Access: The trailhead is on the east side of State Highway 57, about 10 miles north of Benndale or six miles south of McLain.
Season: Fall or winter.
Wilderness Fees/Permits: None.
Maps: A map that includes the Wilderness is available for $5 from the district ranger.
Management: Black Creek Ranger District, DeSoto National Forest, 1436 West Border and Frontage Road, Box 248, Wiggins, MS 39577; (601) 928-4422.

> "We are a great people because we have been so successful in developing and using our marvelous natural resources, but also, we Americans are the people we are largely because we have had the influence of the wilderness on our lives."
>
> —Congressman John P. Saylor

MISSOURI

Total Wilderness areas: 8
Total Wilderness acreage: 70,860

The intensive harvesting of Missouri's sweeping pine and oak forests began even before the Civil War and continued well into the 1900s. Farmers burned trees left standing by timber companies to the point where the sky grew dark with smoke and ash for weeks on end. Cattle and hogs competed with wildlife until Missouri fell, exhausted—an overgrazed and undernourished farmland.

In the 1930s and 1940s, the U.S. Forest Service joined forces with the state of Missouri and conservation groups, buying up land in hopes of restoring it to its natural condition. Today, herds of deer and flocks of wild turkeys are well established, and more than 300 wildlife species inhabit the forest. Fed by some of the largest springs in America, clear lakes and free-flowing streams highlight the landscape. From the Saint Francois Mountains across the foothills and plateaus of the Ozarks to the glades and bald hills of southwest Missouri, Mark Twain National Forest contains seven small Wilderness areas in about 1.5 million acres. The U.S. Fish and Wildlife Service manages Missouri's eighth Wilderness area.

MISSOURI

Bell Mountain Wilderness

Named for a family that once farmed here, Bell Mountain protects a predominately oak-hickory forest interspersed with pine and elm, scattered grassy glades with lichen-covered granite outcroppings, and a diversity of plant species usually found in old-growth forests. Shut-In Creek, a year-round spring-fed run of water with several gorges ("shut-ins") crosses the area between steep talus slopes. The elevation peaks at 1,702-foot Bell Mountain, then falls to 970 feet at Joe's Creek, another small perennial stream. White-tailed deer, turkeys, and squirrels call this home, but not in abundance. They share the area with pileated woodpeckers, woodthrush, and ovenbirds, all of which thrive in a mature forest.

A maintained pathway, the Bell Mountain Trail, crosses the Wilderness from north to south for approximately six miles and joins a small section of the Ozark Trail in the southwestern corner of the area. When completed, the Ozark Trail will run from Saint Louis, Missouri, to the Arkansas border, where it will join the Ozark Highlands Trail. Another route, the Lindsey Mountain Trail in the southeastern portion, climbs almost 2.5 miles one-way to a dead end on Lindsey Mountain, the second highest point in the Wilderness.

Bell Mountain Essentials

Size: 8,817 acres.
Year Designated: 1980.
Location: Southeastern Missouri.
Easiest Access: From Potosi, take State Highway 21 south for approximately 18 miles. Turn west on State Highway 32 and continue about seven miles, then head south on County Highway a short distance. When you reach Forest Service Road 2228, turn east and proceed two miles to the Bell Mountain Trailhead.
Season: Spring and fall are crowded. Summer and winter are feasible, but summer is hot.
Wilderness Fees/Permits: None.
Maps: A forest map is available for $3 from the district ranger. USGS topographic maps are Banner, Edgehill, Johnson Mountain, and Johnson Shut-ins.
Management: Potosi Ranger District, Mark Twain National Forest, P.O. Box 188, Potosi, MO 63664; (314) 438-5427.

Devils Backbone Wilderness

A long, narrow ridge supports the center of this Wilderness, with 1,020 feet as its highest "vertebra." Thirteen miles of maintained foot and horse trails follow the Devils Backbone and four other ridges, dropping off into surrounding hollows in a forest dominated by oaks, hickories, and shortleaf pines. In spring, the dogwoods, redbuds, and wild azaleas explode in flowering color. Then, in fall, the oaks, sweet gums, and sugar maples turn yellow, orange, and red, respectively and delightfully.

Three springs in the Wilderness (Blue, Amber, and McGarr) feed the North Fork of the White River, which flows through the area. North Fork Recreation Area on the northern boundary offers campsites and a canoe launch for the river. Blue Springs alone produces an average of seven million gallons of water per day. The water flows clear, but the Forest Service recommends disinfecting all springwater before drinking.

The deer, fox, bobcats, skunks, squirrels, coyotes, and raccoons that prowl these parts

MISSOURI

are most often seen in limestone glades. The sky is often alive with eagles, hawks, owls, and vultures. Potentially threatening (but easily avoided) copperheads and eastern timber rattlesnakes are likewise commonly seen.

From the North Fork Campground, a spur trail runs about one-fourth mile south to join the McGarr Ridge Trail, which crosses the area for approximately three miles. The McGarr Ridge Trail then joins the Collins Ridge Trail, allowing you to hike a loop that runs about 5.5 miles up and down the Devils Backbone (careful not to tickle). You should find the hiking moderate, and backcountry camping is unrestricted.

Devils Backbone Essentials

Size: 6,595 acres.
Year Designated: 1980.
Location: Central southern Missouri.
Easiest Access: From the junction of U.S. 63 and County Highway CC near West Plains, take Highway CC west for 15 miles to the North Fork of the White River and North Fork Campground.
Season: Spring and fall.

Wilderness Fees/Permits: None.
Maps: A forest map is available for $3 from the district ranger. USGS topographic maps are Cureall NW, Dora, Pottersville, and Siloam Springs.
Management: Willow Springs Ranger District, Mark Twain National Forest, P.O. Box 99, Willow Springs, MO 65793; (417) 469-3155.

Hercules Glades Wilderness

Some of the most scenic country in Missouri, perhaps in the Midwest, lies protected by the Hercules Glades Wilderness: open grassland, forested knobs, steep rocky hillsides, limestone outcroppings, a maze of narrow drainages, and hollows cut by water. The high points of Coy Bald and Pilot Knob stand more than 600 feet above Long Creek, one of only two (along with Cane Creek) year-round sources of water. Redbuds and dogwoods flower beautifully in spring, and smoke tree and maple vividly paint the fall. Glades of prairie grass often open a forest dominated by eastern red cedar and oak. This is a fine home for deer, raccoons, rabbits, squirrels, turkeys, and quail. Rattlesnakes and copperheads may be encountered. Rare but well-documented sightings report roadrunners, tarantulas, and collared lizards.

Missouri's second largest Wilderness is small and easily accessible. Forty-two miles of maintained foot and horse trails cover virtually every ridge and hollow of Hercules Glades. The primary east-west trail, although unnamed, is easily followed from maintained parking lots on either end. The hiking is moderate, and backcountry camping is unrestricted. On or off trail, this is a chance to backpack wild Missouri at its best.

Hercules Glades Essentials

Size: 12,314 acres.
Year Designated: 1976.
Location: Southwestern Missouri.
Easiest Access: From Springfield, take U.S. 60 east for about five miles. When you reach State Highway 125, turn south and continue for another 45 miles to the east-side trailhead.
Season: Spring and fall.

Wilderness Fees/Permits: None.
Maps: A forest map is available for $3 from the district ranger. USGS topographic maps are Hilda and Protem NE.
Management: Ava Ranger District, Mark Twain National Forest, 1103 South Jefferson, Ava, MO 65608; (417) 683-4428.

MISSOURI

Irish Wilderness

Irish Catholic Father John Hogan brought Irish immigrants to this region in the mid-1800s to escape oppression in the big city of Saint Louis, Missouri. His timing was off. The Civil War erupted, and Union and Confederate soldiers raided the settlement. When the war ended, Hogan and his Irish had mysteriously disappeared forever. Nothing remains but the name and the rolling-to-steep topography of Missouri's largest Wilderness.

Here you'll find sinkholes, disappearing streams that reappear downstream, and Whites Creek Cave, a spacious walk-in with numerous crystalline formations. The western boundary of Irish is near the Eleven Point National Scenic River, which you can see from up high.

About 18.6 miles of the Whites Creek Trail provides the main thoroughfare of Irish, a looping path through oak, hickory, shortleaf pine, dogwood, persimmon, and sassafras . . . past Bliss and Fiddler Springs . . . and past Whites Creek Cave. As you hike through these wilds, you may encounter typical Ozark wildlife: deer, squirrel, rabbit, raccoon, fox, bobcat, coyote, turkey, vulture, hawk, and owl. Watch your step lest you disturb a sleeping copperhead, rattlesnake, or eastern cottonmouth.

Irish Essentials

Size: 16,500 acres.
Year Designated: 1984.
Location: Central southern Missouri.
Easiest Access: From Poplar Bluff, take U.S. 160 to 20 miles past Doniphan. Turn north on State Highway J and proceed seven miles to the Whites Creek Trailhead.
Season: Most people come in spring and fall.
Wilderness Fees/Permits: None.
Maps: A forest map is available for $3 from the district ranger. USGS topographic maps are Bardley, Handy, Riverton, and Wilderness.
Management: Doniphan Ranger District, Mark Twain National Forest, 1104 Walnut, Doniphan, MO 63935; (314) 996-2153.

Mingo Wilderness

Eighteen thousand years ago, the Mississippi River swept through this area on its way to the Gulf of Mexico. Then the river shifted east and a swampland formed in the old channel. Settlers drained much of the original swamp, cutting down the cypress and tupelo forest. In 1945, purchase of the land began to create a wildlife refuge. Today, 21,676-acre Mingo National Wildlife Refuge represents swampland restored as food and shelter for migratory waterfowl, an important link in the Mississippi Flyway. Predator-proof nesting boxes, used primarily by the strikingly beautiful wood duck, dot the refuge.

About one-third of the refuge on the western half has been designated Wilderness. A marshy area best seen by canoe, the Mingo River flows gently out of the Wilderness, draining Monopoly Swamp. Many miles of ditches give canoe access to the rest of this sodden spot. Camping is not allowed.

MISSOURI

Mingo Essentials

Size: 7,730 acres.
Year Designated: 1976.
Location: Southeastern Missouri.
Easiest Access: From Poplar Bluff, take U.S. 60 east. Turn north on State Highway 51 and continue to Puxico. The visitors center is just north of Puxico.
Season: March 15 to September 30 during daylight hours only. Visitors may be allowed into the refuge at other times of the year depending on nesting conditions; apply with the refuge manager.
Wilderness Fees/Permits: Permission to visit in the off-season must be obtained from refuge headquarters.
Maps: A free map is available from the refuge manager.
Management: Mingo National Wildlife Refuge, Route 1, P.O. Box 103, Puxico, MO 63960; (314) 222-3589.

Paddy Creek Wilderness

When Sylvester Paddy first logged this region in the early 1800s, many trees floated from here to Saint Louis, Missouri, providing an important supply of building materials for that city. The area was then homesteaded and used as grazing land into the 1930s.

Big Paddy and Little Paddy Creeks drain the area, flowing into the Big Piney River near the eastern Wilderness boundary. With a mixed hardwood forest lining their banks and steep cliffs and rocky outcroppings hanging over the drainages, the creeks run most of the year. Above the drainages is a forest of black, white, and post oaks, along with hickories and shortleaf pines. Wildlife common to the Ozarks prevail in this area: white-tailed deer, wild turkey, squirrel, rabbit, fox, coyote, and bobcat.

The Big Piney Trail starts at the Roby Lake Recreation Area, just outside the southwestern corner, and loops for 17 miles through the heart of the Wilderness along some of the area's finest overlooks. You can leave the Wilderness at the Paddy Creek Campground on the northeastern corner or loop back to where you started.

Paddy Creek Essentials

Size: 6,728 acres.
Year Designated: 1983.
Location: Central southern Missouri.
Easiest Access: From Rolla, take U.S. 63 south for about 35 miles to Licking. Turn west on State Highway 32 and continue for about 20 miles to Success, then drive north on State Highway 17 for approximately nine miles. About three miles past Roby, turn southeast on Forest Service Road 274 and continue to the Roby Lake Recreation Area and the Big Piney Trailhead.
Season: Spring and fall are the most popular times of the year to visit.
Wilderness Fees/Permits: None.
Maps: A forest map is available for $3 from the district ranger. USGS topographic maps are Roby and Slabtown.
Management: Houston-Rolla Ranger District, Mark Twain National Forest, 108 Sam Houston Boulevard, Houston, MO 65483; (417) 967-4194.

Piney Creek Wilderness

Railroad companies were the principal loggers in this area circa the late 1800s, followed by settlers on the ridges who happily discovered that tomatoes and strawberries grew large and juicy here. Nonetheless, in the early 1950s residents abandoned the last permanent household in the vicinity of Piney Creek.

The ridge tops rise 400 or more feet above hollows and drainages that dissect the area. Numerous small springs feed several waterways, but the main stream is Piney Creek itself. All five miles of the Piney Creek watershed lie within the Wilderness. Oak and hickory dominate the ridges today, and along the drainages you'll find hardwoods such as sycamore, ash, elm, buckeye, and walnut. Wildlife species are typical of the Ozarks, and armadillos also live here. Copperheads, eastern timber rattlers, and western pygmy rattlers are common. Great blue herons and pileated woodpeckers add to the local color.

The major east-west trail follows Piney Creek for approximately four miles. From Pineview Tower Trailhead on the north, two paths of approximately 1.5 miles each lead south to Piney Creek. Two other maintained foot and horse trails leave the main trail to head south for a grand total of 13.1 Wilderness miles. Portions of the trail system utilize old roads.

Piney Creek Essentials

Size: 8,087 acres.
Year Designated: 1980.
Location: Southwestern Missouri.
Easiest Access: From U.S. 64 in Branson, take State Highway 76 west for approximately 32 miles. Then turn south on Lake Road 76-6 and drive a short distance to the Pineview Tower Trailhead.
Season: Spring and fall.
Wilderness Fees/Permits: None.
Maps: A forest map is available for $3 from the district ranger. USGS topographic maps are Cape Fair and Shell Knob.
Management: Cassville Ranger District, Mark Twain National Forest, P.O. Box 310, Cassville, MO 65625; (417) 847-2144.

Rock Pile Mountain Wilderness

Private land virtually surrounds the state's smallest Wilderness area, a heavily forested spot within the Saint Francois Mountains. Its name comes from a mountain in the area that sets the stage for an ancient circular pile of granite erected by some long-forgotten inhabitant. Elevations range from about 1,300 feet to 520 feet.

The Wilderness is primarily a broken ridge with steep rocky sides. One sheltered gorge boasts a tiny virgin forest of basswood, butternut, Kentucky coffee tree, walnut, sugar maple, and white and red oak. Limestone bluffs and caves line the Saint Francis River, which touches the southwestern border. Other than the river, no year-round water sources exist, except in five ponds built before Wilderness designation to trap intermittent springwater and provide watering holes for wildlife. Speaking of which, the most

MISSOURI

common creatures here are white-tailed deer, wild turkeys, squirrels, rabbits, hawks, owls, turkey vultures, and pileated woodpeckers. Lizards, turtles, and snakes, including timber rattlers and copperheads, likewise reside in these parts.

Two miles of maintained trail enter from the north at Little Grass Mountain. Then the trail divides several times to follow abandoned and unmaintained roads that access the rest of the area. The old tracks are unmarked. Backcountry exploration and camping are unrestricted. Heavy rains yield a bonus: temporary streams may go on a rampage, tumbling through narrow gorges.

Rock Pile Mountain Essentials

Size: 4,089 acres.
Year Designated: 1980.
Location: Southeastern Missouri.
Easiest Access: From Fredericktown, take U.S. 67 south for approximately five miles. Turn west and drive on County Road C for about 10 miles, then west again on County Road 406 for approximately two miles. When you reach Forest Service Road 2124, turn south and proceed for three-fourths of a mile to the trailhead at the top of Little Grass Mountain.
Season: Most people come in spring and fall.
Wilderness Fees/Permits: None.
Maps: A forest map is available for $3 from the district ranger. USGS topographic map is Rock Pile Mountain.
Management: Fredericktown Ranger District, Mark Twain National Forest, Route 2, Box 175, Fredericktown, MO 63645; (314) 783-7225.

> "The doctrine of the greatest good to the greatest number does not mean that this laudable relationship has to take on every acre. If it did, we would be forced to change our metropolitan art galleries into metropolitan bowling alleys."
>
> —Bob Marshall

MONTANA

Total Wilderness areas: 15
Total Wilderness acreage: 3,436,578

Only Alaska and Wyoming have fewer people per square mile than Montana. The eastern two-thirds of this wild, wide-open state, the fourth largest in the United States, rolls with prairies before it reaches the state's western side, where the Rocky Mountains suddenly soar upward. Mighty rivers flowing through broad valleys divide the mountains into ranges with densely forested slopes that often rise raggedly above the tree line. Federal agencies own most of the western half of the state, which contains 12 of Montana's U.S. Forest Service Wilderness areas, one of which is shared with the Bureau of Land Management. Wildlife refuges preserve three more areas.

Absaroka-Beartooth Wilderness

It was a cold and stormy summer week when I worked my way up the steep rocky mass known as Granite Peak, bare except for lichen, to reach an eye-stretching vista across land as wild as any I've ever seen. At 12,799 feet, Granite Peak is the highest point in Montana. It anchors the Beartooth Range, which stands higher and more rugged than the Absarokas, with many peaks exceeding 12,000 feet (one of them resembles, you guessed it, a bear's tooth).

As I crossed this vast, treeless plateau, which fell off sharply into surrounding canyons, I thought of the Alaska Range. The lakes I saw, much more numerous in Beartooth than in the nearby Absarokas, were small and tucked fabulously into glacial cirques. From bold Mystic Lake, the Froze-To-Death Plateau Trail (don't let the name discourage you) switchbacks up 12 miles to an open plateau, a nontechnical approach to Granite Peak.

MONTANA

The Crow Indians called themselves Absarokas, hence the name of the mountain range that, along with Beartooth, characterizes this Wilderness. Active glaciers, sweeping tundra plateaus, deep canyons, sparkling streams, and hundreds of alpine lakes combine to make this one of the most outstanding Wilderness areas in America.

The Absarokas, unlike Beartooth, have ample vegetative cover, including dense forests and broad mountain meadows crossed by meandering streams. None of the few peaks among these rolling mountains is higher than 11,206-foot Mount Cowan. Bighorn sheep and mountain goats roam about the mostly rugged country, along with elk, deer, moose, marmots, coyotes, black bears, and members of a substantial grizzly population. The harsher Beartooths accommodate far fewer animals. Trout reside in many of the lakes and streams in both ranges.

Adjoining Yellowstone National Park on the park's northern edge, this Wilderness extends down into Wyoming (see Wyoming, Absaroka-Beartooth Wilderness). More than 700 miles of hiking trails provide access to this area, a backpacker's dream. Both ranges, but especially the Absarokas, offer opportunities to wander off-trail for an unsurpassed Wilderness experience.

Absaroka-Beartooth Essentials

Size: 920,310 acres in Montana (944,060 acres total).
Year Designated: 1978; expanded in 1983.
Location: Southern Montana.
Easiest Access: From Red Lodge, take State Highway 78 northwest for approximately 30 miles to Fishtail. Turn south and drive on Forest Service Road 419 for about 10 miles, then continue south on Forest Service Road 425 to the parking lot at Mystic Lake, about 12 miles.
Season: July through September.
Wilderness Fees/Permits: None.
Maps: A Wilderness map is available for $3 from the forest rangers. The Custer National Forest Visitors Map and the Gallatin National Forest Travel Plan Map ($3 each) show the major portals and trail systems in the Wilderness.
Management: Custer National Forest, Box 2556, Billings, MT 59103; (406) 657-6361. Gallatin National Forest, 10 East Babcock Avenue, Federal Building, Box 130, Bozeman, MT 59771; (406) 587-6701.

Anaconda-Pintlar Wilderness

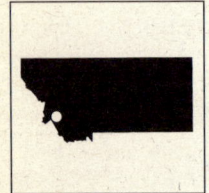

This Wilderness, which straddles the Continental Divide in the Anaconda Range, has it all in terms of mountain grandeur, whether that entails high and rugged peaks, cirques, U-shaped valleys, or glacial moraines. Sparkling lakes and tumbling streams fed by the icy water running off the snowfields above the timberline enhance the beauty and offer excellent fishing for four species of trout, three of char, mountain whitefish, and arctic grayling (although the surfaces are usually frozen until early July). If you have the gear, try your luck in the headwaters of Rock Creek, a blue-ribbon trout stream, or the branches of the Bitterroot and Big Hole Rivers.

Black bears, moose, elk, deer, and mountain goats call this home. Elevations range from about 5,100 feet to 10,793 feet on West Goat Peak, with sagebrush and willow flats in the lower elevations rising to forests of pine, fir, and spruce and eventually to aspen, pine, fir, and larch. The highest slopes are often bare talus, with vegetation limited to lichens.

MONTANA

A 45-mile section of the 3,100-mile Continental Divide National Scenic Trail (here called the Hi-Line Trail) traverses the length of the Wilderness and provides access to many of the most rewarding spots. Horsepackers and backpackers come in approximately equal numbers. Despite the splendor of this Wilderness, hundreds of miles of other trails are rarely used.

Anaconda-Pintlar Essentials

Size: 157,874 acres.
Year Designated: 1964.
Location: Southwestern Montana.
Easiest Access: From Missoula, take U.S. 93 south for approximately 93 miles to Lost Trail Pass. Hike northeast on the Continental Divide Trail to reach the western Wilderness boundary.
Season: Late June through September.
Wilderness Fees/Permits: None.
Maps: A Wilderness map is available for $3 from the district rangers.

Management: Wise River Ranger District, Beaverhead National Forest, P.O. Box 86, Wise River, MT 59762; (406) 839-3178. Wisdom Ranger District, Beaverhead National Forest, P.O. Box 238. Wisdom, MT 59761; (406) 689-3243. Sula Ranger District, Bitterroot National Forest, 7338 Highway 93 South, Sula, MT 59871; (406) 821-3201. Philipsburg Ranger District, Deerlodge National Forest, P.O. Box H, Philipsburg, MT 59858; (406) 859-3211.

Bob Marshall Wilderness

Many credit early forester, Wilderness preservation pioneer, and Wilderness Society cofounder Bob Marshall with singlehandedly protecting at least 5.4 million acres of wildland. The least he deserves is to have this pristine area named for him. This region, in fact, was set aside as the South Fork, Pentagon, and Sun River Primitive Areas in 1941, and designated the "Bob" in 1964. Here is one of the most completely preserved mountain ecosystems in the world, the kind of Wilderness most people can only imagine: rugged peaks, alpine lakes, cascading waterfalls, grassy meadows embellished with shimmering streams, a towering coniferous forest, and big river valleys.

The Wilderness, which includes the North and South Forks of the Sun River and the Middle and South Forks of the Flathead River, runs for 60 miles along the Continental Divide, with elevations ranging from 4,000 feet to more than 9,000 feet. A huge escarpment called the Chinese Wall, a part of the Divide, highlights the Bob's vast untrammeled beauty, with an average height of more than 1,000 feet and a length of 22 miles. The Chinese Wall extends into Scapegoat Wilderness (see below) to the south. The Bob Marshall Wilderness Complex (which emcompasses Bob Marshall, Scapegoat, and Great Bear Wildernesses, see below) is the last holdout habitat south of Canada for the grizzly bear, and in my opinion, nothing speaks of Wilderness as eloquently as griz. Sharing turf with the great bears is every species of mammal indigenous to the northern Rocky Mountains, except bison, which once roamed the lower slopes, and woodland caribou, which live farther north.

You'll find more than 1,000 miles of a well-developed trail system, with maintained paths giving way to less well managed trails as you travel deeper into Montana's largest Wilderness. The Meadow Creek Trail provides a primary access route into the Bob. Approximately half of

MONTANA

the many visitors to the Bob ride in on horseback. Unfortunately, the Wilderness, like many others, is in danger of being loved to death. Eroded trails, trampled vegetation, and abused trees blemish many popular sections. Scarred areas include: Big Prairie, Big River Meadow, Black Bear, Salmon Forks, and the Chinese Wall. Use is heaviest during the fall hunting season.

Bob Marshall Essentials
Size: 1,009,356 acres.
Year Designated: 1964; expanded in 1978.
Location: Northwestern Montana.
Easiest Access: From Hungry Horse on the northern end of Hungry Horse Reservoir, take Forest Service Road 895 south along the west side of the reservoir for approximately 65 miles to Meadow Creek.
Season: July through September.
Wilderness Fees/Permits: None.
Maps: A Wilderness map covering the Bob Marshall Wilderness Complex is available for $3 from the forest ranger.
Management: Flathead National Forest, 1935 Third Avenue East, Kalispell, MT 59901; (406) 755-5401. Lewis and Clark National Forest, 1101 Fifteenth Street North, Great Falls, MT 59403; (406) 791-7700.

Cabinet Mountains Wilderness

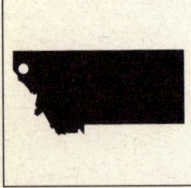

Berries grow in abundance here, sweet treats for the few grizzlies that survive in these parts. This mountainous Wilderness is only about seven miles at its widest point, but packed in its borders you will find dozens of small lakes (most of them stocked with fish) set in scenic basins. The ridge tops above these hidden treasures offer terrific panoramas. The craggy peaks of the Cabinets reach a high point on Snowshoe Peak at 8,738 feet, but the altitude translates into snowfall as late as June and as early as September.

The vegetation here also differs from what characterizes much of western Montana, a result of the wetter climate. Many plant species hail from the Pacific Coast: giant western red cedar in the moister valleys submitting eventually to stunted heath on the open ridges. And the array of wildflowers is exemplary: violets, lupine, trillium, sego lily, buttercups, columbine, clematis, phlox, harebell, and Indian paintbrush to name a few. Elk are the primary game species, but you may see deer, moose, black bears, mountain lions, and a host of small, furry critters.

Trampling by human visitors is apparent on many of the 20-plus trails that lead through alpine meadows and along streams to most of the lakes. The Engle Lake Trail runs about two miles to Engle Lake and provides access to 7,554-foot Engle Peak, where the view ranks among the best in western Montana. But the trails give access to only about 15 percent of the area. Venture off-trail for a truly rich Wilderness experience.

Cabinet Mountains Essentials

Size: 94,272 acres.
Year Designated: 1964.
Location: Northwestern Montana.
Easiest Access: From Trout Creek, take State Highway 200 north for approximately 10 miles. Turn east on Forest Service Road 150 (Rock Creek Road) and continue for approximately five miles, then head south on Forest Service Road 2285 where a series of switchbacks will take you about six miles to the Engle Lake Trailhead.
Season: Midsummer.
Wilderness Fees/Permits: None.
Maps: A Wilderness map is available for $3 from the forest ranger.
Management: Kootenai National Forest, 506 Hwy 2W, Libby, MT 59923; (406) 293-6211.

Gates of the Mountains Wilderness

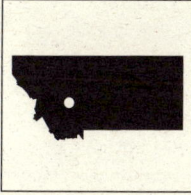

Explorers Meriwether Lewis and William Clark entered the Rocky Mountains through the whitish rocks that tower above the Missouri River to form the official Gates of the Mountains. East of the river and slightly back from the shoreline is Gates of the Mountains Wilderness, which, despite accessible trailheads and easy trails, receives fewer visitors than any other Montana Wilderness. The reason may be its general lack of both water and remarkable scenery in a state rich with the latter. There are, however, plenty of steep canyons, craggy peaks, and wide-open meadows. The habitat is excellent for birds of prey, mountain goats, and bighorn sheep, which hunters come seeking in fall. Late June and often through July a wild array of flowers carpets the meadows, including lupine, larkspur, senecio, fairy slippers, and dogtooth violets.

Trail 259 crosses from east to west about 18 miles from Refrigerator Canyon (where it's always cooler than the open country above) in the southeast corner to Kennedy Springs (where the only reliable water source exists in summer) and on to Meriwether Canyon and the Missouri River. You'll have to leave a car at Meriwether Picnic Area and get a ride to the other side of the Wilderness to make this trip.

Gates of the Mountains Essentials

Size: 28,562 acres.
Year Designated: 1964.
Location: Western central Montana.
Easiest Access: From Helena, take County Road 280 north for approximately 18 miles to York. Turn north on County Road 4 and continue for approximately 7.5 miles to Nelson, then head east on Forest Service Road 138 for about five miles to Refrigerator Canyon.
Season: By May the snow is usually gone. Summers are typically hot and very dry.
Wilderness Fees/Permits: None.
Maps: USGS topographic maps are Candle Mountain, Hogback, and Upper Holter Lake.
Management: Helena Ranger District, Helena National Forest, Federal Building, Drawer 10015, Helena, MT 59626; (406) 449-5490.

MONTANA

Great Bear Wilderness

This Wilderness, on the western side of the Continental Divide, shares its southern border with Bob Marshall Wilderness (see above), which in turn shares its southern border with Scapegoat Wilderness (see below). Together, the three areas form a Wilderness complex of more than 1.5 million acres. Nowhere in the Lower 48 do "great bears" (a.k.a. grizzlies) live in denser populations than in the Great Bear–Bob–Scapegoat complex; their mere presence ensures that this is one of the wildest landscapes on Earth. Glacier National Park lies just across U.S. 2 to the north of Great Bear.

In addition to great bears, there are wolverines, deer, elk, moose, black bears, mountain goats, and mountain sheep roaming about these rugged ridge tops, gently sloping alpine meadows, and thickly forested river bottoms.

The upper Middle Fork of the Flathead River rises here and runs Wild and Scenic through the area for about 50 miles, raging below cliff faces and over boulder-strewn rapids in what some refer to as Montana's wildest waterway. Trout fishing in the Flathead River and in many streams rates as excellent. Elevations range from 4,000 feet on the Middle Fork to 8,705 feet on Great Northern Mountain.

More than 300 miles of trails provide access to virtually unlimited backpacking and horsepacking, hunting and fishing, backcountry skiing, and mountain climbing, but much of the interior has no trail. A primary access route into the area is along the Spotted Bear River. Human use is high.

Great Bear Essentials

Size: 286,700 acres.
Year Designated: 1978.
Location: Northwestern Montana.
Easiest Access: From Hungry Horse on the northern end of Hungry Horse Reservoir, take Forest Service Road 895 south for approximately 55 miles to the Spotted Bear Ranger Station.
Season: July through September.
Wilderness Fees/Permits: None.

Maps: A Wilderness map that includes the Scapegoat Wilderness and the "Bob" is available for $3 from the district rangers.
Management: Hungry Horse Ranger District, Flathead National Forest, Hungry Horse, MT 59919; (406) 387-5243. Spotted Bear Ranger District, Flathead National Forest, P.O. Box 130, Hungry Horse, MT 59919; (406) 752-7345 (in the summer); (406) 387-5243 (in the winter).

Lee Metcalf Wilderness

This Wilderness consists of not one hunk of wildland, but four separate units in the Madison Range of Montana, a huddle of high peaks rising above 10,000 feet from exquisite subalpine meadows, managed by the BLM and the Gallatin and Beaverhead National Forests.

The BLM manages all 6,000 acres of the Bear Trap Canyon Unit, a stretch of wild canyon country along the Madison River. This was the BLM's first designated Wilderness.

The Monument Mountain Unit lies on the northwest boundary of Yellowstone National

MONTANA

Park, an isolated piece of territory rarely visited but rich in wildlife, including a large population of grizzly bears. All 30,000-plus acres lie within Gallatin National Forest.

The 78,000-acre Spanish Peaks Unit encompasses steeply rugged, glaciated peaks rising more than 11,000 feet above scenic cirques and gemlike lakes. This heavily used area, popular with bighorn sheep hunters, boasts a well-developed trail system. From near Big Sky, Montana, the North Fork Trail provides access for more than five miles into the heart of the area.

At about 141,000 acres, the Taylor-Hilgard Unit is the largest. It runs along the crest of the Madison Range, with several peaks exceeding 11,000 feet above the Hilgard Basin, with its meadows and lakes surrounded by snowcapped summits in Beaverhead National Forest.

Trails link these four units. Deer, elk, moose, mountain lions, mountain goats, black bears, and grizzly bears abound. The lakes and streams are home to cutthroats, graylings, rainbows, and brookies. Camping and campfires are not allowed within 200 feet of any body of water.

Lee Metcalf Essentials

Size: 254,944 acres.
Year Designated: 1983.
Location: Southwestern Montana.
Easiest Access: From Bozeman, take U.S. 191 south for approximately 40 miles. Turn west on State Highway 64 and continue for about two miles to one mile past Meadow Village, then turn north at the sign to the North Fork Trail and continue one more mile to the trailhead.
Season: Late spring through early fall.
Wilderness Fees/Permits: None.
Maps: A Wilderness map is available for $3 from the district rangers.
Management: BLM Butte District Office, P.O. Box 3388, Butte, MT 59701; (406) 494-5059 (Bear Trap Canyon Unit). Hebgen Lake Ranger District, Gallatin National Forest, P.O. Box 520, West Yellowstone, MT 59758; (406) 646-7369 (Monument Mountain Unit). Bozeman Ranger District, Gallatin National Forest, 3710 Fallon Street, Bozeman, MT 59715; (406) 587-6920 (Spanish Peaks Unit). Madison Ranger District, Beaverhead National Forest, Route 2, Box 5, Ennis, MT 59729; (406) 683-3900 (Taylor-Hilgard Unit).

Medicine Lake Wilderness

Medicine Lake National Wildlife Refuge, established in 1935, contains 31,467 acres of water, marsh, and uplands bordering the great prairie pothole duck production region, an area within the ancestral flight path of ducks, geese, swans, sandhill cranes, and sometimes whooping cranes. The terrain, once scoured by glaciation, varies in elevation from 1,935 feet to 2,025 feet. White pelicans, great blue herons, double-crested cormorants, ring-billed gulls, California gulls, and other breeding birds use the area extensively. More than 100,000 individual birds stop here in spring and fall, down from 250,000 in the peak population. More than 200 winged species and 44 mammalian species have been identified on the refuge. White-tailed deer, mule deer, and antelope are hunted here. Waterfowl hunting is permitted on the east end of the refuge, and sportfishing is allowed on the waters of at least eight lakes, including Medicine Lake.

Two sections of Medicine Lake National Wildlife Refuge are designated together as Montana's smallest Wilderness: (1) Medicine Lake and all the islands within the lake, and (2) a trailless

MONTANA

upland portion just southeast of the lake called the Sandhill Unit, 2,320 acres of rolling hills, grassland, cactus, and clumps of chokecherry, buffalo berry, and buck brush. Foot and boat travel is unrestricted in the Wilderness except when it might endanger wildlife, such as during spring nesting season. The refuge is open from sunrise to sunset. Camping is not allowed.

Medicine Lake Essentials

Size: 11,366 acres.
Year Designated: 1976.
Location: Northeastern Montana.
Easiest Access: From Williston, North Dakota, take U.S. 2 west for 35 miles to Culbertson, Montana. Turn north on State Highway 16 and continue 25 miles, then turn at the refuge sign.
Season: May and October provide the best opportunities for observing wildlife.
Wilderness Fees/Permits: None, but foot travel may be restricted during specific time periods to protect wildlife.
Maps: A refuge map is available from the refuge manager.
Management: Medicine Lake National Wildlife Refuge, HC 51, Box 2, Medicine Lake, MT 59247; (406) 789-2305.

Mission Mountains Wilderness

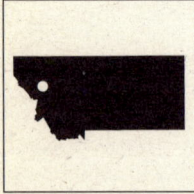

Flathead and Pend Oreille Indians once hunted, fished, gathered berries, and sought visions (they would go into the Wilderness alone, often depriving themselves of food and water, in hopes of seeing a vision) in the rough and broken Mission Mountains. The first organized exploration of this area did not occur until 1922, after which part of the region was set aside as the Mission Mountains Primitive Area in 1931 and then expanded in 1939. The Wilderness you see today stretches for about 30 miles and varies from two to six miles in width.

Here is a land of ragged peaks with snow on them most of the year, small active glaciers, alpine lakes, meadows, clear streams that run icy cold, slablike boulders, vertical cliff faces, and talus slopes. The average elevation is 7,000 feet. In the northern portion you'll find the terrain less severe and more heavily timbered. The southern portion, however, receives more visitors, primarily around the lakes (most of which do not thaw until mid-June). The dense forest includes pine, fir, larch, and western red cedar. The array of summer wildflowers that grows in high basins will delight you.

Wildlife lives in abundant numbers in the Missions: elk and deer, black bears and grizzly bears, mountain goats and mountain lions, a few gray wolves, and a wealth of smaller furbearing animals. Approximately 50 species of birds have been identified, including bald eagles. A small population of fish is generally confined to the lakes.

About 45 miles of maintained trails are used almost exclusively by backpackers, the terrain being generally unsuitable for horses. None of the trails are easy, and many are tremendously steep. The trail to Glacier Lake Trail is perhaps the least demanding hike. Take Trail 690 up one mile to the junction with Trail 742, then take 742 one-quarter mile to Glacier Lake. To reach the region of Heart, Island, and Crescent Lakes, stay on Trail 690 for three more miles. These lakes are periodically stocked with cutthroat trout. The area shares its entire western and southern boundaries with the Flathead Indian Reservation (you must have a permit to walk onto their tribal land).

MONTANA

Mission Mountains Essentials

Size: 73,877 acres.
Year Designated: 1975.
Location: Northwestern Montana.
Easiest Access: From Condon, take State Highway 83 south for approximately six miles. Turn west on Forest Service Road 561 (Kraft Creek Road) and continue for 11 miles to the end of the road and the head of Trail 690.
Season: July through September.

Wilderness Fees/Permits: None. Permits to visit the wildland on the Flathead Indian Reservation may be obtained by calling the Confederated Salish and Kootenai Tribal Recreation Department at (406) 675-2700.
Maps: A Wilderness map is available for $3 from the district ranger.
Management: Swan Lake Ranger District, Flathead National Forest, Bigfork, MT 59911; (406) 837-5081.

Rattlesnake Wilderness

With its southern boundary just four miles north of Missoula, Montana, the Rattlesnake National Recreation Area (RNRA) receives heavy human use, but primarily in the South Zone. Far fewer people venture into its remote northern portion—the Rattlesnake Wilderness Area. A primitive track leaves the main entrance to snake along Rattlesnake Creek and head up a non-Wilderness corridor to within approximately three miles of a scenic Wilderness cluster of high alpine lakes. Near the RNRA entrance at about 3,600 feet, the elevation rises to 8,620 feet on McLeod Peak and a picturesque mountain setting. You'll find relatively gentle western slopes in the Rattlesnake Mountains and steeper east-facing slopes.

Deer, elk, coyotes, mountain goats, black bears, moose, and mountain lions reside in the Rattlesnake, with feathered "friends" such as eagles, hawks, ospreys, and numerous songbirds roosting above. Grizzly bears reportedly live in the upper Wilderness. You may catch trout in the lakes and streams. The northern boundary of the Wilderness abuts the Flathead Indian Reservation, upon whose sacred ground only members of the Confederated Salish and Kootenai Tribes are allowed (nonmembers may visit if they first obtain a permit).

Eight trailheads give access to Wilderness backpacking and horsepacking. From the parking lot in the South Zone, you can hike up the Stuart Peak Trail, entering the Wilderness after approximately four miles near Stuart Peak. Continue on this trail to the spur trail that descends to the Rattlesnake Creek Trail for a loop back to the car of about 35 miles total. Camping and campfires are unrestricted in the Wilderness, but this watershed supplies Missoula with water and the law requires that the streams and lakes must be kept clean. You are advised not to camp near water sources.

MONTANA

Rattlesnake Essentials

Size: 29,824 acres.
Year Designated: 1980.
Location: Western Montana.
Easiest Access: From Missoula, take Exit 104 from Interstate 90 and head four miles north on Van Buren Street and Rattlesnake Drive to the main entrance of the South Zone.
Season: Late spring through early fall.
Wilderness Fees/Permits: None. Permits to visit the wildland on the Flathead Indian Reservation may be obtained by calling the Confederated Salish and Kootenai Tribal Recreation Department at (406) 675-2700.
Maps: The Lolo Forest Visitors Map shows the trails and is available for $3 from the district ranger.
Management: Missoula Ranger District, Lolo National Forest, Building 24A–Fort Missoula, Missoula, MT 59801; (406) 329-3814.

Red Rock Lakes Wilderness

Back in 1935, fewer than 70 trumpeter swans in the Lower 48 had survived the pursuit of human hunters. Two-thirds of these rare birds, the largest of North America's waterfowl and, to some, the most beautiful, then lived in Montana's remote Centennial Valley. In an effort to save the swans, the Red Rock Lakes National Wildlife Area was established there.

Higher in elevation than most waterfowl refuges (6,600 feet to 9,000 feet), the Centennial Mountains border the south and east. Of the refuge's total of about 43,500 acres, roughly three-fourths has been designated Wilderness, including the major bodies of water and surrounding marsh and grassland. Snow melting off the mountains fills the refuge's 14,000 acres of lakes, marshes, and creeks.

Don't have your heart set on seeing the trumpeter swans, as they nest in the most remote marshes. But you can see many other species of birds, including sandhill cranes, great blue herons, willets, avocets, long-billed curlews, and at least 17 species of ducks. Other year-round residents include moose and porcupine, red fox, badger, skunks, and Richardson's ground squirrels. Elk, deer, and antelope pass through in summer, and a riot of wildflowers blooms in the growing season, when mosquitoes likewise swarm in great multitudes.

The refuge has two free campgrounds, but no camping is allowed in the Wilderness. Hiking is permitted everywhere except for certain areas during periods when wildlife is most sensitive to human interference. Boating is limited to canoes except during waterfowl hunting seasons in the fall. Some of the creeks and ponds are generally open to fishing for cutthroat and rainbow trout from May to November.

MONTANA

Red Rock Lakes Essentials

Size: 32,350 acres.
Year Designated: 1976.
Location: Southwestern Montana.
Easiest Access: From Lima, take Interstate 15 south for about 15 miles to the Monida exit and the refuge sign. Take the gravel road about 28 miles east to the refuge at Lakeview.
Season: Mid-May through September.
Wilderness Fees/Permits: None.
Maps: A free refuge map is available from the refuge manager.
Management: Red Rock Lakes National Wildlife Refuge, Monida Star Route, Box 15, Lima, MT 59739; (406) 276-3536.

Scapegoat Wilderness

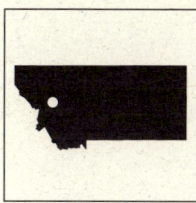

The long northwest border of Scapegoat Wilderness is shared with Bob Marshall Wilderness (see above), and the massive limestone cliffs that dominate 9,204-foot Scapegoat Mountain are an extension of the "Bob's" Chinese Wall. Scapegoat's rugged ridge tops slope down onto alpine meadows, heavily forested hillsides, and timbered river bottoms. Fish are plentiful in the 14 lakes (most abundant in the northern and southern portions) and 89 miles of streams. You will have to hike several miles to get to the less visited central portion. Elevations range from about 5,000 feet on the Blackfoot River to about 9,400 feet on Red Mountain. Wildlife includes wolverines, moose, deer, elk, mountain goats, mountain sheep, mountain lions, black bears, and numerous grizzly bears. Hunting season, opening the second half of September, draws the most visitors to this area.

Hundreds of miles of trails are suitable for backpacking and horsepacking, and most of them follow drainages. The Wilderness lies along the Continental Divide and contains this section of the Continental Divide National Scenic Trail (CDT), a length of approximately 50 miles. The Alice Creek Basin Trail climbs through lovely Alice Creek Basin to join the CDT after approximately four miles of uphill hiking. Alice Creek is considered the easiest access to the Divide in the Scapegoat.

Scapegoat Essentials

Size: 239,296 acres.
Year Designated: 1972.
Location: Northwestern Montana.
Easiest Access: From Lincoln, take State Highway 200 west for approximately eight miles. Turn north on Alice Creek Road and continue for approximately 15 miles, where the road dead-ends and the Alice Creek Basin Trail begins.
Season: July through mid-September.
Wilderness Fees/Permits: None.
Maps: A Wilderness map that includes Bob Marshall and Great Bear Wildernesses is available for $3 from the forest rangers.
Management: Helena National Forest, 2880 Skyway Drive, Helena, MT 59601; (406) 449-5201. Lewis and Clark National Forest, P.O. Box 869, Great Falls, MT 59403; (406) 791-7700. Lolo National Forest, Building 24A–Fort Missoula, Missoula, MT 59801; (406) 329-3750.

MONTANA

Selway-Bitterroot Wilderness

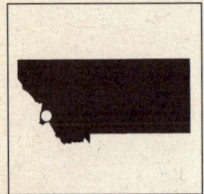

Selway-Bitterroot is the third largest Wilderness in the Lower 48, surpassed in size only by California's Death Valley Wilderness and Idaho's Frank Church–River of No Return Wilderness (RONR). But less than one-fifth of the area lies in Montana (see Idaho, Selway-Bitterroot Wilderness). Only the 600-foot-wide Nez Perce Trail (The Magruder Corridor), an unimproved dirt road, separates the Selway-Bitterroot from the Frank Church-RONR. The Wilderness straddles both sides of the Bitterroot Range, which stands along the Montana-Idaho border and includes the Wild and Scenic Selway River, all of which flows through Idaho.

This vast wildland is one of the roughest mountain areas on earth, a country of high ridges dropping off into steep-walled canyons. The barren peaks don't hint at the dense forests below, where a number of streams and more than 100 lakes offer excellent trout fishing. Hardly any humans visit the huge trailless portions of this Wilderness, which makes it all the more appealing for the large Selway elk herd, plus deer, moose, black bears, and mountain lions.

Many miles of trails provide access to the Montana side of the Selway-Bitterroot, but large sections are unmaintained and rugged. The Divide Trail (Trail 16) follows the Bitterroot Divide for approximately seven miles north of Nez Perce Pass, offering outstanding views across the Montana and Idaho portions of the Wilderness. Hunting brings the most visitors.

Selway-Bitterroot Essentials

Size: 248,893 acres in Montana (1,337,910 acres total).
Year Designated: 1964.
Location: Western Montana.
Easiest Access: From Darby, take U.S. 93 south for approximately eight miles to Conner. Turn southwest on Forest Service Road 473 and continue for approximately 12 miles, then go west on Forest Service Road 468 (The Magruder Corridor) for 16.4 miles to Nez Perce Pass.
Season: Late spring through fall.

Wilderness Fees/Permits: None.
Maps: A Wilderness map is available for $3 from the forest rangers.
Management: Bitterroot National Forest, 1801 North First Street, Hamilton, MT 59840; (406) 363-7121. Lolo National Forest, Building 24A–Fort Missoula, Missoula, MT 59801; (406) 329-3750. West Fork Ranger District, Bitterroot National Forest, Darby, MT 59829; (406) 821-3269.

MONTANA

UL Bend Wilderness

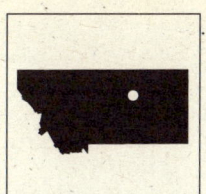

For approximately one million acres and 125 miles up the Fort Peck Reservoir and the Missouri River from the Fort Peck Dam, you'll find the Charles M. Russell National Wildlife Refuge. This area is characterized by breaks (badlands), steep-sided forested coulees, prairie grasslands, cottonwood river bottoms, and an abundance of wildlife: elk, mule deer, white-tailed deer, pronghorn antelope, bighorn sheep, coyotes, badgers, bobcats, Canada geese, grouse, and a wide variety of raptors. Prairie dogs have established "towns" here, complex systems of interconnected burrows that cover thousands of acres. *Tyrannosaurus rex* once hunted these grounds, and in many areas of the refuge little has changed since those forgotten days.

Some of the remotest regions of the refuge are seldom seen and virtually unexplored by humans. Foremost among those regions is UL Bend Wilderness, which is a part of the UL Bend National Wildlife Refuge that is in turn swallowed by the vast Charles M. Russell National Wildlife Refuge (CMRNWR). You'll find UL Bend north of a tight U-shaped bend in the Missouri River in the western section of the CMRNWR. The Wilderness is divided into four units: three small northern units and the large southern unit that borders the river. The area is almost entirely open grassland and sagebrush, without water and exposed to the whimsy of prairie winds. There are no maintained trails, but hiking and camping within the Wilderness are unrestricted, scenic, and rugged. Horses, hunting, and fishing (in season) are allowed.

As the Missouri enters the refuge it is designated Wild and Scenic, and many paddlers continue down past the Wilderness on placid waters. High winds may make open areas of water dangerous. You'll be paddling in the long-gone wake of Lewis and Clark.

UL Bend Essentials

Size: 20,819 acres.
Year Designated: 1976; expanded in 1983.
Location: Northern central Montana.
Easiest Access: Cross the Fred Robinson Bridge over the Missouri River and continue north on U.S. 191 for approximately 20 miles. Turn east on Dry Fork Road until the road ends at a T, approximately 26 miles. Turn south and continue for approximately 15 miles to a second T. The open grassland to the west is the largest northern unit of the Wilderness. Turn east at the second T and drive for about eight miles to Dry Lake. The main section of the Wilderness lies south, east, and west of Dry Lake.
Season: Open all year, but spring is probably the best time.
Wilderness Fees/Permits: None.
Maps: A free map is available from the refuge manager.
Management: Charles M. Russell National Wildlife Refuge, P.O. Box 110, Lewistown, MT 59457; (406) 538-8707.

353

MONTANA

Welcome Creek Wilderness

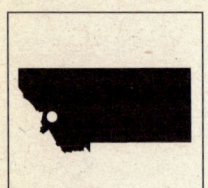

A hardy setting for the Sapphire Mountains, which lie just west of this area, Welcome Creek Wilderness measures nine miles by seven miles. The ridges are steep and the valleys narrow and uneven, hardly encouraging news to anyone interested in pitching a tent. Most of the land is heavily timbered (pine, fir, larch), although the south-facing mountains boast a few open and grassy slopes. Welcome Creek flows south and east, providing a home to native trout. Hunters of big game (elk, deer, bighorn sheep, mountain goats, and the like) are the most common visitors. Gray wolves may live here; rest assured that bears do.

About 25 miles of strenuous trails provide foot and horse access, but overnight backpackers are few and far between. The main pathway is the Welcome Creek Trail, which crosses the area east-west for approximately seven miles, passing no lakes (this Wilderness has none).

Welcome Creek Essentials

Size: 28,135 acres.
Year Designated: 1978.
Location: Western Montana.
Easiest Access: From Missoula, take Interstate 90 east for about 20 miles. Exit at Rock Creek and travel about 14 miles south on Rock Creek Road. Just across a suspension bridge, park at the eastern end of the Welcome Creek Trail.

Season: Late spring through early fall.
Wilderness Fees/Permits: None.
Maps: A Wilderness map is available for $3 from the district ranger.
Management: Missoula Ranger District, Lolo National Forest, Building 24A–Fort Missoula, Missoula, MT 59801; (406) 329-3814.

> *"Wilderness is an idea as much as a place, with modern man learning to pass like a shadow of a cloud across what he did not make and cannot improve."*
>
> —Gilbert H. Grosvenor

NEBRASKA

Total Wilderness areas: 2
Total Wilderness acreage: 12,735

Less than two centuries ago, only the wooded banks of streams and rivers cut through the wild sea of grass that eventually became known as Nebraska. Sioux Indians followed great herds of buffalo, their chief source of food, clothing, and shelter. As they moved westward, settlers confined the Native Americans to reservations and all but wiped out the buffalo population. Today, Nebraska contains only about 351,000 acres of national forestland: Samuel R. McKelvie National Forest in the north and Nebraska National Forest in the central and western parts of the state. Only one modest area in Nebraska National Forest qualifies as Wilderness. An even smaller section of a wildlife refuge has been designated as Wilderness.

Fort Niobrara Wilderness

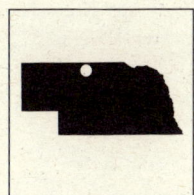

Growing herds of buffalo, elk, and Texas longhorns have found a sanctuary in the rolling sand hills of the 19,123-acre Fort Niobrara National Wildlife Refuge, but nothing much remains of the fort that once protected northern Nebraska settlers. The only surviving colonists, prairie dogs, have taken up residence in large "towns" beneath the wildflower-scattered grasses. The Niobrara River flows swiftly through about nine miles of the refuge, creating a canyon riverine ecosystem of trees and bushes and attracting summer canoeists. North of the river you'll find the Fort Niobrara Wilderness, a unique mix of prairie and wooded valleys. Buffalo winter here, then head south of the river for the summer. No maintained trails offer access north of the river. The refuge is open only during daylight hours, and camping is prohibited. Day-hikers, most of whom follow the river, can at least get a sense of the nature of the land. Fires are forbidden in the refuge.

NEBRASKA

Fort Niobrara Essentials

Size: 4,635 acres.
Year Designated: 1976.
Location: Central northern Nebraska.
Easiest Access: From Valentine, take State Highway 12 east for about four miles to the refuge visitors center.
Season: Summer.
Wilderness Fees/Permits: None.
Maps: Contact the refuge manager to obtain a free map.
Management: Fort Niobrara National Wildlife Refuge, Hidden Timber Route, HC 14, Box 67, Valentine, NE 69201; (402) 376-3789.

Soldier Creek Wilderness

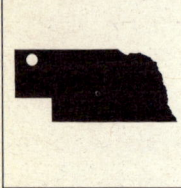

From the 1870s to after World War II, Fort Robinson soldiers pastured their horses, gathered wood, and relaxed along Soldier Creek, now a playground for white-tailed deer, mule deer, turkeys, coyotes, bobcats, eagles, and hawks. Here the ponderosa pine–covered ridges of northwest Nebraska give way to grassy upland parks. And while the Wilderness is recovering from a wildfire that destroyed about 90 percent of the pine trees in July 1989, the devastation wrought by those raging flames will be evident for a long time to come. Several well-developed trails loop through the area, which shares a border with Fort Robinson State Park, but the 10-mile Trooper Trail rewards your hiking efforts with a bit of history: two windmills that haven't stopped pumping since the turn of the century. Old windmills spaced around Soldier Creek likewise continue to draw up water. Horsepackers can saddle up at the Soldier Creek Trailhead corral.

Soldier Creek Essentials

Size: 8,100 acres.
Year Designated: 1986.
Location: Northwestern Nebraska.
Easiest Access: From Chadron, take U.S. 20 west for about eight miles past Crawford to the Fort Robinson State Park access road. Signs within the park will direct you to Soldier Creek.
Season: Summer.
Wilderness Fees/Permits: None.
Maps: A detailed map is available for free from the forest supervisor.
Management: Forest Supervisor, Nebraska National Forest, 125 North Main, Chadron, NE 69337; (308) 432-3367.

> *"In Wildness is the preservation of the World. Every tree sends its fibers forth in search of the Wild. The cities import it at any price. Men plow and sail for it. From the forest and wilderness come the tonics and barks which brace mankind."*
>
> —Henry David Thoreau

NEVADA

Total Wilderness areas: 14
Total Wilderness acreage: 798,067

Between 1964 and 1989, Nevada contained only one small Wilderness—Jarbidge in Humboldt National Forest. Yet here, in the driest and arguably the least explored and least visited of the Lower 48, 2.5 million acres of the Humboldt lie fragmented in northern and western Nevada. And here stands Toiyabe National Forest, the largest chunk of national forestland outside of Alaska, splattered in sections across the eastern, central, and southern parts of the state. (The Toiyabe also includes a piece of eastern California.) The Nevada Wilderness Protection Act of 1989 recognized the worth of Nevada Wilderness by creating five Wilderness areas in the Toiyabe and seven more in the Humboldt. Inyo National Forest lies mostly in California, but it reaches over the boundary just enough to include another Wilderness Area created by the 1989 act. The BLM manages sections of three Nevada Wildernesses.

Alta Toquima Wilderness

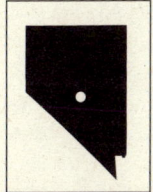

Steep and sharply cut with many rocky canyons, the Toquima Mountain Range lies between Big Smoky Valley on the west and Monitor Valley on the east. In the central portion of the range you'll find Alta Toquima Wilderness, rising from gentler terrain in the northern section to more rugged ground that peaks in the south on Mount Jefferson. This massif stands boldly prominent, a collection of three summits on a ridge eight miles long and two miles wide, with a high point of 11,949 feet. On a clear day, you can stand on this ridge and see all the way to the mountains in California and Utah. In 1978, an archaeological site was discovered on Jefferson, the highest-known Indian village in North America,

NEVADA

built some 7,000 years ago. Why, archaeologists wondered, did entire families scale the steep slopes of Mount Jefferson to build their homes?

From sagebrush and grass at lower elevations, the vegetation turns to piñon-juniper woodlands and finally to limber pine and a few patches of aspen in the higher country. Pine Creek supports a native population of trout, and the slopes are home to deer, bighorn sheep, grouse, and chukar.

The six-mile Pine Creek Trail leaves Pine Creek Campground on the eastern boundary and gives relatively easy access to Jefferson and a clear, cold mountain pond. The trail is steep only near the top. Pine Creek Campground is primitive; sites are free. A 16-mile trail follows the crest of the Wilderness, from Charnock Pass on the north to a guard station outside the area on the south. Trails cross the eastern side of the Wilderness. The western side is seldom seen.

Alta Toquima Essentials

Size: 38,000 acres.
Year Designated: 1989.
Location: Central Nevada.
Easiest Access: From Tonopah, drive east on U.S. 6 for approximately six miles, then turn north on State Route 376 and continue for approximately 14 miles. Go north on State Route 82 for approximately 45 miles, then west on Forest Service Road 009 for three miles to Pine Creek Campground.
Season: In fall and winter, rain can suddenly turn to snow. Spring probably rates as the all-around best season. Summer weather can be marvelously hot.
Wilderness Fees/Permits: None.
Maps: A Toiyabe National Forest map can be ordered or picked up for $3 from the ranger.
Management: Tonopah Ranger District, Toiyabe National Forest, P.O. Box 3940, Tonopah, NV 89049; (702) 482-6286.

Arc Dome Wilderness

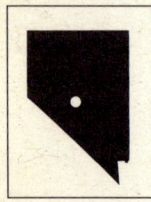

The largest of Nevada's Wildernesses, Arc Dome comprises the southern third of the Toiyabe Range, a rugged spine of mountains with difficult access, and includes the range's highest summits. Much of the Wilderness lies above 10,000 feet, but Arc Dome itself, at 11,775 feet, dominates the area. On the west side, the ground rises gradually from the Reese River Valley; on the east, rocky canyons break up steep inclines. Vegetation consists of sagebrush and grass lower down, and gives way to piñon-juniper higher up, with occasional stands of pine and aspen.

Desert bighorn sheep, once abundant in the state, seldom appear except in the Jett Canyon-Twin Rivers region in the eastern section. Mountain lions, bobcats, deer, beavers, grouse, and raptors are more established, but it's the trout in the Reese River, South Twin Creek, and North Twin Creek that qualify as a bona fide wildlife attraction (among anglers, at least).

Trails from the eastern boundary give access to both Twin Creeks and some beautiful country. The Toiyabe Crest Trail, a 72-mile designated National Recreation Trail, sweeps through more than 30 miles of the area, from a parking lot at Ophir Summit to a parking lot at South Twin, offering access to the summit of Arc Dome. This trail boasts great views but little water, and subsequently feels the tread of few human feet. The Cow Canyon Trail, from the western boundary, follows the Reese River for about a mile, then splits to give access to other trails and anywhere in the area you'd care to visit. Of all the trails, it generates the most human use. Twenty acres of Arc Dome Wilderness lie on BLM land.

NEVADA

Arc Dome Essentials
Size: 115,000 acres.
Year Designated: 1989.
Location: Central Nevada.
Easiest Access: From Tonopah, take U.S. 6 east for approximately six miles. Turn north on State Route 376 and continue driving for about 63 miles, then go west on Road 080 for another three miles until you reach the parking lot at South Twin.
Season: Spring and fall for the best weather.
Wilderness Fees/Permits: None.
Maps: A detailed map is available for $3 from the district ranger.
Management: Tonopah Ranger District, Toiyabe National Forest, P.O. Box 3940, Tonopah, NV 89049; (702) 482-6286. BLM Battle Mountain District Office, P.O. Box 911, Tonopah, NV 89049; (702) 885-6000.

Boundary Peak Wilderness

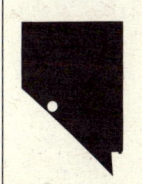

Of the 11.86 million acres of the heavily visited Inyo National Forest split between Nevada and California, only 60,654 lie in Nevada. In that portion, you will find this one lonely Wilderness, the state's smallest. But this Wilderness makes up in height what it lacks in size, with Boundary Peak, at 13,140 feet, rating as the highest point in Nevada. The peak overlooks, as might be expected, the California border, and rises above the White Mountains, a high and dry range from which colorful canyons descend eastward into desertland. Hiking up these precipitous canyons will often lead you to an abrupt end, where waterfalls (now dry) once carved the rock. Rising dramatically from the floor of Nevada, the mountains are primarily of granite, with an overlay of old sedimentary rock and exposed fossils dating back 600 million years. Boundary Peak and nearby Montgomery Peak pair up in an impressive massif with a grand view. Most climbers approach Boundary from Nevada, and find the trail easy to follow and the 4,400-foot elevation gain strenuous.

Boundary Peak Essentials
Size: 10,000 acres.
Year Designated: 1989.
Location: Western Nevada.
Easiest Access: From Bishop, California, take U.S. 6 north approximately 60 miles. You'll now be in Nevada and over Montgomery Pass. Turn south on State Route 264 and continue for 13.9 miles, then head west on an unmarked dirt road on the north side of Chiatovich Creek. Continue for 12.2 miles, taking all the right forks in the road until you reach a small meadow and the Boundary Peak Trailhead.
Season: July through September.
Wilderness Fees/Permits: None.
Maps: USGS topographic maps covering the White Mountains are Mount Barcroft and White Mountain Peak.
Management: White Mountain Ranger District, Inyo National Forest, 798 North Main Street, Bishop, CA 93514; (619) 873-4207.

Currant Mountain Wilderness

Volcanic-deposited sediments uplifted into a fault-block mountain range, now called the White Pine Range, which peaks at 11,513-foot Currant Mountain near the center of the Wilderness. Sagebrush, piñon pine, and juniper dot the lower elevations, deferring to white fir, limber pine, and bristlecone pine higher up. Portions of the area are important to upland game birds, especially partridge, and sometimes to members of the northernmost herd of desert bighorn sheep. The southern section provides ideal habitat for raptors. Monte Cristo Wild Horse and Burro Territory extends into the western section of the area, but wild horses are not frequently seen here. Elk use the northeastern section, and mule deer are common. Extremely rugged terrain and limited access (especially from the east) make this an odds-on favorite for solitude in a Nevada Wilderness.

The 10.6 miles or so of trail are in poor condition and receive light use. You'll find little to no water in this region. The Broom Canyon Trail enters on the western side, follows an old road for about 2.5 miles, and, although it disappears, probably provides the best access. Three acres of the Wilderness lie in the Ely District on BLM land.

Currant Mountain Essentials

Size: 36,000 acres.
Year Designated: 1989.
Location: Eastern central Nevada.
Easiest Access: From Ely, take U.S. 6 south and west for approximately 50 miles before turning north and west on State Highway 379. After about 10 miles, when you reach Forest Service Road 646 (four-wheel drive is recommended), turn north and east up Broom Canyon and proceed approximately three miles to the Broom Canyon Trailhead.
Season: Spring for the most water, but always carry plenty anyway.
Wilderness Fees/Permits: None.
Maps: Detailed maps are available for $3 from the district ranger.
Management: Ely Ranger District, Humboldt National Forest, 350 Eighth Street, Ely, NV 89301; (702) 289-3031. BLM Ely District Office, 702 North Industrial Way, Ely, NV 89301; (702) 289-1800.

East Humboldt Wilderness

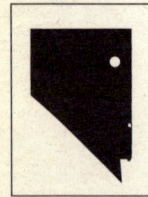

Anchored in the center by 11,127-foot Hole in the Mountain Peak, the East Humboldt Range and this Wilderness are generally sparse in vegetation: grasses and sage lower down, mountain mahogany and aspen in dense stands higher up. Here in the high country, including 11,020-foot Humboldt Peak in the southern portion, you'll find a very remote area with limited access, appealing to large mammals such as mountain lions, bobcats, deer, and mountain goats. Several trails enter from the west side, usually following small drainages such as First, Second, Third, and Fourth Boulder Creeks. Six lakes accommodate cutthroat and brook trout, an attraction to anglers. Most visitors are found at Angel Lake Campground just outside the northeastern boundary, a facility that requires a fee ($6 per night) and offers fishing, water, sites for tents or RVs, and a trailhead leading to Greys Lake in the north of the Wilderness. The round-trip to Greys Lake is a possible day hike.

NEVADA

East Humboldt Essentials
Size: 36,900 acres.
Year Designated: 1989.
Location: Northeastern Nevada.
Easiest Access: From Interstate 80 about one mile west of Wells, take State Highway 231 south approximately six miles to Angel Lake Campground.
Season: Spring and fall.
Wilderness Fees/Permits: None.
Maps: A detailed map is available for $4 from the forest supervisor's office.
Management: Forest Supervisor, Humboldt National Forest, 976 Mountain City Highway, Elko, NV 89801; (702) 738-5171.

Grant Range Wilderness

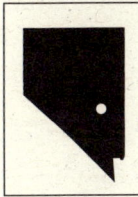

Raptors flock to this area, which falls away from 11,298-foot Troy Peak to a few firs and bristlecone pines and on down to dryland piñon-juniper with a sagebrush understory. Hikers won't find any maintained trails, just abandoned four-wheel-drive tracks that extend into the area from the east and west. Water is virtually impossible to find, except when snow melts and runs off from higher elevations. Only a dirt road separates this land from Quinn Canyon Wilderness (see below) to the south. Few people ever explore this region of Nevada, although it is relatively easy to get to the high country.

Grant Range Essentials
Size: 50,000 acres.
Year Designated: 1989.
Location: Southern central Nevada.
Easiest Access: From Ely, take U.S. 6 south for approximately 50 miles. Just past Currant, turn south on a well-used dirt road (a sign, if it's still standing, will direct you to Blue Eagle Ranch). Take the dirt road approximately 36 miles, then, before Nyala, turn east on another dirt road, which will take you approximately 10 miles to a saddle (low point on the ridge). Park at the saddle and hike northeast.
Season: Spring.
Wilderness Fees/Permits: None.
Maps: Detailed maps are available for $3 from the district ranger.
Management: Ely Ranger District, Humboldt National Forest, 350 Eighth Street, Ely, NV 89301; (702) 289-3031.

Jarbidge Wilderness

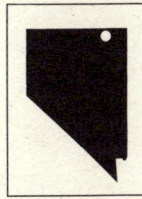

According to legend, a hardy band of Shoshone braves kept the original *jarbidge* (their word for "a weird beastly creature") in a cave in Jarbidge Canyon. Now this Wilderness merits attention as one of the most remote spots in America. You can't even see its peaks (eight of which exceed 10,000 feet) from the highway. But with air as unpolluted as you will find anywhere, the view from these heights goes on for 150 miles. Look down from the peaks and you will see 4,000 feet into the valleys.

This area is unusually wet for Nevada, with seven to eight feet of snow falling annually, ideal for vegetation that varies from northern desert plants to alpine plants. Snow often clogs high trails from mid-October to mid-June. Two small basins guard Jarbidge Lake and Emerald Lake (brook trout swim about this pretty gem), true hidden Wilderness treasures. Elk graze on the eastern side of the area, attracting their fair share of hunters, and the deer herd has grown quite large. Mountain lions also prowl these grounds.

The Snowslide Gulch Trail enters on the northwest end of the area and provides the most used access. This trail leads to Jarbidge Lake in about six miles and over the mountains about one more mile to Emerald Lake. Trailheads also exist at Slide Creek and Three Day Creek. As you approach the mountains, you may be reminded of the splendor of the European Alps. Although more than 125 miles of trails exist, remoteness and rugged mountain terrain place this area among the least visited of all Wildernesses.

Jarbidge Essentials

Size: 113,167 acres.
Year Designated: 1964; expanded in 1989.
Location: Northeastern Nevada.
Easiest Access: From Twin Falls, Idaho, take U.S. 93 south approximately 30 miles to Rogerson, Idaho. Turn west on Three Creek Highway and drive approximately 40 miles to the Idaho/Nevada state line. Continue about nine miles to Jarbidge, Nevada, then another four miles past Jarbidge to the Snowslide Gulch Trailhead on the east side of the road.
Season: The Fourth of July and the hunting season in late October bring the most visitors to this region. Depending on snowpack, the upper elevations may not be easy to travel until midsummer.
Wilderness Fees/Permits: None.
Maps: A detailed map is available for $4 from the district ranger.
Management: Jarbidge Ranger District, Humboldt National Forest, 1008 Buhl, ID 83316; (208) 543-4129.

Mount Charleston Wilderness

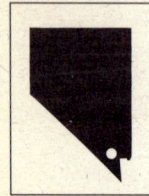

Here in the high country you'll find a forested oasis—relief from the heat of southern Nevada, where summer temperatures often rise above 100 degrees Fahrenheit. However, don't expect to find much water (there are no running streams and precious few springs). This area, extending completely across the crest of the Spring Mountain Range, includes its high point on Charleston Peak at 11,918 feet. Short, steep-walled canyons penetrate the range, which is characterized by some 18,000 acres of bristlecone pine, the largest such stand in the Intermountain West. Some 40 miles of trails include the Bonanza Trail, which runs along the spine of the Spring Mountains for approximately 14 miles. Elevation changes and the virtual absence of flat terrain make for strenuous hiking.

Mount Charleston Essentials

Size: 43,000 acres.
Year Designated: 1989.
Location: Southern Nevada.
Easiest Access: From Las Vegas, take Interstate 95 north for approximately 30 miles, then turn west on State Highway 156 and proceed for approximately 15 miles until you reach the Bonanza Trailhead.
Season: Summer temperatures are cool compared to those in Las Vegas.
Wilderness Fees/Permits: None.
Maps: A detailed map is available for a nominal charge from the district ranger.
Management: Las Vegas Ranger District, Toiyabe National Forest, 550 East Charleston, Las Vegas, NV 89104; (702) 477-7782.

Mount Moriah Wilderness

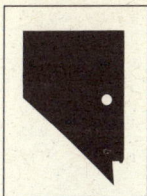

Shallow caves, many of which show evidence of prehistoric habitation, are common in this Wilderness. And those who would know suspect that many more caves have yet to be discovered. If you set out to explore this territory, you will be in the northern Snake Range, bounded on the east by Snake Valley and on the west by Spring Valley. Stretching north and west of 12,050-foot Mount Moriah is a plateau known as The Table, a unique world of subalpine vegetation lined with bristlecone and limber pine. Dry piñon-juniper forestland dominates a large part of the lower elevations here.

Four year-round creeks provide watery homes for Bonneville cutthroat trout, but the heart of the area tends toward the parched, requiring you to carry all your water. Rocky Mountain bighorn sheep scramble around Mount Moriah, but visitors are few (most come to hunt mule deer or grouse). The rugged topography is at least partially to blame.

About 50 miles of fair to very poor trails give access to the area. Trailheads on the east side are accessible by passenger car along roads that follow Hampton Creek, Hendry's Creek, and Smith Creek. Some of Mount Moriah Wilderness (6,435 acres in the north) lies on BLM land and is managed by the Ely District Office. Great Basin National Park lies just to the south.

Mount Moriah Essentials

Size: 82,000 acres.
Year Designated: 1989.
Location: Eastern central Nevada.
Easiest Access: From Ely, take U.S. 50 east approximately 58 miles. Turn north on the road to Gandy and Trout Creek and continue for approximately 10 miles, then go west on Forest Service Road 429 for about three miles to the Hendry's Creek Trail.
Season: Spring and fall.
Wilderness Fees/Permits: None.
Maps: A detailed map is available for $3 from the district ranger.
Management: Ely Ranger District, Humboldt National Forest, 350 Eighth Street, Ely, NV 89301; (702) 289-3031. BLM Ely District Office, 702 North Industrial Way, Ely, NV 89301; (702) 289-1800.

Mount Rose Wilderness

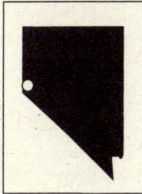

Nestled between Lake Tahoe, California, and Reno, Nevada, Mount Rose encompasses most of the high country of the Carson Range. The Hunter Lake jeep road splits the area into two distinct sections: the 5,000-acre northern section includes Hunter Creek Canyon and the two-mile Hunter Creek Trail, while the 23,000-acre southern section contains 10,776-foot Mount Rose and most of the major canyons and ridges. Due to its proximity to urban centers (the area almost shares a border with Reno), Mount Rose is easily the state's most heavily used Wilderness. An estimated 100 hikers per day tramp along the Mount Rose Trail (200 per day on weekends). But portions of the interior hide small meadows and smaller lakes seldom seen by humans. Wander off the three-mile Thomas Creek Trail and you will find hidden camping spots and a more primitive experience.

NEVADA

Mount Rose Essentials
Size: 28,000 acres.
Year Designated: 1989.
Location: Western Nevada.
Easiest Access: From Reno, take U.S. 395 south for about 10 miles, then turn west on State Route 431 and continue for about seven miles to find the Mount Rose Trailhead and a parking lot on the north side of the road.
Season: Spring.
Wilderness Fees/Permits: None.
Maps: A detailed map is available for $3 from the district ranger.
Management: Carson Ranger District, Toiyabe National Forest, 1536 South Carson Street, Carson City, NV 89701; (702) 882-2766.

Quinn Canyon Wilderness

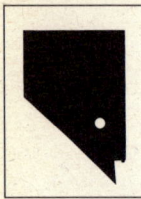

Extreme isolation defines Quinn Canyon. From the main ridgeline of the area, cresting at more than 10,000 feet, many smaller ridges and narrow canyons extend out east and west. In the V-shaped drainages, snowmelt along with summer rains collect in four year-round streams. Several springs usually provide water. From piñon pine and juniper, the vegetation gives way to sagebrush with scattered white fir, aspen, and mahogany higher up. Small stands of bristlecone pine can be found here, too. Mule deer move into the higher elevations in summer.

About 20.8 miles of trails in poor to very poor condition access the area and receive light or no use. Rough hiking on the Little Cherry Trail, the only path in fair condition, will lead you to the 10-mile Hooper Canyon Trail, which offers a semi-loop through the Wilderness that must be connected by shuttle.

Quinn Canyon Essentials
Size: 27,000 acres.
Year Designated: 1989.
Location: Southern central Nevada.
Easiest Access: From Ely, take U.S. 6 south for approximately 50 miles. Just past Currant, turn south on a well-used dirt road (a sign, if it's still standing, will direct you to Blue Eagle Ranch) and proceed for approximately 36 miles. Before Nyala, turn east on another well-used dirt road that leads approximately 10 miles to a saddle. Hike southwest from the saddle and down into Hooper Canyon.
Season: Spring.
Wilderness Fees/Permits: None.
Maps: A detailed map is available for $3 from the district ranger.
Management: Ely Ranger District, Humboldt National Forest, 350 Eighth Street, Ely, NV 89301; (702) 289-3031.

Ruby Mountains Wilderness

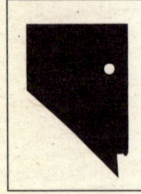

Glaciers scoured the northern end of the Rubies during the last ice age, creating the U-shaped Lamoille Canyon, also known as Nevada's Yosemite. Hanging valleys, towering summits, and year-round snowfields characterize this Wilderness.

South of Lamoille you'll encounter seven miles of lake basins and meadows before the terrain south of Furlong Lake turns into a narrow, grassy ridge that runs 20 miles to the Overland Lake basin. The Rubies contain 10 peaks above 10,000 feet (including Ruby Dome at 11,387 feet) and more than two dozen alpine lakes, rare treats in this arid state. You'll also find here one of the largest herds of mule deer in Nevada, numbers of mountain goats and bighorn sheep, and streams teeming with trout (including the threatened Lahontan cutthroat). Himalayan snow cocks and Hungarian partridges have been introduced and are doing well. Prehistoric hunting blinds and once-inhabited caves on high ridges indicate that this area has been in use for a long time.

The Ruby Crest National Recreation Trail crawls along the top of this Wilderness for 40 miles. Shorter side trails climb to the crest from several trailheads.

Ruby Mountains Essentials

Size: 90,000 acres.
Year Designated: 1989.
Location: Northeastern Nevada.
Easiest Access: From Elko, take State Road 227 south for approximately 25 miles. Turn south on Forest Service Road 660 (Lamoille Canyon Scenic Byway) and continue for 12 miles to the Roads End Trailhead, which opens onto the Ruby Crest Trail.
Season: Mid-June until October, when the snow falls.
Wilderness Fees/Permits: None.
Maps: A Wilderness topographic map is available for a nominal fee from the district ranger. A free trail guide is available.
Management: Ruby Mountains Ranger District, Humboldt National Forest, 428 South Humboldt, Wells, NV 89825; (702) 738-3357.

Santa Rosa–Paradise Peak Wilderness

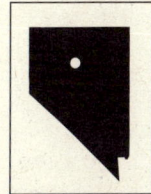

Lonely, rarely visited, and subtle, this area is quintessential basin and range country: no lakes, no alpine meadows, no large coniferous forests. It encompasses the south end of the Santa Rosa Mountains, with 9,701-foot Santa Rosa Peak in the northern section as its highest point. Paradise Peak in the southern section overlooks rugged granite, a profusion of spring wildflowers, sweeping basins above pockets of quaking aspen, and an abundance of wildlife. Mountain lions and bobcats are elusive but common inhabitants, and California bighorn sheep have been introduced. Eagles and hawks soar with the wind in the higher country, while upland game birds, grouse, and partridge dominate lower elevations. Cold streams provide a home for many trout, including the threatened Lahontan cutthroat. Rattlesnakes and hornets threaten the unobservant in summer.

The Summit Trail, with a trailhead at Singas Creek on the east side, crosses the northern section, slips outside the boundary on the east side, and reenters to cross the southern section. The Buffalo Canyon Trail, on the west side, climbs through rock outcroppings for 4.5 miles to join the Summit Trail at the top of the range. The Falls Canyon Trail passes a small waterfall about one-half mile into its 1.5-mile length. The two-mile McConnell Creek Trail offers a rewarding view of Santa Rosa Peak, whose summit can be reached with some strenuous hiking.

NEVADA

Santa Rosa–Paradise Peak Essentials

Size: 31,000 acres.
Year Designated: 1989.
Location: Northern Nevada.
Easiest Access: From Winnemucca, take U.S. 95 north for approximately 37 miles, then turn east on Buffalo Canyon Road and continue driving for about one mile to the Buffalo Canyon Trailhead.
Season: Spring for the wildflowers.
Wilderness Fees/Permits: None.
Maps: A map is available for $3 from the district ranger.
Management: Santa Rosa Ranger District, Humboldt National Forest, 1200 Winnemucca Boulevard East, Winnemucca, NV 89445; (702) 623-5025.

Table Mountain Wilderness

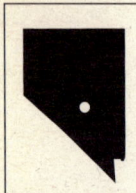

A unique high plateau, or tableland, distinguishes this Wilderness. On the plateau west of Lower Dry Lake, a strange network of low-lying stone walls gives evidence of prehistoric human activity of undetermined purpose. This rolling, semiforested region attracts hikers and horsepackers. The Monitor Range, in which Table Mountain stands, rises above 10,000 feet and provides a home for one of the largest mule deer herds in the state. A well-established elk herd introduced in 1979 adds incentive for hunters. Five major streams attract anglers seeking trout, especially Mosquito Creek (sound inviting?) in the northern central section. Large stands of aspen over much of the mountainsides are unusual in this region of Nevada (some of the aspens in Waterfall Canyon are carved with dates dating back as early as 1907). Waterfall Canyon also features well-preserved samples of Basque sheepherder art, hence its nickname, Pornographic Grove.

The Barley Creek Trail, entering from the south, is the most used access. After five miles of hiking, you can take a steep one-mile side trail to the top of Table Mountain. Before you get to the side trail you'll pass alongside beaver ponds with good fishing. From where the Barley Creek Trail splits the west fork will take you to Dry Lake and all the way across the Wilderness to the Morgan Creek Trailhead on the north end, for a total walking distance of about 20 miles. Other trailheads can be accessed at Mosquito Creek on the west side, Clear Creek (which goes to Clear Lake) on the east side, and Green Monster Canyon on the east side.

Table Mountain Essentials

Size: 98,000 acres.
Year Designated: 1989.
Location: Central Nevada.
Easiest Access: From Tonopah, take U.S. 6 approximately five miles east, then turn north on State Highway 376 and continue for approximately 12 miles. Take the Belmont turnoff (northeast) and continue for 34 miles, which will take you seven miles north of Belmont. When you reach Barley Creek Road, drive east for about 6.5 miles to the end of the road and the Barley Creek Trailhead.
Season: Spring and fall.
Wilderness Fees/Permits: None.
Maps: A map is available for $3 from the district ranger.
Management: Tonopah Ranger District, Toiyabe National Forest, P.O. Box 3940, Tonopah, NV 89049; (702) 482-6286.

> "It is not enough to fight for the land: it is even more important to enjoy it. While you can. While it's still there. So get out there and hunt and fish and mess around with our friends, ramble out yonder and explore the forests, encounter the grizz, climb the mountains, bag the peaks, run the rivers, breathe deep of that yet sweet and lucid air, sit quietly for a while and contemplate the precious stillness, that lovely, mysterious and awesome space."
>
> —Edward Abbey

NEW HAMPSHIRE

Total Wilderness areas: 4
Total Wilderness acreage: 102,932

The Granite State boasts 182 mountains rising above 3,000 feet, more than 10,000 miles of rivers and brooks, at least 1,000 lakes and ponds, and 18 miles of Atlantic coastline. In the White Mountain National Forest of northern New Hampshire, you'll find the largest alpine area east of the Rocky Mountains, the highest point in New England, a vast hardwood forest, and four untrammeled areas deemed worthy of Wilderness designation.

Great Gulf Wilderness

You may find yourself humming "Hail to the Chief" as you take in New Hampshire's Presidential Range. This peaked carpet begins at Mount Washington, unfurling north and east to cover Mounts Jefferson, Adams, and Madison. Then, finally, it enfolds the Great Gulf, the largest cirque in the White Mountains of New Hampshire, and a steep-walled bowl drained eastward by the West Fork of the Peabody River. Many rivulets tumble into the Peabody. From the headwall rising 1,100 feet to 1,600 feet above the bowl's bottom, the gulf drops ruggedly east for about 3.5 miles, then flattens into more open country for another 1.5 miles.

Mount Washington, just south of the Wilderness boundary, stands at 6,288 feet, the highest point in New England. Let the records show that it was here, on April 12, 1934, that winds howled past at 231 miles per hour, the highest wind velocity ever documented on Earth. The southern Wilderness boundary lies just north of the Mount Washington Auto Road, which provides paved access to the summit. Mount Adams anchors the northwestern Wilderness boundary, and at 5,774 feet garners second place in the New England height tourney. Mount Madison, at the northernmost point of the Wilderness, tops out at 5,367 feet then plummets 4,000 feet to river valleys below. The views from the ridge and summits of the Presidentials, and from the floor of the bowl, rank among New England's best.

Six spur trails hook up to the Great Gulf Trail, which cuts roughly east-west through the center of New Hampshire's oldest and smallest Wilderness. Beginning about 1.5 miles east of the state boundary, the trail crosses approximately five miles of Wilderness and beyond to Mount Washington. The Appalachian Trail runs perpendicular to the Great Gulf Trail. I hiked the four-mile path early one spring only to find myself wandering alone through deep snowbanks that absorbed sound and created a heavy silence. Having lived for several years in Conway, New Hampshire, I've hiked the Great Gulf in every season, and have found the forest most appealing when autumn leaves weave their vivid tapestry of color and the voracious black flies of early summer buzz off to other grounds.

Camping is prohibited above the tree line except in winter, when temperatures typically drop to bitter cold and snow buries everything in sight. Other portions of the Wilderness are seasonally closed to camping. Fires are not permitted.

Great Gulf Essentials

Size: 5,552 acres.
Year Designated: 1964.
Location: Northern New Hampshire.
Easiest Access: From North Conway, take State Highway 16 north for approximately 25 miles to the meeting point of the West Branch of the Peabody River and the Peabody River. You can park your vehicle in the lot there and start at the trailhead for the Great Gulf Trail.
Season: All seasons offer splendid Wilderness travel. Winters are often ferocious. Fall is the nicest time of year to visit.
Wilderness Fees/Permits: None.
Maps: A free Wilderness map is available from the district ranger. The *AMC White Mountain Guide* provides excellent trail information (Appalachian Mountain Club, 5 Joy Street, Boston, MA 02108; $16.95). DeLorme's *Trail Map & Guide to the White Mountain National Forest* also covers the area.
Management: Androscoggin Ranger District, White Mountain National Forest, 80 Glen Road, Gorham, NH 03581; (603) 466-2713.

Pemigewasset Wilderness

Nary a road blemishes New Hampshire's largest Wilderness, a bastion of hardwoods further insulated by a series of raggedly beautiful peaks that extend beyond the tree line and drain into the East Branch of the Pemigewasset River. If you make it past these welcome obstacles, prepare to enjoy New England backpacking at its best. The "Pemi" is so secluded, in fact, that I've run across many a moose, deer, even a fox and a black bear. Loggers removed almost the entire forest cover between 1890 and 1940, but 55 years of regeneration have eliminated virtually all signs of that era. The sharp, narrow Franconia Range and Twin Range form a horseshoe around the western portion of the area, with the Franconia threatening to challenge the Presidential Range for the title of Premier Peak. Mount Bond's crags and ledges demarcate the central northern boundary, and the Bondcliffs, just southwest of Mount

NEW HAMPSHIRE

Bond, quietly flaunt a vista across mountains and forests that show no trace of human interference. This is one of the few places in New Hampshire that can confess to boasting such a flawless view. The Wilderness flattens in the eastern portion, an area sometimes referred to as the Desolation Region for having withstood devastating logging operations. But despite the bad rap, the Desolation Region contains lovely Thoreau Falls, Ethan Pond, and Shoal Pond.

The Lincoln Woods Trail leaves a parking lot on the Kancamagus Highway, then crosses the East Branch of the Pemigewasset River on a 160-foot-long suspension bridge. At that point it turns east to enter the Wilderness and become the Wilderness Trail, which continues to travel upstream for a combined total of about nine miles along the East Branch. This trail, possibly the most trekked upon in the White Mountains, follows an old railway bed. Camping is forbidden within one-quarter mile of the Wilderness Trail. At least nine well-maintained trails leave the Wilderness Trail to provide foot access to the area. The Appalachian Trail follows the northern border.

Pemigewasset Essentials

Size: 45,000 acres.
Year Designated: 1984.
Location: Northern New Hampshire.
Easiest Access: From Lincoln, just off Interstate 93, drive along State Highway 112 (the Kancamagus Highway) east for approximately five miles to the 160-car parking lot and the Lincoln Woods Trailhead.
Season: Fall for the dramatic foliage. To help time your visit for peak color, phone (800) 258-3608 for a foliage update.
Wilderness Fees/Permits: None.
Maps: A map and thorough trail information are available in the *AMC White Mountain Guide* (Appalachian Mountain Club, 5 Joy Street, Boston, MA 02108; $16.95). DeLorme's *Trail Map & Guide to the White Mountain National Forest* also covers the area.
Management: Pemigewasset Ranger District, White Mountain National Forest, RFD 3, P.O. Box 15, Route 175, Plymouth, NH 03264; (603) 536-1310.

Presidential Range–Dry River Wilderness

South of Mount Washington, the Presidential Range embraces a few more granite "chiefs," including Mounts Monroe and Eisenhower. Beyond these peaks, the Presidential Range–Dry River Wilderness extends down the central valley of the Dry River to the Saco River, then farther south to numerous babbling brooks and the heavily forested lower mountains. Although the Dry River flows meagerly in the dry season, floods brought on by heavy rain and swift runoff have killed several hikers. Access to the Presidentials is arduous, with several water crossings required, but roughing your way up the Isolation Trail to the top of Mount Isolation (7.3 miles to the summit from State Highway 16) guarantees views well worth the exertion, as well as sweet, rare solitude.

You can access all other trails in the area from the 9.4-mile Dry River Trail, which constitutes the main pathway across the Wilderness and up Oakes Gulf and on to Mount Washington, outside the Wilderness area. Until the trail crawls above the tree line, it sticks close to an old railway bed and the river, always in heavy timber and scrub. The southern portion of the area is virtually trailless, steep, and much less visited.

NEW HAMPSHIRE

Presidential Range–Dry River Essentials

Size: 27,380 acres.
Year Designated: 1975; expanded in 1984.
Location: Northern New Hampshire.
Easiest Access: From North Conway, take U.S. 302 north for approximately 20 miles to the Dry River Campground. The Dry River Trailhead lies 0.3 miles north of the campground entrance on the east side of U.S. 302.
Season: Fall.
Wilderness Fees/Permits: None.

Maps: The *AMC White Mountain Guide* provides first-rate maps and trail information (Appalachian Mountain Club, 5 Joy Street, Boston, MA 02108; $16.95). DeLorme's *Trail Map & Guide to the White Mountain National Forest* also covers this Wilderness area.
Management: Saco Ranger District, White Mountain National Forest, RFD 1, Box 94, Conway, NH 03818; (603) 447-5448.

Sandwich Range Wilderness

Although this area may not rise to great New England heights, its peaks and cliff faces and long ridges are no less striking, embellished with a dense forest of tall hardwoods and brooks spilling over waterfalls. The country is relatively rugged, especially to the north, with climbs up the mountainsides qualifying as strenuous. The ruggedness mellows out toward the center and then sharpens again in the south. Despite gentler inclines, the more isolated central portion has fewer pathways.

Rough and shaggy Mount Paugus dominates the eastern arm of the Wilderness. Be cautious if you venture onto one of the slippery mountain ledges—the views are less appealing if you're nursing a sprained ankle. As a volunteer backcountry rescuer I've carried several hikers with broken ankles out of the Sandwich Range.

The Oliverian Brook Trail (4.4 miles), one of six trails that enter from the north, joins a network of heavily used paths, especially busy with cross-country skiers in winter. Trails lead to Mount Paugus, Mount Whiteface, Sandwich Mountain, and other Wilderness highlights.

Sandwich Range Essentials

Size: 25,000 acres.
Year Designated: 1984.
Location: Northern New Hampshire.
Easiest Access: From Conway, take State Highway 112 (the Kancamagus Highway) west for approximately 12 miles, to one mile past Bear Notch Road. The Oliverian Brook Trailhead is located on the south side of the highway.
Season: Fall.
Wilderness Fees/Permits: None.

Maps: The *AMC White Mountain Guide* (Appalachian Mountain Club, 5 Joy Street, Boston, MA 02108; $16.95) provides maps and trail information. DeLorme's *Trail Map & Guide to the White Mountain National Forest* covers the area.
Management: Saco Ranger District, White Mountain National Forest, RFD 1, Box 94, Conway, NH 03818; (603) 447-5448. Pemigewasset Ranger District, White Mountain National Forest, RFD 3, Box 15, Route 175, Plymouth, NH 03264; (603) 536-1310.

> "Wilderness settles peace on the soul because it needs no help; it is beyond human contrivance. Wilderness is a metaphor of unlimited opportunity, rising from the tribal memory of a time when humanity spread across the world . . . godstruck, firm in the belief that virgin land went on forever."
>
> —E. O. Wilson

NEW JERSEY

Total Wilderness areas: 2
Total Wilderness acreage: 10,341

When thoughts turn to New Jersey, they often beat a hasty retreat at the imagined crowds of people. Of the 50 states, New Jersey ranks 46th in size and ninth in population. That's not to say natural areas can't be found within these borders; in fact, both a coastal wetland and an inland swamp qualify as Wilderness.

Brigantine Wilderness

In 1984, to posthumously honor a New Jersey conservationist congressman, Brigantine National Wildlife Refuge (established in 1939) and Barnegat National Wildlife Refuge (established in 1967) were combined to create the Edwin B. Forsythe National Wildlife Refuge.

Although the refuge consists of more than 39,000 acres, less than 7,000 acres in the southern division (the Brigantine) qualify as Wilderness. This trailless area, a tidal wetland and shallow bay habitat, is one of the most active flyways for migratory waterbirds in North America. Bird-watchers, binoculars in hand, have zoomed in on close to 300 species, including Atlantic brant and American black duck.

The Wilderness also protects Holgate and Little Beaches, two of the few remaining barrier beaches in New Jersey. Grasses on these shores stabilize the fragile dunes and safeguard the rare piping plover, black skimmer, and least tern.

The refuge is open during daylight hours, but there are prohibitions on camping, fires, horses, kite flying, swimming, flower picking, or anything else that might endanger the wildlife and their habitat. During nesting season (mid-April to mid-July), the area is closed to all public use. In the same protective vein, access to some portions is restricted to people with special-use permits for research and education.

NEW JERSEY

Brigantine Essentials

Size: 6,681 acres.
Year Designated: 1975.
Location: Coastal southeastern New Jersey.
Easiest Access: From the junction of U.S. 9 and U.S. 30 northwest of Atlantic City, take U.S. 9 north for about 4.5 miles to Oceanville. When you reach Great Creek Road, turn east and continue a short distance to the refuge office.
Season: Wildlife viewing is best in spring and fall. In warmer months, you may encounter swarms of biting insects.
Wilderness Fees/Permits: A refuge entrance fee is required every day at the Brigantine Division. Children under 16 may enter for free. Check with the refuge manager for permission to visit the Wilderness.
Maps: A free map is available from the refuge manager.
Management: Edwin B. Forsythe National Wildlife Refuge, Great Creek Road, P.O. Box 72, Oceanville, NJ 08231; (609) 652-1665.

Great Swamp Wilderness

About 25,000 years ago the Wisconsin glacier receded from northern New Jersey, leaving extensive wetlands in its icy wake. The glacier's southernmost point became Great Swamp, which is far more attractive than its name might imply. With cattail marshes, wet grassland, swampy woodland, and ridges thick with oak, beech, and laurel, Great Swamp provides a home for mice, moles, skunks, raccoons, otters, foxes, and white-tailed deer. Migratory birds see Great Swamp as a "nest and rest" (bird-watchers have identified 222 species). Numerous reptiles and amphibians have taken up residence, including rare bog turtles, wood turtles, and blue-spotted salamanders.

Almost half of the Great Swamp National Wildlife Refuge, the eastern portion, is designated Wilderness. About eight miles of trail provide access during daylight hours only, and camping and picnicking are not permitted.

Great Swamp Essentials

Size: 3,660 acres.
Year Designated: 1968.
Location: Northern central New Jersey.
Easiest Access: Great Swamp lies about 26 miles west of Times Square in New York City. Take the Lincoln Tunnel to the New Jersey Turnpike, then take Exit 14 to Interstate 78 west followed by Interstate 287 north. From 287 take Exit 26 at Basking Ridge onto North Maple Avenue, then turn left on Madisonville Road (which becomes Lee's Hill Road). To reach the refuge headquarters, turn right on Long Hill Road, then right on White Bridge Road, and right again on Pleasant Plains Road.
Season: Spring and fall for the birds. From May to September the area is "swamped" with biting insects.
Wilderness Fees/Permits: None.
Maps: Free maps are available from the refuge manager.
Management: Great Swamp National Wildlife Refuge, 152 Pleasant Plains Road, Basking Ridge, NJ 07920; (201) 425-1222.

> "A thing is right only when it tends to preserve the integrity, stability and beauty of the community; and the community includes the soil, water, fauna and flora, as well as the people."
>
> —Aldo Leopold

NEW MEXICO

Total Wilderness areas: 24
Total Wilderness acreage: 1,609,797

Although references to New Mexico may call to mind images of cacti and parched land, only the south and west parts of the state can own up to having real deserts, or at least small portions of the Chihuahuan and Great Basin Deserts. The southern Rocky Mountains anchor central and western New Mexico, with splendid mountains characterizing more than half the state. About one-third of New Mexico lies on federal ground, primarily where the Rockies stake their claim, including roughly nine million acres of national forestland. Most of the state's eastern third lies in flat rangeland. There are 16 Wilderness areas in national forests, 4 on BLM land, 2 on wildlife refuges, and 2 managed by the National Park Service.

Aldo Leopold Wilderness

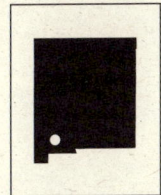

This Wilderness, which straddles the crest of the Black Range and contains the most rugged and wild portion of these mountains, pays tribute to one of the greatest pioneers of Wilderness preservation. Only Forest Service Road 150 separates it from the even larger Gila Wilderness (see below), recognized on June 3, 1924, as the world's first designated Wilderness area, a direct result of Leopold's efforts.

The Black Range shoots out of the desert sands in a network of deep canyons and precipitous timbered ridges, rincons, and forested benches—a land of superlative beauty and unbroken serenity. Juniper, piñon pine, and oak dominate up to about 7,000 feet, at which point other pines, fir, spruce, and aspen take over the woodland.

Vista points here sometimes drop off as much as 1,000 feet to rivers and streams verdantly outlined by cottonwoods, willows, and elders. And while numerous springs usually

NEW MEXICO

bubble to the surface throughout the Wilderness year-round, the streams dry up from time to time.

One thing that never dwindles is the wealth of critters, from bats to bears, coyotes, foxes, skunks, raccoons, coatimundis, ringtail cats, weasels, bobcats, mountain lions, squirrels, rats, mice, and voles, along with a multitude of songbirds, plus turtles, frogs, lizards, and snakes.

The Continental Divide cuts across the center ridgeline of the Wilderness, and a 33-mile-plus section (with many miles of trails) of the Continental Divide National Scenic Trail (CDT) forms a portion of the southern boundary. Consider devoting a large chunk of time to exploring this area—when you discover the bounty that awaits you won't regret it.

Aldo Leopold Essentials

Size: 201,966 acres.
Year Designated: 1980.
Location: Southwestern New Mexico.
Easiest Access: From San Lorenzo, take State Highway 152 north and west for about 18 miles to Emory Pass, and hike north on the CDT. You'll enter the Wilderness in about two miles.
Season: March through October, with spring and fall being the best times to visit.
Wilderness Fees/Permits: None.
Maps: A Wilderness map is available for $4 from the district rangers.
Management: Black Range Ranger District, Gila National Forest, 1804 Date Street, P.O. Box 431, Truth or Consequences, NM 87901; (505) 894-6677. Mimbres Ranger District, Gila National Forest, P.O. Box 79, Mimbres, NM 88049; (505) 536-2250.

Apache Kid Wilderness

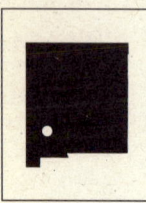

Angered by his relentless raids, local ranchers hunted down and killed the Apache Kid on these grounds. To mark the site of the Kid's undoing, the vengeful posse blazed a tree, the hacked remains of which you can see to this day.

Narrow, steep canyons bisect the peaks of the southern San Mateo Mountains, where elevations exceed 10,000 feet. The vegetation is typical of the region, with piñon-juniper woodland down low, spruce and fir and aspen up high, and ponderosa pine in between. Human visitors are few, but other creatures commonly seen making their way across this rugged terrain range from Coue's white-tailed deer and mule deer to elk, black bears, bobcats, cougars, antelope, javelina, coyotes, rabbits, squirrels, and quail.

Hiking is easy if you manage to stay on the 68-mile trail system (the pathways are not always maintained). The main trail, which leads to the Kid's gravesite, follows about 13 miles of mountain crest, which translates into ample photo opportunities. Water is limited to less than a dozen semi-dependable springs, most of which dry up in summer. July and August rains keep small streams periodically filled.

NEW MEXICO

Apache Kid Essentials

Size: 44,650 acres.
Year Designated: 1980.
Location: Western central New Mexico.
Easiest Access: From Truth or Consequences, take Interstate 25 north approximately 14 miles. Take Exit 89 and the frontage road north for four more miles, then turn west on Forest Service Rd. 139 and continue to Springtime Campground and the crest trailhead, about 17 miles.

Season: Spring offers the most agreeable weather and the best opportunities to see the running springs of water.
Wilderness Fees/Permits: None.
Maps: A Wilderness map is available for $4 from the district ranger.
Management: Magdalena Ranger District, Cibola National Forest, Box 45, Magdalena, NM 87825; (505) 854-2281.

Bandelier Wilderness

From the ninth to the thirteenth centuries, a large population of prehistoric people (known today as the Anasazi) flourished among the cream and tan cliffs and piñon-juniper-forested mesas of the Four Corners region. The dramatic setting, now Bandelier National Monument, showcases deep gorges sculpted by running water, and canyons slashing the slopes of the Pajarita Plateau. The people eventually disappeared, but they left a fine legacy: exquisite ruins in a desert oasis. Access to the oasis, known as Frijoles Canyon, is easy from within the monument.

With 90 percent of the monument beyond the oasis designated Wilderness—equal to some 50 square miles with 70-plus miles of trails—Bandelier offers a mixed bag of scenery. Hikers will inevitably encounter challenging terrain, sweeping mesa tops, lush canyons, and isolated ruins. Hiking choices vary wildly: three miles one-way to the gorges of Alamo Canyon; five miles one-way to the pueblo ruins of Yapashi; a 20-mile loop to the Stone Lions Shrine and the Painted Cave; and about eight miles one-way to the densely forested upper Frijoles Canyon along El Rito de los Frijoles (Bean Creek), where a stay at a silent camp under tall ponderosa pines has become one of my fondest memories. Three westbound trails leave the monument to enter Dome Wilderness (see below). Pets and campfires are not allowed in the monument's Wilderness.

Bandelier Essentials

Size: 23,267 acres.
Year Designated: 1976.
Location: Northern central New Mexico.
Easiest Access: From Santa Fe, take U.S. 285 north to State Highway 502, approximately 16 miles. To get to the visitors center, travel west on State Highway 502 for about 11 miles, then continue south on State Highway 4 for another 14 miles.

Season: Spring and fall have the most pleasant weather.
Wilderness Fees/Permits: An entrance fee of $5 per car or $3 per individual is charged. A free overnight backcountry permit is required.
Maps: Trails Illustrated's *Topographic Map and Hiking Guide to Bandelier* is available for $7.95 at the visitors center.
Management: Bandelier National Monument, Los Alamos, NM 87544; (505) 672-3861.

NEW MEXICO

Bisti Wilderness

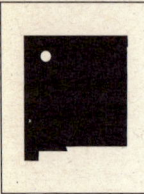

An eerie otherworldliness surrounds Bisti Badlands, especially when the moon casts shadows across the hoodoos, weird rock formations with mazelike passages. Difficult as it is to believe, this stark landscape, once buried beneath an ancient sea, used to have ample water. As the water slowly receded, prehistoric animals roamed about, living off of each other and the lush foliage that flourished along the many riverbanks. Eventually, the water disappeared, leaving behind a 1,400-foot-thick layer of jumbled sandstone, shale, and coal that lay undisturbed for 50 million years. Then, 6,000 years ago, the last ice age receded, exposing fossils and eroding the rock into the fantastic hoodoos you see today. The soil underfoot now lies soft and yielding, wrinkled like the surface of stale popcorn. But the ominous silence reflects the absence of wildlife, for very few animals—save a handful of lizards, snakes, tarantulas, and scorpions, and an occasional hawk or eagle—have taken up residence on this somewhat forbidding land.

Camping is unrestricted here on New Mexico's smallest Wilderness, but you'll find no water, no trails, and virtually no shady escape from the relentless sun. Campfires are not permitted. From the parking lot, the land lies flat across an expanse of desert that rises suddenly into convolutions with hidden and twisty paths carved by erosion. After squirming through one narrow passageway after another, you come upon an explosion of hoodoos stretched above and before you like a sculpted playground on a world you never knew existed. I found a map and compass unnecessary in this area.

Bisti Essentials

Size: 3,968 acres.
Year Designated: 1984.
Location: Northwestern New Mexico.
Easiest Access: From Interstate 40, approximately 30 miles east of Gallup, take State Highway 371 north for about 70 miles (46 miles past Crown Point) until a BLM sign directs you to turn east on a gravel road. The gravel road leads about three miles to a parking lot.
Season: April and May are pleasant, but fall is the best time to visit.
Wilderness Fees/Permits: None.
Maps: USGS topographic maps are Alamo Mesa West, Bisti Trading Post, and Tanner Lake.
Management: BLM Farmington District Office, 1235 La Plata Highway, Farmington, NM 87401; (505) 599-8900.

Blue Range Wilderness

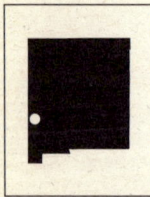

Combine New Mexico's Blue Ridge Wilderness with Arizona's Blue Range Primitive Area and you have two pieces of earth that encompass a wild, generally dry, and seemingly endless expanse of rough but beautiful terrain. The state line is all that separates the two areas, with New Mexico's Wilderness tucked into the Blue Range Mountains and halved by the Mogollon Rim, a dramatic edge of the Colorado Plateau that runs east to west.

Grassland foothills rise to juniper woodland and higher up to peaks forested in ponderosa pine, spruce, and fir. On occasion, just when you can't see the trees for the forest, the dense woods will give way to a mountain meadow or a cool aspen glade. The rock-walled canyons are narrow and steep, sometimes plummeting as much as 1,000 feet from their forested rims. By contrast, the sweeping reaches of stark land offer tremendous solitude and soul-stretching quiet, a silence broken only visually by ragged rock towers.

Hikers may be discouraged by Forest Service reports that the few trails of the Blue Range have no dependable, potable water source, and the fact that trail markers aren't always easy to follow. If that doesn't deter you, consider crossing the Wilderness via the 8.8-mile WS Mountain Trail, which starts at Pueblo Park Campground, continues along the rugged Pueblo Creek and Bear Creek drainages, and ends in Arizona. Chances are you won't run into a single person, and there's something to be said for that.

Blue Range Essentials

Size: 30,000 acres.
Year Designated: 1980.
Location: Western New Mexico.
Easiest Access: From Silver City, take U.S. 180 north. Drive approximately 85 miles, then turn west on Forest Service Road 232 and continue 5.6 miles to Pueblo Park Campground.
Season: Spring, summer, and fall.
Wilderness Fees/Permits: None.
Maps: USGS topographic maps covering the trail system are Blue SE and Saliz Pass.
Management: Luna Ranger District, Gila National Forest, Box 91, Luna, NM 87824; (505) 547-2611.

Bosque del Apache Wilderness

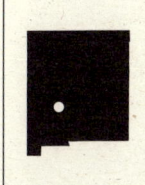

On a quiet day in November you'll hear the haunting cry of sandhill cranes echoing across the marsh and grasslands of 57,191-acre Bosque del Apache National Wildlife Refuge. Amazing to think that in 1939, when the refuge was established, the crane count averaged a sobering 17. That figure has since soared to 17,000. Add to that impressive tally 30,000 snow geese, 20,000-plus ducks (at least 14 species), endangered whooping cranes, Canada geese, Gambel's quail, pheasants, roadrunners, and more than 300 other winged species and banner birding is a given.

A few landlubbers have strayed into this bona fide bird society, including mule deer, coyotes, porcupines, and western diamondback rattlesnakes. If your eyes aren't glued to binoculars, you may want to study the thirteenth-century pueblo ruins of the Piro Indians or the vestiges of El Camino Real ("The Royal Road"), the route between Mexico and Santa Fe from the late 1500s to the mid-1800s. The refuge, sheltered by the Magdalena Mountains, is split in two by the hushed flow of the Rio Grande. Apache Indians once camped along the river in cottonwood and willow bosques, little stands of trees long since lost to human development.

The three designated Wilderness areas within the refuge are the 5,289-acre Chupadera Unit, walled off from the rest of the refuge by Interstate 25; the 5,139-acre Indian Well Unit, just across the interstate from the Chupadera Unit; and the Little San Pascual Unit, which covers 19,859 acres just east of the Rio Grande.

The units hold in common a lack of water, but otherwise offer distinctive terrains. Arroyos divide the Chupadera's series of small ridges and mesas, while Indian Well has rounded mountains along its western side and arroyos and mesas on its gentler eastern side. The largest unit rolls gently across desert terrain, sharpening to a peak at Little San Pascual Mountain and again at San Pascualito Mountain. Day hiking is allowed, but campers must obtain advance permission, usually granted only to educational groups.

NEW MEXICO

Bosque del Apache Essentials

Size: 30,287 acres.
Year Designated: 1975.
Location: Central New Mexico.
Easiest Access: From Albuquerque, take Interstate 25 south for 90 miles. To get to the ranger headquarters, take Exit 139 east at San Antonio, then turn south on State Highway 1 and continue eight miles.
Season: The most fascinating birds show up from November through early February.
Wilderness Fees/Permits: An entry fee of $2 per vehicle is charged.
Maps: A free map is available from the refuge.
Management: Bosque del Apache National Wildlife Refuge, P.O. Box 1246, Socorro, NM 87801; (505) 835-1828.

Capitan Mountains Wilderness

The birthplace of Smokey the Bear, discovered here as a cub in 1951, is a rugged piece of mountain real estate that straddles something that's unusual in New Mexico: an east-west-running range. Numerous canyons cut into the north side of the rocky range, while rocky outcroppings distinguish the region to the south. The terrain flattens now and then along the main ridge, and then opens out into meadows and groves of aspen.

The Wilderness measures 12 miles long and two to six miles wide, with elevations varying from about 5,500 feet near the eastern boundary to 10,083 feet on Capitan Peak (sometimes called El Capitan Mountain). At the lower elevations, piñon and juniper woodland flourishes, with ponderosa pine making an appearance midslope, followed by mixed conifers (Douglas fir, Engelmann spruce, corkbark fir, and pine) on the main ridge.

The original Smokey, the world-famous symbol of forest fire prevention, lies buried in nearby Capitan, but plenty of his kinfolk still reside in these woods. Other denizens include large populations of mule deer and wild turkey, both of which attract hunters in the fall (as do the black bears). Anglers can try to catch small brook trout at Pine Lodge, Copeland Canyon, Kelly Canyon, and Seven Cabins Canyon.

Of the dozen or so hikes in the Wilderness, 8.2-mile Summit Trail follows the main ridge and probably offers some of the best views. Foot traffic is usually heaviest on the Capitan Peak Trail, which takes 5.7 miles of steep switchbacks to reach El Capitan's summit.

Capitan Mountains Essentials

Size: 34,513 acres.
Year Designated: 1980.
Location: Southern central New Mexico.
Easiest Access: From Roswell, follow U.S. 380 west for just over 40 miles. Turn north on State Route 368 and continue about 17 miles to the Capitan Peak Trailhead.
Season: Spring and fall. Summers are hot and winters usually cold with snow.
Wilderness Fees/Permits: None.
Maps: A Wilderness map is available for $4 from the district ranger.
Management: Smokey Bear Ranger District, Lincoln National Forest, 901 Mechem Drive, Ruidoso, NM 88345; (505) 257-4095.

NEW MEXICO

Carlsbad Caverns Wilderness

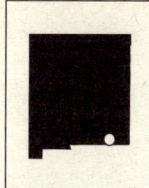

With at least 76 caves, including one of the largest underground chambers ever discovered, 46,775-acre Carlsbad Caverns National Park deserves its international reputation. Way back when, the limestone of the caverns was laid down beneath the edge of an ancient sea and then covered with eons' worth of sediment. Cracks in the sediment eventually allowed water loaded with carbonic acid to filter in and dissolve the limestone into colorful caves filled with elaborate formations. Be sure to dress warmly before venturing into these chilly underground caves. I also recommend rubber-soled shoes for walking on the slick surfaces.

The landscape above the caverns is just as rugged, with steep, rocky ridges and craggy canyons. Elevations range from 3,600 feet to 6,350 feet, providing ample room and variety for flora and fauna. The species tally so far is 740 plants, 273 resident and transient birds, 44 reptiles and amphibians, and 59 mammals. The latter includes the main attraction, an astounding colony of 300,000 Mexican free-tailed bats who live in the caves from late spring through early fall, emerging in a cloud at dusk for their moonlit feeding frenzy. And don't worry that a furry bat will try to feed on you. The only nourishment they're interested in comes in the form of flying insects. Almost three-fourths of the park, the southwestern portion, has been designated Wilderness. Trails provide foot access.

Carlsbad Caverns Essentials

Size: 33,125 acres.
Year Designated: 1978.
Location: Southeastern New Mexico.
Easiest Access: From Carlsbad, take U.S. 62/180 south about 20 miles to the park entrance and a visitors center.
Season: The caverns stay open year-round, but you should go in late spring and early fall for the bats and accommodating weather. Winters are usually mild but can turn suddenly cold.
Wilderness Fees/Permits: A variable park fee is charged, usually $5 or $6. Some cavern tours are offered for an additional charge. Overnight backcountry permits are required and available at the visitors center.
Maps: A map is available from the park ranger.
Management: Carlsbad Caverns National Park, 3225 National Parks Highway, Carlsbad, NM 88220; (505) 785-2232.

Cebolla Wilderness

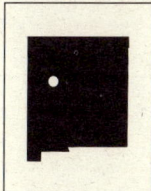

Part of El Malpais National Conservation Area, Cebolla Wilderness lies just across State Highway 117 from West Malpais Wilderness (see below) but offers easier traveling than the ominously raw volcanic terrain of the badlands. Cebolla shares its eastern border with the Acoma Indian Reservation, but you should avoid crossing the border without first checking with the reservation manager. Abandoned roads provide effortless hiking up Cebolla Canyon, Sand Canyon, and Armijo Canyon, all of which feature sandstone bluffs and sandy side washes beneath high mesas. Look for evidence of past habitation, from ancient petroglyphs to the ruins of Depression-era homesteads. La Ventana Natural Arch, eroded from sandstone laid down when dinosaurs ruled this territory, anchors the northern portion of what is now primarily forested rimrock. Carry plenty of water, as you won't find any here.

NEW MEXICO

Cebolla Essentials

Size: 60,000 acres.
Year Designated: 1987.
Location: Western central New Mexico.
Easiest Access: From Interstate 40, about five miles east of Grants, take State Highway 117 south another 17 miles to a marked parking lot for Cebolla Canyon.
Season: Spring and fall.
Wilderness Fees/Permits: A backcountry permit is required. Check in at El Malpais Information Center, 620 East Santa Fe Street, Grants, NM 87020; (505) 285-5406.
Maps: USGS topographic maps are Arrosa Ranch, Bonine Canyon, Cebollita Peak, Laguna Honda, Los Pilares, North Pasture, and Sand Canyon.
Management: El Malpais National Conservation Area, P.O. Box 846, Grants, NM 87020; (505) 285-5406.

Chama River Canyon Wilderness

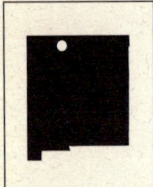

The Wild and Scenic Chama River, popular among river rafters and canoeists, runs through six miles of the Wilderness. Its beauty is so impressive that most people don't bother visiting the relatively unspectacular grassland that dominates the upland portion of the area. Trail access is poor here above the colorful sandstone bluffs and lovely rock formations that rise to high rims on both riverbanks.

Water levels reflect releases from the upstream El Vado Lake Dam, but you can usually float the river, with portages, all the way from the Colorado border to the Rio Grande through the rainbow-hued Chama River Canyon. Backpackers can hike along portions of the Chama River, then pitch their tents in a secluded wooded campsite above one of the canyon's high-water beaches. Trout often flourish in the river (so bring your gear), and onshore residents include mule deer, black bears, elk, coyotes, and mountain lions. Varying canyon elevations also provide a wide range of vegetation, from low-lying piñon-juniper woodland to ponderosa pine and fir. Most of the Wilderness lies in Santa Fe National Forest, with a portion in Carson National Forest.

Chama River Canyon Essentials

Size: 50,260 acres.
Year Designated: 1978.
Location: Northern New Mexico.
Easiest Access: Head north on U.S. 84 from Santa Fe. After about 90 miles, turn west on State Route 112 (El Vado Reservoir Road) and drive another 14 miles to El Vado Dam, the most popular put-in for the river. The Wilderness boundary lies several miles downstream.
Season: Late April through early July to run the river.
Wilderness Fees/Permits: None for most of the Wilderness, but to use the river you must get a permit from the BLM Taos District Office; phone (505) 758-8851. Applications must be received by March 15.
Maps: Contact the U.S. Forest Service, Public Affairs Office, 517 Gold Avenue SW, Albuquerque, NM 87102; (505) 842-3292. This office sells maps of all the national forestland in New Mexico.
Management: Coyote Ranger District, Santa Fe National Forest, P.O. Box 160, Coyote, NM 87012; (505) 638-5526. Canjilon Ranger District, Carson National Forest, P.O. Box 488, Canjilon, NM 87515; (505) 684-2486.

NEW MEXICO

Cruces Basin Wilderness

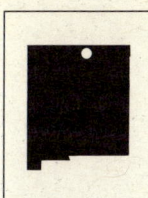

Some of New Mexico's most pristine high country, as of yet virtually undiscovered, lies in the center of the state, just south of Colorado. I've been to Cruces Basin Wilderness a number of times, only to find boundless solitude and lonely, expansive beauty.

A mountain plateau sets the stage, with backdrops ranging from ridges covered in spruce, fir, and aspen up to 10,900 feet to a grass carpet that extends down to 8,600 feet. About 2,000 elk graze here in summer.

Just southeast of northeast-flowing Beaver Creek is San Antonio Mountain, the largest free-standing mountain (not a part of a range) in the Lower 48. You will find few trails.

Cruces Basin Essentials

Size: 18,000 acres.
Year Designated: 1980.
Location: Northern New Mexico.
Easiest Access: From Tres Piedras, take U.S. 285 north approximately 18 miles. Just before you reach San Antonio Mountain, turn west on Forest Service Road 87. Continue 20 miles to the campground on the southern boundary.
Season: Spring through fall.
Wilderness Fees/Permits: None.
Maps: A topographic Wilderness map is available for $2 from the district ranger.
Management: Tres Piedras Ranger District, Carson National Forest, P.O. Box 728, Tres Piedras, NM 87577; (505) 758-8678.

De-Na-Zin Wilderness

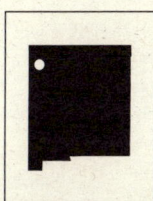

De-Na-Zin Wilderness preserves badlands, but it achieves a greater natural diversity than Bisti Wilderness (see above), its neighbor to the east. You won't find many animals in this Wilderness, just rolling grasslands and slopes of piñon and juniper mixed here and there with yucca, cacti, sagebrush, snakeweed, and Mormon tea. The intricately wind-carved sandstone bluffs, spires, and mushrooms display a palette of creams, buffs, maroons, and purples that put on a colorful sideshow at dusk and dawn.

Precipitation in this Wilderness averages a mere eight inches a year, and that typically holds off until July and August temperatures rise to screaming highs. When a downpour does occur, the soil, typically baked to ceramic hardness by the sun, softens into a slippery, yielding substance. Cottontail rabbits, coyotes, badgers, and prairie dogs have been able to eke out a living in this unusually harsh environment, and the avian life is downright prosperous, with piñon jays, ravens, and, of course, several species of birds of prey. Although I've seen evidence of heavy deer traffic, I have never seen a deer here. Researchers believe that dinosaurs passed into extinction around these parts, so keep an eye out for fossils (if you find one, remember that removing fossils is illegal).

Although there are no formal trails at De-Na-Zin, the hiking is easy along the washes and an old jeep track leading into the region from the parking lot. Elevation averages around 6,300 feet, and the most striking scenery is in the southern two-thirds of the area. The Wilderness boundaries enclose three parcels of private Navajo land. Carry a map, a compass, and plenty of water. Backpacking and horsepacking are unrestricted, but campfires are forbidden. Chances are you won't encounter a soul here.

NEW MEXICO

De-Na-Zin Essentials

Size: 23,872 acres.
Year Designated: 1984.
Location: Northwestern New Mexico.
Easiest Access: From Bloomfield, take State Highway 44 south about 30 miles. When you reach County Road 7500 (look for El Huerfano Trading Post), turn southwest and continue 11 more miles until you find a marked place to park.
Season: Late fall to early spring. Winters can be surprisingly cold.
Wilderness Fees/Permits: None, but sections are closed seasonally to protect nesting raptors. Check with the BLM before you enter this Wilderness.
Maps: USGS topographic maps are Alamo Mesa East, Alamo West, and Huerfano Trading Post SW.
Management: BLM Farmington District Office, 1235 La Plata Highway, Farmington, NM 87401; (505) 599-8900.

Dome Wilderness

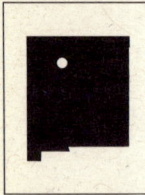

Dome Wilderness seems dwarfed by the adjacent Bandelier Wilderness (see above), but sometimes the best gifts come in small packages. In this case, be prepared for primitive canyonlands and prehistoric ruins (and take care not to disturb the latter).

You'll also find an abundance of wildflowers and strawberries in spring, countered, unfortunately, by hordes of horseflies and deerflies. From high points near Saint Peters Dome you'll be able to see all the way east to the Sangre de Cristo Mountains and south to the Cochita Lake region. Elevations peak at 8,200 feet, then drop to 5,800 feet at Sanchez Canyon.

The Saint Peters Dome Trail (6.1 miles) gives access to this Wilderness, starting on the north end near the Dome and losing elevation as it runs south past canyon walls and through stands of large pines, then across Sanchez Creek, a fishless stream that endures periods of extremely low water. The Capulin Trail (two miles) also begins in the northern portion of the area, but it runs east past pueblo ruins and into Bandelier Wilderness before veering south to return to Dome Wilderness and hook up with the Saint Peters Dome Trail. The Capulin Trail follows a creek with year-round water and cutthroat trout.

Dome Essentials

Size: 5,200 acres.
Year Designated: 1980.
Location: Northern central New Mexico.
Easiest Access: At the junction of State Routes 4 and 126, take State Route 4 east (toward Los Alamos) for approximately 18 miles. Turn south on Forest Service Road 289 and continue for another six miles, then turn east on Forest Service Road 142. Continue three more miles to the Dome Lookout Tower and the Saint Peters Dome Trailhead.
Season: Spring and fall.
Wilderness Fees/Permits: None.
Maps: USGS topographic maps are Bland, Canada, Chochiti Dam, and Frijoles.
Management: Jemez Ranger District, Santa Fe National Forest, Jemez Springs, NM 87025; (505) 829-3535.

Gila Wilderness

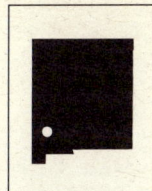

On June 3, 1924, at Aldo Leopold's insistence, Gila became the world's first designated Wilderness area (and also New Mexico's largest Wilderness). Today this is one of the best destinations for backpackers in America.

High mesas, rolling hills, and deep canyons distinguish the eastern portions, as do piñon and juniper woodland and a few grassland areas. Ponderosa pines blanket the central portion, with sheer cliffs outlining the Gila River. The west and southwest portions boast high mountains, particularly the Mogollon Range, with elevations up to 10,895 feet and steep canyons carved from the drainages of Turkey Creek and Mogollon Creek. The star attraction, Gila Cliff Dwellings National Monument, is in the heart of the area.

Even if you choose to skip the cliff dwellings, you will almost undoubtedly find ruins of the prehistoric Indians who once lived here. Disturbing these sites is strictly prohibited.

The three forks and the Gila River run year-round, with creeks, springs, and tanks serving as alternative water sources. Searching for hot springs is worthwhile, but don't dunk your head in the water if you find one—some of the springs contain a microorganism that can enter the brain and cause death.

An extensive trail system provides access to the Wilderness: the 36-mile Middle Fork Trail follows the Middle Fork of the Gila River from the Gila Visitors Center to Snow Lake. The West Fork Trail follows the West Fork of the Gila River from the Gila Cliff Dwellings (near the visitors center) to Willow Creek, about 33.25 miles.

Winter temperatures are mild during the day, but they fall to well below freezing at night. July and August suffer the hottest temperatures, along with frequent heavy rains that can produce flash floods.

Gila Essentials

Size: 557,819 acres.
Year Designated: 1964; expanded in 1980.
Location: Southwestern New Mexico.
Easiest Access: From Silver City, take State Highway 15 44 miles north to the visitors center at Gila Cliff Dwellings National Monument.
Season: May and June attract the most backpackers. Fall brings hunters.
Wilderness Fees/Permits: None.
Maps: A Wilderness map is available for $4 from the Gila National Forest, or from the Gila Visitors Center, Box 100, Silver City, NM 88061; (505) 536-9461.
Management: Gila National Forest, 3005 East Camino del Bosque, Silver City, NM 88061; (505) 388-8201.

Latir Peak Wilderness

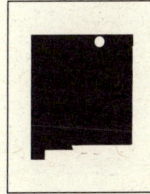

This remote, seldom-seen area is a land of lakes and streams, with deep forest cover interrupted only by pleasant meadows and alpine tundra on the northern portion's Latir Mesa. With three peaks exceeding 12,500 feet in elevation, including a portion of the Sangre de Cristo Mountains, this Wilderness showcases the very finest of New Mexico's high country.

An abundance of southern Rocky Mountain wildlife takes advantage of the region's riches, including mule deer, black bears, badgers, beavers, bobcats, coyotes, ferrets, foxes, mountain lions, marmots, martens, and muskrats. Heart Lake, named for its romantic shape, is the source of Cabresto Creek.

The Lake Fork Trail is the most popular of the main trails. It begins at Cabresto Lake and continues five miles to Heart Lake, which is 11,520 feet above sea level. More ambitious hikers can head five miles past Heart Lake to enter the magnificent country of Latir Peak and the alpine mesas. Two other trails, Midnight and Bull Creek, run west and receive much less use.

Latir Peak Essentials

Size: 20,000 acres.
Year Designated: 1980.
Location: Northern New Mexico.
Easiest Access: From Questa, take Highway 38 east for two-tenths of a mile. Drive six miles north on State Highway 563 (Cabresto Road). Turn east on Forest Service Road 134A for two miles of rough driving to Cabresto Lake.
Season: Summer and fall.
Wilderness Fees/Permits: None.
Maps: A topographic Wilderness map is available for $4 from the district ranger.
Management: Questa Ranger District, Carson National Forest, P.O. Box 110, Questa, NM 87556; (505) 586-0520.

Manzano Mountain Wilderness

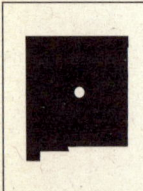

Don't let this area deceive you. It looks devoid of scenery from a distance, but is full of surprises the farther in you hike. The same held true in the early 1700s, when explorers visiting a small village on the eastern edge of these mountains discovered very old *manzanos* (apple trees), a fruit tree not native to this country. No one has ever figured out where these trees came from, but the name stayed with the region.

Spread out across the western slope of the Manzano Mountain Range, this Wilderness varies in elevation from about 6,000 feet to 10,098 feet atop Manzano Peak. Piñon and juniper grow low, gradually submitting to ponderosa pine and then spruce, fir, and aspen higher up. This is steep and rugged terrain for the most part, cut with canyons and marked with outcroppings of rock. Thousands of raptors migrate along the Manzanos in spring and fall as they work their way between Canada and Mexico.

More than 64 miles of a well-developed trail system provide access to the Wilderness, although the lack of reliable water sources and campsites may explain why so few people take advantage. One hike starts at Fourth of July Campground near the eastern boundary and leads 1.5 miles to the crest of the area. From there, a trail runs along the crest for 22 miles to Manzano Peak.

Manzano Mountain Essentials

Size: 36,650 acres.
Year Designated: 1978.
Location: Central New Mexico.
Easiest Access: From Mountainair, take State Secondary Highway 55 north to Tajique, a distance of approximately 20 miles. When you get to Forest Service Road 55, turn west and drive to Fourth of July Campground, approximately eight miles.
Season: Spring and fall.
Wilderness Fees/Permits: None.
Maps: A Wilderness map is available for $4 from the district rangers.
Management: Mountainair Ranger District, Cibola National Forest, P.O. Box 69, Mountainair, NM 87036; (505) 847-2990. Sandia Ranger District, Cibola National Forest, 11776 Highway 337, Tijeras, NM 87059; (505) 281-3304.

NEW MEXICO

Pecos Wilderness

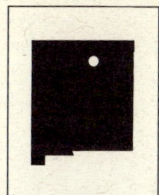

To date, this is my favorite piece of New Mexico. Unfortunately, people who aren't as careful as they should be about leaving no trace seem to feel the same way. Abuse has led to restrictions pertaining to camping on most of the lakeshores.

Aside from that, at least 15 of the lakes offer first-rate fishing, as do 150-plus miles of sparkling streams. These waters head the Wild and Scenic Pecos River. Here at the southern end of the Sangre de Cristo Mountains, elevations range from 8,400 feet to 13,103 feet atop South Truchas Peak, the state's second highest point.

The scenery varies (although it's always extraordinary) from 100-foot-drop waterfalls and crumbled talus slopes to dramatic rock cliffs, towering peaks, and wildflower meadows best caught in July and August. Engelmann spruce, corkbark fir, ponderosa pine, Douglas fir, white fir, limber pine, bristlecone pine, and aspen pack the forest. Equally diverse is the wildlife, with enough elk, deer, bears, and turkeys to satisfy any hunter. Rocky Mountain bighorn sheep have actually grown tame enough that they feel comfortable walking into camps in the Pecos.

The northern section includes about 25,000 acres in Carson National Forest, the least visited portion of the Wilderness. The rest of this large area lies in Santa Fe National Forest, and accommodates close to 500,000 trekkers per year. Most hikers come during the summer months to explore the extensive system of at least 34 trails.

From Santa Barbara Campground (with campsites and corrals) near the northern boundary, the Middle Fork Trail travels 12 miles up to the Santa Barbara Divide. The Middle Fork Trail accesses the East Fork and West Fork Trails, both of which run about 12 miles to the divide. Off-trail you'll discover virtually unlimited amounts of untrammeled terrain.

Pecos Essentials

Size: 223,333 acres.
Year Designated: 1964; expanded in 1980.
Location: Northern central New Mexico.
Easiest Access: From State Highway 68 between Taos and Chimayo, take State Highway 75 about 17 miles east to Penasco. Turn south on State Highway 73 (Forest Service Road 116) and continue a few miles to Santa Barbara Campground.
Season: Spring through fall.
Wilderness Fees/Permits: None.
Maps: A Wilderness map is available for $4 from the district ranger.
Management: Pecos/Las Vegas Ranger District, Santa Fe National Forest, P.O. Drawer 429, Pecos, NM 87552; (505) 757-6121. Espanola Ranger District, Santa Fe National Forest, P.O. Box R, 222 Los Alamos Highway, Espanola, NM 87532; (505) 753-7331. Camino Real Ranger District, Carson National Forest, P.O. Box 68, Penasco, NM 87553; (505) 587-2255.

Salt Creek Wilderness

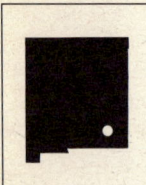

Migratory waterfowl may consider this a sufficient winter home, but birders will see it as paradise. From October through February, the seasonal wetlands of 24,526-acre Bitter Lake National Wildlife Refuge play host to 5,000 to 20,000 ducks, 20,000 to 40,000 geese, as many as 70,000 cranes, and countless white pelicans and snowy egrets. The uplands, by contrast, are chock-full of quail, roadrunners, pheasant, desert cottontail rabbits, and black-tailed jackrabbits. More secretive but still to be found are mule deer, coyotes, bobcats, and badgers.

Three tracts make up the refuge: the South Tract is primarily farmland; the Middle Tract holds refuge headquarters and Bitter Lake (named for its water, which tastes sour to many people and often dries up in summer, leaving nothing but a white alkaline bed); and most of the North Tract is designated Wilderness. Salt Creek itself runs through the center of the Wilderness, an area of native grassland, sand dunes, brushy bottomlands, and a northern boundary distinguished by its red-rimmed plateau, all just west of the Pecos River. With Cannon Air Force Base and Roswell Airport nearby, you may find silence a rare pleasure. Exploring is limited to daylight hours, as camping is not allowed.

Salt Creek Essentials

Size: 9,621 acres.
Year Designated: 1970.
Location: Southeastern New Mexico.
Easiest Access: From Roswell, take U.S. 380 (Second Street) east for approximately three miles until you reach a sign directing you to refuge headquarters. Continue driving for about eight miles north until you reach the Wilderness.
Season: Open year-round. Early fall through February brings the most birds, with cranes usually reaching peak populations in November.
Wilderness Fees/Permits: None.
Maps: A free map is available from the refuge manager.
Management: Bitter Lake National Wildlife Refuge, P.O. Box 7, Roswell, NM 88202; (505) 622-6755.

San Pedro Parks Wilderness

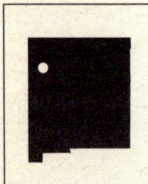

Although the elevation averages 10,000 feet above sea level, San Pedro Parks Wilderness is bereft of the usual dramatic peaks and picturesque cliffs. Instead, expect high, relatively moist, rolling mountaintops with numerous meadows and large grassy "parks." Dense stands of Engelmann spruce and mixed conifers compete for space with small stands of aspen. Clear streams wander through the forest openings and rarely send trout-seeking anglers away empty-handed. Frequent rainfall in July and August enables the meadows to flourish with bluegrass, oat grass, sedge, rush, and the extravagant Rocky Mountain iris, only to be covered with snow come November.

Campsites with abundant water appeal to backpackers, as do the nine major trails. Trails receiving the heaviest use are the Vacas Trail to San Pedro Park (10.69 miles) and the Palomas Trail (3.63 miles), which joins the Vacas Trail. Fall brings hunters seeking elk, deer, bears, and grouse. Heavy human use, especially from horsepackers, has damaged much of this area.

San Pedro Parks Essentials

Size: 41,132 acres.
Year Designated: 1964.
Location: Northern central New Mexico.
Easiest Access: From State Highway 44, turn east on State Highway 126 (just north of Cuba) and drive about 11 miles. When you reach Forest Service Road 70, turn north and continue for 2.7 miles to the parking lot at the Vacas Trailhead.
Season: Summer and early fall.

Wilderness Fees/Permits: A Wilderness permit is required. Contact the district ranger.
Maps: A Wilderness map is available for $3 from the district ranger.
Management: Coyote Ranger District, Santa Fe National Forest, P.O. Box 160, Coyote, NM 87012; (505) 638-5547. Cuba Ranger District, Santa Fe National Forest, P.O. Box 130, Cuba, NM 87013; (505) 289-3264. Jemez Ranger District, Santa Fe National Forest, Jemez Springs, NM 87025; (505) 829-3535.

Sandia Mountain Wilderness

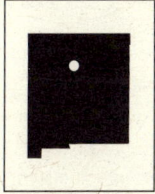

Despite the fact that these mountains tower above the very nearby sprawl of Albuquerque and despite the fact that the trails of this Wilderness may be more heavily used than any other trail system in the state, Sandia Mountain Wilderness still provides an opportunity to get out of town . . . but be prepared to work for your solitude. An estimated two million people visit this Wilderness each year, though many of them simply ride the Sandia Peak Tramway to the top of the mountain to watch the lights of Albuquerque twinkle in the night.

The area lies primarily on the western slope of the Sandia Mountains, but it crosses over to the eastern side at the north and south ends. Spruce and fir dominate the high country, with stands of mixed conifers just below. Many raptors migrate through these mountains in spring and fall, sharing their territory with a few mule deer and black bears. Accessible from the tram is the Crest Trail, which runs along 22 miles of the main ridge of the Sandias at an elevation averaging 10,000 feet. There are 117 miles of well-maintained trails here, but you have the best chance of avoiding other hikers if you stick to side trails. Carry water, as there is very little in this region.

Sandia Mountain Essentials

Size: 37,028 acres.
Year Designated: 1978.
Location: Central New Mexico.
Easiest Access: From Interstate 25 just north of Albuquerque, take the Tramway exit and follow the signs east about seven miles to the foot of the tram.
Season: Summer temperatures are much cooler than down below. Spring and fall offer more solitude and pleasant weather.

Wilderness Fees/Permits: None. The charge for the round-trip tram ride is $13 per adult, or $9.50 if you eat at the summit restaurant. A one-way ticket is $7.50.
Maps: A Wilderness map is available for $4 from the district ranger.
Management: Sandia Ranger District, Cibola National Forest, 11776 Highway 337, Tijeras, NM 87059; (505) 281-3304.

West Malpais Wilderness

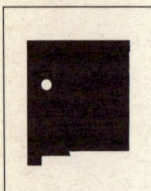

El Malpais is Spanish for "the badlands," a name that perfectly describes this region of New Mexico, where countless volcanic eruptions sent rivers of molten rock and flying cinders over what is now a bleak valley of three million years' worth of hardened lava. Native American settlers probably witnessed the last of the eruptions. Their former home is now a land of craters and lava tubes, cinder cones and spatter cones, ice caves and pressure ridges, and a surprising amount of vegetation. Even on terrain that one would presume to be barren, wind-deposited debris has thickened enough to support grasses, cacti, aspen, pine, juniper, and fir.

Preserved as El Malpais National Monument (managed by the NPS) and Conservation Area (managed by the BLM), two Wildernesses lie within the boundaries of BLM land: Cebolla and West Malpais. The latter Wilderness is home to Hole-In-The-Wall, the largest islandlike depression in these lava fields. Over the years, moisture and soil collected on some of the oldest lava to form this 6,000-acre park of ponderosa pine.

About 10 miles of hiking on the Hole-In-The-Wall Trail gives access to this parkland, but the trail is rugged (cutting across the exposed lava will be hazardous to your boots and, if you stumble, to your health). You may want to opt for the abandoned jeep roads that course through this Wilderness—your feet will thank you.

Be prepared for heat and high winds. I escaped a fierce dry wind cutting across the lava beds by dropping into the shadowy pleasantness of a convenient lava tube (formed by molten lava cooling faster on the surface while a hot river of lava continued to flow underneath, thus leaving a cave).

You may see antelope here, and during summer a large colony of Mexican free-tailed bats migrates between some of the caves. I missed them, but I've heard it's quite wonderful to sit at dusk and watch the colony emerge to hunt the night sky. Bring several flashlights and protective clothing to explore the miles of lava tubes, but stay out of the bat caves. No groundwater exists in the entire area, so pack plenty.

West Malpais Essentials

Size: 38,210 acres.
Year Designated: 1987.
Location: Western central New Mexico.
Easiest Access: From Interstate 40 about five miles west of Grants, turn south on State Highway 117 and continue for approximately 35 miles. When you reach Road 42, turn north. The Hole-In-The-Wall Trailhead is nearby.
Season: Spring and fall.
Wilderness Fees/Permits: A backcountry permit is required. Check in at El Malpais Information Center, 620 East Santa Fe Street, Grants, NM 87020; (505) 285-5406.
Maps: Topographic maps covering the area may be purchased from the managing agency.
Management: El Malpais National Conservation Area, P.O. Box 846, Grants, NM 87020; (505) 285-5406.

Wheeler Peak Wilderness

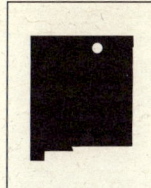

About 135 million years ago a tremendous geologic uplift created the Sangre de Cristo Mountains. Wheeler Peak Wilderness now marks the top of this rugged range, with Wheeler Peak, at 13,161 feet, standing higher than any other point in New Mexico. Alpine tundra, rare in the American Southwest, covers Wheeler and other nearby Wilderness mountains. Below the tundra, from cottonwoods on the Rio Hondo to bristlecone pines in the high country, you'll find at least a few of almost every tree native to the northern part of the state.

As for wildlife, the most activity takes place in the short four-month "summer," when elk and mule deer visit, golden eagles soar in the clear skies, songbirds are ubiquitous, and marmots and pikas have their run of the place. Mountain lions and black bears have been seen here, too. Less obvious, perhaps, but no less abundant are the trout swimming the three stocked lakes. Anglers who prefer moving water can likewise find trout in the Rio Hondo and Sawmill Creek.

Taos Ski Valley abuts the northern boundary, and a trailhead there (specifically at Twining Campground, which has a parking lot) accesses a trail system leading to myriad peaks and lakes and long talus slopes. The Wheeler Peak Trail starts near here and travels a well-defined path that leads to the summit of the state, a distance of approximately eight miles. You'll need no technical gear to attempt this hike. From the summit you can choose to take the steep, rocky descent to Williams Lake; continue on a trail to Horseshoe Lake; or follow the ridge to Simpson Peak and Taos Cone and on into Sawmill Park, where you can exit the Wilderness on the East Fork of the Red River.

About half the annual precipitation of 40 inches falls in summer and half in winter (when it appears in the form of fluffy white flakes). Cross-country skiing and snowshoeing are popular, but beware the danger of avalanche. This is an attractive, easily accessible, and heavily used area.

Wheeler Peak Essentials

Size: 19,661 acres.
Year Designated: 1964; expanded in 1980.
Location: Northern New Mexico.
Easiest Access: From Taos, take U.S. 64 north for about four miles. Then turn east on State Highway 150 and drive another 16 miles to Taos Ski Valley. Continue driving through the ski area parking lot to Twining Campground and the trailhead.
Season: Fourth of July through Labor Day are most crowded. Late June and early September are typically pleasant and less crowded.
Wilderness Fees/Permits: None.
Maps: A topographic Wilderness map is available for $4 from the district ranger.
Management: Questa Ranger District, Carson National Forest, P.O. Box 110, Questa, NM 87556; (505) 586-0520.

NEW MEXICO

White Mountain Wilderness

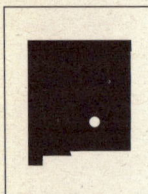

With elevations reaching 11,580 feet, up to six feet of snow blankets these mountains from the middle to latter part of November until as late as June, hence the name White Mountains. The White Mountains run generally north-south, with the Mescalero Apache Reservation anchoring the southern end. The steep west side is extremely rugged, with extensive rocky outcroppings, while the gentler east side is distinguished by broad forested canyons and a few tiny streams.

The Wilderness measures roughly 12.5 miles long and 4 to 12 miles wide, and includes many ridges branching off the main crest. Meadows and grassy oak savannas break the continuity of the forest, especially along the crest. Abrupt elevation changes with accompanying variations in vegetation, tall escarpments, avalanche chutes, and bold rock promontories combine to create dramatic but scenic contrasts. Several of the streams flow year-round and may hold a few small trout. You'll see terrestrial wildlife in abundance: mule deer, elk, black bears, wild turkeys, porcupines, badgers, bobcats, foxes, coyotes, skunks, squirrels, and many species of the "little people" (mice, voles, rats). Although many types of birds live in the White Mountains, it's a critical habitat for five specific species: northern three-toed woodpeckers, Clark's nutcrackers, red-breasted nuthatches, Townsend's solitaires, and golden-crowned kinglets.

About 50 miles of easy-to-strenuous trails trace the ridges and canyon bottoms. The Three Rivers Trail (5.6 miles) follows what is probably the best fishing stream in the area. Many older pathways, kept open by use, can be found throughout the area. Almost all the paths eventually join the 21-mile-long Crest Trail, which offers views worth the lengthy hike. Water, though not plentiful, can almost always be located with a bit of looking.

White Mountain Essentials

Size: 48,366 acres.
Year Designated: 1964; expanded in 1980.
Location: Southern central New Mexico.
Easiest Access: From Alamagordo, take U.S. 54 north 17 miles to Three Rivers. Turn east at the sign to Three Rivers Petroglyph Site, and go approximately eight miles to the Three Rivers Trailhead at Three Rivers Campground.
Season: Spring and fall, and even summer, can be cool and refreshing.
Wilderness Fees/Permits: None.
Maps: A Wilderness map is available for $4 from the district ranger.
Management: Smokey Bear Ranger District, Lincoln National Forest, 901 Mechem Drive, Ruidoso, NM 88345; (505) 257-4095.

Withington Wilderness

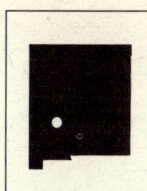

In the northern extreme of the San Mateo Mountains and almost entirely on their eastern slopes lies the little-known Withington Wilderness, a land of precious and often parched solitude. Elevations range from 6,800 feet to 10,100 feet atop Mount Withington, which marks the center of the western boundary. Mixed conifers (pine, spruce, fir) vegetate the shady bottoms of the area's steep-walled canyons, then give way to a woodland of piñon and juniper as the ground becomes more open and drier and the vistas stretch eastward toward the Rio Grande. In the lowest land, near the eastern boundary, you'll find small stands of ocotillo.

None of the several miles of trail receive many human footfalls. Winters bring snow, and summers dry the land to the quality of old sandpaper. During the desert "monsoon" season, July and August, rainwater may flood the narrow canyons, but most of the year offers little or nothing in the way of water sources, relegating most of the few visitors to day hikes. If you want to hike in, you can begin at Bear Trap Campground (and park your vehicle there), about one mile from the western boundary.

Withington Essentials

Size: 18,869 acres.
Year Designated: 1980.
Location: Western central New Mexico.
Easiest Access: From Socorro, take U.S. 60 west approximately 38 miles. Turn south on Forest Service Road 549 (Bear Trap Canyon Road) and continue to Bear Trap Campground, about 15 miles.
Season: Spring for the most easily available water.
Wilderness Fees/Permits: None.
Maps: A Wilderness map is available for $4 from the district ranger.
Management: Magdalena Ranger District, Cibola National Forest, Box 45, Magdalena, NM 87825; (505) 854-2281.

> "How many generations will pass before it will have become nearly impossible to be alone even for an hour... to see anywhere nature as she is without man's improvement?"
> —Joseph Wood Krutch

NEW YORK

Total Wilderness areas: 1
Total Wilderness acreage: 1,363

Precious little remains of the wild, forested seashore that so impressed the first European settlers 400 years ago. What remains on federal land, in fact, in the people-heavy region we call the state of New York, is one small designated Wilderness managed by the National Park Service.

Fire Island Wilderness

Almost within sight of New York City's skyscrapers, herons stalk through grassy wetlands and startled white-tailed deer leap over thickets of catbrier and the ubiquitous poison ivy. Their home is the 32-mile barrier known as Fire Island, now protected as Fire Island National Seashore. The island, which shields Long Islanders from the raging Atlantic Ocean, attracts springtime rafts of migratory waterfowl bobbing on mainland-side waters and summer swimmers basking on the white beaches bordering the Atlantic.

Fire Island traces a thin line along the coast, ranging from 200 yards to one-half mile wide. A seven-mile stretch on the northern half has been designated Wilderness, from Smith Point West south to Watch Hill. From patches of seaside plants among the ocean-side dunes, the area extends across pine forest with hidden hardwood groves to the sheltered mainland side. Bellport Beach splits the Wilderness in two, but, excepting a short boardwalk for the handicapped into the north section from Smith Point West Visitors Center, the area has no roads, no trails, and no developed campsites. Year-round fishing attracts anglers who cast for bluefish, striped bass, winter flounder, and other saltwater species.

Fire Island Essentials

Size: 1,363 acres.
Year Designated: 1980.
Location: Off the southeastern New York coast.
Easiest Access: From Interstate 495 on Long Island, turn south on County Highway 46 (William Floyd Parkway) and continue about nine miles to the Smith Point West Visitors Center.
Season: Summer for sun and the best weather; winter for storms and solitude.
Wilderness Fees/Permits: None. Reservations are required at the Watch Hill Campground, just south of the Wilderness, from May 15 to October 15.
Maps: A free map is available from the seashore ranger.
Management: Fire Island National Seashore, 120 Laurel Street, Patchoque, NY 11772; (516) 289-4810.

> *"Wilderness exists for its own intrinsic values. Economy, user comfort and convenience, or commercial value are not standards of wilderness management or use. Where a choice must be made between wilderness values and human use, preserving the wilderness resource is the overriding value. The guiding principle is to allow the natural processes to shape the environment."*
>
> —United States Forest Service

NORTH CAROLINA

Total Wilderness areas: 12
Total Wilderness acreage: 109,003

From the forested mountains of the west to the estuarine seashores of the Atlantic Coast, the state of North Carolina contains four national forests: 516,000-acre Nantahala, 495,000-acre Pisgah, 157,000-acre Croatan, and 46,000-acre Uwharrie. These forests have more than 1,300 miles of trails, more than 800 campsites, 7 swimming beaches—and 11 Wildernesses. A 12th Wilderness is preserved by a wildlife refuge.

Birkhead Mountains Wilderness

Most people haven't even heard of the Uwharrie Mountains, much less seen these ancient volcanic landforms, considered the oldest range on the North American continent. Although eroded by eons of time and weather, the Uwharries are still the highest uplift in the eastern half of North Carolina. Birkhead Mountains Wilderness marks their northern end.

Covered primarily in old-growth hardwoods, the Wilderness consists of several long, wooded ridges and surrounding drainages of moderately steep terrain. Small, clear streams run past rocky outcroppings down to the Uwharrie River and outside the western boundary. An understory of wildflowers, shrubs, ferns, mosses, and other plant species flourish on their sodden banks. Elevations range from about 450 feet on drainage bottoms to around 950 feet on Cedar Rock Mountain in the northeastern section.

When explorers first landed here in the late 1600s, they found Native American tribes that had been inhabiting the area for more than 12,000 years. European settlement began in earnest in the 1760s, and the natives were

393

NORTH CAROLINA

pushed westward. The Birkhead family moved in around 1850, leaving their name and mark on the land. Among the trees of Birkhead you may see remnants of old homesteads, farms, gold mining operations, old roads, and evidence of timber harvesting.

The Birkhead Mountain Trail crosses the heart of the area for approximately 4.5 miles from north to south (but you won't find a parking lot on either end). From a parking lot on the western boundary of the Wilderness, the Robbins Branch Trail (about three miles) enters the area to fork at the Hannah's Creek Trail (about 1.5 miles). Both trails join the Birkhead Mountain Trail. Group size is limited to 10, a regulation enforced in all North Carolina Wildernesses.

Birkhead Mountains Essentials

Size: 4,790 acres.
Year Designated: 1984.
Location: Central North Carolina.
Easiest Access: From Greensboro, take U.S. 220 south for approximately 25 miles. Turn west on State Highway 49 and continue approximately five miles, then go south on Secondary Highway 1107 another five miles. When you reach Forest Service Road 6532, turn east and proceed approximately one-half mile to the parking lot and the Robbins Branch Trailhead.
Season: Spring and fall are the best.
Wilderness Fees/Permits: None.
Maps: A Wilderness map is available for $3.75 from the district ranger.
Management: Uwharrie Ranger District, Uwharrie National Forest, Route 3, Box 470, Troy, NC 27371; (919) 576-6391.

Catfish Lake South Wilderness

North Carolina's Croatan National Forest is a unique coastal ecosystem set between the Atlantic Ocean and the Neuse River and interlaced with the sea's nurseries, called estuaries, where oysters, shrimp, and crab reproduce and grow to maturity. Croatan's Catfish Lake South Wilderness is primarily raised bogland, where biting insects try to steal the spotlight from the American alligator and the cottonmouth, canebrake rattler, eastern diamondback rattler, pygmy rattler, copperhead, and other poisonous snakes. Five genera of insectivorous plants live here, a combination rarely seen elsewhere: the erect pitcher plant; the hairy, sticky round-leafed sundew; the waxy, "buttery" butterwort; the hinged-leafed Venus flytrap; and the aquatic, floating bladderwort. You may see deer, bears, squirrels, rabbits, and raccoons, all of which may be hunted according to state law. Sleek muskrats, minks, and otters are common. On the Atlantic Flyway, Catfish Lake attracts ducks and geese. Bird lovers have also spotted egrets, flycatchers, woodpeckers, hawks, woodcocks, owls, and ospreys.

The Wilderness, which is bordered by roads and on the northeast by Catfish Lake, offers nothing in the way of trails—just lots of chances to find yourself the victim of some hungry pest. The lake draws a few anglers who hope to hook bass, redbreast, bluegill, chain pickerel, warmouth, yellow perch, and, of course, catfish. If you brought your pole, prepare to be disappointed due to the lake's high acidity.

NORTH CAROLINA

Catfish Lake South Essentials

Size: 7,600 acres.
Year Designated: 1984.
Location: Eastern North Carolina.
Easiest Access: From Jacksonville, take U.S. 17 north for 21 miles to Pollocksville. Turn west on Secondary Highway 1100 (Bender Road), which becomes Catfish Lake Farm Road for a drive of approximately nine miles to Catfish Lake. The Wilderness lies southwest of the lake.

Season: Summer for fishing. Fall for migratory birds. Winter for fewer critters interested in biting you.
Wilderness Fees/Permits: None.
Maps: USGS topographic map is Catfish Lake.
Management: Croatan Ranger District, Croatan National Forest, 141 East Fisher Avenue, New Bern, NC 28560; (919) 638-5628.

Ellicott Rock Wilderness

This is America's only designated Wilderness to extend into three states (see Georgia and South Carolina, Ellicott Rock Wilderness). In North Carolina, the bowl-shaped Wilderness drops to the Wild and Scenic Chattooga River and attracts numerous visitors, most of whom have yet to grasp or appreciate the principles of Leave No Trace. The dense overstory vegetation may appear virgin to the uninformed.

Although the area is rugged and mountainous, trails to the river are relatively easy going in, more strenuous coming back out, and day hiking constitutes the main human use. Ellicott Rock Trail typifies the footpaths. It follows an abandoned road from a parking lot for two miles before gently dropping into the Wilderness, then follows the old road another mile before bearing left steeply down one-half mile to the Chattooga River and Ellicott Rock. This site bears the inconspicuous mark of Andrew Ellicott, the surveyor who in 1811 determined the border between Georgia and North Carolina.

Ellicott Rock Essentials

Size: 4,022 acres in North Carolina (9,012 acres total).
Year Designated: 1975.
Location: Western North Carolina.
Easiest Access: From Highlands, take Horse Cove Road south for four miles before turning east on Bull Pen Road. Continue for approximately three miles, past a primitive campground. Turn south on Forest Service Road 441-F and you will soon find a parking lot for Ellicott Rock Trail.
Season: Winter for chilly weather and far fewer people.
Wilderness Fees/Permits: None.
Maps: A Wilderness map is available for $3 from the district ranger.
Management: Highlands Ranger District, Nantahala National Forest, 2010 Flat Mountain Road, Highlands, NC 28741; (704) 526-3765.

NORTH CAROLINA

Joyce Kilmer–Slickrock Wilderness

Preserving the northwestern corner of Nantahala National Forest, this rugged and mountainous Wilderness crosses the state line into Tennessee, where you will find the northern section of the area (see Tennessee, Joyce Kilmer–Slickrock Wilderness). Spared the keen edge of the ax when bankruptcy closed the local logging company in 1890, this Wilderness contains some magnificent old-growth forest, where oaks, hemlocks, and tulip poplars have reached six feet in diameter.

You can see some of the best of the old growth along the Joyce Kilmer National Recreation Trail, a 1.2-mile path ambling through the Joyce Kilmer Memorial Forest. This forest, a living monument to the poet Joyce Kilmer, covers some 3,800 acres on the southern end of the Wilderness. A picnic area and parking lot lie on the edge of the forest, and the trail begins there.

Walk beyond Joyce Kilmer Memorial Forest and you will discover that the area runs north into two basins separated by a high ridge: the Little Santeetlah Creek watershed and the Slickrock Creek watershed. More than 60 miles of trails provide access into the Wilderness, trails that wander along the tops of ridges or down beside streams of cool mountain water. These trails lead into one of the most remote regions of North Carolina. The Slickrock Creek Trail (13.3 miles) crosses the Wilderness generally in a north-south direction, providing a broad look at the area, and can be accessed from the Joyce Kilmer National Recreation Trail.

Joyce Kilmer–Slickrock Essentials

Size: 13,181 acres in North Carolina (17,013 acres total).
Year Designated: 1975.
Location: Western North Carolina.
Easiest Access: From Robbinsville, take U.S. 129 north for one mile, then turn north on State Highway 1127 and continue for 12 miles. Just past Santeetlah Lake, turn west on Forest Service Road 416 and drive for one mile to where the Joyce Kilmer National Recreation Trail begins.
Season: Spring and fall.
Wilderness Fees/Permits: None.
Maps: A Wilderness map is available for $3.75 from the district ranger.
Management: Cheotah Ranger District, Nantahala National Forest, Route 1, Box 16-A, Robbinsville, NC 28771; (704) 479-6431.

Linville Gorge Wilderness

Native Americans scalped explorers William Linville and his son in 1766, an unhappy ending for a family whose name is now associated with one of the most scenic river gorges in the eastern United States. From its headwaters high on Grandfather Mountain, the powerful Linville River patiently carves the rugged, steep-walled gorge that encloses it for approximately 12 miles. Within the gorge, the river drops a dramatic 2,000 feet before leveling out in the Catawba Valley.

East of the gorge is Jonas Ridge; west is Linville Mountain. The gorge's rim extends 3,400 feet, compared to the river's average of 2,000 feet. Plant communities range from lichens and shrubs on the cliffs to laurel and rhododendron along the riverbanks. In some spots, the gorge shelters stands of virgin timber.

NORTH CAROLINA

Assorted odd rock formations along Jonas Ridge—Sitting Bear, Hawksbill, Table Rock, and the Chimneys—attract beginner, intermediate, and advanced rock climbers. With 39 miles of challenging trails, backpackers come to Linville Gorge in substantial numbers. If you want more solitude during your visit, go to the southern half of the Wilderness, south of Conley Cove Trail (1.35 miles) in the western portion and south of the Chimneys in the eastern portion. The rough northern section surrounding Brushy Ridge also receives few visitors. A large black bear population attracts hunters between late October and early January.

Linville Gorge Essentials

Size: 10,975 acres.
Year Designated: 1964.
Location: Western North Carolina.
Easiest Access: From Marion just north of Interstate 40, take U.S. 70 east for approximately five miles to Nebo. Turn north on State Highway 126 across Lake James and continue eight miles, then turn west on State Highway 1238 (Kistler Memorial Highway), a gravel road that is rough in places and not recommended for two-wheel-drive vehicles. You will soon come to several west-side trailheads with parking lots.
Season: Weekdays from November through March to avoid the crowds.
Wilderness Fees/Permits: Free camping permits are required on weekends and holidays from the first of May through October. Early registration is recommended. Contact the district ranger.
Maps: A Wilderness map is available for $3.75 from the district ranger.
Management: Grandfather Ranger District, Pisgah National Forest, P.O. Box 519, Marion, NC 28752; (704) 652-2144.

Middle Prong Wilderness

Pioneers grabbed up this area, once part of the Cherokee Nation, starting in 1796. After settlement, most of the land was purchased, first by a paper company in the early 1900s, then by a lumber company. A town shaped up at the junction of the Right Prong, Middle Prong, and Left Prong of the West Fork of the Pigeon River. The town was later relocated, but the lumber company continued its quest for timber, removing vast stands of red spruce, Fraser fir, hemlocks, and hardwoods from 1906 to 1926 and building an extensive system of logging railroads. Four of these old railroad beds are now used as hiking trails in today's Middle Prong Wilderness.

The Wilderness rests on high ridges southeast of Richland Balsam, a steep and rugged terrain forested with second-growth spruce and fir, and opened by grass-heath "balds" on the ridges. Mixed hardwoods cover the lower slopes. Elevations range from 3,200 feet on the West Fork of the Pigeon River to 6,400 feet near Richland Balsam. Numerous streams work their way down to the river. Only a road separates this Wilderness from Shining Rock Wilderness (see below) to the north.

Middle Prong is a small Wilderness with a limited and primitive trail system. The hiking rates as difficult, but ample opportunities exist for solitude. The most used trail is a four-mile portion (approximate distance) of the Mountains-to-Sea route to the extreme south. The Green Mountain Trail (approximately six miles) crosses the area from north to south. No campfires are permitted, and group size is limited to 10. The Blue Ridge Parkway parallels the southern Wilderness boundary.

397

NORTH CAROLINA

Middle Prong Essentials
Size: 7,900 acres.
Year Designated: 1984.
Location: Western North Carolina.
Easiest Access: From near Asheville, take the Blue Ridge Parkway west for about 40 miles. A parking lot and the Mountains-to-Sea Trailhead (which leads to the Green Mountain Trail) lie at Buckeye Gap.
Season: Spring and fall typically offer the best weather.
Wilderness Fees/Permits: None.
Maps: A Wilderness map is available for $3.75 from the district ranger.
Management: Pisgah Ranger District, Pisgah National Forest, 1001 Pisgah Highway, Pisgah Forest, NC 28768; (704) 877-3265.

Pocosin Wilderness

Native Americans called it a *pocosin*, which in their language means "swamp on a hill." A more accurate assessment of this seemingly flat area that rises slightly in the center might be "raised bog." Over thousands of years, organic matter (basically black muck) accumulated to form a pocosin, an area highly acidic and deficient in nutrients that produces a unique biological occurrence. The thickness of the muck varies from several inches at the edge to several feet at the center. Growth on the outer rim is typically pond pine with a dense understory of titi, the shrub Zenobia (unique to pocosins), and an impenetrable jungle of greenbrier vines. Toward the center of the waterlogged goo, trees thin and grow more stunted, and shrubs and vines diminish, their tangled roots providing the only footing. Thus you'll find the trailless Pocosin Wilderness in Croatan National Forest near the coast of North Carolina. People come to see the flora (no other national forest boasts the insectivorous Venus flytrap) and fauna, but there is no place to camp or even easily hike through the muck.

Avian life abounds here on the Atlantic Flyway, with many water-related birds, hawks, owls, woodpeckers, and flycatchers. Biting insects also thrive, along with alligators and poisonous snakes.

Pocosin Essentials
Size: 11,000 acres.
Year Designated: 1984.
Location: Eastern North Carolina.
Easiest Access: From Jacksonville, take U.S. 17 north for approximately 15 miles to Maysville. Turn southeast on State Highway 58 and continue for approximately 12 miles, then drive east on Secondary Highway 1104 for 1.5 miles. When you reach Forest Route 127, turn east again and head 2.5 miles to the western boundary.
Season: Fall for migratory birds, and winter for fewer insects.
Wilderness Fees/Permits: None.
Maps: USGS topographic maps are Hadnot Creek and Masontown.
Management: Croatan Ranger District, Croatan National Forest, 141 East Fisher Avenue, New Bern, NC 28560; (919) 638-5628.

NORTH CAROLINA

Pond Pine Wilderness

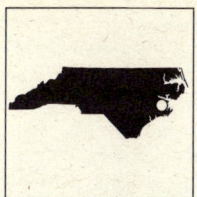

The smallest of North Carolina's designated Wildernesses is just south of Great Lake in the middle of Croatan National Forest. The lake is acidic, the Wilderness a trailless pocosin (see Pocosin Wilderness, above), and the few who visit are a hardy breed who can cope with the deep muck, alligators, biting insects, poisonous snakes, and tangled masses of vines and shrubs. People come to see the wildlife and plants, but they rarely stay long. In case you fancy yourself to be the exception to that rule, be forewarned that there are no campsites.

Pond Pine Essentials

Size: 1,860 acres.
Year Designated: 1984.
Location: Eastern North Carolina.
Easiest Access: From Jacksonville, take U.S. 17 north for approximately 15 miles to Maysville. Turn southeast on State Highway 58 and continue for approximately 10 miles, then head east on Forest Route 126 (Great Lake Road), which runs four miles to the western boundary of Pond Pine.
Season: Fall and winter.
Wilderness Fees/Permits: None.
Maps: USGS topographic map is Hadnot Creek.
Management: Croatan Ranger District, Croatan National Forest, 141 East Fisher Avenue, New Bern, NC 28560; (919) 638-5628.

Sheep Ridge Wilderness

All that remains of Sir Walter Raleigh's lost colony is the word *croatan*, Algonquian for "council town," carved on a tree on Roanoke Island. This raised bogland or pocosin (see Pocosin Wilderness, above) lies in the heart of Croatan National Forest, with Catfish Lake Road to the north and Great and Long Lakes to the south. A high water table keeps the black muck of the pocosin wet and agreeable enough to grow dwarf swamp vegetation. Hazards include biting insects, poisonous snakes, and alligators. The reptiles are generally shy, retiring, and uninterested in humans, but the biting pests will be happy to greet you. Visitors who venture in to see the plants and animals usually make it a quick trip, as the Wilderness doesn't offer campsites or trails.

Sheep Ridge Essentials

Size: 9,540 acres.
Year Designated: 1984.
Location: Eastern North Carolina.
Easiest Access: From Jacksonville, take U.S. 17 north for about 21 miles to Pollocksville. Turn east on Secondary Highway 1100 (Bender Road). It becomes Catfish Lake Road and runs about 12 miles total to the northern boundary.
Season: Fall or winter.
Wilderness Fees/Permits: None.
Maps: USGS topographic maps are Catfish Lake and Havelock.
Management: Croatan Ranger District, Croatan National Forest, 141 East Fisher Avenue, New Bern, NC 28560; (919) 638-5628.

Shining Rock Wilderness

Named for the mountain from which Moses first viewed the Promised Land, Shining Rock became one of the original components of the National Wilderness Preservation System in September 1964, a few months after garnering designation as a Wild area. It is now the largest Wilderness in North Carolina, separated by only a road from Middle Prong Wilderness (see above) to the southwest. Standing at an elevation of more than 5,000 feet and boasting five peaks exceeding 6,000 feet (three within the Wilderness boundaries), Shining Rock Ledge forms the backbone of this area.

Here in this series of high ridges on the north slopes of Pisgah Ridge, you'll find extremely steep and rugged terrain ranging in elevation from 3,200 feet on the banks of the West Fork of Pigeon River, a major tributary of the Tennessee River, to 6,030 feet on Cold Mountain. Streams abound, cutting narrow passages through the mountains on their way to either the East or West Forks of the Pigeon River. Loggers cut down the forest between 1906 and 1926 (see Middle Prong Wilderness, above) and fires raged through the area in 1925 and 1942. These two factors account for Shining Rock's grassy "balds" and unique vegetation.

Almost all the trails in the area rate as difficult, and they can be hard to follow. Nevertheless, this Wilderness is one of the most trampled in the state, especially along the trails of Art Loeb (11.6 miles), Ivester Gap (1.6 miles), and Shining Creek (3.4 miles). The entry at the Big East Fork Trailhead also sees heavy use. Off-trail you will see few other humans. No campfires are permitted, and group size is limited to 10.

Shining Rock Essentials

Size: 18,450 acres.
Year Designated: 1964; expanded in 1984.
Location: Western North Carolina.
Easiest Access: From Waynesville, take U.S. 276 south for approximately 19.5 miles until you reach a parking lot at the Big East Fork Trailhead.
Season: Spring and fall.
Wilderness Fees/Permits: None.
Maps: A Wilderness map is available for $3.75 from the district ranger.
Management: Pisgah Ranger District, Pisgah National Forest, 1001 Pisgah Highway, Pisgah Forest, NC 28768; (704) 877-3265.

Southern Nantahala Wilderness

The Cherokee Indians thought of the Blue Ridge Mountains as the Great Blue Hills of God. These original inhabitants named the shady forests and deep, dark gorges *Nantahala*, or Land of the Noonday Sun. Later settlers saw this same area as fodder for their mills. They removed virtually every piece of good timber that was at least 15 inches in diameter from the main drainages of the southern end of the Blue Ridge Mountains, what is today Southern Nantahala Wilderness and shared by North Carolina and Georgia (see Georgia, Southern Nantahala Wilderness). It is a land characterized by steep, rugged terrain dissected by many streams and old drainages. Numerous peaks exceed 4,000 feet. Streams feed into one of three rivers: the Nantahala, the

Tallulah, and the Hiwassee. Now regrown, the forest cover is lush with spruce and fir on the ridges, broken by grass-heath "balds" and mixed hardwoods lower down.

Almost all of the developed trails are steep and strenuous, with a rough tread that is sometimes a challenge to find. But few places in the southern United States offer such outstanding backpacking opportunities. Many people wander into the area from the popular adjacent Standing Indian Basin. Thirty-two miles of the Appalachian Trail (AT) pass through the Southern Nantahala, following the ridge crest of the Nantahala Range. In addition to the AT, the most used trails are the Lower Ridge Trail (4.1 miles), Big Indian Loop (8 miles), and Beech Gap (2.8 miles), but I have hiked here in the chill of January in utter silence, seeing nary another human.

Southern Nantahala Essentials

Size: 10,900 acres in North Carolina (23,339 total).
Year Designated: 1984.
Location: Western North Carolina.
Easiest Access: From Franklin, take U.S. 64 south and west for approximately 11 miles. Turn east on Forest Route 67 (Old U.S. 64) and then continue for approximately seven miles to a parking lot on the Big Indian Loop.
Season: Fall and spring for the best weather. Winter for solitude.
Wilderness Fees/Permits: None.
Maps: A Wilderness map is available for $3.75 from the district ranger.
Management: Wayah Ranger District, Nantahala National Forest, 8 Sloan Road, Franklin, NC 28734; (704) 524-6441.

Swanquarter Wilderness

In colonial days, large flocks of whistling swans came to the nearby community of Swan Quarter. The swans have since disappeared, but the area still attracts diving ducks in winter and raptors (primarily ospreys, red-shouldered hawks, and marsh hawks), marsh birds, and shorebirds at other times of the year.

Established in 1932, Swanquarter National Wildlife Refuge, a satellite of Mattamuskeet National Wildlife Refuge, encompasses 16,411 acres of islands and coastal marshland on the north side of Pamlico Sound. Another 27,082 acres of nearby open water protects migratory birds under Presidential Proclamation.

You have to come in by boat to get to most of Swanquarter. One road, outside the Wilderness, leads to the refuge's 1,100-foot-long Bell Island fishing pier in the northern portion off U.S. 264. More than one-half of the refuge has been designated Wilderness: Judith Island, Swanquarter Island, Great Island, Marsh Island, and portions of the mainland along Juniper Bay. Judith, Swanquarter, and Great Islands are entirely estuarine, dominated by black needlerush, intermittently under water usually due to wind tides. Marsh Island is almost entirely estuarine, with a small upland forest section on the extreme northern boundary. Along the mainland of Juniper Bay, the Wilderness is approximately half estuarine and half upland forest.

In uplands forested in loblolly pine you may catch a glimpse of white-tailed deer, opossums, raccoons, and squirrels. Yellow-bellied turtles and water snakes skulk about the needlerush and saw grass that blankets the refuge, and a few of the northernmost North American alligators

NORTH CAROLINA

(around 30 individuals) live here in brackish water. Most visitors come to fish from May through November for croaker, spot, gray trout, flounder, puppydrum, and bluefish. Crabbing is a popular sport in the warmer months. Portions of the refuge open seasonally for waterfowl hunting.

Swanquarter Essentials

Size: 8,785 acres.
Year Designated: 1976.
Location: Eastern North Carolina.
Easiest Access: From Greenville, take U.S. 264 east for approximately 70 miles. Just before the town of Swan Quarter, turn south on the access road to Bell Island Recreation Area.
Season: Winter for bird watching, and summer for fishing.
Wilderness Fees/Permits: Waterfowl hunting is governed by state and federal regulations. Contact the refuge manager.
Maps: A free map is available from the refuge manager.
Management: Mattamuskeet National Wildlife Refuge, Route 1, Box N-2, Swan Quarter, NC 27885; (919) 926-4021.

> "Selected portions [of the wilderness] have been kept here and there in a state of nature, not merely for the sake of preserving the forests and the water, but for the sake of preserving all its beauties and wonders unspoiled by greedy and short-sighted vandalism."
> —Theodore Roosevelt

NORTH DAKOTA

Total Wilderness areas: 3
Total Wilderness acreage: 39,652

Heading west from Minnesota, the North Woods lean out into the Great Plains, giving way to tallgrass and then shortgrass prairies. North Dakota—once a land of the wild and free, the Lakota Indians, and endless herds of buffalo—now preserves Wilderness only in two portions of wildlife refuges and part of a national park. Still, the sunsets are often blinding, the sound of distant thunder rumbles enchantingly, and Arctic winds can chill you to the bone.

Chase Lake Wilderness

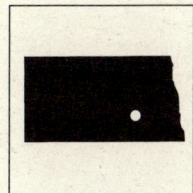

If you were to tally up all of the white pelicans that nest on two islands in this isolated alkali lake, you'd find more than 12,000, the largest colony in North America. That figure is all the more impressive (and heartening) when you consider that only 50 birds inhabited the region when the area was officially slated for protection in 1908. Birders may observe these creatures from a rise near the lake, but the islands themselves are strictly off-limits. In addition to pelicans, you may encounter ducks, geese, swans, sharp-tailed grouse, ring-necked pheasants, gulls, cormorants, white-tailed deer, and many smaller mammals. An old, unimproved trail circles the lake. The refuge is not monitored, off-trail travel is discouraged, and camping is not allowed.

Of the 4,385 acres of Chase Lake National Wildlife Refuge, 230 (separated from the rest of the refuge by a powerline) were not designated as Wilderness. The lake itself takes up more than half of the area; the remaining acreage is grassland and wetland with very few trees.

NORTH DAKOTA

Chase Lake Essentials

Size: 4,155 acres.
Year Designated: 1975.
Location: Southern central North Dakota.
Easiest Access: From Bismarck, take Interstate 94 east to Medina. Follow County Road 68 north for 10 miles, then turn west onto the refuge access route and go about 12 miles. Turn south at the refuge sign for a short drive that leads to a viewing point at its northwest corner. Cars are not allowed in the refuge.

Season: Summer temperatures have reached 118 degrees Fahrenheit, and winter temperatures have dipped to minus 42. June is probably best for observing the birds.
Wilderness Fees/Permits: None.
Maps: Free maps are available from the Chase Lake Prairie Project office.
Management: Chase Lake Prairie Project, R.R. 1, P.O. Box 144, Woodworth, ND 58496; (701) 752-4218.

Lostwood Wilderness

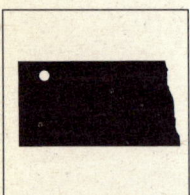

When the last glaciers receded from North Dakota approximately 10,000 years ago, they scoured out potholes and smoothed the terrain, forging the vast "prairie pothole" region. Today the area supports an abundance of wildlife among an open expanse of grasslands and watery marshes. The land is especially suited to numerous waterfowl and other water-dependent birds, such as ducks, rails, phalaropes, avocets, and godwits.

The 26,747-acre Lostwood National Wildlife Refuge protects the best surviving example of prairie-pothole land. Approximately 70 percent of the refuge is considered virgin prairie. In its northern section lies Lostwood Wilderness, whose established trails are open year-round to hiking, snowshoeing, and cross-country skiing. No camping, fire building, or use of motorized vehicles are allowed.

Lostwood Essentials

Size: 5,577 acres.
Year Designated: 1975.
Location: Northwestern North Dakota.
Easiest Access: From Minot, take U.S. 52 approximately 60 miles northwest to Kenmare. Turn west on County Road 2 and drive about 12 miles to the Wilderness.

Season: Spring, summer, and fall are all good for bird-watching. Winter can be mercilessly cold, with subzero temperatures.
Wilderness Fees/Permits: None.
Maps: A free map is available from the refuge.
Management: Lostwood National Wildlife Refuge, R.R. 2, Kenmare, ND 58746; (701) 848-2722.

Theodore Roosevelt Wilderness

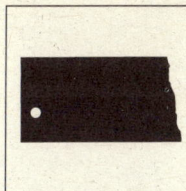

Divided into two units set 70 miles apart, Theodore Roosevelt National Park encompasses more than 70,000 acres, including a big hunk of scenic North Dakota badlands along the Little Missouri River. Eons ago, when the Rocky Mountains emerged, material washed off the range and was deposited here, forming a plain. Centuries of wind and rain eroded the plain into the naked, broken, colorful, and moonlike splendor of today's badlands. Teddy himself once owned and lived on a cattle ranch here, the Elkhorn, which is protected as a third unit of the park. The park bears the former president's name in honor of his devotion to practical conservation.

Most of the North and South Units west of the river have been designated Wilderness, and they provide a home for a multitude of wildlife. Many of the buffalo, coyotes, and prairie dogs that roam here have lost their natural fear of people; do not feed them. And whatever you do, don't pet the rattlesnakes.

Eighty-five miles of trails offer ample opportunity for solitude, as most visitors stay on park roads and in established campgrounds. In the South Unit, west of the river, the Petrified Forest Loop Trail (11 miles) is an especially popular route. Off-trail the terrain is wide open, but identifiable landmarks make cross-country hiking easy.

In spring, when snowmelt fills the river, paddling can be excellent. Put in at Medora on the South Unit and paddle the 110 miles to a takeout at Long X Bridge on U.S. 85 near the North Unit to see everything the river has to offer. Excellent campsites exist all along the waterway. Gathering firewood is prohibited.

Theodore Roosevelt Essentials

Size: 29,920 acres.
Year Designated: 1978.
Location: Western North Dakota.
Easiest Access: The South Unit runs along Interstate 94 with park headquarters in Medora. The North Unit lies on U.S. 85, 53 miles north of the Belfield exit off Interstate 94. Elkhorn Ranch can be accessed from the South Unit.
Season: Most visitors come from May through September, but even then sudden storms may bring hail and high winds.
Wilderness Fees/Permits: From May through September an entrance fee is charged: $4 per car, $2 per person, or $10 per season. No fees are required during the rest of the year. A free backcountry overnight permit must be obtained.
Maps: Free maps are available from park headquarters, but they are not topographic. A topographic map is available for $4 from the Theodore Roosevelt Nature and History Association, P.O. Box 167, Medora, ND 58645; (701) 623-4884.
Management: Theodore Roosevelt National Park, P.O. Box 7, Medora, ND 58645; (701) 623-4466.

> "The universe of the wilderness is disappearing like a snowbank on a south-facing slope on a warm June day."
>
> —Bob Marshall

OHIO

Total Wilderness areas: 1
Total Wilderness acreage: 77

Geologically, the islands of Lake Erie were carved from solid limestone by the last glaciers that blanketed this region in ice so long ago. Far from the lakeshore, the islands aren't subject to the wide fluctuations in daily temperatures experienced on the mainland. For this reason, many birds make their homes there. One small lake isle claims all the Wilderness in Ohio.

West Sister Island Wilderness

When sailing ships first plied the waters of Lake Erie, they were guided safely on their way by a lighthouse perched on the westernmost point of West Sister Island. Keepers operated the light until 1937, when it became automated. Thanks to the Coast Guard, the lighthouse and the surrounding three acres are now part of the designated Wilderness of West Sister Island National Wildlife Refuge, managed as a satellite of Ottawa National Wildlife Refuge.

The island rises from the water to a not-very-high point of 35 feet. More than 75 percent of the land is shaded by 40- to 50-foot-tall hackberry, an almost pure stand. The upper reaches of the hackberry trees cradle more than 1,100 active nests that contain the eggs of great blue herons, black-crowned night herons, and common egrets in season. A food shortage on the island sends these birds on an 18-mile round-trip flight to mainland marshes several times a day. Rock ledges along the island's shore provide sunning spots for many of West Sister's dense snake population. This island is strictly for the birds, and human visitors are not allowed to step ashore. You may cruise around the perimeter and view the inhabitants from a respectful distance. Don't forget your binoculars.

West Sister Island Essentials

Size: 77 acres.
Year Designated: 1975.
Location: Southern Lake Erie.
Easiest Access: From Toledo, take State Route 2 east about 12 miles to Ottawa National Wildlife Refuge. West Sister Island lies about nine miles offshore.
Season: June to see nesting birds from a boat.
Wilderness Fees/Permits: None, but visitors must remain in their boats.
Maps: Any nautical chart of Lake Erie. Ask the refuge manager.
Management: Ottawa National Wildlife Refuge, 14000 West State Route 2, Oak Harbor, OH 43449; (419) 898-0014.

> "[Wilderness] is a part of the earth that many of us are beginning to view as vital to our survival, necessary for our mental and spiritual health, and intrinsically valuable regardless of its importance to us."
>
> —Chad Henderson

OKLAHOMA

Total Wilderness areas: 3
Total Wilderness acreage: 22,524

Once known as "Indian Territory," Oklahoma today is home to more Native Americans than any other state, and they live primarily in the wind-swept grasslands and the eastern evergreen forest/lake country. Unfortunately, Oklahoma does not claim much Wilderness space. Here you'll find one national forest, shared with Arkansas, that protects two small Wildernesses created by the Oklahoma Wilderness Area Act of 1988. A third Wilderness stands on a wildlife refuge.

Black Fork Mountain Wilderness

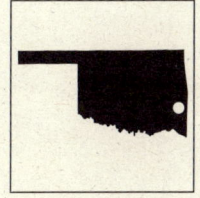

Shared by Oklahoma and Arkansas (see Arkansas, Black Fork Mountain Wilderness), this area contains the 13-mile-long, rugged ridge of Black Fork Mountain. Large rock flows or "glaciers" and sandstone bluffs stand above a forest dominated by oak and shortleaf pine. The northern slopes support hardwoods with an open understory. A forest of dwarf oaks adds to the cover of vegetation, which includes several unique plant species, such as serviceberry and granddaddy graybeard, hidden away in small coves.

There are no maintained trails on the Oklahoma side, and you'll find the hiking to be challenging. You'll also find the headwaters of Big Creek along the southern boundary. Once you're deep in the interior, water sources are either slim or none. Two small springs on the mountain flow most of the year. Few humans ever walk on Black Fork Mountain. On the northern side the sound of traffic from a nearby highway fades away and leaves you as alone as you can get in an Oklahoma Wilderness.

OKLAHOMA

Black Fork Mountain Essentials

Size: 4,583 acres in Oklahoma (12,151 acres total).
Year Designated: 1988 in Oklahoma.
Location: Eastern Oklahoma.
Easiest Access: From U.S. 59/270 at Page, take County Road 1040 north about two miles to a parking lot.
Season: Spring and summer.

Wilderness Fees/Permits: None.
Maps: USGS topographic maps are Mountain Fork, Page, and Rich Mountain. A Wilderness map is available for $3 from the Ozark Interpretive Association, P.O. Box 1279, Mountain View, AR 72560.
Management: Choctaw Ranger District, Ouachita National Forest, HC 64, Box 3467, Heavener, OK 74937; (918) 653-2991.

Charons Garden–North Mountain Wilderness

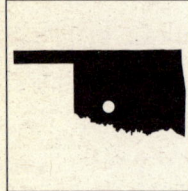

The American buffalo once roamed in uncountable numbers here among the grasslands that rise to lakes, streams, and stunning canyons. Today there's a small but growing herd. Something about seeing these near-extinct creatures, grazing in apparent contentment, makes conflicting emotions well up in my heart at once: sadness for the loss of the restless sea of shaggy beasts, yet excitement that a few still remain with us. Here in the Wichita Mountains life must be close to the way it was in the Old West.

Although the National Wildlife Refuge System technically was born when it claimed Florida's Pelican Island in 1903, practically speaking the system began here just after the turn of the century, in what is now known as Wichita Mountains National Wildlife Refuge. In 1901 this area was proclaimed a "Forest Preserve," and in 1905 President Theodore Roosevelt signed a law creating the first "Game Sanctuary" here for the almost-extinct *Bison bison*. Thanks to careful management, a remnant bunch of 15 buffalo has grown to a maintained herd of more than 500, who live among the rugged rocky outcroppings, oak forests, and the mixed-grass prairie of the refuge.

Rare in this area, a herd of about 300 Texas longhorn cattle are kept wild, sharing the region with elk, deer, and buffalo. Open range allows the animals to wander through your camp, but they are not tame. At night you will probably hear coyotes howl and owls hoot, and you may be visited by the resident population of overly friendly raccoons.

Of the refuge's 59,019 acres, 22,400 acres are open to public use. The rest of the refuge is a special-use area reserved for the wild animals. Within the northern portion of the special-use area lies North Mountain Wilderness, which appears on some lists as a separate Wilderness. The southwestern corner of the refuge is protected as Charons Garden Wilderness and is open to the public. Two trails of the Elk Mountain Trail System cross Charons Garden, one wandering through the heart of the Wilderness (three miles one-way), the other climbing 900 feet to the summit of Elk Mountain (one mile one-way). No fires and no alcohol are permitted.

OKLAHOMA

Charons Garden–North Mountain Essentials

Size: 5,723 acres of Charons Garden, 2,847 acres of North Mountain (8,570 acres total).
Year Designated: 1970.
Location: Southwestern Oklahoma.
Easiest Access: From Medicine Park, located on Interstate 44, take State Route 49 west for approximately five miles to the refuge.
Season: Spring to see the baby animals.
Wilderness Fees/Permits: No permit is necessary for day hikes. Overnighters must have a permit; only 10 people are allowed per day. Three days and two nights is the maximum stay. Advance reservations are recommended and cost $2 per person.
Maps: A topographic refuge map that includes the Wilderness is available for a nominal price from the refuge manager.
Management: Wichita Mountains National Wildlife Refuge, Route 1, Box 448, Indiahoma, OK 73552; (405) 429-3222.

Upper Kiamichi River Wilderness

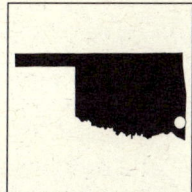

Long ridges called Pine Mountain and Rich Mountain, with a high point of approximately 2,600 feet, shelter this Wilderness, and on Pine Mountain the Kiamichi River is born. *Kiamichi* is derived from the French word for "waterbird." Unusual for Oklahoma, you'll find groves of beech along the Kiamichi's headwaters, giving way to a dense forest of pine and hardwoods. The ridges are steep and the valleys below are relatively flat but narrow. In several places the ridges are broken by rock flows or "glaciers." Several creeks drain the area, often creating miniature and picturesque waterfalls.

On the northern boundary runs the Talimena Scenic Byway (Oklahoma Highway 1) with overlooks of the area. The Arkansas state line forms the eastern boundary. The western boundary lies along the Kiamichi Electric powerline, and the southwestern boundary begins at a parking lot on Pashubbe Creek where the Ouachita National Recreation Trail has a trailhead. Oklahoma holds a total of about 57 miles of the Ouachita Trail. Stretching nearly 200 miles from Talihina, Oklahoma, to Hot Springs, Arkansas, here the trail follows the Upper Kiamichi River all the way across the Wilderness to a second trailhead at Stateline Monument. The Ouachita is the only maintained trail in the area; it crosses through the river several times, so you should plan on getting your feet wet. The Wilderness may be accessed off State Highway 63 near the southern boundary, and there is a parking lot near the southeastern corner where Horsepen Creek flows out of the area.

Upper Kiamichi River Essentials

Size: 9,371 acres.
Year Designated: 1988.
Location: Eastern Oklahoma.
Easiest Access: From Poteau, take U.S. 59/259 south for approximately 40 miles, then turn east on Forest Service Road 6032 and drive three miles to the parking lot at Pashubbe Creek.
Season: Spring and fall.
Wilderness Fees/Permits: None.
Maps: A free Wilderness map is available from the district ranger.
Management: Kiamichi Ranger District, Ouachita National Forest, P.O. Box 577, Talihina, OK 74571; (918) 567-2326.

> "In the past, pioneers saw the open prairies and were filled with dreams of dominating nature with the glories of man. Now we know different: We must preserve the wilds for our very survival."
>
> —Deng Ming-Dao

OREGON

Total Wilderness areas: 38
Total Wilderness acreage: 2,093,888

Although logging has taken a vast swipe out of Oregon's forests, large portions of the state remain remarkably close to what early pioneers settled. The terrain varies dramatically, ranging from thrusting mountains to high desert to a ragged Pacific coastline.

Three mountain ranges distinguish Oregon: the Coastal Range near the sea, the Cascade Mountains dominating roughly the entire center from north to south, and the Blue Mountains in the northeast. Most Oregonians live in the fertile Willamette Valley between the Coastal and Cascade Ranges, where part of an ancient forest—perhaps the most magnificent on earth—once stretched from California to Alaska.

The Oregon Wilderness is preserved primarily on national forestland, with small pieces on lands overseen by the Bureau of Land Management and the U.S. Fish and Wildlife Service.

Badger Creek Wilderness

For the most commanding view of the Cascades and the high desert country to the east, you'll have to hike up Lookout Mountain, the highest point in the area at 6,525 feet. The mountain itself and the high ridgeland extending east feature a subalpine ecosystem, with hardy trees and rocky terrain. Then, farther east in the Wilderness, where the climate is warm and dry, you'll find a forest of ponderosa pines and extensive growths of Oregon white oak and grasslands.

Three creeks—Badger, Little Badger, and Tygh—drain Badger Creek Wilderness, where slope inclines range from 30 to 70 degrees. Rocks chiseled smooth by glaciers distinguish the upper reaches of Badger Creek, and mountain hemlock dominates all three streams.

There are about 55 miles of trails in the Wilderness, including the Badger Creek National Recreation Trail, which follows the length of the creek in the Wilderness, a distance of 11.9 miles. From Robin Hood Campground near the western boundary, the steep 2.4-mile Gumjuwac Saddle Trail climbs to the confluence of four trails, including a spur route that ultimately connects to the Badger Creek Trail and a fine view of Mount Hood to the northwest. Mount Hood Wilderness (see below) lies just across State Highway 35.

Badger Creek Essentials

Size: 24,000 acres.
Year Designated: 1984.
Location: Northwestern Oregon.
Easiest Access: From just east of the town of Hood River on Interstate 84, take State Highway 35 south approximately 30 miles to Robin Hood Campground on the east side of the road.
Season: Spring through fall.
Wilderness Fees/Permits: None.
Maps: A Wilderness map that includes Columbia Wilderness is available for $2 from the district ranger.
Management: Barlow Ranger District, Mount Hood National Forest, P.O. Box 67, Dufur, OR 97021; (541) 467-2291.

Black Canyon Wilderness

Thickets of willow and brush line the banks of Black Canyon Creek, which drops from 6,483 feet to 2,850 feet as it drains the Black Canyon Wilderness easterly into the South Fork John Day River. Cliffs line the creek's winding lower gorge.

North-south ridges and steep side slopes along the waterway defer to rolling and then flat benches on the Wilderness edges. Dry sagebrush covers these exposed ridge tops as well as the lowlands, with a dense forest of mixed conifers (fir and pine), including parklike stands of ponderosa pine, flourishing in between.

Elk and deer graze openly year-round, with black bears, coyotes, and mountain lions spotted less often. If you visit in summer, beware the danger of rattlesnakes. Snow falls by mid-November and usually melts by April, with access sometimes blocked by the fluffy white stuff well into May. Summer months typically tend to be hot and dry.

The 12-mile Black Canyon Trail cuts through a narrow gorge, requiring hikers to cross rushing water at least a dozen times. Prepare for wet feet, and expect to find the creek unfordable at high water, usually January through March. Three short side trails join the Black Canyon Trail. Cross-country hiking on the ridges rates as relatively easy (and dry). A large piece of undesignated wildland lies to the north. Opportunities for solitude are splendid, with approximately 18 miles of maintained trails on which to lose yourself.

OREGON

Black Canyon Essentials

Size: 13,400 acres.
Year Designated: 1984.
Location: Central Oregon.
Easiest Access: From one mile east of Prineville, on U.S. 26, head south and east on State Highway 380 for approximately 59 miles until you are four miles past Paulina. Drive north on Road 42 until you reach Road 58, about eight miles. Turn east on Road 58, then north again on Road 5810 after one mile. When you reach Road 5840, about 10 miles, turn east and drive three more miles to the upper Black Canyon Trailhead.
Season: Late spring through early fall.
Wilderness Fees/Permits: None.
Maps: USGS topographic maps of the Wilderness and surrounding wildland are Aldrich Gulch, Antone, Day Basin, Dayville, Six Corners, and Wolf Mountain.
Management: Paulina Ranger District, Ochoco National Forest, 6015 Paulina Star Route, Paulina, OR 97751; (541) 742-7511.

Boulder Creek Wilderness

Small waterfalls and rapids connect the series of quiet pools (suitable for summer swimming) that make up Boulder Creek, a tributary of the North Umpqua River. The rapids run south and west, channeling through the heart of the Wilderness. Numerous streams feed into Boulder Creek, quenching the thirst of the old-growth timber that towers over its banks. Ponderosa pines flourish on Pine Bench, near the lower end of the Wilderness, and are thought to be the largest such stand this far northwest of the crest of the Cascade Mountains.

The rocky monoliths and outcroppings attract (and challenge) technical rock climbers, especially in the southern portion's Umpqua Rocks Special Interest Geologic Area. Elevations range from 1,600 feet to 5,600 feet. If you choose to go underground rather than scale a rock, you may find evidence of early Indian use within several caves in the area.

Low elevation means the 30 miles of trails remain clear and can provide access to the Wilderness year-round. The Soda Springs Trail rambles about two miles to Pine Bench and joins the Boulder Creek Trail, which crosses about seven miles of the Wilderness in a generally north-south direction. From Pine Bench, you can get a terrific view of Boulder Creek's canyon.

Boulder Creek Essentials

Size: 19,100 acres.
Year Designated: 1984.
Location: Southwestern central Oregon.
Easiest Access: From Roseburg, take State Highway 138 east about 48 miles. Eight miles east of Dry Creek Store, turn north on paved Medicine Creek Road 4775 and then west immediately on the Soda Springs Dam access road. The Soda Springs Trailhead is in 1.2 miles.
Season: Spring through fall.
Wilderness Fees/Permits: None.
Maps: A Wilderness map that includes Rogue-Umpqua Divide Wilderness and Mount Thielsen Wilderness is available for $1 from the district ranger.
Management: Steamboat Ranger District, Umpqua National Forest, Toketee Star Route, Idleyld, OR 97447; (541) 498-2511.

OREGON

Bridge Creek Wilderness

Bridge Creek drains northeasterly from the edge of the summit of the Ochoco Mountains, essentially dividing the Wilderness into two meadow-filled plateaus. The peaks of East Point and North Point look across this small Wilderness from 6,625 feet and 6,607 feet, respectively. The view from North Point's 600-foot cliff face is particularly breathtaking.

Most of the 30 inches of annual precipitation falls as winter snow on a forest dominated by fir and larch with streaks of pine and clearings of sagebrush and bunchgrass. In the central core of the area, you'll find stands of white fir and lodgepole pine nearing 100 years in age. Water gurgles perennially from five springs: Thompson, Pisgah, Masterson, Nelson, and Maxwell. Mule deer and elk seek the densest thickets when hunters come in fall.

You will not find much in the way of trails (about 3.5 poorly maintained miles), and off-trail hiking (through a tangled understory) tends to be difficult. Wind has stunted the trees and opened the country around North Point; an easy hike of about 1.2 miles from near Pisgah Springs along an abandoned jeep track will take you to the summit. Another trail leads about 1.5 miles to the summit of East Point. You may very well have this area all to yourself.

Bridge Creek Essentials

Size: 5,400 acres.
Year Designated: 1984.
Location: Central Oregon.
Easiest Access: From Prineville, take U.S. 26 east and north about 16 miles. Turn south on Ochoco Creek Road (which becomes Road 22) and continue 8.5 miles past the ranger station. Then turn left on Road 150 and continue for one-half mile. When you reach Forest Service Road 2630, turn right and drive seven more miles to Bridge Creek near Pisgah Springs and the trailhead to North Point. The last two miles of road are rough.
Season: Summer and fall.
Wilderness Fees/Permits: None.
Maps: USGS topographic map is Mount Pisgah.
Management: Big Summit Ranger District, Ochoco National Forest, Mitchell Star Route, Box 255, Prineville, OR 97754; (541) 416-6645.

Bull of the Woods Wilderness

This isolated Wilderness boasts about a dozen lakes measuring at least one acre and chock-full of trout. These blue jewels are nestled throughout the mountains, accessible by trail but separated by high ridges. The mountain slopes are quite steep, with lower inclines ranging from 30 to 60 degrees and upper inclines from 60 to 90 degrees. Numerous streams cut through the peaks, including the major headwaters of the Collawash, Breitenbush, and Little North Santiam Rivers.

The vegetation varies according to the elevation, from sparse subalpine forestland that extends to 5,700 feet to dense old-growth Douglas fir and western hemlock, one of the last stands of old growth in western Oregon. The northern spotted owl shares these lofty branches with at least five other species of owls. Chances are slim that you'll ever encounter one of these

413

OREGON

nocturnal creatures; you're much more likely to see deserted mine shafts and old equipment, relics of past mining activity. Not far west lies Table Rock Wilderness (see below).

At 5,523 feet, Bull of the Woods Peak marks the hub of a relatively challenging 68-mile trail system, with several loop opportunities for overnight or long weekend hikes. An old lookout at the summit still commands an astounding view of the surrounding area. The Pansy Lake Trail to the lookout tower travels about 1.2 easy miles to pretty-as-a-flower Pansy Lake before starting to climb. The Hot Springs Trail leads about 1.5 miles to Bagby Hot Springs, where you can melt into one of the steamy soaking tubs. Rangers don't allow camping here, so after your soak you can pick up the same trail and head more than 13 miles across the middle of the Wilderness. Twin Lakes and Elk Lake are the most popular, and show the impact of poor camping habits.

Bull of the Woods Essentials

Size: 34,900 acres.
Year Designated: 1984.
Location: Northwestern Oregon.
Easiest Access: From Estacada, take State Highway 224 southeast about 26 miles. Near the Ripplebrook Campground, head south on Forest Service Road 46 for 3.6 miles. When you reach Forest Service Road 63, turn south and continue for 5.6 miles. Turn south again at Forest Service Road 70, which leads six miles to the Hot Springs Trailhead.
Season: Late spring through fall.
Wilderness Fees/Permits: None.
Maps: A Wilderness map that includes Salmon-Huckleberry Wilderness is available for $2 from the district rangers.
Management: Estacada Ranger District, Mount Hood National Forest, 595 NW Industrial Way, Estacada, OR 97023; (503) 630-6861. Detroit Ranger District, Willamette National Forest, HC 73, Box 320, Mill City, OR 97360; (503) 854-3366.

Columbia Wilderness

Known as the Columbia Gorge Recreation Area prior to Wilderness designation, this area lies just south of the sheer cliffs of the Columbia River Gorge. Most of the land adjacent to the river and along Interstate 84 is privately owned and often developed and, of course, outside the Wilderness boundary. The breaks of the gorge are spectacular basalt cliffs, rocky slopes, and rock outcroppings. Rugged and steep, the slopes of the Wilderness rise to a slightly uneven plateau and on to mountain peaks, talus slopes, and lakes with elevations ranging from approximately 100 feet near the river to 4,900 feet on Mount Defiance. Sparkling waterfalls and mossy-green cliff faces often highlight the deep drainages slashing through the broad, flat ridge tops. The main waterways—Herman Creek, Eagle Creek, and Tanner Creek—flow north toward the river, supporting borders of western hemlock and fir.

Most of the 200 miles of trails follow drainages. Approximately 14 miles of the Pacific Crest Trail and the Eagle Creek Trail receive the most use. The Eagle Creek Trail, with seven waterfalls, a tunnel, and designated campsites, can be hiked in a 16-mile-plus loop that hurdles Tanner Butte. Its proximity to Portland translates into lots of people. If you require solitude, take one of the quieter trails: Tanner Butte, Herman Creek, and Nick Eaton Ridge. Each of these is approximately 10 to 12 miles round-trip.

Columbia Essentials

Size: 39,000 acres.
Year Designated: 1984.
Location: Northwestern Oregon.
Easiest Access: From Portland, take Interstate 84 approximately 40 miles east to find the Eagle Creek Trailhead near Eagle Creek Campground on the south side of the highway.
Season: With mild winters, this area is accessible all year.

Wilderness Fees/Permits: None.
Maps: A Wilderness map that includes Badger Creek Wilderness is available for $2 from the district ranger.
Management: Columbia Gorge Ranger District, Mount Hood National Forest, 31520 SE Woodard Road, Troutdale, OR 97060; (503) 695-2276.

Cummins Creek Wilderness

Overhung with alder and maple, Cummins and Bob Creeks drain west through this dense rainforest Wilderness, where Sitka spruce sometimes reach nine feet in diameter. Both creeks spill into the Pacific Ocean, whose salty water almost reaches the western Wilderness boundary. Salmon, steelhead, and cutthroat trout spawn in the cool creek waters. Spruce-covered Cummins Ridge, which peaks at almost 2,000 feet, splits the rain forest in two. Yellow monkey flower, purple aster, white candy flower, and red foxglove brighten summer days, which otherwise tend toward the wet and foggy. Winters never see snow.

Just north of the Wilderness, Cape Perpetua offers you a chance to see migrating whales from December to May, and Perpetua Campground offers campsites. The Cummins Creek Trail follows the creek for a couple of deep forest miles, then turns north and circles back toward Cape Perpetua along Gwynn Creek outside the Wilderness. You may keep following Cummins Creek along a pleasant but unofficial path. The Cummins Ridge Trail follows the entire 6.2-mile ridge between Cummins and Bob Creeks, crossing old-growth Sitka spruce. This ridge-crest trail can be connected at both ends by vehicle.

Cummins Creek Essentials

Size: 9,300 acres.
Year Designated: 1984.
Location: Central coastal Oregon.
Easiest Access: From Florence, take U.S. 101 north approximately 22 miles to Cape Perpetua and Perpetua Campground.
Season: Spring and fall for the clearest days.

Wilderness Fees/Permits: None.
Maps: A Wilderness map is available for $2 from the district ranger. USGS topographic maps are Cummins Peak and Yachats.
Management: Waldport Ranger District, Siuslaw National Forest, 1049 SW Pacific Highway, Waldport, OR 97394; (541) 563-3211.

OREGON

Diamond Peak Wilderness

Great glaciers carved Diamond Peak after volcanic activity created the mountain. Today, at 8,744 feet, it surpasses every other summit in this region of the Cascade Mountains. Diamond Peak Wilderness, which straddles the crest of the Cascades, rests largely beneath a dense forest of mountain hemlock, lodgepole and western pine, and silver, noble, and other true firs. Snowfields remain most of the year in pockets above the tree line, and dozens of small lakes, one to 28 acres in size, bejewel the high country. Pikas and marmots scurry about the numerous scree slopes, along with Roosevelt elk, at least until November snows drive them out. Stinging hordes of mosquitoes hatch from the first of July through much of August. Excluded from Wilderness designation but on the eastern and southern boundaries you'll find three large scenic lakes: Summit, Crescent, and Odell.

Approximately 14 miles of the Pacific Crest National Scenic Trail pass through the area and near Diamond Peak itself, and another 38 miles of trails give access to many lovely lakeside campsites. Mountain climbers scaling Diamond Peak's nontechnical summit often set up base camps at Marie Lake, Divide Lake, and Rockpile Lake. Much of this area is worthy of off-trail exploration.

Diamond Peak Essentials
Size: 52,337 acres.
Year Designated: 1964; expanded in 1984.
Location: Southwestern central Oregon.
Easiest Access: From Interstate 5 south of Eugene, take State Highway 58 southeast approximately 63 miles to Willamette Pass and the Pacific Crest Trailhead. Hike south.
Season: Summer and fall.
Wilderness Fees/Permits: None.
Maps: A Wilderness map is available for $5 from the district rangers. PCT maps are available for $2 per section from the rangers. PCT Central Oregon Portion covers the Wilderness.
Management: Crescent Ranger District, Deschutes National Forest, P.O. Box 208, Crescent, OR 97633; (541) 433-2234. Rigdon Ranger District, Willamette National Forest, 49098 Salmon Creek Road, Oakridge, OR 97463; (541) 782-2283.

Drift Creek Wilderness

Towering Sitka spruce and western hemlock that sometimes reach seven feet in diameter shade the Coast Range's largest rainforest stand of old growth. The steep canyons of rock-splattered Drift Creek may give you the impression of mountainous country, but the forested hills rise only slightly above 2,000 feet. Soaked by as much as 120 inches of annual rainfall, moss and ferns as thick as six inches cushion the ground along numerous streams shadowed by overhanging bigleaf maples. Roosevelt elk and black bears share this lush territory with two endangered Oregon species: northern spotted owls and bald eagles. In fall, Drift Creek comes alive with spawning chinook and coho salmon as well as steelhead and cutthroat trout.

Three trails descend through the forest to the soft green banks of Drift Creek: the Horse

Creek Trail from the north (about three miles) and east (about two miles), and the Harris Ranch Trail (about two miles) from the south. These paths can be connected if you're willing to wade the creek, a dangerous undertaking during winter and spring high water. The Horse Creek Trail from the north crosses some of the best old-growth forest. Faded trails laid down by anglers follow most of Drift Creek itself. Bushwhacking here is difficult enough to almost ensure solitude.

Drift Creek Essentials

Size: 5,800 acres.
Year Designated: 1984.
Location: Central coastal Oregon.
Easiest Access: From U.S. 101 turn east on North Beaver Creek Road at Ona Beach State Park and drive 3.8 miles. When you reach North Elkhorn Road 51, turn south and continue six more miles, then proceed 1.3 miles east on Forest Service Road 50. Turn south on Forest Service Road 5087, which leads 3.4 miles to the northern Horse Creek Trailhead.
Season: Summer and fall.
Wilderness Fees/Permits: None.
Maps: USGS topographic maps are Hellion Rapids and Tidewater.
Management: Waldport Ranger District, Siuslaw National Forest, 1049 SW Pacific Highway, Waldport, OR 97394; (541) 563-3211.

Eagle Cap Wilderness

Oregon's largest Wilderness encompasses the heart of the Wallowa Mountains, once home to the Nez Perce Indians. It also qualifies as the state's largest continuous alpine area and encompasses Legore Lake, at 8,880 feet the highest lake above sea level in the state.

This vast region has almost 60 high alpine lakes, which are surrounded by open meadows, bare granite peaks and ridges, and classical U-shaped glacial valleys thickly forested in their lower sections and rising to scattered stands of alpine timber.

Elevations start at about 5,000 feet and top out at 9,845 feet on Matterhorn Peak near the center of the area. Thirty-one summits exceed 8,000 feet. Trout fishing can be fair to excellent in the 37-plus miles of streams. And if your luck there is lousy, you can always drop a line in one of the lakes. The upper four miles of the Wild and Scenic Eagle Creek flow here. Backpacking and horsepacking are very popular pursuits in this area. Hunters come for elk, deer, mountain goats, and bighorn sheep. Black bears, bobcats, and mountain lions prowl these parts, too. High summer temperatures guarantee swarms of mosquitoes and horseflies in wet areas.

The Lakes Basin Area, a series of sparkling sapphires surrounded by peaks, ranks as the most impacted by humans and the most fragile region of the Wilderness. Huge portions of Eagle Cap are virtually unseen. Ridges radiate out like the spokes of a wagon wheel from the 9,595-foot hub known as Eagle Cap Mountain, which overlooks the Lakes Basin and anchors the southern portion of the area. The waters flowing down these ridges join together to form the Wild and Scenic Imnaha River, the Wild and startlingly Scenic Lostine River, the entire designated length of the Wild and Scenic Minam River, and the Wallowa River.

Approximately 534 miles of trails give access to this area. An estimated nine out of 10 visitors enter from either Wallowa Lake State Park, Hurricane Creek Campground, or Two Pan Campground. Hikers may find the rough terrain strenuous, but many glorious mountaintops can

OREGON

be reached without technical climbing skill. My memories of the Wallowas recall majestic summits lightly dusted with early October snow around lovely Chimney Lake, after a 4.4-mile hike from Lillyville Campground up the Chimney Lake Trail switchbacks.

Eagle Cap Essentials

Size: 358,461 acres.
Year Designated: 1964; expanded in 1972 and 1984.
Location: Northeastern Oregon.
Easiest Access: From Enterprise, take State Highway 82 north and east about 16 miles to Lostine. Turn south on Forest Service Road 8210 and continue to Lillyville Campground, approximately 12 miles.
Season: July through October.
Wilderness Fees/Permits: None.
Maps: A Wilderness map is available for $3 from the district ranger.
Management: Eagle Cap Ranger District, Wallowa-Whitman National Forest, P.O. Box M, Enterprise, OR 97828; (541) 426-3104.

Gearhart Mountain Wilderness

At 8,364 feet, Gearhart Mountain stands higher than all the other volcanic domes in this Wilderness of high mountain meadows, cirques, and U-shaped valleys. Picturesque rock formations cap most of the ridgelines, offering sweeping views of the artistic sculpturings of long-vanished glaciers. Lodgepole pine, ponderosa pine, and white fir dominate the vegetation. Sadly, the only lake in the Wilderness, Blue Lake, shows the impact of careless human use. The Wild and Scenic North Fork Sprague River sweeps past the northern boundary of the area.

The main thoroughfare, Gearhart Mountain Trail, provides about 12 miles of access for foot and horse traffic along the main ridge and to the well-visited shores of Blue Lake. Joining the main trail from the southwest is the 3.7-mile Boulder Spring Trail. The region's fairly gentle terrain and open forestland invite bushwhacking, but snow may linger until early July. Snowshoeing and backcountry skiing are increasingly popular sports here.

Gearhart Mountain Essentials

Size: 22,809 acres.
Year Designated: 1964; expanded in 1984.
Location: Central southern Oregon.
Easiest Access: From Paisley, take Mill Street west for one mile, then turn right and follow Road 3315 south for 20.5 miles. When you reach Road 28, turn south, proceed for one-half mile, then turn west on Forest Service Road 3411. After six miles you will reach Forest Service Road 3372. Turn south and continue 1.5 miles to Forest Service Road 015. Continue south a little more than a mile to the end of the road, the northern terminus of the Gearhart Mountain Trail.
Season: July through October.
Wilderness Fees/Permits: None.
Maps: A Wilderness map is available for $3 from the district ranger. USGS topographic maps are Coffeepot Creek, Coleman Point, Cougar Peak, and Lee Thomas Crossing.
Management: Bly Ranger District, Fremont National Forest, P.O. Box 25, Bly, OR 97622; (541) 353-2427.

OREGON

Grassy Knob Wilderness

Covered in a tangled rain forest of coniferous evergreens thick with an ankle-grabbing understory, Grassy Knob Wilderness lies rugged and steep. Elevations vary from almost sea level to more than 2,000 feet on summits that include Grassy Knob, at 2,342 feet, on the western boundary. This Wilderness nurtures the fragrant Port Orford cedar, drooping with its characteristic twisting limbs in rare stands of old growth with some trunks exceeding six feet in diameter. The primary drainage of misnamed Dry Creek provides habitat for a remarkable population of spawning salmon. Many small, turbulent, and virtually pure streams tumble for short distances over emerald waterfalls and through ravines cool with shade during typically sunny summers. The red of vine maple brightens moss-laden glens come autumn, while winter brings an average of 130 inches of chilly rain born in the nearby Pacific. Weather changes may be remarkable and rapid.

Off-trail hiking rates as an extremely rough experience, hence the general absence of visitors. The route along Dry Creek is passable and wondrously deep with old-growth Douglas fir and cedar. The Grassy Knob Trail follows an abandoned road for about 1.3 miles and continues (moderate to difficult) one last mile to the top of Anvil Mountain, where you can take in bird's-eye views of the area and perhaps get a peek at the distant sea rolling restlessly against rocky little islands. Elk River forms part of the southern boundary and offers Class IV white water.

Grassy Knob Essentials

Size: 17,200 acres.
Year Designated: 1984.
Location: Southwestern coast of Oregon.
Easiest Access: From Port Orford, take U.S. 101 north about four miles. Turn east on Grassy Knob Road and continue to the barricade marking the Wilderness boundary, about seven miles.
Season: Summer and early fall.
Wilderness Fees/Permits: None.
Maps: USGS topographic maps are Father Mountain, Mount Butler, Port Orford, and Sixes. A topographic map is available for $3 from the district ranger.
Management: Powers Ranger District, Siskiyou National Forest, Powers, OR 97466; (541) 439-3011.

Hells Canyon Wilderness

White-water rafters can rage through this Wilderness on the Snake River, 68 miles of which have been designated Wild and Scenic. With Class IV drops, this river is far too turbulent for open canoes, short rafts, or unskilled paddlers. Most of the wild water is packed into the first 17 miles below the Hells Canyon Dam.

Cut by the Snake River to a depth greater than any other canyon in North America, Hells Canyon exceeds 8,000 feet in places. The 652,488-acre Hells Canyon National Recreation Area (HCNRA), managed by the U.S. Forest Service, straddles both the border of northeastern Oregon–western Idaho and the Snake River. Approximately one-third of HCNRA has been designated Wilderness.

The Idaho side of the Wilderness lies in parts of Nez Perce and Payette National Forests (see

OREGON

Idaho, Hells Canyon Wilderness). Clear creeks dissect the larger but more isolated and less visited Oregon side. Its higher elevations are thinly treed, with occasional dense stands of Douglas fir and ponderosa pine. Grassy benches dominate the lower elevations.

The Nee Me Poo Trail, 3.7 miles of the old Nez Perce Trail, scales the northern section of the area to garner the view from Lone Pine Saddle before descending to Dug Bar on the river. Three miles of the Snake River Trail from Dug Bar follow the Oregon side of the Snake River south, providing access to several other trails. More than 1,500 prehistoric sites have been identified here, including petroglyphs and depressions that once marked pit houses; federal law requires they be left alone. Elk, deer, and chukar (a partridge) are hunted here.

I was deceived looking over the edge of Hells Canyon. It just does not seem as deep as they say it is. But birds of prey swooped about in the windy, clean air, the sound of the river swept up the slope, and I will be ever glad I stopped for at least one day.

Hells Canyon Essentials

Size: 131,133 acres in Oregon (214,933 total).
Year Designated: 1975; expanded in 1984.
Location: Northeastern Oregon.
Easiest Access: From Copperfield, take County Road 454 (Idaho Power Company Road) west across the river and 20 miles to Hells Canyon Dam and the launch site. From Imnaha, take Forest Service Road 4260 north and east approximately 20 miles. Two miles past the Imnaha Bridge, you'll find the Nee Me Poo Trailhead.
Season: Trails begin to open in June and may stay open into October. The river-rafting season is mid-May until mid-September.
Wilderness Fees/Permits: None for backcountry use of the Wilderness. River use requires a permit, which can be obtained from Wallowa-Whitman National Forest. A fee of $6 is charged for a river permit application, with no guarantee of being chosen.
Maps: The Wilderness appears on the Hells Canyon Map ($2) and the Wallowa-Whitman National Forest Map ($3), both available from the forest rangers.
Management: Hells Canyon National Recreation Area Headquarters, P.O. Box 490, Enterprise, OR 97828; (541) 426-4978. Wallowa-Whitman National Forest, P.O. Box 907, Baker, OR 97814; (541) 523-6391. BLM Vale District Office, 100 Oregon Street, Vale, OR 97918; (541) 473-3144.

Kalmiopsis Wilderness

This harsh and ragged piece of territory, Oregon's third largest Wilderness, has earned a reputation for being inhospitable—aficionados of great myths consider it a likely hideout for Bigfoot. Chill rains (100 or more inches per year) beat against the very rugged and steep terrain, rocky and outrageously dense with brush, especially in the river and low creek canyons, where cold rushing water rises with dangerous speed after storms.

Most of the headwater basin and 25.5 miles of the Wild and Scenic Chetco River lies within the Wilderness, as does the beginning of the extraordinary Wild and Scenic North Fork of the Smith River. Twenty-two miles of the Wild and Scenic Illinois River, considered by many whitewater enthusiasts to be Oregon's most difficult river run, flow through a rugged gorge in the area, with rapids that reach towering Class V proportions. Elevations range from about 1,800 feet to 5,098 feet on Pearsoll Peak. This area rewards botanists with plentiful plant species, including rare species such as the carnivorous pitcher plant.

Although much of the interior is seldom if ever seen, about 30 trails varying from five to 30 miles provide limited foot access. The 27-mile Illinois River Trail descends into the bowels of the gorge and ranks high as a well-maintained path. For views from the heights and a hike dry enough at times to warrant carrying plenty of water, take the 42-mile loop from four-acre Vulcan Lake west over Dry Butte, then north to Taggarts Bar and Emily Cabin, where you will swing back south to Doe Gap and over Chetco Peak. This is Oregon at its wildest and, at least in the interior, its most undiscovered.

Kalmiopsis Essentials

Size: 179,700 acres.
Year Designated: 1964; expanded in 1978.
Location: Southwestern Oregon near the coast.
Easiest Access: From Selma, on U.S. 199, take Forest Service Road 4103 west approximately 13 miles to the Oak Flat launch site on the Illinois River. From Brookings, turn east after crossing the Chetco River Bridge and follow Chetco River Road for 16.5 miles. When you reach Forest Service Road 1909, turn west and proceed to the end of the road and the Vulcan Lake Trailhead, about 12 miles.
Season: Spring through fall.
Wilderness Fees/Permits: Obtain a free permit for the Illinois River from the district ranger. No permit is required for the backcountry.
Maps: A Wilderness map that includes Wild Rogue Wilderness is available for $3 from the district rangers.
Management: Chetco Ranger District, Siskiyou National Forest, 555 Fifth Street, Brookings, OR 97415; (541) 469-2196. Galice Ranger District, Siskiyou National Forest, 1465 NE Seventh Street, Grants Pass, OR 97526; (541) 476-3830. Gold Beach Ranger District, Siskiyou National Forest, 1225 South Ellensburg Avenue, Gold Beach, OR 97444; (541) 247-6651. Illinois Valley Ranger District, Siskiyou National Forest, 26569 Redwood Highway, Cave Junction, OR 97532; (541) 592-2166.

Menagerie Wilderness

Technical rock climbers travel substantial distances to test their skills on the series of weird rock pinnacles that dominates Menagerie Wilderness. Each is named after a different animal—Roosters Tail, Chicken Rock, Hen Rock, Turkey Monster, and North and South Rabbit Ears are a few examples. Most popular is Rooster Rock, which you can ascend with 5.4 climbing skills (the routes on these stony towers rate to at least 5.9).

This area is used year-round by day-trippers. Elevations range from 1,600 feet to 3,900 feet, with a thick forest of Douglas fir, western hemlock, and western red cedar. Not far north lies Middle Santiam Wilderness (see below).

Two main routes—the Rooster Rock Trail (2.1 miles) and the Trout Creek Trail (3.3 miles)—lead eventually to Rooster Rock. To see the rest of the "menagerie," you'll have to hike cross-country over rugged terrain.

OREGON

Menagerie Essentials

Size: 4,725 acres.
Year Designated: 1984.
Location: Western Oregon.
Easiest Access: From Sweet Home, take U.S. 20 east approximately 22 miles to Trout Creek Campground and the Trout Creek Trailhead.
Season: Year-round, with spring and fall being most pleasant.
Wilderness Fees/Permits: None.
Maps: A Wilderness map that includes Middle Santiam Wilderness is available for $2 from the district ranger.
Management: Sweet Home Ranger District, Willamette National Forest, 3225 Highway 20, Sweet Home, OR 97386; (541) 367-5168.

Middle Santiam Wilderness

Mature old-growth trees shadow virtually all of this Wilderness, with Douglas fir, western red cedar, and western hemlock at lower elevations and true firs higher up. Some of the trees, estimated to be 450 years old, tower to more than 200 feet. Gently sloping, benchy terrain in the lower country starts at about 1,600 feet and rises to steep slopes, ridges, and peaks that reach 5,022 feet above sea level. The most prominent geological feature is 4,965-foot Chimney Peak, a lava plug in the northwestern portion.

The Middle Santiam River flows through the area, slowing into quiet pools with mossy banks. Both the river and Donaca Lake teem with native fish, including chinook salmon during spawning season. Not far to the south lies Menagerie Wilderness (see above).

Three seldom-hiked trails provide access routes to the area: McQuade Creek (6.1 miles); Chimney Peak, a short spur leading almost to the summit of Chimney Peak; and Middle Santiam (11.4 miles), which allows you to cross the area.

Middle Santiam Essentials

Size: 7,500 acres.
Year Designated: 1984.
Location: Western Oregon.
Easiest Access: From Sweet Home, take U.S. 20 east about four miles. Turn north on Quartzville Road and continue for 24.7 miles, then head east on Forest Service Road 11 for 2.6 miles. When you reach Forest Service Road 1142, turn south and continue four miles to the McQuade Creek Trailhead.
Season: Year-round, with spring and fall being most pleasant.
Wilderness Fees/Permits: None.
Maps: A Wilderness map that includes Menagerie Wilderness is available for $2 from the district ranger.
Management: Sweet Home Ranger District, Willamette National Forest, 3225 Highway 20, Sweet Home, OR 97386; (541) 367-5168.

Mill Creek Wilderness

The southwest-tending drainage of Mill Creek makes up 85 percent of the Wilderness, with Marks Creek drainage accounting for the difference. Both creeks are tributaries of Ochoco Creek, and home to small trout. The steep, broken ridges that drop into Mill Creek rise to Bingham Prairie in the northwest corner, a virtually flat plateau with open meadows and a lodgepole pine forest. Although some of the ridges are barren, an exemplary climax forest (one that has reached its peak of growth) of ponderosa pine dominates most of the area, habitat for elk, mule deer, bobcats, mountain lions, and the occasional black bear.

Two eroded volcanic plugs distinguish the northwest-central portion: Twin Pillars, with vertical walls rising 200 dramatic feet above the forest, and 400-foot Steins Pillar, just outside the southwestern boundary. Both pillars pose rock-climbing challenges, with routes rated to at least 5.7.

North of Twin Pillars lies rugged, rocky Desolation Canyon, aptly named since its lack of trails discourages most human visitors. Summer months are usually hot and dry. Snowfall typically blankets the ground from mid-November through March.

Four trailheads ramble out into about 27 miles of trails: Bingham Prairie, White Rock Campground, Whistler Point, and Wildcat Campground. From the Wildcat Campground Trailhead, the East Fork Mill Creek Trail climbs past Twin Pillars to Bingham Prairie, about eight miles in all. If you want to stay overnight, there are plenty of pleasant campsites near the water.

Mill Creek Essentials

Size: 17,400 acres.
Year Designated: 1984.
Location: Central Oregon.
Easiest Access: From Prineville, take U.S. 26 east for nine miles to the Ochoco Reservoir. Turn north on Forest Service Road 33 (Mill Creek Road) and continue for nine miles to Wildcat Campground.
Season: Late spring and early fall.
Wilderness Fees/Permits: None.
Maps: USGS topographic maps are Steins Pillar and Whistler Point.
Management: Prineville Ranger District, Ochoco National Forest, 2321 East Third, Prineville, OR 97754; (541) 447-3825.

Monument Rock Wilderness

In the southern Blue Mountains of eastern Oregon, Monument Rock, Bullrun Rock, and Table Rock tower over the many streams that form the headwaters of the Little Malheur River and the upper drainages of the South Fork of the Burnt River. Elevations range from 5,120 feet on the Little Malheur to 7,815 feet on Table Rock, with subalpine fir growing in the higher elevations. Ponderosa pine, Douglas fir, white fir, lodgepole pine, and quaking aspen cover the more moderate slopes. Large, grassy meadows bright with summer wildflowers appear willy-nilly, a sunny contrast to the shadowy forest. Black bears, deer, elk, badgers, and, albeit rarely, a wolverine or two still find a reclusive hideaway in this quiet Wilderness. Hawks commonly swoop overhead, and grouse scurry down below. Summers are dry here, hence the fire-lookout station on Table

Rock; snow usually falls by December and melts by the end of March.

About 15 miles of relatively easy trails provide access to the area and to excellent viewpoints. From Table Mountain, the Bullrun Rock Trail takes you an easy two miles to Bullrun Rock, from where you can bushwhack your way south about one mile to Monument Rock itself. Strawberry Mountain Wilderness (see below) lies not far to the east.

Monument Rock Essentials

Size: 19,800 acres.
Year Designated: 1984.
Location: Eastern Oregon.
Easiest Access: From Unity, Forest Service Road 6005 leads west up the drainage of the South Fork of the Burnt River. After about 16 miles, turn south on Road 2652 and proceed two miles. When you reach Road 1370, turn east to find Table Rock, approximately five miles.
Season: Spring through fall.
Wilderness Fees/Permits: None.
Maps: A Wilderness map that includes Strawberry Mountain is available for $4 from the district ranger.
Management: Prairie City Ranger District, Malheur National Forest, Prairie City, OR 97869; (541) 820-3311. Unity Ranger District, Wallowa-Whitman National Forest, Unity, OR 97884; (541) 446-3351.

Mount Hood Wilderness

Mount Hood, Oregon's highest summit at 11,240 feet, is a dormant volcano covered with 11 active glaciers. This sleeping giant dominates a Wilderness of glaciated peaks with forested slopes and alpine meadows. More than 10,000 climbers a year come seeking the top of the state, making Mount Hood's summit the most visited snowclad peak in America. With crevassed glaciers to cross, rotten rock to negotiate, and inclement weather the norm, Mount Hood also boasts one of the highest accident rates of all the earth's peaks. The most popular and easiest route on the mountain climbs the South Side from Timberline Lodge, a route most climbers complete in less than 10 hours. At least 12 other routes up the mountain have been well established. Dormant but not dead, Mount Hood still vents sulfurous steam near the summit.

Much of the area's annual precipitation of 150 inches falls as snow between October and April, but sudden snowstorms may surprise you any time of year, a fact that has led to numerous fatalities on Mount Hood. A forest of Douglas fir covers much of the lower elevations, supported by an understory of Oregon grape, salal, rhododendron, and huckleberries (they ripen deliciously in August). More than a dozen waterfalls brighten river valleys that lie in the shade of the deep forest. Listen for the chirps and whistles of pikas and marmots on the rocky slopes at the tree line.

The majestic and very popular Timberline Trail encircles the mountain for 38 miles, often crossing panoramic alpine meadows painted with summer wildflowers and through creeks that may rise dangerously in June and July when snow melts rapidly. At least 21 trails zig and zag their way through the Wilderness to join the Timberline Trail. Cross-country skiing attracts many winter visitors.

Overuse has led to a ban on camping in many portions of the Wilderness, but careful hikers will discover some of the most splendid mountain terrain in the Lower 48.

OREGON

Mount Hood Essentials
Size: 46,520 acres.
Year Designated: 1964; expanded in 1978.
Location: Northwestern Oregon.
Easiest Access: From Portland, take U.S. 26 east approximately 46 miles. Just past Government Camp, turn north on the well-marked Timberline Lodge Road, and drive about six miles to the lodge.
Season: May through September.
Wilderness Fees/Permits: None. Registration at Timberline Lodge is required for climbing.
Maps: A Wilderness map is available for $2 from the district ranger.
Management: Hood River Ranger District, Mount Hood National Forest, 6780 Highway 35 South, Mount Hood-Parkdale, OR 97041; (541) 352-6002. Zigzag Ranger District, Mount Hood National Forest, 70220 East Highway 26, Zigzag, OR 97049; (503) 666-0704 (a climbing ranger is often available to provide information at the Zigzag office).

Mount Jefferson Wilderness

Five glaciers mantle the slopes of stately Mount Jefferson, the dominant feature in this region of the High Cascades: Whitewater, Waldo, Milk Creek, Russell, and Jefferson Park. At 10,497 feet, Mount Jefferson challenges hikers with the steepest, most difficult climb of Oregon's high summits. The southern portion of the area rests beneath 7,841-foot Three Fingered Jack. Most of the high country of this Wilderness is wide open, almost like a park, with scattered tree cover, long talus slopes, rocky outcroppings, alpine meadows, and year-round patches of snow. Between 5,000 feet and 6,000 feet you'll find more than 150 small lakes, about half of them stocked with trout. A grand forest of Douglas fir, silver fir, subalpine fir, mountain hemlock, lodgepole pine, ponderosa pine, and cedar mix with vine maple, huckleberry, and rhododendron to distinguish the lower elevations. The vast Warm Springs Indian Reservation shares a long northeastern border.

Hikers can wend their way through approximately 190 miles of very heavily used trails, including about 40 miles of the Pacific Crest National Scenic Trail. Jefferson Lake, Marion Lake, Pamelia Lake, and Jack Lake are the most impacted by human traffic. Special restrictions apply to this Wilderness, including no campfires within 100 feet of water, no camping in posted rehabilitation zones, and no groups consisting of more than 12 people.

OREGON

Mount Jefferson Essentials

Size: 107,008 acres.
Year Designated: 1968; expanded in 1984.
Location: Western Oregon.
Easiest Access: From Sisters, take U.S. 20 north and west approximately 25 miles to Santiam Pass and the Pacific Crest Trailhead at the southern end of the Wilderness.
Season: Mid-June through October.
Wilderness Fees/Permits: Entering this area without a free permit is illegal. Applications for a Wilderness permit are available from the district ranger. Some trails allow you to register at the trailhead. Contact the ranger.
Maps: A Wilderness map is available for $7 from the district ranger. Pacific Crest Trail (PCT) maps are available for $2 per section from the district rangers. PCT Northern Oregon Portion covers the Wilderness.
Management: Clackamas Ranger District, Mount Hood National Forest, 61431 East Highway 224, Estacada, OR 97023; (503) 834-2275. Detroit Ranger District, Willamette National Forest, HC 73, Box 320, Mill City, OR 97360; (541) 854-3366. Sisters Ranger District, Deschutes National Forest, P.O. Box 249, Sisters, OR 97759; (541) 549-2111.

Mount Thielsen Wilderness

Carved majestically by glacial activity and rising 9,182 feet to a spire-shaped summit referred to sometimes as the "Lightning Rod of the Cascades," Mount Thielsen anchors the southern portion of this Wilderness. To the south is Crater Lake National Park, and on the periphery is flat to moderately rolling country, which changes to very steep and sharply dissected ridges toward the crest of the Cascade Mountains.

Timberline stands at about 7,200 feet, just above a forest of mountain hemlock and fir mixed with whitebark pine. Lodgepole pine dominates the vegetation lower down. Many streams carry a substantial amount of snowmelt in spring, giving rise to an abundance of early summer mosquitoes. You'll find both lovely Lake Lucille and Maidu Lake near the center of the area.

A 34-mile segment of the Pacific Crest National Scenic Trail crosses the Wilderness from Tolo Mountain in the north to near Summit Rock in the south. The Mount Thielsen Trail enters for approximately five miles from the west side to rise above the tree line and, after 200 feet of hand-over-hand scrambling, finally reaches to within 80 feet of the summit and a breathtaking view. The summit itself requires a short technical climb. The trail system totals about 78 miles. The land on the eastern side of the crest ranks among the most pristine in the state, a region far less visited by humans.

Mount Thielsen Essentials

Size: 55,100 acres.
Year Designated: 1984.
Location: Southwestern Oregon.
Easiest Access: From Roseburg, take State Route 138 east approximately 77 miles to Diamond Lake and the Mount Thielsen Trailhead.
Season: Late spring through fall.
Wilderness Fees/Permits: None.
Maps: Free trail guides are available from the district ranger. A Wilderness map costs $1.
Management: Chemult Ranger District, Winema National Forest, P.O. Box 150, Chemult, OR 97731; (541) 365-2229. Diamond Lake Ranger District, Umpqua National Forest, HC 60, Box 101, Idleyld Park, OR 97447; (541) 498-2531.

OREGON

Mount Washington Wilderness

This geological wonderland of rugged terrain topped by jagged peaks includes, near its center, the 6,872-foot cinder and ash cone of Belknap Crater, whose eruptions created one of the largest sheets of lava in the United States. The summit of the 7,794-foot dissected volcano named after our first president, scraped bare by ancient glaciation (the peak, not the president), overlooks some 75 miles of black lava-strewn plains. A dense forest of lodgepole pine and mountain hemlock covers much of the Wilderness. There are 28 lakes and wildlife enough to attract hunters. Only State Highway 242 separates Mount Washington Wilderness from Three Sisters Wilderness to the south (see below).

The primary trail through this area is 16.6 miles of the Pacific Crest National Scenic Trail, which enters at McKenzie Pass in the south, crosses a section of the lava, skirts the Belknap Crater, climbs the western slopes of Mount Washington, passes through a region of high lakes, and then leaves the Wilderness to hit U.S. 20 to the north. Tenas Lake and Benson Lake in the southwest corner receive substantial human use, as does Patjens Lake in the north. All three lakes are accessible via short trails.

Mount Washington Essentials

Size: 52,516 acres.
Year Designated: 1964; expanded in 1984.
Location: Western central Oregon.
Easiest Access: From Sisters, take State Highway 242 about 15 miles west to McKenzie Pass, where you will find the Pacific Crest Trail near the Dee Wright Observatory. Hike north.
Season: Mid-June through October.
Wilderness Fees/Permits: A Wilderness permit is required to legally enter this area. Contact a district ranger in person, by mail, or by telephone.
Maps: A Wilderness map is available for purchase from the district rangers. Pacific Crest Trail (PCT) maps are available for $2 per section from the district rangers. PCT Northern Oregon Portion covers the Wilderness.
Management: McKenzie Ranger District, Willamette National Forest, McKenzie Bridge, OR 97413; (541) 822-3381. Sisters Ranger District, Deschutes National Forest, P.O. Box 249, Sisters, OR 97759; (541) 549-2111.

Mountain Lakes Wilderness

Before its eruption and subsequent transformation into a large caldera (a broad, craterlike basin formed by volcanic violence), the area we call Mountain Lakes Wilderness was a 12,000-foot mountain, one of the giants of the southern Cascades. Glaciation then carved up the caldera, leaving a scattering of small alpine lakes instead of one enormous body of water, such as Crater Lake National Park to the north. Only eight prominent peaks remain of the caldera's rim. Unique to the National Wilderness Preservation System, this area is the only Wilderness with a perfectly square boundary. Long appreciated for its wonder, Mountain Lakes was one of the three original Primitive areas created in 1930 in the Washington-Oregon region. Mosquitoes fly thickly from snowmelt to mid-August, snack food for the rainbow and brook trout in the lakes.

OREGON

The 10.5-mile Mountain Lakes Loop Trail winds along the southern rim of the caldera, connecting three trails in the interior of the Wilderness: the Clover Creek Trail (4 miles) from the south, the Mountain Lakes Trail (6.5 miles) from the west, and the Varney Creek Trail (4.5 miles) from the north. Two other trails, Moss Creek and South Pass, provide access to the eastern portion. Beyond the eastern boundary lies private land.

Mountain Lakes Essentials

Size: 23,071 acres.
Year Designated: 1964.
Location: Southwestern Oregon.
Easiest Access: From Klamath Falls, take State Highway 140 northwest about 20 miles. Turn south on Forest Service Road 3637 and continue for 1.8 miles, then head east on Forest Service Road 3664 for another two miles to the Varney Creek Trailhead.
Season: June through October.
Wilderness Fees/Permits: None.
Maps: A Wilderness map is available for $2 from the district ranger.
Management: Klamath Ranger District, Winema National Forest, 1936 California Avenue, Klamath Falls, OR 97601; (541) 885-3400.

North Fork John Day Wilderness

The North Fork John Day drainage bustled with gold and silver mining operations in the mid-1800s, and traces of the thousands of hopefuls who made off with an estimated 10 million dollars in ore are still visible in this Wilderness: old mining structures, building foundations, dredged ditches. But the rolling benchlands, granite outcroppings, and the rugged gorge of the North Fork John Day River have recovered enough to provide an excellent Wilderness setting here in the Blue Mountains.

The Wilderness encompasses two entire subranges: the Greenhorn Mountains and the ragged Elkhorn Mountains. A 39-mile segment of the North Fork John Day River has been designated Wild and Scenic. This area deserves its fame for big-game animals, which currently include a herd of Rocky Mountain elk estimated to number beyond 50,000 and a herd of mule deer that reportedly exceeds 150,000. Bull elk here sometimes weigh more than 800 pounds and sport antlers spreading beyond five feet. The area's anadromous fish population (fish that spawn in fresh water and swim to the sea) include vast numbers of chinook salmon and steelhead with runs that peak in August. More than 130 miles of perennial streams provide at least 40 miles of spawning habitat.

This Wilderness consists of four separate units: the main 85,000-acre unit of the North Fork John Day drainage, the Greenhorn Unit to the south, the Tower Mountain Unit to the north, and the Baldy Creek Unit to the east in the Wallowa-Whitman National Forest. Approximately 6,000 acres of cirque basins and steep cliffs within the Vinegar Hill-Indian Rock Scenic Area also lie within the Wilderness.

Hikers can access roughly 133 miles of trails from several trailheads on the perimeter of the area, three of which—Elkhorn Crest, Winom Creek, and North Fork John Day—are National Recreation Trails. The Elkhorn Crest Trail soars for 24 miles through alpine scenery. The North Fork John Day Trail follows the river gorge for 25 serpentine miles. You should expect a significant amount of elevation gain and loss.

OREGON

North Fork John Day Essentials

Size: 121,400 acres.
Year Designated: 1984.
Location: Northeastern Oregon.
Easiest Access: From Ukiah, take State Highway 244 east approximately 16 miles. Turn south on Forest Service Road 51 and continue about 28 miles to North Fork John Day Campground and the North Fork John Day Trailhead.
Season: Early spring through late fall.
Wilderness Fees/Permits: None.
Maps: A Wilderness map is available for $2 from the district ranger.
Management: North Fork John Day Ranger District, Umatilla National Forest, P.O. Box 158, Ukiah, OR 97880; (541) 427-3231. Baker Ranger District, Wallowa-Whitman National Forest, Route 1, Box 1, Baker, OR 97814; (541) 523-6391.

North Fork Umatilla Wilderness

Instead of rising into high peaks to offer a somewhat unique Wilderness experience, the gently sloping hills of North Fork Umatilla Wilderness fall into extremely steep, timbered canyons below a high plateau. Down along the river you'll probably feel more isolated than the small acreage of the area would indicate. Vegetation ranges from juniper and sagebrush to fir, spruce, pine, and western larch. Elevations drop from 6,000 feet to 2,000 feet in a relatively short distance to provide a substantial physical workout. The North Fork Umatilla River supports large runs of anadromous fish, including steelhead, a major force in pushing for designation of this area as well as an attraction to anglers. Several streams are home to native trout. Hunters come for big-game animals, including a fairly large population of Rocky Mountain elk. Here in the northern Blue Mountains the weather tends to change radically and unpredictably any day of the year, but snow usually melts by early spring.

The 27 miles of trails attract both backpackers and horsepackers. You can connect the route up Buck Creek by crossing a bit of non-Wilderness tableland to go down Buck Mountain's ridge for a lovely 15-mile loop. The trail along North Fork Umatilla River is popular. To reach it, drop down the trail following Lick Creek.

North Fork Umatilla Essentials

Size: 20,200 acres.
Year Designated: 1984.
Location: Northeastern Oregon.
Easiest Access: From Pendleton, take State Highway 11 north to Weston. Turn east on State Highway 204 and south on Forest Service Road 3715 to find Lick Creek.
Season: Early spring to late fall.
Wilderness Fees/Permits: None.
Maps: A Wilderness map is available for $6 from the forest ranger. USGS topographic maps are Andies Prairie, Bingham Springs, Drumhill Ridge, Thimbleberry Mountain, and Tollgate.
Management: Umatilla National Forest, 2517 SW Hailey Avenue, Pendleton, OR 97801; (541) 278-3716. Walla Walla Ranger District, Umatilla National Forest, 1415 West Rose, Walla Walla, WA 99362; (541) 522-6290.

OREGON

Oregon Islands Wilderness

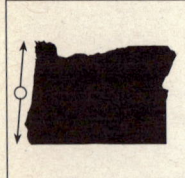

A string of some 1,477 wave-washed rocks and tiny islands mirror almost the entire length of the Oregon coast from Tillamook Head to the California border. These precious chunks of land, protected as the Oregon Islands National Wildlife Refuge, equal less than 800 acres, but those relatively few acres provide a nesting habitat for an estimated 1.1 million seabirds, more than nest along the coastlines of California and Washington combined. Beginning in April, black-and-white murres throng the islands. Summer brings tufted puffins, auklets, and murrelets, who stay here with the murres until August. Loons, scoters, and grebes arrive for winter. Five species of gulls and two of cormorants reside here year-round. These rocky islands also serve as haul-outs for seals and sea lions, who heave themselves up to give birth, to rest, and to molt. You'll see few plants other than sea palms and bobbing bulbous heads of kelp. Some of the islands support meager growths of twinberry, salal, and stunted spruce. The threatened seacliff stonecrop flowers here occasionally and nowhere else in Oregon.

Approximately 64 percent of the island acreage has been designated Wilderness, including five acres managed by the BLM in the Coos Bay District.

Oregon Islands Essentials

Size: 485 acres.
Year Designated: 1970; expanded in 1978 (expansion included BLM land).
Location: Off the coast of Oregon.
Easiest Access: William L. Sullivan's fine book *Exploring Oregon's Wild Areas* suggests that the best viewing points are from the Yaquina Head Lighthouse, three miles north of Newport; the Cape Meares Loop Road west of Tillamook; Cape Kiwanda near Pacific City; the state park on Cape Blanco; Boardman State Park north of Brookings; and the shoreline near Brookings itself. The islands are closed to all public entry, and all watercraft should remain at least 500 feet away.
Season: April to August for the most birds.
Wilderness Fees/Permits: None.
Maps: A free map is available from the refuge manager.
Management: Oregon Coastal National Wildlife Refuges, 2030 South Marine Science Drive, Newport, OR 97365; (541) 867-4550. BLM Coos Bay District Office, 1300 Airport Lane, North Bend, OR 97459; (541) 756-0100.

Red Buttes Wilderness

This Wilderness straddles the crest of the Siskiyou Mountains but has more acreage in California (see California, Red Buttes Wilderness) than in Oregon. The twin peaks of Red Buttes anchor the southern extreme of the area in California, red peridotite nudged up from a 425-million-year-old seafloor by plate shifts in the earth's crust. Some 3.5 miles of the Pacific Crest Trail passes by Lilypad Lake at the foot of the Buttes.

Rocky buttes, forested ridges, and small lakes characterize this area, with a confounding jumble of manzanita, snowbrush, and other brushy plants carpeting the dry south-facing slopes. Pines, spruces, and massive old cedars dominate the vegetation, providing habitat for black bears, cougars, deer, and coyotes. Unsubstantiated sightings of the infamous Bigfoot date back over the last century.

On the eastern side of Oregon's portion, from the grassy dale of Sucker Creek Gap, a trail leads three miles through heavy tree cover along the merry tumble of Steve Fork. If you're looking for a cool dip after a summer hike, take the Tannen Lakes Trail one-quarter of a mile to Tannen Lakes, where you can swim below the rockslides of Tannen Mountain. You will probably see few other people. Although summers are typically dry, snow buries much of the higher country from November until May. Just to the north is Oregon Caves National Monument.

Red Buttes Essentials

Size: 3,750 acres in Oregon (19,900 total).
Year Designated: 1984.
Location: Southwestern Oregon.
Easiest Access: From Cave Junction, take State Highway 46 east toward Oregon Caves National Monument for 14.5 miles. Turn south on Forest Service Road 4612 and go nine miles, then head east on Forest Service Road 098 for four miles to the Sucker Creek Gap Trailhead.
Season: May through early fall.
Wilderness Fees/Permits: None.
Maps: A Wilderness map is available for $2 from the district ranger.
Management: Illinois Valley Ranger District, Siskiyou National Forest, 26568 Redwood Highway, Cave Junction, OR 97532; (541) 592-2166.

Rock Creek Wilderness

Pristine rain forest canyons run with crystalline water pouring into either Rock Creek itself in the heart of the Wilderness or Big Creek on the southern boundary. Mossy bigleaf maple and red alder hang suspended over both creeks as they make their way toward the salty waves of the Pacific Ocean. Look carefully for Oregon silverspot butterflies on the tall ridge between Rock and Big Creeks; these orange-and-brown butterflies live only here and in two other places on earth.

Near the coast, tremendous old-growth Sitka spruce sometimes reach nine feet in diameter, giving way to old Douglas fir farther inland. Pink-blossomed rhododendron bloom in May, joining salal, salmonberry, and swordfern in their efforts to keep the ground perpetually shaded. Salmon, steelhead, and cutthroat trout migrate upcreek to spawn in vast numbers. Fog cools the area almost all of every summer; and winters are snowless.

The only path, Rock Creek Trail, starts at Rock Creek Campground on the coast and travels about one-half mile to end in a meadow. All other routes call for bushwhacking. You will probably find an old elk trail tracing the ridge between Rock and Big Creeks (passable for about five miles) by taking Forest Service Road 1055 east from U.S. 101 to a saddle on the ridge. Otherwise, most hikers just walk in the chilly, shallow water of Rock Creek. About two miles to the north lies Cummins Creek Wilderness (see above).

OREGON

Rock Creek Essentials
Size: 7,400 acres.
Year Designated: 1984.
Location: Central coastal Oregon.
Easiest Access: From Florence, take U.S. 101 north approximately 16 miles to Rock Creek Campground.
Season: Spring and fall for the clearest days.

Wilderness Fees/Permits: None.
Maps: USGS topographic maps are Cannibal Mountain and Heceta Head.
Management: Waldport Ranger District, Siuslaw National Forest, 1049 SW Pacific Highway, Waldport, OR 97394; (541) 563-3211.

Rogue-Umpqua Divide Wilderness

Ten miles northwest of Crater Lake National Park, this Wilderness falls in the Western Cascade geologic province and encompasses the Rogue-Umpqua Divide Scenic Area. Notable features include Elephant Head (with walls of vertical rock), 90-acre Fish Lake, and Highrock Mountain. Grasshopper Mountain looms over the latter attraction, along with its richly meadowed Fish Lake Basin. Among the other beautiful lakes in this Wilderness are Cliff, Buckeye, and Wolf.

The Civilian Conservation Corps built shelters that still stand at Rocky Ridge, Cripple Camp, and Fish Creek Valley, mountain valleys timbered in Douglas fir that climb to subalpine meadows mixed with stands of true fir. Several large streams originate in the Wilderness, the largest being Castle Rock Fork Creek. Elevations peak at 6,783 feet on Fish Mountain, where you'll be treated to views that range from the Three Sisters to Mount Shasta.

An extensive trail system gives access to the wonders of this area from 10 trailheads. The Fish Lake Trail follows Fish Lake Creek and ascends across Beaver Swamp to reach the lake in three miles. This trail traces the northwest shore and offers fine views of the rock formations along Rocky Ridge. You can loop back via Buckeye and Cliff Lakes for a hike totaling 6.5 miles, or you can leave the lake to travel about 2.5 miles through scattered timber and large meadows typical of the Wilderness to join the 25-mile Rogue-Umpqua Divide National Recreation Trail, which weaves along the divide and attracts the most foot traffic.

Rogue-Umpqua Divide Essentials
Size: 33,200 acres.
Year Designated: 1984.
Location: Southwestern Oregon.
Easiest Access: From Canyonville, on Interstate 5, take the road toward Crater Lake for approximately 23 miles to Tiller. Head north on South Umpqua Road, which becomes Forest Service Road 28, for 23 miles, then go 2.3 miles east on Forest Service Road 2823. When you reach Forest Service Road 2830, drive south for 1.7 miles, then east again on Forest Service Road 2840. The Fish Lake Trailhead is a short distance from here.
Season: June through October.
Maps: A Wilderness map that includes Boulder Creek and Mount Thielsen Wildernesses is available for $1 from the district rangers.
Management: Tiller Ranger District, Umpqua National Forest, 27812 Tiller-Trail Highway, Tiller, OR 97484; (541) 825-3201. Prospect Ranger District, Rogue River National Forest, Prospect, OR 97536; (541) 560-3623.

OREGON

Salmon-Huckleberry Wilderness

The main attraction in this Wilderness, the Salmon River dives splendidly over numerous waterfalls, luring fishers hoping to hook steelhead and chinook and coho salmon. The drainages of the South Fork Salmon River and Eagle Creek stand cloaked in a dense rain forest of Douglas fir, true firs, western red cedar, and western hemlock with a thick understory. Volcanic plugs, pinnacles, and cliffs distinguish the area's sharply dissected ridges.

Much of the water in this area runs off of Huckleberry Mountain in the northern portion. To the south is Salmon Butte, a striking 4,877-foot landmark with a fine view from the top that can be reached by trail. Mule deer and black bears find winter range hidden in the area's wild off-trail country.

The Salmon River National Recreation Trail cuts through more than 10 miles of this Wilderness, part of a trail system that totals about 70 miles. Maps typically imply that this trail parallels the river, but it actually travels several hundred feet above the banks, except for a couple of miles at the lower end of the gorge. At least five trails begin with long climbs and trace ridges with panoramic views, including the Wildcat Mountain Trail (five miles), which is probably the easiest to access.

Salmon-Huckleberry Essentials

Size: 44,560 acres.
Year Designated: 1984.
Location: Northwestern Oregon.
Easiest Access: From Sandy, southeast of Portland, take U.S. 26 east for about 11 miles, then go south on East Wildcat Creek Road for 4.1 miles to the Wildcat Mountain Trailhead.
Season: Spring through fall.
Wilderness Fees/Permits: None.
Maps: A Wilderness map that includes Bull of the Woods Wilderness is available for $2 from the district ranger.
Management: Zigzag Ranger District, Mount Hood National Forest, 70220 East Highway 26, Zigzag, OR 97049; (503) 622-3191.

Sky Lakes Wilderness

With a name like Sky Lakes, this Wilderness is obliged to deliver at least one impressive sapphire pool, and it does. In fact, it takes in three major lake basins as it stretches along the crest of the Cascade Mountains from the southern border of Crater Lake National Park to State Highway 140: Sky Lakes, Seven Lakes, and Blue Canyon. All of southern Oregon seems to lay at your feet from the summit of Mount McLoughlin, which peaks at 9,495 feet then levels out northward into a broad plateaulike ridge dotted with many of the lakes. You'll find creeks and ice-cold springs, and scores of crystalline alpine lakes stocked every other year with either rainbow trout, brook trout, cutthroat trout, or kokanee. This is arguably some of the best alpine fishing in America, set against a backdrop of tall trees that reach to the edge of the lakes. A forest of lodgepole pine and mountain hemlock holds an Engelmann spruce here and there.

433

OREGON

The large elk herd spends much of the year here, along with numerous other species of wildlife. During October and November, migrating birds pass over in the hundreds of thousands, often stopping at the high lakes. Mosquitoes hatch from snowmelt until mid-August.

The Pacific Crest National Scenic Trail crosses the entire area north-south for about 35 miles, amazingly missing almost every drop of water. From the Sevenmile Marsh Trailhead you can hike 4.7 miles to Grassy Lake and have several major lakes within a day-hike radius. Numerous other trails enter the Wilderness from the east and west, including the Cold Springs Trail, which leads a mere two miles to the shores of the exceptionally tranquil Heavenly Twin Lakes. Human use is heavy in this extremely popular fishing, hiking, and camping destination.

Sky Lakes Essentials

Size: 116,300 acres.
Year Designated: 1984.
Location: Southwestern Oregon.
Easiest Access: From Fort Klamath, on State Highway 62, take the Nicholson Road west for 4.3 miles. Turn west on Forest Service Road 3334 and continue for approximately five miles to its end at the Sevenmile Marsh Trailhead.
Season: June through October.
Wilderness Fees/Permits: None.
Maps: A Wilderness map is available for $2 from the district ranger.
Management: Klamath Ranger District, Winema National Forest, 1936 California Avenue, Klamath Falls, OR 97601; (541) 885-3400. Ashland Ranger District, Rogue River National Forest, 654 Washington, Ashland, OR 97520; (541) 482-3333.

Strawberry Mountain Wilderness

For diversity, this high-country rugged Wilderness has few equals, containing five of the seven major life zones in North America. Glaciation hollowed out beds in U-shaped valleys that today hold seven alpine lakes, rare treasures in Oregon's arid west. Elevation ranges from about 4,000 feet to 9,038 feet atop Strawberry Mountain in the east-central portion. Large numbers of larch, the only conifer to lose its needles, turn to spun gold in fall, highlighting a forest of spruce, pine, and fir. Accenting the gold hues are wild strawberries that ripen to juicy redness in July, and mountain basins blooming with summer wildflowers. A native population of Rocky Mountain elk reside here with mule deer, antelope, black bears, cougars, mink, and beavers. Martens, hawks, and eagles watch the wildlife action from on high.

A long trail system offers room for backpacking trips of a week or more. Trails to the lakes are popular, but thoughtless campers have scarred many of the waterside campsites. The craggy backdrop of Strawberry Lake is especially pretty. From Strawberry Campground, the hike is 1.2 miles up to Strawberry Lake. Above the lake, about one mile, Strawberry Falls plummets about 40 feet over mossy rocks. This trail continues on for about 3.7 arduous miles to the top of Strawberry Mountain.

Strawberry Mountain Essentials

Size: 68,303 acres.
Year Designated: 1964; expanded in 1984.
Location: Western central Oregon.
Easiest Access: From Prairie City, on U.S. 26, take Main Street south and follow the signs about 11 miles to Strawberry Campground and the trail to Strawberry Lake.
Season: July through September.

Wilderness Fees/Permits: None.
Maps: A Wilderness map that includes Monument Rock Wilderness is available for $4 from the forest ranger.
Management: Malheur National Forest, 139 NE Dayton Street, John Day, OR 97845; (541) 575-1731.

Table Rock Wilderness

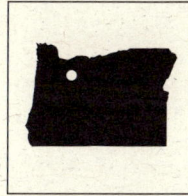

A remnant of a lava flow that once covered this region along the western foothills of the Cascades, the "fortress" of Table Rock stands at 4,881 feet above the northeastern portion of this small Wilderness. On this steep and rugged terrain you'll find a quiet forest of Douglas fir and western hemlock, with noble fir at higher elevations and crowds of rhododendron on many of the upper slopes, an island of old growth in an ocean of forest development. At least two endangered plants bloom here: Oregon sullivantia and Gorman's aster. Deer and elk wander about in winter, and the northern spotted owl has been spotted among the old trees.

From four trailheads, about 17 miles of trails give access to the Wilderness. A relatively easy hike of 2.3 miles from Table Rock Road will take you up the Table Rock Trail to the sweeping vista from the summit of Table Rock, where the land falls suddenly away in basalt cliffs on the north face. From this high point, Mount Rainier looms far to the north, Bull of the Woods Wilderness (see above) beckons from the east, and the Willamette Valley spreads out to the south.

You will not find any reliable sources of potable water on the trails, so pack along your own. Horses may find dangerous footing on some of the talus slopes.

Table Rock Essentials

Size: 5,500 acres.
Year Designated: 1984.
Location: Northwestern central Oregon.
Easiest Access: From Mollala, about 30 miles south of Portland, take State Highway 211 east about one-half mile. Drive south on South Mathias Road for four-tenths of a mile, then bear east onto South Feyrer Park Road for 1.6 miles. When you reach South Dickey Prairie Road, head south for 5.3 miles, until you get to an unmarked junction. At the junction, turn to cross the Mollala River and go 12.8 miles to Middle Fork Road. The Table Rock Trailhead is at this junction.
Season: Spring through fall.
Wilderness Fees/Permits: None.
Maps: USGS topographic maps are Gawley Creek and Rooster Rock. A free Wilderness map is available from the BLM office.
Management: BLM Salem District Office, 1717 Fabry Road Southeast, Salem, OR 97306; (503) 375-5646.

OREGON

Three Arch Rocks Wilderness

Three Arch Rocks National Wildlife Refuge, the first wildlife refuge established west of the Mississippi River, consists of a group of wildly arched islands two miles south of and visible from Cape Meares National Wildlife Refuge (on a headland off Tillamook Bay). These rocky points shelter one of the most populous bird colonies on the continent during nesting season: 200,000 common murres, 2,000 to 4,000 tufted puffins, guillemots, petrels, Brandt's cormorants, and pelagic cormorants. While harbor seals and a large herd of northern sea lions haul out here, the refuge is off-limits to humans except via special permits granted for scientific work. But observation points onshore allow you to observe the birds. According to the *Guide to the National Wildlife Refuges*, you'll get your best view "from a pleasant motel on a hill just beside Oceanside where the proprietors seem to enjoy having birdwatching visitors." Bring a spotting scope.

Three Arch Rocks Essentials

Size: 15 acres.
Year Designated: 1970.
Location: Along the northwestern coast of Oregon.
Easiest Access: From Tillamook, take the access road a short distance west to the Cape Meares National Wildlife Refuge and then two miles south to Oceanside. All watercraft should stay at least 500 feet away from the rocks.
Season: For peak concentrations of birds, consult the refuge suboffice at the Marine Science Center, 2030 South Marine Science Drive, Newport, OR 97365; (541) 867-4550.
Wilderness Fees/Permits: None.
Maps: Free maps are available from the refuge.
Management: Western Oregon Refuge Complex, 26208 Finley Refuge Road, Corvallis, OR 97333; (541) 757-7236.

Three Sisters Wilderness

Many would argue, including me, that this is Oregon at its finest. The high, snowcapped Three Sisters (North Sister at 10,085 feet, Middle Sister at 10,047 feet, and South Sister at 10,358 feet) embellish the eastern side of this Wilderness, the second largest in Oregon. If you include Broken Top at 9,175 feet just to the south, you have 14 glaciers offering perhaps the best example of the effects of glaciation in the Pacific Northwest. Collier Glacier, between North and Middle Sister, is the largest sheet of ice in Oregon.

Here is a fabulous volcanically formed landscape of lava fields, waterfalls, alpine meadows, lakes and streams teeming with brook and rainbow trout, and a lush forest of Douglas fir, silver fir, subalpine fir, mountain hemlock, western hemlock, lodgepole pine, ponderosa pine, and true fir. The headwaters of the Wild and Scenic Squaw Creek likewise emerge here. Only State Highway 242 separates Three Sisters Wilderness from Mount Washington Wilderness (see above) to the north. Waldo Lake Wilderness (see below) shares the southern boundary.

You'll find about 260 miles of trails, including 40 miles of the Pacific Crest Trail running north-south, and human traffic in multitudes

OREGON

estimated to exceed every other Wilderness in the state. Green Lakes, Obsidian, Sunshine, Erma Bell Lakes, and the climbing trail to South Sister are especially used and abused. The Chambers Lakes Trail leads 7.1 miles from Pole Creek to Chambers Lakes, all the while encompassed by the dramatic glaciers of South and Middle Sister, where ice can appear year-round, the growth is limited to wind-twisted pines, and the rock-rimmed beauty will take your breath away.

Human impact has created a need for special-use restrictions here: no campfires within 100 feet of water, no trespassing within posted rehabilitation zones, and no groups larger than 12.

Three Sisters Essentials

Size: 285,202 acres.
Year Designated: 1964; expanded in 1978 and 1984.
Location: Western Oregon.
Easiest Access: From Sisters, take State Highway 242 west for 1.4 miles. Turn south on Forest Service Road 15 and continue for five miles, then go south and east on Forest Service Road 1524 for approximately five miles to the Chambers Lakes Trailhead.
Season: Mid-June through October.
Wilderness Fees/Permits: You must carry a free permit in order to legally enter this Wilderness. Contact a district ranger in person, over the phone, or by mail.
Maps: A Wilderness map is available for $3 from the district ranger. Pacific Crest Trail (PCT) maps are available for $2 per section from the district ranger. PCT Northern Oregon Portion covers the Wilderness.
Management: Bend Ranger District, Deschutes National Forest, 1230 NE Third Street, Bend, OR 97701; (541) 388-5664. Sisters Ranger District, Deschutes National Forest, P.O. Box 249, Sisters, OR 97759; (541) 549-2111. Blue River Ranger District, Willamette National Forest, Blue River, OR 97413; (541) 822-3317. McKenzie Ranger District, Willamette National Forest, McKenzie Bridge, OR 97413; (541) 822-3381. Oakridge Ranger District, Willamette National Forest, 46375 Highway 58, Westfir, OR 97492; (541) 782-2291.

Waldo Lake Wilderness

Oregon's second-largest body of natural water dwells in a basin scooped out by ancient glaciers, covers 10 square miles (6,700 acres), and is 420 feet deep at some points. On a bright day, you can see 100 feet down into the water, as this is one of the purest lakes left in the world. Waldo Lake lies just outside the eastern boundary of the Wilderness, hinting at the impressive array of beautiful trout-filled lakes scattered within, including the Six Lakes Basin, Eddeeleo Lakes, and Quinn Lakes. Here in the High Cascades the terrain is characterized by moderate to steep dissected slopes with many basins, small meadows, and rocky outcroppings peaking at 7,144 feet. Roughly 98 percent of the area stands forested in Douglas fir, western hemlock, western fir, and some true fir. The northern border of Waldo Lake Wilderness is the southern border of the very popular Three Sisters Wilderness (see above).

Some 84 miles of trails lead to many of the lakes. The Waldo Lake Trail is a 22-mile loop trail around Waldo Lake itself (outside the Wilderness), and a 2.7-mile stretch of the Pacific

437

OREGON

Crest National Scenic Trail crosses the eastern portion. From North Waldo Campground, the Rigdon Lakes Trail travels 2.4 miles to peaceful Rigdon Lakes, with a rocky butte nearby that you can climb for a fine view. The trails to Six Lakes and Wahanna Lakes receive the most traffic.

Waldo Lake Essentials

Size: 39,200 acres.
Year Designated: 1984.
Location: Western Oregon.
Easiest Access: From Oakridge, take State Highway 58 east for approximately 23 miles. Turn north on Forest Service Road 5897 and continue for approximately 10 miles, then go west on Forest Service Road 5898 for approximately three miles to North Waldo Campground.
Season: Late spring through fall.
Wilderness Fees/Permits: None.
Maps: A Wilderness map is available for $2 from the district ranger.
Management: Oakridge Ranger District, Willamette National Forest, 46375 Highway 58, Westfir, OR 97492; (541) 782-2291.

Wenaha-Tucannon Wilderness

Straddling both Oregon and Washington, with the larger portion in Washington (see Washington, Wenaha-Tucannon Wilderness), this Wilderness distinguishes the northern section of the expansive Blue Mountains, a region of rugged basaltic ridges and outcroppings and broad tablelands separated by deep canyons with steep gravelly sides. From bunchgrass communities on the slopes to higher regions of lodgepole pine and subalpine fir, you'll find habitat for almost every wildlife species present in the Blue Mountains, including Rocky Mountain elk (in huge numbers), bighorn sheep, mule deer, white-tailed deer, black bears, cougars, coyotes, and pine martens. Anglers will find anadromous chinook salmon and steelhead in both the Wild and Scenic Wenaha River and the Tucannon River. Many streams support trout, especially Crooked Creek, Rock Creek, and Butte Creek. Elevations range from about 2,000 feet on the Wenaha River to 6,401 feet on Oregon Butte (which is, ironically, in the state of Washington).

Traditionally, the primary human use of this area has been for elk hunting, and many hunters horsepack in every fall. Several trailheads are well equipped to handle horses, including Elk Flats on the Oregon side. Special regulations apply to horsepackers in order to maintain low-impact travel: carrying feed that's free of weed seed, using tree-saver straps and highlines to keep stock in camp, and preventing stock from skirting puddles to reduce erosion.

But backpacking has increased in popularity here, especially in summer and early fall, on more than 200 miles of maintained trails. From Troy, the Wenaha River Trail wanders for 31.3 miles, providing an exemplary route through the Oregon side of the area.

OREGON

Wenaha-Tucannon Essentials

Size: 66,375 acres in Oregon (177,423 total).
Year Designated: 1978.
Location: Northeastern Oregon.
Easiest Access: From Enterprise, take State Highway 3 north approximately 50 miles before turning west on the access road to the ghost town of Flora. Take this road approximately 21 miles to Troy. From just south of Troy, take Forest Service Road 62 west approximately 18 miles to Elk Flats.
Season: July through fall.
Wilderness Fees/Permits: None.
Maps: A Wilderness map is available for $2 from the forest ranger.
Management: Pomeroy Ranger District, Umatilla National Forest, Route 1, Box 53-F, Pomeroy, WA 99347; (541) 843-1891.

Wild Rogue Wilderness

Designated Wild and Scenic, the Rogue River churns its way through adamant old lava down a canyon that reaches 4,000 feet in depth, attracting thousands of river runners every year to Oregon's most popular and most famous waterway. Between frothy rapids, the river lies quietly in green pools. But when it rages, it does so magnificently, over drops as far as 15 feet that will stand a boat on end, through chasms so narrow a raft will rub both sides of the canyon at once, and over the white tops of treacherous Class IV rapids. If you do the entire 40-mile stretch, which includes non-Wilderness riverway, plan on the following: a three-day trip, pleasant campsites on river bars and benches where creeks spill into the main flow, and a long wait for a chance since only one applicant in 10 gets a permit.

At 4,319 feet, Mount Bolivar anchors the extreme northeastern corner of the area, offering a first-rate view from the summit. Away from the water, the land lies steep and dense with brush, attracting surprisingly few people. The forest stands dominated by Douglas fir in the wetter west but gives way to oak and madrona in the east. The eastern two-sevenths of the Wilderness lies on BLM land, and the western five-sevenths on USFS land.

Along the river you may see deer and otters, or even black bears looking for a meal of salmon. Bears, grown accustomed to easy pickings from boaters, may prove a nuisance in numerous campsites. You may see nocturnal ringtail cats living at their northernmost extreme. Birds abound and lizards hasten over the dry slopes above the water, especially in the eastern portion. Fishing tends to be excellent for trout, salmon, and steelhead (only Oregon's Columbia River gives a greater annual yield of fish). Ticks and rattlesnakes, poison ivy, and pestiferous insects are a nuisance during the typically hot, rainless summer days.

The Rogue River Trail (47 miles total, with approximately 12 miles in the Wilderness), closed to horse traffic, sometimes crosses steep terrain hundreds of feet above the river.

OREGON

Wild Rogue Essentials

Size: 35,818 acres.
Year Designated: 1978.
Location: Southwestern Oregon.
Easiest Access: From Wolf Creek, on Interstate 5, take Grave Creek Road west approximately 13 miles to the Grave Creek launch site on the river, where you can also access the Rogue River Trail.
Season: Summer for the best water and warmest weather. Spring and fall for fewer people and cooler temperatures.
Wilderness Fees/Permits: No fees or permits are needed for the backcountry. A permit must be acquired in advance to run the Rogue River between May 15 and October 15. For an application, which must be submitted before the end of January, contact Tioga Resources, Inc., at (541) 672-4168.
Maps: A Wilderness map that includes Kalmiopsis Wilderness is available for $2 from the district ranger. A waterproof Rogue River map/booklet is also available for $10.
Management: Gold Beach Ranger Station, Siskiyou National Forest, 1225 South Ellensburg Avenue, Gold Beach, OR 97444; (541) 247-6651. BLM Medford District Office, 3040 Biddle Road, Medford, OR 97504; (541) 770-2200.

> "To a vast number of American citizens life's most splendid moments come in the opportunity to enjoy undefiled nature."
>
> —Bob Marshall

PENNSYLVANIA

Total Wilderness areas: 2
Total Wilderness acreage: 9,705

Pennsylvania, so rich in American history, no longer boasts the wealth of natural treasures it once did. Long plundered by the ax, the hoe, and the plow, little of the state's vast woodland remains as it was. In Allegheny National Forest of western Pennsylvania stand a pair of small designated Wildernesses, one a forest and the other a string of islands dotting the Allegheny River.

Allegheny River Islands Wilderness

Between Buckaloons Recreation Area and the town of Tionesta, a distance of approximately 56 miles, seven islands in the Allegheny River have been designated Wilderness. Eighty-five miles of the river have been designated Wild and Scenic. The accent is decidedly on "scenic" rather than "wild," and the calm water here extends an irresistible invitation to many placid-water canoeists.

Alluvial in origin, the islands were formed from deposits of sand, mud, and clay that the river carried down from the Allegheny Mountains.

Old river-bottom trees—willow, sycamore, and silver maple—characterize these little hunks of land. Crull's, at 96 acres, is the largest, followed by Thompson's and Baker (both 67 acres), Courson (62 acres), King (36 acres), R. Thompson's (30 acres), and No-Name (10 acres).

Although trailless, the islands are relatively easy to explore on foot, except where brush is dense (as is the case on at least half of No-Name) or downfall has formed a matrix of dead trees (as on parts on Baker). Camping is permitted on any island unless otherwise posted. At night you may hear the "who cooks for you allll!" cry of barred owls. Woodpeckers and flying squirrels live here, too.

PENNSYLVANIA

Allegheny River Islands Essentials

Size: 368 acres.
Year Designated: 1984.
Location: Northwestern Pennsylvania.
Easiest Access: From Warren, follow U.S. 62 west for six miles to Buckaloons Recreation Area. Continue on U.S. 62 as it winds south and west along the Allegheny River. The first Wilderness island, Crull's, lies about one mile south of Buckaloons. Thompson's Island is approximately one mile south of Crull's, and R. Thompson's lies about one mile south of Thompson's. Courson Island is located near Tidioute, about 29 miles south of Buckaloons. King Island is situated near East Hickory, about seven miles north of Tionesta. Baker and No-Name Islands lie close together, approximately two miles south of King Island.
Season: Fall for color.
Wilderness Fees/Permits: None.
Maps: A 30-by-36-inch map of the forest is available for $3 from the district ranger.
Management: Sheffield Ranger District, Allegheny National Forest, U.S. 6, Sheffield, PA 16347; (814) 968-3232.

Hickory Creek Wilderness

Drained by East Hickory and Middle Hickory Creeks, this Wilderness's gentle to moderate terrain rises from 1,273 feet to a plateau at 1,900 feet. Heavy forest cover is composed of northern hardwoods: hickory (of course), oak, beech, birch, and hemlock, with an understory of abundant flowers, shrubs, and mosses. Middle Hickory flows through bog-meadows slowed by beaver ponds. Bear, deer, and turkey are common, and barred owls often break the night stillness with their distinctive hooting. Anglers can catch small native brook trout in the creeks.

The Hickory Creek Trail, a loop of 11.1 miles, starts at Hearts Content Recreation Area on the eastern boundary. It circles the center of the Wilderness, passing through an old artillery range. The trail is the only maintained path here, except for about one-quarter mile of the Tanbark Trail, which cuts across the extreme southeastern corner. Two old railroad grades run north-south and east-west, meeting near the southern end of the area to provide additional access.

Hickory Creek Essentials

Size: 9,337 acres.
Year Designated: 1984.
Location: Northwestern Pennsylvania.
Easiest Access: From Warren, take Warren-Tidioute Road south for about 11 miles. Turn onto Township Road 61031 and drive four miles to Hearts Content Recreation Area and the Hickory Creek Trailhead.
Season: Year-round, but fall is best for color.
Wilderness Fees/Permits: None.
Maps: USGS topographic maps, available from the district ranger, are Cherry Grove and Cobham.
Management: Sheffield Ranger District, Allegheny National Forest, U.S. 6, Sheffield, PA 16347; (814) 968-3232.

> *"I look at the venerable trees around me and I know that I must not dishonor them."*
>
> —General Francis Marion

SOUTH CAROLINA

Total Wilderness areas: 7
Total Wilderness acreage: 60,539

Despite the honor that American Revolution notable Francis "The Swamp Fox" Marion wished for the trees of South Carolina, by 1936 large-scale logging operations had removed almost all the timber from the national forest that bears his name. Today Francis Marion National Forest shows few signs of human intervention, aside from a few old canals, dikes, and earthen railroad trams, and Congress has established four Wilderness areas here. South Carolina's oldest Wilderness lies on Sumter National Forest. Of the two remaining areas, one stands on a wildlife refuge and the other on a national monument.

Cape Romain Wilderness

For 22 miles, the Cape Romain National Wildlife Refuge stretches wild and free along the coastline of South Carolina, protecting sanctuaries of open water, sandy beaches, freshwater and saltwater marshes, and tens of thousands of water-loving birds. No other place on Earth attracts as many oystercatchers during winter. Waiting patiently until an oyster opens up, these splendid black and white birds strike suddenly, using their long red beaks to rip at the oyster's muscle. Here in winter you'll find thousands of terns and brown pelicans, and black skimmers flying with their black and red bills gaping to skim food from the surface of the ocean. Hundreds of herons and egrets pace on long legs looking for food, and the beaches stir under the feet of godwits, whimbrels, and dowitchers, who often share the sand with alligators. In the marshes, the clapper rails, sometimes more than 25,000 of them, fill the air with their strange clattering. Colorful songbirds migrate through in spring, joining year-round residents such as flickers and yellow-throated warblers.

SOUTH CAROLINA

The shorelines rise to uplands of live oak dripping with long gray beards of Spanish moss. Owls haunt the forestland, flying at night over an abundant population of white-tailed deer, wild turkeys, black fox squirrels, and rare red wolves.

During my last visit, I failed to see a loggerhead sea turtle, even though they lay more eggs in these beaches than anywhere else along South Carolina's coast. Don't be surprised if you miss them as well, since they most often choose the night, when the refuge is closed, to drag their great broad backs from the ocean.

Sea kayaking is the best way to see Cape Romain. Overnight camping is prohibited. Most of the refuge has been designated Wilderness, and much of it was altered drastically by Hurricane Hugo in 1989. (Blustery Hugo even tore down the visitors center.) Although decades will pass before it returns to its past condition, the land that remains is glorious and appealing.

Cape Romain Essentials

Size: 29,000 acres.
Year Designated: 1975.
Location: Off the eastern South Carolina coast.
Easiest Access: From Charleston, take U.S. 17 north about 20 miles to refuge headquarters along the sea side of the road.
Season: March and April are best, when the bird migration peaks and alligators lay sunning on warm beaches. Cape Romain is open year-round, from sunrise to sunset.
Wilderness Fees/Permits: A free permit is required for sea kayaking. Hunting is allowed for deer, rail, and raccoon in season with a state permit. Contact the refuge manager for more information.
Maps: NOAA Chart 11531 covers the refuge including all the adjoining islands.
Management: Cape Romain National Wildlife Refuge, 5801 U.S. 17 North, Awendaw, SC 29429; (803) 928-3368.

Congaree Swamp Wilderness

Almost entirely a designated Wilderness area, Congaree Swamp National Monument protects an unsurpassed old-growth riverbottom hardwood forest that miraculously managed to escape the rampaging saws and axes of the post–Civil War South. The Congaree River and its tributaries flood the parkland an average of 10 times each year, bringing rich silt that encourages tree growth. And do the trees of Congaree ever grow! Approximately 90 species attain heights and girths found nowhere else in the state. You'll find bald cypress with circumferences of 27.5 feet and extensive root systems that rise above the water in "knees" that reach as high as 7.5 feet. Loblolly pines, rarely associated with hardwood swamps, have stood here for about 300 years, soaring to record-breaking altitudes of 169 feet.

Sweet gums are the most ubiquitous trees, along with swamp chestnuts, laurel oaks, green ash, hickories, elms, sugarberries, and sycamores. Poison ivy and wild grapevines climb the tree trunks to disappear into the high forest canopy. Most of these swampland trees have shallow roots, and their great cathedral heights often cause them to topple, sometimes leaving a hole in the canopy up to a half acre wide. In these deadfall openings, brambles quickly grow and, in summer and fall, swarms of wasps surround unwary hikers. Standing dead trees offer homes to all eight species of Southeastern woodpeckers, including the endangered red-cockaded woodpecker.

Through this floodplain forest flows slow-moving Cedar Creek, dropping only 10 feet in

13 linear miles. A marked 20-mile canoe trail on Cedar Creek provides the best way to see Congaree. The southern boundary of the Wilderness is over 25 miles of the lazy, looping river, another fine canoe route. I often fished the Congaree as a boy, long before Wilderness designation. The shoreline, shadowed by giant trees, was a place as wild as any I can remember.

Six trails provide access to the northwestern portion of the swamp. All originate near park headquarters, and some traverse boardwalks above the shallow murky water. The Weston Lake Loop Trail circles for 4.2 miles to offer a "quick peek" at the swamp. The secret central and southeastern portions are trailless, inviting the brave and the bold.

Congaree Swamp Essentials

Size: 15,010 acres.
Year Designated: 1988.
Location: Central South Carolina.
Easiest Access: From Columbia, take State Highway 48 east about 11 miles. Turn south on County Road 1288 and soon after turn west on County Road 734 (Old Bluff Road) to reach the park entrance.
Season: The park is open year-round, except Christmas Day. Early spring and late fall are the most comfortable and least humid times to visit.
Wilderness Fees/Permits: A free backcountry camping permit is required.
Maps: Get a free trail map from the park ranger.
Management: Congaree Swamp National Monument, 200 Caroline Sims Road, Hopkins, SC 29061; (803) 776-4396.

Ellicott Rock Wilderness

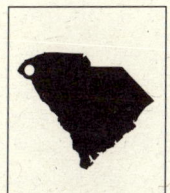

In 1811, surveyor Andrew Ellicott determined the starting point for the North Carolina–Georgia state line and chiseled an inconspicuous mark on a rock on the east bank of the Chattooga River. Here the mountainous regions of South Carolina, North Carolina, and Georgia converge, and this is where the Ellicott Rock Wilderness straddles the Wild and Scenic Chattooga River. This is the only Wilderness area lying in three states (see the Ellicott Rock Wildernesses in Georgia and North Carolina). Unlike many pristine areas in the western United States (but like many other southeastern Wildernesses), Ellicott Rock has been heavily impacted by humans in the not too distant past. Nevertheless, enough time has passed since the logging operations of yesteryear for impressive second-growth forests, typical of the Appalachian greenbelt, to reclaim Ellicott Rock Wilderness. Today dense stands of white pine and hemlock occupy the lower coves and areas along streams, upland hardwoods thrive on slopes, and scrub oaks and pitch pines grow on dry ridges. The region lies just south of the area that receives the highest rainfall in the eastern United States; expect some wet weather.

In South Carolina the Wilderness rises from the river to a high point on Fork Mountain at 3,294 feet. Several trails originate in the South Carolina portion. From the Sloan Bridge Picnic Area on the eastern border, 6.3 miles of the Ellicott Rock Trail will take you down to Ellicott Rock itself. This trail joins the Chattooga River Trail, which follows the South Carolina side of the river south for 4.4 miles to Burrell's Ford Campground. Ellicott Rock stands relatively near millions of Americans, and use of the area is high. Along the river you'll find more solitude.

SOUTH CAROLINA

Ellicott Rock Essentials

Size: 2,809 acres in South Carolina (9,012 acres total).
Year Designated: 1975 in South Carolina.
Location: Extreme western South Carolina.
Easiest Access: From Walhalla, take State Highway 28/107 north approximately seven miles to the Sloan Bridge Picnic Area.
Season: Year-round; winter weekdays bring fewer visitors.
Wilderness Fees/Permits: None.
Maps: Free maps showing the hiking trails are available from the district ranger.
Management: Andrew Pickens Ranger District, Sumter National Forest, Star Route, Walhalla, SC 29691; (803) 638-9568. Highlands Ranger District, Nantahala National Forest, P.O. Box 749, Highlands, NC 28741; (704) 562-3765. Tallulah Ranger District, Chattahoochee National Forest, Clayton, GA 30525; (770) 782-3320.

Hell Hole Bay Wilderness

Swamps and wetlands—that's what you'll find on all four Wildernesses in the Francis Marion National Forest. From June through August (the wettest season) much of the ground is usually submerged in 2 to 18 inches of standing water. On September 21, 1989, Hurricane Hugo swept through with winds in excess of 135 miles per hour, devastating decades-old second-growth forest. Virtually every tree that reached nine inches in diameter fell to earth, and trails and old roads were washed away. Wildlife suffered greatly, especially the endangered red-cockaded woodpecker. On the four Wilderness areas, nature has begun to rebuild without human interference. Insects abound, with mosquitoes, chiggers, and ticks reaching peak irritability from summer through fall. Many snakes, including poisonous water moccasins, copperheads, and rattlesnakes, make their homes here. Within most of the areas visibility is poor due to dense vegetation, and getting lost is easy. There are precious few spots dry enough for camping. If you desire a true South Carolina Wilderness adventure, bring shoes that will hold up when wet, insect repellent, and courage.

Hell Hole Bay, one of the four Francis Marion Wildernesses, takes its name from a large opening in the forest probably formed by wildfires dating back to before the 1700s. For much of the year the Hell Hole Canoe Trail (6 to 12 inches deep, 6 to 8 feet wide, and just over a mile long) crosses the bay, but during the "dry" season it becomes a mushy hiking trail. The trail passes bald cypress, tupelo, and spreading maple. There are no other trails in the area.

SOUTH CAROLINA

Hell Hole Bay Essentials

Size: 1,980 acres.
Year Designated: 1980.
Location: Eastern South Carolina.
Easiest Access: From Charleston, take State Highway 41 north approximately 20 miles. Turn east on Forest Service Road 158 and drive two miles to the Hell Hole Canoe Trail sign.
Season: Winter for cooler temperatures and less standing water. Summer and fall for heat, humidity, and canoeing.
Wilderness Fees/Permits: A free permit is required for backcountry camping. Ask the district ranger about water levels in Hell Hole Bay Wilderness.
Maps: A free map is available from the district ranger.
Management: Witherbee Ranger District, Francis Marion National Forest, P.O. Box 1532, Moncks Corner, SC 29461; (803) 336-3248.

Little Wambaw Swamp Wilderness

Another of the four Wildernesses within Francis Marion National Forest (see Hell Hole Bay Wilderness, above), Little Wambaw Swamp is a river-bottom land of hardwoods and sloughs. Bald cypress and tupelo grow impressively large, and about 60 acres of forest in the southwestern portion of the swamp are believed to be virgin timber. The dense understory consists primarily of wild orchids, bladderwort, and pickerel weed. Old, earthen railroad trams cross the area and provide high ground for foot traffic and possible spots to camp. Bridges where the trams spanned the many sluggish waterways are long gone; prepare to wade in the water. Camping is available at bordering Buck Hall Recreation Area, where the earthen tram system can be accessed.

Little Wambaw Swamp Essentials

Size: 5,000 acres.
Year Designated: 1980.
Location: Eastern South Carolina.
Easiest Access: From Awendaw, take U.S. 17 east and north about three miles to Buck Hall Recreation Area and the Wilderness boundary.
Season: Winters tend to be somewhat drier.
Wilderness Fees/Permits: A free permit is required for backcountry camping.
Maps: A free map is available from the district ranger.
Management: Wambaw District Ranger, Francis Marion National Forest, P.O. Box 788, McClellanville, SC 29458; (803) 887-3257.

Wambaw Creek Wilderness

Wilderness designation protects 11 miles of Wambaw Creek, another area in Francis Marion National Forest (see Hell Hole Bay and Little Wambaw Swamp, above). Old dikes and canals bear evidence of attempts made by early European settlers to tame this region for agriculture. Giant cypress and gum trees line the creek, which flows down the heart of this long, slender Wilderness. The creek varies in width from 20 to 80 feet and provides a home for a few alligators who are seen only occasionally by humans. There are no hiking trails; to see Wambaw Creek you will need a canoe and tide table. Proximity to the Atlantic Ocean causes the creek to be greatly altered by tides. During low tide, the upper creek, especially the first two miles, can be blocked by logs. Passage should be attempted only after heavy rainfall or during high tides, which occur here approximately 4.5 hours after high tide listed in tables for Charleston, South Carolina.

Wambaw Creek Essentials

Size: 1,640 acres.
Year Designated: 1980.
Location: Eastern South Carolina.
Easiest Access: From McClellanville, take State Highway 45 west approximately 16 miles. Turn north on Forest Service Road 211 and drive approximately six miles. Turn north on Forest Service Road 204 and continue about one mile to the put-in on Wambaw Creek.
Season: Water levels vary throughout the year with tides and rain. Winters are cooler.
Wilderness Fees/Permits: A free permit is required for backcountry camping.
Maps: A free map is available from the district ranger.
Management: Wambaw Ranger District, Francis Marion National Forest, P.O. Box 788, McClellanville, SC 29458; (803) 887-3257.

Wambaw Swamp Wilderness

Wambaw Swamp offers no trails and little dry ground. Here, in another of the four Wildernesses in Francis Marion National Forest (see the previous listings), you'll find river-bottom hardwood swamp edged with small stands of pine. Wild orchids, lizard's tail, pickerel weed, sedges, and ferns dominate the understory. The water level is generally too low for canoeing. Insects, snakes, muck, and lack of dry campsites keep most humans away. This may be the least visited spot in South Carolina.

Wambaw Swamp Essentials

Size: 5,100 acres.
Year Designated: 1980.
Location: Eastern South Carolina.
Easiest Access: From Awendaw, take State Highway 133 west for about six miles. Turn north on State Highway 98 and drive one mile. For the next three miles State Highway 98 parallels the northwestern boundary of the swamp.
Season: Winter for cooler temperatures.
Wilderness Fees/Permits: A free permit is required for backcountry camping.
Maps: A free map is available from the district ranger.
Management: Wambaw Ranger District, Francis Marion National Forest, P.O. Box 788, McClellanville, SC 29458; (803) 887-3257.

> "The lover of nature could here find his soul's delight; the invalid regain his health; the old, be rejuvenated; the weary find sweet repose and invigoration; and all who could come and spend the heated season here would find it the pleasantest summer home in America."
> —A. B. Donaldson (Custer's Black Hills Expedition)

SOUTH DAKOTA

Total Wilderness areas: 2
Total Wilderness acreage: 74,074

The Lakota Sioux called them *Paha Sapa*, the "hills that are black," and indeed the spruce-covered Black Hills do appear dark when viewed from a distance. This forested island rises several thousand feet high in the midst of a sea of prairie grasslands and covers a region 125 miles long and 65 miles wide in western South Dakota and a portion of eastern Wyoming. One small Wilderness is located in the Black Hills. Not far to the east, Badlands National Park protects another, much larger designated area.

Black Elk Wilderness

Within the heart of the Black Hills lies a region long held sacred by Native Americans and appreciated for its splendid beauty by many others. On its northeastern border towers Mount Rushmore National Memorial and to the south roams the buffalo herd of Custer State Park. Most of the area now bears the name Norbeck Wildlife Preserve. Of its 35,000 acres, 27,800 are managed by Black Hills National Forest, while Custer State Park oversees most of the rest. In the center of this sprawling preserve you'll find Black Elk Wilderness, named for an Oglala Sioux holy man. Here you can see elk, deer, and mountain goats among the rugged granite formations and cliffs and beside small lakes.

At least five trails lead to the summit of Harney Peak in the west-central portion, at 7,242 feet the highest point east of the Rocky Mountains. From a stone "lookout" on Harney, visitors enjoy panoramic views across South Dakota, Wyoming, Nebraska, and Montana. Eight miles of the Centennial Trail (which crosses the entire Black Hills) runs through the eastern portion of the area. From Iron Creek Horse Camp outside the southern boundary, the Norbeck Trail heads into the Wilderness to meet the Grizzly Creek Trail for a loop trip of 15 miles back to your starting point.

SOUTH DAKOTA

Black Elk Essentials

Size: 9,824 acres.
Year Designated: 1980.
Location: Southwestern South Dakota.
Easiest Access: From the town of Custer, take State Route 89 north for approximately six miles. Then turn east on the Needles Highway and drive approximately five miles. Turn north at the sign indicating the Orphan Trailhead on the Norbeck Trail.
Season: Summer is the most popular time. Come in spring or fall to avoid crowds.
Wilderness Fees/Permits: None.
Maps: A detailed map is available for $2 from the forest supervisor's office and all the nearby forest ranger, park, and monument offices.
Management: Forest Supervisor, Black Hills National Forest, R.R. 2, Box 200, Custer, SD 57730; (605) 673-2251.

Sage Creek (Badlands) Wilderness

About 38 million years ago this region was a marshy jungle filled with saber-toothed cats, camels no bigger than dogs, turtles the size of Volkswagens, and other long-extinct life-forms. Their bones were buried in mud washed down from the Black Hills and beneath gray and white ash from later volcanic periods. The jungle turned to grassland, and eons of wind, rain, and frost carved the land into a moonscape of cliffs, gorges, mesas, soaring spires, keen-edged ridges, and fossil-filled canyons. To the Dakota Indians it was *Mako Sica*, "bad lands to travel through." Early pioneers hastily filled their wagons with thousands of bleached bones as they migrated west.

Almost one-half million acres of the land lie within Badlands National Park, and the most spectacular parkland is within Sage Creek Wilderness in its northern section. A tortured, mystical land, Sage Creek still changes with the elements. It represents the largest mixed-grass prairie wildland in the United States. Deer, rattlesnakes, coyotes, bighorn sheep, and a large herd of buffalo live here. You'll find isolated backpacking opportunities with unrestricted camping. There are no established trails in this little-used wild area.

Sage Creek (Badlands) Essentials

Size: 64,250 acres.
Year Designated: 1976.
Location: Southwestern South Dakota.
Easiest Access: From Rapid City, take Interstate 90 east for approximately 57 miles to the Pinnacles entrance on the north side of the Wilderness.
Season: Crowds gather in the summer. Fall is usually best.
Wilderness Fees/Permits: All visitors are required to pay a park entrance fee of $5 per vehicle or $3 per person.
Maps: Topographic maps are necessary and available for a small charge from the Badlands Natural History Association, P.O. Box 6B, Interior, SD 57750.
Management: Badlands National Park, P.O. Box 6, Interior, SD 57750; (605) 433-5361.

> "I have a hunger for nonhuman spaces, not out of any distaste for humanity, but out of a need to experience my humanness the more vividly . . . by confronting stretches of the earth that my kind has had no part in making."
>
> —Scott Russell Sanders

TENNESSEE

Total Wilderness areas: 11
Total Wilderness acreage: 66,714

The salt water of the Gulf of Mexico once covered western Tennessee, now a relatively flat land of rich farm fields sometimes referred to as delta country. Bluegrass (you've heard of the music, but this is the real thing) characterizes middle Tennessee, where wooded hills shadow idyllic pastures. The eastern portion of the state, by contrast, is downright mountainous. Anchored by the Cumberland Plateau, a part of the vast Appalachian Plateau that stretches from New York to central Alabama, this region offers high cliffs, tumbling rivers, deep caves, and the Big South Fork National Recreation Area. But the small area still worthy of Wilderness designation lies along the North Carolina border, where Great Smoky Mountains National Park divides 625,000-acre Cherokee National Forest into southern and northern halves.

Bald River Gorge Wilderness

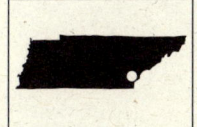

Bald River is a small wild trout stream flowing cold and clear northward through the middle of the steep-sided Bald River Gorge and hence down the middle of this Wilderness. The Wilderness ends just before the river plunges dramatically over what is arguably the loveliest waterfall in the state, Bald River Falls. Southern Appalachian hardwoods, pine, dog hobble, and other flora cloak the mountain slopes above the river, home to black bears, deer, wild turkeys, and wild hogs. Fall turns the area into a quilt of color. Summer wildflowers are plentiful.

The Bald River Trail climbs steeply from a parking lot on the northern edge of the Wilderness at the Bald River Falls Picnic Area, descends

TENNESSEE

past a series of waterfalls and along an old logging railway bed, then rises to follow the side of the gorge. Alternating between riverbank and gorge rim, the trail eventually passes through thick stands of laurel and rhododendron before climbing briefly to the Cantrell Parking Area on the southern boundary. The distance is less than six miles, the hiking fairly easy, and campsites exist in several sheltered spots. Two additional trails provide shorter hikes. Human use is heavy. Anglers are limited to fly-fishing and must have a special fishing permit.

Bald River Gorge Essentials

Size: 3,887 acres.
Year Designated: 1984.
Location: Southeastern Tennessee.
Easiest Access: From the intersection of State Highway 165 and State Highway 68 on the west side of Tellico Plains, take Highway 165 east up the Tellico River for 5.3 miles. Continue east on Forest Service Road 210 (Tellico River Road) for 6.3 miles to the Bald River Falls Picnic Area.
Season: Spring and fall.
Wilderness Fees/Permits: None.
Maps: USGS topographic map is Bald River Falls. Maps that include the Wilderness are available for $3 from the district ranger.
Management: Tellico Ranger District, Cherokee National Forest, Route 3, Tellico River Road, P.O. Box 339, Tellico Plains, TN 37385; (423) 253-2520.

Big Frog Wilderness

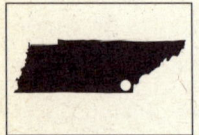

Distinguished by 4,224-foot Big Frog Mountain, this Wilderness not only lies over the state line in Georgia (see Georgia, Big Frog Wilderness), it borders the Cohutta Wilderness (see Georgia, Cohutta Wilderness). The Big Frog–Cohutta combination, with adjacent Primitive areas, creates the largest tract of Wilderness on USFS land in the eastern United States. Virginia pine covers the lower elevations, and hardwoods, including white oak, red oak, and hickory, shade the upper. The Wilderness is home to a few deer, wild turkeys, and a mixture of Russian wild hogs released in the 1960s and domestic hogs gone wild. Timber rattlesnakes commonly slither across these trails.

Hikers can enjoy the most diverse and the best hiking in Cherokee National Forest in this Wilderness, choosing from pathways that wander easily with little elevation changes; long, contouring trails; and strength-sapping up-and-down routes. Although rugged, most of the trails are well maintained. The 4.5-mile Wolf Ridge Trail climbs from a trailhead near the western boundary to enter the Wilderness and ascend to the top of Big Frog Mountain, where the 5.6-mile Big Frog Trail, perhaps the most scenic in Tennessee, descends northward. The Big Frog Trail provides access to several other trails that cross the Wilderness along ridges and streams. From the top of Big Frog Mountain you can hike south into Cohutta Wilderness on the Hemp Top Trail (eight-tenths of a mile). Even in the wet season (spring and early summer), water may be hard to find. Carry plenty.

TENNESSEE

Big Frog Essentials

Size: 7,972 acres in Tennessee (8,055 total).
Year Designated: 1984; expanded in 1986.
Location: Southeastern Tennessee.
Easiest Access: From Ocoee and the junction of U.S. 411 and U.S. 64, take U.S. 64 east for 18.6 miles until you are past Ocoee Lake to Ocoee Number 3 Powerhouse. Turn south on Forest Service Road 45 (look for a sign for Thunder Rock Campground) and continue for approximately three miles, then proceed west on Forest Service Road 221 for 7.3 miles. Turn east on Road 221E and go about 100 feet to a parking lot and the Wolf Ridge Trailhead.
Season: Spring through fall.
Wilderness Fees/Permits: None.
Maps: USGS topographic maps are Caney Creek and Ducktown.
Management: Ocoee Ranger District, Cherokee National Forest, Route 1, Box 348D, Benton, TN 37307; (423) 338-5201.

Big Laurel Branch Wilderness

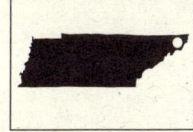

Numerous streams drain from a major northeast-southwest-trending ridge crest in Big Laurel Branch Wilderness, which includes the completely forested southern end of Iron Mountain. Hidden behind Iron Mountain's double parallel crests are the valleys of Big Laurel Branch and Little Laurel Branch. The former, on the western side of the crest, eases out of seclusion until it runs into Wilbur Lake on the edge of the Wilderness. Sheer rock walls herald the blue jewel, and Big Laurel Branch gracefully plunges 50 feet to join the lake. Waterways here typically plummet over cascades, slides, and short falls into hollows (choked with rhododendron and laurel) separated by narrow ridges that run east-west from the main ridge. Mixed second-growth hardwoods dominate the forest cover, occasionally sharing turf with yellow and white pines and eastern hemlocks. From Watauga Lake, which forms most of the southern Wilderness boundary, you can see many of the cliffs along the eastern side of the main crest. Just south of Watauga Lake lies Pond Mountain Wilderness (see below). Hunters come here seeking deer and grouse.

The Appalachian National Scenic Trail (AT) follows the entire length of the crest of the Wilderness, a distance of about 5.8 miles, with a shelter about midway. Off-trail bushwhacking is a possibility and your sense of isolation should be worth the effort, especially in the valley of Big Laurel Branch. Along the Wilderness shore of Watauga Lake you'll find at least 10 pleasant campsites accessible by boat.

Big Laurel Branch Essentials

Size: 6,251 acres.
Year Designated: 1986.
Location: Northeastern Tennessee.
Easiest Access: From Elizabethton, on the east end of Broad Street, take U.S. 321 south for one-half mile. Turn east on Siam Road and continue for about five miles to the Watauga River (but don't cross the river), then turn east on Watauga Dam Road, which will take you across Wilbur Lake to the Appalachian Trailhead, approximately 3.6 miles.
Season: Spring and fall.
Wilderness Fees/Permits: None.
Maps: USGS topographic maps are Carter and Watauga Dam. An AT map is available for $5 from the district ranger.
Management: Watauga Ranger District, Cherokee National Forest, Route 9, Box 2235, Elizabethton, TN 37643; (423) 542-2942.

TENNESSEE

Citico Creek Wilderness

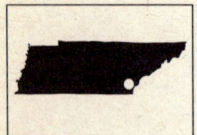

Natural splendor has regained a strong foothold in this Wilderness, the largest in Tennessee, ever since fire put an end to a devastating logging period. You can actually find stands of virgin forest in some of the more isolated regions. Three steep-sided ridges run west from the long, high ridge of the Unicoi Mountains: Brush Mountain, Pine Ridge, and Sassafras Ridge. Narrow steep-walled valleys of streams divide these smaller ridges, draining swiftly westward.

Elevations range from 1,400 feet to about 4,600 feet, with only a few of the rugged upper terrain's slopes inclined less than 30 degrees. The Wilderness contains the entire upper drainage of Citico Creek, which consists of the North and South Forks and at least eight clear-running tributaries. The Wilderness shares its eastern border with Joyce Kilmer-Slickrock Wilderness of Tennessee and North Carolina.

Thirteen trails totaling 57.4 miles provide access to much of the Wilderness. Most of the paths at lower elevations follow old tramways or roads with gentle inclines, but may require "wet" crossings (typically streams). Upper-elevation trails grow faint and sometimes remarkably steep. The 10.6-mile Fodderstack Trail, often used by horsepackers, runs along the Unicoi Mountains, passing near the crests of Big Fodderstack and Little Fodderstack. Several trails lead into the neighboring Joyce Kilmer–Slickrock Wilderness and North Carolina.

Citico Creek Essentials

Size: 16,000 acres.
Year Designated: 1984.
Location: Southeastern Tennessee.
Easiest Access: From just west of Tellico Plains, and the junction of State Highway 165 and State Highway 68, take Highway 165 east for 13.7 miles. Turn north on Forest Service Road 365 and continue for approximately four miles, then go north on Forest Service Road 59 (Doublecamp Road) for approximately seven miles to Farr Gap and the Fodderstack Trailhead.

Season: Spring and fall.
Wilderness Fees/Permits: None.
Maps: USGS topographic maps are Big Junction and Whiteoak Flats. A Wilderness map that shows all the trails is available for $3 from the district ranger.
Management: Tellico Ranger District, Cherokee National Forest, Route 3, Tellico River Road, P.O. Box 339, Tellico Plains, TN 37385; (423) 253-2520.

Cohutta Wilderness

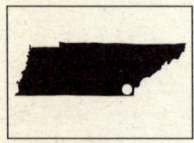

Most of mountainous Cohutta lies within Tennessee's Cohutta Wildlife Management Area, but a small portion runs over the southern border (see Georgia, Cohutta Wilderness). Immediately northeast of Tennessee's portion, and sharing a border, lies Big Frog Wilderness (see above). Cohutta and Big Frog combine with 1,460 acres of the West Big Frog Primitive Area bordering Cohutta on the north to form the largest tract of Wilderness on national forestland in the eastern United States.

Although timber companies made off with 70 percent of the trees between 1915 and 1930—evidence of logging is apparent in a few spots—oak and pine have returned and now blanket the forest. Virginia pine thickly dominate the forest floor at lower elevations, deferring to upland hardwoods that include hickory, red oak, and white oak. Beech, basswood, birch, red maple, black gum, and silver bell shade four species of plants designated rare in this region: catchfly, purple hyssop, cow parsnip, and rattlesnake root. Spring and summer bring a riot of colorful blooms to many flowering shrubs, vines, and herbaceous plants, including the brilliant orange of flame azalea, the pink and yellow of lady's slippers, the blue cohosh, and the scarlet cardinal flower.

But summer also brings heat, high humidity, biting insects, and heavy foliage blocking some of the must-see fall and spring views. You may glimpse domestic hogs gone wild, as well as wild turkeys and bobcats. Many species of snakes, including unusually large copperheads and timber rattlesnakes lurk in the shadows.

One short piece of Trail 74 crosses the Tennessee portion for less than one-half mile, with junctions onto Georgia's Jacks River Trail and onto trails leading into Big Frog Wilderness. To explore most of this small piece of Tennessee, you will have to wander off-trail.

Cohutta Essentials

Size: 1,795 acres in Tennessee (37,042 acres total).
Year Designated: 1975.
Location: Southeastern Tennessee.
Easiest Access: From Ocoee and the junction of U.S. 411 and U.S. 64, take U.S. 64 east for 18.6 miles until you are past Ocoee Lake to Ocoee Number 3 Powerhouse. Turn south on Forest Service Road 45 (look for a sign for Thunder Rock Campground) and continue for about three miles, then proceed west on Forest Service Road 221 for 9.8 miles. Drive south on Forest Service Road 62 until you reach the trailhead for Trail 74, about seven miles, on the south side of the road.
Season: Spring and fall.
Wilderness Fees/Permits: None.
Maps: USGS topographic map is Caney Creek.
Management: Ocoee Ranger District, Cherokee National Forest, Route 1, Box 348D, Benton, TN 37307; (423) 338-5201.

Gee Creek Wilderness

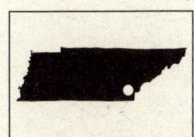

To the early settlers in South Carolina, the Cherokee Indians lived "over the hills" in eastern Tennessee. People today refer to the region, which includes the southern portion of Cherokee National Forest, as Tennessee Overhill Country. Small Gee Creek Wilderness marks the forest's western border, with the long rise of Starr Mountain to the west and north and Chestnut Mountain to the south.

South-flowing Poplar Springs Branch and Gee Creek drain the Wilderness. From a distance, the two waterways appear to cut a V in the otherwise continuous face of the mountains where the drainage lies. Peaceful trails follow Poplar Springs Branch and Gee Creek through hollows dense with hemlock, buckeye, white pine, beech, and rhododendron. Both creeks teem with native trout, and the fishing can be excellent. Loggers once devastated the forest, but that was 80 years ago. Lush trees have long since returned, even though some have had to contend with old mining sites (one of which you can still see on Gee Creek) and other abandoned relics of the past.

The semiprimitive Gee Creek Trail starts at a parking lot outside the southwestern corner

TENNESSEE

and follows an old forest road about one-half mile before entering the Wilderness to trace the creek for a total of approximately two miles to a dead end. This is a place where you'll feel isolated from the rest of the world and as immersed in wildness as you can get in Tennessee. The trail branches at the confluence of Poplar Springs Branch to go a short distance up Gee Creek and a long distance up the branch. The terrain steepens in the northern section. The Chestnut Mountain Trail follows the slopes of Chestnut Mountain in the south and east for 5.6 miles and is used primarily by horseback riders. The total trail equals about eight miles.

Gee Creek Essentials

Size: 2,493 acres.
Year Designated: 1975.
Location: Southeastern Tennessee.
Easiest Access: From Etowah, take U.S. 411 south until you are about five miles south of the old Etowah train depot. Turn east on the paved road marked by a Gee Creek Wilderness sign, then continue until the road turns to dirt for a total of 2.2 miles to the Gee Creek Trailhead.
Season: Spring and fall.
Wilderness Fees/Permits: None.
Maps: USGS topographic maps are Etowah, Mecca, and Oswald Dome.
Management: Hiwassee Ranger District, Cherokee National Forest, 274 Highway 310, Box D, Etowah, TN 37331; (423) 263-5486.

Joyce Kilmer–Slickrock Wilderness

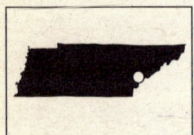

Joyce Kilmer acquired some fame as a journalist, serving on the staff of the *New York Times* from 1913 to 1918, but most people remember him as the author of the poem "Trees" ("I think that I shall never see/A poem lovely as a tree"). He died in action in World War I. The 3,800 acres of North Carolina's Joyce Kilmer Memorial Forest—perhaps the single most impressive growth of eastern virgin forest in the United States, with many trees hundreds of years old—is a part of Joyce Kilmer–Slickrock Wilderness. Except for its northwestern section, this Wilderness is in North Carolina (see North Carolina, Joyce Kilmer–Slickrock Wilderness). The Tennessee section borders Citico Creek Wilderness (see above).

The forest includes yellow pine, hemlock, sycamore, basswood, dogwood, beech, and oak, with a wild understory of shrubs, vines, ferns, mosses, lichens, liverworts, and herbaceous plants. Wildflowers bloom in spring sunshine but fade when the trees leaf out, darkening the forest floor.

Six trailheads provide access to more than 60 miles of trail (in the entire Wilderness), which typically follow ridge tops or drop into the shady drainages. Camping is permitted anywhere in the small Tennessee portion of the Wilderness, but sections in North Carolina are closed. The Stiff Knee Trail (3.4 miles) follows Little Slickrock Creek across the Tennessee portion to a junction with the Slickrock Creek Trail (13.3 miles), longer and more beautiful than any trail in the entire Wilderness.

TENNESSEE

Joyce Kilmer–Slickrock Essentials
Size: 3,832 acres in Tennessee (17,013 total).
Year Designated: 1975.
Location: Southeastern Tennessee.
Easiest Access: From just west of Tellico Plains, and the junction of State Highway 68 and State Highway 165, take Highway 165 east for 13.7 miles. Turn north on Forest Service Road 365 and continue driving for approximately four miles, then go north on Forest Service Road 59 (Doublecamp Road) for approximately seven miles to Farr Gap and the Stiff Knee Trailhead.
Season: Spring and fall.
Wilderness Fees/Permits: None.
Maps: USGS topographic maps are Tapoco and Whiteoak Flats. A Wilderness map is available for $3.75 from the district ranger.
Management: Tellico Ranger District, Cherokee National Forest, P.O. Box 339, Tellico Plains, TN 37385; (423) 253-2520.

Little Frog Mountain Wilderness

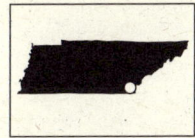

Little Frog Mountain Wilderness, now covered in second-growth forest, encompasses a horseshoe-shaped valley, Pressley Cove. It is formed by Little Frog Mountain on the southeast and Dry Pond Lead on the northwest. Panoramic views are the main attraction atop Sassafras Knob near the northern boundary, the highest point in the area at 3,322 feet. The terrain bottoms out at approximately 1,200 feet near the Ocoee River, which flows just outside the southern boundary. You'll see flame azalea, mountain laurel, rhododendron, trailing arbutus, crested dwarf iris, mayapple, bloodroot, toothwort, magnolia, dogwood, redbud, and many other flowering plants, shrubs, and trees.

The Rock Creek Trail, the only path here, winds through the heart of the Wilderness for 5.5 miles into the valley of Pressley Cove. Just outside the Wilderness, the Dry Pond Lead Trail follows the northwestern boundary for 4.5 miles along well-forested Dry Pond Lead.

Little Frog Mountain Essentials
Size: 4,800 acres.
Year Designated: 1986.
Location: Southeastern Tennessee.
Easiest Access: Take U.S. 64 approximately 21.3 miles east of the intersection of U.S. 64 and U.S. 411 to find the Rock Creek Trailhead on the north side of the highway.
Season: Spring and fall.
Wilderness Fees/Permits: None.
Maps: USGS topographic map is Ducktown.
Management: Ocoee Ranger District, Cherokee National Forest, Route 1, Box 348D, Benton, TN 37307; (423) 338-5201.

Pond Mountain Wilderness

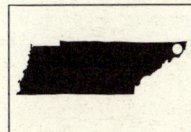

If this Wilderness were a dartboard, players would aim for a 4,329-foot bull's-eye known as Pond Mountain, the highest point in the area. Rugged and steep, the terrain has numerous inclines that exceed 60 degrees and support seven major streams. Elevation bottoms out at unusual Buckled Rock (1,900 feet), a 150-foot vertical cliff named for the pattern of bends in the strata near Hampton, Tennessee.

Upland hardwoods dominate the tree cover, along with a few cove hardwoods and yellow pines. In the center of the Wilderness you'll find the upright cliffs and rocky outcroppings of the Watauga Scenic Area. This is a rare discovery indeed, with small stands of virgin timber, scarce in Tennessee, including scarlet oak dating from the late 1800s. Several cascading waterfalls spill down the Laurel Fork Gorge in the southwestern corner of the area, where cliffs stand 100 to 200 feet above trout-teeming Laurel Fork Creek. Hunters are attracted in season to deer, grouse, and wild turkeys. Big Laurel Branch Wilderness (see above) lies just north of Watauga Lake.

The Appalachian Trail (AT) crosses the area for about 6.6 miles, including a trek through the Laurel Fork Gorge, where a shelter stands. Several other trails provide access to the area. The Watauga Scenic Trail travels about 2.2 miles up Dry Branch into the heart of the scenic area. And the Pond Mountain Trail crawls up some steep and rocky terrain for about 4.5 miles along the top of Pond Mountain in a generally north-south direction.

Pond Mountain Essentials

Size: 6,665 acres.
Year Designated: 1986.
Location: Northeastern Tennessee.
Easiest Access: From Hampton, take U.S. 321 east for 5.5 miles to find the Pond Mountain Trailhead on the south side of the road and parking on the north side of the road.
Season: Spring and fall.
Wilderness Fees/Permits: None.
Maps: USGS topographic maps are Elizabethton and Watauga Dam. Maps may be ordered for $4 from the district rangers.
Management: Unaka Ranger District, Cherokee National Forest, 1205 North Main Street, Erwin, TN 37650; (423) 743-4452. Watauga Ranger District, Cherokee National Forest, Route 9, Box 2235, Elizabethton, TN 37643; (423) 542-2942.

Sampson Mountain Wilderness

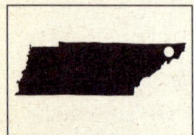

The five clear, swift, rocky streams that course through this Wilderness, which drain secluded hollows shadowed by steep and open ridges, plunge over several waterfalls, some of them dramatic cascades. Buckeye Falls drops 475 feet, reputedly more than any other waterfall in the eastern United States. A heavy forest cover of pine and hardwoods includes 536 acres of old growth that has been flourishing for more than a century. Wildflowers proliferate, and flowering shrubs include laurel, rhododendron, and flame azalea. Trout fishing may be excellent in the streams, but if your line keeps coming up empty, you can always snack on native blueberries. Problem is, you have to share the sweet fruit with black bears, who live here in greater numbers than anywhere else north of Great Smoky Mountains National Park.

Several trails crawl faintly up creek valleys until they gradually fade away altogether. Confusing old roadbeds appear and disappear just as suddenly, leading nowhere. None of the trails are well maintained. The Squibb Creek Trail, in the extreme western section, travels 2.2 miles up Squibb Creek to a picturesque waterfall where the path dead-ends. The East Fork of Cassi Creek Trail leads 3.4 miles after it branches off of the Cassi Creek Trail (2.5 miles) to dead-end at Painter Creek Falls, a lovely cascading drop of approximately 200 feet. This could be your best opportunity to wander in solitude in a Tennessee Wilderness. Sampson Mountain, which peaks at 4,060 feet, anchors the Wilderness.

TENNESSEE

Sampson Mountain Essentials

Size: 8,319 acres.
Year Designated: 1986.
Location: Northeastern Tennessee.
Easiest Access: From Greeneville, take State Highway 107 east from the junction with the U.S. 11E bypass for 11.4 miles before heading south on Maple Swamp Road for 1.1 miles. At County Road 5404 (Cassi Creek Road), go straight through the intersection onto Cassi Creek Road and continue for 3.2 miles, where the pavement ends. Park your car here and continue up the road, which narrows to the Cassi Creek Trail.
Season: Spring and fall.
Wilderness Fees/Permits: None.
Maps: USGS topographic maps are Flag Pond, Greystone, and Telford.
Management: Unaka Ranger District, Cherokee National Forest, 1205 North Main Street, Erwin, TN 37650; (423) 743-4452.

Unaka Mountain Wilderness

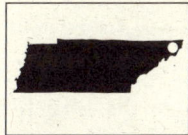

This Wilderness spills down the western slopes of the Unaka Mountains, which form part of the boundary between Tennessee and North Carolina. Birch, beech, maple, oak, cherry, poplar, hickory, pine, hemlock, spruce, and fir forest the slopes. Some of the hemlocks are almost 100 years old, but loggers worked their way through most of the original forest prior to designation.

The deciduous trees paint a glorious fall tapestry best appreciated from high elevations such as the 4,800-foot Unaka Mountain Overlook. More than 10 waterfalls tumble down 20-foot-plus drops along seven major streams, with Red Fork Falls, the highest, shooting water over a 60-foot drop in the eastern portion of the area.

The Limestone Cove Trail, about 2.8 miles total, climbs steeply then levels off slightly along an old logging road to the top of Stamping Ground Ridge. It meets the Unaka Mountain Road, where you can easily ascend to the overlook. The Rattlesnake Ridge Trail descends for three miles across the Wilderness from near the overlook. The Red Fork Falls Trail dead-ends after less than a quarter mile at the falls near the eastern boundary. Foot and horse access are offered.

Unaka Mountain Essentials

Size: 4,700 acres.
Year Designated: 1986.
Location: Northeastern Tennessee.
Easiest Access: From Unicoi, northeast of Erwin, take State Highway 107 about three miles east to the Limestone Cove Recreation Area on the south side of the road. Take the USFS road that goes east from the camping area about one-half mile to the Limestone Cove Trailhead.
Season: Fall for the color.
Wilderness Fees/Permits: None.
Maps: USGS topographic maps are Erwin, Huntdale, and Unicoi. Maps are available for $4 from the district ranger.
Management: Unaka Ranger District, Cherokee National Forest, 1205 North Main Street, Erwin, TN 37650; (423) 743-4452.

> "We simply need wild country available to us, even if we do no more than drive to its edge and look in. For it can be a means of reassuring ourselves of our sanity as creatures, a part of the geography of hope."
>
> —Wallace Stegner

TEXAS

Total Wilderness areas: 6
Total Wilderness acreage: 81,196

The Lone Star State was once an independent republic, which meant the state owned the land and private hands snatched it up. That left Texas with zilch in the way of federal land, and about the same amount of Wilderness. In relation to its vast size, this state preserves extremely tiny pieces of the National Wilderness Preservation System: barely more than 700,000 acres in four small national forests in eastern Texas and two national grasslands in northeastern Texas. The U.S. Government purchased this real estate in the 1930s, after loggers made off with the forestland trees. Five small Wildernesses now exist on the national forests, a result of the Texas Wilderness Act of 1984. Another Wilderness, with more acreage than the five U.S. Forest Service (USFS) lands combined, lies within a national park.

Big Slough Wilderness

Logging operations that began in the late 1800s left only scrub hardwoods and a few isolated "islands" of young pines on the land now known as Big Slough, the smallest Wilderness in Texas. You'll still encounter large stumps and evidence of the narrow-gauge trams that supported tree-hauling railroads. You'll also see a regrown forest, 66 percent of which is composed of hardwoods (oak, hickory, sweet gum, willow) and 26 percent of shortleaf and loblolly pine. Hardwoods and pines cover 4 percent of the area, and Big Slough's waters cover the remaining 4 percent.

Warmth and moisture characterize the Gulf Coastal Plain climate, encouraging poison ivy, poisonous snakes, chiggers, ticks, mosquitoes, and irritable, ground-nesting yellowjackets. Deer and smaller mammals live here, too.

Despite the large number of dead trees that were killed by the Southern pine beetle, some USFS employees rate this as one of the most interesting Wilderness areas on Texas national forestland. The Neches River forms the entire eastern boundary and joins the idle water of Big Slough to create the seven-mile Big Slough Canoe Trail, a paddling loop with a trailhead in the northern portion. Bear in mind that the canoe trail has not been maintained and wading will be required. Hickory Creek drains hills along the western boundary and eases eastward to meet the river. Well-marked hiking trails crisscross the area, including the 20-mile Four C National Recreation Trail, which runs north-south and cuts through two miles of the higher southern portion. Try to wear bright outer clothing in the fall season, as hunting (for deer, wild hogs, and squirrels) is allowed. Anglers don't pose any threat, except perhaps to the catfish, bass, crappie, and sunfish.

Big Slough Essentials

Size: 3,000 acres.
Year Designated: 1984.
Location: Eastern Texas.
Easiest Access: From Crockett, take State Highway 103 to Ratcliff, about 20 miles east. Near Ratcliff lies Ratcliff Lake, where you can pick up the Four C National Recreation Trail or take one of the forest roads that continue north about five miles to the Wilderness.
Season: Late fall to early spring for cooler weather and fewer insects.
Wilderness Fees/Permits: None.
Maps: A topographic map is available for $3 from the district ranger.
Management: Neches Ranger District, Davy Crockett National Forest, 1240 East Loop 304, Crockett, TX 75835; (409) 544-2046.

Guadalupe Mountains Wilderness

Approximately 250 million years ago, a 350-mile reef formed along the edge of the great sea that covered this area. With time, the sea receded and the reef died, only to be buried by sediment. Eons later an uplift created the arid Guadalupe Mountains and erosion wore down the sediment, eventually revealing what is now the most extensive exposed fossil reef on the earth. The most outstanding stretch of exposed reef is within 86,415-acre Guadalupe Mountains National Park, 55 miles southwest of Carlsbad, New Mexico. More than half of the park is Wilderness, the largest and oldest in the state and the only one in western Texas.

Rugged mountainous terrain here reaches 8,749 feet on Guadalupe Peak, the highest point in Texas. More than 80 miles of trail, some in the Wilderness, give access to the mountains. You can hike the Guadalupe Peak Trail to the "Top of Texas" (a strenuous 8.4-mile round-trip), where on a clear day the view will be magnificent. Whatever the time of year, you'll want sturdy boots for rough hiking all over the Guadalupes, plus a tent, rain gear, and a strong back to haul water. You'll find no sure water in the area except at the visitors center and two campgrounds that charge a fee. Flora and fauna don't seem to mind the water shortage. Resident species tally up at more than 900 plants (watch out for those with needle-tipped spines), 60 mammals, 289 birds, and 55 reptiles (some poisonous) and amphibians.

Extreme weather is characteristic of the area: hurricane winds in spring and sometimes fall, severe thunderstorms and flash floods in summer, and snow and rain in winter.

TEXAS

Guadalupe Mountains Essentials

Size: 46,850 acres.
Year Designated: 1978.
Location: Western Texas.
Easiest Access: From El Paso, take U.S. 62/180 east for approximately 110 miles to the visitors center.
Season: Year-round possibilities, but fall tends to have the best weather.

Wilderness Fees/Permits: A free backcountry permit is required for overnight trips.
Maps: A thorough topographic map is available for $8 from the Carlsbad Caverns Guadalupe Mountains Association, P.O. Box 1417, Carlsbad, NM 88221-1417; (505) 785-2318.
Management: Guadalupe Mountains National Park, HC 60, Box 400, Salt Flat, TX 79847-9400; (915) 828-3251.

Indian Mounds Wilderness

Prior to 1930, before loggers had worked their way through the area, longleaf pine, beech, oak, and magnolia trees supported a vigorous turpentine industry. Today, Indian Mounds Wilderness safeguards a few acres of lovely old-growth trees near the edge of the Toledo Bend Reservoir, close enough to the state line to lose a few pinecones to Louisiana with a favoring wind.

The trees around the reservoir vary, with loblolly and shortleaf pines on the periphery and hardwoods marking drainages created by Indian Creek, Bull Creek, and Hurricane Bayou. You may even find a mature grove of American beech trees or the fabulous yellow lady's slipper (a member of the orchid family). One thing you probably won't see is the endangered red-cockaded woodpecker—the colony that lies in the area has been inactive for years.

Both the Indian Mounds Recreation Area, outside the southeastern border, and the Wilderness are named for their unusual "hills," once thought to be the handiwork of a prehistoric people and later confirmed to be the result of natural processes. The Wilderness is cut like a jigsaw puzzle into seven sections along three non-Wilderness roads and a gas-pipeline corridor. Abandoned roads offer hiker and horse access, and boats can get to parts of the area via the reservoir. You can camp for $4 a night and launch a boat for free at the recreation area.

Indian Mounds Essentials

Size: 9,946 acres.
Year Designated: 1984.
Location: Eastern Texas.
Easiest Access: From Hemphill, take State Highway 83 east for eight miles. Turn south on Farm-to-Market Road 3382 and drive four miles, then turn east on Forest Service Road 130. Indian Mounds Recreation Area is a mile away.
Season: Fall to spring for a quieter visit.

Wilderness Fees/Permits: None.
Maps: A topographic map is available for $3 from the district ranger.
Management: Yellowpine Ranger District, Sabine National Forest, Highway 83, P.O. Box F, Hemphill, TX 75948; (409) 787-3870. Tenaha Ranger District, Sabine National Forest, 101 South Bolivar, San Augustine, TX 75972; (409) 275-2632.

Little Lake Creek Wilderness

Years after loggers' saws tore through these hills, hardwoods again dominate Little Lake Creek Wilderness. Three major drainages—Pole Creek, Sand Branch, and Little Lake Creek—divide the area, which sits perched on the western edge of the Gulf Coastal Plain. The latter waterway runs the entire length of this relatively narrow Wilderness. On ridges above the drainages, loblolly and shortleaf pines thrive beneath the plentiful sunlight. But many of the pines are now dead, victims of the Southern pine beetle epidemic of the mid-1980s.

Colonies of the endangered red-cockaded woodpecker share their home here with deer, owls, and armadillos. There are also less hiker-friendly critters: snakes slither through poison ivy, ticks wait patiently for their next meal, and mosquitoes whine hungrily (campers: consider this fair warning to bolster your tent with intact mosquito netting). Deer hunters come in their season.

An abandoned pipeline right-of-way marks the entire western boundary. The Lone Star Hiking Trail crosses the pipeline twice (for about two miles in the north and 1.5 miles in the center) as it loops through the area. The southern portion offers an additional five to six miles of trail. The three parking lots are easily accessible.

Little Lake Creek Essentials

Size: 4,000 acres.
Year Designated: 1984.
Location: Eastern Texas.
Easiest Access: From Interstate 45 south of Huntsville, take Farm-to-Market Road 1375 west from New Waverly until it dead-ends, about 10 miles. At Farm-to-Market Road 149, turn south and continue 3.5 miles to where the Lone Star Hiking Trail crosses the road.
Season: Late fall to early spring.
Wilderness Fees/Permits: None.
Maps: A topographic map is available for $3 from the district ranger.
Management: San Jacinto Ranger District, Sam Houston National Forest, 308 North Belcher, Cleveland, TX 77327; (713) 592-6461. Raven Ranger District, Sam Houston National Forest, FM Road 1375, P.O. Drawer 1000, New Waverly, TX 77358; (409) 344-6205.

Turkey Hill Wilderness

You might expect to find a few gobblers running about these hills, but you will have to settle for deer (hunters don't seem to mind), snakes, stinging insects, ticks, and chiggers. Turkey Hill Wilderness belongs to the Bannister Wildlife Management Area on the Gulf Coastal Plain. A forest dense with hardwoods and pine covers the relatively gentle hills, as well as steeper slopes to the north and east. Turkey Hill anchors the southeastern corner, peaking at 298 feet above sea level. The wide, flat ridge tops around Turkey Hill exceed 300 feet in some places.

From Forest Service Road 307 on the southern boundary, the fairly easy to follow Wash Branch Trail runs north along Wash Branch (near the center of the area) and over a ridge, a distance of about 3.5 miles. Other trails, some of which fade out on ridges, access the eastern and western portions. You can usually find water in Sandy Creek, Clear Branch, and Wash Branch.

TEXAS

Turkey Hill Essentials

Size: 5,400 acres.
Year Designated: 1984.
Location: Eastern Texas.
Easiest Access: From Jasper, take U.S. 96 north for about 25 miles to Pineland. Turn west on State Highway 83 and continue to Broadus, about 20 miles. When you reach State Highway 147, turn north and drive another seven miles to Wash Branch Road, where you will turn east. The trailhead is just a few hundred yards away.
Season: Late fall to early spring offer the coolest temperatures.
Wilderness Fees/Permits: None.
Maps: A topographic map is available for $3 from the district ranger.
Management: Angelina Ranger District, Angelina National Forest, 1907 Atkinson Drive, P.O. Box 756, Lufkin, TX 75901; (409) 639-8620.

Upland Island Wilderness

By 1930, loggers had chopped down almost all the pine with any commercial value, leaving behind a few small "islands" of immature trees and remnants of sawmill sites. A dense cover of second-growth pines and hardwoods now fills out the Wilderness, while the more stately longleaf pines have established fiefdoms on the wide, flat ridge tops. The "upland" portion, to the south, rises only a few hundred feet above sea level. The terrain flattens in the northern section, and again in a small southern section bordered by the Neches River and separated from the remainder of the Wilderness by a non-Wilderness road corridor.

Upland Island may be the most interesting Texas national forestland acreage, with flora ranging from the carnivorous pitcher plant to wild azaleas and rose pogonias, a member of the orchid family. Water flows in Cypress Creek, Salt Branch, Oil Well Creek, Big Creek, and Graham Creek. Numerous trails give access to the area, some along abandoned roads, and hiking and horseback riding are relatively easy. From a trailhead on Forest Service Road 303 you can hike in one-half mile to join the primary north-south pathway, which crosses the area for approximately six miles.

Upland Island Essentials

Size: 12,000 acres.
Year Designated: 1984.
Location: Eastern Texas.
Easiest Access: From Jasper, take State Highway 63 north for about 20 miles across the Angelina River and turn west at Forest Service Road 302, where a sign designates the Wilderness area. Follow 302 a couple of miles until it dead-ends, then turn south on Forest Service Road 303 and follow the eastern Wilderness boundary until you reach the eastern trailhead, about two miles.
Season: Late fall to early spring.
Wilderness Fees/Permits: None.
Maps: A topographic map is available for $3 from the district ranger.
Management: Angelina Ranger District, Angelina National Forest, 1907 Atkinson Drive, P.O. Box 756, Lufkin, TX 75901; (409) 639-8620.

> "Man could be a lover and defender of wilderness without ever in his lifetime leaving the boundaries of asphalt, power lines, and right-angled surfaces. . . . We need the possibility of escape as surely as we need hope."
>
> —Edward Abbey

UTAH

Total Wilderness areas: 15
Total Wilderness acreage: 802,189

Utah, the second driest of the 50 states, covers about 54.4 million acres, 33.5 million of which are owned by the federal government. The Bureau of Land Management manages 22 million acres, the U.S. Forest Service oversees more than eight million acres, and about two million acres are managed by the National Park Service. Out of all this land, fewer than one million acres are designated Wilderness.

Western Utah lies almost entirely within the Great Basin, flat and barren except for the vast Great Salt Lake, a few mountain ranges, and one Wilderness area. Throughout eastern and central Utah are towering mountain ranges dotted with narrow valleys that lead into the desert. These mountains contain 10 Wilderness areas.

The broad plateaus of southern Utah, which comprise a substantial section of the vast Colorado Plateau, are deeply cleft with canyons and gorges. Most of this region is pristine and unspoiled. Don't be misled by the fact that southern Utah contains only four relatively small Wilderness areas. It is well worth visiting.

UTAH

Ashdown Gorge Wilderness

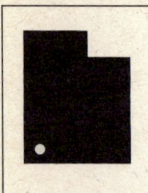

Sharing the western and northern borders of the desertlike Cedar Breaks National Monument, Ashdown Gorge Wilderness displays eroded, multicolored Wasatch limestone, meadows, and forestland including a significant stand of bristlecone pine, known as the Twisted Forest, in the northern corner. Bristlecones are among the oldest living life-forms, and some of the trees in this Wilderness were alive during the time of Christ. The area is home to a diversity of wildlife that includes mule deer, yellow-bellied marmots, chipmunks, golden-mantled ground squirrels, voles, and mice. Creeks run year-round.

Elevations range from 8,000 feet to 10,400 feet, and winter snows often add spectacular highlights to the colorful stone formations.

Within the Wilderness, you'll find less than 10 miles of trails. The Rattlesnake Trail (five miles) traces the northern boundary of the national monument and follows Rattlesnake Creek on an east-to-west path across the Wilderness to meet the Potato Hollow Trail. The latter trail continues south to a trailhead at Cedar Springs. The Potato Hollow Trail (2.5 miles) forks before the trailhead to become the Blowhard Trail, which climbs Blowhard Mountain. There is ample opportunity to find solitude, especially if you hike off-trail (taking care, of course, to create as little impact on the land as possible).

Ashdown Gorge Essentials

Size: 7,000 acres.
Year Designated: 1984.
Location: Southwestern Utah.
Easiest Access: From Cedar City, take Interstate 15 north for 15 miles. Turn south on State Highway 143 and continue for about 20 miles. The Rattlesnake Trailhead lies just outside the northern boundary of the national monument.
Season: Spring and fall.
Wilderness Fees/Permits: None.
Maps: Trails Illustrated's Map 702 documents the Wilderness. It is an excellent resource available for $8.99.
Management: Dixie National Forest, 82 North 100 East, P.O. Box 627, Cedar City, UT 84721-0627; (801) 865-3700.

Beaver Dam Mountains Wilderness

The rugged mountains and gently sloping alluvial plain of Beaver Dam Mountains Wilderness straddles the Arizona-Utah border. Administration of the site is shared by the Bureau of Land Management in both states (see Arizona, Beaver Dam Mountains Wilderness). The Wilderness is further divided into northeastern and southwestern units by Cedar Pockets Road in Arizona. On the Utah side, this area is the state's smallest Wilderness.

The region is covered with Joshua trees and desert shrubs set among scattered grasses. Several rare plant species have been identified in this area. Notable wildlife species include desert bighorn sheep, the endangered desert tortoise, and large numbers of raptors. The endangered woundfin minnow lives in the Virgin River, which flows through the eastern section of the Wilderness for several miles.

River rafters and kayakers have been increasingly attracted to the Virgin River, and primitive recreation in the Wilderness has increased in recent years. Virgin River Campground offers 115 sites year-round for $6 per night. There are no trails in the area so hone your cross-country skills before heading out to canvass the land off-trail.

Beaver Dam Mountains Essentials

Size: 2,597 acres in Utah (19,600 total).
Year Designated: 1984.
Location: Southwestern Utah.
Easiest Access: From Saint George, take Interstate 15 south for approximately 15 miles. Take the Cedar Pockets Rest Area exit. Right next to it, you'll see Virgin River Campground.
Season: Fall to spring.

Wilderness Fees/Permits: None.
Maps: USGS topographic maps are Castle Cliff, Jarvis Peak, Littlefield, and Mountain Sheep Spring. The Cedar City District Map, available for $4 from the BLM, also shows the area.
Management: BLM Shivwits Resource Area, 225 North Bluff Street, Saint George, UT 84770; (801) 628-4491.

Box-Death Hollow Wilderness

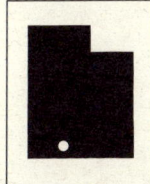

Vertical gray-orange walls of Navajo sandstone stand above two canyon tributaries of the Escalante River in Box-Death Hollow Wilderness. This is canyon country, home to numerous monoclines—places where fault lines have made layers of earth rise and fall sharply, exposing the colorful strata of sediment. Running north-south through a steeply dipping monocline, Pine Creek forms the area known as "The Box." Death Hollow Creek, east of The Box, has carved its way through a gently dipping monocline. The threat of death probably refers to the sudden, towering wall of raging waters that often floods these canyon narrows after a rain. Piñon and juniper cover many of the plateaus above the canyons. Brown and rainbow trout are plentiful in Pine Creek. Along the creek banks, you may see mule deer, an occasional cougar, or even elk in winter. Three of Utah's sensitive bird species—Lewis woodpecker, western bluebird, and mountain bluebird—live here. The BLM's Phipps-Death Hollow Outstanding Natural Area lies adjacent to the Wilderness. Although it has been years since I hiked this barren yet beautiful country, the two trips I made to this region are among my most cherished memories.

From Hell's Backbone Bridge in the extreme northern portion of the area, you can hike the length of Death Hollow all the way across the Wilderness to the Escalante River on Bureau of Land Management land. The 21-mile trip is recommended only for the adventurous. You'll find no maintained trails, and it's about 11 miles to the first reliable water source. Start early and bring a map. By the time you reach the Upper Narrows you'll find plenty of water, enough to inspire thoughts of a quick plunge. There are even more opportunities for swimming in the Lower Narrows. At Box-Death Hollow Wilderness, I guarantee you will experience canyonland that has few equals.

Box-Death Hollow Essentials

Size: 26,000 acres.
Year Designated: 1984.
Location: Southwestern central Utah.
Easiest Access: From the east side of Escalante, take the Hell's Backbone Road north approximately 15 miles toward Hell's Backbone Bridge. Two miles before the bridge you'll find the trailhead into Death Hollow.
Season: Spring and fall.

Wilderness Fees/Permits: None.
Maps: Trails Illustrated's Map 710 is an excellent resource. You will find the BLM's *Escalante Resource Area Recreation Map and Visitor Information* useful.
Management: Dixie National Forest, 82 North 100 East, P.O. Box 627, Cedar City, UT 84721-0627; (801) 865-3700.

Dark Canyon Wilderness

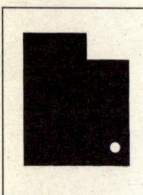

With narrow, steep walls that block the light, Dark Canyon is aptly named. Once home to a small segment of the widespread Anasazi Indians, Dark Canyon, nearby Woodenshoe Canyon, and their tributary canyons make up the roughly horseshoe-shaped Dark Canyon Wilderness. This is an extraordinarily beautiful section of the Colorado Plateau where sculpted and colored walls of sandstone rise above the shadowed sandy floors. You'll see evidence of Anasazi culture in ruined homes, granaries, and paintings.

The upper reaches of the canyons are wide and meadowed. As you move down into the deeper sections, spruce and fir give way to ponderosa pine, piñon pine, juniper, and cottonwood. The feeling of timelessness and solitude increases as the majestic canyon walls rise higher and higher above you. In the lower section of Dark Canyon is a marvelous hidden world of waterfalls and deep, clear pools.

All the trails dropping into the canyons are easy to moderate, but they are often difficult, if not impossible, to find and follow. Be sure to carry a very good map and a compass. Once you're on the floor of Dark Canyon, however, you'll have no trouble following the Dark Canyon Trail through the length of the canyon, a distance of approximately 30 miles. You may continue past the western Wilderness boundary into the BLM-managed Dark Canyon Primitive Area and on down to the upper end of Lake Powell.

Dark Canyon Essentials

Size: 45,000 acres.
Year Designated: 1984.
Location: Southeastern Utah.
Easiest Access: From Blanding, take State Route 95 west approximately 27 miles. Turn northwest on Road 275 (the entrance to Natural Bridges National Monument) and continue for approximately one mile. Head north on Road 088 for approximately 20 miles to the Dark Canyon Trailhead at The Notch. In some seasons, the Wilderness is easier to access via the BLM's Dark Canyon Primitive Area. Contact the BLM San Juan Resource Area, P.O. Box 7, Monticello, UT 84535; (801) 587-2141.
Season: Spring and late fall have the most water and appealing temperatures.
Wilderness Fees/Permits: None.
Maps: A combined Wilderness and Primitive area waterproof map is available for $8.47 (tax included) from the district ranger. Trails Illustrated's Map 703 also covers the area well.
Management: Monticello Ranger District, Manti-La Sal National Forest, P.O. Box 820, Monticello, UT 84535; (801) 587-2041.

Deseret Peak Wilderness

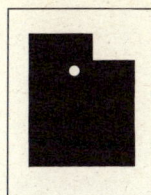

Semiarid Deseret Peak Wilderness, not far south of the Great Salt Lake, contains rugged terrain and high peaks that include Deseret Peak itself at 11,030 feet, and many steep-walled canyons shadowed by rocky outcroppings. Here in the Stansbury Mountains, with barren Skull Valley to the west, you'll find numerous springs and intermittent creeks despite the general dryness of the area.

Much of the higher country is alpine, with open basins and barren rocky ridges. From December through May, you can expect the high country to be covered in snow. Fir and aspen are commonly found growing in patches at higher elevations. Juniper, mountain brush, sagebrush, and grass cover much of the lower territory. Cattle are still allowed to graze in portions of the area.

From the east, the Deseret Peak Trail (approximately 3.5 miles) will take you to the summit of Deseret Peak and a splendid 360-degree view. Backpackers and horsepackers enjoy this area, but they don't come in droves. In fact, hikers often find themselves alone on the trails, especially on weekdays. Some extremely rough terrain is covered on the trails. Hunters come in search of mule deer.

Deseret Peak Essentials

Size: 25,500 acres.
Year Designated: 1984.
Location: Northern central Utah.
Easiest Access: From the west side of Grantsville, take West Street south for five miles. Turn west on South Willow Canyon Road. Drive for approximately four miles to the end of the road and the Deseret Peak Trailhead.
Season: Summer and early fall.
Wilderness Fees/Permits: None.
Maps: USGS topographic maps are Deseret Peak East, Deseret Peak West, North Willow, and Salt Mountain.
Management: Salt Lake Ranger District, Wasatch-Cache National Forest, 6944 South 3000 East, Salt Lake City, UT 84121; (801) 943-1794.

High Uintas Wilderness

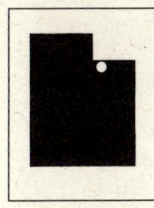

By far Utah's largest Wilderness, the High Uintas boasts the tallest mountains in the state. Numerous summits rise grandly above the tree line. At 13,528 feet, Kings Peak is the highest point in Utah. The main crest of the High Uintas runs in an east-west direction for more than 60 miles, with few mountains wider than one mile at the base. Many secondary ridges, often higher than the main ridge, extend north and south from the main crest.

Much of the exposed rock is tinted a deep vermilion. Within the mountains are lovely alpine basins splashed with picturesque lakes and meadows. The fishing is excellent in the many lakes and streams, but overfishing has hurt some of the more popular areas. Rivers plunge from the basins into U-shaped canyons carved by glacial activity. Waterways raging with spring runoff and melted snow can be dangerous to cross.

Snow usually lingers through June, and temperatures in the high country rarely top 70 degrees Fahrenheit. Below the timberline (about 10,000 feet) are forests of conifers (mostly

Engelmann spruce), lodgepole pine, and subalpine fir. These mountains are the summer home to elk, mule deer, moose, and an occasional mountain sheep. It is not uncommon for visitors to see black bears.

Many trails crisscross the Wilderness, which has trailheads on all four sides. All are easy to follow, and the lower pathways make excellent paths for horsepackers. Higher up, the trails sometimes cross extremely rugged terrain. The High Line Trail enters from the east and west to travel the crest of the High Uintas through the very heart of this area, approximately 28 miles of mountain splendor. Human use is light to moderate except at a few high-traffic areas, notably the lake basins on the western side.

High Uintas Essentials

Size: 460,000 acres.
Year Designated: 1984.
Location: Northeastern Utah.
Easiest Access: From Kamas, take State Route 150 (a scenic byway) east about 34 miles to serene and picturesque Mirror Lake and the western High Line Trailhead.
Season: July through mid-September.
Wilderness Fees/Permits: None.
Maps: A Wilderness map is available for $3 from the national forest rangers. Trails Illustrated's Map 711 is an excellent resource available for $8.99.
Management: Ashley National Forest, 1680 West Highway 40, Vernal, UT 84078; (801) 789-1181. Wasatch-Cache National Forest, 8230 Federal Building, 125 South State Street, Salt Lake City, UT 84138; (801) 524-5030.

Lone Peak Wilderness

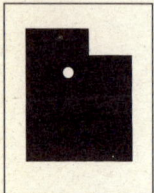

The largest of a trio of Wilderness areas just southeast of Salt Lake City, Lone Peak Wilderness contains very rugged terrain with narrow canyons and high peaks. Among the highest are Little Matterhorn at 11,326 feet and Lone Peak at 11,253 feet, where snow often remains until midsummer. Much of the higher elevation is alpine, with large, open cirque basins and exposed rocky ridges.

The region is geologically complex. You'll see sedimentary, metamorphic, and igneous rock formations in dramatic relief, as well as colorful bands stretching for great wavering distances across mountainsides. A few small lakes, including Red Pine Lakes, add to the scenic beauty. Douglas fir, subalpine fir, and aspen grow in isolated patches on north-facing slopes. Dense mountain brush dominates the lower altitudes.

State Route 92 follows the American Fork Canyon. With the short stretch of State Route 144, it forms the southern-southeastern boundary of the Wilderness. State Route 144 provides access to trailheads and campgrounds. This Wilderness shares its southern border with Timpanogos Cave National Monument. State Route 210, along Little Cottonwood Creek Canyon, forms the northern boundary and separates Lone Peak Wilderness from Twin Peaks Wilderness (see below) just to the north.

The trails are easy to follow but many are strenuously difficult. From the White Pine Trailhead you can hike in and join the Red Pine Trail to Red Pine Lakes for a total distance of three miles. No camping is allowed within 200 feet of water sources or trails. Many people from the Salt Lake City area visit here, especially in summer, requiring additional restrictions in some areas, such as the Silver Lake drainage. Please check with the forest rangers before arriving.

Lone Peak Essentials

Size: 30,088 acres.
Year Designated: 1978.
Location: Northern central Utah.
Easiest Access: From Interstate 215 southeast of Salt Lake City, take the Solitude/Brighton Ski Areas exit. Head south for approximately two miles. Continue southeast on State Route 210. After you enter Little Cottonwood Creek Canyon, go 5.3 miles to the White Pine Trailhead.
Season: Summer and early fall.

Wilderness Fees/Permits: None.
Maps: USGS topographic maps are Draper, Dromedary Peak, Lehi, and Timpanogos Cave.
Management: Salt Lake Ranger District, Wasatch-Cache National Forest, 6944 South 3000 East, Salt Lake City, UT 84121; (801) 943-1794 (manages the northern third). Pleasant Grove Ranger District, Uinta National Forest, 390 North 100 East, P.O. Box 228, Pleasant Grove, UT 84062; (801) 785-3563 (manages the southern two-thirds).

Mount Naomi Wilderness

Boasting some of most spectacular alpine scenery in the Intermountain West, Mount Naomi Wilderness lies between the Logan River and the Utah-Idaho state line. At 9,980 feet, Naomi Peak, near the eastern boundary, is the area's highest point, although this mountainous country contains several peaks towering above 9,000 feet. On the western side, there are many deep, scenic canyons. This area is less rugged and easier to hike than much of the terrain in Wasatch-Cache National Forest. Wildflowers carpet the large mountain meadows during summer blooms, and five of the flowers are unique to this region. You'll find large populations of moose, elk, and deer, and beavers are well established in several glacial lakes and streams.

Trails meander up the major canyons on the western side of the Wilderness from trailheads near U.S. 91. Most of these canyons are undesignated, including an extensive non-Wilderness intrusion around Green Canyon in the southern portion. The trails join with others to link the area to U.S. 89. The Smithfield Canyon Trail (about three miles in the Wilderness), the Cherry Peak Trail (about four miles in the Wilderness), and the High Creek Trail (about five miles in the Wilderness) provide access to Naomi Peak.

Mount Naomi Essentials

Size: 44,350 acres.
Year Designated: 1984.
Location: Northern Utah.
Easiest Access: From Smithfield, take the Smithfield Canyon Road east approximately three miles to the trailhead.
Season: Summer and early fall.

Wilderness Fees/Permits: None.
Maps: A Wilderness map that includes Wellsville Mountains Wilderness is available for $3 from the district ranger.
Management: Logan Ranger District, Wasatch-Cache National Forest, 1500 East Highway 89, Logan, UT 84321; (801) 755-3620.

Mount Nebo Wilderness

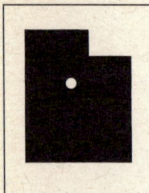

The centerpiece of the southern portion of this Wilderness, Mount Nebo rises to a majestic 11,877 feet—the highest point in the entire Wasatch Range. The peak looms above a swatch of mountain scenery located between Interstate 15 and the Nebo Scenic Loop Byway (one of my favorite drives). Wilderness elevation starts at 5,400 feet and climbs through mountain valleys and meadows broken by moderate to steep ridges. The climb will take you through great biological diversity, beginning with a sagebrush-cliffrose association, to mountain brush (oakbrush and mahogany), aspen, and white fir, then spruce and alpine fir, until you reach the timberline and an alpine zone with primrose, alpine moss, and tundra plants. Bobcats, mule deer, elk, and moose are commonly seen here; black bears and mountain lions are more elusive. Numerous streams are rich with rainbow trout. Wildflowers abound in late spring and summer. Devil's Kitchen Geologic Site, adjacent to the eastern Wilderness boundary, will remind you of a miniature (but not as grand) Bryce Canyon.

More than 100 miles of maintained trails provide access to the area. The Nebo Bench Trail (approximately 12 miles) and the Andrews Ridge Trail (approximately four miles) are popular. Both lead to the summit of Mount Nebo's center peak and the ridge to the high point on the north peak.

Mount Nebo Essentials

Size: 28,000 acres.
Year Designated: 1984.
Location: Central Utah.
Easiest Access: From Nephi, take State Route 132 east for approximately five miles. Turn north on the Nebo Scenic Loop Byway and continue for approximately five miles to Bear Canyon and the Nebo Bench Trailhead.
Season: Summer and early fall.
Wilderness Fees/Permits: None.
Maps: USGS topographic maps covering the area are available from the U.S. Geological Survey, 8105 Federal Building, 125 South State Street, Salt Lake City, UT 84138. Trails Illustrated's Map 701 shows this Wilderness, plus Mount Timpanogos and Lone Peak. It's an excellent resource available for $8.99.
Management: Spanish Fork Ranger District, Uinta National Forest, 44 West 400 North, Spanish Fork, UT 84660; (801) 798-3571.

Mount Olympus Wilderness

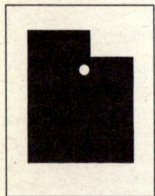

One of three Wilderness areas that form a spectacular backdrop for the Salt Lake Valley southeast of Salt Lake City, Mount Olympus Wilderness consists of narrow canyons and rugged terrain varying from moderate to severe. High peaks include Mount Raymond, Gobbler's Knob, and Mount Olympus itself, topping off at 9,793 feet. Elevations range approximately from 5,000 feet to 10,000 feet. The higher country is characterized by large, alpine cirque basins and bare rocky ridges. This land often has snow until midsummer.

Patches of various firs and aspen grow in stands, mainly on north-facing slopes. Lower elevations are covered in dense mountain brush mixed with sagebrush and grass. I have gazed up at these craggy and colorful heights from the floor of Salt Lake Valley and felt a mysterious allure that is all but irresistible.

UTAH

State Route 190 follows the scenic canyon of Big Cottonwood Creek along the southern boundary, and the canyon separates this Wilderness from Twin Peaks Wilderness (see below) to the south. Mill Creek Canyon and its road form the northern boundary. From both roads you can enter the area at several trailheads. The trails may be easy to follow, but they are rigorous and difficult. The Butler Creek Trail allows you to cross the entire Wilderness, a distance of more than six miles. No camping is allowed within 200 feet of water sources or trails. Crowds from the Salt Lake City area flood into here, especially on summer weekends.

Mount Olympus Essentials

Size: 16,000 acres.
Year Designated: 1984.
Location: Northern central Utah.
Easiest Access: From Interstate 215 southeast of Salt Lake City, take the Solitude/Brighton Ski Areas exit and travel south approximately two miles. Turn east on State Route 190 and continue through Big Cottonwood Creek Canyon for 8.2 miles to the Butler Creek Trailhead.
Season: Summer and early fall.
Wilderness Fees/Permits: None.
Maps: USGS topographic maps are Draper, Mount Aire, and Sugarhouse.
Management: Salt Lake Ranger District, Wasatch-Cache National Forest, 6944 South 3000 East, Salt Lake City, UT 84121; (801) 943-1794.

Mount Timpanogos Wilderness

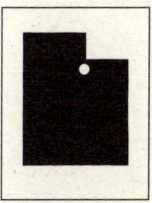

On the front range of the Wasatch Mountain Range, just south of Lone Peak Wilderness (see above), and situated between American Fork Canyon on the north and Provo Canyon on the south, Mount Timpanogos Wilderness offers abundant rugged terrain embellished with waterfalls and summer wildflowers. You'll find forget-me-nots, alpine buttercups, bluebells, and columbine blooming in high canyon meadows. There are also outstanding glacial cirques and moraines (rocks formed into loose ridges by glacial activity).

Below the tree line are forests of aspen, Douglas fir, subalpine fir, limber pine, Gambel oak, maple, and chokecherry. You'll have an excellent chance of spotting Rocky Mountain goats in the Emerald Lake region, as well as numerous mule deer and elk, moose and mountain lions, black bears, and several species of raptors. In early summer the rush of rapidly melting snow can cause dangerous flash floods.

There are about 17 miles of maintained trails from two trailheads: Timpooneke and Aspen Grove. Both lead to the summit of Mount Timpanogos, otherwise known as "Timpy," at 11,753 feet. The stretch between Timpooneke and Aspen Grove is 12 miles long and passes through the heart of the area. Horses are allowed only on the Timpooneke Trail to Emerald Lake. No campfires are allowed in this heavily frequented area.

UTAH

Mount Timpanogos Essentials

Size: 10,750 acres.
Year Designated: 1984.
Location: Northern central Utah.
Easiest Access: From Orem, on Interstate 15 south of Salt Lake City, take the Eighth North Exit and go east approximately four miles. Turn east on U.S. 189 and continue for approximately 10 miles, then head north on State Route 92 for approximately five miles to Theater in the Pine and the Aspen Grove Trailhead.
Season: Mid-June through September.
Wilderness Fees/Permits: None.
Maps: USGS topographic maps are Aspen Grove and Timpanogos Cave.
Management: Pleasant Grove Ranger District, Uinta National Forest, 390 North 100 East, Pleasant Grove, UT 84062; (801) 785-3563.

Paria Canyon-Vermilion Cliffs Wilderness

This colorful Wilderness snakes through northern Arizona (see Arizona, Paria Canyon-Vermilion Cliffs Wilderness) northeast along the gorgeous Vermilion Cliffs and swings northwest along the not-to-be-missed Paria Canyon before eventually leading into Utah, where a much smaller portion of the area is preserved. Paria Canyon is considered one of the best canyon-backpacking destinations in the world. Soaring walls are streaked with desert varnish, and serpentine canyons are so narrow in places that the sky is reduced to a ribbon of faded blue. Vast red-rock amphitheaters, sandstone arches, intricate erosion-carved sculptures, woodland terraces, and hanging gardens of ferns and orchids are found here. The heart of the earth is laid bare in this region, and few places so convincingly compel me to return. Beyond the canyon, the Vermilion Cliffs, massive and multicolored, rise as much as 3,000 feet, an escarpment dominating the rest of the Wilderness with its thick Navajo sandstone face, boulder-bound slopes, and rugged arroyos.

The main canyon is usually entered from the Utah end of the Wilderness at the White House Trailhead, but some backpackers choose the more laborious Buckskin Gulch route. This canyon is about 12 miles long and enters Paria approximately seven miles from White House. At some points, the route narrows to only three feet in width. A 30-foot climb down a rock jam is required before entering Paria Canyon. Flash floods may cause a 20-foot wall of water to pour down Buckskin. To safely travel Buckskin an accurate weather forecast is a necessity.

Buckskin Gulch may be entered from the west via Wire Pass, a 1.7-mile hike through a slot canyon that slims to shoulder-width at times. Wire Pass allows you to avoid the laborious first 4.5 miles of Buckskin, and makes a fine day hike.

No campfires are allowed in Paria Canyon Gulch or Buckskin. Group size is limited to 10 but smaller groups are recommended. All garbage and trash, except human waste products, must be carried out.

Paria Canyon-Vermilion Cliffs Essentials

Size: 19,954 acres in Utah (110,000 total).
Year Designated: 1984.
Location: Southern Utah.
Easiest Access: From Kanab, take U.S. 89 south about 44 miles and turn south at the sign to the Paria Information Station. Continue on this dirt road for two miles to the White House Trailhead. You must hike about 2.5 miles before entering the Wilderness and more than seven miles before entering Arizona.
Season: Fall to spring; May and June are most popular.
Wilderness Fees/Permits: Registration at the ranger station is required.
Maps: USGS topographic maps for Utah are Bridger Point, Glen Canyon City, Pine Hollow Canyon, and West Clark Bench. USGS topographic maps for Arizona are The Big Knoll, Bitter Springs, Coyote Buttes, Emmett Wash, Ferry Swale, House Rock Emmett Hill, House Rock Spring, Lees Ferry, Navajo Bridge, One Toe Ridge, Poverty Flat, Water Pockets, and Wrather Arch. Ask the BLM about their excellent *Hiker's Guide to Paria Canyon* ($8, plus $2 postage).
Management: BLM Interagency Offices, 345 East Riverside Drive, Saint George, UT 84790; (801) 628-4491.

Pine Valley Mountain Wilderness

A mountain island surrounded by desert, Pine Valley Mountain Wilderness preserves numerous lush meadows (up to 50 acres in size) and a beautiful forest of Engelmann spruce in the south, and spruce mixed with fir, pine, and large stands of aspen in the north. The Pine Valley Mountains rise through the entire center of the area and provide habitat for chipmunks, marmots, red squirrels, and a large herd of deer in summer. Elevations rise to a high point at 10,365 feet on Signal Peak in the southern portion. On a clear day at this site, you can see Zion National Park across Interstate 15 to the west, and some of Arizona's highest mountains to the south.

Several springs fill numerous perennial creeks. Snow falls October through March, followed by a relatively dry and pleasant period that ends with a season marked by typically violent storms from July through September.

The Summit Trail follows the crest of the Pine Valley Mountains in their north-south ramble for a distance of about 18 miles, and at least eight other trails climb the mountains to join the crest, including the easily accessible Whipple Trail (six miles). The Wilderness, Utah's second largest, lies within a much larger undesignated wild and free recreation area, bringing the total mileage of maintained trails to more than 151.

UTAH

Pine Valley Mountain Essentials

Size: 50,000 acres.
Year Designated: 1984.
Location: Southwestern Utah.
Easiest Access: From Saint George, take State Highway 18 north approximately 15 miles to Central. Turn east on the road to Pine Valley and go through Pine Valley to the Whipple Trailhead, a distance from Highway 18 of approximately 12 miles.

Season: Spring through fall.
Wilderness Fees/Permits: None.
Maps: A free trail map without much detail is available from the forest ranger. USGS topographic maps are available from the U.S. Geological Survey, 8105 Federal Building, 125 South State Street, Salt Lake City, UT 84138.
Management: Dixie National Forest, 82 North 100 East, P.O. Box 627, Cedar City, UT 84721-0627; (801) 865-3700.

Twin Peaks Wilderness

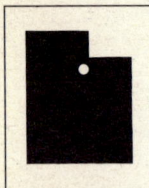

Twin Peaks Wilderness forms a part of the dramatic backdrop you see on the east side of the Salt Lake Valley, southeast of Salt Lake City. Originally carved by glaciation and currently remodeled by erosion, this area consists of narrow canyons and high peaks (including Twin Peaks, Superior Peak, and Dromedary Peak) that combine to form a rugged and spectacular display. Elevations range from just under 5,000 feet to 11,319 feet on Twin Peaks. Much of the higher terrain is classified as alpine and characterized by large cirque basins and exposed rocky ridges.

Dense mountain brush mixed with sagebrush and grass dominates the vegetation. There are stands of firs and aspen in isolated patches on some north-facing slopes. You'll also find a few small lakes. Extreme temperatures are common, with a typical 50-degree difference between summer highs and lows. Snow remains in some regions until midsummer.

State Route 190 follows Big Cottonwood Creek along the northern boundary and separates this Wilderness from Mount Olympus Wilderness (see above) to the north. State Route 210 follows Little Cottonwood Creek along the southern boundary and stands between Twin Peaks and Lone Peak Wilderness (see above) to the south. The canyons of both these creeks are highly scenic, and you'll find trailheads along both routes. Trails are easy to follow, but they become extremely strenuous in the higher country. The Lake Branch Trail leads 2.75 miles to scenic Lake Branch. No camping is allowed within 200 feet of a water source or a trail. Crowds of people are common, especially on weekends, and visitors tend to congregate around the lakes.

UTAH

Twin Peaks Essentials
Size: 13,100 acres.
Year Designated: 1984.
Location: Northern central Utah.
Easiest Access: From Interstate 215 southeast of Salt Lake City, take the Solitude/Brighton Ski Areas exit and travel south approximately two miles. Turn east on State Route 190 and go up Big Cottonwood Creek Canyon for 4.5 miles to the Lake Branch Trailhead.
Season: Summer and early fall.
Wilderness Fees/Permits: None.
Maps: USGS topographic maps are Draper, Dromedary Peak, Mount Aire, and Sugarhouse.
Management: Salt Lake Ranger District, Wasatch-Cache National Forest, 6944 South 3000 East, Salt Lake City, UT 84121; (801) 943-1794.

Wellsville Mountains Wilderness

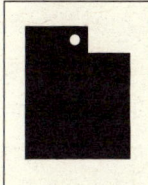

Extending along the high north-south ridge and both sides of the Wellsville Mountains for about 14 miles, the Wellsville Mountains Wilderness encompasses extremely rugged and picturesque terrain. These mountains are among the highest on earth to rise from such a narrow base, no more than one mile in many places. The U.S. Forest Service calls the Wellsvilles "the steepest range in the United States." The tallest summits are Wellsville Cone at 9,356 feet and Box Elder Peak at 9,372 feet. Canyons cut into the mountains from the east and west. The water that runs out of the Wellsvilles is enough to supply 16 small Utah communities. Once devastated by overgrazing, the Wilderness is on the road to recovery and now supports populations of deer, moose, and mountain lions, not to mention the occasional bighorn sheep. Raptors use the mountain range as a major flyway. Day hikers and hunters are the primary human users.

The Deep Canyon Trail, one of three routes, enters from approximately the northeastern tip to climb the main ridge. The trail then crawls south to Stewart Pass, a distance of about five miles. A short path from Coldwater Lake on the eastern side also leads to Stewart Pass, about 1.5 miles. From Stewart Pass, a waterless trail, marked on some maps as the Box Elder Trail, descends from the pass and then rises again to Wellsville Cone and Box Elder Peak to finish the last six-mile, hilly stretch south to U.S. 89. The western side, lacking trails, contains the most rugged terrain.

Wellsville Mountains Essentials
Size: 23,850 acres.
Year Designated: 1984.
Location: Northern Utah.
Easiest Access: From Mendon, take Third North Street west approximately two miles to the Deep Canyon Trailhead.
Season: Summer and early fall.
Wilderness Fees/Permits: None.
Maps: A Wilderness map that includes Mount Naomi Wilderness is available for $3 from the district ranger.
Management: Logan Ranger District, Wasatch-Cache National Forest, 1500 East Highway 89, Logan, UT 84321; (801) 755-3620.

"The Mountains enter into our lives as we enter into theirs. We are lifted up in the high places, not beyond ourselves, but to our best selves."

—Chester Rowell

VERMONT

Total Wilderness areas: 6
Total Wilderness acreage: 58,539

A land of steep, forested mountains, Vermont gets snowy winters, muddy springs, deep green summers, and splendidly colored falls. Green Mountain National Forest, which stretches north-south for almost two-thirds the length of the state, stands split into two sections. The northern section is further divided into the Middlebury and Rochester Districts, and protects two Wilderness areas. The Manchester District makes up the larger southern section and holds four more Wilderness areas. These great tracks of Wilderness were set aside as a result of the Eastern Wilderness Act of 1975.

Big Branch Wilderness

Named after Big Branch Stream, this area provides a home for wild turkeys, beavers, and moose. Wildlife photographers come here to shoot the latter (providing attention the moose have been known to resent, quite aggressively, during the fall rut). Gun-toting hunters track the substantial populations of white-tailed deer and black bears, while trout lure anglers to Big Branch Stream and Lake Brook. Approximately 80 percent of the forest leafs out in northern hardwoods—maple, beech, and birch—and straddles the steep slopes and summits of the Green Mountains. Red spruce, balsam fir, and hemlock pretty much fill out the rest of the trees. Elbow Swamp, a large wetland, lies on the eastern edge of the Wilderness, and hikers who intend to wander there must don rubber boots. The weather is cool from spring through fall, followed by long, frigid winters that attract cross-country skiers.

The Appalachian Trail/Long Trail crosses the area for approximately five miles and, with side trails, allows you to explore Big Branch with numerous camping opportunities. Bring a map and compass and wander off-trail for a more vivid Vermont Wilderness experience.

VERMONT

Big Branch Essentials

Size: 6,720 acres.
Year Designated: 1984.
Location: Southern central Vermont.
Easiest Access: From Rutland, take U.S. 7 south for approximately 20 miles to Danby. Turn east and drive a short distance to Mount Tabor. After Mount Tabor, turn up Forest Service Roads 10, 30, 58, or 259, where parking lots mark access to the Appalachian Trail/Long Trail.
Season: In the higher elevations, snow arrives usually by late November and doesn't melt until early April. By early October, the colorful tapestry of fall has begun to settle over the Green Mountains.
Wilderness Fees/Permits: None.
Maps: A free map is available from the district ranger. USGS topographic map is Wallingford Southwest.
Management: Manchester Ranger District, Green Mountain National Forest, Routes 11 and 30, RR 1, Box 1940, Manchester Center, VT 05255; (802) 362-2307.

Breadloaf Wilderness

The largest of the Wildernesses in Green Mountain National Forest, Breadloaf takes its name from Breadloaf Mountain, the highest point in the area at 3,835 feet. Within the boundaries you'll be able to climb Vermont's Presidential Range: Mounts Wilson, Roosevelt, Cleveland, and Grant. Although evidence of past logging operations can still be seen, the forest is slowly regenerating and numerous wildlife species take cover in these cutover sections. Moose and black bears live here in considerable numbers. Breadloaf contains the headwaters of the New Haven and White Rivers, both well stocked with small brook trout.

Seventeen miles of the Long Trail run the length of Breadloaf and pass over 11 peaks above 3,000 feet. The views in fall and winter are spectacular, and you'll find some of the few loop hikes in the national forest here. From a parking lot on the western side, Cooley Glen Trail (approximately 3.5 miles) rises to meet about four miles of the Long Trail, allowing a return to the same parking lot via the Emily Proctor Trail (approximately 3.5 miles).

In the southern portion, you can hike up the Long Trail and down the Burnt Hill Trail (approximately 2.5 miles), with a cutoff path that leads to Crystal Brook and Crystal Brook Glacial Kettle. When glaciers last retreated from this region more than 12,000 years ago, a block of ice was left stuck in the ground, eventually melting to form the "kettle," a big hole in the earth. Once you've seen that, hike the road a short distance back to where you started. Skiers will appreciate the Norske Trail, accessible off Forest Service Road 59.

VERMONT

Breadloaf Essentials

Size: 21,480 acres.
Year Designated: 1984.
Location: Northern central Vermont.
Easiest Access: From Middlebury, take U.S. 7 south for approximately four miles to East Middlebury. Turn east on State Highway 125 and continue about 16 miles to Middlebury Gap where the Long Trail leads into the Wilderness. Other access points include Lincoln Gap Road and Forest Service Roads 39, 55, 59, and 201.

Season: It's beautiful in fall. The winters are uniformly cold.
Wilderness Fees/Permits: None.
Maps: A free map is available from the district ranger. USGS topographic maps are Breadloaf, Lincoln, and Warren.
Management: Middlebury Ranger District, Green Mountain National Forest, Route 7, RD 1, Box 1260, Middlebury, VT 05753; (802) 388-4362.

Bristol Cliffs Wilderness

Bristol Cliffs, Vermont's smallest Wilderness, takes its name from the overhanging cliffs on the huge rocky slopes within the western portion of the area. From their 1,500-foot summit, you can gaze across Champlain Valley, over Lake Champlain, and into the Adirondacks of New York. A bulge of quartzite called Devil's Pulpit, probably used by early Native American toolmakers, dominates the cliff face. The face is considered unsafe for climbing.

The forest of Bristol Cliffs provides habitat for beavers, white-tailed deer, black bears, and grouse. If you're lucky, you might spot a peregrine falcon on the cliffs. Two secluded ponds, North and Gilmore, are nestled deep in the interior. Numerous streams tumble musically over low waterfalls.

The area has no established trails, and the occasional footpaths to the cliffs are faint and hard to follow. But with a map and compass in hand, you can explore the area and find one of the least visited spots in Vermont.

Bristol Cliffs Essentials

Size: 3,738 acres.
Year Designated: 1975.
Location: Northern central Vermont.
Easiest Access: In the town of West Lincoln, a Wilderness sign located at the junction of Atkins Road and York Hill Road points south onto York Hill Road. Travel 1.7 miles to a 10-car parking lot. There you'll see a footpath that disappears into the brush.

Season: Fall for the best color.
Wilderness Fees/Permits: None.
Maps: A free map is available from the district ranger. USGS topographic maps are Bristol and South Mountain.
Management: Middlebury Ranger District, Green Mountain National Forest, Route 7, RD 1, Box 1260, Middlebury, VT 05753; (802) 388-4362.

VERMONT

George D. Aiken Wilderness

The late Vermont senator George D. Aiken was a strong advocate of preservation and a leader in securing the Eastern Wilderness Act of 1975. Situated on a plateau rising as high as 2,300 feet, the area named in his honor differs from the state's other designated Wildernesses. Wet and marshy, the ground surface of Aiken Wilderness is covered with a great deal of water from either rain or melted snow. In spring and summer, I have found the air to be swarming with mosquitoes and black flies. Without rubber boots, your feet are going to get soaked. Beavers are very active here, chewing trees down to stumps and building dams. Brook trout live in their ponds and make for excellent fishing opportunities. Bears, moose, deer, otters, and many smaller mammals and birds share the area. Although not mountainous, this land of ponds, meadows, and brushy forest has no established trails, and bushwhacking can be tough and messy. Old logging roads, evident in some places, disappear quickly.

George D. Aiken Essentials

Size: 5,060 acres.
Year Designated: 1984.
Location: Southwestern Vermont.
Easiest Access: From Bennington, take State Highway 9 south for approximately eight miles to Forest Service Road 74, which runs along the eastern boundary of the Wilderness.
Season: Fall for a bug-free visit.
Wilderness Fees/Permits: None.
Maps: A free map is available from the district ranger. USGS topographic maps are Stamford and Woodford.
Management: Manchester Ranger District, Green Mountain National Forest, Routes 11 and 30, RR 1, Box 1940, Manchester Center, VT 05255; (802) 362-2307.

Lye Brook Wilderness

In the heart of the Wilderness, water drops in a series of cascades over Lye Brook Falls, the area's star attraction. The brook has trout for the catching. The surrounding forest is primarily northern hardwoods: birch, beech, and maple. Thickets of small spruce dot the area. Bourn Pond, a shallow body of water, opens the forest canopy and is surrounded by marshy ground. Prospect Rock—actually a series of cliffs—provides a sky-top view of the Wilderness. On the cliff top and in the marshy areas, the ecological balance is quite fragile. Try to walk softly. Hunting opportunities for deer bring many seasonal visitors, as do snowshoeing and cross-country skiing in the winter months.

A long-abandoned railroad bed, now choked with deadfall, crosses the Wilderness, and remnants of the railroad trestle spanning Lye Brook are visible. The falls are 2.3 miles into the area. The trail starts at a parking lot, and a section of the path follows the old railroad bed. To see most of Lye Brook Wilderness, you'll need a map, a compass, and the willingness to bushwhack.

VERMONT

Lye Brook Essentials

Size: 14,621 acres.
Year Designated: 1975; expanded in 1984.
Location: Southwestern Vermont.
Easiest Access: From the Manchester Ranger Station, drive west one-half mile on State Highways 11 and 30 to East Manchester Road. Turn south on East Manchester Road and continue to Glen Road, then turn southwest. Just past the first bridge, Glen Road bears left. Do not go left but continue straight ahead about one-half mile to the parking lot.
Season: Fall is the best time.
Wilderness Fees/Permits: None.
Maps: USGS topographic maps are Manchester and Stratton Mountain for about 90 percent of the Lye Brook Wilderness Area. Two other USGS topographic maps, Peru and Sunderland, cover the rest.
Management: Manchester Ranger District, Green Mountain National Forest, Routes 11 and 30, RR 1, Box 1940, Manchester Center, VT 05255; (802) 362-2307.

Peru Peak Wilderness

Resting just east of Big Branch Wilderness, Peru Peak Wilderness takes its name from the highest mountain in the area. In the more remote, trailless northern half stands Pete Parent Peak, a 3,000-footer that, unlike most in Vermont, has no marked path to the top. Two networks of beaver ponds in the northern section (below Big Mud and Little Mud Ponds) yield excellent trout fishing. Black bear and white-tailed deer attract hunters in the fall. Deer are more numerous in the eastern section along Utley Brook. Cross-country skiers like the deep, hard snow deposited in winter.

The Appalachian Trail/Long Trail crosses the southern end of the Wilderness for about three miles, taking in the summits of Peru and Styles Peak, both topping 3,000 feet. Styles Peak provides the best view.

Peru Peak Essentials

Size: 6,920 acres.
Year Designated: 1984.
Location: Southern central Vermont.
Easiest Access: From Rutland, take U.S. 7 south for approximately 20 miles to Danby. Turn east and drive a short distance to Mount Tabor. Continue to USFS Road 21, which generally follows the southern boundary of the Wilderness. The Appalachian Trail/Long Trail crosses USFS Road 21. USFS Road 58 accesses the western side of Peru Peak (and the eastern side of Big Branch).
Season: Fall is the best time.
Wilderness Fees/Permits: None.
Maps: USGS topographic map is Danby.
Management: Manchester Ranger District, Green Mountain National Forest, Routes 11 and 30, RR 1, Box 1940, Manchester Center, VT 05255; (802) 362-2307.

> "The earth does not argue, is not pathetic, has no arguments, does not scream, haste, persuade, threaten, promise, makes no discriminations, has no conceivable failures."
>
> —Walt Whitman

VIRGINIA

Total Wilderness areas: 16
Total Wilderness acreage: 169,453

Virginia, so very rich in American history, is impoverished in the way of Wilderness, especially when you compare the current preserved holdings with the vast wealth of wild forestland and mountains that once covered the state from border to border. What remains is primarily second-growth forests that teem with the chatter of squirrels, the alert gracefulness of deer, the restless foraging of black bears, the gobble of wild turkeys, and the songs of a multitude of birds. This is a legacy well worth preserving.

Two national forests, stretching along the boundary between Virginia and West Virginia, protect 15 small areas, 10 of which were designated by the Virginia Wilderness Act of 1984 (the act also identified four of the other areas, which were granted designation in 1988). One more area, almost equal in size to all of the others combined, is found within a national park.

Barbours Creek Wilderness

The rugged and remote mountain terrain of Barbours Creek Wilderness drops down the southeastern slope of Potts Mountain to Barbours Creek along the southern boundary. Elevations range from about 3,800 feet on the mountain to about 1,700 feet at the creek. The creek has carved a slim valley between Potts and Bald Mountains. You'll have a chance to find solitude here in a hardwood forest interspersed with yellow pine where the slopes face south and west. Some hemlock and white pine grow in the drainages, including the major cross-Wilderness waterway, Lipes Branch, in which you may catch native brook trout. Barbours Creek itself is a popular trout-fishing spot. Much of the year the area is colored with flowering vegetation. You'll be sharing the region with an abundance of wildlife including deer, black bears, wild turkeys, grouse, quail, doves, and squirrels. More than 160 species of birds have been identified here. Thunderstorms

VIRGINIA

are common between May and September, and snow falls two to three feet deep in winter.

One maintained trail within the Wilderness, the Lipes Branch Trail, allows north-south travel by horse or on foot for approximately two miles across the area and to the top of Potts Mountain. The trailhead begins on the creek at Pines Campground, complete with 17 campsites, fireplaces, and tent pads. The Barbours Creek Trail follows Barbours Creek for about five miles along the Wilderness border.

The area lies within Jefferson National Forest, except for 25 eastern acres that are part of George Washington National Forest.

Barbours Creek Essentials

Size: 5,700 acres.
Year Designated: 1988.
Location: Western Virginia.
Easiest Access: From Roanoke, take State Highway 311 north for approximately 30 miles; turn east on State Highway 617 and continue approximately 10 miles to Pines Campground.
Season: Spring and fall.
Wilderness Fees/Permits: None.
Maps: USGS topographic maps are Jordan Mines, New Castle, and Potts Creek.
Management: New Castle Ranger District, Jefferson National Forest, Box 246, New Castle, VA 24127; (703) 864-5195.

Beartown Wilderness

Some of Virginia's most remote territory is nestled in Beartown Wilderness. No improved roads lead here, and the old dirt roads are being reclaimed by native vegetation. This country is steep and rugged, particularly at the heads of the drainages, and reaches elevations of almost 5,000 feet. The principal waterways are Roaring Fork Creek, Bark Camp Creek, and Cove Branch, which runs off Beartown Ridge. The creeks feed several beaver ponds. For native trout, fish Roaring Fork. The vegetation is diverse, featuring Appalachian hardwoods, northern spruce-fir, northern hardwoods, hemlock, a sphagnum bog, and a few rare plants. You may see bears, you may see deer, and you're certain to see many smaller mammals and a great variety of birds.

The Appalachian Trail (AT) traces the southern boundary for about four miles, providing access for backpackers. There are no other maintained trails. Parking lots exist at two locations: one on the southwestern boundary at the end of a primitive road, one roughly two miles from the southeastern corner, both on the AT.

Beartown Essentials

Size: 6,375 acres.
Year Designated: 1984.
Location: Western Virginia.
Easiest Access: From Wytheville, take U.S. 52 north approximately 15 miles. Head west on State Highway 42 for approximately 13 miles. Turn north on County Road 635 and continue for about four miles, then go north on Forest Service Road 631 for another mile to a parking lot on the AT.
Season: Spring and fall.
Wilderness Fees/Permits: None.
Maps: USGS topo map is Hutchinson Rock.
Management: Wythe Ranger District, Jefferson National Forest, 1625 West Lee Highway, Wytheville, VA 24382; (703) 228-5551.

VIRGINIA

James River Face Wilderness

The first (and for two years, the only) designated Wilderness in Virginia, James River Face is bounded to the northeast by the James River and to the south by Forest Service Road 35. Immediately south of Road 35 lies Thunder Ridge Wilderness (see below), the two areas separated by a thin strip of dirt. James River Face reaches a high point of 3,073 feet on Highcock Knob near the southern boundary, and a low point of about 650 feet near the river. You'll find unusually diverse vegetation, especially in the James River Gorge, dominated by a typical Appalachian hardwood forest.

The Appalachian Trail (AT) meanders across the Wilderness for about 11 miles, from the region's easternmost corner to the southwestern corner. Matts Creek Shelter lies approximately three miles in from the east. Five other trails are maintained within or partially within this area. The Sulphur Springs Trail (three miles), the Balcony Falls Trail (2.5 miles), and the Piney Ridge Trail (1.5 miles) are open to foot and horse traffic. The Belfast Creek Trail (two miles), the Gunter Ridge Trail (three miles), and the AT are only open to foot traffic. You'll find the off-trail terrain rugged and difficult to hike. There are four parking lots near the Wilderness border—two at either end of the AT, one at Sulphur Springs, and another at Belfast Creek.

James River Face Essentials

Size: 8,903 acres.
Year Designated: 1975.
Location: Central Virginia.
Easiest Access: From Lynchburg, take U.S. 501 north about 25 miles to the parking lot on the James River where the AT crosses the road.

Season: Spring and fall.
Wilderness Fees/Permits: None.
Maps: USGS topographic map is Snowden.
Management: Glenwood Ranger District, Jefferson National Forest, P.O. Box 10, Natural Bridge Station, VA 24579; (703) 291-2189.

Kimberling Creek Wilderness

Very few people visit Kimberling Creek Wilderness, which has no parking lots and no maintained trails. In fact, save for a couple of old, long-abandoned dirt tracks there is little evidence that anyone has ever walked this land. Kimberling Creek, fed by Kimberling Springs by way of Sulphur Spring Fork, just touches the southernmost portion of the area. The Wilderness lies at its lowest elevation on the creek at 2,282 feet and rises to 3,200 feet in the northern portion on Hogback Mountain. Most of the terrain is steep and not hiker-friendly.

You'll find a forest of mixed hardwoods with white and yellow pine scattered throughout, and an understory of dogwood, sourwood, red maple, mountain laurel, and rhododendron. Wildlife, primarily deer, wild turkeys, grouse, and smaller nongame species, is abundant. None of the streams support trout. It's just a piece of wild Virginia at its untrammeled finest.

VIRGINIA

Kimberling Creek Essentials

Size: 5,580 acres.
Year Designated: 1984.
Location: Western Virginia.
Easiest Access: From Wytheville, take Interstate 77 north about 10 miles to Bland. Exit onto U.S. 52 and travel approximately five miles to the top of Brushy Hill. Then turn east on County Road 612 and continue until you cross back over Interstate 77. After a mile, turn north on the first unmarked dirt road, which will take you to the Wilderness boundary in about six miles.
Season: Spring and fall.
Wilderness Fees/Permits: None.
Maps: USGS topographic map is Rocky Gap.
Management: Wythe Ranger District, Jefferson National Forest, 1625 West Lee Highway, Wytheville, VA 24382; (703) 228-5551.

Lewis Fork Wilderness

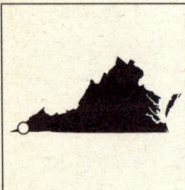

According to the U.S. Forest Service, Lewis Fork is "one of the most heavily used Wilderness areas in the Southeast." As a section of the 114,000-acre Mount Rogers National Recreation Area (Jefferson National Forest), Lewis Fork Wilderness includes Mount Rogers, Virginia's highest point at 5,729 feet. The scenery is typical of Appalachia, with the expected forest and wildlife.

The Appalachian Trail (AT) wanders north-south for about two miles through the northeast section of Lewis Fork, and Old Orchard Shelter is situated near the north end. The trail weaves out and back into the area twice more along the southern boundary for approximately five more miles within the Wilderness. The Thomas Knob Shelter sits at the head of the Mount Rogers Spur Trail, a mile-long path to the summit. If you want solitude, avoid the AT here except perhaps during midweek in low-use seasons (call the ranger before scheduling your trip).

You should also avoid the Mount Rogers Trail, the Mount Rogers Spur Trail, and the Virginia Highlands Horse Trail. You will have the best chance of finding peace on either the Grassy Branch Trail (about three miles within the area), the Helton Creek Trail (less than a mile within the area), or the Sugar Maple Trail (about two miles within the area). Of the network of trails in the area, all are open to foot and horse traffic except the "foot only" trails of the AT, which include the Mount Rogers Trails, and the Cliffside, Pine Mountain, and Lewis Fork Spur Trails. If real Virginia solitude is your goal, respect Lewis Fork but go somewhere else.

Lewis Fork Essentials

Size: 5,802 acres.
Year Designated: 1984.
Location: Western Virginia.
Easiest Access: From Interstate 81 at Marion, take State Highway 16 south approximately 20 miles to Troutdale. Turn west on County Road 603 and continue for approximately 10 miles to the Grassy Branch Trailhead. On the way you'll pass trailheads for the AT and Mount Rogers.
Season: Spring and fall for pleasant weather and more fellow visitors.
Wilderness Fees/Permits: None.
Maps: The Mount Rogers High Country and Wilderness Map is available for $3 from Mount Rogers National Recreation Area.
Management: Mount Rogers National Recreation Area, Route 1, Box 303, Marion, VA 24354; (703) 783-5196.

VIRGINIA

Little Dry Run Wilderness

On the eastern end of Mount Rogers National Recreation Area (Jefferson National Forest), Little Dry Run Wilderness gets very few visitors, despite the fact that the area is easily accessible. Most hikers and horsepackers pass through on the Virginia Highlands Horse Trail, which traces the southern boundary for approximately five miles. A land of small ridges and drainages, hardwood forested slopes, and opportunities for genuine solitude, the terrain ranges in elevation from 2,440 feet on Little Dry Run itself to 3,614 feet at a point near the middle of the area. Wildlife is diverse, abundant, and typical of Appalachia. You can fish for native trout in Little Dry Run.

Access to the area centers along one trail, the Little Dry Run Trail (about four miles). It starts at a parking lot on the northeast corner and follows the run up and over a ridge and down across the Virginia Highlands Horse Trail to Comers Rock Campground south of the Wilderness.

Little Dry Run Essentials

Size: 3,400 acres.
Year Designated: 1984.
Location: Western Virginia.
Easiest Access: From Wytheville, take U.S. 21 south. Two miles south of Speedwell you'll find the Little Dry Run Trailhead.
Season: Spring and fall.
Wilderness Fees/Permits: None.
Maps: USGS topographic map is Speedwell. The area is well displayed on the Mount Rogers High Country and Wilderness Map, available for $3 from the Mount Rogers National Recreation Area.
Management: Mount Rogers National Recreation Area, Route 1, Box 303, Marion, VA 24354; (703) 783-5196.

Little Wilson Creek Wilderness

Adjoining Grayson Highlands State Park, Little Wilson Creek Wilderness is a part of Mount Rogers National Recreation Area (Jefferson National Forest). It's located near a region of the NRA noted for its open, bald crests. Elevations range from 3,280 feet near the southern border to 4,857 near the northern. The vegetation is primarily upland hardwoods with sugar maple, beech, yellow birch, and some stands of red spruce and Fraser fir. Deer and bears, grouse and quail, and numerous small mammals and birds are found here. You can try to hook native trout in Big Wilson Creek and in the lower section of Little Wilson Creek.

Several maintained trails draw large numbers of visitors. The First Peak Trail, the Bearpen Trail, and the Appalachian Trail, which makes a brief appearance in the western section, are especially popular. The Big Wilson Creek Trail is fairly well used. You'll find less traffic on the Little Wilson Creek Trail (1.5 miles), the Kabel Trail (1.5 miles), and the Hightree Rock Trail (about three miles within the area). The Appalachian and Little Wilson Creek Trails are "foot only" pathways. There are no parking lots immediately adjacent to the area.

VIRGINIA

Little Wilson Creek Essentials

Size: 3,855 acres.
Year Designated: 1984.
Location: Western Virginia.
Easiest Access: From Marion, take State Highway 16 south for approximately 28 miles. Turn west on U.S. 58 and continue for approximately five miles to Grayson Highlands State Park, where you'll find access to trailheads.

Season: Spring and fall.
Wilderness Fees/Permits: None.
Maps: The Mount Rogers High Country and Wilderness Map is available for $3 from Mount Rogers National Recreation Area.
Management: Mount Rogers National Recreation Area, Route 1, Box 303, Marion, VA 24354; (703) 783-5196.

Mountain Lake Wilderness

Mountain Lake, the only natural body of water in western Virginia, actually sits just outside the southwestern Wilderness boundary. Inside the boundary you'll find a highland plateau resting squarely on the Eastern Continental Divide, isolated stands of virgin spruce and hemlock in a typical Appalachian hardwood forest, a mountain bog, and War Spur Overlook, which yields a panoramic view of this Wilderness. Elevations range from over 4,000 feet on Lone Pine Peak near the middle of the area to about 2,200 feet. Deer, bears, squirrels, and grouse run wild in the forest.

Several trails provide access to primitive Wilderness. The Appalachian Trail (AT) crosses from a parking lot on the west to the War Spur Shelter on the east, a distance of approximately five miles. The War Spur Trail runs less than a mile to the overlook. On this wide and flat mountaintop, you'll be treated to a panoramic 270-degree view of the Wilderness. The Johns Creek Trail wanders in from the south for about three miles, and the Potts Mountain Trail crosses the northern section for about five miles, briefly following the Virginia-West Virginia state line. Approximately one-fourth of the Wilderness lies in West Virginia (see West Virginia, Mountain Lake Wilderness). Backcountry hiking and camping are unrestricted.

Mountain Lake Essentials

Size: 8,253 acres in Virginia (10,753 total).
Year Designated: 1984.
Location: Western Virginia.
Easiest Access: From Blacksburg, take U.S. 460 west about 12 miles. Turn north on County Road 700 and go about five miles to Mountain Lake. Head north on Road 613 for approximately 3.3 miles to the War Spur parking lot.

Season: Spring and fall.
Wilderness Fees/Permits: None.
Maps: USGS topographic maps are Eggleston, Interior, Newport, and Waiteville.
Management: Blacksburg Ranger District, Jefferson National Forest, 110 Southpark Drive, Blacksburg, VA 24060; (703) 552-4641.

VIRGINIA

Peters Mountain Wilderness

Small Peters Mountain Wilderness, lying on the east slope of Peters Mountain, ranges in elevation from 3,956 feet on the mountaintop to 3,000 feet on Stony Creek, the southern border. State Highway 635 also helps determine the southern border. The terrain rises fairly steeply from the creek, then smooths out somewhat toward higher ground. Hikers who have made it to the summit report that the view is rewarding. Up high, the vegetation is primarily upland oak with yellow poplar, red oak, and hickory standing lower down. Numerous sandstone outcroppings along the crest of the mountain highlight this area, and a number of high mountain bogs can be found on Pine Swamp Ridge.

The Appalachian Trail (AT) drops about 1.5 miles from north to south near the middle of the area with the Pine Swamp Shelter near the southern boundary. Two other trails cross the area on the eastern and western sides.

Peters Mountain Essentials

Size: 3,326 acres.
Year Designated: 1984.
Location: Western Virginia.
Easiest Access: From Blacksburg, take U.S. 460 west for about 22 miles. Turn north on State Highway 635 and 10 miles later park at a trailhead that leads to the AT.
Season: Spring and fall.
Wilderness Fees/Permits: None.
Maps: USGS topographic maps are Interior and Lindside.
Management: Blacksburg Ranger District, Jefferson National Forest, 110 Southpark Drive, Blacksburg, VA 24060; (703) 552-4641.

Ramseys Draft Wilderness

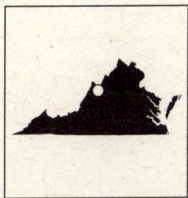

A "draft," according to local custom, is a creek. This area is named after its main drainage, a native eastern brook trout stream. Ramseys Draft Wilderness is a rugged and steep piece of land on the eastern side of Shenandoah Mountain, a region redolent with memories of America's Civil War. One of the largest tracts of virgin forest left in the eastern United States has been preserved here. Among the variety of plants you may see are some virgin hardwoods and hemlocks standing in the upper elevations and a more typical Appalachian forest of tulip poplar, red oak, and basswood. Watch for deer and the many smaller mammals that inhabit the woods of Virginia.

Eight trails lie within or along the border of this Wilderness. Inside the area's boundaries, the trails receive only minimal maintenance. You may find them difficult to travel. But the chance for solitude increases with the difficulty, and the rewards, so says the U.S. Forest Service, are well worth the effort. The Ramseys Draft Trail (6.8 miles) provides the primary and best access. This trail crosses the draft several times, which can be a problem when the water level runs high.

VIRGINIA

Ramseys Draft Essentials
Size: 6,725 acres.
Year Designated: 1984.
Location: Northern Virginia.
Easiest Access: From Staunton, take State Route 250 west for 24 miles. Turn north on Forest Development Road 68 and you'll immediately find the Mountain House Picnic Area. About one-tenth of a mile past the picnic area is a parking lot and the Ramseys Draft Trailhead.
Season: Spring and fall.
Wilderness Fees/Permits: None.
Maps: USGS topographic maps are Palo Alto and West Augusta.
Management: Deerfield Ranger District, George Washington National Forest, West Beverley Street, Route 6, Box 419, Staunton, VA 24401; (703) 885-8028.

Rich Hole Wilderness

In the late 1800s and early 1900s iron ore was mined from some of the hillsides in this area, and trees were cut to make charcoal for the iron ore furnaces. Traces of this activity, including an old mountain homestead with a small orchard, remain today in Rich Hole Wilderness.

The Wilderness consists primarily of Brushy Mountain and portions of Mill Mountain with their drainages, the North Branch of Simpson Creek and Alum Creek. You'll find a mature hardwood ecosystem with large old hemlocks in the drainage bottoms, and chestnut oaks and pines on south-facing slopes where the Virginia sun warms them. Wildlife watchers have a good chance of seeing black bears, deer, wild turkeys, and many smaller species.

The six-mile Rich Hole Trail passes through the southern half of the Wilderness, most of it along the North Branch of Simpson Creek. A parking lot is located at the trailhead.

Rich Hole Essentials
Size: 6,450 acres.
Year Designated: 1988.
Location: Northern Virginia.
Easiest Access: From Lexington, take Interstate 64 west to Exit 43. Follow Forest Development Road 447 for two-tenths of a mile. Turn on State Route 850 and continue for about three miles to the Rich Hole Trailhead.
Season: Spring and fall.
Wilderness Fees/Permits: None.
Maps: USGS topographic maps are Collierstown, Longdale Furnace, Millboro, and Nimrod Hall.
Management: James River Ranger District, George Washington National Forest, 810-A Madison Avenue, Covington, VA 24426; (703) 962-2214.

VIRGINIA

Rough Mountain Wilderness

Approximately six miles long and two miles wide, Rough Mountain Wilderness is an area of steep ridges and dry drainages with elevations reaching from 1,150 feet along the Cowpasture River to 2,842 feet on Griffin Knob. The ridges often afford great views across the Allegheny Mountains, the Blue Ridge, and the valley of the Cowpasture River. Upland hardwoods dominate the ridges, and the drainages sport oaks as the primary growth. On the south-facing slopes you'll probably see some southern yellow pines.

Rough Mountain gets light visitor use, mainly because getting there is so difficult. Most of the area borders CSX Railroad land and other privately owned acreage without legal access. One short trail, the Crane Trail, runs through the middle of the Wilderness, but there is no legal access to it either. If you want to visit Rough Mountain you'll need to travel cross-country from the north to reach the boundary (see Easiest Access, below). You'll still be bushwhacking when you enter the area, and you'll have to carry water, but you probably will not see another human (unless it's hunting season). Appropriately named, Rough Mountain Wilderness offers excellent opportunities for physical challenge and solitude.

Rough Mountain Essentials

Size: 9,300 acres.
Year Designated: 1988.
Location: Northern Virginia.
Easiest Access: From Millboro Springs, northwest of Lexington, take State Highway 42 south for 1.5 miles. Turn east on Forest Development Road 462 (Coffee Pot Road), drive about 100 yards, and park by the gate. Walk the closed road about 1.5 miles. Proceed cross-country on the ridge between Pads Creek and the Cowpasture River about 1.5 miles more to the Wilderness boundary.
Season: Spring, and fall before the hunting season.
Wilderness Fees/Permits: None.
Maps: USGS topographic maps are Longdale Furnace and Nimrod Hall.
Management: Warm Springs Ranger District, George Washington National Forest, Highway 220 South, Route 2, Box 30, Hot Springs, VA 24445; (703) 839-2521.

Saint Mary's Wilderness

Saint Mary's, the largest Virginia Wilderness on national forestland, is located in the Blue Ridge Mountain Range. It has elevations ranging from 1,700 feet to 3,400 feet and includes the drainages of Cellar Hollow, Spy Run, and the upper part of the Saint Mary's River. Along the Saint Mary's you can fish for native trout, walk through rhododendron and mountain laurel, and discover a lovely waterfall. The area was mined for iron ore and manganese until the mid-1900s, and evidence of those bygone days remains along the Saint Mary's River Gorge.

The area comprises a typical southern Appalachian hardwood ecosystem that, unfortunately, has been impacted heavily by an infestation of gypsy moths.

A total of approximately 17 miles of trails exists on five pathways. Primary access is gained from the Saint Mary's parking lot and trailhead. This trail leads around one mile to Saint Mary's Falls, a sparkling ribbon that drops about 100 feet and a popular destination for day hikers.

Saint Mary's Essentials

Size: 10,090 acres.
Year Designated: 1984.
Location: Northern Virginia.
Easiest Access: From Staunton, take Interstate 81 south about 18 miles to Exit 205. Turn east on State Route 606 and continue about two miles. Go north on U.S. 11 a very short distance, then head east on State Route 56 for 1.5 miles to State Route 608. Follow 608 north about 2.3 miles to Forest Development Road 41, which leads to the Saint Mary's parking lot.
Season: Spring and fall.
Wilderness Fees/Permits: None.
Maps: USGS topographic maps are Big Levels and Vesuvius.
Management: Pedlar Ranger District, George Washington National Forest, 2424 Magnolia Ave, Buena Vista, VA 24416; (703) 261-6105.

Shawvers Run Wilderness

No maintained trails give access to little Shawvers Run Wilderness. This is an area of rugged and remote mountain terrain on the northwestern slope of Potts Mountain, just over the hill from Barbours Creek Wilderness (see above). Elevations range from 2,000 feet on Shawvers Run in the extreme north to 3,800 feet on the top of Hanging Rock in the extreme south. Hanging Rock is a 240-acre geologic attraction. Rough hiking will take you through a hardwood forest interspersed with yellow pine, hemlock, and white pine growing in some of the drainages. Within the Wilderness, the headwaters of Valley Branch contain native brook trout, as does Shawvers Run. There is plenty of wildlife: deer, bears, gray squirrels, wild turkeys, grouse, and a myriad of other small creatures.

Although most of the area lies within Jefferson National Forest, the northern tip (95 acres) falls on George Washington National Forestland. Here is a genuine chance for a quiet Virginia Wilderness experience.

Shawvers Run Essentials

Size: 3,665 acres.
Year Designated: 1988.
Location: Western Virginia.
Easiest Access: From New Castle, north of Roanoke, take State Highway 311 north approximately six miles to the top of Potts Mountain. Turn east on Forest Service Road 177.1 and go three miles to find the boundary on the north side of the road. You'll also find a parking lot and an information sign.
Season: Spring and fall.
Wilderness Fees/Permits: None.
Maps: USGS topographic map is Potts Creek.
Management: New Castle Ranger District, Jefferson National Forest, Box 246, New Castle, VA 24127; (703) 864-5195.

Shenandoah Wilderness

The 195,000 acres of Shenandoah National Park stretch for 80 miles along the Blue Ridge Mountains, which form the eastern boundary of the Appalachian Range. The valley to the west holds the Shenandoah River and lends its name to the park. Settlement began here in the early 1700s, and early settlers discovered rich soil in the region and outstanding vistas from the Blue Ridge. By the twentieth century, the land had been thoroughly abused: the topsoil was eroded, the forests cleared, the wildlife depleted.

Established in 1926, the park contained croplands and pastures that were gradually overgrown with pine and locust trees that in turn gave way to a mature deciduous woodland of oak, hickory, and other hardwoods. Today, 95 percent of the park is forested with approximately 100 species of trees. It was this regeneration of the natural order that led to Wilderness designation for about two-fifths of the park.

Deer, bears, and bobcats have returned to the homes their ancestors knew. Chipmunks, groundhogs, squirrels, skunks, raccoons, and opossums are frequently seen. Approximately 200 species of birds have been identified in Shenandoah, with ruffed grouse, ravens, juncos, barred owls, and wild turkeys counted among the permanent residents. Timber rattlesnakes and copperheads are occasionally sighted, but they rarely pose a threat to humans.

More than 500 miles of trails provide access to the park, including 95 miles of the Appalachian Trail (AT). The Riprap Hollow Trail offers 10 miles of great views with cascading streams and one of the largest "swimming pools" in the entire park. Long and slender in shape, the most untrammeled portions can be found in the mid-northern and mid-southern sections.

Shenandoah Essentials

Size: 79,579 acres.
Year Designated: 1976.
Location: Northern Virginia.
Easiest Access: From Harrisonburg, take Interstate 81 north approximately 20 miles. Turn east on U.S. 211 and drive approximately 22 miles to Shenandoah National Park headquarters, located four miles east of Luray. Most of the trailheads lie on Skyline Drive, which runs the length of the park.
Season: April and May for the wildflowers. Fall colors usually peak from October 10 to 25.
Wilderness Fees/Permits: An entrance fee of $5 per vehicle or $3 per person is charged. A free backcountry camping permit is required.
Maps: Free Wilderness trail maps are available from the park ranger.
Management: Shenandoah National Park, Route 4, P.O. Box 348, Luray, VA 22835; (540) 999-2243.

VIRGINIA

Thunder Ridge Wilderness

The smallest of Virginia's Wildernesses, Thunder Ridge sits high on the northeastern slope of the Blue Ridge, separated from James River Face Wilderness (see above) by Forest Service Road 35. It's bordered on the south by the famous Blue Ridge Parkway ("America's most scenic drive"), which runs from Shenandoah National Park to Great Smoky Mountains National Park. Elevations range from 1,320 feet on the northwest corner to 4,200 feet on Apple Orchard Mountain at the southern tip. Thunder Ridge dominates the center of the area, falling away sharply on the north slope and not as steep on the south. Up high, the vegetation is primarily mixed upland and cove hardwoods. In this section, you may see black bears and deer, squirrels and rabbits, raccoons and foxes, wild turkeys and grouse. The U.S. Forest Service says the area may harbor several endangered or threatened species.

The Appalachian Trail runs through the Wilderness for approximately six miles from a parking lot on the eastern boundary, along Thunder Ridge. It takes in Thunder Ridge Overlook and leaves the area briefly on the south to reenter the southern corner. A second trail crosses a short piece of the northern section.

Thunder Ridge Essentials

Size: 2,450 acres.
Year Designated: 1984.
Location: Western Virginia.
Easiest Access: Take U.S. 60 west from Buena Vista for approximately three miles to the Blue Ridge Parkway. Turn south and continue for approximately 25 miles to the parking lot and trailhead on the eastern boundary.
Season: Spring and fall.
Wilderness Fees/Permits: None.
Maps: USGS topographic maps are Arnold Valley and Snowden.
Management: Glenwood Ranger District, Jefferson National Forest, P.O. Box 10, Natural Bridge Station, VA 24579; (703) 291-2189.

> "We are part of the earth, and it is a part of us. The perfumed flowers are our sisters; the deer, the horse, the great eagle, these are our brothers. The rocky crests, the juices in the meadows, the body heat of the pony, and man—all belong to the same family."
>
> —Chief Seattle

WASHINGTON

Total Wilderness areas: 30
Total Wilderness acreage: 4,252,344

Only Alaska, California, and Arizona have more designated Wilderness acreage than Washington. The terrain in this state varies from rain forest in the west to desert in the east, with the Cascade Range dividing the two. Much of this formidable mountain barrier, which extends from Canada to Oregon, is public land, whether national park or national forest. And a large part of it is protected as designated Wilderness areas. Four more designated areas can be found in the eastern part of the state—forested and mountainous to the north, arid and desertlike in the middle, and forested again to the south. The remaining Wilderness areas—comprised of rain forest, rain shadow (when mountains rise up near the sea, the side farthest from the water tends to have cloud cover but little rain, as the moisture is squeezed out on the ocean side), steep terrain, and wild beaches—are found on the Olympic Peninsula of northwestern Washington, a world unto itself.

Alpine Lakes Wilderness

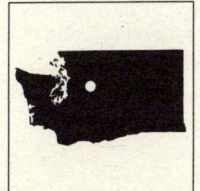

More than 700 lakes and mountain ponds fill practically every low spot in the glacier-carved terrain of this Wilderness. Valleys thick with trees give way to rocky ridges and rugged peaks along the crest of the Cascades, some slopes permanently cloaked with snowfields. Diverse is the word that best describes the Alpine Lakes: from wet forests of Douglas fir, cedar, and western hemlock understoried with salal and berries at lower elevations on the western side; to true firs and mountain hemlock opened by extensive meadows matted with low growth; to the crest and 180 inches of precipitation per year (largely as snow); countered by spruce, whitebark pine, and

WASHINGTON

larch on the eastern side; and ending farther down with a dry forestland of ponderosa pine and lodgepole pine understoried by grasses and dampened by as little as 10 inches of annual precipitation.

Prior to designation, aggressive mining and logging operations punched numerous access roads into the area, creating a wildly irregular boundary to this very popular (read: overcrowded) area, but one still deserving of its Wilderness classification.

The Enchantment Lakes region of the southeast portion boasts the Cashmere Crags, which rate among the best rock-climbing sites in the western United States. Dozens of solid granite spires offer routes from the low Class 5s to 5.11, from faces as long as one lead (the length of the rope used for climbing) to 1,500 feet. Some of the names may cause you to think twice before heading up: Bloody Tower, Cruel Thumb, Cynical Pinnacle, and Crocodile Fang.

The Pacific Crest National Scenic Trail (PCT) enters from Stevens Pass on the north to follow the crest south, with a long westward bend to Snoqualmie Pass, a distance of 67 trail miles. Hordes of people take advantage of the PCT's 450 miles or so of excellent trails. Subsequent use and abuse of the area has resulted in a permit system, which is applied to some regions of the Wilderness between June 15 and October 15. No dogs are permitted, and campfires are banned above 5,000 feet.

Alpine Lakes Essentials

Size: 305,407 acres.
Year Designated: 1976.
Location: Eastern central Washington.
Easiest Access: From Interstate 5 at Everett, take U.S. 2 east for approximately 60 miles to Stevens Pass and head south on the PCT.
Season: Spring through fall.
Wilderness Fees/Permits: Permits for access to certain regions of the area must be applied for in advance. A fee is charged, if your name is drawn, based on the number of days you wish to visit ($1 per person per day). Permits are required for the Enchantment Lakes, Stuart Lake, Colchuck Lake, and Snow Lakes areas. Contact district rangers for more information.
Maps: USGS topographic maps are Bandera, Big Jim Mountain, Big Snow Mountain, Blewett, Cashmere Mountain, Chikamin Peak, Chiwaukum Mountains, The Cradle, Davis Peak, Devils Slide, Enchantment Lakes, Grotto, Index, Jack Ridge, Lake Phillipa, Leavenworth, Mount Daniel, Mount Howard, Mount Phelps, Mount Si, Mount Stuart, Polallie Ridge, Scenic, Skykomish, Snoqualmie Lakes, Snoqualmie Pass, and Stevens Pass.
Management: North Bend Ranger District, Mount Baker-Snoqualmie National Forest, 42404 North Bend Way, North Bend, WA 98045; (206) 888-1421. Skykomish Ranger District, Mount Baker-Snoqualmie National Forest, P.O. Box 305, Skykomish, WA 98288; (360) 677-2414. Cle Elum Ranger District, Wenatchee National Forest, 803 West Second Street, Cle Elum, WA 98922; (509) 674-4411. Lake Wenatchee Ranger District, Wenatchee National Forest, 22976 Highway 207, Star Route, Box 109, Leavenworth, WA 98826; (509) 763-3103. Leavenworth Ranger District, Wenatchee National Forest, 600 Sherbourne Street, Leavenworth, WA 98826; (509) 782-1413.

Boulder River Wilderness

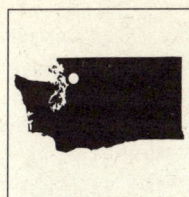

Three narrow spires—North, Middle, and South Peaks—known collectively as Three Fingers anchor the center of this Wilderness. Boulder River, the primary drainage, runs northwesterly from a north-south ridge that rises to a high point of 6,850 feet on South Peak. South Peak is also home to an old, precariously perched fire lookout. The high central ridge bears a narrow saw-toothed profile with several sharp summits, which include Liberty, Big Bear, and Whitehorse Mountains and Salish and Buckeye Peaks, all above 5,600 feet in elevation and flaunting sheer faces that attract rock climbers. Several steep and heavily wooded ridges thrust out east and west from the central crest of the Wilderness.

Alder, willow, devil's club, and other brushy plants (encouraged by as much as 100 inches of annual precipitation) make off-trail travel tremendously arduous. Climbers often wait until winter, when snow covers the brush. Along the river you'll find ancient trees: Douglas fir, true fir, western hemlock, and western red cedar. Some old trees have reached beyond 100 feet in height. Black bears, black-tailed deer, and elk inhabit the forest, with mountain goats staking out the rocky shelves above the tree line.

The great central core of the area remains rough and trailless. A short trail extends up Boulder River for 4.3 miles through old-growth forest. Three short trails climb toward the high crest and peter out. Another trail crosses the northeast corner of the Wilderness over Squire Creek Pass, with outstanding views of the high crest. Total trail miles come to about 25.

Boulder River Essentials

Size: 49,000 acres.
Year Designated: 1984.
Location: Northwestern central Washington.
Easiest Access: From Darrington, take State Highway 530 west for approximately 10 miles. Turn south on Forest Service Road 2010 and continue for approximately four miles to the Boulder River Trailhead.
Season: Year-round, depending on your choice of activities.
Wilderness Fees/Permits: None.
Maps: USGS topographic maps are Helena Ridge, Mallardy Ridge, Meadow Mountain, Mount Higgins, Silverton, and Whitehorse Mountain.
Management: Darrington Ranger District, Mount Baker-Snoqualmie National Forest, Darrington, WA 98241; (360) 436-1155.

The Brothers Wilderness

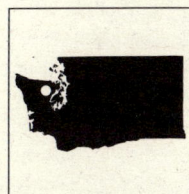

Between moss- and fern-laden banks, the Dosewallips and Hamma Hamma Rivers run cold and clear north and south, respectively, of the borders of The Brothers Wilderness. Only the Dosewallips separates The Brothers from Buckhorn Wilderness (see below), and only an imaginary line separates The Brothers from Olympic National Park to the west. At 6,866 feet, The Brothers is the highest peak in the area, with a distinct double summit that ranks among the most popular climbs (a Class 4 scramble) in Washington. Through the center of the Wilderness the Duckabush River splashes down a wide and lovely glacier-carved valley shadowed by tall hemlock, fir, and cedar.

WASHINGTON

From the Duckabush the terrain rises steeply into a mazelike network of forested ridges that peak on The Brothers to the south and 5,701-foot Mount Jupiter to the north. In the rain shadow of the Olympic Mountains, the area collects about 80 inches of precipitation each year, and temperatures stay temperate, rarely rising above 80 degrees Fahrenheit and seldom freezing along the river. The higher elevations get their fair share of snow.

I have hiked the pleasant Duckabush Trail that follows the Duckabush River for 6.2 miles into the park several times, always seeing black-tailed deer and occasionally spotting a black bear or a mountain goat. The Brothers Trail (4.5 miles) entering from the south provides access to the foot of The Brothers, and the steep Jupiter Ridge Trail (7.1 miles) entering from the north gives access to the nontechnical summit of Mount Jupiter.

The Brothers Essentials

Size: 16,682 acres.
Year Designated: 1984; expanded in 1986.
Location: Northwestern Washington on the Olympic Peninsula.
Easiest Access: From U.S. 101 about five miles south of Brinnon, turn west on Forest Service Road 2510 and continue approximately six miles to the Duckabush Trailhead.
Season: Early spring through late fall.
Wilderness Fees/Permits: None.
Maps: USGS topographic maps are The Brothers, Mount Jupiter, and Mount Washington.
Management: Hood Canal Ranger District, Olympic National Forest, P.O. Box 68, Hoodsport, WA 98548; (360) 877-5254. Quilcene Ranger District, Olympic National Forest, Highway 101, P.O. Box 280, Quilcene, WA 98376; (360) 765-3368.

Buckhorn Wilderness

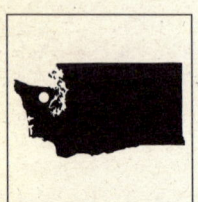

Bordering the northeast corner of Olympic National Park, just to the north of The Brothers Wilderness (see above), Buckhorn Wilderness stands divided into northern and southern portions by the Dungeness River and a parallel road.

The smaller northern portion, drained by the Gray Wolf River and its tributaries, descends from higher mountainous terrain to lowlands heavily forested in fir, hemlock, and cedar with an understory of moss, ferns, and berry bushes. Two trails provide access to northern Buckhorn: the 9.1-mile Gray Wolf Trail follows the river up its steep-sided gorge and into the park, while the 3.1-mile Slab Camp Trail descends a tributary of the river to join the Gray Wolf Trail about halfway across the Wilderness. South of the river and south of the trails, the terrain soars skyward to a ragged ridge with difficult access and few human visitors.

Drained by the Dungeness and Quilcene Rivers down glacier-carved valleys and fed by deep canyon tributaries, the larger southern portion is even more rugged than the northern. A dense and stately forest covers the lower elevations, while the higher country often opens into large alpine meadows rich with summer grasses and bright wildflowers. In hiking most of the 60 or so miles of trails in southern Buckhorn, I have found that they typically follow drainages, where the walking is easiest but still strenuous. The Big Quilcene Trail (5.3 miles) follows the Quilcene River up to Marmot Pass and then continues down the Dungeness River. At Marmot Pass the Big Quilcene Trail meets the 8.8-mile Tubal Cain Trail, offering you a worthwhile opportunity to hike into the park over Constance Pass.

WASHINGTON

Buckhorn Essentials
Size: 44,474 acres.
Year Designated: 1984; expanded in 1986.
Location: Northwestern Washington on the Olympic Peninsula.
Easiest Access: From U.S. 101 about one mile south of Quilcene, take Penny Creek Road west about one mile. When the road splits, take the south fork and you will be on County Road 27. Proceed about 10 miles before turning west on Forest Service Road 2750, which follows the Quilcene River approximately five miles to the Big Quilcene Trailhead.
Season: Late spring through early fall.
Wilderness Fees/Permits: None.
Maps: USGS topographic maps are The Brothers, Mount Deception, Mount Jupiter, Mount Townsend, Mount Zion, and Tyler Peak.
Management: Quilcene Ranger District, Olympic National Forest, Highway 101, P.O. Box 280, Quilcene, WA 98376; (360) 765-3368.

Clearwater Wilderness

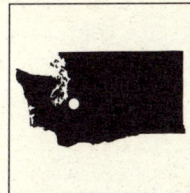

At about 6,089 feet, Bearhead Mountain stands higher above the headwaters of the Clearwater River than any other point in this Wilderness. Streams and small lakes (few of which you can reach by trail) quench the thirst of the old-growth Douglas fir, western red cedar, and western hemlock that shade these ridges. Most of the streams drain northward toward the north-flowing river. Ferns and mosses form a large part of the understory. Ninety percent of the annual precipitation falls between October and May, as much as 25 feet of it as snow that often lingers up high until late July. Wildlife here is typical of the Cascades: bears, deer, squirrels, skunks, raccoons, marmots, and a small number of elk. Just to the south lies Mount Rainier National Park.

The Summit Lake Trail roams the forest for 2.5 miles and gradually ascends to Summit Lake, not a bad trail for horsepackers, with a view of Mount Rainier to the south. The Clearwater Trail (8.1 miles) descends east to the Clearwater River, then crosses Lily Creek and climbs to a small lake and on to the western Wilderness boundary. From the same trailhead as the Clearwater Trail, the Carbon Trail wanders south in a long bend for 9.4 miles to join the Summit Lake Trail. You may see quite a few other people, especially on weekends.

Clearwater Essentials
Size: 14,300 acres.
Year Designated: 1984.
Location: Southwestern central Washington.
Easiest Access: From Enumclaw, take State Highway 410 east and south for approximately 40 miles. Turn west on Forest Service Road 74 and continue for approximately 15 miles, then head west on Road 7450 for approximately 3.5 miles to the trailheads for the Clearwater and Carbon Trails.
Season: Midsummer into early fall.
Wilderness Fees/Permits: None.
Maps: USGS topographic maps are Bearhead Mountain, Clear West Peak, and Old Baldy Mountain.
Management: White River Ranger District, Mount Baker-Snoqualmie National Forest, 857 Roosevelt Avenue East, Enumclaw, WA 98022; (360) 825-6585.

WASHINGTON

Colonel Bob Wilderness

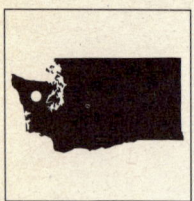

Off-trail travel in this Wilderness is nothing short of nightmarish thanks to the truly majestic but oh-so-dense rain forest that covers its steep mountainsides. Rain falls every month of the year, maximizing the lushness of the area even as it accumulates to depths that exceed 120 inches. The terrain is otherwise steep, rising suddenly from the Quinault River to gain more than 4,000 feet in little over a mile. Marking the center of the area is 4,492-foot Colonel Bob, the second highest point in the Wilderness (after a 4,509-foot peak that has no name). Two relatively parallel ridges join near the Colonel to continue southwesterly with a ragged profile. Several creeks run off the crest of the ridge either north to meet the Quinault River or south to meet the Humptulips River. Both waterways lie outside of the Wilderness, which shares a border with Olympic National Park near the park's southwest corner. Magnificent solitude fills cliff-sided Fletcher Canyon as it drops away from the summit of Colonel Bob toward the northeast.

The few miles of trails here are, for the most part, terrifically strenuous. The Colonel Bob Trail (7.2 miles) climbs steeply from the northern boundary to the top of Colonel Bob past the juncture with the Petes Creek Trail (1.8 miles), which runs down Petes Creek and out of the area in a southerly direction. You will likely encounter no other hikers.

Colonel Bob Essentials

Size: 12,120 acres.
Year Designated: 1984.
Location: Northwestern Washington on the Olympic Peninsula.
Easiest Access: From U.S. 101 on Lake Quinault, take South Shore Road east past Quinault for approximately six miles to the Colonel Bob Trailhead.
Season: Mid-June to October.
Wilderness Fees/Permits: None.
Maps: USGS topographic maps are Bunch Lake, Colonel Bob, Finley Creek, and Lake Quinault East.
Management: Quinault Ranger District, Olympic National Forest, South Shore Road, P.O. Box 9, Quinault, WA 98575; (360) 288-2525.

Glacier Peak Wilderness

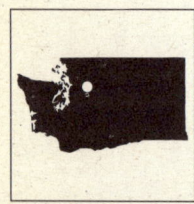

To me, Glacier Peak Wilderness, which shares its northern border with North Cascades National Park, has few equals in terms of sheer ruggedness. Glacier Peak, the highest summit in the area at 10,541 feet, is more remote than any of the state's other famous old volcanoes. Above the tree line (5,000 feet to 6,000 feet), lovely meadows stretch out below the tattered ridges and the dozen or so summits draped with active glaciers, while below the tree line you will wander through dense forest cover. Ultimately, the steep fractured walls and ragged peaks lead to deep U-shaped valleys tangled with huckleberry and other woody plants. Numerous ice-cold creeks splash gloriously through the valleys from their sharp drainages.

Other bodies of water include more than 200 lakes, many unnamed and tremendously difficult to access, in various cirques and hidden basins. Wildlife species include several that epitomize

WASHINGTON

Wilderness: grizzly bears, wolverines, gray wolves. Snows accumulate to depths of 45 feet on the west side of the crest. The paths of old avalanches mark some of the forested hillsides.

The 450 or so miles on as many as 100 trails vary from relatively easy hiking on maintained footpaths to starkly strenuous and seldom-used old animal trails. The Pacific Crest National Scenic Trail (PCT) follows the crest through the area for about 60 miles. The Suiattle River Trail acts as the main route from the west side, a pathway that travels 10.8 miles and joins the PCT. Above timberline, the land opens invitingly to cross-country travel. The Ptarmigan Traverse, probably the most famous untrailed route, combines rock climbing and glacier travel across 15 miles of the northern section of the Wilderness.

Climbers have put up routes on at least 140 peaks and faces in the area, and the rock climbing rates among the best in America. Blue Mountain, for example, in the northern portion of the area, boasts a 700-foot granite face with routes rated as high as 5.10. Some of the faces in the Wilderness exceed 1,000 feet.

Glacier Peak Essentials

Size: 576,648 acres.
Year Designated: 1964; expanded in 1968 and 1984.
Location: Northwestern central Washington.
Easiest Access: From Rockport, take State Highway 530 south for approximately 15 miles. Turn east on Forest Service Road 26 and continue to the Suiattle River Trailhead, approximately 20 miles.
Season: Summer.
Wilderness Fees/Permits: None.
Maps: USGS topographic maps are Agnes Mountain, Bench Mark Mountain, Cascade Pass, Clark Mountain, Dome Peak, Downey Mountain, Gamma Peak, Glacier Peak East, Glacier Peak West, McGregor Mountain, Mount David, Mount Lyall, Pinnacle Mountain, Prairie Mountain, Pugh Mountain, Pyramid Mountain, Saska Peak, Schaefer Lake, Sloan Peak, Snowking Mountain, Sonny Boy Lakes, Stehekin, Suiattle Pass, Trinity, and White Chuck Mountain.
Management: Mount Baker Ranger District, Mount Baker-Snoqualmie National Forest, 2105 Highway 20, Sedro Wooley, WA 98284; (360) 856-5700. Darrington Ranger District, Mount Baker-Snoqualmie National Forest, Darrington, WA 98241; (360) 436-1155. Chelan Ranger District, Wenatchee National Forest, 428 Woodin Avenue, P.O. Box 189, Chelan, WA 98816; (509) 682-2576. Entiat Ranger District, Wenatchee National Forest, 2108 Entiat Way, P.O. Box 476, Entiat, WA 98822; (509) 784-1511. Lake Wenatchee Ranger District, Wenatchee National Forest, 22976 Highway 207, Star Route, Box 109, Leavenworth, WA 98826; (509) 763-3103.

Glacier View Wilderness

For an extravagant look at the glacier-covered west side of Mount Rainier, hike to the top of 5,450-foot Glacier View in the northwest corner of this Wilderness, which, coincidentally, shares a portion of the western boundary of Mount Rainier National Park. Look west and you will see vast areas of unsightly clear-cuts, a reminder of what can happen to undesignated land. I crossed this area one fall prior to Wilderness designation and found that a considerable amount of its annual snowfall (which exceeds 30 feet) had stuck to the ground. The snowmelt here tumbles down eventually into the South Puyallup River, filling nine small alpine lakes in a rich meadowed basin

WASHINGTON

hidden by long ridges on both sides. Some of these lakes dry up in summer. You'll find cold water in Goat Lake, Lake West, and Lake Christine year-round. The forest cover is heavy with fir, pine, hemlock, and cedar, and thick with an understory of ferns, mosses, beadlily, trillium, and other sweet wildflowers. Elk and mountain goats graze the basin in the summer.

The 1.8-mile Lake Christine Trail enters near the southern end of the area and passes Lake Christine to hook up with the Puyallup Trail, which goes 2.5 miles north and east to Goat Lake and then into the park or west to join the 2.9-mile Glacier View Trail. A side trail off the Lake Christine Trail allows you to climb 5,475-foot Mount Beljica for another breathtaking view. The Glacier View Trail continues north, with side trails to Glacier View itself and Lake West, and proceeds to Lake Helen, which is outside the Wilderness boundary.

Glacier View Essentials

Size: 3,050 acres.
Year Designated: 1984.
Location: Southwestern central Washington.
Easiest Access: From Ashford, take State Highway 706 east approximately two miles toward the Nisqually entrance to Rainier National Park. Turn north on Forest Service Road 59 and continue for approximately four miles, then head east on Forest Service Road 5920 for about two miles to the end of the road and the Lake Christine Trailhead.
Season: Late summer and early fall.
Wilderness Fees/Permits: None.
Maps: USGS topographic map is Mount Wow.
Management: Packwood Ranger District, Gifford Pinchot National Forest, Highway 12, Packwood, WA 98361; (360) 494-0600.

Goat Rocks Wilderness

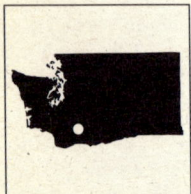

When I first visited the non-Wilderness shores of Packwood Lake, one midsummer long ago, and hiked into the Wilderness on the Packwood Lake Trail about two miles to Mosquito Lake, I thought the air contained more skeeters than oxygen. My first night I endured a survival-oriented mad rush to set up the tent and get inside.

Glaciation and erosion have worn away at the terrain here, leaving moderate summits on both sides of the crest of the Cascades. The deep east-west drainages below the ridges often open into parklike alpine meadows dotted with small lakes and even smaller ponds, all clouded over with mosquitoes in summer.

In winter, however, snow typically accumulates to more than 25 feet, not melting entirely until August and keeping the ponds and lakes full when it does give in to the sun. Pikas and marmots scurry about above timberline, while the more reserved deer and elk have been spotted lower down. Mountain goats frequently show up in the higher country, especially along Upper Lake Creek, which feeds Packwood Lake at the northwest boundary, and in Nannie Basin in the southern portion of the area.

Much of the 120-mile trail system stays on the ridges at or above timberline. The Pacific Crest National Scenic Trail (PCT) wanders north-south through the middle of the Wilderness for 31.1 miles, past 7,930-foot Old Snowy Mountain, where glaciers persist. At least 14 other trails climb to eventually join the PCT.

WASHINGTON

Goat Rocks Essentials

Size: 105,023 acres.
Year Designated: 1964; expanded in 1984.
Location: Southwestern central Washington.
Easiest Access: From U.S. 12 about one-half mile north of Packwood, turn east on Forest Service Road 1260 and continue for approximately 1.5 miles. Head north on Forest Service Road 1262 for approximately six miles to Packwood Lake (and Packwood Lake Resort) and the Packwood Lake Trailhead.
Season: Fall, before the snow falls and after the mosquitoes have died.

Wilderness Fees/Permits: None.
Maps: USGS topographic maps are Hamilton Buttes, Jennies Butte, Ohanapecosh Hot Springs, Old Snowy Mountain, Packwood Lake, Pinegrass Ridge, Spiral Butte, Walupt Lake, and White Pass.
Management: Packwood Ranger District, Gifford Pinchot National Forest, Highway 12, Packwood, WA 98361; (360) 494-0600. Naches Ranger District, Wenatchee National Forest, 10061 Highway 12, Naches, WA 98937; (509) 653-2205.

Henry M. Jackson Wilderness

Senator Henry Jackson of Washington was instrumental in the designation of many of the state's Wildernesses, and this "forest" of fabled peaks recalls his efforts. Straddling more than 30 miles of the craggy north-south trending crest of the Cascade Mountains, with deep glacial valleys spreading out east and west from the crest, this Wilderness is perhaps most distinctive in its northwest section. Here you will find terrain reminiscent of the Swiss Alps: glacial basins surrounded by raggedy ridgelines supporting sharp spires and imposing rock towers, attractions to many mountain climbers. Snow often accumulates to a depth of 20 feet in the higher country, and remains well into summer, eventually melting into the 60-plus lakes, which range from small pools of water to Blanca Lake's approximately 180 acres in the northwest section. A tall forest covers the lower elevations, then thins out and changes in species to eventually open into broad meadows on many ridge tops. This Wilderness shares its northeast border with the huge Glacier Peak Wilderness (see above).

The Pacific Crest National Scenic Trail (PCT) winds down the high heart of the area for about 32 miles. Other trails snake up from the east and west to join the PCT. The Blanca Lake Trail leads 3.5 miles to Blanca Lake, and five short pathways approach the center of the northwest section and fade to bushwhacking terrain.

WASHINGTON

Henry M. Jackson Essentials

Size: 102,671 acres.
Year Designated: 1984.
Location: Northwestern central Washington.
Easiest Access: From Everett, take U.S. 2 east approximately 65 miles. After crossing Stevens Pass, turn north on County Road 67 and continue for about three miles to the Smithbrook Trailhead for a 1.5-mile hike, the easiest east-side approach to the PCT.
Season: Late spring through early fall.
Wilderness Fees/Permits: None.
Maps: USGS topographic maps are Bedal, Bench Mark Mountain, Blanca Lake, Captain Point, Evergreen Mountain, Labyrinth Mountain, Monte Cristo, Poe Mountain, Scenic, Skykomish, Sloan Peak, and Stevens Pass.
Management: Darrington Ranger District, Mount Baker-Snoqualmie National Forest, Darrington, WA 98241; (360) 436-1155. Skykomish Ranger District, Mount Baker-Snoqualmie National Forest, 74920 Northeast Stevens Pass Highway, Box 305, Skykomish, WA 98288; (360) 677-2414. Lake Wenatchee Ranger District, Wenatchee National Forest, 22976 Highway 207, Star Route, Box 109, Leavenworth, WA 98826; (509) 763-3103.

Indian Heaven Wilderness

A forested plateau dominated by fir (Pacific silver, noble, subalpine) opens often into meadows splattered with at least 150 small lakes, ponds, and marshes in this Wilderness. Most of the larger lakes contain rainbow and brook trout. Lava once flowed from almost every knobby rise above the plateau, which averages 4,500 feet in elevation. The numerous volcanic cones reach their highest point on Lemei Rock (5,927 feet), where a broad crater now contains Lake Wapiki. A wealth of summer wildflower color is negated by the swarms of biting insects born in the ubiquitous water. Deer and elk reside here until winter snows drive them lower, along with black bears attracted to the abundant ripening of fall huckleberries. Periodically over the past 9,000 years Indians (including the Yakima, Klickitat, Cascades, Wasco, Wishram, and Umatilla tribes) gathered here for berry picking, fishing, and hunting.

The Pacific Crest National Scenic Trail (PCT) crosses the entire Wilderness north-south for a distance of 16.4 miles, with several side trails to some of the larger lakes and to the Indian Racetrack, a 2,000-foot-long field where horse racing once provided a break from the tribal food-gathering routine. Seven other trails enter from the east and west to join the PCT. In winter, the gentle terrain is buried under four to six feet of snow, an increasing attraction to cross-country skiers.

Indian Heaven Essentials

Size: 20,650 acres.
Year Designated: 1984.
Location: Southwestern Washington.
Easiest Access: From Carson, near Interstate 84, take County Road 65 north about 30 miles. Turn east on County Road 60 and drive about three miles to Crest Horse Camp and the Pacific Crest Trailhead near the south boundary.
Season: Fall.
Wilderness Fees/Permits: None.
Maps: USGS topographic maps are Gifford Peak, Lone Butte, and Sleeping Beauty.
Management: Mount Adams Ranger District, Gifford Pinchot National Forest, 2455 Highway 141, Trout Lake, WA 98650; (509) 395-2501.

WASHINGTON

Juniper Dunes Wilderness

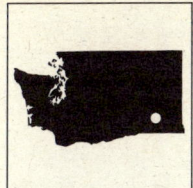

The Juniper Dunes Wilderness preserves the northernmost growth of western juniper, some of which have been around for 150 years, along with windswept sand dunes measuring 130 feet in height and 1,000 feet in width. Other than junipers, no trees grow in significant numbers here, but many bushes and flowers bloom wondrously come spring, although the mountains that separate western and eastern Washington generally wring the moisture from the air. The landscape here takes quite a battering, in fact, with strong southwest winds to build the dunes, seven to eight inches of precipitation to moisten them, a foot or so of snow that drifts down in winter, and summer temperatures that occasionally rise above 100 degrees Fahrenheit. Elevations range from 750 feet to 1,130 feet above sea level. But plenty of animals thrive despite the extremes: mule deer, bobcats, coyotes, badgers, skunks, weasels, porcupines, pocket gophers, kangaroo rats, several species of mice, hawks, owls, ravens, quail, partridge, pheasants, doves, numerous songbirds, and rattlesnakes.

Currently no legal access to Juniper Dunes exists, as the entire surrounding land is privately owned. With permission, you can travel on about six old jeep trails that end near the boundary. You'll find no maintained trails and no water.

Juniper Dunes Essentials

Size: 7,140 acres.
Year Designated: 1984.
Location: Southeastern Washington.
Easiest Access: The area lies about 1.5 miles northwest of Pasco-Kahlotus Road between Mile 15 and Mile 18. At least two jeep trails start from the road heading northwest.
Season: Spring and fall.
Wilderness Fees/Permits: Contact the BLM for specific information about contacts for access permission.
Maps: USGS topographic maps are Levey NE, Levey SE, Levey SW, and Rye Grass Coulee.
Management: BLM Spokane District Office, East 4217 Main Avenue, Spokane, WA 99202; (509) 353-3144.

Lake Chelan–Sawtooth Wilderness

Long, lean, and lovely best describes Lake Chelan. From Chelan's northeastern shore, this secluded Wilderness rears rapidly skyward to the crest of bold Sawtooth Range, which cuts diagonally through the area, rising serenely from the south to fall off dramatically on the north faces. Northeast of the crest, the terrain drops into the valley of the Twisp River only to climb again into a subrange. Wolf Creek and other creek drainages have cut deep ravines through much of the area, with elevations ranging from 1,100 feet to 9,000 feet. You'll find 63 lakes, many too small to have ever been named, often tucked into scenic cirques in the high country and without trail access. A pleasant forest covers the ground below the tree line, home to bears and mule deer. Winters are colder and summers hotter than in western Washington.

To me, one appealing aspect of this Wilderness is its lack of direct road access. All trailheads on the south side, on Lake Chelan, must be gained via a regularly scheduled ferry boat

WASHINGTON

or a private craft. From the roadless town of Stehekin, the northern terminus of the ferry, the Lakeshore Trail follows the lake south for 18 miles, with 14 miles within the Wilderness. Trails entering from the west first cross North Cascades National Park or Lake Chelan National Recreation Area. Trails from the north and east cross miles of national forestland before entering the Wilderness. Parklike ridges and open forests encourage you to leave the trail for relatively easy bushwhacking travel. A high-quality Wilderness experience awaits.

Lake Chelan-Sawtooth Essentials

Size: 150,704 acres.
Year Designated: 1984.
Location: Northern central Washington.
Easiest Access: From Wenatchee, take U.S. 97 north approximately 40 miles to Chelan, where the ferry boat leaves regularly for the long ride to Stehekin on the northern tip of Lake Chelan. Arrange for a drop at a trailhead in advance. Call the Lake Chelan Boat Company at (509) 682-2224.
Season: Spring through fall.
Wilderness Fees/Permits: None.
Maps: USGS topographic maps are Big Goat Mountain, Gilbert, Lucerne, Martin Peak, Mazama, McAlester Mountain, Midnight Mountain, Oval Peak, Prince Creek, Rendezvous Mountain, Silver Star Mountain, Sun Mountain, Thompson Ridge, and Washington Pass.
Management: Chelan Ranger District, Wenatchee National Forest, 428 Woodin Avenue, P.O. Box 189, Chelan, WA 98816; (509) 682-2576. Twisp Ranger District, Okanogan National Forest, 502 Glover, P.O. Box 188, Twisp, WA 98856; (509) 997-2131. Winthrop Ranger District, Okanogan National Forest, West Chewuch Road, P.O. Box 579, Winthrop, WA 98862; (509) 996-2266.

Mount Adams Wilderness

Second in height only to Mount Rainier statewide, 12,276-foot Mount Adams looms over at least 10 impressive glaciers and a Wilderness of forested slopes and subalpine meadows. The huge volcanic bulk of the mountain takes up a considerable portion of the Wilderness and rises to its only peak. As many as 25 climbing routes, from nontechnical to technically challenging, provide access to this very popular summit. Elevation gain is approximately 6,000 feet. Approaching the mountain from the south you will find relatively gentle terrain, a nice contrast for hikers in comparison to the treacherous ice and sharp ridges on the west and the treacherous ice and vertical cliffs on the east. The glaciated north face is less imposing. On the east, the lower reaches of the mountain fall within the Yakima Indian Reservation, open only to those with a special permit (available for a fee).

The Pacific Crest National Scenic Trail (PCT) crosses the Wilderness generally north-south for about 21 miles on the west side of Mount Adams. Some 45 additional miles of trails join the PCT, allowing you to hike about three-fourths of the way around the base of Mount Adams. Extensive, careless human use shows in this well-trodden area, especially where camps have marred fragile meadowlands. Walk with great care.

WASHINGTON

Mount Adams Essentials

Size: 46,776 acres.
Year Designated: 1964; expanded in 1984.
Location: Southwestern Washington.
Easiest Access: From Trout Lake, take County Road 23 north 15 miles to where the PCT crosses the road. Hike north into the Wilderness.
Season: Late spring through early fall.
Wilderness Fees/Permits: A free Wilderness permit is required and available from the ranger.

Maps: USGS topographic maps are Glaciate Butte, Green Mountain, Jungle Butte, King Mountain, Mount Adams East, Mount Adams West, Steamboat Mountain, and Trout Lake. A Wilderness map that shows climbing routes is available for $2 from the district ranger.
Management: Mount Adams Ranger District, Gifford Pinchot National Forest, 2455 Highway 141, Trout Lake, WA 98650; (509) 395-2501.

Mount Baker Wilderness

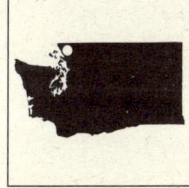

Mount Baker has shown steamy signs of life as recently as 1975. The volcanic mountain stands at 10,778 feet, making it the fourth highest summit in the state and the dominant feature in the southern portion of this Wilderness. Fourteen glaciers blanket the immediate region of the mountain. Add to that the frozen sheets on nearby peaks and the total perpetual ice in the area surpasses 10,000 acres. Precipitation on the heights of Mount Baker sometimes reaches 150 inches per year, with up to 18 feet of snow accumulating. Many of the ridges stand above fir- and cedar-forested drainages, dividing the sky and opening often into large heather-filled meadows that showcase riots of summer alpine wildflowers, huckleberries, and blueberries. Devil's club, salmonberry, skunk cabbage, and ferns brighten the banks of creeks and rivers. Black bears and black-tailed deer share the area, while mountain goats clamber about in the rocky high country. Just south of Mount Baker, outside the Wilderness, elk congregate in numbers rarely seen in this part of the state. The Wilderness shares its eastern border with North Cascades National Park, and lovely Mount Shuksan looms just over the boundary inside the park.

Rock climbers flood onto Mount Baker in spring and summer before fall opens numerous large crevasses. Hundreds of climbers may be seen on the mountain in a single day. The Heliotrope Ridge Trail winds 2.7 miles to the Coleman Glacier, the most popular climbing route on the mountain. A well-developed and very busy trail system provides access to the lower country.

WASHINGTON

Mount Baker Essentials

Size: 117,580 acres.
Year Designated: 1984.
Location: Northwestern Washington.
Easiest Access: From Bellingham, take State Highway 542 east about 40 miles to Glacier. Turn south on Forest Service Road 37 and continue south on Road 39 for approximately seven miles to find the Heliotrope Ridge Trailhead.
Season: Spring and summer for climbing. Summer and fall for hiking.
Wilderness Fees/Permits: None, but climbers are strongly encouraged to register.
Maps: USGS topographic maps are Bacon Peak, Baker Pass, Bearpaw Mountain, Cavanaugh Creek, Glacier, Groat Mountain, Mount Baker, Mount Larrabee, Mount Sefrit, Mount Shuksan, Shuksan Arm, Twin Sisters Mountain, and Welker Peak. A climbing route brochure is available for $1.95 from the district ranger.
Management: Mount Baker Ranger District, Mount Baker-Snoqualmie National Forest, 2105 Highway 20, Sedro Wooley, WA 98284; (360) 856-5700.

Mount Rainier Wilderness

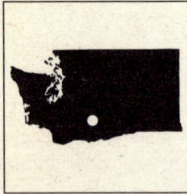

No peak in the state of Washington stands higher than Mount Rainier. At 14,410 feet, this handsome summit crowns the central region of Mount Rainier National Park, although between October and April, clouds often hide it from view. Twenty-seven named glaciers spill down the slopes, covering approximately 37 square miles, making it the largest field of glaciers in the Lower 48. The distinguishing aspects of the park only begin with the mountain. You'll find 300 miles of maintained trails, 382 bodies of water, almost 500 miles of rivers and streams, 54 species of mammals, 787 of plants, 130 of birds, and 17 of reptiles and amphibians. Most of the 235,612 acres of the park are designated Wilderness. Within the park but outside the Wilderness you can pitch a tent at one of about 600 regulated campsites.

I have been to Paradise, where a lodge and a starting point for most climbers exists, when snow lay more than 20 feet deep. On my three climbs of Rainier the wind thundered near the top, as is its habit, I am told. Climbers are almost as conspicuous as the wind, with as many as 10,000 attempting the summit every year. Due to rapid weather changes and altitude gain, only about half of those who attempt to reach the top actually make it.

One of the most scenic hikes I have ever taken is the 93-mile Wonderland Trail, which completes a loop around the base of Mount Rainier. It ascends to alpine meadows aflame with summer wildflowers, past clear lakes, then down into canyons cut deeply by streams into the old lava that once flowed from the mountain's crater.

WASHINGTON

Mount Rainier Essentials

Size: 216,855 acres.
Year Designated: 1988.
Location: Southwestern central Washington.
Easiest Access: From Tacoma, take State Highway 7 south for approximately 40 miles to Elbe. Turn east on State Highway 706 and continue for approximately 15 miles to the Nisqually entrance to the park and on about seven miles to the Wonderland Trailhead.
Season: Summer and early fall.
Wilderness Fees/Permits: The park charges an entrance fee of $5 per auto or $3 per individual (hikers, bikers, etc.). A free permit is required for backcountry camping and climbing.
Maps: USGS topographic maps are Chinook Pass, Cougar Lake, Golden Lakes, Mount Rainier East, Mount Rainier West, Mount Wow, Mowich Lake, Ohanapecosh Hot Springs, Sawtooth Ridge, Sunrise, Tatoosh Lakes, Wahpenayo Peak, White Pass, and White River Park. Trails Illustrated's Map 217, Mount Rainier National Park, covers the area well.
Management: Mount Rainier National Park, Tahoma Woods, Star Route, Ashford, WA 98304; (360) 569-2211.

Mount Skokomish Wilderness

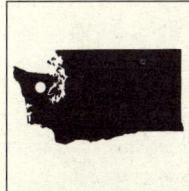

This Wilderness marks the southeast corner of Olympic National Park, just north of Lake Cushman. Two long ridges here, running roughly northeast to southwest, support several bold rocky summits and numerous sharp spires. Elevations range from about 2,000 feet to 6,434 feet on Mount Skokomish, which anchors the northwest boundary. The northern ridge rises to Mounts Skokomish, Lincoln, and Cruiser, with ragged Sawtooth Ridge, popular for its excellent rock-climbing opportunities, stretching between Lincoln and Cruiser. The southern ridge includes the summits of Mounts Pershing, Washington, Rose, Elinor, Jefferson Peak, and Tran Spire, all interesting and often challenging climbs. Between the ridges lies the headwaters basin of the Hamma Hamma River, which gathers its waters from Mildred Lakes and tributary streams in the western portion to flow east across the Wilderness.

Magnificent old-growth western hemlock, western red cedar, and Douglas fir dominate the forest in the lower elevations, providing a shady home for elk, black-tailed deer, black bears, and mountain lions. Higher elevations display firs, pines, and dwarf juniper, and open rock faces alive with marmots and mountain goats (which look like pockets of old snow from a distance).

Most of the area is wild and ruggedly free, penetrated only by four short and wondrously neglected trails. The Putvin Trail (3.7 miles) crosses the northeast corner of the Wilderness, climbing steeply up Whitehorse Creek to gorgeous Lake of the Angels inside the park. The faint Mildred Lakes Trail (4.5 miles) runs to Mildred Lakes below the Sawtooth Ridge. Short, unmaintained trails provide access to Mounts Rose and Elinor in the southern portion of the area. Lakesides have suffered abuse, and campfires are not allowed near bodies of water.

WASHINGTON

Mount Skokomish Essentials

Size: 13,015 acres.
Year Designated: 1984; expanded in 1986.
Location: Northwestern Washington on the Olympic Peninsula.
Easiest Access: From Hoodsport, take U.S. 101 north for 14 miles. Turn west on Forest Service Road 25 and continue up the Hamma Hamma River for 14 miles to the end of the line and the Mildred Lakes Trailhead.
Season: Summer offers the best access to the peaks.
Wilderness Fees/Permits: None.
Maps: USGS topographic maps for the area are Lightning Peak, Mount Skokomish, and Mount Washington.
Management: Hood Canal Ranger District, Olympic National Forest, P.O. Box 68, Hoodsport, WA 98548; (360) 877-5254.

Noisy-Diobsud Wilderness

Noisy Creek flows north through this Wilderness and Diobsud Creek drifts south, both bolstering a foot-entangling understory of ferns, mosses, salal, elderberry, and salmonberry, mixed with nasty devil's club along the banks. Staggeringly steep ridges rise abruptly to the northeast and southwest of the creeks, topping out at 6,234 feet on Mount Watson, which anchors the center of the area. The Wilderness shares the border of the southwest corner of North Cascades National Park, just south of Baker Lake. Deep drainages carve its forested slopes, the lower portions of which consist of old-growth fir, cedar, and hemlock. Black-tailed deer, black bears, elk, and northern spotted owls all seek refuge in the dense, shadowy forest. Some alpine meadows open the ridge tops. Annual precipitation reaches 150 inches. National forestland—roadless, primitive, and undesignated—surrounds the Wilderness to the east, west, and south.

You won't find much at all in the way of trails or people, so expect to have to cross-country scramble if you want to reach one of the 12 or so lakes. If you must use a trail, you can choose from two short routes: Trail 609 goes less than one mile up Noisy Creek from Baker Lake, and the 2.3-mile Watson Lakes Trail courses across non-Wilderness land from near Maple Grove Campground to the Anderson Lakes and Watson Lakes regions.

Noisy-Diobsud Essentials

Size: 14,300 acres.
Year Designated: 1984.
Location: Northwestern Washington.
Easiest Access: From Concrete, on State Highway 20 near Baker Dam, take Forest Service Road 11 north for approximately 10 miles. Turn east on Forest Service Road 1107 and continue for approximately 10 miles to the end of the line and the Watson Lakes Trailhead.
Season: Summer.
Wilderness Fees/Permits: None.
Maps: USGS topographic maps are Bacon Peak, Damnation Peak, Lake Shannon, Marblemount, Sauk Mountain, and Welker Peak.
Management: Mount Baker Ranger District, Mount Baker-Snoqualmie National Forest, 2105 Highway 20, Sedro Wooley, WA 98284; (360) 856-5700.

WASHINGTON

Norse Peak Wilderness

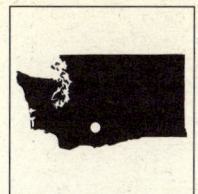

Just northeast of Mount Rainier National Park, Norse Peak Wilderness reaches down both sides of the crest of the Cascade Mountain Range. Narrow drainages below rockbound ridges slice deeply into the area, which opens here and there into scenic basins dotted with lakes. A typical western Cascades forest of Douglas fir, western hemlock, and cedar understoried with ferns and mosses characterizes the western side of the crest, giving way to mountain hemlock, subalpine fir, and lovely meadows before dropping down on the eastern side to drier country and a forest of larch, spruce, and pine. Remnants of the old gold-seeking days recall the past in the southwest corner: mine shafts, tailings, derelict cabins. The bold faces of Fifes Peaks in the southeast portion attract rock climbers. Only the corridor of State Highway 410 and the American River separate Norse Peak from William O. Douglas Wilderness (see below) to the south.

Norse Peak (6,856 feet) anchors the southwestern boundary. Hike the 5.2-mile Trail 1191 (also known as the Norse Peak Trail) that leads to the summit and you will be rewarded with panoramic views. Carry water and you can pitch a tent on top and watch the sunrise. The Pacific Crest Trail (PCT) crosses the Wilderness in a north-south direction for about 27 miles. Other trails enter from all four sides of the Wilderness to join the PCT.

Norse Peak Essentials

Size: 50,902 acres.
Year Designated: 1984.
Location: Southwestern central Washington.
Easiest Access: From Enumclaw, take State Highway 410 east and south approximately 45 miles to Chinook Pass, where the PCT crosses the road. Hike north.
Season: Late spring through early fall.
Wilderness Fees/Permits: None.
Maps: USGS topographic maps are Goose Prairie, Mount Clifty, Noble Knob, Norse Peak, and Raven Roost.
Management: Naches Ranger District, Wenatchee National Forest, 10061 Highway 12, Naches, WA 98937; (509) 653-2205. White River Ranger District, Mount Baker-Snoqualmie National Forest, 857 Roosevelt Ave. East, Enumclaw, WA 98022; (360) 825-6585.

Olympic Wilderness

The years I spent living near Washington's largest Wilderness area, which includes most of Olympic National Park, allowed me the opportunity to explore a large portion of this remarkable piece of the earth. The area, a complex jumble of rocky ridges, covers approximately 50 miles east to west and 40 north to south. Small glaciers and permanent snowfields drape the ridges, broken up at lower elevations by the tangled vegetation bordering the long drainages and the old growth that forests the utterly spectacular valleys.

Ridges and drainages radiate from the high central region of the park like a pinwheel topped by glacier-cloaked Mount Olympus, an irresistible attraction to climbers at 7,965 feet. If you're willing to search all the high and secret places of the park, you may discover more than 300 lakes. The forest is fantastically verdant and filled

WASHINGTON

to abundance with wildlife, including the world's largest herd of Roosevelt elk. Black bears are everywhere. Mountain goats wander into camps. The nearby ocean and the sudden rise of the Olympic Mountains together create unpredictable weather conditions that tend toward the sodden. Winter snows smother the high country.

Separate from the vast interior portion, the park includes 57 miles of beach, most of it grandly isolated, splendidly wild, and wracked by waves and storms. The northern beach is one of my all-time favorite hikes.

Almost 600 miles of trails lead into the interior of the park. The Hoh Trail comes in from the west side to follow the Hoh River (which has excellent fishing) for 18 miles with relative ease. Ferns, lush and otherworldly, carpet the hushed rain forest. The Hoh Trail provides the easiest access to Mount Olympus. The Enchanted Valley Trail (18.9 miles) crosses much of the southeast corner along one of the most scenic paths I've ever hiked.

Overuse threatens some of the park, and the easily accessible and popular Flapjack Lakes and Lake Constance require advance camping permits. Whenever you come, visit with care. You'll find that the delights of the Olympic Wilderness are never-ending.

Olympic Essentials

Size: 876,669 acres.
Year Designated: 1988.
Location: Northwestern Washington on the Olympic Peninsula.
Easiest Access: From Forks, take U.S. 101 south for approximately 15 miles. Turn east on Hoh River Road and continue to the Hoh River Trailhead, a distance of approximately 18 miles.
Season: Summer and early fall.
Wilderness Fees/Permits: Free backcountry permits are required and available at ranger stations.
Maps: Trails Illustrated's Map 216, Olympic National Park, covers the area well. USGS topographic maps for the interior of the park are Bob Creek, Bogachiel Peak, The Brothers, Bunch Lake, Chimney Peak, Colonel Bob, Elwha, Finley Creek, Hunger Mountain, Indian Pass, Kimta Peak, Kloochman Rock, Lake Crescent, Lake Quinault East, Lake Quinault West, Lake Sutherland, Maiden Peak, Matheny Ridge, McCartney Peak, Morse Creek, Mount Angeles, Mount Carrie, Mount Christie, Mount Deception, Mount Hoquiam, Mount Muller, Mount Olson, Mount Olympus, Mount Queets, Mount Skokomish, Mount Steel, Mount Tom, Mount Townsend, Mount Washington, Owl Mountain, Port Angeles, Queets, Salmon River East, Salmon River West, Slide Peak, Spruce Mountain, Stequaleho Creek, Tyler Peak, Wellesley Peak, Winfield Creek, and Wynooche Lake.

USGS maps for the beach are Allens Bay, Destruction Island, Dickey Lake, Hoh Head, La Push, Makah Bay, Ozette, Queets, Quillayute Prairie, Toleak Point, and Umbrella Creek.
Management: Olympic National Park, 600 East Park Avenue, Port Angeles, WA 98362; (360) 452-0330.

WASHINGTON

Pasayten Wilderness

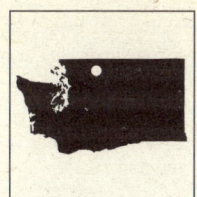

Skirting more than 50 miles of Canada's border and encompassing the crest of the Cascades, this big piece of very wild country is home to the largest population of lynx in the Lower 48. The Wilderness boasts almost 150 peaks over 7,500 feet in elevation, 160 or more bodies of water, and at least as many waterways, some fierce enough to have carved incisive canyons with sheer walls. Rugged ridges in the west flatten into parklike plateaus toward the east, with deep drainages on both sides. Its diverse forest changes from vegetation typical of western Washington (fir, cedar, western hemlock) to growth typical of eastern Washington (fir, pine, larch).

Deer, moose, mountain goats, bighorn sheep, the fabled gray wolf, and the intimidating grizzly bear steal through these woods. Snow falls between October and May, and the hardpack may block the high western-side trails sometimes until early August. Eastern-side trails are usually free of snow by early July. Although part of the Wilderness lies in Mount Baker-Snoqualmie National Forest, the largest section (and its management) falls within the boundaries of Okanogan National Forest.

More than 600 miles of trails provide access to the Wilderness, many of them deceptively gentle at the start and progressively labor-intensive as they crawl up endless switchbacks into the higher country. The Pacific Crest Trail (PCT) crosses the area north-south for about 32 miles. The Boundary Trail moves north from the southeast corner to ramble near the Canadian border for a total of more than 73 miles (making it the longest route in the Wilderness) before eventually joining the PCT.

Pasayten Essentials

Size: 529,850 acres.
Year Designated: 1968; expanded in 1984.
Location: Northern Washington.
Easiest Access: From one mile north of Loomis, on the eastern side of the Wilderness, turn west on Forest Service Road 39 and continue for approximately 10 miles. Turn north on Forest Service Road 500 and go approximately three miles to Iron Gate Campground and the Boundary Trailhead.
Season: July through September.
Wilderness Fees/Permits: None.
Maps: USGS topographic maps are Ashnola Mountain, Ashnola Pass, Bauerman Ridge, Billy Goat Mountain, Castle Peak, Coleman Peak, Crater Mountain, Frosty Creek, Horseshoe Basin, Hozomeen Mountain, Hurley Peak, Jack Mountain, Lost Peak, McLeod Mountain, Mount Barney, Mount Lago, Pasayten Peak, Pumpkin Mountain, Remmel Mountain, Shull Mountain, Slate Peak, Sweetgrass Butte, and Tatoosh Buttes. A Wilderness map is available for $3 from the district rangers.
Management: Tonasket Ranger District, Okanogan National Forest, 1 West Winesap, P.O. Box 466, Tonasket, WA 98855; (509) 486-2186. Winthrop Ranger District, Okanogan National Forest, West Chewuch Road, P.O. Box 579, Winthrop, WA 98862; (509) 996-2266.

WASHINGTON

Salmo-Priest Wilderness

Tucked into the extreme northeastern corner of the state, sharing borders with Idaho and British Columbia, this Wilderness consists of two very long ridges, generally running north-south and connected at their northern ends by an east-west ridge crowned by 6,828-foot Salmo Mountain. The eastern ridge stands lower, more wooded, and more rounded off than the steep-sided, rocky-crested western ridge. Streams have cut deep drainages into both ridges, and much of the water from the eastern side of the eastern ridge ends up in Idaho's Priest River. Sullivan Creek and its tributaries drain the wide non-Wilderness area between the ridges.

Below the ridge tops you'll find the largest growth of virgin forest left in eastern Washington: western red cedar, western hemlock, Douglas fir, grand fir, larch. The forest houses mule deer and white-tailed deer, elk, black bears, cougars, bobcats, wolverines, badgers, pine martens, lynx, bighorn sheep, and moose. This is one of the few places in the Lower 48 where you might see a woodland caribou. Grizzly bears have been spotted in the Wilderness, as have rare gray wolves. Winter snows may blanket the ground until midsummer at higher elevations. Some of the land around the western ridge, and some east of the eastern ridge (in Idaho) is worthy of Wilderness designation.

The Shedroof Divide Trail, the longest path in the area at 21.8 miles, follows the extent of the eastern ridge through open timber and alpine meadows, while the 7.8-mile Crowell Ridge Trail traces the narrower western ridge, offering splendid overviews. A dozen other trails climb drainages to join the two primary ridge trails.

Salmo-Priest Essentials

Size: 41,335 acres.
Year Designated: 1984.
Location: Northeastern Washington.
Easiest Access: From Metaline, take State Highway 31 north for approximately four miles before heading east on County Road 9345 toward Sullivan Lake for approximately four miles. Turn east again on Forest Service Road 22 and continue for approximately 15 miles to Pass Creek Pass and the southern terminus of the Shedroof Divide Trail.
Season: Late spring through early fall.
Wilderness Fees/Permits: None.
Maps: USGS topographic maps are Boundary Dam, Gypsy Peak, Helmer Mountain, Metaline Falls, Pass Creek, and Salmo Mountain.
Management: Sullivan Lake Ranger District, Colville National Forest, 12461 Sullivan Lake Road, Metaline, WA 99153; (509) 775-3305. Priest River Ranger District, Kaniksu National Forest, Route 5, Box 207, Priest River, ID 83856; (208) 443-2512.

San Juan Islands Wilderness

The tips of submerged mountains collectively thrust above the sea where two straits—Georgia and Juan de Fuca—meet up with Puget Sound. Of the 700 or so islands, islets, rocks, and reefs that make up the San Juan Islands, fewer than 200 have garnered official names. The large islands of San Juan, Lopez, Orcas, and Shaw make up more than 80 percent of the landmass. Of the rest of the land, much of it wave-drenched, 84 pieces are included in the San Juan Islands

WASHINGTON

National Wildlife Refuge, a sanctuary for gulls, cormorants, guillemots, puffins, brants, oystercatchers, and auklets. Of these 84 specks of land, 81 have been designated Wilderness: Aleck Rocks, Bare Island, Barren Island, Battleship Island, Bird Rock, Black Rock, Boulder Island, Brown Rock, Buck Island, Castle Island, Center Reef, Clements Reef, Colville Island, Crab Island, Davidson Rock, Dot Island, Eliza Rock, Flattop Island, Flower Island, Fortress Island, Four Bird Rocks, Gull Reef, Gull Rock, Half Tide Rock, Hall Island, Harbor Rock, Lawson Rock, Little Sister Island, two named Low Island, Matia Island (with the exception of five acres of state parkland), Mouatt Reef, Mummy Rocks, Nob Island, North Pacific Rock, North Peapod Rocks, Parker Reef, Peapod Rocks, Pointer Island, Puffin Island, Rim and Rum Islands, Ripple Island, Secar Rock, Sentinel Island, Shag Rock, Shark Reef, Skipjack Island, Skull Island, Small Island, South Peapod Rocks, Swirl Island, The Sisters, Three Williamson Rocks, Tift Rocks, Turn Rock, Viti Rocks, White Rocks, and Willow Island, along with various unnamed islands, islets, rocks, and reefs.

Small boats are allowed to pass near enough to the Wilderness to observe the wildlife (I found the sea kayaking excellent), but public access to the designated land itself is not permitted, with the exception of Matia Island. On Matia you will find four small coves with limited anchorage, moorage in a cove accessing the state park where camping is allowed on the island, and a hiking trail skirting the shoreline.

San Juan Islands Essentials

Size: 353 acres.
Year Designated: 1976.
Location: Off the northwest coast of Washington in Puget Sound.
Easiest Access: Ferries from Anacortes run regularly to San Juan, Orcas, Lopez, and Shaw Islands.
Season: Mid-May until mid-September.
Wilderness Fees/Permits: None.
Maps: USGS topographic maps are Anacortes North, Blakely Island, Deception Pass, Eastsound, Eliza Island, False Bay, Friday Harbor, Lopez Pass, Lummi Island, Mount Constitution, Richardson, Roche Harbor, Shaw Island, Stuart Island, Sucia Island, and Waldron Island.
Management: Nisqually (San Juan Islands) National Wildlife Refuge, 100 Brown Farm Road, Olympia, WA 98506; (360) 753-9467.

Stephen Mather Wilderness

If you're looking for sheer wildness and first-rate alpine climbing, this area may be your best choice in the Lower 48. The North Cascades National Park "Complex" consists of three units: 505,000-acre North Cascades National Park, which boasts 504,614 acres of designated Wilderness; 117,600-acre Ross Lake National Recreation Area, a slim piece of land just east of the park that has 74,000 acres of designated Wilderness; and 62,000-acre Chelan Lake National Recreation Area, at the southeast corner of the park, with 56,000 acres of designated Wilderness.

These three components are combined into Stephen Mather Wilderness, a huge and tremendously rugged piece of earth with jagged glaciated peaks above narrow stream drainages and densely forested U-shaped valleys. The snowfall, which may exceed your imagination in the virtually inaccessible heights, stays on the ground for a long, long time.

WASHINGTON

The Pacific Crest Trail (PCT) crosses the southeastern corner of the park for about 13 miles, but most of the trails tend to be long and crudely rambling. Maps show about 390 miles of pathways, but if trail access determines what you see, you'll see little of the Wilderness. Reaching huge sections of the area can entail multiday hikes, often combined with mountaineering, through remote, trailless territory. I have been grandly "almost lost" here several times. A Wilderness experience of the highest order awaits the prepared.

Stephen Mather Essentials

Size: 634,614 acres.
Year Designated: 1988.
Location: Northwestern Washington.
Easiest Access: From Sedro Wooley, take State Highway 20 east for approximately 100 miles to Rainy Pass and hike south on the PCT. Highway 20 divides the park and provides access to several trailheads.
Season: Summer.
Wilderness Fees/Permits: A free backcountry permit is required and available from the rangers in Sedro Wooley or Marblemount.
Maps: USGS topo maps are Bacon Peak, Big Devil Peak, Cascade Pass, Copper Mountain, Crater Mountain, Damnation Peak, Diablo Dam, Eldorado Peak, Forbidden Peak, Gilbert, Goode Mountain, Hozomeen Mountain, Jack Mountain, Marblemount, McAlester Mountain, McGregor Mountain, Mount Arriva, Mount Blum, Mount Challenger, Mount Logan, Mount Lyall, Mount Prophet, Mount Redoubt, Mount Sefrit, Mount Shuksan, Mount Spickard, Mount Triumph, Pinnacle Mountain, Pumpkin Mountain, Ross Dam, Shuksan Arm, Skagit Peak, Sonny Boy Lakes, Stehekin, and Sun Mountain. Trails Illustrated's Map 223, North Cascades National Park, is an excellent resource.
Management: North Cascades National Park, 2105 Highway 20, Sedro Wooley, WA 98284; (360) 856-5700.

Tatoosh Wilderness

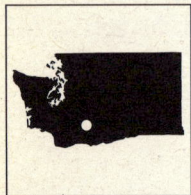

One of five Wilderness areas near Mount Rainier National Park, the Tatoosh shares a portion of the park's southern boundary. Tatoosh Ridge, a long, formidably rugged ridge, runs north-south out of the park to cross the Wilderness near the middle. On the eastern side of the area you'll find the southern tail end of another rocky spine, Backbone Ridge, which also hails from the park. Numerous streams cascade off the ridges into the Muddy Fork of the Cowlitz River or into Butter Creek, both of which in turn funnel down to the Cowlitz River south of the Wilderness. Deer and elk winter along the Muddy Fork, then wander into the higher country in warmer seasons. Black bears may be seen foraging in the forest of hemlock, fir, and red cedar, and mountain goats scramble along the upper elevations, which top out at 6,310-foot Tatoosh Lookout. About 40 feet of snow falls on Tatoosh Ridge during the winter, dusting a half-dozen small lakes (including three that thoroughly satisfy the meaning of "tiny").

The 8.6-mile Tatoosh Trail climbs wickedly steep up Tatoosh Ridge but then mellows out substantially for a long descent off the ridge top and down through subalpine meadows afire with summer wildflowers. I found this ridge to be most definitely worth the effort, and the view of Mount Rainier to the north breathtaking. Side trails will take you to Tatoosh Lakes and Tatoosh Lookout. Camping is not allowed beside the fragile Wilderness lakes.

WASHINGTON

Tatoosh Essentials

Size: 15,720 acres.
Year Designated: 1984.
Location: Southwestern central Washington.
Easiest Access: From Packwood, take U.S. 12 north approximately six miles. Turn west and north on Forest Service Road 52 and continue for approximately four miles, then go east and north on Forest Service Road 5270 for approximately nine miles to find the northern trailhead to the Tatoosh Trail.
Season: Midsummer through early fall.
Wilderness Fees/Permits: None.
Maps: USGS topographic maps are Ohanapecosh Hot Springs, Tatoosh Lakes, and Wahpenayo Peak.
Management: Packwood Ranger District, Gifford Pinchot National Forest, Highway 12, Packwood, WA 98361; (360) 494-5515.

Trapper Creek Wilderness

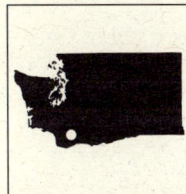

Trapper Creek drains this unspoiled paradise, which consists of heavily forested ridges surrounding a clear turbulent waterway that, with its tributaries, flushes through deep canyons and over sparkling waterfalls on its journey to the Wind River outside the southeast boundary. Soda Peaks Lake, the area's single body of water, gleams from a cirque below Soda Peaks in the southwest corner. Douglas fir, western hemlock, western red cedar, white pine, and true firs grow at lower elevations, giving way higher up to whitebark pine, mountain hemlock, and subalpine fir. Wildflowers literally carpet the mountain meadows in summer. The forest is home to black-tailed deer, black bears, cougars, bobcats, and pine martens, with pikas and marmots abundant on upper rocky slopes. As much as 100 inches of precipitation falls primarily between September and May, much of it as snow. At the northwest corner you'll find Sister Rocks and the Sister Rocks Natural Research Area, which is preserved for the study of subalpine ecosystems. Immediately to the northeast lies the drainage of Bourbon Creek, worthy but undesignated as of today.

The Trapper Creek Trail follows the length of the creek for six miles across the Wilderness, joining other trails to loop back to itself or take you north into the Bourbon Creek drainage. The 5.6-mile Soda Peaks Lake Trail travels to Soda Peaks Lake, and meets the Trapper Creek Trail.

Trapper Creek Essentials

Size: 6,050 acres.
Year Designated: 1984.
Location: Southwestern Washington.
Easiest Access: From Carson, just off Interstate 84, take County Road 8C north approximately 15 miles to Government Mineral Springs Campground and the Trapper Creek Trailhead.
Season: Summer.
Wilderness Fees/Permits: None.
Maps: USGS topographic maps are Bare Mountain and Termination Point. A Trapper Creek Wilderness map is available for $3.25 from the district ranger.
Management: Wind River Ranger District, Gifford Pinchot National Forest, 1262 Hemlock Road, Carson, WA 98610; (509) 427-3200.

WASHINGTON

Washington Islands Wilderness

I have spent many an afternoon perched on a driftwood log, binoculars in hand, watching the birds and marine mammals that inhabit the beach portion of Olympic National Park. Approximately 870 islands, rocks, and reefs comprise Washington Islands National Wildlife Refuges (WINWR). The islands range in size from less than one acre to about 36 acres, and most drop abruptly into the sea. The three refuges combined in WINWR are 125-acre Flattery Rocks, 300-acre Quillayute Needles, and 60-acre Copalis, stretching from Cape Flattery all the way south to Copalis.

Dozens of seabird species (murres, puffins, cormorants, gulls, auklets, petrels, oystercatchers) breed on these fragments of earth and thousands of migratory birds use them as rest stops. The heads of numerous harbor and fur seals, northern and California sea lions, and even whales (including rights, grays, and humpbacks) take turns breaking through the surface of the surrounding water. But if I had to choose a favorite, it would be the infinitely-at-ease sea otters, whose pleasant faces I often saw bobbing playfully among the kelp beds.

All of this wild sea-washed land has been designated Wilderness, and all of it is closed to public entry in order to protect the wildlife, which live with great sensitivity to human trespass.

Washington Islands Essentials

Size: 485 acres.
Year Designated: 1970.
Location: Off the western coast of the Olympic Peninsula.
Easiest Access: You can view the wildlife from the mainland with access points that include Ozette, La Push, and Pacific Beach. Pacific Beach lies on State Highway 109, approximately 30 miles north of Aberdeen.
Season: Year-round.
Wilderness Fees/Permits: None are required to just watch.
Maps: USGS topographic maps are Allens Bay, Bodelteh Islands, Cape Flattery, Destruction Island, Hoh Head, La Push, Makah Bay, Moclips, Ozette, Quillayute Prairie, Shale Slough, Taholah, Toleak Point, and Tunnel Island.
Management: Washington Islands National Wildlife Refuges, 33 South Barr Road, Port Angeles, WA 98362; (360) 457-8451.

Wenaha-Tucannon Wilderness

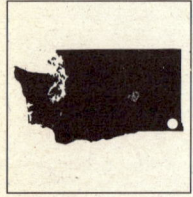

This Wilderness is a maze of deep, sheer-walled canyons that cut into what was once a flat and expansive plateau at the northernmost reach of the Blue Mountains. The plateau has since eroded into long ridge tops and wide, forest-covered mesas that now stand as much as 2,000 feet above the drainages. Following ridges will often bring you to dead ends that fall away vertically into a confluence of drainages. Much of the area's water runs south into Oregon's Wild and Scenic Wenaha River, although some of it slips north into Washington's Tucannon River. Ponderosa pine dominates the lower drainages, then defers to a forest of lodgepole pine above about 4,500 feet, with some larch, fir, and spruce. Subalpine fir reigns supreme at the highest elevations, with grasses covering the ground. Large herds of Rocky Mountain elk thrive in this area, which subsequently attracts more hunters than hikers. Rattlesnakes love the area, too, and you may

WASHINGTON

see mule deer, white-tailed deer, black bears, coyotes, cougars, bobcats, marmots, and snowshoe hares. Snow falls and accumulates about two feet deep between November and April. Summers are typically very hot and very dry. Approximately one-third of the Wilderness lies in Oregon (see Oregon, Wenaha-Tucannon Wilderness).

Most of a fairly extensive trail system stays high on the open ridges, winding and connecting often enough to provide long loops through the Washington side and down into Oregon. Several trailheads are equipped for easy unloading and loading of horses, including the Washington campgrounds of Panjab, Godman, and Tepee, and horsepackers will find few areas more suitable. The Rattlesnake Trail climbs steeply for the first half of its five miles to level out in the second half, where it joins four other trails.

Wenaha-Tucannon Essentials

Size: 111,048 acres in Washington (177,423 acres total).
Year Designated: 1978.
Location: Southeastern Washington.
Easiest Access: From Dayton, take U.S. 12 north approximately 14 miles. Turn east and south on Forest Service Road 47, which follows the Tucannon River for about 30 miles to where Forest Service Roads 4712 and 4713 split. The Panjab Campground and the Rattlesnake Trailhead are near the split on the 4713 side.
Season: Spring or fall.
Wilderness Fees/Permits: None.
Maps: USGS topographic maps are Deadman Peak, Diamond Peak, Godman Spring, Panjab Creek, Saddle Butte, and Stentz Spring in Washington. (Bone Spring, Eden, Elbow Creek, and Wenaha Forks in Oregon.) A Wilderness map is available for $2 from the district ranger.
Management: Pomeroy Ranger District, Umatilla National Forest, Route 1, Box 53-F, Pomeroy, WA 99347; (509) 843-1891.

William O. Douglas Wilderness

This magnificent region pays tribute to the Wilderness-loving Supreme Court justice who often explored the area on foot. It lies bordered to the west by Mount Rainier National Park, with Norse Peak and Goat Rocks Wildernesses just to the north and south, respectively. Non-Wilderness roads drive into the area from the north, up Bumping River to a non-Wilderness central section around Bumping Lake. From the lake, the wild terrain rises west and east to high, broad ridges capped with rock summits. Subalpine meadows and thick old-growth forestland of fir, hemlock, and cedar distinguish the lower elevations. Beyond the east ridge, the land descends to open ridges and tall ponderosa pine. The southern portion of the Wilderness spreads out into a large parklike plateau, where the forest thins and 59 lakes lie among another 200 or so ponds and pools. You may see members of large herds of elk and mule deer, who reside here with fishers and foxes, mountain goats and grouse. As much as 120 inches of precipitation per year drowns the western side of the area, while the eastern side may get as little as 20 to 24 inches. Snow usually starts to fall by November, and often lingers in patches up high until midsummer.

Sixty-six trails crisscross the Wilderness for a total of about 250 miles, providing access to just about everything the Wilderness has to offer. All but two trails are open to horsepackers (the exceptions being the Ironstone Mountain Trail and the Goat Peak Trail). Indeed, the land may be best appreciated from a saddle. The Pacific Crest Trail (PCT) traces the western ridge and rambles across the southern plateau for a total of 13.5 miles.

WASHINGTON

William O. Douglas Essentials

Size: 166,603 acres.
Year Designated: 1984.
Location: Southwestern central Washington.
Easiest Access: From Yakima, take U.S. 12 west approximately 45 miles to White Pass Campground, where the PCT heads north into the Wilderness.
Season: June through October.
Wilderness Fees/Permits: None.
Maps: USGS topographic maps are Bumping Lake, Chinook Pass, Cougar Lake, Goose Prairie, Meeks Table, Norse Peak, Old Scab Mountain, Rimrock Lake, Spiral Butte, Timberwolf Mountain, and White Pass.
Management: Naches Ranger District, Wenatchee National Forest, 10061 Highway 12, Naches, WA 98937; (509) 653-2205. Packwood Ranger District, Gifford Pinchot National Forest, Highway 12, Packwood, WA 98361; (360) 494-5515.

Wonder Mountain Wilderness

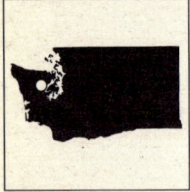

From near the southeast corner of Olympic National Park, little Wonder Mountain Wilderness extends south roughly in the shape of a triangle. A high ridge encompasses the southern point of the triangle, rising to the abrupt rocky peak of 4,848-foot Wonder Mountain. Below the summit, a heavy forest of western hemlock, Douglas fir, and silver fir reaches northward into the park. Within the Wilderness, the headwaters of McKay Creek and Five Stream emerge from four tiny secluded lakes, the only bodies of water in the area, that bear no names. A thick jungle of alder, willow, and vine maple grows along the creeks. A year's worth of precipitation sometimes reaches 60 inches, often falling as snow, and summer temperatures seldom top 80 degrees Fahrenheit.

No trails cross this rarely visited Wilderness, nor do any trails lead to its boundaries. Two forest roads that run relatively near the southeast and southwest borders close in fall and winter to provide protection for wildlife. Difficult hiking over steep forested slopes and along exposed ridges through tangles of huckleberry and thimbleberry will give you a Wilderness experience seldom surpassed in primitive solitude and exertion.

Wonder Mountain Essentials

Size: 2,320 acres.
Year Designated: 1984.
Location: Northwestern Washington on the Olympic Peninsula.
Easiest Access: From Hoodsport, take State Route 119 north approximately five miles to Lake Cushman. Continue north on Forest Service Road 24 for approximately five miles, then head west on Forest Service Road 2451 for nine miles to the end of the line, and start bushwhacking south.
Season: Spring and summer.
Wilderness Fees/Permits: None.
Maps: USGS topographic maps are Mount Olson and Mount Tebo.
Management: Hood Canal Ranger District, Olympic National Forest, P.O. Box 68, Hoodsport, WA 98548; (360) 877-5254.

> "Within these plantations of God a decorum and sanctity reign, a perennial festival is dressed, and the guest sees not how he could tire of them in a thousand years. In the woods we return to reason and faith."
>
> —Ralph Waldo Emerson

WEST VIRGINIA

Total Wilderness areas: 5
Total Wilderness acreage: 80,631

Prior to 1920, when Monongahela National Forest was established, most of the woods of West Virginia had been destroyed by loggers. Today, a thick new cover of second-growth trees stands on the scenic mountains of the eastern part of the state. Rich forestland covers the headwaters of five major rivers (some are favorites of white-water enthusiasts) and hundreds of miles of streams that are alive with native and stocked trout. There are four U.S. Forest Service–managed Wilderness areas in the region. A fifth Wilderness lies on U.S. Forest Service land in the southern part of the state.

Cranberry Wilderness

Broad mountains are dissected by deep and narrow valleys with elevations ranging from 2,400 feet to more than 4,600 feet in Cranberry Wilderness, the largest such area in West Virginia. Here on the Allegheny Plateau, the Wilderness contains the entire drainage of the Middle Fork of the Williams River and the North Fork of the Cranberry River. The Williams River forms the northern Wilderness boundary, and the South Fork of the Cranberry River marks the southwestern boundary. You'll find primarily Appalachian hardwoods, but there are also stands of red spruce at the highest elevations. Cranberry Wilderness is contained within the Black Bear Sanctuary. Black bears are abundant and share the Wilderness with white-tailed deer, wild turkeys, grouse, rabbits, mink, bobcats, and foxes. Naturally acidic water limits the fish populations, and the streams are not stocked. Frost may occur any month of the year. Precipitation (rain or snow) falls in winter, spring, and fall. Winter snow may block road access.

More than 50 miles of maintained hiking trails provide access to the area on at least 10 named paths. Trails follow both the rivers. The Middle Fork Trail runs for nine miles, and the North Fork Trail for 7.5 miles. There are no trails maintained for horses and no bridges over streams. You'll have to wade across them. This works fine during dry months, but it is not advisable during periods of high water.

WEST VIRGINIA

Cranberry Essentials

Size: 35,864 acres.
Year Designated: 1983.
Location: Eastern West Virginia.
Easiest Access: Take the Highland Scenic Highway (Route 150) west from U.S. 219 for approximately 12 miles. Turn west on Forest Service Road 86, which follows the Williams River to two trailheads on the south side of the road, one within approximately one mile, the second within about five miles.

Season: Summer.
Wilderness Fees/Permits: None.
Maps: USGS topographic maps are Hillsboro, Lobelia, Webster Springs SE, Webster Springs SW, and Woodrow, all of which are available for $4 from the district ranger.
Management: Gauley Ranger District, Monongahela National Forest, Box 110, Richwood, WV 26261; (304) 846-2695.

Dolly Sods Wilderness

In the mid-1800s, the Dalhe family used open grassy fields called "sods" for grazing sheep in this area, which now bears the name Dolly Sods Wilderness. The region, located high on the Allegheny Plateau, is known for its extensive rocky plains, upland bogs, and sweeping vistas. In the lower elevations, you'll find a forest of northern hardwoods and laurel thickets. Higher up, groves of wind-stunted red spruce stand near heath barrens where azaleas, mountain laurels, rhododendron, and blueberries grow. The bogs are unique depressions of sphagnum moss, cranberries, and the insect-eating sundew plant—an ecosystem you'd expect to see in northern Canada. Beaver ponds dot the Wilderness and the headwaters of Red Creek spill out of the area.

Nine trails crisscross this Wilderness. They are relatively rough and wet most of the year. The Red Creek Trail runs north-south for approximately eight miles, moist and rocky across the entire area, and splashes through Red Creek at least twice. The Breathed Mountain Trail climbs abruptly from the west side of Red Creek to level off in the high plateau country. Solitude may be difficult to find unless you wander off-trail. This is easily the most popular Wilderness in West Virginia, and the amount of foot traffic proves it. Maximum group size is 10.

Dolly Sods Essentials

Size: 10,215 acres.
Year Designated: 1975.
Location: Eastern West Virginia.
Easiest Access: From Elkins, take U.S. 33 east for approximately 25 miles. Turn north on State Route 32 at Harmon and continue driving for approximately five miles. Then turn east on State Route 45 (Laneville Road) and drive for 10 miles to the Dolly Sods Picnic Area. This road becomes quite rough and gravelly. You'll find a parking lot at the south end of the Red Creek Trail as you cross Red Creek before the picnic area.

Season: May through July.
Wilderness Fees/Permits: None.
Maps: USGS topographic maps are Blackbird Knob, Blackwater Falls, Hopeville, and Laneville; all can be ordered for $4 from the district ranger.
Management: Potomac Ranger District, Monongahela National Forest, Route 3, Box 240, Petersburg, WV 26847; (304) 257-4388.

WEST VIRGINIA

Laurel Fork North/ Laurel Fork South Wilderness

Although sometimes listed as two areas, Laurel Fork Wilderness straddles the Laurel Fork of the Cheat River and only the corridor of Route 40 separates the north and south portions. The narrow river valley runs north-south below regularly dissected slopes and long, slim ridges, fed by numerous side streams. Immediately to the east stands Rich Mountain; to the west looms Middle Mountain, with elevations over 3,700 feet. An almost continuous forest cover dominated by beech, maple, black cherry, birch, and yellow poplar is broken only by grassy meadows along the Laurel Fork itself. White-tailed deer live here with wild turkeys, bobcats, and beavers. You might occasionally spot a few black bears, although you're more likely to see some of the myriad resident bird species. You may catch native brook and brown trout in the river, but heavy brush can make casting difficult. Winters typically bring heavy snows; temperatures are pleasant in summer.

The Laurel River North and Laurel River South Trails, both five miles long, follow the river from a central trailhead. Seven side trails—three in the north portion and four in the south—leave the Wilderness west on Forest Service Road 14. No trails exist on the east side of the area.

Laurel Fork North/Laurel Fork South Essentials

Size: 6,055 acres in the north; 5,997 acres in the south (12,052 acres total).
Year Designated: 1983.
Location: Eastern West Virginia.
Easiest Access: From Elkins, take U.S. 33 east for about 15 miles to Wymer. Turn south on Forest Service Road 14 and continue driving for approximately 10 miles. Head east on Route 40 for approximately one mile to Laurel Fork Campground and the main trailhead.
Season: Summer.
Wilderness Fees/Permits: None.
Maps: USGS topographic maps are Glady and the Sinks of Gandy.
Management: Greenbrier Ranger District, Monongahela National Forest, Box 67, Bartow, WV 24920; (304) 456-3335.

Mountain Lake Wilderness

Three-fourths of Mountain Lake Wilderness is situated in Virginia and consists of highland plateau sitting squarely on the Eastern Continental Divide (see Mountain Lake Wilderness in Virginia). You'll find stands of virgin spruce and hemlock, some bogland, and elevations ranging from 2,200 feet to 4,100 feet. The diversity of flora and fauna is significant. Little Mountain dominates the West Virginia portion, and crisscrossing trails access this part of the area. From the Appalachian Trail, which passes through the area on the Virginia side, the Potts Mountain Trail enters West Virginia, providing a route to the top of Little Mountain. At this point, the trail splits off and drops down to two hollows and then leaves the northern boundary, for a distance (in West Virginia) of about three miles. You should find ample opportunities for solitude and primitive recreation.

523

WEST VIRGINIA

Mountain Lake Essentials

Size: 2,500 acres in West Virginia (10,753 acres total).
Year Designated: 1988.
Location: Southern West Virginia.
Easiest Access: From Blacksburg, Virginia, take U.S. 460 north and west for approximately 10 miles. Then turn north on State Route 613 and continue driving for approximately 12 miles until the Appalachian Trail crosses the road. Hike east on the Appalachian Trail into Mountain Lake Wilderness.
Season: Summer.
Wilderness Fees/Permits: None.
Maps: USGS topographic maps are Eggleston, Interior, Newport, and Waiteville.
Management: Blacksburg Ranger District, Jefferson National Forest, 110 Southpark Drive, Blacksburg, VA 24060; (703) 552-4641.

Otter Creek Wilderness

In a natural bowl between Shavers Mountain (on the east side) and McGowan Mountain (on the west side) lies Otter Creek Wilderness. Most of the numerous streams in the area flow into Otter Creek, which runs north across the Wilderness into the Dry Fork River. These streams frequently flash flood during periods of heavy rain. From the mouth of Otter Creek, the terrain rises to about 3,900 feet on McGowan Mountain. The area, logged extensively between 1897 and 1914, now sports a second-growth forest, dense thickets of rhododendron and mountain laurel along the streams, and a variety of mosses in damper regions. Spruce dominate the higher country and give way to hardwoods such as black cherry and yellow birch lower down. Black bears have returned and are reunited with white-tailed deer, wild turkeys, hares, rabbits, grouse, and several species of squirrels. Beavers are active in several spots. Timber rattlesnakes may be seen, and Otter Creek shelters a small population of brook trout.

You can explore the Wilderness on 42 miles of trails, many following old railroad grades. The longest and most used path is the Otter Creek Trail, more than 11 miles long, which follows Otter Creek with bridge access across Dry Fork River on the north end. Once on the trail, you'll have to ford the creek several times. Two slowly deteriorating shelters exist in the area: one near Devil's Gulch, one on Shavers Mountain.

Otter Creek Essentials

Size: 20,000 acres.
Year Designated: 1975.
Location: Eastern West Virginia.
Easiest Access: From Elkins, take U.S. 219 north for approximately 20 miles. Turn south on Forest Route 701 and continue for approximately five miles until you reach the Otter Creek Trailhead.
Season: Summer.
Wilderness Fees/Permits: None.
Maps: USGS topographic maps are Bowden, Harmon, Mozark Mountain, and Parsons. The trails of Otter Creek Wilderness (and the other Wildernesses of West Virginia) are well covered in the *Monongahela National Forest Hiking Guide*, available from West Virginia Highlands Conservancy, P.O. Box 306, Charleston, WV 25321 ($12.85 total).
Management: Cheat Ranger District, Monongahela National Forest, P.O. Box 368, Parsons, WV 26287; (304) 478-3251.

> "Leave [Wilderness] as it is. You cannot improve it. The ages have been at work on it and man can only mar it. What you can do is keep it for your children, your children's children, and for all who come after you."
> —Theodore Roosevelt

WISCONSIN

Total Wilderness areas: 6
Total Wilderness acreage: 43,988

In 1634, the French explorer Jean Nicolet first walked the darkly wooded shores of Lake Superior and Lake Michigan in the area we now call northern Wisconsin. Nicolet National Forest, a 658,000-acre wildland, was named in his memory. Within the Nicolet, three smaller Wilderness areas have been deemed worthy of designation. In addition, the 850,000-acre Chequamegon National Forest protects two more Wildernesses. A sixth tiny Wilderness is managed by the U.S. Fish and Wildlife Service.

Blackjack Springs Wilderness

In the midst of dense tree cover in Nicolet National Forest, typical of the Lake Superior Highlands, four large crystal-clear springs form the headwaters of Blackjack Creek. Here, glaciation from the last ice age has produced a rolling and uneven terrain. In the northeastern section, you will find the delightfully named Whispering Lake, surrounded by forest that provides habitat for black bears, deer, fishers, ruffed grouse, and a variety of sweet-throated songbirds. Three streams drain the area, and produce occasional ponds and wetlands. Visitors come to hunt and fish, paddle and hike.

Ten trails enter the area, with at least one from each of the four directions. From the Whispering Lake Trailhead near Whispering Lake, a path leads one-half mile to the lake itself with one branch leaving the trail and crossing the northern section for approximately two miles. To follow the Blackjack Creek Trail to Blackjack Springs, enter from the northwest corner at a trailhead off Forest Service Road 21990 and hike about one mile. Follow the creek upstream to reach the heart of the Wilderness.

WISCONSIN

Blackjack Springs Essentials

Size: 5,886 acres.
Year Designated: 1978.
Location: Northeastern Wisconsin.
Easiest Access: From Eagle River, take State Route 70 east less than 10 miles toward Anvil Lake Recreation Site. Then turn north on Forest Service Road 2178, and continue driving for approximately six miles to the Whispering Lake Trailhead.

Season: Summer brings the most recreational hikers. In the fall, the hardwood forest turns scarlet and gold.
Wilderness Fees/Permits: None.
Maps: USGS topographic maps are Anvil Lake and Phelps.
Management: Eagle River Ranger District, Nicolet National Forest, 4364 Wall Street, Eagle River, WI 54521; (715) 479-2827.

Headwaters Wilderness

The largest of Wisconsin's Wildernesses is characterized by generally flat terrain with forested swamps and muskeg, and bog lowlands overlooked by a few hardwood ridges. The headwaters of Pine River, a legally protected Wild River, lie within the area. In the southern portion, you'll find the Giant Pine Grove and Shelp Lake, where some of the largest and oldest trees of Nicolet National Forest grow. The quiet waters of Shelp Lake, shadowed by towering pines on the southwest Wilderness boundary, are worth a peek. Deer hunting, bass fishing, hiking, and a chance for solitude lure people to Headwaters.

The area is subdivided into three sections: The northern half for the most part consists of the Kimball Creek Unit, drained by Kimball and several other creeks. The Shelp Lake Unit lies in the southwestern portion, with Shelp Lake in the southwest corner. Finally, Headwaters of the Pine Unit comprises the southeast portion. All three units are crisscrossed with trails off Forest Service roads that border the entire Wilderness.

Headwaters Essentials

Size: 19,950 acres.
Year Designated: 1984.
Location: Northeastern Wisconsin.
Easiest Access: From Eagle River, take State Route 70 east about 10 miles. Turn south on Forest Service Road 2178 and continue for approximately 17 miles to find Shelp Lake.

Season: Spring, when the wildflowers bloom.
Wilderness Fees/Permits: None.
Maps: USGS topographic maps are Alvin NW, Alvin SW, and Julia.
Management: Eagle River Ranger District, Nicolet National Forest, 4364 Wall Street, Eagle River, WI 54521; (715) 479-2827.

WISCONSIN

Porcupine Lake Wilderness

The North Country National Scenic Trail carves a path for approximately eight miles through the very heart of this forest, half of which is rich with sugar maples, red maples, and yellow birches, while the other half supports aspen, red oak, hemlocks, white pine, balsam fir, cedar, spruce, and tamarack. Touching the northern tip of Porcupine Lake itself, the trail is part of the proposed system that will eventually reach from New York to North Dakota. Within the Wilderness, only two other short trails, entering from the northern boundary, are maintained, and both join the North Country Trail.

During the ice age, glaciers covered this area, scouring it into mild to moderate hiking terrain: rolling hills in the west dropping to swampland in the east. Black bears are frequently seen; store your food off the ground and well away from campsites. Many lakes dot the area—six of them larger than five acres. Most of them are located in the western portion. Fishing and paddling attract visitors to 75-acre Porcupine Lake, which is filled with northern pike, largemouth bass, and bluegill. All of the major streams in this area contain trout. Cross-country skiers enjoy this Wilderness in winter.

Porcupine Lake Essentials

Size: 4,195 acres.
Year Designated: 1984.
Location: Northern Wisconsin.
Easiest Access: From the junction of U.S. 2 and U.S. 63 west of Ashland, go south on U.S. 63 for about 15 miles. Turn south on County Highway D at Grand View and continue for about 4.5 miles to reach the North Country Trail at East Davis Lake.
Season: Fall for the color; winter for the artistry of snowfall.
Wilderness Fees/Permits: None.
Maps: USGS topographic maps are Diamond Lake and Grand View.
Management: Hayward Ranger District, Chequamegon National Forest, Route 10, Box 508, Hayward, WI 54843; (715) 634-4821.

Rainbow Lake Wilderness

Slightly more than six miles of the North Country National Scenic Trail cross this Wilderness from northwest to southeast, passing close to Rainbow Lake itself. Anderson Grade is the only other maintained pathway, crossing from east to west for about four miles. Rolling terrain stands cloaked in northern hardwoods, balsam fir, pine, and paper birch that provide shelter for deer, black bears, red foxes, and coyotes. Hiking is relatively easy. Bald eagles, hawks, owls, loons, woodpeckers, and songbirds enliven the skies, and waterfowl are often seen on Reynard and Wishbone Lakes. Thousands of migrating birds stop for a rest in spring and fall.

Anglers should find the panfishing excellent on Rainbow Lake, and very good in the 15 other lakes and nine small ponds. The lakes also attract canoeists. Cross-country skiers come for the winter snow. The area is tightly bordered by Forest Service roads, providing easy access.

WISCONSIN

Rainbow Lake Essentials

Size: 6,583 acres.
Year Designated: 1975.
Location: Northern Wisconsin.
Easiest Access: From Drummond on U.S. 63, take Forest Service Road 35 north about three miles. Turn west on Forest Service Road 392 and continue for three-fourths of a mile to the North Country Trailhead on the southern Wilderness boundary.

Season: Most hikers come in summer. In winter, cross-country skiers flock here.
Wilderness Fees/Permits: None.
Maps: USGS topographic maps are T45N, R8W and T46N, R8W.
Management: Washburn Ranger District, Chequamegon National Forest, 113 South Bayfield Street, Washburn, WI 54891; (715) 373-2667.

Whisker Lake Wilderness

Located on the Michigan-Wisconsin border, this area takes its name from the large trees near the shoreline of Whisker Lake. These old pines were called "chin whiskers" by locals. Surprisingly, they were unscathed by logging and wildfires, both of which ravaged the region in the early 1900s. Here you'll find rolling uplands falling away to wetlands flooded by beaver activity. Six small lakes and three major streams provide trout fishing that can be worth the effort, most notably Riley Lake, Edith Lake (which is split by the eastern boundary), Wakefield Creek, and the Brule River. The Brule forms the northern boundary and separates Nicolet National Forest from Michigan.

Hiking and camping, as in the other forestland Wildernesses of Wisconsin, are unrestricted. Six trails enter from the western side, and two of them exit from the eastern side. The Whisker Lake Trail crosses the entire Wilderness in an east-west direction, a distance of approximately 2.5 miles, with access to the lake itself. Deer hunting is allowed in season, and winter brings cross-country skiers.

Whisker Lake Essentials

Size: 7,345 acres.
Year Designated: 1978.
Location: Northeastern Wisconsin.
Easiest Access: From U.S. 2 at Florence, take State Route 70 west approximately 20 miles. Turn north on Forest Service Road 2150 and continue approximately four miles to a parking area and the Whisker Lake Trailhead.

Season: Many visitors come in late summer to pick berries. Fall brings hunters.
Wilderness Fees/Permits: None.
Maps: A topographic map of Whisker Lake is available for $4.50 from the district ranger.
Management: Florence Ranger District, Nicolet National Forest, HC 1, Box 83, Florence, WI 54121; (715) 528-4464.

WISCONSIN

Wisconsin Islands Wilderness

Three small limestone outcroppings in Lake Michigan—Gravel Island, by far the largest at 27 acres, and tiny Spider and Hog Islands—are managed as national wildlife refuges. Designated protected areas, they provide important nesting grounds for colonial birds, especially herring gulls, ring-billed gulls, and double-crested cormorants. Because human contact could easily destroy these fragile and threatened communities, the public is not permitted to set foot on the islands. Boaters are asked to stay at least a quarter-mile offshore so as not to endanger the nesting areas. Bring your binoculars if you want to take a peek. Hazardous shoals surround the Wilderness trio, which further protects the safety of the birds and preserves the wildness of the islands.

Wisconsin Islands Essentials

Size: 29 acres.
Year Designated: 1970.
Location: One mile off the northeastern shore of Wisconsin.
Easiest Access: From Green Bay, take State Highway 57 northeast to Sturgeon Bay, a distance of approximately 46 miles. From the town of Sturgeon Bay, take State Highway 42 north for approximately 40 miles to the end of the road. From there, take the ferry across to Washington Island. Cross the island (which only has one road) to Rock Island State Park on its northern side. Launch your boat for a 10-mile trip to Saint Martin Island. From the east side of Saint Martin, you should have a clear view of the protected Wilderness area. Boaters and kayakers should take care not to paddle too close to the island. In no case should anyone attempt to land on shore. One unintended footfall can destroy a generation of endangered birds.
Season: Spring and early summer for the nesting birds.
Wilderness Fees/Permits: No permits are available.
Maps: Ask the refuge manager.
Management: Horicon National Wildlife Refuge, W4279 Headquarters Road, Mayville, WI 53050; (414) 387-2658.

> "Wilderness itself is the basis of all our civilization. I wonder if we have enough reverence for life to concede to wilderness the right to live on?"
>
> —Margaret Murie

WYOMING

Total Wilderness areas: 15
Total Wilderness acreage: 3,084,640

Although Yellowstone and Grand Teton National Parks are the most prominent natural attractions, wild Wyoming is by no means limited to these scenic and often overcrowded places. National forestland in the state encompasses more than four times the acreage of these two national parks, and includes Bridger-Teton National Forest, the second largest forest outside of Alaska. Wyoming's Wilderness areas are extraordinarily vast, diverse, and scenic. Big-game hunting and fishing have been the primary draws for visitors, but the hiking trails—rapidly growing in popularity—are unparalleled in the United States, providing access to virtually untouched wilderness for mile after mile.

Absaroka-Beartooth Wilderness

Only a relatively small portion of the extensive Absaroka-Beartooth Wilderness lies in Wyoming (see Montana, Absaroka-Beartooth Wilderness). The area—just the southern tip of the Eastern Unit—is dominated by the high granitic alpine plateaus of the Beartooth Mountains, a starkly beautiful country of expansive views, hidden lakes among bald rocks, and wildly unpredictable weather. Cold and wind may strike any day of the year.

Boulder-strewn Beartooth Plateau lies between 9,000 and 10,000 feet below bare crags and peaks streaked with red and yellow. The plateau is cut by deep canyons and carpeted in wildflowers when the snow melts in June. This is an extremely fragile environment.

The lakes are rich in trout, and the air teems with mosquitoes in summer. Wildlife is abundant in the forested valleys: moose, elk, and mule deer live here with grizzly bears. On barren ridges you'll see little except pikas and the occasional mountain goat and bighorn sheep. An extensive network of trails is often under snow in mid-June.

Absaroka-Beartooth Essentials

Size: 23,750 acres in Wyoming (944,060 acres total).
Year Designated: 1984.
Location: Northwestern Wyoming.
Easiest Access: From Cody, take State Highway 120 north for 17 miles. Turn west on the exceptionally scenic, partly gravel Sunlight Basin Road (State Highway 296) and continue for 51 miles. Turn east on U.S. 212, which runs along the southern boundary. Within approximately 10 miles, you'll find two campgrounds from which you can hike into the Wilderness to the north.
Season: Summer and early fall. Snow often closes the roads before November.
Wilderness Fees/Permits: None.
Maps: A Wilderness map is available for $3.75 from the Grand Teton Natural History Association, P.O. Box 170, Moose, WY 83012.
Management: Clarks Fork Ranger District, Shoshone National Forest, 1002 Road 11, Powell, WY 82435; (307) 754-7207.

Bridger Wilderness

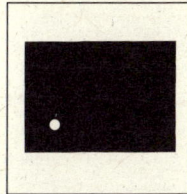

Jim Bridger, certainly one of the most famous mountain men in American history, is memorialized by this popular Wilderness area in the Wind River Range of Wyoming. Here is scenic wildland at its finest, a rugged piece of the Rocky Mountains on the western slope of the Continental Divide. It holds 7 of the 10 largest glaciers in the Lower 48, and at least 1,300 cold crystalline lakes and numerous glacier-carved cirques, kettles, valleys, and hanging troughs. Many clear streams feed the Green and Sweetwater Rivers. Gannett Peak (on the shared border with Fitzpatrick Wilderness, see below), the highest point in Wyoming at 13,804 feet, towers above a vast area of stark granite summits that were once thrust violently into the sky by enormous compressional forces within the earth. I have spent some of the best weeks of my life here, awestruck by the views, cowering in dense stands of trees during late summer thunderstorms, feasting on huge trout, and wandering aimlessly for miles well beyond the nearest trail in country that Wilderness dreams are made of.

More than 600 miles of trails provide access to this seemingly boundless area. One of my favorite trails enters from Big Sandy and crosses Jackass Pass into the Cirque of the Towers, a hike of six or seven miles. The Cirque is an almost circular rise of bold rock faces with virtually unlimited routes for rock climbing.

The majority of the visitors come to backpack. Horsepacking, fly-fishing, and hunting bring the others. Campfires are allowed only below timberline and may only be fueled by down and dead material. Snow usually lingers on the high trails until mid-July, but the lower pathways are open by late spring or early summer. It can freeze any night of the year, even after warm, sunny summer days.

In July and August, mosquitoes and biting flies are inescapable anywhere near water. But you'll also encounter more appealing wildlife, including moose, elk, bighorn sheep, mule deer, and badgers. Other Wilderness denizens that you are likely to see include yellow-bellied marmots whistling from sun-washed rocks, little round-eared pikas, and beavers working busily in their pearl-like ponds. Visitors should take precautions against black bears, who are becoming uncharacteristically bold.

WYOMING

Bridger Essentials

Size: 428,169 acres.
Year Designated: 1964; expanded in 1984.
Location: Western Wyoming.
Easiest Access: From Pinedale, take U.S. 191 south about 14 miles to Boulder. Turn east on State Route 353 and continue for approximately 20 miles to Big Sandy. Head east on Forest Service Road 116 for approximately 20 miles to Big Sandy Campground.
Season: Summer and fall. I prefer fall.
Wilderness Fees/Permits: None, unless you are part of an organized group, such as a school or club, or an overnight horsepacking group, in which case you must obtain a permit (they are available for free). Those visiting Bridger Wilderness for commercial purposes are required to pay a fee.
Maps: A district map that includes the Wilderness is available for $3.75 from the Grand Teton Natural History Association, P.O. Box 170, Moose, WY 83012.
Management: Pinedale Ranger District, Bridger-Teton National Forest, P.O. Box 220, Pinedale, WY 82941; (307) 367-4326.

Cloud Peak Wilderness

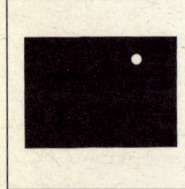

Long recognized as having some of the most majestic alpine scenery in America, this region was managed as the Cloud Peak Primitive Area as far back as 1932. For 27 miles along the spine of the Bighorn Mountain Range, Cloud Peak Wilderness preserves many sharp summits and towering sheer rock faces standing above glacier-carved U-shaped valleys. Named for the tallest mountain in Bighorn National Forest—Cloud Peak at 13,167 feet—the Wilderness is blanketed in snow for a large part of the year. Most of the higher ground doesn't show bare ground until July. On the east side of Cloud Peak itself, a deeply inset cirque holds the last remaining glacier in this range. Several hundred beautiful lakes, many offering excellent trout fishing, cover the landscape and drain into miles of trout streams. The forest is an attractive mix of pine and spruce opened by meadows and wetlands.

Although rugged in appearance, the Bighorns are actually more gentle than other mountains in Wyoming. Once used primarily by hunters and anglers, the area is now visited each year by thousands and thousands of backpackers who hike along more than 100 miles of maintained trails. The Misty Moon Trail (6.5 miles) climbs steadily north from the subalpine timber near West Tensleep Lake to open alpine meadows and a number of striking lakes, with access to Florence Pass and Cloud Peak to the north.

Cloud Peak Essentials

Size: 195,500 acres.
Year Designated: 1984.
Location: Northern Wyoming.
Easiest Access: From Tensleep, take U.S. 16 east for approximately 18 miles. Turn north on Forest Route 604 (West Tensleep Lake Road) and continue driving for seven miles to West Tensleep Lake Campground and the Misty Moon Trailhead.
Season: July through September.
Wilderness Fees/Permits: None.
Maps: A free Wilderness map is available from the district rangers. USGS topographic maps are Caribou Creek, Cloud Peak, Dome Lake, Hunter Mesa, Lake Angeline, Lake Helen, Lake Solitude, Little Goose Peak, Meadowlark Lake, Park Reservoir, Powder River Pass, Shell Lake, Shell Reservoir, Spanish Point, and Willow Park Reservoir.
Management: Buffalo Ranger District, Bighorn National Forest, 300 Spruce Street, Buffalo, WY 82834; (307) 684-7981. Paintrock Ranger District, Bighorn National Forest, 1220 North Eighth Street, Greybull, WY 82462; (307) 765-4435. Tensleep Ranger District, Bighorn National Forest, 2009 Big Horn Avenue, Worland, WY 82401; (307) 347-8291. Tongue Ranger District, Bighorn National Forest, 1969 South Sheridan Avenue, Sheridan, WY 82801; (307) 672-0751.

Encampment River Wilderness

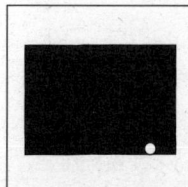

Here in the northernmost extension of the Southern Rocky Mountains, the Encampment River flows north out of Colorado, past the town of Encampment and into the North Platte River. Along part of the river's canyon lies Wyoming's smallest Wilderness, approximately 16 square miles, a strip less than one mile wide in the southern portion that widens to about five miles near the northern boundary. Throughout the canyon, the river runs from wild rapids to peacefully placid stretches, and is home to brook, rainbow, and brown trout (the fishing can be worth the hike). Sagebrush grows on the open slopes, and the canyon is full of riparian vegetation.

The Encampment River Trail runs the length of this narrow, rugged river canyon, one of the main attractions of the Wilderness. The lower five miles are relatively easy to hike, although the terrain becomes increasingly difficult in the remaining 10 upper miles. The trail receives moderate use by hikers. Along the way you'll pass ruins of old cabins and mining operations. You may see members of a large wildlife population: mule deer, elk, Rocky Mountain bighorn sheep. The river runs wildly over rocks, creating rapids that only expert kayakers dare to attempt.

WYOMING

Encampment River Essentials

Size: 10,400 acres.
Year Designated: 1984.
Location: Central southern Wyoming.
Easiest Access: From the west edge of Encampment, turn south on the signed gravel road. Take a short drive to the BLM's Encampment River Campground and trailhead. Follow the trail down the canyon about five miles.
Season: From snowmelt in spring until the first snow in the fall.

Wilderness Fees/Permits: None.
Maps: Topographic maps for this area (as well as any area of Wyoming) may be ordered from the Geological Survey of Wyoming, P.O. Box 3008, University Station, Laramie, WY 82071-3008; (307) 766-2286.
Management: Hayden Ranger District, Medicine Bow National Forest, 204 West Ninth Street, P.O. Box 187, Encampment, WY 82325; (307) 327-5481.

Fitzpatrick Wilderness

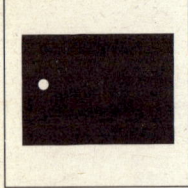

Originally called the Glacier Primitive Area, this Wilderness now holds 44 active glaciers (one spanning 1,220 acres) and many ragged mountain peaks in the northern half of the Wind River Mountains. Lying on the east side of the Continental Divide, this area displays incomparable beauty and grandeur. You can climb Gannett Peak–at 13,804 feet it's the highest point in Wyoming–for what seems to be unlimited mountaineering challenges. The western border is the Continental Divide, shared with Bridger Wilderness. The eastern border is shared with the Wind River Indian Reservation. Carved by glaciers from granite and limestone rock, the area contains splendid alpine meadows, rocky plateaus, and stands of virgin timber. Precipitous canyons shadow tumbling streams, and at least 60 crystalline lakes are full of fish. More than 75 miles of streams offer excellent trout fishing. Many species utilize these mountains as summer habitat, including elk, mule deer, moose, bighorn sheep, black bears, bobcats, and coyotes. Fall brings many big-game hunters.

Named for Tom "Half-Hand" Fitzpatrick, a mountain man and sometime partner of Jim Bridger, the Wilderness is extremely rugged with miles of bare granite rock. No season is free of frost and snowfall is possible any day of the year. Many miles of trails provide access, and one of the main routes enters the Wilderness from Trail Lake. For a hardy backpacking or horsepacking trip, this is wild Wyoming at its best. After an arduous scramble, I once camped beside a hidden lake in the Fitzpatrick. Surrounded by bold rock faces, I remember thinking that surely no human had ever set foot here before. Undoubtedly, I was wrong, but it was certainly a compelling fantasy.

WYOMING

Fitzpatrick Essentials

Size: 198,838 acres.
Year Designated: 1976; expanded in 1984.
Location: Western Wyoming.
Easiest Access: From Dubois, take U.S. 287 south approximately 10 miles. Turn south on the Whiskey Basin access road. This dirt road leads approximately eight miles to Trail Lake and a major trailhead.
Season: Mid-June to late October.

Wilderness Fees/Permits: None.
Maps: A Wilderness map is available for $3.75 from the Grand Teton Natural History Association, P.O. Box 170, Moose, WY 83012.
Management: Washakie Ranger District, Shoshone National Forest, 333 Highway 789 South, Lander, WY 82520; (307) 332-5460. Wind River Ranger District, Shoshone National Forest, P.O. Box 186, Dubois, WY 82513; (307) 455-2466.

Gros Ventre Wilderness

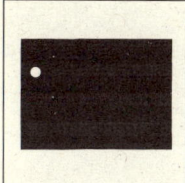

With Wyoming's two national parks and the Wildernesses of Bridger and Teton nearby, Gros Ventre receives relatively light human use. In fact, few people can claim any real familiarity with the area. Even the name is not well understood. *Gros ventre* is French for "big belly" and may refer to the Indians who once inhabited the area. But *gros vente* means "big wind," and the similarity may have created some confusion among mountain men who stood here and looked across the Wind River Mountains.

From the town of Kelly, I've watched alpenglow gloriously dwindle into darkness from the mountain called Sleeping Indian. The Indian, in full warbonnet, lies on his back, while behind him hides this wild, steep, and rugged Wilderness interspersed with rolling, luxuriant meadows. Meandering streams occasionally roar through narrow chasms when the snow melts on the 20 or so peaks that rise above 10,000 feet.

Doubletop Peak, the highest point in the Wilderness, reaches 11,750 feet. Elk and moose live here, along with black bears, mule deer, and bighorn sheep. Great fishing is available in a half-dozen alpine lakes and miles of streams. In July and August, colorful wildflowers bloom in the meadows near forests of quaking aspen, lodgepole pine, Engelmann spruce, and alpine fir.

Many paths lead into the area from numerous trailheads. Approaches from the northern (Gros Ventre River) side are generally easier than those from the southern (Hoback River) side. A great introduction to Gros Ventre Wilderness is a loop on the Goodwin Lake–Cache Creek Trail (approximately eight miles in length). This route passes the scenic Goodwin Lake and traverses a high plateau with extraordinary views before dropping down Cache Creek. A shuttle is required to complete the loop. On the south side, four trailheads leave the region of Granite Creek Hot Springs, including the Swift Creek Trail, which offers excellent scenery. The first three miles of Swift Creek are relatively easy, but the final three-mile stretch is extremely steep.

WYOMING

Gros Ventre Essentials

Size: 287,000 acres.
Year Designated: 1984.
Location: Western Wyoming.
Easiest Access: From Jackson, drive south and east on U.S. 189 for 28 miles. Turn north at the sign directing you to Granite Creek Hot Springs and drive nine miles.
Season: Summer and early fall.
Wilderness Fees/Permits: None.

Maps: USGS topographic maps are Blue Miner Lake, Bull Creek, Cache Creek, Camp Davis, Crystal Peak, Darwin Peak, Doubletop Peak, Granite Falls, Grizzly Lake, Ouzel Falls, Tosi Peak, Turquoise Lake, and Upper Slide Lake.
Management: Jackson Ranger District, Bridger-Teton National Forest, P.O. Box 1689, Jackson, WY 83001; (307) 739-5400.

Huston Park Wilderness

With approximately 48 square miles of high forested land, Huston Park Wilderness rises beyond 10,500 feet and contains alpine bogs and stands of lodgepole pine, spruce, fir, and aspen, interspersed with open parks and brushy meadows. The streams are small and their water drains into the Little Snake and North Platte Rivers. Some of the streams harbor trout that are there for the catching. Straddling the Continental Divide, this area includes 45.9 miles of the Continental Divide National Scenic Trail, at an average elevation of 9,750 feet. This section of the Divide Trail is called the Huston Park Trail, undeveloped and marked with rock cairns and blazed trees. Many views are panoramic and spectacular. The Baby Lake, Verde Mine, and Roaring Fork Trails offer side trips, but these pathways are also undeveloped and lack well-marked trailheads. Human use of Huston Park is low except during elk hunting season.

Huston Park Essentials

Size: 31,300 acres.
Year Designated: 1984.
Location: Southern Wyoming.
Easiest Access: From Encampment, take Forest Service Road 11 west for six miles. Turn southwest on Forest Service Road 550 and continue for 24.5 miles to access the Huston Park Trail at its south end.
Season: Late spring through fall.

Wilderness Fees/Permits: None.
Maps: USGS topographic maps are Bridger Peak, Fletcher Peak, Red Mountain, and Solomon Creek.
Management: Hayden Ranger District, Medicine Bow National Forest, 204 West Ninth Street, P.O. Box 187, Encampment, WY 82325; (307) 327-5481.

WYOMING

Jedediah Smith Wilderness

Jedediah Smith Wilderness was named in honor of one of the most energetic and talented young mountain men, one of the first to explore this area. The wilderness spreads over high mountainous slopes on the west side of Grand Teton National Park, wondrous country "behind" the Grand Teton itself. Here you'll find magnificent glacier-carved subalpine lake basins, limestone cave systems, outstanding views, and abundant wildlife in a relatively long, narrow area near the Idaho state line that stretches from Yellowstone National Park in the south almost to Teton Pass.

At least 16 well-maintained trails provide miles of access to some of the best scenery in the Rockies. Several of the trails lead over the watershed divide at approximately 10,000 feet and spill into Grand Teton National Park.

Two years before the Wilderness was designated in 1984, I hiked the South Teton–Alaska Basin Trail along South Teton Creek for about eight easy miles. I passed the lakes and smooth rock ledges of lovely Alaska Basin and set up a Wilderness camp that still warms my heart with memories of splendor and solitude.

Today, overuse threatens the health of this region. Neither campfires nor horses are permitted in the area. But there are still pathways, such as the steep Andy Stone Trail (2.7 miles) with its terrific views from 10,000 feet, that receive few human visitors. Pack a load of Leave No Trace wisdom and venture off-trail for a true Wilderness experience.

Jedediah Smith Essentials

Size: 116,535 acres.
Year Designated: 1984.
Location: Western Wyoming.
Easiest Access: From Driggs, Idaho, take Forest Service Road 009 east seven miles to Teton Campground and the South Teton Trailhead.
Season: Summer and early fall.
Wilderness Fees/Permits: None.
Maps: A Wilderness map is available for $3 from the district ranger.
Management: Ashton Ranger District, Targhee National Forest, 30 South Yellowstone Highway, P.O. Box 228, Ashton, ID 83420; (208) 652-7442. Teton Basin Ranger District, Targhee National Forest, North Main Street, Driggs, ID 83422; (208) 354-2312.

North Absaroka Wilderness

Yellowstone National Park lies along the northeastern boundary of North Absaroka Wilderness, which also shares a border with Montana and contains one of the areas least desecrated by humanity's insatiable thirst for development, a fact evidenced throughout the Lower 48. Several summits rise above 10,000 feet with the highest point on Dead Indian Peak at 12,216 feet. Dead Indian Peak stands about eight miles from Dead Indian Meadows and about 15 miles from other landmarks, such as Dead Indian Pass, Dead Indian Hill, Dead Indian Creek, and Dead Indian Campground. It makes you wonder if this region was hazardous to Native Americans. This remote and rugged country contains large regions of virtually inaccessible terrain. Volcanic in origin, the land is dissected by numerous creeks forming huge drainages (containing tons of erodible topsoil) that turn into frenzied rivers of mud during summer rainstorms.

WYOMING

There are 217 miles of rough and minimally marked trails, and hikers run a high risk of getting lost or hurt. The Wilderness receives few visitors, especially before hunting season opens. The trails are generally long, steep, and narrow. They tend to follow drainages and have few places to cross from one drainage to another except at the headwaters. From easily accessible Pahaska Campground, a trail runs north along Crow Creek to meet other trails. Only a few lakes exist, but the streams contain cutthroat, brown, brook, and rainbow trout.

The region is home to grizzly bears, so precautions are in order. Big-game hunters come by the hundreds for bighorn sheep, elk, and moose. Marmots and pikas reign on numerous talus slopes.

Summers are relatively dry, and flies and gnats may disturb your serenity. Mosquitoes are generally few, I'm happy to report, and far between. Some of the trails will take you far from water. A limited number of appealing campsites has created some overuse at the desirable places.

North Absaroka Essentials

Size: 350,538 acres.
Year Designated: 1964.
Location: Northern Wyoming.
Easiest Access: From Cody, take U.S. 20/16/14 (North Fork Scenic Byway) west for approximately 47 miles to Pahaska.
Season: Summer and early fall.
Wilderness Fees/Permits: None.
Maps: A map is available for $3.75 from the Grand Teton Natural History Association, P.O. Box 170, Moose, WY 83012.
Management: Clarks Fork Ranger District, Shoshone National Forest, 1002 Road 11, Powell, WY 82435; (307) 754-7207. Wapiti Ranger District, Shoshone National Forest, 203A Yellowstone Avenue, P.O. Box 1840, Cody, WY 82414; (307) 527-6921.

Platte River Wilderness

About 36 square miles of forested land lying primarily north and east of the North Platte River is included in this Wyoming Wilderness, with a small segment in Colorado's Routt National Forest (see Colorado, Platte River Wilderness). The North Platte River enters Routt National Forest about four miles south of the Wyoming state line and flows north through a portion of the Wilderness and North Gate Canyon, a popular white-water rafting section of water. Elevations average 7,700 feet with the wide and relatively flat Platte Ridge rising in the middle of the area between the river and Douglas Creek. Elk and deer winter here. Both the creek and the river are noted for their excellent trout fishing opportunities.

The Platte River Trail gently parallels the river on the west bank after a steep descent from the Platte River Trailhead. During high water, the trail dead-ends after five miles. During low water (usually in late July and August), you can ford the river and continue on the east bank. The Douglas Creek Trail follows the creek for 9.5 miles through an open canyon with trailheads at both ends. You can hike a loop from the Pelton Creek Trailhead by exiting the Douglas Creek Trail to return via the Platte River Trail.

WYOMING

Platte River Essentials

Size: 22,230 acres in Wyoming (23,000 total).
Year Designated: 1984.
Location: Southern Wyoming.
Easiest Access: From Laramie, take State Highway 230 southwest about 40 miles. Turn northwest on Forest Service Road 898 and continue driving nine miles to Pelton Creek Campground.
Season: Late spring through fall.
Wilderness Fees/Permits: None.
Maps: USGS topographic maps are Elkhorn Point, Horatio Rock, and Overlook Hill.
Management: Hayden Ranger District, Medicine Bow National Forest, 204 West Ninth Street, P.O. Box 187, Encampment, WY 82325; (307) 327-5481. Laramie Ranger District, Medicine Bow National Forest, 2468 Jackson Street, Laramie, WY 82070; (307) 745-8971.

Popo Agie Wilderness

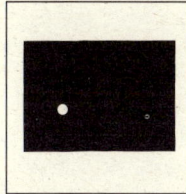

This piece of land is one of the loveliest in Wyoming. So rich in wildlife, it definitely ranks among my favorites. Along the western boundary, which Popo Agie (pronounced "po-*po*-zsha") shares with Bridger Wilderness, stands Wind River Peak, at 13,255 feet the highest point in the area. More than 20 other summits rise above 12,000 feet. The lowest elevation in the Popo Agie is the Middle Fork of the Popo Agie River at 8,400 feet on the eastern boundary. Bordering the north side is the Wind River Indian Reservation, outstanding country where visitors must first obtain a permit before entering.

More than 300 alpine and subalpine lakes and ponds, many filled with trout, send their waters down sparkling streams and over waterfalls to the Middle Fork and North Fork of the Popo Agie River and the South Fork of the Little Wind River. All the water eventually ends up in the Wind River. This rough land features high, jagged peaks; deep, narrow valleys and canyons; sheer granite walls; cirque basins; talus slopes; and perennial snowfields along its eastern side. The area, which abuts the Continental Divide, encompasses about 25 miles of the southern Wind River Mountain Range, with forests of lodgepole pine and Douglas fir, Engelmann spruce, and subalpine fir.

In a Smithsonian Institute report issued in 1879, it was said of the Wind River Mountains, "when a good Indian dies, he falls into a beautiful stream of bright, fresh water, and is carried to the pleasant grounds [of the Winds]...." The temperature rarely exceeds 80 degrees Fahrenheit, but it may plunge to 40 below zero in the winter. Snow may fall any day of the year, and most of the precipitation is snow. There are occasional heavy rains in summer, and light afternoon thunderstorms are common.

Many miles of trails attract a relatively large number of visitors, which has led to a few restrictions on camping in some areas. Check with the district ranger. The Popo Agie Falls Trail quickly takes you into the silence of the Wilderness. On the first night of a camping trip here a few years ago, I saw moose, mule deer, and beavers at the edge of a wide meadow as dusk set in. Nearby Lander is the site of the international headquarters of the National Outdoor Leadership School (NOLS). In town you can find anything—major and minor—to outfit your Wilderness trip.

WYOMING

Popo Agie Essentials

Size: 101,991 acres.
Year Designated: 1984.
Location: Western Wyoming.
Easiest Access: From Lander, take State Road 131 south approximately 15 miles through Sinks Canyon State Park to a large parking lot and the well-marked Pogo Agie Falls Trailhead.
Season: Late spring through early fall.

Wilderness Fees/Permits: None.
Maps: A map is available for $3.75 from the Grand Teton Natural History Association, P.O. Box 170, Moose, WY 83012.
Management: Washakie Ranger District, Shoshone National Forest, 600 North Highway 287, Lander, WY 82520; (307) 332-5460.

Savage Run Wilderness

Steep-sided canyons rest at the lower elevations (around 8,000 feet) of this forested Wilderness, which covers about 23 square miles on the west side of the Medicine Bow Range. The land rises to about 10,000 feet and rolling plateaulike terrain. At the tree line you'll find Engelmann spruce, ponderosa pine, limber pine, Douglas fir, subalpine fir, cottonwood, and quaking aspen. Anglers come for the creek's brook trout, while a resident elk population attracts hunters.

Savage Run Creek tumbles through the heart of the area in roughly an east-west direction. The "more difficult" Savage Run Trail follows the creek for about nine miles, with an elevation change of 2,400 feet. Along the way you'll pass through stands of virgin timber. The strenuous Cottonwood Trail enters from the southern boundary and travels two miles to join the Savage Run Trail.

Savage Run Essentials

Size: 14,940 acres.
Year Designated: 1978.
Location: Central southern Wyoming.
Easiest Access: From Albany, take Forest Service Road 500 west for about 12 miles. At that point, turn south on an old logging road and drive for two miles to the north end of the Savage Run Trail.
Season: Late spring through fall.

Wilderness Fees/Permits: None.
Maps: Topographic maps may be ordered from the Geological Survey of Wyoming, P.O. Box 3008, University Station, Laramie, WY 82071-3008; (307) 766-2286.
Management: Laramie Ranger District, Medicine Bow National Forest, 2468 Jackson Street, Laramie, WY 82070-6535; (307) 745-8971.

WYOMING

Teton Wilderness

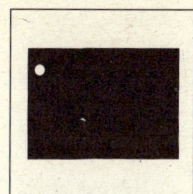

The state's second largest Wilderness area straddles the Continental Divide deep in the heart of Wyoming. It is bordered on the north by Yellowstone National Park, on the east by Washakie Wilderness, and on the west by Grand Teton National Park. To the west of the Great Divide the land is dominated by timbered ridges, mountain meadows, and grassy slopes with elevations from 7,500 feet to 9,675 feet. To the east are high plateaus broken by ridges and extensive mountain meadows with elevations from 8,000 feet to 12,165 feet (on Younts Peak). On Two Ocean Pass, the famous Two Ocean Creek splits to send water to both the Atlantic and the Pacific. You'll see evidence of the great fire from the summer of 1988 that burned here and in Yellowstone. You'll also see ruined trees from 1987's summer tornado that mowed a 20-mile-long, two-mile-wide swath through the area. But in general, this area is vast, spectacular, and relatively unspoiled.

Teton Wilderness ranks among this nation's best wildlife areas. Summer brings trumpeter swans, sandhill cranes, ducks, geese, and grouse. Grizzly bears and bison wander across meadows. Golden and bald eagles, hawks, coyotes, beavers, martens, bobcats, porcupines, otters, and mink live here year-round. Hunting season opens in fall for elk, mule deer, black bears, moose, antelope, and bighorn sheep. Hundreds of miles of streams and hundreds of lakes attract anglers. About half of the visitors to this area come expressly to hunt and fish. I strongly recommend that all visitors take precautions to protect themselves against the threat of bears.

Many miles of trails provide access to this popular area. The primary trailheads are on the west and southwest boundaries. From Bridger Lake in the northern section, the popular Thorofare Trail follows the Yellowstone River into the park to Yellowstone Lake, a distance of approximately 15 miles. From Flagg Ranch, a trail climbs toward Huckleberry Mountain for about five miles, where it joins a central network of pathways.

Teton Essentials

Size: 585,468 acres.
Year Designated: 1964; expanded in 1984.
Location: Western Wyoming.
Easiest Access: From Jackson, take U.S. 191 north approximately 54 miles to Flagg Ranch.
Season: Memorial Day to Labor Day is most popular. I prefer fall for cool weather and fewer backpackers.
Wilderness Fees/Permits: None.
Maps: Thirty-four USGS topographic maps cover the area. They can be ordered for $2.50 each from Bridger-Teton National Forest, P.O. Box 1888, Jackson, WY 83001.
Management: Buffalo Ranger District, Bridger-Teton National Forest, P.O. Box 278, Moran, WY 83013; (307) 543-2386.

Washakie Wilderness

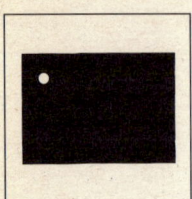

Chief Washakie was the most famous of the Shoshone Indians. In 1972, the Stratified Primitive Area was joined with South Absaroka Wilderness to form the Wilderness area (Wyoming's largest) that now bears his name. Yellowstone National Park borders to the northwest, Teton Wilderness to the west, and the Wind River Indian Reservation to the southeast—a combination of lands that stretches across a tremendous part of western Wyoming and is one of the greatest wild regions of America.

In the southern Absarokas you'll find broad, flat-topped mountains and plateaus separating narrow valleys that have been deeply incised with exposed volcanic strata. This volcanic material lies primarily horizontal and has been eroded into irregular steplike cliffs and buttes. I have sat for hours staring at the Pinnacles around Brooks Lake. These unique geological formations, in addition to petrified forests and many fossils of long-gone plants and animals, are among the most attractive attributes of this area. Elevations range from about 6,600 feet to 13,153 feet, and peaks exceeding 12,000 feet are scattered throughout the Wilderness. Large portions are rough and barren, and vegetation is sparse. Approximately half the area is forested.

With fewer lakes than the Wind River Mountains, the fishing is less active here, but large streams do support trout. Nonetheless, the wildlife population and diversity is extraordinary. I've spotted bobcats, coyotes, foxes, beavers, and numerous smaller furbearers, as well as bald eagles and peregrine falcons. I've watched bull elk sparring here, and waited while moose leisurely crossed the trail ahead of me. Hunters come for elk, moose, bighorn sheep, mule deer, and black bears. Grizzly bears are numerous and on the increase. Travelers should take appropriate precautions, as these are no teddy bears.

There are many miles of trails and the relative openness of much of the area encourages off-trail hiking. Snow may fall any day of the year in the higher country, and summer temperatures rarely rise above 80 degrees Fahrenheit. Be prepared for rain showers in late summer.

Washakie Essentials

Size: 703,981 acres.
Year Designated: 1964; expanded in 1972 and 1984.
Location: Western Wyoming.
Easiest Access: From Cody, head southwest on State Highway 291, a non-Wilderness road that penetrates into the area and provides access to several trailheads. After approximately 35 miles, the road ends at a major trailhead and parking lot.
Season: Summer and early fall. I prefer fall.
Wilderness Fees/Permits: None.
Maps: Wilderness maps are available from the Grand Teton Natural History Association, P.O. Box 170, Moose, WY 83012.
Management: Greybull Ranger District, Shoshone National Forest, 2044 State Street, P.O. Box 158, Meeteetse, WY 82433; (307) 868-2379. Wapiti Ranger District, Shoshone National Forest, 203A Yellowstone Avenue, P.O. Box 1840, Cody, WY 82414; (307) 527-6921. Wind River Ranger District, Shoshone National Forest, 209 East Ramshorn, P.O. Box 186, Dubois, WY 82513; (307) 455-2466.

WYOMING

Winegar Hole Wilderness

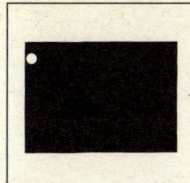

This Wilderness, the second smallest in Wyoming, huddles near the southwest corner of Yellowstone National Park (the area's northern boundary), with the Wyoming state line and Fall River on the west and Ashton-Flagg Ranch Road on the south. The landform is volcanic in origin. Encompassing relatively flat terrain of low rolling hills with numerous lakes, streams, and wetlands, Winegar Hole ranges in elevation from 6,020 feet to 6,985 feet. A forest of lodgepole pine, Douglas fir, subalpine fir, and Engelmann spruce covers much of the area. Winegar, Bog, and Boone Creeks support trout, and you will find a range of animals, including trumpeter swans. This is prime habitat for the powerful and often ferocious grizzly bear, so campers are strongly encouraged to take extreme bear precautions.

Less than 10 percent of the area can be accessed by the two maintained and seldom-used trails: Calf Creek and Fish Lake, both less than five miles long. Easily followed, the Fish Lake Trail joins the South Boundary Trail of Yellowstone National Park. A permit is required to enter the park. Winegar may look tiny on the map, but the place truly has retained a big piece of its wild nature.

Winegar Hole Essentials

Size: 14,000 acres.
Year Designated: 1984.
Location: Northwestern Wyoming.
Easiest Access: From Ashton, Idaho, take Ashton-Flagg Ranch Road west about 27 miles to find both trailheads.
Season: Summer and early fall. Wilderness cross-country skiing is also excellent.

Wilderness Fees/Permits: None.
Maps: A Wilderness map is available for $3 from the district ranger.
Management: Ashton Ranger District, Targhee National Forest, P.O. Box 858, Ashton, ID 83420; (208) 652-7442.

Author's Choice:
Buck's Top Ten Wilderness Areas

Best All-Around Wilderness Areas

- Alaska, Wrangell–Saint Elias—page 74
- California, Golden Trout—page 174
- Colorado, Weminuche—page 264
- Idaho, Frank Church–River of No Return—page 295
- Montana/Wyoming, Absaroka–Beartooth—page 341, 530
- New Mexico, Pecos—page 385
- Oregon, Three Sisters—page 436
- Utah, High Uintas—page 469
- Washington, Alpine Lakes—page 495
- Wyoming, Popo Agie—page 539

Best Backpacking (Rockies and West)

- California, Trinity Alps—page 232
- Colorado, South San Juan—page 262
- Colorado, Weminuche—page 264
- Idaho, Frank Church–River of No Return—page 295
- Montana, Bob Marshall—page 343
- Montana/Wyoming, Absaroka–Beartooth—page 341, 530
- New Mexico, Gila—page 383
- Oregon, Three Sisters—page 436
- Washington, Olympic—page 511
- Wyoming, Fitzpatrick—page 534

Best Backpacking (East of the Rockies)

- Arkansas, Richland Creek—page 145
- Georgia/Tennessee, Big Frog and Cohutta—page 283, 452, 454
- Kentucky, Clifty—page 310
- Maine, Caribou–Speckled Mountain—page 313
- Michigan, Isle Royale—page 320
- Michigan, Sylvania—page 327
- Missouri, Hercules Glades—page 336
- New Hampshire, Pemigewasset—page 368
- North Carolina/Georgia, Southern Nantahala—page 289, 400
- Virginia, Shenandoah—page 493

Best Bird Watching

- Alaska, Aleutian Islands—page 37
- Alaska, Endicott River—page 45
- Alaska, Selawik—page 63
- Arizona, Aubrey Peak—page 78
- Arizona, Chiricahua National Monument—page 83
- Florida, Everglades—page 271
- Louisiana, Lacassine—page 312
- Maine, Moosehorn—page 314
- North Dakota, Chase Lake—page 403
- Oregon, Oregon Islands—page 430

AUTHOR'S CHOICE

Best Canoeing

- Alaska, Gates of the Arctic—page 47
- Alaska, Kobuk Valley—page 54
- Alaska, Noatak—page 59
- Arkansas, Buffalo National River—page 140
- Florida, Everglades—page 271
- Georgia, Okefenokee—page 286
- Minnesota, Boundary Waters—page 329
- Mississippi, Black Creek—page 331
- North Dakota, Theodore Roosevelt—page 405
- South Carolina, Congaree Swamp—page 444

Best Canyon Hiking

- Arizona, Aravaipa Canyon—page 76
- Arizona, Cottonwood Point—page 85
- Arizona, Grand Wash Cliffs—page 92
- Arizona, Kanab Creek—page 100
- Arizona, Sycamore Canyon—page 130
- Arizona, West Clear Creek—page 134
- Arizona/Utah, Paria Canyon-Vermilion Cliffs—page 115, 474
- Utah, Ashdown Gorge—page 466
- Utah, Box-Death Hollow—page 467
- Utah, Dark Canyon—page 468

Best Desert Hiking

- Arizona, Cabeza Prieta—page 81
- Arizona, Havasu (Needles)—page 95
- Arizona, Kofa—page 102
- Arizona, Organ Pipe Cactus—page 112
- Arizona, Superstition—page 128
- California, Death Valley—page 166
- California, Mojave—page 196
- California, North Algodones Dunes—page 200
- California, Palen-McCoy—page 205
- California, Turtle Mountains—page 233

Best Fishing

- Alaska, Togiak—page 69
- Arizona/California, Imperial—page 98, 180
- California, Sequoia-Kings Canyon—page 221
- California, Thousand Lakes—page 230
- Colorado, Cache la Poudre—page 241
- Florida, Little Lake George—page 276
- Idaho, Frank Church-River of No Return—page 295
- Mississippi, Gulf Islands—page 332
- North Carolina, Swanquarter—page 401
- Oregon, Sky Lakes—page 433

Best Horsepacking

- California, Snow Mountain—page 225
- California, South Warner—page 227
- California, Yolla Bolly-Middle Eel—page 235
- Colorado, Flat Tops—page 244
- Colorado, La Garita—page 249
- Colorado, West Elk—page 265
- Idaho, Frank Church-River of No Return—page 295
- Oregon/Washington, Wenaha-Tucannon—page 438, 518
- Utah, High Uintas—page 469
- Washington, William O. Douglas—page 519

Best Hunting

- Alaska, Becharof (brown bear & moose)—page 40
- Alaska, Koyukuk (moose)—page 55
- Alaska, Nunivak Island (musk ox)—page 60
- Alaska, Wrangell-Saint Elias (Dall sheep)—page 74
- Arizona, Pine Mountain (javelina)—page 117
- Arkansas, Upper Buffalo (squirrel)—page 146
- California, North Fork (black-tailed deer)—page 201
- Colorado, West Elk (elk & mule deer)—page 265
- Oregon, North Fork John Day (elk & mule deer)—page 428
- Oregon/Washington, Wenaha-Tucannon (elk)—page 438, 518

AUTHOR'S CHOICE

Best Mountaineering

- Alaska, Denali—page 44
- Alaska, Wrangell–Saint Elias—page 74
- California, John Muir—page 184
- California, Mount Shasta—page 198
- Colorado, Collegiate Peaks—page 241
- Colorado, Maroon Bells–Snowmass—page 251
- Oregon, Mount Hood—page 424
- Washington, Mount Baker—page 507
- Washington, Mount Rainier—page 508
- Wyoming, Fitzpatrick—page 534

Best Rock Climbing

- California, Joshua Tree—page 185
- California, Pinnacles—page 208
- California, San Jacinto—page 216
- California, Yosemite—page 236
- Colorado, Black Canyon of the Gunnison—page 238
- Oregon, Menagerie—page 421
- Oregon, Mill Creek—page 423
- Washington, Alpine Lakes—page 495
- Washington, Glacier Peak—page 500
- Wyoming, Bridger—page 531

Best Sea Kayaking

- Alaska, Glacier Bay—page 48
- Alaska, Kootznoowoo (Admiralty Island)—page 54
- Alaska, Misty Fiords—page 58
- Alaska, South Baranof—page 66
- Alaska, Tebenkof Bay—page 69
- Alaska, West Chichagof–Yakobi—page 73
- Florida, Florida Keys—page 272
- Michigan, Isle Royale—page 320
- South Carolina, Cape Romain—page 443
- Washington, San Juan Islands—page 514

Best White-Water Rafting

- Alaska, Lake Clark—page 57
- Arizona, Salt River Canyon—page 124
- California, Golden Trout—page 174
- California, Yolla Bolly–Middle Eel—page 235
- Idaho, Frank Church–River of No Return—page 295
- Idaho/Oregon, Hells Canyon—page 298, 419
- Idaho/Montana, Selway-Bitterroot—page 299, 352
- Michigan, Sturgeon River Gorge—page 326
- Oregon, Kalmiopsis—page 420
- Oregon, Wild Rogue—page 439

Wilderness Areas At-A-Glance
(by State, Acreage, and Managing Agency)

Below are all of the Wilderness areas in the United States, listed from largest to smallest within each state. The managing agency follows each listing: Bureau of Land Management (BLM); National Park Service (NPS); U.S. Forest Service (USFS); and U.S. Fish and Wildlife Service (USF&WS). Note that Connecticut, Delaware, Iowa, Kansas, Maryland, and Rhode Island contain no Wilderness areas.

Alabama
Total Wilderness acreage: 33,396
1. **Sipsey:** 25,906 acres (USFS)
2. **Cheaha:** 7,490 acres (USFS)

Alaska
Total Wilderness acreage: 56,770,766
1. **Wrangell–Saint Elias:** 8,700,000 acres (NPS)
2. **Arctic:** 8,000,000 acres (USF&WS)
3. **Gates of the Arctic:** 7,052,000 acres (NPS)
4. **Noatak:** 5,800,000 acres (NPS)
5. **Katmai:** 3,473,000 acres (NPS)
6. **Glacier Bay:** 2,770,000 acres (NPS)
7. **Lake Clark:** 2,470,000 acres (NPS)
8. **Togiak:** 2,270,000 acres (USF&WS)
9. **Misty Fiords:** 2,142,243 acres (USFS)
10. **Denali:** 1,900,000 acres (NPS)
11. **Kenai:** 1,350,000 acres (USF&WS)
12. **Aleutian Islands:** 1,300,000 acres (USF&WS)
13. **Andreafsky:** 1,300,000 acres (USF&WS)
14. **Innoko:** 1,240,000 acres (USF&WS)
15. **Kootznoowoo (Admiralty Island):** 945,569 acres (USFS)
16. **Unimak:** 910,000 acres (USF&WS)
17. **Tracy Arm–Fords Terror:** 653,179 acres (USFS)
18. **Nunivak:** 600,000 acres (USF&WS)
19. **Stikine-LeConte:** 448,841 acres (USFS)
20. **Becharof:** 400,000 acres (USF&WS)
21. **Koyukuk:** 400,000 acres (USF&WS)
22. **Russell Fiord:** 348,701 acres (USFS)
23. **South Baranof:** 319,568 acres (USFS)
24. **Izembek:** 300,000 acres (USF&WS)
25. **West Chichagof–Yakobi:** 264,747 acres (USFS)
26. **Semidi:** 250,000 acres (USF&WS)
27. **Selawik:** 240,000 acres (USF&WS)
28. **Kobuk Valley:** 190,000 acres (NPS)
29. **Endicott River:** 98,729 acres (USFS)
30. **South Prince of Wales:** 90,996 acres (USFS)
31. **South Etolin Island:** 83,642 acres (USFS)
32. **Bering Sea:** 81,340 acres (USF&WS)
33. **Chuck River:** 72,503 acres (USFS)
34. **Tebenkof Bay:** 66,839 acres (USFS)
35. **Kuiu:** 60,576 acres (USFS)
36. **Petersburg Creek–Duncan Salt Chuck:** 46,777 acres (USFS)
37. **Karta River:** 38,046 acres (USFS)

WILDERNESS AREAS AT-A-GLANCE

38. **Simeonof Island:** 25,855 acres (USF&WS)
39. **Pleasant/Lemusurier/Inian Islands:** 23,140 acres (USFS)
40. **Coronation Island:** 19,232 acres (USFS)
41. **Warren Island:** 11,181 acres (USFS)
42. **Tuxedni:** 5,566 acres (USF&WS)
43. **Maurelle Islands:** 4,937 acres (USFS)
44. **Forrester Island:** 2,832 acres (USF&WS)
45. **Chamisso Island:** 455 acres (USF&WS)
46. **Bogoslof Island:** 175 acres (USF&WS)
47. **Saint Lazaria Island:** 65 acres (USF&WS)
48. **Hazy Islands:** 32 acres (USF&WS)

Arizona

Total Wilderness acreage: 4,470,948

1. **Cabeza Prieta:** 803,418 acres (USF&WS)
2. **Kofa:** 516,200 acres (USF&WS)
3. **Organ Pipe Cactus:** 312,600 acres (NPS)
4. **Mazatzal:** 251,912 acres (USFS)
5. **Superstition:** 159,757 acres (USFS)
6. **Arrastra Mountain:** 126,760 acres (BLM)
7. **Warm Springs:** 90,600 acres (BLM)
8. **Paria Canyon–Vermilion Cliffs:** 90,046 acres, with more acreage in Utah (BLM)
9. **Eagletail Mountains:** 89,000 acres (BLM)
10. **Chiricahua:** 87,700 acres (USFS)
11. **Paiute:** 84,700 acres (BLM)
12. **Kanab Creek:** 77,100 acres (BLM and USFS)
13. **Galiuro:** 76,317 acres (USFS)
14. **Saguaro:** 71,400 acres (NPS)
15. **North Maricopa Mountains:** 63,600 acres (BLM)
16. **Woolsey Peak:** 61,000 acres (BLM)
17. **South Maricopa Mountains:** 60,800 acres (BLM)
18. **Pusch Ridge:** 56,933 acres (USFS)
19. **Sycamore Canyon:** 55,937 acres (USFS)
20. **Four Peaks:** 53,500 acres (USFS)
21. **Petrified Forest:** 50,620 acres (NPS)
22. **Red Rock–Secret Mountain:** 43,950 acres (USFS)
23. **Rawhide Mountains:** 41,600 acres (BLM)
24. **Saddle Mountain:** 40,600 acres (USFS)
25. **Rincon Mountain:** 38,590 acres (USFS)
26. **Wabayuma Peak:** 38,400 acres (BLM)
27. **Hellsgate:** 36,780 acres (USFS)
28. **Grand Wash Cliffs:** 36,300 acres (BLM)
29. **Table Top:** 34,400 acres (BLM)
30. **Salt River Canyon:** 32,800 acres (USFS)
31. **Mount Tipton:** 31,070 acres (BLM)
32. **Hummingbird Springs:** 30,170 acres (BLM)
33. **Trigo Mountains:** 29,095 acres (BLM)
34. **Upper Burro Creek:** 27,900 acres (BLM)
35. **Mount Nutt:** 27,530 acres (BLM)
36. **Santa Teresa:** 26,780 acres (USFS)
37. **Castle Creek:** 26,030 acres (USFS)
38. **Harcuvar Mountains:** 25,287 acres (BLM)
39. **Mount Wrightson:** 25,260 acres (USFS)
40. **Mount Wilson:** 23,600 acres (BLM)
41. **Harquahala:** 22,865 acres (BLM)
42. **New Water Mountains:** 21,680 acres (BLM)
43. **Sierra Ancha:** 20,850 acres (USFS)
44. **Big Horn Mountains:** 20,600 acres (BLM)
45. **Miller Peak:** 20,190 acres (USFS)
46. **Pine Mountain:** 20,061 acres (USFS)
47. **Aravaipa Canyon:** 19,700 acres (BLM)
48. **Peloncillo Mountains:** 19,650 acres (BLM)
49. **Salome:** 18,950 acres (USFS)
50. **Gibralter Mountain:** 18,805 acres (BLM)
51. **Kachina Peaks:** 18,200 acres (USFS)
52. **Munds Mountain:** 18,150 acres (USFS)
53. **Beaver Dam Mountains:** 17,003 acres, with more acreage in Utah (BLM)
54. **Aubrey Peak:** 15,900 acres (BLM)
55. **Swansea:** 15,755 acres (BLM)
56. **Signal Mountain:** 15,250 acres (BLM)
57. **Cedar Bench:** 14,950 acres (USFS)
58. **East Cactus Plain:** 14,630 acres (BLM)

WILDERNESS AREAS AT-A-GLANCE

59. **Havasu (Needles):** 14,606 acres, with more acreage in California (USF&WS)
60. **Mount Logan:** 14,600 acres (BLM)
61. **Sierra Estrella:** 14,500 acres (BLM)
62. **West Clear Creek:** 13,600 acres (USFS)
63. **Dos Cabezas Mountains:** 11,998 acres (BLM)
64. **Hassayampa River Canyon:** 11,840 acres (BLM)
65. **Fossil Springs:** 11,550 acres (USFS)
66. **Bear Wallow:** 11,080 acres (USFS)
67. **Fishhooks:** 10,833 acres (BLM)
68. **Chiricahua National Monument:** 10,290 acres (NPS)
69. **Strawberry Crater:** 10,140 acres (USFS)
70. **Granite Mountain:** 9,800 acres (USFS)
71. **Imperial:** 9,220 acres, with more acreage in California (USF&WS)
72. **Needle's Eye:** 9,201 acres (BLM)
73. **Hells Canyon:** 9,200 acres (BLM)
74. **Muggins Mountains:** 8,855 acres (BLM)
75. **Tres Alamos:** 8,700 acres (BLM)
76. **Mount Trumbull:** 7,900 acres (BLM)
77. **Juniper Mesa:** 7,600 acres (USFS)
78. **Pajarita:** 7,420 acres (USFS)
79. **Mount Baldy:** 7,079 acres (USFS)
80. **Wet Beaver:** 6,700 acres (USFS)
81. **Redfield Canyon:** 6,600 acres (BLM)
82. **North Santa Teresa:** 6,590 acres (BLM)
83. **Kendrick Mountain:** 6,510 acres (USFS)
84. **Cottonwood Point:** 6,500 acres (BLM)
85. **White Canyon:** 5,800 acres (BLM)
86. **Woodchute:** 5,600 acres (USFS)
87. **Apache Creek:** 5,420 acres (USFS)
88. **Escudilla:** 5,200 acres (USFS)
89. **Coyote Mountains:** 5,080 acres (BLM)
90. **Baboquivari Peak:** 2,065 acres (BLM)

Arkansas

Total Wilderness acreage: 128,362

1. **Leatherwood:** 16,956 acres (USFS)
2. **Hurricane Creek:** 15,177 acres (USFS)
3. **Caney Creek:** 14,344 acres (USFS)
4. **Richland Creek:** 11,822 acres (USFS)
5. **Upper Buffalo:** 11,746 acres (USFS)
6. **Poteau Mountain:** 10,884 acres (USFS)
7. **East Fork:** 10,777 acres (USFS)
8. **Buffalo National River:** 10,529 acres (NPS)
9. **Flatside:** 10,105 acres (USFS)
10. **Black Fork Mountain:** 7,568 acres, with more acreage in Oklahoma (USFS)
11. **Dry Creek:** 6,310 acres (USFS)
12. **Big Lake:** 2,144 acres (USF&WS)

California

Total Wilderness acreage: 13,987,677

1. **Death Valley:** 3,158,038 acres (NPS)
2. **Sequoia–Kings Canyon:** 736,980 acres (NPS)
3. **Mojave:** 695,200 acres (NPS)
4. **Yosemite:** 677,600 acres (NPS)
5. **John Muir:** 580,675 acres (USFS)
6. **Joshua Tree:** 561,470 acres (NPS)
7. **Trinity Alps:** 500,000 acres (USFS)
8. **Golden Trout:** 303,287 acres (USFS)
9. **Palen-McCoy:** 270,629 acres (BLM)
10. **Marble Mountain:** 241,744 acres (USFS)
11. **Ansel Adams:** 229,334 acres (NPS and USFS)
12. **Sespe:** 219,700 acres (USFS)
13. **Kingston Range:** 209,608 acres (BLM)
14. **Inyo Mountains:** 205,020 acres (BLM and USFS)
15. **Ventana:** 202,144 acres (USFS)
16. **San Rafael:** 197,010 acres (USFS)
17. **Sheephole Valley:** 174,800 acres (BLM)
18. **Carson-Iceberg:** 160,000 acres (USFS)
19. **Yolla Bolly–Middle Eel:** 153,904 acres (BLM and USFS)
20. **Siskiyou:** 153,000 acres (USFS)

WILDERNESS AREAS AT-A-GLANCE

21. **Old Woman Mountains:** 146,020 acres (BLM)
22. **Turtle Mountains:** 144,500 acres (BLM)
23. **Domeland:** 130,986 acres (BLM and USFS)
24. **Kelso Dunes:** 129,580 acres (BLM and NPS)
25. **Emigrant:** 112,191 acres (USFS)
26. **Nopah Range:** 110,860 acres (BLM)
27. **Mokelumne:** 104,461 acres (USFS)
28. **San Gorgonio:** 94,702 acres (BLM and USFS)
29. **Kiavah:** 88,290 acres (BLM and USFS)
30. **Santa Rosa:** 84,500 acres (BLM and USFS)
31. **Stepladder Mountains:** 81,600 acres (BLM)
32. **Chuckwalla Mountains:** 80,770 acres (BLM)
33. **Lassen Volcanic:** 78,982 acres (NPS)
34. **Resting Spring Range:** 78,868 acres (BLM)
35. **Whipple Mountains:** 77,520 acres (BLM)
36. **Argus Range:** 74,890 acres (BLM)
37. **Pahrump Valley:** 74,800 acres (BLM)
38. **Owens Peak:** 74,060 acres (BLM)
39. **Piper Mountain:** 72,575 acres (BLM)
40. **South Warner:** 70,385 acres (USFS)
41. **Bristol Mountains:** 68,515 acres (BLM)
42. **Dick Smith:** 65,130 acres (USFS)
43. **Chemehuevi Mountains:** 64,320 acres (BLM)
44. **Desolation:** 63,475 acres (USFS)
45. **South Sierra:** 63,000 acres (USFS)
46. **Sacatar Trail:** 51,900 acres (BLM)
47. **Coso Range:** 50,520 acres (BLM)
48. **Dead Mountains:** 48,850 acres (BLM)
49. **Hoover:** 48,601 acres (USFS)
50. **Big Maria Mountains:** 47,570 acres (BLM)
51. **Mesquite Mountains:** 47,330 acres (BLM)
52. **Monarch:** 45,000 acres (USFS)
53. **Sheep Mountain:** 43,600 acres (USFS)
54. **Ishi:** 41,840 acres (USFS and BLM)
55. **Rice Valley:** 40,820 acres (BLM)
56. **Orocopia Mountains:** 40,735 acres (BLM)
57. **Cadiz Dunes:** 39,740 acres (BLM)
58. **San Mateo Canyon:** 39,540 acres (USFS)
59. **Bighorn Mountains:** 39,185 acres (BLM and USFS)
60. **Chumash:** 38,150 acres (USFS)
61. **Golden Valley:** 37,700 acres (BLM)
62. **Mount Shasta:** 37,000 acres (USFS)
63. **Snow Mountain:** 37,000 acres (USFS)
64. **Piute Mountains:** 36,840 acres (BLM)
65. **San Gabriel:** 36,118 acres (USFS)
66. **Sawtooth Mountains:** 35,080 acres (BLM)
67. **Cleghorn Lakes:** 33,980 acres (BLM)
68. **Indian Pass:** 33,855 acres (BLM)
69. **Jacumba Mountains:** 33,670 acres (BLM)
70. **Little Picacho Peak:** 33,600 acres (BLM)
71. **Malpais Mesa:** 32,360 acres (BLM)
72. **Palo Verde Mountains:** 32,310 acres (BLM)
73. **North Algodones Dunes:** 32,240 acres (BLM)
74. **San Jacinto:** 32,040 acres (USFS)
75. **Grass Valley:** 31,695 acres (BLM)
76. **Trilobite:** 31,160 acres (BLM)
77. **Dinkey Lakes:** 30,000 acres (USFS)
78. **Little Chuckwalla Mountains:** 29,880 acres (BLM)
79. **Matilija:** 29,600 acres (USFS)
80. **Surprise Canyon:** 29,180 acres (BLM)
81. **Lava Beds:** 28,460 acres (NPS)
82. **Funeral Mountains:** 28,110 acres (BLM)
83. **Rodman Mountains:** 27,690 acres (BLM)
84. **Ibex Hills:** 26,460 acres (BLM)
85. **Clipper Mountains:** 26,000 acres (BLM)
86. **Fish Creek Mountains:** 25,940 acres (BLM)

WILDERNESS AREAS AT-A-GLANCE

87. **North Mesquite Mountains:** 25,540 acres (BLM)
88. **Phillip Burton:** 25,370 acres (NPS)
89. **Granite Chief:** 25,000 acres (USFS)
90. **Mecca Hills:** 24,200 acres (BLM)
91. **El Paso Mountains:** 23,780 acres (BLM)
92. **Newberry Mountains:** 22,900 acres (BLM)
93. **Kaiser:** 22,700 acres (USFS)
94. **Riverside Mountains:** 22,380 acres (BLM)
95. **Hollow Hills:** 22,240 acres (BLM)
96. **Bucks Lake:** 21,000 acres (USFS)
97. **Caribou:** 20,625 acres (USFS)
98. **Santa Lucia:** 20,412 acres (BLM and USFS)
99. **Machesna Mountain:** 20,000 acres (USFS and BLM)
100. **Sylvania Mountains:** 17,820 acres (BLM)
101. **Coyote Mountains:** 17,000 acres (BLM)
102. **South Nopah Range:** 16,780 acres (BLM)
103. **Thousand Lakes:** 16,335 acres (USFS)
104. **Red Buttes:** 16,150 acres, with more acreage in Oregon (USFS)
105. **Manly Peak:** 16,105 acres (BLM)
106. **Agua Tibia:** 15,933 acres (USFS)
107. **Carrizo Gorge:** 15,700 acres (BLM)
108. **Silver Peak:** 14,500 acres (USFS)
109. **Garcia:** 14,100 acres (USFS)
110. **Black Mountain:** 13,940 acres (BLM)
111. **Chimney Peak:** 13,700 acres (BLM)
112. **Pine Creek:** 13,100 acres (USFS)
113. **Cucamonga:** 12,981 acres (USFS)
114. **Pinnacles:** 12,952 acres (NPS)
115. **Russian:** 12,000 acres (USFS)
116. **Jennie Lakes:** 10,500 acres (USFS)
117. **Bigelow Cholla Garden:** 10,380 acres (BLM)
118. **Bright Star:** 9,520 acres (BLM)
119. **Darwin Falls:** 8,600 acres (BLM)
120. **Chanchelulla:** 8,200 acres (USFS)
121. **North Fork:** 8,100 acres (USFS)
122. **Hauser:** 8,000 acres (USFS)
123. **Picacho Peak:** 7,700 acres (BLM)
124. **Castle Crags:** 7,300 acres (USFS)
125. **Stateline:** 7,050 acres (BLM)
126. **Imperial:** 5,836 acres, with more acreage in Arizona (USF&WS)
127. **Havasu:** 3,195 acres, with more acreage in Arizona (USF&WS)
128. **Saddle Peak Hills:** 1,440 acres (BLM)
129. **Farallon:** 141 acres (USF&WS)

Colorado

Total Wilderness acreage: 3,256,594

1. **Weminuche:** 488,544 acres (USFS)
2. **Flat Tops:** 235,035 acres (USFS)
3. **Sangre de Cristo:** 226,455 acres (USFS)
4. **Maroon Bells–Snowmass:** 181,138 acres (USFS)
5. **West Elk:** 176,092 acres (USFS)
6. **Collegiate Peaks:** 166,654 acres (USFS)
7. **Mount Zirkel:** 160,568 acres (USFS)
8. **South San Juan:** 158,790 acres (USFS)
9. **Eagles Nest:** 133,325 acres (USFS)
10. **La Garita:** 129,626 acres (USFS)
11. **Holy Cross:** 122,037 acres (USFS)
12. **Lost Creek:** 119,790 acres (USFS)
13. **Uncompahgre:** 102,525 acres (USFS)
14. **Hunter-Fryingpan:** 82,580 acres (USFS)
15. **Mount Evans:** 74,401 acres (USFS)
16. **Indian Peaks:** 73,296 acres (NPS and USFS)
17. **Rawah:** 73,020 acres (USFS)
18. **Comanche Peak:** 66,791 acres (USFS)
19. **Raggeds:** 65,019 acres (USFS)
20. **Powderhorn:** 60,100 acres (BLM and USFS)
21. **Sarvis (Service) Creek:** 47,140 acres (USFS)
22. **Buffalo Peaks:** 43,410 acres (USFS)

WILDERNESS AREAS AT-A-GLANCE

23. **Lizard Head:** 41,189 acres (USFS)
24. **Great Sand Dunes:** 33,450 acres (NPS)
25. **Fossil Ridge:** 33,060 acres (USFS)
26. **Mount Massive:** 30,540 acres (USFS and USF&WS)
27. **Greenhorn Mountain:** 22,040 acres (USFS)
28. **Never Summer:** 20,692 acres (USFS)
29. **Mount Sneffels:** 16,505 acres (USFS)
30. **Ptarmigan Peak:** 13,175 acres (USFS)
31. **Vasquez Peak:** 12,300 acres (USFS)
32. **Black Canyon of the Gunnison:** 11,180 acres (NPS)
33. **Neota:** 9,924 acres (USFS)
34. **Cache la Poudre:** 9,238 acres (USFS)
35. **Mesa Verde:** 8,100 acres (NPS)
36. **Byers Peak:** 8,095 acres (USFS)
37. **Platte River:** 770 acres, with more acreage in Wyoming (USFS)

Florida

Total Wilderness acreage: 1,420,335

1. **Everglades:** 1,296,500 acres (NPS)
2. **Bradwell Bay:** 24,602 acres (USFS)
3. **Chassahowitzka:** 23,580 acres (USF&WS)
4. **Saint Marks:** 17,350 acres (USF&WS)
5. **Big Gum Swamp:** 13,600 acres (USFS)
6. **Juniper Prairie:** 13,260 acres (USFS)
7. **Mud Swamp/New River:** 7,800 acres (USFS)
8. **Alexander Springs:** 7,700 acres (USFS)
9. **Florida Keys:** 6,197 acres (USF&WS)
10. **Billies Bay:** 3,120 acres (USFS)
11. **J. N. "Ding" Darling:** 2,619 acres (USF&WS)
12. **Little Lake George:** 2,500 acres (USFS)
13. **Lake Woodruff:** 1,066 acres (USF&WS)
14. **Cedar Keys:** 379 acres (USF&WS)
15. **Passage Key:** 36 acres (USF&WS)
16. **Island Bay:** 20 acres (USF&WS)
17. **Pelican Island:** 6 acres (USF&WS)

Georgia

Total Wilderness acreage: 486,055

1. **Okefenokee:** 353,981 acres (USF&WS)
2. **Cohutta:** 35,247 acres, with more acreage in Tennessee (USFS)
3. **Mark Trail:** 16,880 acres (USFS)
4. **Brasstown:** 12,565 acres (USFS)
5. **Southern Nantahala:** 12,439 acres, with more acreage in North Carolina (USFS)
6. **Tray Mountain:** 9,702 acres (USFS)
7. **Rich Mountain:** 9,649 acres (USFS)
8. **Cumberland Island:** 8,840 acres (NPS)
9. **Raven Cliffs:** 8,562 acres (USFS)
10. **Blood Mountain:** 7,800 acres (USFS)
11. **Wolf Island:** 5,126 acres (USF&WS)
12. **Blackbeard Island:** 3,000 acres (USF&WS)
13. **Ellicott Rock:** 2,181 acres, with more acreage in North Carolina and South Carolina (USFS)
14. **Big Frog:** 83 acres, with more acreage in Tennessee (USFS)

Hawaii

Total Wilderness acreage: 142,370

1. **Hawaii Volcanoes:** 123,100 acres (NPS)
2. **Haleakala:** 19,270 acres (NPS)

Idaho

Total Wilderness acreage: 4,001,617

1. **Frank Church–River of No Return:** 2,362,569 acres (BLM and USFS)
2. **Selway-Bitterroot:** 1,089,017 acres, with more acreage in Montana (USFS)
3. **Sawtooth:** 217,088 acres (USFS)
4. **Gospel Hump:** 205,900 acres (USFS)
5. **Hells Canyon:** 83,800 acres (USFS)
6. **Craters of the Moon:** 43,243 acres (NPS)

WILDERNESS AREAS AT-A-GLANCE

Illinois

Total Wilderness acreage: 30,316
1. **Bald Knob:** 5,918 acres (USFS)
2. **Lusk Creek:** 4,796 acres (USFS)
3. **Clear Springs:** 4,730 acres (USFS)
4. **Crab Orchard:** 4,050 acres (USF&WS)
5. **Burden Falls:** 3,723 acres (USFS)
6. **Garden of the Gods:** 3,293 acres (USFS)
7. **Bay Creek:** 2,866 acres (USFS)
8. **Panther Den:** 940 acres (USFS)

Indiana

Total Wilderness acreage: 12,935
1. **Charles C. Deam:** 12,935 acres (USFS)

Kentucky

Total Wilderness acreage: 18,056
1. **Clifty:** 13,300 acres (USFS)
2. **Beaver Creek:** 4,756 acres (USFS)

Louisiana

Total Wilderness acreage: 17,046
1. **Kisatchie Hills:** 8,700 acres (USFS)
2. **Breton Island:** 5,000 acres (USF&WS)
3. **Lacassine:** 3,346 acres (USF&WS)

Maine

Total Wilderness acreage: 19,392
1. **Caribou–Speckled Mountain:** 12,000 acres (USFS)
2. **Moosehorn:** 7,392 acres (USF&WS)

Massachusetts

Total Wilderness acreage: 2,420
1. **Monomoy:** 2,420 acres (USF&WS)

Michigan

Total Wilderness acreage: 248,724
1. **Isle Royale:** 131,880 acres (NPS)
2. **Seney:** 25,150 acres (USF&WS)
3. **Sylvania:** 18,327 acres (USFS)
4. **McCormick:** 16,850 acres (USFS)
5. **Sturgeon River Gorge:** 14,500 acres (USFS)
6. **Mackinac:** 12,230 acres (USFS)
7. **Delirium:** 11,870 acres (USFS)
8. **Big Island Lake:** 5,500 acres (USFS)
9. **Rock River Canyon:** 4,640 acres (USFS)
10. **Horseshoe Bay:** 3,790 acres (USFS)
11. **Nordhouse Dunes:** 3,450 acres (USFS)
12. **Round Island:** 378 acres (USFS)
13. **Huron Islands:** 147 acres (USF&WS)
14. **Michigan Islands:** 12 acres (USF&WS)

Minnesota

Total Wilderness acreage: 804,489
1. **Boundary Waters:** 798,309 acres (USFS)
2. **Agassiz:** 4,000 acres (USF&WS)
3. **Tamarac:** 2,180 acres (USF&WS)

Mississippi

Total Wilderness acreage: 7,300
1. **Black Creek:** 4,560 acres (USFS)
2. **Gulf Islands:** 1,800 acres (NPS)
3. **Leaf:** 940 acres (USFS)

Missouri

Total Wilderness acreage: 70,860
1. **Irish:** 16,500 acres (USFS)
2. **Hercules Glades:** 12,314 acres (USFS)
3. **Bell Mountain:** 8,817 acres (USFS)
4. **Piney Creek:** 8,087 acres (USFS)
5. **Mingo:** 7,730 acres (USF&WS)

WILDERNESS AREAS AT-A-GLANCE

  6. **Paddy Creek:** 6,728 acres (USFS)
  7. **Devils Backbone:** 6,595 acres (USFS)
  8. **Rock Pile Mountain:** 4,089 acres (USFS)

Montana

Total Wilderness acreage: 3,436,578
  1. **Bob Marshall:** 1,009,356 acres (USFS)
  2. **Absaroka-Beartooth:** 920,310 acres, with more acreage in Wyoming (USFS)
  3. **Great Bear:** 286,700 acres (USFS)
  4. **Lee Metcalf:** 254,944 acres (BLM and USFS)
  5. **Selway-Bitterroot:** 248,893 acres, with more acreage in Idaho (USFS)
  6. **Scapegoat:** 239,296 acres (USFS)
  7. **Anaconda-Pintlar:** 157,874 acres (USFS)
  8. **Cabinet Mountains:** 94,272 acres (USFS)
  9. **Mission Mountains:** 73,877 acres (USFS)
  10. **Red Rock Lakes:** 32,350 acres (USF&WS)
  11. **Rattlesnake:** 29,824 acres (USFS)
  12. **Gates of the Mountains:** 28,562 acres (USFS)
  13. **Welcome Creek:** 28,135 acres (USFS)
  14. **UL Bend:** 20,819 acres (USF&WS)
  15. **Medicine Lake:** 11,366 acres (USF&WS)

Nebraska

Total Wilderness acreage: 12,735
  1. **Soldier Creek:** 8,100 acres (USFS)
  2. **Fort Niobrara:** 4,635 acres (USF&WS)

Nevada

Total Wilderness acreage: 798,067
  1. **Arc Dome:** 115,000 acres (USFS)
  2. **Jarbidge:** 113,167 acres (USFS)
  3. **Table Mountain:** 98,000 acres (USFS)
  4. **Ruby Mountains:** 90,000 acres (USFS)
  5. **Mount Moriah:** 82,000 acres (USFS)
  6. **Grant Range:** 50,000 acres (USFS)
  7. **Mount Charleston:** 43,000 acres (USFS)
  8. **Alta Toquima:** 38,000 acres (USFS)
  9. **East Humboldt:** 36,900 acres (USFS)
  10. **Currant Mountain:** 36,000 acres (USFS)
  11. **Santa Rosa–Paradise Peak:** 31,000 acres (USFS)
  12. **Mount Rose:** 28,000 acres (USFS)
  13. **Quinn Canyon:** 27,000 acres (USFS)
  14. **Boundary Peak:** 10,000 acres (USFS)

New Hampshire

Total Wilderness acreage: 102,932
  1. **Pemigewasset:** 45,000 acres (USFS)
  2. **Presidential Range–Dry River:** 27,380 acres (USFS)
  3. **Sandwich Range:** 25,000 acres (USFS)
  4. **Great Gulf:** 5,552 acres (USFS)

New Jersey

Total Wilderness acreage: 10,341
  1. **Brigantine:** 6,681 acres (USF&WS)
  2. **Great Swamp:** 3,660 acres (USF&WS)

New Mexico

Total Wilderness acreage: 1,609,797
  1. **Gila:** 557,819 acres (USFS)
  2. **Pecos:** 223,333 acres (USFS)
  3. **Aldo Leopold:** 201,966 acres (USFS)
  4. **Cebolla:** 60,000 acres (BLM)
  5. **Chama River Canyon:** 50,260 acres (USFS)
  6. **White Mountain:** 48,366 acres (USFS)
  7. **Apache Kid:** 44,650 acres (USFS)
  8. **San Pedro Parks:** 41,132 acres (USFS)
  9. **West Malpais:** 38,210 acres (BLM)
  10. **Sandia Mountain:** 37,028 acres (USFS)
  11. **Manzano Mountain:** 36,650 acres (USFS)
  12. **Capitan Mountains:** 34,513 acres (USFS)
  13. **Carlsbad Caverns:** 33,125 acres (NPS)

WILDERNESS AREAS AT-A-GLANCE

14. **Bosque del Apache:** 30,287 acres (USF&WS)
15. **Blue Range:** 30,000 acres (USFS)
16. **De-Na-Zin:** 23,872 acres (BLM)
17. **Bandelier:** 23,267 acres (NPS)
18. **Latir Peak:** 20,000 acres (USFS)
19. **Wheeler Peak:** 19,661 acres (USFS)
20. **Withington:** 18,869 acres (USFS)
21. **Cruces Basin:** 18,000 acres (USFS)
22. **Salt Creek:** 9,621 acres (USF&WS)
23. **Dome:** 5,200 acres (USFS)
24. **Bisti:** 3,968 acres (BLM)

New York

Total Wilderness acreage: 1,363

1. **Fire Island:** 1,363 acres (NPS)

North Carolina

Total Wilderness acreage: 109,003

1. **Shining Rock:** 18,450 acres (USFS)
2. **Joyce Kilmer–Slickrock:** 13,181 acres, with more acreage in Tennessee (USFS)
3. **Pocosin:** 11,000 acres (USFS)
4. **Linville Gorge:** 10,975 acres (USFS)
5. **Southern Nantahala:** 10,900 acres, with more acreage in Georgia (USFS)
6. **Sheep Ridge:** 9,540 acres (USFS)
7. **Swanquarter:** 8,785 acres (USF&WS)
8. **Middle Prong:** 7,900 acres (USFS)
9. **Catfish Lake South:** 7,600 acres (USFS)
10. **Birkhead Mountains:** 4,790 acres (USFS)
11. **Ellicott Rock:** 4,022 acres, with more acreage in Georgia and South Carolina (USFS)
12. **Pond Pine:** 1,860 acres (USFS)

North Dakota

Total Wilderness acreage: 39,652

1. **Theodore Roosevelt:** 29,920 acres (NPS)
2. **Lostwood:** 5,577 acres (USF&WS)
3. **Chase Lake:** 4,155 acres (USF&WS)

Ohio

Total Wilderness acreage: 77

1. **West Sister Island:** 77 acres (USF&WS)

Oklahoma

Total Wilderness acreage: 22,524

1. **Upper Kiamichi River:** 9,371 acres (USFS)
2. **Charons Garden–North Mountain:** 8,570 acres (USF&WS)
3. **Black Fork Mountain:** 4,583 acres, with more acreage in Arkansas (USFS)

Oregon

Total Wilderness acreage: 2,093,888

1. **Eagle Cap:** 358,461 acres (USFS)
2. **Three Sisters:** 285,202 acres (USFS)
3. **Kalmiopsis:** 179,700 acres (USFS)
4. **Hells Canyon:** 131,133 acres, with more acreage in Idaho (BLM and USFS)
5. **North Fork John Day:** 121,400 acres (USFS)
6. **Sky Lakes:** 116,300 acres (USFS)
7. **Mount Jefferson:** 107,008 acres (USFS)
8. **Strawberry Mountain:** 68,303 acres (USFS)
9. **Wenaha-Tucannon:** 66,375 acres, with more acreage in Washington (USFS)
10. **Mount Thielsen:** 55,100 acres (USFS)
11. **Mount Washington:** 52,516 acres (USFS)
12. **Diamond Peak:** 52,337 acres (USFS)
13. **Mount Hood:** 46,520 acres (USFS)
14. **Salmon-Huckleberry:** 44,560 acres (USFS)
15. **Waldo Lake:** 39,200 acres (USFS)
16. **Columbia:** 39,000 acres (USFS)
17. **Wild Rogue:** 35,818 acres: (BLM and USFS)
18. **Bull of the Woods:** 34,900 acres (USFS)
19. **Rogue-Umpqua Divide:** 33,200 acres (USFS)
20. **Badger Creek:** 24,000 acres (USFS)

WILDERNESS AREAS AT-A-GLANCE

21. **Mountain Lakes:** 23,071 acres (USFS)
22. **Gearhart Mountain:** 22,809 acres (USFS)
23. **North Fork Umatilla:** 20,200 acres (USFS)
24. **Monument Rock:** 19,800 acres (USFS)
25. **Boulder Creek:** 19,100 acres (USFS)
26. **Mill Creek:** 17,400 acres (USFS)
27. **Grassy Knob:** 17,200 acres (USFS)
28. **Black Canyon:** 13,400 acres (USFS)
29. **Cummins Creek:** 9,300 acres (USFS)
30. **Middle Santiam:** 7,500 acres (USFS)
31. **Rock Creek:** 7,400 acres (USFS)
32. **Drift Creek:** 5,800 acres (USFS)
33. **Table Rock:** 5,500 acres (BLM)
34. **Bridge Creek:** 5,400 acres (USFS)
35. **Menagerie:** 4,725 acres (USFS)
36. **Red Buttes:** 3,750 acres, with more acreage in California (USFS)
37. **Oregon Islands:** 485 acres (BLM and USF&WS)
38. **Three Arch Rocks:** 15 acres (USF&WS)

Pennsylvania

Total Wilderness acreage: 9,705

1. **Hickory Creek:** 9,337 acres (USFS)
2. **Allegheny River Islands:** 368 acres (USFS)

South Carolina

Total Wilderness acreage: 60,539

1. **Cape Romain:** 29,000 acres (USF&WS)
2. **Congaree Swamp:** 15,010 acres (NPS)
3. **Wambaw Swamp:** 5,100 acres (USFS)
4. **Little Wambaw Swamp:** 5,000 acres (USFS)
5. **Ellicott Rock:** 2,809 acres, with more acreage in Georgia and North Carolina (USFS)
6. **Hell Hole Bay:** 1,980 acres (USFS)
7. **Wambaw Creek:** 1,640 acres (USFS)

South Dakota

Total Wilderness acreage: 74,074

1. **Sage Creek (Badlands):** 64,250 acres (NPS)
2. **Black Elk:** 9,824 acres (USFS)

Tennessee

Total Wilderness acreage: 66,714

1. **Citico Creek:** 16,000 acres (USFS)
2. **Sampson Mountain:** 8,319 acres (USFS)
3. **Big Frog:** 7,972 acres, with more acreage in Georgia (USFS)
4. **Pond Mountain:** 6,665 acres (USFS)
5. **Big Laurel Branch:** 6,251 acres (USFS)
6. **Little Frog Mountain:** 4,800 acres (USFS)
7. **Unaka Mountain:** 4,700 acres (USFS)
8. **Bald River Gorge:** 3,887 acres (USFS)
9. **Joyce Kilmer–Slickrock:** 3,832 acres, more acreage in North Carolina (USFS)
10. **Gee Creek:** 2,493 acres (USFS)
11. **Cohutta:** 1,795 acres, with more acreage in Georgia (USFS)

Texas

Total Wilderness acreage: 81,196

1. **Guadalupe Mountains:** 46,850 acres (NPS)
2. **Upland Island:** 12,000 acres (USFS)
3. **Indian Mounds:** 9,946 acres (USFS)
4. **Turkey Hill:** 5,400 acres (USFS)
5. **Little Lake Creek:** 4,000 acres (USFS)
6. **Big Slough:** 3,000 acres (USFS)

Utah

Total Wilderness acreage: 802,189

1. **High Uintas:** 460,000 acres (USFS)
2. **Pine Valley Mountain:** 50,000 acres (USFS)
3. **Dark Canyon:** 45,000 acres (USFS)

WILDERNESS AREAS AT-A-GLANCE

4. **Mount Naomi:** 44,350 acres (USFS)
5. **Lone Peak:** 30,088 acres (USFS)
6. **Mount Nebo:** 28,000 acres (USFS)
7. **Box–Death Hollow:** 26,000 acres (USFS)
8. **Deseret Peak:** 25,500 acres (USFS)
9. **Wellsville Mountains:** 23,850 acres (USFS)
10. **Paria Canyon–Vermilion Cliffs:** 19,954 acres, with more acreage in Arizona (BLM)
11. **Mount Olympus:** 16,000 acres (USFS)
12. **Twin Peaks:** 13,100 acres (USFS)
13. **Mount Timpanogos:** 10,750 acres (USFS)
14. **Ashdown Gorge:** 7,000 acres (USFS)
15. **Beaver Dam Mountains:** 2,597 acres, with more acreage in Arizona (BLM)

Vermont

Total Wilderness acreage: 58,539

1. **Breadloaf:** 21,480 acres (USFS)
2. **Lye Brook:** 14,621 acres (USFS)
3. **Peru Peak:** 6,920 acres (USFS)
4. **Big Branch:** 6,720 acres (USFS)
5. **George D. Aiken:** 5,060 acres (USFS)
6. **Bristol Cliffs:** 3,738 acres (USFS)

Virginia

Total Wilderness acreage: 169,453

1. **Shenandoah:** 79,579 acres (NPS)
2. **Saint Mary's:** 10,090 acres (USFS)
3. **Rough Mountain:** 9,300 acres (USFS)
4. **James River Face:** 8,903 acres (USFS)
5. **Mountain Lake:** 8,253 acres, with more acreage in West Virginia (USFS)
6. **Ramseys Draft:** 6,725 acres (USFS)
7. **Rich Hole:** 6,450 acres (USFS)
8. **Beartown:** 6,375 acres (USFS)
9. **Lewis Fork:** 5,802 acres (USFS)
10. **Barbours Creek:** 5,700 acres (USFS)

11. **Kimberling Creek:** 5,580 acres (USFS)
12. **Little Wilson Creek:** 3,855 acres (USFS)
13. **Shawvers Run:** 3,665 acres (USFS)
14. **Little Dry Run:** 3,400 acres (USFS)
15. **Peters Mountain:** 3,326 acres (USFS)
16. **Thunder Ridge:** 2,450 acres (USFS)

Washington

Total Wilderness acreage: 4,252,344

1. **Olympic:** 876,669 acres (NPS)
2. **Stephen Mather:** 634,614 acres (NPS)
3. **Glacier Peak:** 576,648 acres (USFS)
4. **Pasayten:** 529,850 acres (USFS)
5. **Alpine Lakes:** 305,407 acres (USFS)
6. **Mount Rainier:** 216,855 acres (NPS)
7. **William O. Douglas:** 166,603 acres (USFS)
8. **Lake Chelan–Sawtooth:** 150,704 acres (USFS)
9. **Mount Baker:** 117,580 acres (USFS)
10. **Wenaha-Tucannon:** 111,048 acres, with more acreage in Oregon (USFS)
11. **Goat Rocks:** 105,023 acres (USFS)
12. **Henry M. Jackson:** 102,671 acres (USFS)
13. **Norse Peak:** 50,902 acres (USFS)
14. **Boulder River:** 49,000 acres (USFS)
15. **Mount Adams:** 46,776 acres (USFS)
16. **Buckhorn:** 44,474 acres (USFS)
17. **Salmo-Priest:** 41,335 acres (USFS)
18. **Indian Heaven:** 20,650 acres (USFS)
19. **The Brothers:** 16,682 acres (USFS)
20. **Tatoosh:** 15,720 acres (USFS)
21. **Clearwater:** 14,300 acres (USFS)
22. **Noisy-Diobsud:** 14,300 acres (USFS)
23. **Mount Skokomish:** 13,015 acres (USFS)
24. **Colonel Bob:** 12,120 acres (USFS)
25. **Juniper Dunes:** 7,140 acres (BLM)
26. **Trapper Creek:** 6,050 acres (USFS)

WILDERNESS AREAS AT-A-GLANCE

27. **Glacier View:** 3,050 acres (USFS)
28. **Wonder Mountain:** 2,320 acres (USFS)
29. **Washington Islands:** 485 acres (USF&WS)
30. **San Juan Islands:** 353 acres (USF&WS)

West Virginia

Total Wilderness acreage: 80,631

1. **Cranberry:** 35,864 acres (USFS)
2. **Otter Creek:** 20,000 acres (USFS)
3. **Laurel Fork North/Laurel Fork South:** 12,052 acres (USFS)
4. **Dolly Sods:** 10,215 acres (USFS)
5. **Mountain Lake:** 2,500 acres, with more acreage in Virginia (USFS)

Wisconsin

Total Wilderness acreage: 43,988

1. **Headwaters:** 19,950 acres (USFS)
2. **Whisker Lake:** 7,345 acres (USFS)
3. **Rainbow Lake:** 6,583 acres (USFS)
4. **Blackjack Springs:** 5,886 acres (USFS)
5. **Porcupine Lake:** 4,195 acres (USFS)
6. **Wisconsin Islands:** 29 acres (USF&WS)

Wyoming

Total Wilderness acreage: 3,084,640

1. **Washakie:** 703,981 acres (USFS)
2. **Teton:** 585,468 acres (USFS)
3. **Bridger:** 428,169 acres (USFS)
4. **North Absaroka:** 350,538 acres (USFS)
5. **Gros Ventre:** 287,000 acres (USFS)
6. **Fitzpatrick:** 198,838 acres (USFS)
7. **Cloud Peak:** 195,500 acres (USFS)
8. **Jedediah Smith:** 116,535 acres (USFS)
9. **Popo Agie:** 101,991 acres (USFS)
10. **Huston Park:** 31,300 acres (USFS)
11. **Absaroka-Beartooth:** 23,750 acres, with more acreage in Montana (USFS)
12. **Platte River:** 22,230 acres, with more acreage in Colorado (USFS)
13. **Savage Run:** 14,940 acres (USFS)
14. **Winegar Hole:** 14,000 acres (USFS)
15. **Encampment River:** 10,400 acres (USFS)

Wilderness Resources

Preservation-Oriented Organizations

Defenders of Wildlife
1101 Fourteenth Street NW
Washington, DC 20005
(202) 682-9400

Leave No Trace
288 Main Street
Lander, WY 82520
(800) 332-4100

National Audubon Society
700 Broadway
New York, NY 10003
(212) 979-3000

National Wildlife Federation
1400 Sixteenth Street NW
Washington, DC 20036
(202) 797-6800

Note: The National Wildlife Federation publishes the annual Conservation Directory *with addresses and phone numbers for all of America's organizations, agencies, and officials concerned with natural resource use and management. It costs about $24.*

The Nature Conservancy
1815 North Lynn Street
Arlington, VA 22209
(703) 841-5300

Sierra Club
85 Second Street
San Francisco, CA 94105
(415) 977-5500

The Wilderness Society
900 Seventeenth Street NW
Washington, DC 20006
(202) 833-2300

Management Agencies

Bureau of Land Management (BLM)
U.S. Department of the Interior
1849 C Street NW
Washington, DC 20240
(202) 452-5125

National Park Service (NPS)
U.S. Department of the Interior
P.O. Box 37127
Washington, DC 20013
(202) 208-6843

U.S. Fish and Wildlife Service (USF&WS)
U.S. Department of the Interior
1849 C Street NW
Washington, DC 20240
(202) 208-4717

U.S. Forest Service (USFS)
U.S. Department of Agriculture
P.O. Box 96090
Washington, DC 20090
(202) 205-0957

BOLD PAGE NUMBERS INDICATE MAIN REFERENCES

Index

A

Abbey, Edward 367, 465
Abel, Mount 161
Aberdeen, WA 518
Absaroka Range 341, 342
Absaroka-Beartooth Wilderness (Montana) **341**, 342
Absaroka-Beartooth Wilderness (Wyoming) 342, **530**, 531 (Eastern Unit) 530
Abyss Lake 253
Acoma Indian Reservation 379
Ada, Mount 66
Adak, AK 38
Adak Island **37**, 38
Adams, Ansel 148
Adams, Mount 367, 506
Adirondacks 480
Admiralty Island 54, 55
Admiralty Island National Monument 55
Affleck Canal 56
Affleck Canal Bay 56
Agassiz National Wildlife Refuge 328, 329
Agassiz Wilderness **328**, 329
Agattu Island 37, 38
Aghileen Pinnacles 51
Aghiluk Island 64
Agligadak Island 38
Agua Fria River 82, 83
Agua Tibia Mountain 148
Agua Tibia Wilderness **148**
Ahklun Mountains 70
Aiken, George D. 481
Ajo, AZ 82, 113
Ajo, Mount 112
Ajo Range 112
Alabama 33-35
Alaid Island 37
Alamagordo, NM 390
Alamar Canyon 168
Alamar Trail 168
Alamo Canyon 375
Alamo Dam 118
Alamo Lake State Park 119
Alamosa, CO 246, 261
Alaska 36-74
Alaska Basin 537
Alaska Maritime National Wildlife Refuge 37, 38, 41, 42, 43, 46, 47, 49, 63, 64, 65, 71, 72 (Alaska Peninsula Unit) 38, 64, 65; (Aleutian Islands Unit) 37, 38, 42, 72; (Bering Sea Unit) 41; (Bogoslof Island Unit) 42; (Chukchi Sea Unit) 42, 43; (Gulf of Alaska Unit) 46, 47, 49, 63, 71
Alaska National History Association 49
Alaska National Interest Lands Conservation Act 36
Alaska Panhandle 58
Alaska Peninsula 40, 51, 65, 72
Alaska Peninsula National Wildlife Refuge 51
Alaska Range 45, 57, 341
Alatna River (Wild and Scenic River) 47

Albany, WY 540
Albuquerque, NM 76, 82, 83, 89, 90, 91, 97, 100, 103, 104, 108, 110, 114, 117, 118, 119, 121, 123, 124, 125, 128, 129, 130, 135, 137, 378, 380, 387
Aldo Leopold Wilderness **373**, 374
Aleck Rocks 515
Aleutian Islands 38, 42, 72
Aleutian Islands National Wildlife Refuge 37
Aleutian Islands Wilderness **37**, 38
Aleutian Range 57
Alexander Springs 267
Alexander Springs Campground (Billies Bay Wilderness) 269
Alexander Springs Creek 267, 268
Alexander Springs Wilderness **267**, 268
Alexandria, LA 312
Algodones Sand Dunes 200
Algonquin Trail 82
Alice Creek 351
Alice Creek Basin Trail 351
Allegheny Mountains 441, 491
Allegheny National Forest 441, 442
Allegheny Plateau 521, 522
Allegheny River (Wild and Scenic River) 441, 442
Allegheny River Islands Wilderness **441**, 442
Almond Mountains 175
Alpine, AZ 79, 89
Alpine, CA 177, 208
Alpine Lake 329
Alpine Lakes Wilderness **495**, 496
Alpine Meadows Ski Area 176
Alta Toquima Wilderness **357**, 358
Altoona, FL 267
Alturas, CA 228
Alum Creek 490
Amak Island 38
Amargosa Desert 173
Amargosa River 211
Amatignak Island 37
Amber Springs 335
AMC White Mountain Guide (book) 368, 369, 370
Amchitka Island 37
American Canyon 191
American Canyon Trail 191
American Flats 263
American Fork Canyon 470, 473
American River 511 (Granite Chief Wilderness) 175, (Middle Fork) 175
Amlia Island 38
AMNWR (see Alaska Maritime National Wildlife Refuge)
Amot Creek 157
Amukta Island 38
Anaconda Range 342
Anaconda-Pintlar Wilderness **342**, 343
Anacortes, WA 515
Anagaksik Island 38
Anaktuvuk Pass, AK 48
Anchorage, AK 36, 38, 39, 42, 45, 50, 51, 52, 53, 54, 57, 60, 64

Anderson Grade 527
Anderson Lakes 510
Andreafsky River 39 (East Fork) 39
Andreafsky Wilderness **38**, 39
Andreanof Islands 37
Andrews Ridge Trail 472
Androscoggin River 313
Andy Stone Trail 537
ANF Interpretive Association 34
Angel Lake Campground (East Humboldt Wilderness) 360, 361
Angeles Crest 215
Angeles Forest Service Facility 216
Angeles National Forest 164, 215, 223
Angelina National Forest 464
Angelina River 464
Angels, Lake of the 509
Angoon, AK 55
ANILCA (see Alaska National Interest Lands Conservation Act)
Animas River 264
Annette Key 273
Ansel Adams Wilderness **148**, 149
Antarctica 39
Anthracite Creek 259
Antonito, CO 262
Anvil Lake Recreation Site 526
Anvil Mountain 419
Anza-Borrego Desert State Park 156, 163, 172
Apache Creek Wilderness **76**
Apache Junction, AZ 129
Apache Kid Wilderness **374**, 375
Apache Maid Trail 135
Apache-Sitgreaves National Forest 79, 89, 104
Apalachee Bay 279
Apalachicola National Forest 277
Appalachian Flyway 283
Appalachian greenbelt 445
Appalachian Mountain Club 368, 369, 370
Appalachian Mountains 280, 493
Appalachian National Scenic Trail 282, 286, 288, 289, 290, 368, 369, 401, 478, 479, 482, 485, 523, 524 (Beartown Wilderness) 484; (Big Laurel Branch Wilderness) 453; (James River Face Wilderness) 485; (Lewis Fork Wilderness) 486; (Little Wilson Creek Wilderness) 487; (Mountain Lake Wilderness) 488; (Peters Mountain Wilderness) 489; (Pond Mountain Wilderness) 458; (Shenandoah Wilderness) 493; (Southern Nantahala Wilderness) 401; (Thunder Ridge Wilderness) 494
Appalachian Plateau 451
Apple Orchard Mountain 494
Applegate Lake 210
Applegate River 210
Arapaho Lake 248
Arapaho National Forest 240, 249, 253, 257, 264

560   INDEX

BOLD PAGE NUMBERS INDICATE MAIN REFERENCES

Aravaipa Canyon Wilderness **76**, 77, 124
Aravaipa Creek 76
Arc Dome Wilderness **358**, 359
Archer Key 273
Arco, ID 295
Arctic Circle 47, 54, 59, 63, 253
Arctic National Wildlife Refuge 39, 40
Arctic Village, AK 40
Arctic Wilderness **39**, 40
Argonne Island 37
Argus Range Wilderness **149**, 150
Arica Range 205
Arizona 75-137
Arizona Trail 103
Arkansas 138-146
Arkansas River 238
Arkansas River Valley 239
Arkansas Wilderness Act (1984) 138
Arkaqua National Recreation Trail 282
Armijo Canyon 379
Arrastra Mountain Wilderness **77**
Arrigetch Peaks 47
Arroyo Grande, CA 173
Arroyo Seco Creek 148
Art Loeb Trail 400
Artillery Mountains 77
Artillery Peak 77
Ashdown Gorge Wilderness **466**
Asheville, NC 398
Ashford, WA 502, 509
Ashland, OR 434
Ashland, WI 527
Ashley National Forest 470
Ashton, ID 537, 543
Aspen, CO 242, 248, 252
Aspen Grove Trailhead 473, 474
Asuksak Island 38
Atka Island 38
Atkin Spring 113
Atkins, AR 142
Atlanta, GA 282, 283, 284, 288
Atlantic City, NJ 372
Atlantic Flyway 314, 394, 398
Attu Island 37
Aubrey Peak Wilderness **78**
Aucilla River 279
Ava, MO 336
Avalanche Gulch 199
Avalanche Gulch Route 198
Avatanak Island 38
Avenales Trail 173
Avoss Lake 66
Awendaw, SC 444, 447, 448
Azalea Lake 210
Aziak Island 38
Aztec Peak 125
Azucar Mine 199

B

Baboquivari Peak Wilderness **78**, 79
Baboquivari Range 78
Baby Lake Trail 536
Backbone Ridge 516
Backbone Trail 312
Baden-Powell, Mount 223
Badger Creek National Recreation Trail 411

Badger Creek Wilderness **410**, 411, 415
Badger Pass 237
Badlands National Park 449, 450
Badlands Natural History Association 450
Badwater (Death Valley Wilderness) 166
Bagby Hot Springs 414
Bagdad, AZ 133
Bagley Ice Field 74
Bahia Honda Key 273 (West) 273
Bailey, CO 251
Baird Mountains 54
Baker, CA 178, 179, 188, 196, 202, 214
Baker Dam 510
Baker Island 441, 442
Baker Lake 510
Baker, OR 298, 420, 429
Baker Spring 134
Bakersfield, CA 160, 169, 188, 192, 204, 214, 219
Balcony Falls Trail 485
Bald Knob Wilderness **301**, 302, 303
Bald Mountain 483
Bald River 451
Bald River Falls 451
Bald River Falls Picnic Area 451, 452
Bald River Gorge Wilderness **451**, 452
Bald River Trail 451
Baldy, Mount (Arizona) 104
Baldy, Mount (California) 164, 223
Balm of Gilead (Garcia Wilderness/campground) 173
Bandelier National Monument 375
Bandelier Wilderness **375**, 382
Bangor, ME 315
Bangs, Mount 113
Bankhead National Forest 35
Bannister Wildlife Management Area 463
Bar Harbor, ME 313
Baranof, Alexander 66
Baranof Island 66
Barbours Creek Trail 484
Barbours Creek Wilderness **483**, 484, 492
Bare Island 515
Bark Camp Creek 484
Barnegat National Wildlife Refuge 371
Barnhardt Trail 103
Barracouta Keys 273
Barren Island 515
Barrett Lake 177
Barrier Islands 67
Barry M. Goldwater Air Force Range 81
Barstow, CA 152, 153, 162, 173, 178, 179, 187, 188, 196, 199, 200, 205, 211, 213, 214, 226, 231
Bartlett Cove 49
Bartow, WV 523
Basin Province 92, 120
Basin, the (Granite Chief Wilderness) 175

Basking Ridge, NJ 372
Bassett Peak 91
Bat Mountain 173
Baton Rouge, LA 312
Battery Rock 305
Battleship Island 515
Baxter Mine 211
Bay Creek Wilderness **302**
Bayfield, CO 265
Bayou Cypre 312
Bayou Misere 312
Bean Creek (see also El Rito de los Frijoles) 375
Bean Point 278
Bear Canyon 472
Bear Canyon Trail 168
Bear Creek (Blue Range Wilderness) 377
Bear Creek (San Gabriel Wilderness) 215
Bear Creek Oasis 219
Bear Hollow 142
Bear Trap Campground (Withington Wilderness) 391
Bear Valley Trail 206
Bear Valley Visitors Center 207
Bear Wallow Creek 79
Bear Wallow Trail 79
Bear Wallow Wilderness **79**
Bearce Lake 315
Beardslee Islands 48
Bearhead Mountain 499
Bearpen Trail 487
Beartooth Mountains (Montana) 341, 342
Beartooth Mountains (Wyoming) 530
Beartooth Plateau 530
Beartown Ridge 484
Beartown Wilderness **484**
Beaver Campground (Sespe Wilderness) 222
Beaver Creek (Cruces Basin Wilderness) 381
Beaver Creek Ranger Station 135
Beaver Creek Wilderness **309**, 310
Beaver Creek Wildlife Management Area 309
Beaver Dam Mountains Wilderness (Arizona) **80**, 113
Beaver Dam Mountains Wilderness (Utah) **466**, 467
Beaver Swamp 432
Beaverhead National Forest 343, 346, 347
Becharof Lake 40
Becharof National Wildlife Refuge 40, 41
Becharof Wilderness **40**, 41
Bedford, IN 308
Beech Gap Trail 401
Behm Canal 58
Belfast Creek 485
Belfast Creek Trail 485
Belford, Mount 241
Beljica, Mount 502
Belknap Crater 427
Bell Island 401
Bell Island Recreation Area 402
Bell Meadow Trailhead 170
Bell Mountain Trail 335
Bell Mountain Wilderness **335**

INDEX 561

BOLD PAGE NUMBERS INDICATE MAIN REFERENCES

Bell Rock 109
Bell Trail 135
Bellingham, WA 508
Bellport Beach 392
Bend, OR 437
Benndale, MS 333
Bennington, VT 481
Benson, AZ 120
Benson Lake 427
Benton, TN 280, 453, 455, 457
Bering Land Bridge 63
Bering Sea 41, 42, 51
Bering Sea Wilderness **41**
Bering, Vitus 74
Bethel, AK 39, 50, 60, 70
Bethel, ME 314
Bettles, AK 48, 60
Bickford Brook Trail 313, 314
Big Agnes Mountain 255
Big Bar, CA 232
Big Bay 320
Big Bear (peak) 497
Big Blue Creek 263
Big Blue Wilderness Area 263
Big Branch Stream 478
Big Branch Wilderness **478**, 479, 482
Big Cinder Butte 295
Big Cottonwood Creek 473, 476
Big Cottonwood Creek Canyon 473, 477
Big Creek (Black Fork Mountain Wilderness) 139, 407
Big Creek (Rock Creek Wilderness) 431
Big Creek (Upland Island Wilderness) 464
Big East Fork Trailhead 400
Big Falls 219
Big Fodderstack 454
Big Fog Saddle 300
Big Frog Mountain 452
Big Frog Trail 452
Big Frog Wilderness (Georgia) 280
Big Frog Wilderness (Tennessee) 280, **452**, 453, 454, 455
Big Gum Swamp Wilderness **268**
Big Hazy Island 49
Big Hole River 342
Big Horn Mountains Wilderness 80, 81, 97
Big Horn Peak 80
Big Indian Loop 401
Big Island Lake Wilderness **317**, 318
Big Lake National Wildlife Refuge 138, 139
Big Lake Wilderness **138**, 139
Big Laurel Branch Wilderness **453**, 458
Big Maria Mountains 150, 211
Big Maria Mountains Wilderness **150**
Big Mud Pond 482
Big Muddy River 303
Big Muddy River Levee 303
Big Mullet Key 273
Big Oak Flat 237
Big Paddy Creek 338
Big Pine, CA 209, 230
Big Pine Key, FL 273
Big Pine Mountain 218

Big Piney River 338
Big Piney Trail 338
Big Piney Trailhead (Hurricane Creek Wilderness) 144
Big Prairie 344
Big Quilcene Trail 498, 499
Big River Meadow 344
Big Sandy Campground (Bridger Wilderness) 532
Big Sandy River 77
Big Sandy, WY 531, 532
Big Sky, MT 347
Big Slough Canoe Trail 461
Big Slough Wilderness **460**, 461
Big Smoky Valley 357
Big South Fork National Recreation Area 451
Big Spanish Key 273
Big Sur 224
Big Sur River (Wild and Scenic River) 234
Big Sur State Park 234
Big Wash 150, 212
Big Wilson Creek 487
Big Wilson Creek Trail 487
Bigelow Cholla Garden Wilderness **151**
Bigfork, MT 349
Bighorn Crags 295
Bighorn Mountains 151, 532
Bighorn Mountains Wilderness **151**, 152
Bighorn National Forest 532, 533
Bill Williams Gorge 118
Bill Williams River 118, 119, 129
Billies Bay Wilderness **268**, 269
Billings, MT 342
Billy Lawrence Trailhead 125
Biloxi, MS 332
Bingham Prairie 423
Bingham Prairie Trailhead 423
Birch Island 314
Birchead Mountain Trail 394
Birkhead Mountains Wilderness **393**, 394
Bishop, CA 182, 185, 359
Bismarck, ND 404
Bisti Badlands 376
Bisti Wilderness **376**, 381
Bitter Lake 386
Bitter Lake National Wildlife Refuge 386
Bitterroot Divide 352
Bitterroot Mountains 299, 352
Bitterroot National Forest 296, 300, 343, 352
Bitterroot River 342
Black Bear (Bob Marshall Wilderness) 344

Black Bear Sanctuary 521
Black Canyon 152, 238
Black Canyon Creek 411
Black Canyon of the Gunnison National Monument 239
Black Canyon of the Gunnison Wilderness **238**, 239
Black Canyon Trail 411, 412
Black Canyon Wilderness **411**, 412
Black Cinder Rock 155
Black Creek National Recreation Trail 331, 332
Black Creek Wilderness **331**, 332, 333
Black Elk Wilderness **449**, 450
Black Fork Mountain Trail 139
Black Fork Mountain Wilderness (Arkansas) **139**, 407
Black Fork Mountain Wilderness (Oklahoma) 139, **407**, 408
Black Hills (Black Elk Wilderness) 449, 450
Black Hills (El Paso Mountains Wilderness) 170
Black Hills National Forest 449, 450
Black Lake 298
Black Mesa 111, 129, 134
Black Mountain (El Paso Mountains Wilderness) 170
Black Mountain Wilderness **152**
Black Mountains (Arizona) 105, 106, 131
Black Mountains (California) 179
Black Mountains (New Mexico) 373
Black Rock (North Santa Teresa Wilderness) 112
Black Rock (San Juan Islands Wilderness) 515
Blackbeard Creek 281
Blackbeard Island National Wildlife Refuge 281
Blackbeard Island Wilderness **281**
Blackfoot River 351
Blackjack Creek 525
Blackjack Creek Trail 525
Blackjack Springs Wilderness **525**, 526
Blacksburg, VA 488, 489, 524
Blackwell Campground (Charles C. Deam Wilderness) 308
Blairsville, GA 282, 283, 286, 288, 290
Blanca Lake 503
Blanca Lake Trail 503
Blanco River 262
Bland, VA 486
Blanding, UT 468
Blankenship Bend 177
Bliss Spring 337
BLM (see Bureau of Land Management)
Blood Mountain Wilderness **281**, 282, 287
Bloomfield, NM 382
Blowhard Mountain 466
Blowhard Trail 466
Blue Canyon 433
Blue Eagle Ranch 361, 364
Blue Hole (Mokelumne Wilderness) 197
Blue Lake (Gearhart Mountain Wilderness) 418

562 INDEX

BOLD PAGE NUMBERS INDICATE MAIN REFERENCES

Blue Lake (South San Juan Wilderness) 262
Blue Lake Trail 260
Blue Lakes 255
Blue Lakes Trail 254, 255
Blue Mountain (Glacier Peak Wilderness) 501
Blue Mountain (Mark Trail Wilderness) 286
Blue Mountains (Oregon) 410, 423, 428, 429, 438; (Washington) 518
Blue Range Mountains 376, 377
Blue Range Wilderness **376**, 377
Blue Ridge (Georgia) 282, 286, 288, 289
Blue Ridge (Virginia) 491, 494
Blue Ridge, GA 288
Blue Ridge Mountains (Georgia) 289
Blue Ridge Mountains (North Carolina) 400
Blue Ridge Mountains (Virginia) 491, 493
Blue Ridge Parkway 397, 494
Blue Ridge Wilderness 376
Blue River, OR 437
Blue Springs 335
Bly, OR 418
Blythe, CA 150, 160, 190, 205, 206, 212
Blytheville, AR 139
Boardman State Park 430
boating (Alaska) 42-44, 46-50, 52-56, 58-74; (Arizona) 95-96, 98; (California) 171-172, 178, 221; (Florida) 267, 270-274, 276-279; (Georgia) 281, 285, 290; (Idaho) 296; (Illinois) 304; (Louisiana) 311-312; (Massachusetts) 316; (Michigan) 320-321, 325; (Minnesota) 329; (Mississippi) 332; (Montana) 348, 350; (North Carolina) 401; (Ohio) 406; (Oregon) 439; (Tennessee) 453; (Texas) 462; (Washington) 505-506, 515; (Wisconsin) 529
Bob Creek 415
Bob Marshall Wilderness **343**, 344, 346, 351
Bob Marshall Wilderness Complex 343, 344
Bob, the (see Bob Marshall Wilderness)
Bobrof Island 37
Boca Crande Key 273
Bog Creek 543
Boggs Creek 287
Bogoslof National Wilderness **42**
Bois Blanc Island 325
Boise, ID 296
Boise National Forest 296, 299
Boise River 299 (Middle Fork) 299, (North Fork) 299
Bolivar, Mount 439
Bonanza Trail 362
Bond, Mount 368
Bondcliffs 368
Boneyard Canyon 177
Boone Creek 543
Boone, Daniel 309

Booneville, AR 142
Borden Creek 34
Border Trail 114
Boreal Mountain 47
Bosque del Apache National Wildlife Refuge 377, 378
Bosque del Apache Wilderness **377**, 378 (Chupadera Unit) 377; (Indian Well Unit) 377; (Little San Pascual Unit) 377
Boston Mountains 140, 142, 143, 145
Bottle Pass 240
Bottomless Pit 292
Boulder, CO 249
Boulder Creek (Indian Peaks Wilderness) 248, (South Fork) 248
Boulder Creek Trail 412
Boulder Creek Wilderness **412**, 432
Boulder Island 515
Boulder River Wilderness **497**
Boulder Spring Trail 418
Boulder, WY 532
Boundary Peak Trailhead 359
Boundary Peak Wilderness **359**
Boundary Trail 513
Boundary Waters Canoe Area Wilderness **329**
Bourbon Creek 517
Bourn Pond 481
Bouse, AZ 88
Bowen Gulch 256
Bowen Gulch Trail 256, 257
Bowie, AZ 87
Box Canyon 212
Box Elder Peak 477
Box Elder Trail 477
Box–Death Hollow Wilderness **467**, 468
Bozeman, MT 342, 347
Brabazon Range 62
Bradenton, FL 278
Bradshaw Mountains 82
Bradwell Bay Wilderness **269**, 277
Branson, MO 339
Brasstown Bald Mountain 282
Brasstown Bald Visitors Center 282, 283
Brasstown Wilderness **282**, 283
Brawley, CA 201
Breadloaf Mountain 479
Breadloaf Wilderness **479**, 480
Breathed Mountain Trail 522
Breitenbush River 413
Breton Island Wilderness **311**
Breton National Wildlife Refuge 311
Brickhill Bluff 284
Bridalveil Falls 236
Bridge Creek Wilderness **413**
Bridgeport, CA 157, 179
Bridger, Jim 531, 534
Bridger Lake 541
Bridger Wilderness **531**, 532, 534, 535, 539
Bridger-Teton National Forest 530, 532, 536, 541
Bridgeville, CA 201
Brigantine National Wildlife Refuge 371

Brigantine Wilderness **371**, 372
Bright Star Canyon 152, 153
Bright Star Wilderness **152**, 153
Brinnon, WA 498
Bristol Cliffs Wilderness **480**
Bristol, FL 277
Bristol Mountains 153, 187
Bristol Mountains Wilderness **153**
Broadus, TX 464
Broken Top Glacier 436
Bronco Flats 177
Brook, Lake 478
Brookings, OR 421, 430
Brook, Lake 478
Brooks Lake 542
Brooks Lodge 52
Brooks Range 39, 40, 47, 54, 59
Broom Canyon 360
Broom Canyon Trail 360
Brothers, The (peak) 497, 498
Brothers Trail, The 498
Brothers Wilderness, The **497**, 498
Brower, David 33, 311
Brown Rock 515
Brown's Cabin 233
Brown's Canyon 94
Brown's Peak 90
Brown's Spring 83
Brown's Spring Trailhead 83
Brown's Trail 90, 91
Brule River 528
Brush Mountain 454
Brushy Hill 486
Brushy Mountain 490
Brushy Ridge 397
Bryce Canyon 472
Buck Creek 429
Buck Hall Recreation Area 447
Buck Island (Aleutian Islands Wilderness) 38
Buck Island (San Juan Islands Wilderness) 515
Buck Lake (Emigrant Wilderness) 171
Buck Mountain 429
Buckaloons Recreation Area 441, 442
Buckeye (Garcia Wilderness/campsite) 173
Buckeye Canyon 86
Buckeye Falls 458
Buckeye Gap 398
Buckeye Lake 432
Buckeye Mountain 141
Buckeye Peak 497
Buckeye Trail 141
Buckhorn Wilderness **497**, **498**, 499
Buckled Rock 457
Bucks Lake Wilderness **154**
Buckskin Gulch 474
Buckskin Gulch Trail 474
Buckskin Mountains 92, 118, 129
Budweiser Wash 153
Buena Vista, CO 240, 242
Buena Vista, VA 492, 494
Buffalo Canyon Trail 365
Buffalo City, AR 140
Buffalo Hump 297
Buffalo Meadows Trail 239, 240

INDEX 563

BOLD PAGE NUMBERS INDICATE MAIN REFERENCES

Buffalo National River 140, 144, 146
Buffalo National River Wilderness **140**, 144
 (Lower Buffalo Unit) 140, 144,
 (Upper Buffalo Unit) 140
Buffalo Peaks Wilderness **239**, 240
Buffalo Point Ranger Station 140
Buffalo River Trail 140
Buffalo, WY 533
Buhl, ID 362
Buldir Island 37
Bull Creek 462
Bull Creek Trail 384
Bull of the Woods Peak 414
Bull of the Woods Wilderness **413**, 414, 433, 435
Bull Pen Ranch 134, 135
Bullion Mountains 161
Bullrun Rock 423, 424
Bullrun Rock Trail 424
Bumping Lake 519
Bumping River 519
Bunchgrass Trailhead 230, 231
Burden Creek 302
Burden Falls Trail 303
Burden Falls Wilderness **302**, 303
Bureau of Biological Survey 281
Bureau of Land Management 75, 77, 78, 79, 80, 81, 85, 86, 87, 88, 89, 92, 94, 95, 96, 98, 101, 105, 106, 107, 108, 109, 110, 111, 112, 114, 115, 116, 119, 120, 124, 126, 127, 129, 131, 132, 133, 134, 136, 137, 150, 151, 152, 153, 155, 156, 159, 160, 162, 163, 164, 165, 166, 169, 170, 172, 173, 175, 176, 178, 179, 181, 182, 183, 187, 188, 190, 191, 192, 193, 195, 196, 199, 200, 201, 202, 203, 204, 205, 206, 207, 209, 210, 211, 212, 213, 214, 215, 216, 219, 220, 224, 226, 228, 229, 230, 231, 232, 233, 235, 236, 238, 258, 263, 294, 295, 296, 341, 346, 347, 357, 358, 359, 360, 363, 373, 376, 380, 382, 388, 410, 420, 430, 435, 439, 440, 465, 466, 467, 468, 475, 505
Burnt Hill Trail 479
Burnt River (South Fork) 423, 424
Burrell's Ford Campground (Ellicott Rock Wilderness) 445
Burro Flats 96
Butler Creek Trail 473
Butte Creek 438
Butte Fork Canyon 210
Butte, MT 347
Butter Creek 516
Butterfield Stage Route 116
Butterfly Mountain 126
BWCA (see Boundary Waters Canoe Area)
Byers Peak Trail 240
Byers Peak Wilderness **240**, 264

C

Cabeza Prieta National Wildlife Refuge 81, 82
Cabeza Prieta Wilderness **81**, 82

Cabinet Mountains Wilderness **344**, 345
Cabresto Creek 383
Cabresto Lake 384
Cache Creek 535
Cache la Poudre River (Wild and Scenic River) 241, 242, 256 (Big South Fork) 242, (Little South Fork) 241, 242, (Main Fork) 241
Cache la Poudre Wilderness **241**
Cactus Flat 163
Cactus Plain 88
Cactus Spring Trail 219, 220
Cadiz Dry Lake 154
Cadiz Dunes Wilderness **154**, 155
Cadiz Valley 211
Cahuilla, Lake 172
Cairn, North 316
Calais, ME 315
Caldwell Mesa 173
Caldwell Mesa Trail 173
Calf Creek 543
Calf Creek Plateau 257
Calf Pen Canyon 90
California 147-237
California Department of Parks and Recreation 216
California Desert Information Center 187, 196
California Desert Protection Act (1994) 36, 147, 166, 169, 185, 196, 214, 219
California Valley 204, 226
California Wilderness Act (1984) 232
Callahan, CA 232
Calumet Mountains 223
Camino, CA 151, 167, 197
Camp Verde, AZ 83, 117, 135, 137
Campbell Lake 193
Canaan Mountain Wilderness Study Area 85
Cane Creek 336
Cane Spring Trail 90
Canebrake Canyon 220
Caney Creek Trail 141
Caney Creek Wilderness **141**
Canjilon, NM 380
Cannibal Plateau 257
Cannon Air Force Base 386
canoeing (Alaska) 40, 53-56, 59; (Arizona) 95, 98; (Arkansas) 140; (California) 180; (Florida) 269, 271-272, 275, 277; (Georgia) 287; (Illinois) 306; (Kentucky) 310; (Michigan) 317, 320-321, 326-327; (Minnesota) 328-329; (Mississippi) 331; (Missouri) 335-337; (Montana) 350; (Nebraska) 355; (New Mexico) 380; (Oregon) 419; (Pennsylvania) 441; (South Carolina) 445-448; (Texas) 461; (Wisconsin) 527
Canon City, CO 246, 261
Canyonville, OR 432
Cape Bingham 73
Cape Blanco 430
Cape Cod 316
Cape Cross 73
Cape Flattery 518
Cape Kiwanda 430

Cape Meares National Wildlife Refuge 436
Cape Perpetua 415
Cape Romain National Wildlife Refuge 443, 444
Cape Romain Wilderness **443**, 444
Cape Saint Elias 74
Capitan Mountains Wilderness **378**
Capitan Peak 378
Capitan Peak Trail 378
Capulin Trail 382
Carbon Trail 499
Carbondale, CO 248, 252, 259
Carefree, AZ 103
Carhart, Arthur 244
Caribou Lake Trail 155
Caribou Mountain 313
Caribou Trail 313
Caribou Wilderness **155**, 189
Caribou–Speckled Mountain Wilderness **313**, 314
Carlisle Island 38
Carlsbad Caverns Guadalupe Mountains Association 462
Carlsbad Caverns National Park 379
Carlsbad Caverns Wilderness **379**
Carlsbad, NM 379, 461
Carnegie, Thomas 284
Carp River 321
Carr Bridge 277
Carrizo Badlands 163
Carrizo Falls 207
Carrizo Gorge Wilderness **156**
Carrizo Mountain 163
Carrizo Wash 207
Carson City, NV 157, 197
Carson, Kit 156
Carson National Forest 380, 381, 384, 385, 389
Carson Pass–Round Top (Mokelumne Wilderness) 197
Carson Peak 264
Carson Range 363
Carson River 156
 (East Fork) 156
Carson, WA 504, 517
Carson-Iceberg Wilderness **156**, 157, 170
Carson's Well (Turtle Mountains Wilderness) 233
Carter, Jimmy 36
Carterville, IL 304
Cascade, ID 296
Cascade Mountains 155, 198, 227, 410, 412, 416, 425, 426, 427, 432, 433, 435, 437, 495, 499, 502, 503, 511, 513
Cashmere Crags 496
Cassi Creek Trail 458, 459 (East Fork) 458
Cassville, MO 339
Castle Crags State Park 157, 158
Castle Crags Wilderness **157**, 158, 199
Castle Creek 265
Castle Creek Trail 82
Castle Creek Wilderness **82**
Castle Dome 162
Castle Dome Mountains 102
Castle Island 515
Castle Pass 265

BOLD PAGE NUMBERS INDICATE MAIN REFERENCES

Castle Rock 42
Castle Rock Fork Creek 432
Castle View 265
Castles, the (West Elk Wilderness) 265
Cataract Lake 243
Catawba Valley 396
Catfish Lake South Wilderness **394**, 395
Catlin, George 280
Caton Island 38
Cave Junction, OR 421, 431
Cayuma Rim 168
Cebolla Canyon 379, 380
Cebolla Wilderness **379**, 380, 388
Cedar Bench Wilderness **83**, 117
Cedar Breaks National Monument 466
Cedar City District Map 467
Cedar City, UT 466, 468, 476
Cedar Creek 444, 445
Cedar Grove Campground (Monarch Wilderness) 198
Cedar Keys National Wildlife Refuge 270
Cedar Keys Wilderness **270**
Cedar Pockets Rest Area 80, 467
Cedar Rock Mountain 393
Cedar Spring 91
Cedar Springs 466
Cedarville, CA 228
Cellar Hollow 491
Cemetery Ridge 87
Centennial Mountains 350
Centennial Trail 449
Centennial Valley 350
Center Mountain Trail 125
Center Reef 515
Central Flyway 312
Central, UT 476
Cerbat Mountains 106
Cerro Gordo Peak 181
Chadron, NE 356
Chagulak Island 37
Challis, ID 296
Challis National Forest 296, 299
Chama River (Wild and Scenic River) 380
Chama River Canyon Wilderness **380**
Chambers Lake 260
Chambers Lakes 437
Chambers Lakes Trail 437
Chamisso Island Wilderness **42**, 43
Champlain, Lake 480
Champlain Valley 480
Chanchelulla Peak 158
Chanchelulla Wilderness **158**
Chandeleur Islands 311
Charles C. Deam Wilderness **307**, 308
Charles M. Russell National Wildlife Refuge 353
Charleston Peak 362
Charleston, SC 444, 447, 448
Charleston, WV 524
Charnock Pass 358
Charons Garden Wilderness 408, 409
Charons Garden–North Mountain Wilderness **408**, 409

Chase Lake National Wildlife Refuge 403
Chase Lake Prairie Project 404
Chase Lake Wilderness **403**, 404
Chassahowitzka National Wildlife Refuge 270, 271, 278
Chassahowitzka River 270, 271
Chassahowitzka Wilderness **270**, 271
Chatham Lighthouse 316
Chatham, MA 316
Chatham, MI 324
Chatham Strait 56, 66
Chatsworth, GA 284
Chattahoochee National Forest 280, 282, 283, 284, 285, 286, 288, 289, 290, 446
Chattahoochee River 286
Chattahoochee Wildlife Management Area 286, 287
Chattooga River (Wild and Scenic River) 285, 395, 445
Chattooga River Trail 445
Cheaha Mountain 33
Cheaha State Park 33, 34
Cheaha Wilderness **33**, 34
Cheat River (Laurel Fork) 523
Chelan, Lake 505, 506
Chelan Lake National Recreation Area 515
Chelan, WA 501, 506
Chemehuevi Mountains Wilderness **159**, 177
Chemehuevi Peak 159
Chemult, OR 426
Chequamegon National Forest 525, 527, 528
Cherokee National Forest 280, 451, 452, 453, 454, 455, 456, 457, 458, 459
Cherry Creek 125
Cherry Peak Trail 471
Chestatee Wildlife Management Area 281, 287
Chester, CA 183
Chestnut Mountain 455, 456
Chestnut Mountain Trail 456
Chetco Peak 421
Chetco River (Wild and Scenic River) 420
Chetco River Bridge 421
Chiatovich Creek 359
Chicago Valley 200
Chichagof Island 62, 73
Chief Shakes Hot Springs 68
Chiefland, FL 270
Chigmit Mountains 57
Chihuahuan Desert 83, 373
Chilikadrotna River (Wild and Scenic River) 57
Chilkat Mountains 45
Chimayo, NM 385
Chimney Creek 159
Chimney Lake 418
Chimney Lake Trail 418
Chimney Peak 159, 422
Chimney Peak Trail 422
Chimney Peak Wilderness **159**, 160
Chimney Rock 141
China Lake Naval Weapons Center 149, 176

Chinese Wall (escarpment) 343, 344, 351
Chinnabee, Lake 33
Chinnabee Silent Trail 33
Chino Valley, AZ 76, 93, 99, 137
Chinook Pass 511
Chip Wash 132
Chiricahua Apache Indian Reservation 84
Chiricahua Mountains 83, 84
Chiricahua National Monument 83, 84, 85
Chiricahua National Monument Wilderness **83**, 84
Chiricahua Peak 84
Chiricahua Wilderness **84**, 85
Chisak Island 38
Chisik Island 71
Chitina, AK 74
Chocolate Mountain 209
Chocolate Mountains 156, 181, 191, 200
Christine, Lake 502
Chuck Mining Camp (Chuck River Wilderness) 43
Chuck River Wilderness **43**
Chuckwalla Mountains Wilderness **160**
Chuckwalla Spring 162
Chugach National Forest 36
Chuginadak Island 38
Chugul Island 38
Chugulak Island 38
Chukchi Sea 54
Chumash Wilderness **161**
Church, Senator Frank 295
Cibola National Forest 375, 384, 387, 391
Cimarron River 263
Cirque of the Towers 531
Cirrus Peak 256
Citico Creek Wilderness **454**, 456
Civilian Conservation Corps 432
Clapp Spring 206
Claremont, CA 164
Clark, Lake 57
Clark Mountains 195, 228
Clark, William 297, 345, 353
Clarkesville, GA 286, 288, 290
Clarksville, AR 144, 146
Claypool, AZ 123
Clayton, GA 285, 289, 290, 446
Cle Elum, WA 496
Clear Branch 463
Clear Creek (Siskiyou Wilderness) 225
Clear Creek (West Clear Creek Wilderness) 134
Clear Creek Canyon 134
Clear Creek National Recreation Trail 225
Clear Lake 227
Clear Springs Wilderness 301, **303**
Clearwater National Forest 300
Clearwater River (Clearwater Wilderness) 499
Clearwater River (Gospel Hump Wilderness) (South Fork) 297
Clearwater Trail 499
Clearwater Wilderness **499**

INDEX 565

Cleghorn Lakes Wilderness **161**, 162
Clements Reef 515
Cleveland, Mount 479
Cleveland National Forest 148, 177, 208, 217
Cleveland, TX 463
Cliff Lake (Marble Mountain Wilderness) 193
Cliff Lake (Rogue-Umpqua Divide Wilderness) 432
Cliffside Trail 486
Clifty Wilderness **310**
Clipper Mountains Wilderness **162**
Cloud Peak Primitive Area 532
Cloud Peak Wilderness **532**, 533
Clover Creek 134
Clover Creek Trail 428
Coachella Canal 195, 201
Coast Campground (Phillip Burton Wilderness) 207
Coast Range 225, 416 (North) 225
Coastal Range 410
Cobscook Bay 314
Cochita Lake 382
Cocks Comb (Saddle Mountain Wilderness) 121
Coconino National Forest 90, 100, 101, 110, 119, 128, 130, 135
Cody, WY 531, 538, 542
Coeur D'Alene, ID 296
Coffin Spring 233
Cohutta Wilderness (Georgia) 280, **283**, 284, 452
Cohutta Wilderness (Tennessee) 283, **454**, 455
Cohutta Wildlife Management Area 283, 454
Colchuck Lake 496
Cold Bay, AK 51
Cold Brook Trail 313
Cold Mountain 400
Cold River Campground (Caribou–Speckled Mountain Wilderness) 314
Cold Springs Trail 434
Coldwater Lake 477
Coleman Glacier 507
Coleman River Wildlife Management Area 289
Collawash River 413
Collegiate Peaks 247
Collegiate Peaks Wilderness 239, **241**, 242
Collier Glacier 436
Collins Ridge Trail 336
Colonel Bob Trail 500
Colonel Bob Wilderness **500**
Colorado 238-266
Colorado City, AZ 85
Colorado City, CO 246
Colorado Desert 156, 160, 183, 185, 219, 233
Colorado Plateau 75, 79, 89, 92, 119, 130, 134, 135, 238, 250, 376, 465, 468
Colorado River 92, 95, 96, 98, 100, 132, 150, 159, 165, 177, 178, 180, 181, 212, 235, 243, 256, 295

Colorado State Forest 259
Colorado Trail 247, 249, 251, 254, 264, 265
Columbia Gorge Recreation Area 414
Columbia, Mount 241
Columbia River 141
Columbia River Gorge 414
Columbia, SC 445
Columbia Wilderness 411, **414**, 415
Colville Island 515
Colville National Forest 514
Comanche Peak Wilderness **242**, 243
Comers Rock Campground (Little Dry Run Wilderness) 487
Conasauga River 283
Concrete, WA 510
Condon, MT 349
Cone Lake Trailhead 155
Conejos Peak 262
Conejos Peak Trail 262
Conejos River 262 (South Fork) 262
Conejos River Trailhead (South Fork) 262
Confederated Salish and Kootenai Tribal Recreation Department 349, 350
Congaree River 444, 445
Congaree Swamp National Monument 444, 445
Congaree Swamp Wilderness **444**, 445
Conley Cove Trail 397
Conner, MT 352
Constance, Lake 512
Constance Pass 498
Continental Divide 241, 242, 247, 248, 249, 254, 255, 256, 262, 264, 342, 343, 346, 351, 374, 531, 534, 536, 539, 541 (Eastern) 488, 523
Continental Divide National Scenic Trail (Aldo Leopold Wilderness) 374; (Anaconda-Pintlar Wilderness) 343; (Huston Park Trail) 536; (Scapegoat Wilderness) 351; (Vasquez Peak Wilderness) 263; (Weminuche Wilderness) 264
Conundrum Creek 252
Conway, NH 368, 370
Cook Inlet 53, 57, 71
Cooley Glen Trail 479
Copalis Refuge 518
Copeland Canyon 378
Copper Harbor, MI 321
Copper World Mine 161, 162
Copperfield, OR 420
Cordes, AZ 82
Corn Springs 160
Corn Springs Wash 160
Corning, CA 236
Corona, CA 217
Coronado Expedition 103
Coronado National Forest 85, 104, 108, 114, 118, 121, 125
Coronado National Memorial 104
Coronation Island 44, 49
Coronation Island Wilderness **44**

Corral Creek 256
Corral Spring 91
Cortez Canyon 152, 153
Cortez, CO 250
Corvallis, OR 436
Cosa Range Wilderness **163**
Cossatot River 141
Cottonwood Campground (Sawtooth Mountains Wilderness) 220
Cottonwood Canyon 85
Cottonwood Lakes 174
Cottonwood Pass (Collegiate Peaks Wilderness) 241
Cottonwood Pass (Golden Trout Wilderness) 174
Cottonwood Pass Trail 174
Cottonwood Peak 124
Cottonwood Point Wilderness **85**
Cottonwood Trail 540
Cottrell Key 273
Cougar Spring 114
Courson Island 441, 442
Courthouse Butte 109
Courthouse Rock 87
Courtright Reservoir 168, 169
Cove Branch 484
Covelo, CA 236
Covington, VA 490
Cow Canyon Trail 358
Cow Creek Canyon 263
Cow Heaven Canyon 187
Cowan, Mount 342
Cowlitz River 516 (Muddy Fork) 516
Cowpasture River 491
Coxcomb Mountains 185
Coy Bald 336
Coyote Mountains Wilderness **86**, 163, 164
Coyote, NM 380, 387
Crab Island 515
Crab Orchard Lake 304
Crab Orchard National Wildlife Refuge 304, 306
Crab Orchard Wilderness **304**, 306
Crabtree Camp Trailhead 171
Craig, AK 44, 47, 58, 68, 73
Cranberry River (North Fork) 521, (South Fork) 521
Cranberry Wilderness **521**, 522
Crane Key 273
Crane Lake, MN 329
Crane Trail 491
Crater Lake (Rawah Wilderness) 259
Crater Lake (Rogue-Umpqua Divide Wilderness) 432
Crater Lake National Park 426, 427, 432, 433
Crater Peak 230
Craters of the Moon National Monument 294, 295
Craters of the Moon Wilderness **294**, 295
Crawfish Key 273
Crawford, NE 356
Crawl Key 273
Creede, CO 250, 265
Crescent Lake (Diamond Peak Wilderness) 416

566 INDEX

BOLD PAGE NUMBERS INDICATE MAIN REFERENCES

Crescent Lake (Mission Mountains Wilderness) 348
Crescent, OR 416
Crest Horse Camp (Indian Heaven Wilderness) 504
Crest Trail 103, 104, 387, 390
Crested Butte, CO 259
Crestone, CO 261
Crestone Needle (peak) 260
Cripple Camp (Rogue-Umpqua Divide Wilderness) 432
Croatan National Forest 393, 394, 395, 398, 399
Crockett, TX 461
Crocodile Lake National Wildlife Refuge 272
Crone Island 38
Crooked Creek 438
Crosley Saddle 148
Cross Creek Trail 247
Crow Creek 538
Crowell Ridge Trail 514
Crown King, AZ 82
Crown Point, NM 376
Cruces Basin Wilderness **381**
Cruiser, Mount 509
Crull's Island 441, 442
Crystal Brook 479
Crystal Brook Glacial Kettle 479
Crystal Creek 245
Crystal Hill 102
Crystal River, FL 271, 278
CSX Railroad 491
Cuba, NM 387
Cucamonga Peak Trail 164
Cucamonga Wilderness **164**
Culbertson, MT 348
Cumberland Island National Seashore 284, 285
Cumberland Island Wilderness **284**, 285
Cumberland, MD 329
Cumberland National Forest 309
Cumberland Plateau 451
Cummins Creek Trail 415
Cummins Creek Wilderness **415**, 431
Cummins Ridge 415
Cummins Ridge Trail 415
Cumulus Peak 256
Currant Mountain Wilderness **360**
Currant, NV 361
Curtis Cemetery (Arkansas) 146
Cushman, Lake 509, 520
Custer National Forest 342
Custer, SD 450
Custer State Park 449
Cutoe Key islands 273
Cutter, AZ 110
Cypress Creek 464
Cypress Trailhead 230

D

Daggett, CA 213
Dahlonega, GA 282, 288
Danby, VT 479, 482
Daniel Boone National Forest 309, 310
Darby, MT 296, 300, 352
Darien, GA 290
Dark Canyon 259, 468

Dark Canyon Primitive Area 468
Dark Canyon Trail 468
Dark Canyon Wilderness **468**
Dark Hollow Creek 226
Darling, Jay Norwood "Ding" 274
Darrington, WA 497, 501, 504
Darwin Canyon 165
Darwin Falls Wilderness **165**
Darwin Plateau 165
Davidof Island 37
Davidof Lake 66
Davidson Rock 515
Davies Valley 183
Davis Bayou Visitors Center 332
Davy Crockett National Forest 461
Dayton, WA 519
De Land, FL 276
De-Na-Zin Wilderness **381**, 382
Dead Indian Campground (North Absaroka Wilderness) 537
Dead Indian Creek 537
Dead Indian Hill 537
Dead Indian Meadows 537
Dead Indian Pass 537
Dead Indian Peak 537
Dead Mountains Wilderness **165**
Dead River 322
Deadman's Key Island 270
Death Hollow 467, 468
Death Hollow Creek 467
Death Valley, CA 166
Death Valley Junction, CA 173, 211
Death Valley National Monument 166
Death Valley National Park 149, 165, 166, 173, 179, 181, 192, 193, 209, 211, 214, 229, 230
Death Valley Wilderness **166**, 295, 352
Dee Wright Observatory 427
Deep Canyon Trail 477
Deer Cove Trail 198
Deer Creek 182
Deer Lake 171
Deer Lick Springs 158
Deer Meadow Trail 198
Deerlodge National Forest 343
Defiance, Mount 414
Del Norte, CO 265
Delaney Gulch 241
Delarof Islands 37
DeLeon Springs, FL 276
Delirium Pond 318
Delirium Wilderness **318**
Denali National Park and Preserve 44, 45
Denali Park, AK 45
Denali Pass 45
Denali Wilderness **44**, 45
Denny Creek Trail 241, 242
Dennysville, ME 315
Denver, CO 240, 243, 248, 251, 253, 254, 258, 264, 295, 298
Deschutes National Forest 416, 426, 427, 437
Deseret Peak Trail 469
Deseret Peak Wilderness **469**
Desert Divide 216
Desolation Canyon 423
Desolation Region (Pemigewasset Wilderness) 369
Desolation Valley Primitive Area 167

Desolation Wilderness **167**
Desor, Mount 320
Desoto Falls Scenic Area 281, 282
DeSoto National Forest 331, 332, 333
Detroit Lakes, MN 330
Devil Canyon 219
Devil's Backbone Park 305
Devils Backbone Wilderness **335**, 336
Devil's Bridge Trail 119
Devil's Canyon 215
Devil's Canyon Trailhead 215
Devil's Fork 145
Devil's Gulch 524
Devil's Highway, The 81
Devil's Kitchen Geologic Site 472
Devil's Kitchen Lake 304, 306
Devil's Lake Trail 258
Devil's Playground 187
Devil's Postpile National Monument 149, 185
Devil's Pulpit 480
Devil's Slide Trailhead 217
Devils Thumb Pass 248
Devils Thumb Trail 248
Dexter, Lake 267
Diamond Bar Spring 89
Diamond Lake 426
Diamond Peak Wilderness **416**
Dick Smith Wilderness **168**, 218
Dick's Creek 282
Dick's Creek Gap 289
Dicks Pass 167
Dillingham, AK 41, 70
Dinkey Lakes Wilderness **168**, 169
Dinkum Rocks Island 37
Diobsud Creek 510
Disenchantment Bay 62
Divide Lake 416
Divide Trail 352
Dixie National Forest 466, 468, 476
Doe Gap 421
Dog Island 314
Dolly Sods Picnic Area 522
Dolly Sods Wilderness **522**
Dolores, CO 250
Dolores Peak 250
Dome Lookout Tower 382
Dome Mountain 175
Dome Wilderness 375, **382**
Domeland Wilderness **169**, 227
Don Victor Canyon 168
Donaca Lake 422
Donaldson, A. B. 449
Doniphan, MO 337
Dora Island 37
Dos Cabezas Mountains Wilderness **86**, 87
Dosewallips River 497
Dot Island 515
Doubletop Peak 535
Douglas, AZ 85
Douglas Creek 538
Douglas Creek Trail 538
Douglas Spring Trail 122
Douglas, William O. 317
Doyles Corner, CA 231
Drift Creek Wilderness **416**, 417
Driggs, ID 537

INDEX 567

BOLD PAGE NUMBERS INDICATE MAIN REFERENCES

Dripping Springs Campground (Agua Tibia Wilderness) 148
Dripping Springs Trail 148
Dromedary Peak 476
Drummond, WI 528
Dry Branch 458
Dry Butte 421
Dry Creek (Dry Creek Wilderness) 141
Dry Creek (Grassy Knob Wilderness) 419
Dry Creek Mountain 141
Dry Creek Trail 141
Dry Creek Wilderness **141**, 142
Dry Fork River 524
Dry Lake 353
Dry Pond Lead 457
Dry Pond Lead Trail 457
Dry River Campground (Presidential Range–Dry River Wilderness) 370
Dry River Trail 369, 370
Dublin Hills 179
Dubois, WY 535, 542
Duck Island 71
Duckabush River 497, 498
Duckabush Trail 498
Dufur, OR 411
Dug Bar 298, 420
Dugas, AZ 117
Duluth, MN 329
Duncan Ridge National Recreation Trail 282
Dungeness Mansion (Georgia) 284
Dungeness River 498
Dunlap, CA 184, 198
Durango, CO 253, 265
Dutch Harbor, AK 38
Dutch Pasture Canyons 89

E

Eagar, AZ 104
Eagle Cap Mountain 417
Eagle Cap Wilderness **417**, 418
Eagle, CO 244
Eagle Crag 148
Eagle Creek (Columbia Wilderness) 414
Eagle Creek (Eagle Cap Wilderness/Wild and Scenic River) 417
Eagle Creek (Salmon-Huckleberry Wilderness) 433
Eagle Creek Campground (Columbia Wilderness) 415
Eagle Creek Trail 414, 415
Eagle Falls Trailhead 167
Eagle Mountain 211
Eagle Mountains 185
Eagle Nest Mines 212
Eagle Peak 227
Eagle River, WI 526
Eagles Nest Wilderness **243**, 264
Eagletail Mountains Wilderness **87**
Eagletail Peak 87
East Baldy Trail 104
East Bellows Creek Trailhead 250
East Cactus Plain Wilderness **88**
East Cowpen Trail 283
East Cuesta Pass 219
East Cuesta Ridge 219
East Davis Lake 527
East Fork Mill Creek Trail 423

East Fork Trail (East Fork Wilderness) 142
East Fork Trail (Pecos Wilderness) 385
East Fork Trail (Sheep Mountain Wilderness) 223
East Fork Wilderness **142**
East Hickory, PA 442
East Humboldt Range 360
East Humboldt Wilderness **360**, 361
East Middlebury, VT 480
East Mojave National Scenic Area 196
East Point 413
Eastern Dry Rocks 273
Eastern National Park and Monument Association 140
Eastern Wilderness Act (1975) 478, 481
Ebbetts Pass 197
Echo Canyon Loop Trail 84
Echo Crater 295
Echo Summit 167
Echo Trailhead 167
Eddeeleo Lakes 437
Eddyville, IL 302, 305
Edith Lake 528
Edwin B. Forsythe National Wildlife Refuge 371, 372
Eel River (Wild and Scenic River) (Middle Fork) 235, (North Fork) 201
Egg Island (Aleutian Islands Wilderness) 38
Egg Island (Wolf Island Wilderness) 290 (Little) 290
Eisenhower, Mount 369
Eisenhower Tunnel 258
Eisley, Loren 301
El Camino del Diablo 81
El Camino Real 377
El Capitan (Yosemite Wilderness) 236
El Capitan Mountain (Capitan Mountains Wilderness) 378
El Centro, CA 156, 164, 172, 181, 183, 191, 201, 206, 207
El Diente (peak) 250
El Huerfano Trading Post 382
El Malpais Information Center 380, 388
El Malpais National Conservation Area 379, 380, 388
El Malpais National Monument 388
El Paso Mountains Wilderness **170**
El Paso, TX 462
El Portal, CA 237
El Rito de los Frijoles (see also Bean Creek) 375
El Vado Lake Dam 380
Elbe, WA 509
Elbert, Mount 241, 254
Elbow Swamp 478
Eldorado National Forest 167, 197
Elephant Head 432
Eleven Point National Scenic River 337
Elf Island 38
Elfin Cove, AK 62
Elinor, Mount 509

Eliza Rock 515
Elizabethton, TN 453, 458
Elizabethtown, IL 305
Elk City, ID 296, 297
Elk Flats, OR 438, 439
Elk Lake 414
Elk Mountain 408
Elk Mountain Trail System 408
Elk Mountains 252, 257
Elk River (Grassy Knob Wilderness) 419
Elk River (Mount Zirkel Wilderness) 255
Elkhorn Crest Trail (National Recreation Trail) 428
Elkhorn Mountains 428
Elkhorn Ranch 405
Elkins, WV 522, 523, 524
Elko, NV 361, 365
Ellicott, Andrew 395, 445
Ellicott Rock Trail (Ellicott Rock Wilderness, North Carolina) 395
Ellicott Rock Trail (Ellicott Rock Wilderness, South Carolina) 445
Ellicott Rock Wilderness (Georgia) **285**, 395
Ellicott Rock Wilderness (North Carolina) 285, **395**
Ellicott Rock Wilderness (South Carolina) 285, 395, **445**, 446
Ellijay, GA 288
Elma Island 38
Ely, MN 329
Ely, NV 360, 361, 363
Emerald Island 38
Emerald Lake (Jarbidge Wilderness) 361, 362
Emerald Lake (Mount Timpanogos Wilderness) 473
Emerson, Ralph Waldo 521
Emigrant Lake (Emigrant Wilderness) 171
Emigrant Lake (Mokelumne Wilderness) 197
Emigrant Pass 170
Emigrant Wilderness **170**, 171
Emily Cabin (Kalmiopsis Wilderness) 421
Emily Proctor Trail 479
Emory Pass, NM 374
Encampment River (Mount Zirkel Wilderness) 255
Encampment River Trail 533, 534
Encampment River Wilderness **533**, 534
Encampment, WY 533, 534, 536, 539
Enchanted Valley Trail 512
Enchantment Lakes 496
Endicott Arm Fiord 70
Endicott River Wilderness **45**, 46
Engle Lake 344
Engle Lake Trail 344, 345
Engle Peak 344
Enterprise, OR 298, 418, 420, 439
Entiat, WA 501
Enumclaw, WA 499, 511
Erie, Lake 406
Erma Bell Lake 437
Erwin, TN 458, 459

568 INDEX

BOLD PAGE NUMBERS INDICATE MAIN REFERENCES

Escalante Resource Area Recreation Map and Visitor Information (guidebook) 468
Escalante River 467
 (Lower Narrows) 467,
 (Upper Narrows) 467
Escalante, UT 468
Escudilla Mountain 88
Escudilla National Recreation Trail 88
Escudilla Wilderness **88**, 89
Espanola, NM 385
Essex, CA 203, 210
Estacada, OR 414, 426
Estes Park, CO 249
Ethan Pond 369
Etna, CA 194, 213, 232
Etna Summit 213
Etolin, Mount 67
Eton, GA 284
Etowah, TN 456
Eugene, OR 416
Eureka, CA 232, 236
Eureka Dunes 187
Eustis, FL 267, 269
Everett, WA 496, 504
Everglades City, FL 271
Everglades National Park 267, 271, 272
Everglades Wilderness **271**, 272
Exploring Oregon's Wild Areas (book) 430

F

Fairbanks, AK 40, 45, 48, 54, 60
Fairplay, CO 240, 251
Fairweather, Mount 48
Fairweather Range 48, 62
Fall Creek Trail 247
Fall River 543
Fall River Mills, CA 231
Fallen Leaf Trailhead 167
Falls Canyon Trail 365
Fancy Pass 247
Faraday Meadows Trail 84
Farallon Islands Wilderness **171**, 172
 (Middle) 171
Farallon National Wildlife Refuge 171
Fargo, ND 330
Farmington, NM 376, 382
Farr Gap 454, 457
Feather River Canyon 154
Feldtmann Ridge–Island Mine Trails 320
Fiddler Spring 337
Fifes Peaks 511
Fire Island (Bogoslof Island Wilderness) 42
Fire Island National Seashore 392
Fire Island Wilderness **392**
First Boulder Creek 360
First Dinkey Lake 168
First Peak Trail 487
First Water Trail 128
Fish Creek 169
Fish Creek Mountains Wilderness **172**
Fish Creek Valley 432
Fish Lake (Rogue–Umpqua Divide Wilderness) 432

Fish Lake (Winegar Hole Wilderness) 543
Fish Lake Basin 432
Fish Lake Creek 432
Fish Lake, ID 300
Fish Lake Trail (Rogue–Umpqua Divide Wilderness) 432
Fish Lake Trail (Winegar Hole Wilderness) 543
Fish Lake Valley 230
Fish Mountain 432
Fisher Caldera 72
Fishhooks Wilderness **89**
fishing (Alabama) 34; (Alaska) 37-39, 41-42, 44, 47, 48, 50-51, 53-54, 56, 59-61, 64, 69, 71-73; (Arizona) 79, 83, 89, 95, 97-98, 134-135; (Arkansas) 138-139, 144; (California) 158, 163, 169, 172, 174, 180, 182, 188-189, 197, 201, 215, 217, 221, 225, 227, 230; (Colorado) 238-239, 241-242, 244, 248, 250, 254, 257-258, 260; (Florida) 271, 276, 278-279; (Georgia) 281-282, 283, 284, 286-287, 289, 290; (Hawaii) 293; (Idaho) 295, 297, 299-300; (Illinois) 303-306; (Kentucky) 309-310; (Louisiana) 311; (Massachusetts) 316; (Michigan) 317, 319-320, 321, 324-325, 327; (Minnesota) 328-330; (Mississippi) 331, 332; (Missouri) 334; (Montana) 342, 344, 346, 348, 350-353; (Nevada) 358, 360, 366; (New Hampshire) 367; (New Mexico) 378, 382, 385, 386, 389, 390; (New York) 392; (North Carolina) 394, 395, 398-399, 401-402; (Oregon) 410, 417, 422, 428-429, 432-434, 438, 439; (Pennsylvania) 442; (South Carolina) 445; (Tennessee) 452, 455, 458; (Texas) 461; (Utah) 469; (Vermont) 478, 481-482; (Virginia) 484, 487, 491; (Washington) 504, 512, 519; (West Virginia) 521; (Wisconsin) 525-528; (Wyoming) 530, 532-535, 538, 540-543
Fishtail, MT 342
Fitzpatrick, Tom "Half-Hand" 534
Fitzpatrick Wilderness 531, **534**, 535
Five Lakes 175
Five Lakes Basin 175, 176
Five Lakes Creek 175
Five Lakes Trail 175, 176
Five Stream 520
Flagg Ranch 541
Flagstaff, AZ 82, 88, 100, 101, 109, 110, 117, 119, 128, 135, 137
Flamingo, FL 272
Flapjack Lakes 512
Flat Tops 206
Flat Tops Wilderness **244**
Flathead Indian Reservation 348, 349, 350
Flathead National Forest 344, 346, 349

Flathead River (Wild and Scenic River) 346
 (Middle Fork) 343, 346, (South Fork) 343
Flatside Pinnacle 143
Flatside Wilderness **143**
Flattery Rocks Refuge 518
Flattop Island 515
Fletcher Canyon 500
Flintridge, CA 223
Flora, OR 439
Florence, OR 415, 432
Florence Pass 532
Florence, WI 528
Florida 267-279
Florida Bay 271
Florida City, FL 272
Florida Keys National Wildlife Refuges 272, 273
Florida Keys Wilderness **272**, 273
Florida National Scenic Trail 268, 269, 275, 279
Florida Parks and Monuments Association 272
Florida Wilderness Act (1983) 267
Flower Island 515
Flume Road Trail 90
Fodderstack Trail 454
Foley Creek Campground (Horseshoe Bay Wilderness) 319
Folkston, GA 287
Fontana, CA 164
Foraker, Mount 45
Foresthill, CA 176
Fork Mountain 445
Forked Mountain 143
Forks, WA 512
Forrester Island Wilderness **46**, 47
Fort Apache Indian Reservation 104, 124
Fort Bowie, AZ 87
Fort Collins, CO 241, 243, 256, 260
Fort Jones, CA 194, 213
Fort Klamath, OR 434
Fort Myers, FL 274
Fort Niobrara National Wildlife Refuge 355, 356
Fort Niobrara Wilderness **355**, 356
Fort Peck Dam 353
Fort Peck Reservoir 353
Fort Robinson 356
Fort Robinson State Park 356
Fort Thomas, AZ 112
Fort Yukon, AK 40
Fortress Island 515
Fossil Ridge Wilderness **244**, 245
Fossil Springs Trail 90
Fossil Springs Wilderness **89**, 90
Four Bird Rocks 515
Four C National Recreation Trail 461
Four Corners region 375
Four Peaks Trail 90, 91
Four Peaks Wilderness **90**, 91
Fourth Boulder Creek 360
Fourth of July Campground (Manzano Mountain Wilderness) 384
Fourth of July Lake 197
Fouts Springs 226
Fox Islands 37, 38
Francis Marion National Forest 443, 446, 447, 448

INDEX 569

BOLD PAGE NUMBERS INDICATE MAIN REFERENCES

Franconia Range 368
Frank Church–River of No Return Wilderness **295**, 296, 297, 352
Franklin, NC 401
Fraser, CO 240
Fraser Experimental Forest 240
Frazier Park, CA 161, 168, 222
Fred Robinson Bridge 353
Fredericktown, MO 340
Fredonia, AZ 101, 105, 107, 122
Fremont National Forest 418
French Meadows Game Refuge 175
Fresno, CA 169, 184, 186, 198, 221
Frigid Crags 47
Frijoles Canyon 375
Frog Lake 197
Front Range (Colorado Rockies) 241, 259
Froze-To-Death Plateau Trail 341
Fryeburg, ME 314
Fryingpan River 247 (South Fork) 248
Fuller Lakes 53
Fuller Lakes Trail 53
Funeral Mountains Wilderness **173**
Furnace Creek Visitors Center 166

G

Gainesville, GA 285
Galena, AK 50, 56
Galiuro Escarpment 120
Galiuro Mountains 76, 91
Galiuro Wilderness **91**
Gallatin National Forest 342, 346, 347
Gallatin National Forest Travel Plan Map 342
Gallup, NM 376
Gandy, NV 363
Gannett, Henry 36
Gannett Peak 531, 534
Gar Lake 66
Garcia Mountain 173
Garcia Wilderness **173**
Garden of the Gods Recreation Area 304
Garden of the Gods Wilderness **304**, 305
Gareloi Island 37
Garfias Mountain 96
Gasquet, CA 225
Gates of the Arctic National Park and Preserve 47, 48, 59
Gates of the Arctic Wilderness **47**, 48, 59
Gates of the Mountains Wilderness **345**
Gavilan Wash 207
Gearhart Mountain Trail 418
Gearhart Mountain Wilderness **418**
Gee Creek Trail 455, 456
Gee Creek Wilderness **455**, 456
Gene Marshall–Piedra Blanca National Recreation Trail 222
George D. Aiken Wilderness **481**
George Washington National Forest 484, 490, 491, 492
Georgia 280-290
Geronimo, AZ 89

Getting Around in the Death Valley Backcountry (book) 166
Gianelli Cabin Trailhead 171
Giant Pine Grove 526
Gibralter Mountain Wilderness **92**
Gifford Pinchot National Forest 502, 503, 504, 507, 517, 520
Gila Bend, AZ 82, 111, 127, 137
Gila Bend Mountains 137
Gila Cliff Dwellings National Monument 383
Gila Indian Reservation 126
Gila Mountains 89
Gila National Forest 374, 377, 383
Gila Peak 89
Gila River 110, 116, 137, 383 (Middle Fork) 383, (West Fork) 383
Gila Visitors Center 383
Gila Wilderness 373, **383**
Gilmore Pond 480
Gilpin Lake 255
Ginpole Lake 324
Glacier Bay 45, 48, 61 (East Arm) 48, (West Arm) 48
Glacier Bay National Park and Preserve 45, 46, 48, 49
Glacier Bay Wilderness **48**, 49
Glacier Lake 348
Glacier Lake Trail 348
Glacier National Park 346
Glacier Peak Wilderness **500**, 501, 503
Glacier Primitive Area 534
Glacier View Trail 502
Glacier View Wilderness **501**, 502
Glacier, WA 508
Glade Mountain 285
Glamis, CA 201
Glen Campground (Phillip Burton Wilderness) 207
Glendora, CA 164, 215, 223
Glennallen, AK 74
Glenwood Springs, CO 244
Globe, AZ 89, 110, 112, 123, 129
Goat Lake 502
Goat Peak Trail 519
Goat Rocks Wilderness **502**, 503, 519
Gobbler Point Trail 79
Gobbler's Knob 472
Godman Campground (Wenaha-Tucannon Wilderness, Washington) 519
Gold Beach, OR 421, 440
Golden Trout Wilderness **174**, 227
Golden Valley Wilderness **175**
Goodnews River 69
Goodwin Lake 535
Goodwin Lake–Cache Creek Trail 535
Goose Creek Campground (Lost Creek Wilderness) 251
Goose Creek Trail 251
Gore Creek 243
Gore Range 243
Gorham, NH 368
Gospel Hump Wilderness **297**
Gospel Peak 297
Goulding Lake 73

Government Camp (Mount Hood Wilderness) 425
Government Mineral Springs Campground (Trapper Creek Wilderness) 517
Government Peak 86
Government Trail 88
Graham Creek 464
Gramp Rock Island 37
Granby, CO 240, 249, 257, 264
Grand Canyon 75, 92, 100, 101, 105, 107, 121, 295
Grand Canyon of the Noatak 59
Grand Marais, MN 329
Grand Portage, MN 321
Grand Teton 537
Grand Teton National Park 530, 537, 541
Grand Teton Natural History Association 531, 532, 535, 538, 540, 542
Grand Wash Cliffs Wilderness **92**
Grandfather Mountain 396
Grangeville, ID 297, 300
Granite Basin Recreation Area 93
Granite Chief Wilderness 153, **175**, 176
Granite Creek Hot Springs 535, 536
Granite Mountain Wilderness **93**
Granite Peak (Absaroka-Beartooth Wilderness) 341
Granite Peak (Bighorn Mountains Wilderness) 151
Granite Peak (Trinity Alps Wilderness) 232
Granite Range 205
Grant, Mount 479
Grant Range Wilderness **361**
Grants, NM 380, 388
Grants Pass, OR 421
Grantsville, UT 469
Grass Valley Wilderness **176**
Grasshopper Mountain 432
Grassy Branch Trail 486
Grassy Knob Trail 419
Grassy Knob Wilderness **419**
Grassy Lake 434
Grassy Pass 260
Grave Creek 440
Gravel Island 529
Gray Wolf River 498
Gray Wolf Trail 498
Grayson Highlands State Park 487, 488
Great Basin 204, 465
Great Basin Desert (Arizona) 75; (California) 196; (New Mexico) 373
Great Basin National Park 363
Great Bear Wilderness 343, **346**, 351
Great Divide 541
Great Falls, MT 344, 351
Great Gulf Trail 368
Great Gulf Wilderness **367**, 368
Great Island 401
Great Kobuk Sand Dunes 54
Great Lake (Pond Pine Wilderness) 399
Great Lake (Sheep Ridge Wilderness) 399

570 INDEX

BOLD PAGE NUMBERS INDICATE MAIN REFERENCES

Great Meadows National Wildlife Refuge Complex 316
Great Northern Mountain 346
Great Plains 403
Great Salt Lake 465, 469
Great Sand Dunes National Monument 245, 246, 260
Great Sand Dunes Wilderness **245**, 246
Great Sitkin Island 38
Great Smoky Mountains National Park 451, 458, 494
Great Swamp National Wildlife Refuge 372
Great Swamp Wilderness **372**
Great White Heron National Wildlife Refuge 272, 273
Greeley, Horace 138
Green Bay, WI 529
Green Canyon 471
Green Island 38
Green Lakes 437
Green Mountain National Forest 478, 479, 480, 481, 482
Green Mountain Trail 397, 398
Green Mountains 478, 479
Green River 531
Greeneville, TN 459
Greenhorn Mountain Wilderness **246**
Greenhorn Mountains 428
Greenhorn Trailhead 246
Greensboro, NC 394
Greenstone Ridge Trail 320
Greentop Harbor 73
Greenville, NC 402
Greenwater Valley 179
Greybull, WY 533
Greys Lake 360
Griffin Knob 491
Griggs, Robert 52
Grizzly Creek Trail 449
Gros Ventre River 535
Gros Ventre Wilderness **535**, 536
Grosvenor, Gilbert H. 355
Groveland, CA 171
Guadalupe Mountains National Park 461, 462
Guadalupe Mountains Wilderness **461**, 462
Guadalupe Peak 461
Guadalupe Peak Trail 461
Guadalupe Canyon 219
Guide to the National Wildlife Refuges (book) 436
Gulf Coastal Plain 460, 463
Gulf Islands National Seashore 332
Gulf Islands Wilderness **332**
Gulf of Alaska 64, 66, 74
Gulf of Mexico 270, 272, 287, 311, 332, 337, 451
Gulkana, AK 74
Gull Keys 273
Gull Reef 515
Gull Rock 515
Gumjuwac Saddle Trail 411
Gunflint Trail 329
Gunnison Basin 257
Gunnison, CO 242, 245, 250, 252, 258, 259, 263, 266
Gunnison National Forest 242, 245, 250, 252, 258, 259, 266

Gunnison River 238, 239
Gunsight Pass 245
Gunter Ridge Trail 485
Gustavus, AK 49, 61, 62
Gwynn Creek 415

H

Hagemeister Island 41
Haigler Creek 97
Haines, AK 46
Haleakala Crater 292
Haleakala, Mount 292
Haleakala National Park 292
Haleakala Wilderness **292**
Halemau'u Trail 292
Haleyville, AL 35
Half Dome 236
Half Tide Rock 515
Hall Canyon 229
Hall Island 41, 515
Hallstone Trail 84
Hamilton, MT 300, 352
Hamma Hamma River 497, 509, 510
Hampton Creek 363
Hampton, TN 458
Hanging Rock 492
Hank and Yank Spring 114
Hankins Pass 251
Hannah's Creek Trail 394
Happy Camp, CA 194, 225
Happy Camp Canyon 86, 87
Happy Canyon 229
Happy Jack, AZ 135
Happy Valley 120
Harbor Rock 515
Harcuvar Mountains Wilderness **94**
Harding Ice Field 53
Harmon, WV 522
Harney Peak 449
Harquahala Mountains Wilderness **94**, 95
Harquahala Peak 94
Harquahala Peak Trail 94
Harris Ranch Trail 417
Harrisburg, IL 302, 303, 305, 306
Harrison, AR 140
Harrisonburg, VA 493
Hart Mine Wash 132
Harvard, Mount 241
Hassayampa River 95
Hassayampa River Canyon Wilderness **95**
Hathaway Pines, CA 157, 171, 197
Hauser Canyon 177
Hauser Creek Trail 177
Hauser Wilderness **177**, 208
Havasu (Needles) Wilderness **95**, 96, 177
Havasu, Lake 96, 129, 159
Havasu National Wildlife Refuge 95, 96, 129, 159, 177, 178
Havasu Palms, CA 235
Havasu Wilderness 159, **177**, 178
Hawaii 291-293
Hawaii (island) 293
Hawaii Volcanoes National Park 293
Hawaii Volcanoes Wilderness **293**
Hay Meadows Trailhead 155
Hayden Pass 260
Hayfork, CA 158

Hayward, WI 527
Hazy Islands National Wildlife Refuge 49
Hazy Islands Wilderness **49**
HCNRA (see Hells Canyon National Recreation Area)
Headwaters Wilderness **526** (Headwaters of the Pine Unit) 526; (Kimball Creek Unit) 526; (Shelp Lake Unit) 526
Heart Lake (Latir Peak Wilderness) 383, 384
Heart Lake (Mission Mountains Wilderness) 348
Hearts Content Recreation Area 442
Heavener, OK 408
Heavenly Twin Lakes 434
Hector, AR 142
Helen, GA 286, 290
Helen, Lake 502
Helena, MT 345, 351
Helena National Forest 345, 351
Heliotrope Ridge Trail 507, 508
Hell Hole Bay Wilderness **446**, 447
Hell Hole Canoe Trail 446, 447
Hell Hole Reservoir 175
Hellgate Mountain 96
Hell's Backbone Bridge 467, 468
Hells Canyon Dam 419, 420
Hells Canyon Map 420
Hells Canyon National Recreation Area 298, 419, 420
Hells Canyon Wilderness (Arizona) **96**
Hells Canyon Wilderness (Idaho) **298**, 420
Hells Canyon Wilderness (Oregon) 298, **419**
Hells Hole (Mount Logan Wilderness) 105
Hell's Hole (Salome Wilderness) 123
Hell's Hole Trail 123
Hells Hollow 105
Hellsgate Ridge 97
Hellsgate Wilderness **97**
Helms Creek 168, 169
Helton Creek Trail 486
Hemp Top Trail (Big Frog Wilderness, Georgia) 280
Hemp Top Trail (Big Frog Wilderness, Tennessee) 452
Hemp Top Trail (Cohutta Wilderness) 283
Hemphill, TX 462
Henderson, Chad 407
Hendry's Creek 363
Hendry's Creek Trail 363
Henry Knob (Mark Trail Wilderness) 286
Henry M. Jackson Wilderness **503**, 504
Henson Creek 263
Herbert Island 38
Hercules Glades Wilderness **336**
Hereford, AZ 104
Herman Creek 414
Herman Creek Trail 414
Hessie Trail 248, 249
Hi Mountain Lookout 219
Hi-Line Trail (see also Continental Divide National Scenic Trail) 343

INDEX 571

BOLD PAGE NUMBERS INDICATE MAIN REFERENCES

Hiawatha National Forest 318, 319, 322, 324, 325
Hickory Creek 461 (East) 442, (Middle) 442
Hickory Creek Trail (Cohutta Wilderness) 283
Hickory Creek Trail (Hickory Creek Wilderness) 442
Hickory Creek Wilderness **442**
Hickory Hill 284
Hidden Springs Canyon 195
Hieroglyphic Mountain Range 96
High Creek Trail 471
High Line Trail 470
High Lonesome Trail 248
High Shoals Scenic Area 289
High Shoals Trail 289
High Sierra Primitive Area 197
High Uintas Wilderness **469**, 470
Highcock Knob 485
Highlands, NC 395, 446
Highrock Mountain 432
Hightree Rock Trail 487
Hiker's Guide to Paria Canyon (book) 115, 475
Hilgard Basin 347
Hilo, HI 293
Hinkley, CA 152
Hiwassee River (Southern Nantahala Wilderness, Georgia) 289
Hiwassee River (Southern Nantahala Wilderness, North Carolina) 401
Hoback River 535
Hog Island 529
Hogan, Father John 337
Hogback Mountain 485
Hogback Peak 198
Hoh River 512
Hoh Trail 512
Holdout Canyon 124
Holdout Spring 91
Hole in the Mountain Peak 360
Hole-In-The-Wall Trail 388
Holgate Beach 371
Hollow Hills Wilderness **178**
Holt, MN 329
Holua Cabin 292
Holy Cross, Mount of the 247
Holy Cross Wilderness **247**
Homer, AK 41, 42, 43, 47, 49, 57, 63, 65, 71, 72
Homestead, FL 272
Homosassa River 270, 271
Hood, Mount 424 (South Side) 424
Hoodsport, WA 498, 510, 520
Hoonah, AK 62
Hoosier National Forest 308
Hoover Wilderness **178**, 179
Hopi Buttes 127
Hopkins Mountain 123
Hopkins, SC 445
Horicon National Wildlife Refuge 529
Horn Island 332
Horn Spring 233
Horse Canyon 187
Horse Creek Trail 416, 417
Horse Mesa 109
Horse Mountain 97
horsepacking (Alabama) 34; (Arizona) 85, 87, 90, 92-93, 95, 103, 111, 117, 129, 131-134; (Arkansas) 144; (California) 174, 210, 225, 227, 236; (Colorado) 249; (Georgia) 288; (Idaho) 296-297; (Indiana) 308; (Kentucky) 309-310; (Montana) 343-344, 349, 351; (Nebraska) 356; (Nevada) 366; (New Mexico) 381, 386; (Oregon) 417, 429, 438; (Tennessee) 454, 456; (Texas) 464; (Utah) 469-470; (Virginia) 487; (Washington) 499, 519; (Wyoming) 531-532, 534
Horse Thief Canyon 209
Horsepen Creek 409
Horseshoe Bay Trail 319
Horseshoe Bay Wilderness **319**
Horseshoe Keys 273
Horseshoe Lake 389
Horsethief Canyon 208
Horsethief Recreation Area 82
Horsethief Trail 208
Horsetrough Falls 286
Horsetrough Mountain 286
Hot Loop Trail 109, 110
hot springs (Alaska) 68, 73; (Arizona) 96; (California) 189, 222; (Colorado) 252, 261; (New Mexico) 383; (Oklahoma) 409; (Oregon) 414; (Virginia) 491; (Washington) 503, 509, 517; (Wyoming) 535-536
Hot Springs, AR 409
Hot Springs Trail 414
Hot Springs, VA 491
Houghton, MI 321
House Rock Valley 121
Houston, MO 338
Howard Mountain 256
Howe Key 273
Howell Canyon 86
Huachuca Mountains 103
Hualapai Mountain County Park 133
Hualapai Mountains 133
Hubbard Glacier 62
Huckleberry Mountain (Salmon-Huckleberry Wilderness) 433
Huckleberry Mountain (Teton Wilderness) 541
Humboldt National Forest 357, 360, 361, 362, 363, 365
Humboldt Peak 360
Hummingbird Spring 162
Hummingbird Springs Wilderness 80, **97**, 98
Humphrey Ranch 78
Humphrey's Peak 99, 100
Humphrey's Trail 100
Humptulips River 500
Hungry Horse, MT 344, 346
Hungry Horse Reservoir 344, 346
Hunter Canyon 182
Hunter Creek 247
Hunter Creek Canyon 363
Hunter Creek Trail 363
Hunter-Fryingpan Wilderness **247**, 248, 254
hunting (Alabama) 34; (Alaska) 40-41, 44, 47, 50-51, 53-56, 59-62, 64, 69, 71-72; (Arizona) 84, 86, 93, 99, 102, 105, 111, 116-117, 121, 124, 126; (Arkansas) 138-139, 144, 146; (California) 154, 158, 170, 182, 186, 199, 201, 208, 226, 235; (Colorado) 242, 247-248, 252, 254, 260, 265-266; (Florida) 268-269, 276, 279; (Georgia) 282-284, 286, 288-289; (Idaho) 297, 299-300; (Illinois) 303-304; (Indiana) 308; (Kentucky) 309-310; (Maine) 314; (Michigan) 318, 325; (Minnesota) 328, 330; (Mississippi) 331, 333; (Montana) 344-348, 350-354; (Nevada) 362-363, 365-366; (New Hampshire) 367; (New Mexico) 374, 378, 383, 385-386, 388; (North Carolina) 394, 397, 402; (Oregon) 413, 417, 420, 427, 429, 438; (South Carolina) 444; (Tennessee) 453, 458-459; (Texas) 461, 463; (Utah) 469, 477; (Vermont) 478, 481-482; (Virginia) 491; (Washington) 504; (Wisconsin) 525-526, 528; (Wyoming) 530-534, 536, 538, 540-542
Huntington Lake 186
Huntsville, TX 463
Huron Islands National Wildlife Refuge 319
Huron Islands Wilderness **319**, 320
Huron, Lake 319, 325
Huron Peak 241
Huron River 322
Huron-Manistee National Forest 324
Hurricane Bayou 462
Hurricane Creek Campground (Eagle Cap Wilderness) 417
Hurricane Creek Valley 143
Hurricane Creek Wilderness **143**, 144
Hurricane Deck 218
Huslia, AK 55, 56
Huston Park Trail 536
Huston Park Wilderness **536**
Hutchins Creek 301, 303

I

Ibex Hills Wilderness **179**
Ibex Pass 179
Ibex Peak 179
Icehouse Saddle 164
Icehouse Trailhead 164
Icy Passage 61
Icy Strait 48, 61
Idaho 294-300
Idaho Outfitters and Guides Association 296
Idaho Primitive Area 295
Idaho Springs, CO 253
Ides Cove Loop Trail 236
Idleyld, OR 412
Idleyld Park, OR 426
Idyllwild, CA 217, 220
Igikpak, Mount 47, 59
Igitkin Island 38
Ikiginak Island 38
Ilak Island 37
Iliamna, AK 57
Iliamna, Lake 40, 57
Iliamna, Mount 57, 71

572 INDEX

BOLD PAGE NUMBERS INDICATE MAIN REFERENCES

Illinois 301-306
Illinois Bayou (East Fork) 142
Illinois River (Wild and Scenic River) 420, 421
 (East Fork) 225
Illinois River Trail 421
Imnaha Bridge 420
Imnaha, OR 420
Imnaha River (Wild and Scenic River) 417
Imperial Dam 98, 180, 191
Imperial National Wildlife Refuge 98, 99, 132, 180, 181
Imperial Wilderness (Arizona) **98**, 99, 180, 181
Imperial Wilderness (California) **180**, 181
In-Ko-Pah Mountains 156
Ina Island 38
Indiahoma, OK 409
Indian Canyon 168
Indian Creek 462
Indian Heaven Wilderness **504**
Indian Kitchen (precipice) 305
Indian Mounds Recreation Area 462
Indian Mounds Wilderness **462**
Indian Pass 181, 207
Indian Pass Wilderness **181**
Indian Peaks Wilderness **248**, 249
Indian Racetrack (field) 504
Indian River 278
Indian Springs Canyon 116
Indiana 307-308
Indio, CA 195, 203
Inian Islands 62
Inian Peninsula 62
Inikla Island 38
Inner Pasture (desert alluvial fan) 220
Innoko National Wildlife Refuge 50
Innoko River 50
Innoko Wilderness **50**
Interior, SD 450
Inyo, Mount 181
Inyo Mountains 181, 192, 209
Inyo Mountains Wilderness **181**, 182
Inyo National Forest 149, 174, 179, 181, 182, 185, 227, 357, 359
Inyokern, CA 188, 204
Irish Wilderness **337**
Iron Creek Horse Camp (Black Elk Wilderness) 449
Iron Gate Campground (Pasayten Wilderness) 513
Iron Mountain (Big Laurel Branch Wilderness) 453
Iron Mountain (Neota Wilderness) 256
Ironstone Mountain Trail 519
Ironwood, MI 327
Isabella, Lake 153
Ishi Wilderness **182**, 183
Island Bay Wilderness **273**, 274
Island Lake (Mission Mountains Wilderness) 348
Island Lake (Rawah Wilderness) 259
Islands of Four Mountains 37, 38
Isle Royale National Park 320, 321
Isle Royale Natural History Association 321
Isle Royale Wilderness **320**, 321

Isolation, Mount 369
Isolation Trail 369
Ives Peak 118
Ivester Gap Trail 400
Izembek Lagoon 51
Izembek National Wildlife Refuge 51, 72
Izembek Wilderness **51**

J

J. N. "Ding" Darling National Wildlife Refuge 274
J. N. "Ding" Darling Wilderness **274**
Jack Lake 425
Jackass Pass 531
Jacks Canyon 109
Jacks Canyon Trail 109
Jack's Knob National Recreation Trail 282
Jack's Knob Trail 286
Jacks River 283
Jacks River Trail (Cohutta Wilderness, Georgia) 283; (Cohutta Wilderness, Tennessee) 455
Jackson Mountain 112
Jackson, Senator Henry 503
Jackson, WY 536, 541
Jacksonville, GA 285
Jacksonville, NC 395, 398, 399
Jacksonville, OR 210
Jacob Lake, AZ 101, 122
Jacumba Mountains Wilderness **183**
Jail Canyon 229
James, Lake 397
James River 485
James River Face Wilderness **485**, 494
James River Gorge 485
Jarbidge Canyon 361
Jarbidge Lake 361, 362
Jarbidge, NV 362
Jarbidge Wilderness 357, **361**, 362
Jasper, AR 144, 146
Jasper Lake 248
Jasper, TX 464
Jawbone-Butterbredt Area of Critical Environmental Concern 153
Jedediah Smith Wilderness **537**
Jefferson Lake 425
Jefferson, Mount (Nevada) 357, 358
Jefferson, Mount (New Hampshire) 367
Jefferson National Forest 484, 485, 486, 487, 488, 489, 492, 494, 524
Jefferson Park Glacier 425
Jefferson Peak 509
Jemez Springs, NM 382, 387
Jennie Lakes Wilderness **184**, 198
Jerome, AZ 137
Jett Canyon 358
Joe Ingram Key 273
Joe Wright Reservoir 256
Joe's Creek 335
John Day, OR 435
John Day River (Wild and Scenic River)
 (North Fork) 428,
 (South Fork) 411

John Muir Trail 148
 (John Muir Wilderness) 184, 185;
 (Sequoia–Kings Canyon Wilderness) 221
John Muir Wilderness 168, **184**, 185, 186, 197, 221
John River (Wild and Scenic River) 47
Johns Creek Trail 488
Johnson Keys islands 273
Johnston, A. D. 327
Jonas Ridge 396, 397
Jonesboro, IL 302, 303
Joseph, Chief 294
Joshua Flat 163
Joshua Tree National Monument 185
Joshua Tree National Park 160, 186, 223
Joshua Tree Wilderness **185**, 186
Joyce Kilmer Memorial Forest (North Carolina) 396, (Tennessee) 456
Joyce Kilmer National Recreation Trail 396
Joyce Kilmer–Slickrock Wilderness (North Carolina) **396**, 454
Joyce Kilmer–Slickrock Wilderness (Tennessee) 396, 454, **456**, 457
Judith Island 401
Julian, CA 172
Julian Wash 181
Juneau, AK 43, 48, 49, 55, 56, 62, 68, 69, 71
Juniper Bay 401
Juniper Creek 275
Juniper Dunes Wilderness **505**
Juniper Mesa Wilderness **99**
Juniper Mountains 99
Juniper Prairie Wilderness **275**
Juniper Ridge 82
Juniper Spring 91
Juniper Springs 275
Juniper Springs Recreation Area Campground (Juniper Prairie Wilderness) 275
Junipero Serra Peak 234
Jupiter, Mount 498
Jupiter Ridge Trail 498

K

Ka'aha Trail 293
Kabel Trail 487
Kachina Peaks Wilderness **99**, 100
Kagalaska Island 38
Kagamil Island 38
Kahiltna Glacier 45
Kahului, HI 292
Kaibab National Forest 101, 122, 130
Kaibab Plateau 100, 121
Kaiser Peak 186
Kaiser Ridge 186
Kaiser Wilderness **186**
Kake, AK 56, 69
Kaktovik, AK 40
Kaligagan Island 38
Kalispell, MT 344
Kalmiopsis Wilderness **420**, 421, 440
Kamas, UT 470
Kanab Creek Wilderness **100**, 101

INDEX 573

BOLD PAGE NUMBERS INDICATE MAIN REFERENCES

Kanab Plateau 100
Kanab, UT 475
Kanaga Island 37, 38
Kanawyer Trail 198
Kanektok River 69
Kaniksu National Forest 514
Kanu Island 38
Karta Bay 51
Karta Lake 51
Karta River Wilderness **51**, 52
Kasaan Bay 51
Kasatochi Island 38
Katmai National Park and Preserve 52
Katmai Wilderness **52**
Ka'u Desert Trail 293
Kaupo Trail 292
Kavalga Island 37
Kaweah River 221
  (Middle Fork) 221
kayaking (Alaska) 38, 48-49, 54-56, 58-59, 62, 66-67, 72-73; (Arizona) 80; (Florida) 272; (Michigan) 320, 326; (South Carolina) 444; (Utah) 466; (Washington) 515; (Wisconsin) 529; (Wyoming) 533
Kea'au, HI 293
Kelly Canyon 378
Kelly River 59
Kelly, WY 535
Kelso Creek 152
Kelso Dunes Wilderness **187**
Kelso Mountains 152
Kelso Peak 152
Kelso Sand Dunes 187
Kenai, AK 57, 71
Kenai Mountains 53
Kenai National Moose Range 53
Kenai National Wildlife Refuge 53
Kenai Peninsula 53, 57
Kenai Wilderness **53**
Kendrick Mountain Trail 101
Kendrick Mountain Wilderness **101**
Kendrick Peak 101
Kenmare, ND 404
Kennedy Creek 171
Kennedy Lake 171
Kennedy Meadows (Chimney Peak Wilderness) 159, 160; (Domeland Wilderness) 169; (Emigrant Wilderness) 171
Kennedy Meadows (South Sierra Wilderness) 227
Kennedy Meadows Trailhead 171
Kennedy Peak 171
Kennedy Springs 345
Kenosha Mountains 251
Kenton, MI 322, 326
Kentucky 309-310
Kern Canyon 174
Kern Plateau 174
Kern River (Wild and Scenic River) 227
  (North Fork) 174, 221,
  (South Fork) 169, 174, 227
Kernville, CA 169, 174, 188, 227
Ketchikan, AK 44, 49, 52, 58, 59, 67, 68, 72, 73
Ketchum, ID 299
Kettenpom Valley 201
Key West 273

Key West National Wildlife Refuge 272, 273
Keynot Peak 181
Khaz Bay 73
Khotol Hills 50
Khvostof Island 37
Kiamichi River 409
Kiavah Wilderness **187**, 188
Kielberg Dam 91
Kigul Island 38
Kilauea Caldera 293
Kilauea Visitors Center 293
Kilmer, Joyce 396, 456
Kimball Creek 526
Kimball Island 267
Kimberling Creek Wilderness **485**, 486
Kimberling Springs 485
King City, CA 224, 234
King Island 441, 442
King Lake 248
King of Arizona Mine 102
King Salmon, AK 41, 52
King Valley 102
Kingman, AZ 77, 78, 106, 108, 133, 134
Kings Canyon 221
Kings Canyon National Park 198, 221
Kings Peak 469
Kings River (Wild and Scenic River) 221
  (North Fork) 184, 221,
  (South Fork) 197, 221
Kingston Peak 188
Kingston Range 188, 204
Kingston Range Wilderness **188**
Kingston Wash 188
Kipahulu Valley 292
Kirk Creek 234
Kisatchie Hills Wilderness **312**
Kisatchie National Forest 311, 312
Kiska Island 37, 38
  (Little) 37
Kit Carson Peak 260
Klamath Falls, OR 428, 434
Klamath National Forest 194, 213, 225, 232
Klawock, AK 58, 73
Klothos Temple (summit) 109
Kluane National Park 74
Knob, The (Pleasant Island) 61
Kobuk River (Wild and Scenic River) 47, 54, 63
Kobuk Valley National Park 54
Kobuk Valley Wilderness **54**
Kodiak, AK 65
Kodiak Island 52
KOFA (see King of Arizona Mine)
Kofa Mountains 102
Kofa National Wildlife Refuge 102
Kofa Queen Canyon 102
Kofa Wilderness **102**, 111
Kootenai National Forest 345
Kootznoowoo (Admiralty Island) Wilderness **54**, 55
Kotzebue, AK 43, 54, 60, 64
Kotzebue Bay 63
Kotzebue Sound 43, 59
Koyukuk National Wildlife Refuge 55, 56

Koyukuk River (Wild and Scenic River) 47, 55
  (lower) 55; (North Fork) 47
Koyukuk Wilderness **55**, 56
Kremmling, CO 240, 258
Krenitzin Islands 37, 38
Krutch, Joseph Wood 291
Kuiu Island 44, 56, 69
Kuiu Wilderness **56**, 69
Kupreanof, AK 61
Kupreanof Island 61
Kuriko Lake 328
Kuskokwim Mountains 50
Kuskokwim River 60
Kyles Landing, AR 140

L

La Canada, CA 215
La Garita Wilderness **249**, 250
La Jara, CO 261, 262
La Panza mountain range 191
La Plata Peak 241
La Push, WA 518
La Ventana Natural Arch 379
Lacassine National Wildlife Refuge 312
Lacassine Pool 312
Lacassine Wilderness **312**
Laguna Mountains 220
Lake Arthur, LA 312
Lake Branch 476
Lake Branch Trail 476, 477
Lake Chelan National Recreation Area 506
Lake Chelan–Sawtooth Wilderness **505**, 506
Lake Chinnabee Recreation Area 34
Lake Christine Trail 502
Lake City, CO 263
Lake City, FL 268
Lake Clark National Park and Preserve 57
Lake Clark Wilderness **57**, 71
Lake Conasauga Recreation Area 284
Lake Fork Trail 384
Lake Havasu City, AZ 88, 92, 94, 96, 119, 129, 177, 178
Lake Mead National Recreation Area 107
Lake Michigan Recreation Area 323, 324
Lake Park Trail 251
Lake Superior Highlands 525
Lake Woodruff National Wildlife Refuge 276
Lake Woodruff Wilderness 276
Lakes Basin 417
Lakeshore Trail 506
Lakeview, MT 351
Lamphier Lake 244, 245
Lamphier Lake Trailhead 245
Lander, WY 535, 540
Laramie, WY 534, 539, 540
Las Vegas, NV 107, 362
Lassen National Forest 155, 183, 230, 231
Lassen Peak 189
Lassen Volcanic National Park 155, 189
Lassen Volcanic Wilderness **189**

574 INDEX

BOLD PAGE NUMBERS INDICATE MAIN REFERENCES

Last Chance Archaeological District 170
Last Chance Range 230
Latir Mesa 383
Latir Peak Wilderness **383**, 384
Laurel Fork Campground (Laurel Fork North/Laurel Fork South Wilderness) 523
Laurel Fork Creek 458
Laurel Fork Gorge 458
Laurel Fork North/Laurel Fork South Wilderness **523**
Laurel River North Trail 523
Laurel River South Trail 523
Lava Beds National Monument 189
Lava Beds Wilderness **189**, 190
Lava Mountains 175
Lave Beds National Monument 190
Lawson Rock 515
Leadville, CO 240, 242, 247, 254
Leadville National Fish Hatchery 254
Leaf River 333
Leaf Trail 333
Leaf Wilderness **333**
Leatherwood Creek 144
Leatherwood Wilderness 140, **144**
Leavenworth, WA 496, 501, 504
Leavitt Peak 170
LeConte Bay 68
LeConte Glacier 68
Lee Metcalf Wilderness **346**, 347 (Bear Trap Canyon Unit) 346, 347; (Monument Mountain Unit) 346, 347; (Spanish Peaks Unit) 347; (Taylor-Hilgard Unit) 347
Lee Vining, CA 149, 179
Lee's Ferry 115
Legore Lake 417
Lemei Rock 504
Lemmon, Mount 118
Lemusurier Island 62
Leopold, Aldo 88, 307, 331, 373, 383
Leveland Mountain 287
Lewis and Clark National Forest 344, 351
Lewis Canyon 214
Lewis Fork Spur Trail 486
Lewis Fork Wilderness **486**
Lewis, Meriwether 297, 345, 353
Lewiston, ID 298
Lewistown, MT 353
Lexington, KY 310
Lexington, VA 490, 491
Libby, MT 345
Liberty (peak) 497
Lick Creek 429
Licking, MO 338
Licklog Ridge Trail 280, 283
Lighthouse Island 319, 320
Ligurta, AZ 109
Lillyville Campground (Eagle Cap Wilderness) 418
Lily Creek 499
Lily Lake 260
Lilypad Lake 430
Lima, MT 351
Limestone Cove Recreation Area 459
Limestone Cove Trail 459
Lincoln, Mount 509

Lincoln, MT 351
Lincoln National Forest 378, 390
Lincoln, NH 369
Lincoln Woods Trail 369
Lindsey Mountain 335
Lindsey Mountain Trail 335
Link Trail 259, 260
Linville Gorge Wilderness **396**, 397
Linville Mountain 396
Linville River 396
Linville, William 396
Lipes Branch 483
Lipes Branch Trail 484
Little Beach 371
Little Cherry Trail 364
Little Chuckwalla Mountains Wilderness **190**
Little Colorado River 128 (East Fork) 104; (West Fork) 104
Little Cottonwood Creek 476
Little Cottonwood Creek Canyon 470, 471
Little Doubtful Canyon 116
Little Dry Run Trail 487
Little Dry Run Wilderness **487**
Little Falls 219
Little Fodderstack 454
Little Frog Mountain Wilderness **457**
Little Grass Mountain 340
Little Grassy Lake 304
Little Lake (Domeland Wilderness) 169
Little Lake (Russian Wilderness) 214
Little Lake (South Sierra Wilderness) 227
Little Lake Creek Wilderness **463**
Little Lake George Wilderness **276**
Little Laurel Branch 453
Little Malheur River 423
Little Maria Range 205
Little Matterhorn 470
Little Missouri River 405
Little Mountain 523
Little Mud Pond 482
Little Mullet Key 273
Little North Santiam River 413
Little Paddy Creek 338
Little Picacho Peak Wilderness **191**
Little Pine Key 273
Little Pine Key Mangrove 273
Little River 138
Little Saline River 302
Little San Bernardino Mountains 185
Little San Pascual Mountain 377
Little Santeetlah Creek 396
Little Silver River 326
Little Sister Island 515
Little Sitkin Island 37
Little Slickrock Creek 456
Little Snake River 536
Little Spanish Key 273
Little Sur River 234
Little Swash Keys 273
Little Wambaw Swamp Wilderness **447**
Little Wilson Creek Trail 487
Little Wilson Creek Wilderness **487**, 488
Lizard Head Pass 250
Lizard Head Peak 250
Lizard Head Trail 250

Lizard Head Wilderness **250**
Logan River 471
Logan, UT 471, 477
Lolo Forest Visitors Map 350
Lolo National Forest 300, 350, 351, 352, 354
Lone Eagle Lake 248
Lone Peak Wilderness **470**, 471, 472, 473, 476
Lone Pine, CA 174, 182, 185, 227
Lone Pine Peak 488
Lone Pine Saddle 420
Lone Star Hiking Trail 463
Lonesome Miner Trail 182
Long Creek 336
Long Devil's Fork Creek 145
Long Island (Aleutian Islands Wilderness) 38
Long Island, NY 392
Long Lake 399
Long Mountain 109
Long Mountain Wash 109
Long Trail 478, 479, 480, 482
Long X Bridge 405
Longleaf Vista Recreation Area 312
Lookout Mountain 410
Lookout Shelter 293
Loomis, WA 513
Lopez Canyon 219
Lopez Canyon Trail 219
Lopez Island 514, 515
Lopez Lake 219
Los Alamos, NM 375, 382
Los Angeles, CA 215, 223
Los Olivos, CA 218
Los Padres National Forest 161, 168, 173, 192, 194, 218, 219, 222, 224, 234
Lost Canyon Oasis 219
Lost Creek Wilderness **251**
Lost Lake Resort 212
Lost Man Creek 248
Lost Man Reservoir 248
Lost Man Trail 248
Lost Trail Pass 343
Lostine, OR 418
Lostine River (Wild and Scenic River) 417
Lostwood National Wildlife Refuge 404
Lostwood Wilderness **404**
Louisiana 311-312
Low Gap 286
Low Island 515
Lowell, ID 300
Lower Coastal Plain (Mississippi) 331
Lower Fishhooks (Canyon) 89
Lower Peninsula (Michigan) 323
Lower Ridge Trail 401
Lowman, ID 296
Lowrie Islands 46
Lucille, Lake 426
Ludlow, CA 196, 231
Lufkin, TX 464
Luna, NM 377
Luray, VA 493
Lusk Creek Canyon 305
Lusk Creek Trail 305
Lusk Creek Wilderness **305**
Lye Brook Falls 481

INDEX 575

BOLD PAGE NUMBERS INDICATE MAIN REFERENCES

Lye Brook Wilderness **481**, 482
Lynchburg, VA 485
Lynn Canal 45, 46
Lytle Creek, CA 223

M

Machesna Mountain Trail 191
Machesna Mountain Wilderness 173, **191**, 192
Mackinac Island 325
Mackinac Wilderness **321**, 322
Mackinaw Trail 319
Mad River, CA 201
Madera Canyon 108
Madison, Mount 367, 368
Madison Range 346, 347
Madison River 346
Madulce Peak 168
Magdalena Mountains 377
Magdalena, NM 375, 391
Magnolia Landing 277
Magruder Corridor, the (see also Nez Perce Trail) 352, 420
Maidu Lake 426
Mail Trail 90
Main Salmon River (Wild and Scenic River) 295, 296
Maine 313-315
Makawao, HI 292
Malaspina Glacier 74
Malheur National Forest 424, 435
Malpais Mesa Wilderness **192**
Mammoth Lakes, CA 149, 185
Man Key 273
Manchester Center, VT 479, 481, 482
Manchester, Mount 165
Manchester Ranger Station 482
Manila, AR 139
Manistee, MI 324
Manly Peak Wilderness **193**
Manteca, CA 237
Manti-La Sal National Forest 468
Manzana Creek 218
Manzano Mountain Wilderness **384**
Manzano Peak 384
Maple Grove Campground (Noisy-Diobsud Wilderness) 510
Marble Canyon Gorge 121
Marble Canyon Rim 121
Marble Islands 48
Marble Mountain Wilderness **193**, 194, 213
Marble Mountains 231
Marblemount, WA 516
Maricopa Mountains 127
Marie Lake 416
Marine Science Center (Newport, OR) 436
Marion, General Francis 443
Marion, IL 304, 306
Marion Lake 425
Marion, NC 397
Marion, VA 486, 487, 488
Mark Trail Wilderness **286**, 289
Mark Twain National Forest 334, 335, 336, 337, 338, 339, 340
Markleeville, CA 197
Markleeville Guard Station 197
Marks Creek 423
Marmot Pass 498

Maroon Bells-Snowmass Wilderness 247, **251**, 252
Maroon Lake 251, 252
Marquesas Keys 273
Marquette, MI 318, 320, 322, 324, 326
Marsh Island 401
Marshall, Bob 47, 341, 343, 406, 441
Martin Canyon 136
Martin Canyon Trail 136
Martinez Lake, AZ 99, 180
Martinez Lake Marina 98, 180
Massachusetts 316
Masterson Springs 413
Matia Island 515
Matilija Canyon Trail 194
Matilija Creek (Wild and Scenic River) 194
(North Fork) 194
Matilija Reservoir 194
Matilija Wilderness **194**
Mattamuskeet National Wildlife Refuge 401, 402
Matterhorn Creek 263
Matterhorn Creek Trailhead 263
Matterhorn Peak 417
Matts Creek Shelter 485
Maui 292
Mauna Loa (mountain) 293
Mauna Ulu Lava Shield 293
Maurelle Islands Wilderness **57**, 58
Maxwell Springs 413
Maxwell Trail 134
Mayer, AZ 82
Mayo Key 273
Maysville, NC 398, 399
Mayville, WI 529
Mazatzal Divide Trail 103
Mazatzal Peak 103
Mazatzal Wilderness **102**, 103
McCall, ID 296
McCarthy, AK 74
McClellanville, SC 447, 448
McCloud, CA 199
McCloud Flat 163
McConnell Creek Trail 365
McCormick, Cyrus 322
McCormick, Gordon 322
McCormick Wilderness **322**
McCoy Range 205
McCurdy Park Trail 251
McDonald Lake 232
McGarr Ridge Trail 336
McGarr Springs 335
McGowan Mountain 524
McGrath, AK 50
McKay Creek 520
McKenzie Bridge, OR 427, 437
McKenzie Pass 427
McKinley, Mount 44, 45
McLain, MS 333
McLeod Peak 349
McLoughlin, Mount 433
McQuade Creek Trail 422
Mead, Lake 107
Meadow Creek 344
Meadow Creek Trail 343
Meadow Village, MT 347
Mecca Hills Wilderness **195**, 203
Medano Pass 260

Medford, OR 210, 440
Medicine Bow Mountains 259, 540
Medicine Bow National Forest 534, 536, 539, 540
Medicine Lake, MT 348
Medicine Lake National Wildlife Refuge 347, 348
Medicine Lake Wilderness **347**, 348
(Sandhill Unit) 348
Medicine Park, OK 409
Medina, ND 404
Medora, ND 405
Meeker, CO 244
Meeteetse, WY 542
Mekoryuk, AK 60
Melbourne, FL 278
Mena, AR 139, 141
Menagerie Wilderness **421**, 422
Mendocino National Forest 226, 236
Mendon, UT 477
Mentone, CA 216
Merced River (Wild and Scenic River) 236
(South Fork) 236
Meriwether Canyon 345
Meriwether Picnic Area (Gates of the Mountains Wilderness) 345
Merritt Island National Wildlife Refuge 278
Mesa, AZ 91, 103, 129
Mesa Springs 161
Mesa Verde National Park 252, 253
Mesa Verde Wilderness **252**, 253
Mescal Mountains 110
Mescalero Apache Reservation 390
Mesquite, AZ 80
Mesquite Dry Lake 195
Mesquite Mountains Wilderness **195**, 196, 202
Mesquite Valley 202, 204
Metaline, WA 514
Meyers Chuck, AK 67
Mi-Wok Wilderness, CA 171
Miami, FL 272, 273
Mica Mountain 122
Mica Peak 207
Michigan 317-327
Michigan Islands National Wildlife Refuge 323
Michigan Islands Wilderness **323**
Michigan, Lake 322, 323, 525, 529
Michigan Wilderness Act (1987) 317
Midas Saddle 158
Middle Fishhooks (canyon) 89
Middle Fork State Wildlife Refuge 307
Middle Fork Trail (Gila Wilderness) 383, (Pecos Wilderness) 385
Middle Fork Trail (Cranberry Wilderness) 521
Middle Hickory Creek 442
Middle Mountain 523
Middle Peak 497
Middle Prong Wilderness **397**, 398, 400
Middle Ridge Trail 309
Middle River, MN 329
Middle Santiam River 422
Middle Santiam Trail 422

576 INDEX

BOLD PAGE NUMBERS INDICATE MAIN REFERENCES

Middle Santiam Wilderness 421, **422**
Middle Sister (mountain) 436, 437
Middlebury Gap 480
Middlebury, VT 480
Midnight Trail 384
Midway Canyon 116
Mildred Lakes 509
Mildred Lakes Trail 509, 510
Miles Ranch Trail 129
Milk Creek Glacier 425
Mill Castle Trail 265, 266
Mill City, OR 414, 426
Mill Creek (East Fork Wilderness) 142
Mill Creek (Ishi Wilderness) 182
Mill Creek Canyon 473
Mill Creek Trail 182, 183
Mill Creek Wilderness **423**
Mill Mountain 490
Millboro Springs, VA 491
Miller Peak Wilderness **103**, 104
Millsite Canyon 116
Mimbres, NM 374
Minam River (Wild and Scenic River) 417
Minarets Range 148
Minarets Wilderness 148
Mine Gulch Trail 223
Mineral, CA 189
Mineral Mountains 136
Ming-Dao, Deng 410
Mingo National Wildlife Refuge 337, 338
Mingo River 337
Mingo Wilderness **337**, 338
Minnesota 328-330
Minong Ridge Trail 320
Minot, ND 404
Minturn, CO 247
Mirror Lake 470
Mission Mountains Primitive Area 348
Mission Mountains Wilderness **348**, 349
Mississippi 331-333
Mississippi Flyway (Arkansas) 138; (Illinois) 304; (Louisiana) 312; (Missouri) 337
Mississippi River 436 (Arkansas) 138; (Illinois) 301, 303, 305; (Louisiana) 311; (Michigan) 327; (Missouri) 337
Mississippi Wash 118
Missoula, MT 300, 343, 349, 350, 351, 352, 354
Missouri 334-340
Missouri Mountain 241
Missouri River (Wild and Scenic River) 345, 353
Misty Fiords National Monument 58, 59
Misty Fiords Wilderness **58**, 59
Misty Moon Trail 532, 533
Mitchell Bay 55
Mitchell Peak 184
Mobile, AZ 126
Modesto, CA 171
Modoc National Forest 228
Modoc War 157
Moffat, CO 261

Mogollon Creek 383
Mogollon Range 383
Mogollon Rim (California) 75, 79, 89, 97, 109, 130, 134; (New Mexico) 376
Mohawk Spring 233
Mojave Desert (Arizona) 75, 78, 92, 113; (California) 152, 160, 185, 187, 196, 204, 231, 233
Mojave National Preserve 153, 162, 187, 188, 195, 196, 228
Mojave Wilderness **196**
Mokelumne Peak 197
Mokelumne River 156, 197
Mokelumne Wilderness **197**
Molas Pass 264, 265
Mole Harbor 55
Mollala, OR 435
Mollala River 435
Monarch Wilderness 184, **197**, 198
Moncks Corner, SC 447
Monitor Valley 357
Mono Canyon 168
Mono Lake 179
Monomoy Island 316 (North) 316; (South) 316
Monomoy National Wildlife Refuge 316
Monomoy Point 316
Monomoy Wilderness **316**
Monongahela National Forest 521, 522, 523, 524
Monongahela National Forest Hiking Guide (book) 524
Monopoly Swamp 337
Monroe, Mount 369
Montana 341-354
Monte Cristo Wild Horse and Burro Territory 360
Monte Vista, CO 250
Monterey, CA 234
Monterey Peninsula 234
Montgomery, AL 34
Montgomery Peak 359
Montana 341-354
Monticello, UT 468
Montrose, CO 239, 255, 263
Monument Rock Wilderness **423**, 424, 435
Mooney Harbor Key 273
Moose Creek 300
Moose, ID 300
Moose, WY 531, 532, 535, 538, 540, 542
Moosehorn National Wildlife Refuge 314, 315 (Baring Unit) 314, 315; (Edmunds Unit) 314, 315
Moosehorn Wilderness **314**, 315
Mopah Spring 233
Moran, WY 541
Morena Village, CA 177
Morongo Valley 215
Morrison, CO 253
Morristown, AZ 96
Morse Canyon 84
Morse Canyon Trail 84, 85
Mosca, CO 246
Mosquito Lake 502
Moss Creek Trail 428

Mouatt Reef 515
Mound Mountain 128
Mount Adams Wilderness **506**, 507
Mount Baker Wilderness **507**, 508
Mount Baker-Snoqualmie National Forest 496, 497, 499, 501, 504, 508, 510, 511, 513
Mount Baldy, CA 164
Mount Baldy Wilderness **104**
Mount Charleston Wilderness **362**
Mount Evans Wilderness **253**
Mount Goliath Natural Area 253
Mount Hood National Forest 411, 414, 415, 425, 426, 433
Mount Hood Wilderness 411, **424**, 425
Mount Hood-Parkdale, OR 425
Mount Jefferson Wilderness **425**, 426
Mount Logan Wilderness **105**
Mount Logan Wilderness Area 107
Mount Massive Wilderness 247, **254**
Mount McConnel Trail 241
Mount McKinley National Park 44
Mount Moriah Wilderness **363**
Mount Naomi Wilderness **471**, 477
Mount Nebo Wilderness **472**
Mount Nutt Wilderness **105**, 106
Mount Olympus Wilderness **472**, 473, 476
Mount Rainier National Park 499, 501, 508, 509, 511, 516, 519
Mount Rainier Wilderness **508**, 509
Mount Rogers High Country and Wilderness Map 486, 487, 488
Mount Rogers National Recreation Area 486, 487, 488
Mount Rogers Spur Trail 486
Mount Rogers Trail 486
Mount Rose Trail 363, 364
Mount Rose Wilderness **363**
Mount Rushmore National Memorial 449
Mount San Jacinto State Park and Wilderness 216
Mount Shasta, CA 158, 199
Mount Shasta Wilderness 158, **198**, 199
Mount Skokomish Wilderness **509**, 510
Mount Sneffels Wilderness **254**, 255
Mount Thielsen Trail 426
Mount Thielsen Wilderness 412, **426**, 432
Mount Timpanogos Wilderness 472, **473**, 474
Mount Tipton Wilderness **106**
Mount Trumbull Trail 107
Mount Trumbull Wilderness 105, **107**
Mount Washington Wilderness **427**, 436
Mount Whitney Trail 185
Mount Wilson Wilderness **107**, 108
Mount Wrightson Wilderness **108**
Mount Zirkel Wilderness **255**
Mountain Home, AR 144
Mountain House Picnic Area (Ramseys Draft Wilderness) 490
Mountain Lake (Russell Fiord Wilderness) 62

INDEX 577

BOLD PAGE NUMBERS INDICATE MAIN REFERENCES

Mountain Lake Wilderness (Virginia) **488**
Mountain Lake Wilderness (West Virginia) **523**, 524
Mountain Lakes Loop Trail 428
Mountain Lakes Wilderness **427**, 428
Mountain View, AR 139, 141, 142, 143, 144, 146, 408
Mountainair, NM 384
Mountains-to-Sea route 397
Mountains-to-Sea Trailhead 398
Mud Lake Refuge 328
Mud Spring 91
Mud Spring Mesas 124
Mud Swamp/New River Wilderness **277**
Muggins Mountains Wilderness **109**
Muggins Peak 109
Muir, John 147, 184, 221, 238, 313
Mulchatna River (Wild and Scenic River) 57
Mule Key 273
Mulkey Pass 174
Mummy Range 242
Mummy Rocks 515
Munds Mountain Trail 109
Munds Mountain Wilderness **109**, 110
Munising, MI 318, 324
Murie, Margaret 530
Myers Valley–Pinto Canyon 183
Mystic Lake 341, 342

N

Naches, WA 503, 511, 520
Nankoweap Rim 121
Nannie Basin 502
Nantahala National Forest 393, 395, 396, 401, 446
Nantahala Range 401
Nantahala River (Georgia) 289, (North Carolina) 400
Naomi Peak 471
Napua Trail 293
Narrows, the (Black Canyon of the Gunnison Wilderness) 239
Narrows, the (Paria Canyon–Vermilion Cliffs Wilderness) 115
National Forest System 138
National Geographic Society 52
National Key Deer Refuge 272, 273
National Outdoor Leadership School 539
National Park Concessions 320
National Park Service 75, 83, 107, 113, 140, 149, 187, 238, 284, 294, 331, 373, 388, 392, 465
National Park System 36, 74, 138, 236
National Recreation Trails 358, 428
National Wilderness Preservation System 36, 51, 74, 75, 156, 178, 193, 218, 278, 294, 295, 323, 400, 427, 460
National Wildlife Refuge System 36, 38, 138, 267, 274, 278, 408
Natural Bridge Station, VA 485, 494
Natural Bridge Trail 84
Natural Bridges National Monument 468
Nature Conservancy, the 78
Near Islands 37
Nebo Bench Trail 472
Nebo, NC 397
Nebo Scenic Loop Byway 472
Nebraska 355-356
Nebraska National Forest 355, 356
Neches River 461, 464
Nederland, CO 249
Nee Me Poo Trail 420
Needle Mountains 264
Needle, The (geologic monolith) 95
Needles, CA 96, 151, 159, 162, 165, 177, 178, 187, 188, 196, 202, 203, 210, 224, 228, 229, 231, 233, 235
Needle's Eye Canyon 110
Needle's Eye Wilderness **110**
Needles Peaks 96
Needles Wilderness Area 96
Neel's Gap 288
Negro Ed (butte) 132
Nellie Creek 263
Nelson Lake 168
Nelson, MT 345
Nelson Springs 413
Nelson Trail 117
Neota Creek 256
Neota Wilderness **256**
Nephi, UT 472
Nettle Spring 161
Nettle Spring Campground (Chumash Wilderness) 161
Neuse River 394
Nevada 357-366
Nevada Wilderness Protection Act (1989) 357
Never Summer Wilderness **256**, 257
New Augusta, MS 332
New Bern, NC 395, 398, 399
New Castle, VA 484, 492
New Hampshire 367-370
New Haven River 479
New Jersey 371-372
New Mexico 373-391
New Orleans, LA 311
New Water and Dripping Springs 111
New Water Mountains Wilderness **111**
New Waverly, TX 463
New York 392
New York Butte 181
New York, NY 372, 392
Newark, CA 172
Newberry Mountains Wilderness **199**, 213
Newport, OR 430, 436
Nez Perce National Forest 296, 297, 298, 300, 419
Nez Perce Pass 352
Nez Perce Trail (see also Magruder Corridor, the) 352, 420
Nick Eaton Ridge Trail 414
Nicolet, Jean 525
Nicolet National Forest 525, 526, 528
Nimbus Peak 256
Ninemile Canyon 204
Niobrara River 355
Nisqually 502, 509
Nisqually (San Juan Islands) National Wildlife Refuge 515
Nixon Spring 107
Nizki Island 37
No Name Canyon 204
No-Name Island 441, 442
Noatak, AK 59
Noatak National Preserve 59, 60
Noatak River (Wild and Scenic River) 47, 59 (lower) 59
Noatak Wilderness **59**, 60
Nob Island 515
Nogahabara Sand Dunes 56
Nogales, AZ 108, 114
Noisy Creek 510
Noisy-Diobsud Wilderness **510**
NOLS (see National Outdoor Leadership School)
Nopah Peak 200
Nopah Range 200, 205, 226
Nopah Range Wilderness **200**, 226
Norbeck Trail 449, 450
Norbeck Wildlife Preserve 449
Nordhouse Dunes Trail 323
Nordhouse Dunes Wilderness **323**, 324
Norfolk, AR 144
Norse Peak Trail 511
Norse Peak Wilderness **511**, 519
Norske Trail 479
North Absaroka Wilderness **537**, 538
North Algodones Dunes Wilderness **200**, 201
North Bend, OR 430
North Bend, WA 496
North Canyon Trailhead 122
North Caribou Peak 155
North Carolina 393-402
North Cascades National Park 500, 506, 507, 510, 515, 516
North Conway, NH 368, 370
North Country National Scenic Trail 321, 326, 527
North Country Trail 527, 528
North Dakota 403-405
North Emerson Lake 227
North Fork, CA 149
North Fork Campground (Devils Backbone Wilderness) 336
North Fork, ID 296, 297
North Fork John Day Campground (North Fork John Day Wilderness) 429
North Fork John Day Trail (National Recreation Trail) 428, 429
North Fork John Day Wilderness **428**, 429 (Baldy Creek Unit) 428; (Greenhorn Unit) 428; (Tower Mountain Unit) 428
North Fork Recreation Area 335
North Fork Trail (Cranberry Wilderness) 521
North Fork Trail (Lee Metcalf Wilderness) 347
North Fork Umatilla Wilderness **429**

BOLD PAGE NUMBERS INDICATE MAIN REFERENCES

North Fork Wilderness **201**
North Gate Canyon 538
North Island 37
North Kaibab Recreation Map 101, 122
North Key Island 270
North Maricopa Mountains Wilderness **111**
North Mesquite Mountains Wilderness 195, **202**
North Mountain Wilderness 408, 409
North Pacific Rock 515
North Palm Springs, CA 150, 155, 160, 190, 195, 203, 205, 212, 216, 220
North Peak 497
North Petit Jean Mountain 141
North Platte River (Colorado) 256, 257; (Wyoming) 533, 536, 538
North Plotnikof Lake 66
North Point 413
North Pond 480
North Santa Teresa Wilderness **112**, 124
North Sister 436
North Umpqua River 412
North Waldo Campground (Waldo Lake Wilderness) 438
North Woods 403
North Yolla Bolly Mountains 235
Norton Sound 41
Norwood, CO 250, 255
Notch, The (Dark Canyon Wilderness) 468
Novarupta Volcano 52
Noyes Island 44
NPS (see National Park Service)
Nunatak Fiord 62
Nunivak Island Wilderness **60**
NWPS (see National Wilderness Preservation System)
NWRS (see National Wildlife Refuge System)
Nyala, NV 361

O

Oak Creek 119
Oak Creek Canyon 101
Oak Flat 421
Oak Flat Trail 90
Oak Harbor, OH 406
Oakes Gulf 369
Oakridge, OR 416, 438
Obsidian Lake 437
Ocala, FL 275
Ocala National Forest 267, 269, 275, 276
Ocean Springs, MS 332
Oceanside, OR 436
Oceanville, NJ 372
Ochoco Creek 423
Ochoco Mountains 413
Ochoco National Forest 412, 413, 423
Ochoco Reservoir 423
Ocoee Lake 453, 455
Ocoee Number 3 Powerhouse 453, 455
Ocoee River 457
Ocoee, TN 453, 455
Ocotillo, CA 164
Odell Lake 416
Odom Trail 33, 34
Ogangen Island 38
Ogchul Island 38
Ogliuga Island 37
Oglodak Island 38
Oh-Be-Joyful Creek Valley 259
Oh-Be-Joyful Pass 259
Oh-Be-Joyful Pass Trail 259
Ohio 406
Ohio City, CO 245
Ohio River 301, 305
OHT (see Ozark Highlands Trail)
Oil Well Creek 464
Ojai, CA 161, 194, 222
Okanogan National Forest 506, 513
Okeechobee, Lake 271
Okefenokee National Wildlife Refuge 286, 287
Okefenokee Swamp 280, 286
Okefenokee Wilderness **286**, 287
Oklahoma 407-409
Oklahoma Wilderness Area Act (1988) 407
Oklawaha River 276
'Ola'a Forest 293
Olancha, CA 163, 165, 166, 192
Olancha Peak 227
Old Horseshoe Canyon 116
Old Orchard Shelter 486
Old Snowy Mountain 502
Old Spanish Trail 121, 123, 226
Old Woman Mountains Wilderness **202**, 203
Old Woman Peak 202
Old Woman Statue (granite monolith) 202
Olema, CA 207
Oliverian Brook Trail 370
Olson, Sigurd F. 328
Olustee, FL 268
Olympia, WA 515
Olympic Mountains 498, 512
Olympic National Forest 498, 499, 500, 510, 520
Olympic National Park 497, 498, 500, 509, 511, 512, 518, 520
Olympic Peninsula 495, 498, 499, 500, 510, 512, 518, 520
Olympic Wilderness **511**, 512
Olympus, Mount (Washington) 511, 512
Ona Beach State Park 417
Onion Portage 54
Ontario Peak 164
Opal Mountain 152
Open Sand Area (Nordhouse Dunes Wilderness) 323
Ophir Summit 358
Orcas Island 514, 515
Oregon 410-440
Oregon Butte 438
Oregon Caves National Monument 431
Oregon Coastal National Wildlife Refuges 430
Oregon Islands National Wildlife Refuge 430
Oregon Islands Wilderness **430**
Orem, UT 474
Organ Pipe Cactus National Monument 81, 112, 113
Organ Pipe Cactus Wilderness **112**, 113
Orleans, CA 194
Orocopia Mountains 195
Orocopia Mountains Wilderness **203**
Orofino, ID 300
Orphan Trailhead 450
Osceola National Forest 268
Ottawa National Forest 322, 326, 327
Ottawa National Wildlife Refuge 406
Otter Creek Trail 524
Otter Creek Wilderness **524**
Ouachita Mountains 141, 143, 145
Ouachita National Forest 139, 141, 142, 143, 145, 408, 409
Ouachita National Recreation Trail 143, 409
Ouachita River 139
Ouray, CO 255
Overlook Loop 226
Owens Lake 181
Owens Peak Wilderness **204**
Owens Valley 163, 181
Oxford, Mount 241
Ozark Highlands Trail 143, 144, 145, 335
Ozark Highlands Trail Guide (book) 143, 145
Ozark Interpretive Association 139, 141, 142, 143, 144, 146, 408
Ozark Mountains 140, 144, 145, 301, 303, 334, 338, 339
Ozark National Forest 140, 145
Ozark Trail 335
Ozark Uplift 301
Ozark–Saint Francis National Forest 142, 144, 146
Ozena Forest Service Facility 168
Ozette, WA 518

P

Pacific Beach, WA 518
Pacific City, OR 430
Pacific Coast 344
Pacific Coast Trail (Russian Wilderness) 213, (South Sierra Wilderness) 227
Pacific Crest National Scenic Trail 148, 154, 157, 159, 167, 169, 170, 174, 204, 223, 426, 427, 437, 496, 501, 502, 503, 504, 506, 507, 511, 513, 516, 520 (Ansel Adams Wilderness) 149; (Bucks Lake Wilderness) 154; (Carson-Iceberg Wilderness) 157; (Columbia Wilderness) 414, 416; (Desolation Wilderness) 167; (Diamond Peak Wilderness) 416; (Domeland Wilderness) 169; (Goat Rocks Wilderness) 502; (Granite Chief Wilderness) 175, 176; (Hauser Wilderness) 177; (Henry M. Jackson Wilderness) 503, 504; (Indian Heaven Wilderness) 504; (John Muir Wilderness) 184; (Kiavah

INDEX 579

BOLD PAGE NUMBERS INDICATE MAIN REFERENCES

Wilderness) 187, 188; (Lassen Volcanic Wilderness) 189; (Marble Mountain Wilderness) 193; (Mokelumne Wilderness) 197; (Mount Adams Wilderness) 506; (Mount Jefferson Wilderness) 425; (Mount Thielsen Wilderness) 426; (Mount Washington Wilderness) 427; (Norse Peak Wilderness) 511; (Owens Peak Wilderness) 204; (Pasayten Wilderness) 513; (Red Buttes Wilderness, Oregon) 430; (Russian Wilderness) 213; (Sacatar Trail Wilderness) 214; (San Jacinto Wilderness) 216, 217; (Sequoia–Kings Canyon Wilderness) 221; (Sky Lakes Wilderness) 434; (South Sierra Wilderness) 227; (Stephen Mather Wilderness) 516; (Three Sisters Wilderness) 436; (Trinity Alps Wilderness) 232; (Waldo Lake Wilderness) 437; (William O. Douglas Wilderness) 519
Pacific Plate (tectonic plate) 291
Packer, Alferd 257
Packwood Lake 502, 503
Packwood Lake Resort 503
Packwood Lake Trail 502, 503
Packwood, WA 502, 503, 517, 520
Paddy Creek Campground (Paddy Creek Wilderness) 338
Paddy Creek Wilderness **338**
Paddy, Sylvester 338
Pads Creek 491
Page, AZ 115
Page, OK 408
Pagosa Springs, CO 262, 265
Pahaska Campground (North Absaroka Wilderness) 538
Pahaska, WY 538
Pahrump Valley Wilderness **204**, 205
Paicines, CA 209
Painted Canyon 195
Painted Cave 375
Painted Desert 116, 127
Painted Gorge 163
Painted Rock Dam 137
Painter Creek Falls 458
Paisley, OR 418
Paiute Wilderness 80, **113**, 114
Pajarita Plateau 375
Pajarita Wilderness **114**
Pakalani, HI 292
Palatka, FL 276
Palen Mountains 205
Palen-McCoy Wilderness **205**
Palm Springs, CA 217, 220
Palo Verde, CA 206
Palo Verde Dam 150
Palo Verde Mountains Wilderness **206**
Palo Verde Peak 206
Palomar-McGee Trail 148
Palomas Trail 386
Pamelia Lake 425
Pamlico Sound 401
Pan Tak Pass 86
Panamint Mountains 166, 193, 229
Panamint Springs 165

Panamint Valley 149, 229
Panjab Campground (Wenaha-Tucannon Wilderness, Washington) 519
Pansy Lake 414
Pansy Lake Trail 414
Panther Den Wilderness **306**
Paonia, CO 266
Papago Indian Reservation 78
Paradise Lake (Marble Mountain Wilderness) 193
Paradise Peak 365
Paradise, WA 508
Paria Canyon (Arizona) 115; (Utah) 474
Paria Canyon Gulch 474
Paria Canyon–Vermilion Cliffs Wilderness (Arizona) **115**
Paria Canyon–Vermilion Cliffs Wilderness (Utah) **474**, 475
Paria Information Station 115, 475
Paria River 115
Parker, AZ 92, 235
Parker Reef 515
Parlin, CO 245
Parson's Spring 130
Parsons, WV 524
Pasayten Wilderness **513**
Pashubbe Creek 409
Paskenta, CA 236
Pass Creek Pass 514
Passage Key Wilderness **277**, 278
Patchoque, NY 392
Patjens Lake 427
Pats Island 275
Patterson Lake 227
Paugus, Mount 370
Paulina, OR 412
Pawnee Lake 248
Payette National Forest 296, 298, 419
Payette River 299 (South Fork) 299
Paynes Lake 213
Paynes Lake Trail 213
Payson, AZ 97, 103
PCT (see Pacific Crest National Scenic Trail)
Peabody River 367, 368 (West Branch) 368, (West Fork) 367
Peaceful Pines Campground (Carson-Iceberg Wilderness) 157
Peapod Rocks 515 (North) 515; (South) 515
Pearsoll Peak 421
Pecos, NM 385
Pecos River (Wild and Scenic River) 385, 386
Pecos Wilderness **385**
Pelican, AK 73
Pelican Island 278, 408
Pelican Island National Wildlife Refuge 278
Pelican Island Wilderness **278**
Peloncillo Mountains 116
Peloncillo Mountains Wilderness **116**
Pelsor, AR 146
Pelton Creek Campground (Platte River Wilderness) 539
Pelton Creek Trailhead 538

Pemigewasset River (East Branch) 368, 369
Pemigewasset Wilderness **368**, 369
Penasco, NM 385
Pendleton, OR 429
Pennsylvania 441-442
Pentagon Primitive Area 343
Peoples Canyon 77
Pepperdine Trailhead 228
Pepperwood Height Trail 220
Peralta Trail 128, 129
Perpetua Campground (Cummins Creek Wilderness) 415
Perryville, AR 143
Pershing, Mount 509
Peru Peak Wilderness **482**
Peshekee River 322
Pete Parent Peak 482
Peters Mountain Wilderness **489**
Petersburg, AK 43, 49, 56, 61, 68, 69, 73
Petersburg Creek–Duncan Salt Chuck Wilderness **61**
Petersburg Lake 61
Petersburg Lake National Recreation Trail 61
Petersburg, WV 522
Petes Creek 500
Petes Creek Trail 500
Petit Bois (island) 332
Petrel Island 46
Petrified Forest Loop Trail 405
Petrified Forest National Monument 116
Petrified Forest National Park 116, 117
Petrified Forest Wilderness **116**, 117
Petrof Bay 56
Peulik, Mount 40
Phelp's Cabin 104
Philipsburg, MT 343
Phillip Burton Wilderness **206**, 207
Phipps–Death Hollow Outstanding Natural Area 467
Phoenix, AZ 81, 82, 87, 88, 89, 92, 95, 96, 98, 110, 111, 112, 117, 124, 126, 127, 130, 131, 136, 137
Picacho Peak Wilderness **207**
Picacho State Recreation Area 98, 180
Picayune Creek 175
Picayune Valley 175
Piedra Area 264
Pigeon Key 273
Pigeon River 400 (East Fork) 400, (West Fork) 397, 400
Pigeon Trail 90, 91
Pike National Forest 240, 251, 253
Pilot Knob 336
Pine Bench 412
Pine Creek (Alta Toquima Wilderness) 358
Pine Creek (Box–Death Hollow Wilderness) 467
Pine Creek Basin 227
Pine Creek Campground (Alta Toquima Wilderness) 358
Pine Creek Trail 358

580 INDEX

BOLD PAGE NUMBERS INDICATE MAIN REFERENCES

Pine Creek Wilderness 177, **208**
Pine Lodge 378
Pine Mountain (Oklahoma) 409
Pine Mountain Trail (Lewis Fork Wilderness) 486
Pine Mountain Trail (Pine Mountain Wilderness) 117
Pine Mountain Wilderness **117**
Pine Ridge 454
Pine Ridge Trail 234
Pine River (Michigan) 318
Pine River (Wisconsin) 526
Pine Swamp Ridge 489
Pine Swamp Shelter 489
Pine Valley, CA 177, 220
Pine Valley Mountain Wilderness **475**, 476
Pine Valley, UT 476
Pinecrest, CA 171
Pinedale, WY 532
Pineland, TX 464
Pines Campground (Barbours Creek Wilderness) 484
Pineview Tower Trailhead 339
Pineville, LA 312
Piney Creek Wilderness **339**
Piney Lake 243
Piney Ridge Trail 485
Pinhook River 279
Pinhoti Trail 33
Pinnacle Island 41
Pinnacles (Mount Tipton Wilderness) 106
Pinnacles (Washakie Wilderness) 542
Pinnacles National Monument 208, 209
Pinnacles Wilderness **208**, 209
Piñon Creek 153
Piñon Flat Campground (Santa Rosa Wilderness) 220
Pinos, Mount 145
Pinto Mountains 185
Piper Mountain 230
Piper Mountain Wilderness **209**
Pisgah Forest, NC 398, 400
Pisgah National Forest 393, 397, 398, 400
Pisgah Ridge 400
Pisgah Springs 413
Pismire Island 323
Pittsburg Landing 298
Piute Mountains 152, 209
Piute Mountains Wilderness **209**, 210
Piute Valley 165
Placer Lakes 43
Platina, CA 158, 236
Platte Ridge 538
Platte River Mountains 251
Platte River Trail 538
Platte River Wilderness (Colorado) **257**
Platte River Wilderness (Wyoming) 257, **538**, 539
Pleasant Grove, UT 471, 474
Pleasant Island 61
Pleasant/Lemusurier/Inian Islands Wilderness **61**, 62
Plumas National Forest 154
Plymouth, NH 369
Poachie Range 77
Pocosin Wilderness **398**, 399
Pogo Agie Falls Trailhead 540
Point Reyes 172
Point Reyes National Seashore 206, 207
Point Reyes Peninsula 206
Point Reyes Station, CA 207
Pointer Island 515
Pole Bridge 84
Pole Bridge Trailhead 85
Pole Creek (Little Lake Creek Wilderness) 463
Pole Creek (Three Sisters Wilderness) 437
Pollocksville, NC 395, 399
Pomeroy, WA 439, 519
Ponca, AR 140
Pond Mountain Trail 458
Pond Mountain Wilderness 453, **457**, 458
Pond Pine Wilderness **399**
Poplar Bluff, MO 337, 338
Poplar Springs Branch 455, 456
Popo Agie Falls Trail 539
Popo Agie River 539 (Middle Fork) 539, (North Fork) 539
Popo Agie Wilderness **539**, 540
Popof Glacier 68
Porcupine Lake Wilderness **527**
Port Alsworth, AK 57
Port Angeles, WA 512, 518
Port Beauclerc Bay 56
Port Malmesbury Bay 56
Port Orford, OR 419
Porterville, CA 174
Portland, OR 414, 415, 425, 433, 435
Portsmouth, ME 313
Portuguese Canyon 214
Posey Creek 145
Potato Hollow Trail 466
Potato Patch Campground (Woodchute Wilderness) 137
Poteau Mountain Wilderness **145**
Poteau, OK 409
Potosi, MO 335
Potts Mountain 483, 484, 492
Potts Mountain Trail 488, 523
Powderhorn Lakes 257
Powderhorn Wilderness **257**, 258
Powell, Lake 468
Powell, WY 531, 538
Power's Garden 91
Powers, OR 419
Pozo Summit 192
Prairie City, OR 424, 435
Prairie Fork 223
Prescott, AZ 82, 93
Prescott National Forest 76, 82, 83, 99, 117, 130, 137
Presidential Range 367, 368, 369, 479
Presidential Range–Dry River Wilderness **369**, 370
Pressley Cove 457
Pribilof Islands 41
Priest River 514
Priest River, ID 514
Primitive areas 125, 128, 178, 193, 218, 234, 452, 468
Prince of Wales Island 44, 51, 58, 67, 72
Prineville, OR 412, 413, 423
Prospect, OR 432
Prospect Rock 481
Provo Canyon 473
Prudhoe Bay, AK 40
Ptarmigan Pass 258
Ptarmigan Peak Trail 258
Ptarmigan Peak Wilderness **258**, 264
Ptarmigan Traverse 501
Puale Bay 40
Pueblo, CO 246
Pueblo Creek 377
Pueblo Park Campground (Blue Range Wilderness) 377
Puerta Suela Trail 168
Puffin Island (Chamisso Island Wilderness) 42
Puffin Island (San Juan Islands Wilderness) 515
Puget Sound 514, 515
Pumpkin Trail 101
Purcell Mountains 64
Pusch Ridge Wilderness **118**
Pustoi Island 38
Putvin Trail 509
Puxico, MO 338
Puyallup Trail 502
Pyramid Island 37

Q

Quartz Peak 181
Questa, NM 384, 389
Quetico Provincial Park 329
Quilcene River 498, 499
Quilcene, WA 498, 499
Quillayute Needles Refuge 518
Quinault, Lake 500
Quinault River 500
Quinault, WA 500
Quincy, CA 154
Quinn Canyon Wilderness 361, **364**
Quinn Lakes 437

R

R. Thompson's Island 441, 442
Rabbit Island 38
Raccoon Key 273
rafting (see river running)
Ragged Mountain 259
Raggeds Wilderness **259**
Rainbow Lake Wilderness **527**, 528
Rainier, Mount 198, 435, 499, 501, 506, 508, 516
Rainier National Park 502
Rainy Pass 516
Raleigh, Sir Walter 399
Ramona, CA 148
Ramseys Draft Trail 489, 490
Ramseys Draft Wilderness **489**, 490
Rancho Nuevo region 168
Ranegras Plain 111
Range Province 92, 120
Rapid City, SD 450
Rat Island 37
Rat Islands 37
Ratcliff Lake 461
Ratcliff, TX 461

INDEX   581

BOLD PAGE NUMBERS INDICATE MAIN REFERENCES

Rattlesnake Canyon (Bighorn Mountains Wilderness) 151, 152
Rattlesnake Canyon (Galiuro Wilderness) 91
Rattlesnake Creek (Ashdown Gorge Wilderness) 466
Rattlesnake Creek (Rattlesnake Wilderness) 349
Rattlesnake Creek Trail 349
Rattlesnake Mountains 349
Rattlesnake National Recreation Area 349
Rattlesnake Ridge Trail 459
Rattlesnake Trail (Ashdown Gorge Wilderness) 466
Rattlesnake Trail (Wenaha-Tucannon Wilderness, Washington) 519
Rattlesnake Wilderness **349**, 350 (South Zone) 349, 350
Rattlesnake Wilderness Area 349
Raven Cliffs Falls Trail 288
Raven Cliffs Scenic Area 288
Raven Cliffs Wilderness 282, **287**, 288
Rawah Trail 259
Rawah Wilderness **259**, 260
Rawhide Mountains Wilderness **118**, 119
Rawlings, Marjorie Kinnan 275
Raymond, Mount 472
Raymond Peak 197
Red Bluff, CA 158, 183
Red Buffalo Pass 243
Red Buttes Wilderness (California) **210**, 430
Red Buttes Wilderness (Oregon) 210, **430**, 431
Red Cinder 155
Red Cloud Wash 132
Red Creek 522
Red Creek Trail 522
Red Dirt National Wildlife Management Preserve 312
Red Fork Falls 459
Red Fork Falls Trail 459
Red Lodge, MT 342
Red Mountain (Grass Valley Wilderness) 176
Red Mountain (Scapegoat Wilderness) 351
Red Pine Lakes 470
Red Pine Trail 470
Red River (Kentucky) 310
Red River (New Mexico) 389 (East Fork) 389
Red River Gorge Geological Area 310
Red Rock Lake 329
Red Rock Lakes National Wildlife Area 350
Red Rock Lakes National Wildlife Refuge 351
Red Rock Lakes Wilderness **350**, 351
Red Rock Trail 313
Red Rock–Secret Mountain Wilderness **119**
Red Spring 165
Redding, CA 158, 189
Redfield Canyon 91, 120
Redfield Canyon Wilderness **120**
Redfish Creek/Baron Creek Trail 299

Redfish Lake 299
Redington, AZ 120
Redlands, CA 216
Redoubt, Mount 57, 71
Redwood Creek 224
Reese River 358
Reese River Valley 358
Refrigerator Canyon 345
Reno, NV 363, 364
Reno Trail 79
Resting Spring Range 200, 211
Resting Spring Range Wilderness **211**
Reward, CA 182
Reynard Lake 527
Reynolds Creek Group Site 123
Reynolds Trailhead 123
Rezanof Lake 66
Rhyolite Canyon Trail 84
Rice Valley Wilderness **211**, 212
Rich Hole Trail 490
Rich Hole Wilderness **490**
Rich Mountain (Laurel Fork North/Laurel Fork South Wilderness) 523
Rich Mountain (Upper Kiamichi River Wilderness) 409
Rich Mountain Wilderness **288**
Rich Mountain Wildlife Area 288
Richland Balsam 397
Richland Creek Campground (Richland Creek Wilderness) 145, 146
Richland Creek Wilderness **145**, 146
Richwood, WV 522
Ridgecrest, CA 150, 153, 160, 163, 165, 170, 175, 176, 188, 192, 193, 204, 209, 214, 229, 230
Rifle, CO 244
Rigdon Lakes 438
Rigdon Lakes Trail 438
Riggins, ID 298
Riley Lake 528
Rim Island 515
Rimrock, AZ 90, 135
Rincon, the (escarpment) 136
Rincon Mountain Wilderness **120**, 121 (Rincon Mountain Unit) 121
Ringgold Island 37
Rio Grande 245, 264, 377, 380, 391
Rio Grande National Forest 250, 261, 262, 265
Rio Grande Valley (upper) 249
Rio Hondo 389
Ripple Island 515
Ripplebrook Campground (Bull of the Woods Wilderness) 414
Riprap Hollow Trail 493
River of No Return 295
river running (Alaska) 57, 63, 69; (Arizona) 80, 118, 124; (California) 174, 216, 221, 235-236; (Colorado) 257; (Georgia) 285; (Idaho) 295-296, 298, 300; (Michigan) 326; (New Mexico) 380; (New York) 392; (Oregon) 419-420, 439; (Utah) 466; (West Virginia) 521; (Wyoming) 538
River-to-River Trail 304, 305

Riverside Mountains Wilderness **212**
RNRA (see Rattlesnake National Recreation Area)
Roads End Trailhead 365
Roanoke Island 399
Roanoke, VA 484, 492
Roaring Fork Creek 484
Roaring Fork Trail 536
Robbins Branch Trail 394
Robbinsville, NC 396
Robin Hood Campground (Badger Creek Wilderness) 411
Roby Lake Recreation Area 338
Roby, MO 338
Rochert, MN 330
Rock Branch Hollow 305
Rock Bridge Nature Trail 310
rock climbing (Alaska) 45, 47; (Arizona) 78, 80, 87, 92-93, 96, 109, 126, 129, 132, 136; (California) 148, 157, 181, 185, 208, 216, 236; (Colorado) 239, 241, 243, 249-250, 252, 254, 260, 263; (Illinois) 304, 306; (Nevada) 359; (North Carolina) 397; (Oregon) 412, 416, 418, 421, 423, 424, 426; (Washington) 496-497, 501, 503, 507-509, 511; (Wyoming) 531
Rock Creek (Anaconda-Pintlar Wilderness) 342
Rock Creek (Poteau Mountain Wilderness) 145
Rock Creek (Rock Creek Wilderness) 431
Rock Creek (Welcome Creek Wilderness) 354
Rock Creek (Wenaha-Tucannon Wilderness, Oregon) 438
Rock Creek Campground (Rock Creek Wilderness) 431, 432
Rock Creek Trail (Little Frog Mountain Wilderness) 457
Rock Creek Trail (Rock Creek Wilderness) 431
Rock Creek Wilderness **431**, 432
Rock Harbor 320
Rock Harbor Lodge 320
Rock Island State Park 529
Rock Key 273
Rock Pile Mountain Wilderness **339**, 340
Rock River 324
Rock River Canyon Wilderness **324**
Rock River Falls 324
Rockhouse Canyon 219
Rockpile Lake 416
Rockport, WA 501
Rocky Mountain National Park 242, 248, 249, 256
Rocky Mountains 238, 240, 251, 256, 259, 341, 343, 345, 367, 373, 383, 405, 449, 531, 537 (Southern) 533
Rocky Ridge 432
Rodman Mountains Wilderness **212**, 213
Rogers, Mount 486
Rogerson, ID 362
Rogue River (Wild and Scenic River) 439, 440

582 INDEX

BOLD PAGE NUMBERS INDICATE MAIN REFERENCES

Rogue River National Forest 210, 432, 434
Rogue River Trail 439, 440
Rogue-Umpqua Divide National Recreation Trail 432
Rogue-Umpqua Divide Scenic Area 432
Rogue-Umpqua Divide Wilderness 412, **432**
Rolla, MO 338
Roosevelt, Franklin Delano 53
Roosevelt, Mount 479
Roosevelt National Forest 241, 243, 249, 256, 260
Roosevelt, Theodore 278, 403, 408, 525
Rooster Rock Trail 421
Rose, Mount (Washington) 509
Rose Spring Trail 79
Roseburg, OR 412, 426
Ross Lake National Recreation Area 515
Roswell Airport 386
Roswell, NM 378, 386
Rough Mountain Wilderness **491**
Round Island Wilderness **325**
Round Top Lake 197
Round Top Peak 197
Routt National Forest 240, 244, 255, 257, 258, 261, 538
Rowell, Chester 478
Rowell Meadow 184
Ruby Crest National Recreation Trail 365
Ruby Dome 365
Ruby Mountains Wilderness **364**, 365
Ruch, CA 210
Ruidoso, NM 378, 390
Rum Island 515
Russell Fiord Wilderness **62**
Russell Glacier 425
Russellville, AR 146
Russian Peak 213
Russian Wilderness 194, **213**
Rutland, VT 479, 482
Rye, CO 246

S

Sabine National Forest 462
Sacatar Canyon 214
Sacatar Trail 159, 214
Sacatar Trail Wilderness **214**
Saco River 313, 369
Sacramento Mountains 151
Sacramento River 182
Saddle Mountain Trail 121
Saddle Mountain Wilderness **121**, 122
(North Canyon) 121;
(South Canyon) 121
Saddle Peak Hills Wilderness **214**
Safford, AZ 77, 87, 89, 112, 116, 125
Sagagik Island 38
Sage Creek (Badlands) Wilderness **450**
Saginaw, MI 323
Saguache, CO 261
Saguaro National Monument 120, 121, 122

Saguaro National Park 123
Saguaro Wilderness **122**, 123
(Rincon Mountain Unit) 122, 123,
(Tucson Mountain Unit) 122, 123
Saijo, Albert 75
Saint Elias Mountains 48
Saint Francis River 339
Saint Francois Mountains 334, 339
Saint George, UT 80, 85, 101, 105, 107, 114, 115, 467, 475, 476
Saint Helens, Mount 52
Saint Ignace, MI 319, 322, 325
Saint Johns River 267, 276
Saint Lazaria Island Wilderness **63**
Saint Louis, MO 335, 337, 338
Saint Louis Peak 240
Saint Marks, FL 279
Saint Marks Lighthouse 279
Saint Marks National Wildlife Refuge 279
(Panacea Unit) 279; (Saint Marks Unit) 279; (Wakulla Unit) 279
Saint Marks Wilderness **279**
Saint Martin Island 529
Saint Mary's, AK 39
Saint Mary's Falls 492
Saint Marys, GA 284, 285
Saint Marys River (Georgia) 287
Saint Mary's River (Virginia) 491
Saint Mary's River Gorge 491
Saint Mary's Trailhead 492
Saint Mary's Wilderness **491**, 492
Saint Matthew Island 41
Saint Matthew Island Group 41
Saint Peters Dome 382
Saint Peters Dome Trail 382
Saint Peters Dome Trailhead 382
Saint Petersburg, FL 271
Salazar Canyon 177
Salem, OR 435
Salida, CO 242, 261
Salinas River 173
Salinas Valley 224
Saline Valley 181
Salish Peak 497
Salmo Mountain 514
Salmo-Priest Wilderness **514**
Salmon Breaks Primitive Area 295
Salmon Butte 433
Salmon Creek 224
Salmon Creek Falls 224
Salmon Creek Trailhead 224
Salmon Forks 344
Salmon, ID 296
Salmon Lake 51
Salmon National Forest 296, 297
Salmon River (Alaska/Wild and Scenic River) 54
Salmon River (California/Wild and Scenic River) 213, 232
Salmon River (Idaho/Wild and Scenic River) 295, 297, 296, 298, 299 (lower) 297; (Middle Fork) 295, 296; (North Fork) 296
Salmon River (Oregon) 433 (South Fork) 433
Salmon River Breaks 297
Salmon River Mountains 295
Salmon River National Recreation Trail 433

Salmon-Huckleberry Wilderness 414, **433**
Salmon-Trinity Alps Primitive Area 232
Salome Canyon 123
Salome Creek 123
Salome Wilderness **123**
Salt Branch 464
Salt Chuck Creek 61
Salt Creek (North Fork Wilderness) 201
Salt Creek Wilderness **386**
Salt Flat, TX 462
Salt Island 38
Salt Lake City, UT 469, 470, 471, 472, 473, 474, 476, 477
Salt Lake Valley 472, 476
Salt River 124
Salt River Canyon Wilderness **124**
Salt Springs Reservoir 197
Salton Sea 156
Sam Canyon 89
Sam Houston National Forest 463
Sam Powell Peak 95
Sample Meadow Campground (Kaiser Wilderness) 186
Sampson Mountain Wilderness **458**, 459
Samuel R. McKelvie National Forest 355
San Andreas Fault 164, 195, 203, 206
San Andreas Rift Zone 208
San Antonio, Mount 223
San Antonio Mountain 381
San Augustine, TX 462
San Bernardino, CA 152
San Bernardino Mountains 151, 215
San Bernardino National Forest 151, 152, 164, 216, 217, 220, 223
San Bernardino Peak 215 (East) 215
San Bernardino Peak Divide Trail 216
San Carlos Apache Indian Reservation 79, 89, 110, 112, 124
San Carlos, AZ 79
San Carlos Tribal Office 79
San Diego, CA 156
San Francisco Bay National Wildlife Refuge Complex 172
San Francisco, CA 207
San Francisco Mountain 101
San Francisco Mountains 127, 136
San Gabriel Mountains 215, 223
San Gabriel River (East Fork) 223; (West Fork) 215
San Gabriel Wilderness **215**
San Gorgonio Mountain 215, 216
San Gorgonio Wilderness **215**, 216
San Isabel National Forest 240, 242, 246, 247, 254, 261
San Jacinto Mountains 216
San Jacinto Wilderness **216**, 217
San Joaquin River (Middle Fork) 148, 184; (North Fork) 148; (South Fork) 148, 184
San Joaquin Valley 221
San Juan Island 514, 515

INDEX 583

BOLD PAGE NUMBERS INDICATE MAIN REFERENCES

San Juan Islands National Wildlife Refuge 514
San Juan Islands Wilderness **514**, 515
San Juan Mountains 250, 254, 257, 263
San Juan National Forest 250, 262, 265
San Juan Range 257
San Juan River 262, 264
San Lorenzo, NM 374
San Luis Obispo, CA 192, 219
San Luis Peak 249
San Luis Valley 245, 249, 260
San Mateo Canyon Trail 217
San Mateo Canyon Wilderness **217**
San Mateo Mountains 374, 391
San Miguel (roadless area) 264
San Pascualito Mountain 377
San Pedro Parks Wilderness **386**, 387
San Rafael Mountains 218
San Rafael Wilderness 168, **218**
San Simeon, CA 224
San Simon, AZ 116
San Simon Valley 86
Sanak Islands 38
Sanchez Canyon 382
Sanchez Creek 382
Sand Branch 463
Sand Canyon (Cebolla Wilderness) 379
Sand Canyon (Owens Peak Wilderness) 204
Sand Flat Trailhead 199
Sand Key 273
Sand Point, AK 65
Sanders, Scott Russell 451
Sandia Mountain Wilderness **387**
Sandia Peak Tramway 387
Sandrock Canyon 90
Sandwich Mountain 370
Sandwich Range Wilderness **370**
Sandy Creek 463
Sandy, OR 433
Sanger, CA 169, 198
Sangre de Cristo Mountains 245, 260, 382, 383, 385, 389
Sangre de Cristo Wilderness **260**, 261
Sanibel, FL 274
Sanibel Island 274
Santa Barbara, CA 168, 218
Santa Barbara Campground (Pecos Wilderness) 385
Santa Barbara Canyon 168
Santa Barbara Divide 385
Santa Catalina Mountains 118
Santa Fe National Forest 380, 382, 385, 387
Santa Fe, NM 375, 380
Santa Lucia Mountains 224, 234
Santa Lucia Wilderness 173, **219**
Santa Maria, CA 173, 192, 218, 219
Santa Maria River 77
Santa Rita Mountains 108
Santa Rosa Island 332
Santa Rosa Mines 192
Santa Rosa Mountains (California) 219; (Nevada) 365

Santa Rosa Peak 365
Santa Rosa Wilderness **219**, 220
Santa Rosa–Paradise Peak Wilderness **365**
Santa Teresa Mountains 124
Santa Teresa Wilderness **124**, 125
Santeetlah Lake 396
Santiam Pass 426
Sapphire Mountains 354
Sarvis (Service) Creek Wilderness **261**
Sassafras Knob 457
Sassafras Ridge 454
Sault Sainte Marie, MI 318, 319
Savage Run Creek 540
Savage Run Trail 540
Savage Run Wilderness **540**
Savannah Coastal Refuges 281, 290
Savannah, GA 281, 290
Sawatch Range 254, 257
Sawmill Creek 389
Sawmill Park 389
Sawtooth Mountains (Idaho) 299; (Washington) 505
Sawtooth Mountains Wilderness **220**
Sawtooth National Forest 299
Sawtooth National Recreation Area 299
Sawtooth Ridge 509
Sawtooth Scenic Route 299
Sawtooth Wilderness **299**
Sawyer Peak 131
Saylor, Congressman John P. 334
Scapegoat Mountain 351
Scapegoat Wilderness 343, 346, **351**
Scarecrow Island 323
Schell Trail 79
Scodie Mountains 187
Scott River 213
Scott River Ranger Station 194
Seagull Lake 329
Seagull Lake-to-Saranaga Lake Loop 329
Seahorse Key Island 270
Sealion Rocks Island 38
Seattle, Chief 495
Secar Rock 515
Second Boulder Creek 360
Secret Canyon 119
Secret Canyon Trail 119
Secret Mountain 119
Sedona, AZ 110, 119, 130
Sedro Wooley, WA 501, 508, 510, 516
Seguam Island 38
Segula Island 37
Selawik Hills 63
Selawik Lake 64
Selawik National Wildlife Refuge 63, 64
Selawik River (Wild and Scenic River) 63
Selawik Wilderness **63**, 64
Seligman, AZ 99
Sellars Potrero Trail 173
Selma, OR 421
Selway River (Wild and Scenic River) (Middle Fork) 295, 300, 352; 300
Selway River Canyon 300

Selway-Bitterroot Wilderness (Idaho) 295, **299**, 300, 352
Selway-Bitterroot Wilderness (Montana) 299, **352**
Semidi Islands National Wildlife Refuge 64
Semidi Islands Wilderness **64**, 65
Semisopochnoi Island 37, 38
Senator Wash 191
Seneca, AZ 124
Seney, MI 320, 323, 326
Seney National Wildlife Refuge 319, 320, 323, 325, 326
Seney Wilderness **325**, 326
Sentinel Island 515
Sequoia National Forest 152, 169, 174, 184, 187, 188, 198, 227
Sequoia National Park 221
Sequoia–Kings Canyon National Park 174, 184, 185, 197, 221
Sequoia–Kings Canyon National Park (map) 221
Sequoia–Kings Canyon Wilderness **221**
Service Creek Trail 261
Sespe Condor Sanctuary 222
Sespe Creek (Wild and Scenic River) 222
(Upper) 222
Sespe Hot Springs 222
Sespe River Trail 222
(Middle) 222
Sespe Wilderness **222**
Seven Cabins Canyon 378
Seven Devils Mountain Range 298
Seven Lakes 433
Sevenmile Marsh Trailhead 434
Seymour Canal 55
Shackleford Creek Trail 193
Shady Lake Campground (Caney Creek Wilderness) 141
Shag Rock 515
Shakes Glacier 68
Shark Reef 515
Shasta, Mount 198, 231, 432
Shasta-Trinity National Forest 158, 199, 232, 236
Shaver Lake, CA 149, 169, 185, 186
Shavers Mountain 524
Shaw Island 514, 515
Shawnee Hills 301, 302
Shawnee National Forest 301, 302, 303, 305, 306
Shawvers Run Wilderness **492**
Shearer, ID 300
Shedroof Divide Trail 514
Sheenjek River (Wild and Scenic River) 40
Sheep Bridge 103
Sheep Creek 242
Sheep Hole Oasis 195
Sheep Mountain Wilderness **223**
Sheep Ridge Wilderness **399**
Sheephole Mountains 223
Sheephole Valley Wilderness **223**, 224
Sheffield, PA 442
Shelikof Strait 52
Shellman Bluff 281
Shelp Lake 526

BOLD PAGE NUMBERS INDICATE MAIN REFERENCES

Shemya, AK 38
Shemya Island 37
Shenandoah Mountain 489
Shenandoah National Park 493, 494
Shenandoah River 493
Shenandoah Wilderness **493**
Sheridan, WY 533
Shiawassee National Wildlife Refuge 323
Shingleton, MI 318
Shining Creek Trail 400
Shining Rock Ledge 400
Shining Rock Wilderness 397, **400**
Shishaldin Volcano 72
Shivwits Plateau 92
Shoal Pond 369
Shoe Island 323
Short Canyon 204
Short Creek 141
Shoshone, CA 200
Shoshone National Forest 531, 535, 538, 540, 542
Shuksan, Mount 507
Shumagin Group 65
Shut-In Creek 335
Sidnaw, MI 326
Sierra Ancha Wilderness **125**
Sierra Estrella Wilderness **126**
Sierra National Forest 149, 169, 185, 186, 198
Sierra Nevada 153, 159, 163, 167, 168, 184, 187, 191, 204, 214, 221, 227, 236 (central) 170, 184, 186
Sierra Nevada Crest 156
Sierra Vista, AZ 103, 104
Signal, Mount 156
Signal Mountain Wilderness **126**, 127, 137
Signal Peak 475
Silurian Valley 214
Silver City, NM 377, 383
Silver Creek 261, 324
Silver Creek Trail 261
Silver Lake (Caribou Wilderness) 155
Silver Lake (Hollow Hills Wilderness) 178
Silver Lake (Lone Peak Wilderness) 470
Silver Park 249
Silver Peak Wilderness **224**
Silver Springs, FL 275, 276
Silverthorne, CO 243, 258
Silverton, CO 265
Simeonof Island Wilderness **65**
Simpson Creek (North Branch) 490
Simpson Peak 389
Singas Creek 365
Sinks Canyon State Park 540
Sipsey River 34
Sipsey River Recreation Site 34, 35
Sipsey Wilderness **34**, 35
Siskiyou Mountains (California) 210; (Oregon) 430
Siskiyou National Forest 419, 421, 431, 440
Siskiyou Wilderness **225**
Sisquoc Condor Sanctuary 218
Sisquoc River (Wild and Scenic River) 218
Sister Rocks 515, 517

Sister Rocks Natural Research Area 517
Sisters, OR 426, 427, 437
Sitka, AK 43, 46, 49, 62, 63, 66, 71, 73, 74
Sitka Sound 63
Situk Lake 62
Situk River 62
Siuslaw National Forest 415, 417, 432
Six Lakes 438
Six Lakes Basin 437
Six Rivers National Forest 201, 225, 232, 236
Skagul Island 37
Skipjack Island 515
Skull Island 515
Skull Valley 183, 469
Skull Valley, AZ 93
Sky Campground (Phillip Burton Wilderness) 207
Sky High Lake 193
Sky Lakes Wilderness **433**, 434
Skykomish, WA 496, 504
Slab Camp Trail 498
Slade, KY 314
Slate Creek 259
Slate River 259
Slavonia Trail 255
Slickrock Creek 396
Slickrock Creek Trail 396, 456
Slide Creek 362
Slidell, LA 311
Sliding Sands Trail 292
Sloan Beach Picnic Area (Ellicott Rock Wilderness) 445, 446
Small Island 515
Smith Creek 363
Smith, Dick 168
Smith, Jedediah 537
Smith Point West 392
Smith Point West Visitors Center 392
Smith River (Wild and Scenic River) (North Fork) 420, (South Fork) 225
Smithbrook Trailhead 504
Smithfield Canyon Trail 471
Smithfield, UT 471
Smithsonian Institute 94, 539
Smugglers Cave 183
Snake Gulch 101
Snake Key Island 270
Snake Range 363
Snake River (Wild and Scenic River) 298, 419, 420
Snake River National Scenic Trail 298, 420
Snake Valley 363
Snoqualmie Pass 496
Snow Lake 383
Snow Lakes 496
Snow Mountain Wilderness **225**, 226
Snowbowl Ski Area 100
Snowmass, CO 252
Snowmass Creek Trail 252
Snowshoe Peak 344
Snowslide Gulch Trail 362
SNRA (see Sawtooth National Recreation Area)

Sobaka Rock Island 37
Socorro, NM 378, 391
Soda Peaks 517
Soda Peaks Lake 517
Soda Peaks Lake Trail 517
Soda Springs Dam 412
Soda Springs Trail 412
Soldier Creek Trailhead 356
Soldier Creek Wilderness **356**
Soldotna, AK 53, 71
Soledad, CA 209
Somerset, KY 310
Sonora Junction 157
Sonora Pass 157
Sonoran Desert (Arizona) 75, 78, 83, 94, 96, 98, 103, 112, 120, 122, 127, 128; (California) 180, 196; (Upper) 90
Sopchoppy River 269
South Absaroka Wilderness 542
South Baranof Wilderness **66**
South Boundary Trail 543
South Canyon Trailhead 122
South Caribou Peak 155
South Carolina 443-448
South Dakota 449-450
South Etolin Island Wilderness **67**
South Field Spring 91
South Fork Pass 248
South Fork Primitive Area 343
South Island 38
South Lake Tahoe, CA 167
South Lottis Creek 245
South Maricopa Mountains Wilderness 111, **127**
South Nopah Range Wilderness **226**
South Park 239
South Pass Trail 428
South Peak 497
South Prince of Wales Wilderness **67**, 68
South Puyallup River 501
South San Juan Wilderness **262**
South Sierra Wilderness 174, **227**
South Sister 436, 437
South Teton Creek 537
South Teton Trailhead 537
South Teton–Alaska Basin Trail 537
South Trail 281
South Truchas Peak 385
South Twin 358, 359
South Twin Creek 358
South Warner Wilderness **227**, 228
South Yolla Bolly Mountains 235
Southeast Louisiana Wildlife Refuges 311
Southern California Gas Pipeline 162
Southern Nantahala Wilderness (Georgia) **289**, 400
Southern Nantahala Wilderness (North Carolina) 289, **400**, 401
Spafariei Bay 42, 43
Spanish Fork, UT 472
Spanish Mountain 197
Spanish Peak 154
Speckled Mountain 313
Speedwell, VA 487
Spencer Hollow 144
Spider Island 529
Spokane, WA 505
Spotted Bear Ranger Station 346

INDEX 585

BOLD PAGE NUMBERS INDICATE MAIN REFERENCES

Spotted Bear River 346
Sprague River (Wild and Scenic River) (North Fork) 418
Spring Lake 321
Spring Lake Creek 321
Spring Mountains 228, 362
Spring Valley 363
Springerville, AZ 89, 104
Springfield, MO 336
Springtime Campground (Apache Kid Wilderness) 375
Spruce Creek 248
Spy Run 491
Square Top Mountain 245
Squaw Creek (Wild and Scenic River) 436
Squibb Creek 458
Squibb Creek Trail 458
Squire Creek Pass 497
Stamping Ground Ridge 459
Standing Indian Basin 401
Stanislaus National Forest 156, 157, 171, 197
Stanislaus River (Clark Fork) 156
Stansbury Mountains 469
Stanton, KY 310
Starr Mountain 455
Stateline Monument 409
Stateline Wilderness **228**
Staten Island 37
Staunton, VA 490, 492
Steamboat Springs, CO 255, 261
Steer Springs 89
Stegner, Wallace 309, 460
Stehekin, WA 506
Stephen Mather Wilderness **515**, 516
Stephens Passage 43
Stepladder Mountains Wilderness **228**, 229
Steuben, MI 318
Steve Fork 431
Stevens Pass 496, 504
Stewart Pass 477
Stewart Peak 211
Stiff Knee Trail 456, 457
Stikine River 68
Stikine-LeConte Wilderness **68**
Stoddard Lake 232
Stone Lions Shrine 375
Stoney Creek 173
Stoney Creek Campground (Garcia Wilderness) 173
Stony Creek (Peters Mountain Wilderness) 489
Stony Creek (Snow Mountain Wilderness) 225 (Middle Fork) 225
Stonyford, CA 226
Storm Pass 265
Stovepipe Wells, CA 150
Strait of Georgia 514
Strait of Juan de Fuca 514
Stratified Primitive Area 542
Stratus Peak 256
Strawberry, AZ 90
Strawberry Campground (Strawberry Mountain Wilderness) 434, 435
Strawberry Crater Wilderness **127**, 128
Strawberry Falls 434

Strawberry Lake 434, 435
Strawberry Mountain Wilderness 424, **434**, 435
Stuart Lake 496
Stuart Peak 349
Stuart Peak Trail 349
Sturgeon Bay, WI 529
Sturgeon Falls 326
Sturgeon River (Wild and Scenic River) 326
Sturgeon River Campground (Sturgeon River Gorge Wilderness) 326
Sturgeon River Gorge Wilderness **326**
Styles Peak 482
Success, MO 338
Sucker Creek Gap 210, 431
Sudbury, MA 316
Sugar Maple Trail 486
Sugar Pine, CA 171
Sugarloaf Key 273
Sugarloaf Mountain 97
Suiattle River Trail 501
Suicide Rock 216
Sula, MT 343
Sullivan Canyon 113
Sullivan Creek 514
Sullivan Lake 514
Sullivan, William L. 430
Suloia Lake 73
Sulphur Spring Fork 485
Sulphur Springs (Dos Cabezas Mountains Wilderness) 86
Sulphur Springs (James River Face Wilderness) 485
Sulphur Springs Trail 485
Summit Lake (Clearwater Wilderness) 499
Summit Lake (Diamond Peak Wilderness) 416
Summit Lake (Marble Mountain Wilderness) 193
Summit Lake Trail 499
Summit Rock 426
Summit Springs Trailhead 226
Summit Trail (Capitan Mountains Wilderness) 378
Summit Trail (Pine Valley Mountain Wilderness) 475
Summit Trail (Santa Rosa–Paradise Peak Wilderness) 365
Summit Trail (South Warner Wilderness) 227, 228
Sumner Strait 56
Sumter National Forest 443, 446
Sun River (North Fork) 343, (South Fork) 343
Sun River Primitive Area 343
Sunset Canyon 94
Sunset Crater National Monument 128
Sunshine Lake 437
Superior, AZ 136
Superior, Lake (Michigan) 319, 320, 321, 322, 327; (Wisconsin) 525
Superior National Forest 328, 329
Superior Peak 476
Superstition Mountains 128

Superstition Wilderness **128**, 129
Surge Bay 73
Surprise Canyon Wilderness **229**, 230
Susan River 155
Susanville, CA 155
Suwanee River 287
Swan Quarter, NC 401, 402
Swanquarter Island 401
Swanquarter National Wildlife Refuge 401
Swanquarter Wilderness **401**, 402
Swansea, AZ 129
Swansea Wilderness **129**
Swanson River Canoe Trail 53
Sweet Home, OR 422
Sweetwater River 531
Swift Camp Creek 310
Swift Camp Creek Trail 310
Swift Creek 535
Swift Creek Trail 535
Swirl Island 515
Sycamore Canyon (Pajarita Wilderness) 114
Sycamore Canyon (Sycamore Canyon Wilderness) 101, 130
Sycamore Canyon Trail 114
Sycamore Canyon Wilderness 119, **130**
Sycamore Creek 130, 142
Sycamore Rim Trail Loop 130
Sylvania Canyon 230
Sylvania Mountains 209, 230
Sylvania Mountains Wilderness **230**
Sylvania Recreation Area 327
Sylvania Wilderness **327**
Sylvester Dam 318
Sylvester Pond 318

T

Table Mountain 424
Table Rock (Linville Gorge Wilderness) 397
Table Rock (Monument Rock Wilderness) 423, 424
Table Rock Trail 435
Table Rock Wilderness 414, **435**
Table Top Mountain 130
Table Top Trail 130
Table Top Wilderness **130**, 131
Tabor, Mount 479, 482
Tacoma, WA 509
Tag Island 37
Tagadak Island 38
Tagalak Island 38
Taggarts Bar 421
Tahoe, Lake 167, 176, 363
Tahoe National Forest 176
Tahquitz Rock 216
Talihina, OK 409
Talimena Scenic Byway 409
Talkeetna, AK 45
Tall Peak 141
Tall Peak Trail 141
Talladega, AL 34
Talladega National Forest 33, 34
Tallahassee, FL 277, 279
Tallulah River (Georgia) 289; (North Carolina) 401
Tamarac Lake 330

586 INDEX

BOLD PAGE NUMBERS INDICATE MAIN REFERENCES

Tamarac National Wildlife Refuge 330
Tamarac Wilderness **330**
Tampa Bay, FL 278
Tanadak Island 37, 38
Tanaga Island 37, 38
 (Little) 38
Tanaklak Island 38
Tanbark Trail 442
Tannen Lakes 431
Tannen Lakes Trail 431
Tannen Mountain 431
Tanner Butte 414
Tanner Butte Trail 414
Tanner Creek 414
Taos Cone 389
Taos, NM 385, 389
Taos Ski Valley 389
Targhee National Forest 537, 543
Tarryall Mountains 251
Tatoosh Lakes 516
Tatoosh Lookout 516
Tatoosh Ridge 516
Tatoosh Trail 516, 517
Tatoosh Wilderness **516**, 517
Teach, Edward "Blackbeard" 281
Tearbritches Trail 283, 284
Tebenkof Bay Wilderness 56, **69**
Tecopa, CA 205, 226
Telegraph Creek (British Columbia) 68
Telescope Peak 166
Tellico Plains, TN 452, 454, 457
Tellico River 452
Temecula, CA 148
Ten Thousand Islands 271
Tenaja Falls 217
Tenaja Falls Trail 217
Tenas Lake 427
Tennessee 451-459
Tennessee River 400
Tensleep, WY 533
Tepee Campground (Wenaha-Tucannon Wilderness, Washington) 519
Teton Campground (Jedediah Smith Wilderness) 537
Teton Pass 537
Teton Wilderness 535, **541**, 542
Texas 460-464
Texas Wilderness Act (1984) 460
Theater in the Pine 474
Theodore Roosevelt National Park 405
Theodore Roosevelt Nature and History Association 405
Theodore Roosevelt Wilderness **405** (North Unit) 405; (South Unit) 405
Thief River Falls, MN 329
Third Boulder Creek 360
Thomas Canyon 78, 79
Thomas Creek Trail 363
Thomas Knob Shelter 486
Thompson Peak 299
Thompson Springs 413
Thompson's Island 441, 442
Thoreau Falls 369
Thoreau, Henry David 357
Thorne Bay, AK 44, 58
Thorofare Trail 541
Thousand Lakes Volcano 230

Thousand Lakes Wilderness **230**, 231
Three Arch Rocks National Wildlife Refuge 436
Three Arch Rocks Wilderness **436**
Three Day Creek 362
Three Fingered Jack (peak) 425
Three Fingers 497
Three Forks Loop Trail 309
Three Forks of Beaver Overlook 309
Three Forks of Beaver Trail 309, 310
Three Points, AZ 86
Three Rivers, CA 221
Three Rivers Campground (White Mountain Wilderness) 390
Three Rivers, NM 390
Three Rivers Petroglyph Site 390
Three Rivers Trail 390
Three Sisters 432, 436
Three Sisters Peak 168
Three Sisters Wilderness 427, **436**, 437
Three Williamson Rocks 515
Thumb Peak 206
Thunder Ridge Overlook 494
Thunder Ridge Wilderness 485, **494**
Thunder Rock Campground (Big Frog Wilderness, Georgia) 280; (Big Frog Wilderness, Tennessee) 453, 455
Tidioute, PA 442
Tift Rocks 515
Tijeras, NM 384, 387
Tillamook Bay 436
Tillamook Head 430
Tillamook, OR 430, 436
Tiller, OR 432
Timberline Lodge 424, 425
Timberline Trail 424
Timpanogos Cave National Monument 470
Timpooneke Trail 473
Tinayguk River (Wild and Scenic River) 47
Tionesta, PA 441, 442
Titusville, FL 278
Tlikakila River (Wild and Scenic River) 57
Tofte, MN 329
Togiak National Wildlife Refuge 69, 70
Togiak River 69
Togiak Wilderness **69**, 70
Toiyabe Crest Trail 358
Toiyabe National Forest 156, 157, 197, 357, 358, 359, 362
Toiyabe Range 358
Toledo Bend Reservoir 462
Toledo, OH 406
Tolo Mountain 426
Tonasket, WA 513
Tongass National Forest 36, 43, 44, 45, 46, 52, 55, 56, 58, 59, 61, 62, 66, 67, 68, 69, 71, 73, 74
Tongass Timber Reform Act (1990) 36
Tonopah Desert 97
Tonopah, NV 358, 359
Tonto Creek 97
Tonto National Forest 91, 97, 103, 117, 123, 124, 125, 129, 136

Topock Gorge 96, 159
Topock Marsh 95
Toquima Mountain Range 357
Toyaibe National Forest 179
Tracy Arm Fiord 70
Tracy Arm–Fords Terror Wilderness 43, **70**, 71
Trail 16 (Selway-Bitterroot Wilderness) 352
Trail 200 (Sipsey Wilderness) 34
Trail 204 (Sipsey Wilderness) 34
Trail 206 (Sipsey Wilderness) 34
Trail 209 (Sipsey Wilderness) 34
Trail 259 (Gates of the Mountains Wilderness) 345
Trail 261 (Granite Mountain Wilderness) 93
Trail 308 (Granite Mountain Wilderness) 93
Trail 690 (Mission Mountains Wilderness) 348, 349
Trail 74 (Cohutta Wilderness, Tennessee) 455
Trail 742 (Mission Mountains Wilderness) 348
Trail 957 (Red Buttes Wilderness) 210
Trail 1191 (Norse Peak Wilderness) 511
Trail Lake 534, 535
Trail Pass 174
Trampas Wash 159
Tramway Trail 134
Tran Spire (peak) 509
Trap Creek 256
Trapper Creek Trail 517
Trapper Creek Wilderness **517**
Trappers Lake 244
Tray Mountain Wilderness 286, **289**, 290
"Trees" (poem) 456
Tres Alamos Wilderness **131**
Tres Piedras, NM 381
Triangle Lake 155
Trigo Mountains Wilderness **132**
Trilobite Wilderness **231**
Trinity Alps Wilderness **232**
Trinity River (Wild and Scenic River) 232
Trona, CA 229
Trooper Trail 356
Trout Creek 363
Trout Creek Campground (Menagerie Wilderness) 422
Trout Creek, MT 345
Trout Creek Trail 421, 422
Trout Lake, WA 504, 507
Troutdale, OR 415
Troutdale, VA 486
Troy, NC 394
Troy, OR 438, 439
Troy Peak 361
Truckee, CA 176
Truth or Consequences, NM 374, 375
Tubal Cain Trail 498
Tucannon River (Oregon) 438; (Washington) 518, 519
Tucson, AZ 79, 86, 108, 118, 120, 121, 122, 123, 125

INDEX 587

BOLD PAGE NUMBERS INDICATE MAIN REFERENCES

Tule Lake 189
Tule Lake National Wildlife Refuge 189
Tule Trail 129
Tulelake, CA 190
Tunawee Canyon 214
Tuolumne Meadows 236, 237
Tuolumne River (Wild and Scenic River) 236
Turkey Creek 383
Turkey Creek Caldera 83
Turkey Hill Wilderness **463**, 464
Turn Rock 515
Turquoise Lake 57
Turquoise Mountains 178
Turtle Mountains Wilderness **233**
Tuxedni Bay 71
Tuxedni Islands Wilderness **71**
20 Lakes Basin 178
Twentynine Palms, CA 155, 162, 186, 224
Twentynine Palms Marine Corps Base 161
Twilight Lake 317
Twin Creeks 358 (North) 358, (South) 358
Twin Falls 145
Twin Falls, ID 362
Twin Lakes 414
Twin Peak Saddle 215
Twin Peaks Trail 82
Twin Peaks Wilderness 470, 473, **476**, 477
Twin Range 368
Twin Rivers 358
Twin Tanks Wash 109
Twining Campground (Wheeler Peak Wilderness) 389
Twisp River 505
Twisp, WA 506
Twisted Forest 466
Two Ocean Creek 541
Two Ocean Pass 541
Two Pan Campground (Eagle Cap Wilderness) 417
Tygh Creek 410

U

U.S. Biological Survey 274
U.S. Coast Guard 319, 406
U.S. Fish and Wildlife Service 138, 238, 254, 272, 274, 278, 287, 311, 316, 334, 410, 525
U.S. Fish and Wildlife Service Wildernesses 38
U.S. Forest Service 43, 58, 62, 66, 68, 70, 71, 73, 75, 76, 82, 83, 88, 89, 90, 91, 97, 99, 100, 103, 104, 108, 110, 114, 117, 118, 119, 121, 123, 124, 125, 128, 129, 130, 134, 135, 137, 149, 164, 177, 185, 216, 219, 220, 232, 238, 244, 251, 263, 282, 296, 298, 299, 309, 322, 327, 334, 335, 377, 380, 393, 419, 439, 460, 465, 486, 489, 494, 521
U.S. Forest Service Wilderness 341
U.S. Geological Survey 472, 476
Ubehebe Crater 166
Ugamak Island 38

Uinkaret Plateau 107
Uinta National Forest 471, 472, 474
Ukiah, CA 183, 232, 236
Ukiah, OR 429
Ukinrek Maars (mountain) 40
Ukonom Lake 193
UL Bend National Wildlife Refuge 353
UL Bend Wilderness **353**
Ulak Island 37, 38
Uliaga Island 38
Umak Island 38
Umatilla National Forest 429, 439, 519
Umatilla River (North Fork) 429
Umla Island 38
Umnak Island 38
Umpqua National Forest 412, 426, 432
Umpqua Rocks Special Interest Geologic Area 412
Unaka Mountain Overlook 459
Unaka Mountain Wilderness **459**
Unalaska, AK 42, 72
Unalaska Island 38, 42
Unalga Island 37
Uncompahgre National Forest 250, 255, 263
Uncompahgre Peak 263
Uncompahgre Wilderness **263**
Uneva Pass 243
Unicoi Gap 289, 290
Unicoi Mountains 454
Unicoi, TN 459
Unimak Island 38, 72
Unimak Island Wilderness **72**
Unity, OR 424
Upland Island Wilderness **464**
Upper Billy Creek Campground (Kaiser Wilderness) 186
Upper Buffalo Wilderness 140, **146**
Upper Burro Creek Wilderness **132**, 133
Upper Fishhooks (canyon) 89
Upper Harbor Key 273
Upper Horrell Trail 129
Upper Kiamichi River Wilderness **409**
Upper Lake, CA 226
Upper Lake Creek 502
Upper Lytle Creek 223
Upper Peninsula (Michigan) 318, 319, 322, 324, 326, 327
Upper Summit City Creek 197
USFS (see U.S. Forest Service)
Utah 465-477
Utah Trail 186
Ute Pass 258
Ute Pass Trail 258
Ute Peak 258
Utley Brook 482
Uwharrie Mountains 393
Uwharrie National Forest 393, 394
Uwharrie River 393

V

Vacas Trail 386, 387
Vail, CO 243
Vale, OR 420
Valentine, NE 356
Vallecito Valley 220

Valley Branch 492
Vancouver, Captain George 48
Varney Creek Trail 428
Vasquez Creek 264
Vasquez Mountains 264
Vasquez Pass 264
Vasquez Pass Trailhead 264
Vasquez Peak Trail 264
Vasquez Peak Wilderness 240, **263**, 264
Venice, LA 311
Ventana Double Cone 234
Ventana Wilderness **234**
Ventura, CA 168
Verde Mine Trail 536
Verde Rim Trail 117
Verde River (Wild and Scenic River) 83, 102, 117, 119, 134, 135
Verde River Bridge 91
Verde River Rim 117
Verde River Trail 103
Verde Valley 130
Vermilion Cliffs (Paria Canyon–Vermilion Cliffs Wilderness, Arizona) 115, 121, (Paria Canyon–Vermilion Cliffs Wilderness, Utah) 474
Vermillion Canyon 163
Vermont 478-482
Vernal, UT 470
Vicente Flat 234
Vidal Valley 233
Vienna, IL 302
Vincent Gap 223
Vinegar Hill–Indian Rock Scenic Area 428
Virgin Mountains 113
Virgin Ridge 114
Virgin Ridge Loop Trail 113
Virgin River (Arizona) 80; (Utah) 466
Virgin River Campground (Beaver Dam Mountains Wilderness, Arizona) 80; (Beaver Dam Mountains Wilderness, Utah) 466, 467
Virginia 483-494
Virginia Highlands Horse Trail 486, 487
Virginia, MN 329
Virginia Wilderness Act (1984) 483
Visalia, CA 221
Viti Rocks 515
Voyageurs National Park 329
Vsevidof Island 38
Vulcan Lake 421
Vulcan Lake Trailhead 421

W

Wabasso, FL 278
Wabayuma Peak Trail 133
Wabayuma Peak Wilderness **133**
Wahanna Lakes 438
Waiska River 318
Wakefield Creek 528
Walden, CO 255, 257
Waldo Glacier 425
Waldo Lake Trail 437
Waldo Lake Wilderness 436, **437**, 438
Waldport, OR 415, 417, 432

BOLD PAGE NUMBERS INDICATE MAIN REFERENCES

Waldron, AR 145
Walhalla, SC 285, 446
Walker Pass 187, 188, 204
Walla Walla, WA 429
Wallowa Lake State Park 417
Wallowa Mountains 417
Wallowa River 417
Wallowa-Whitman National Forest 298, 418, 420, 424, 428, 429
Walnut Creek Work Station 76, 99
Walnut Spring 91
Warnbaw Creek Wilderness **447**, 448
Wambaw Swamp Wilderness **448**
Wanda Island 38
Wapiki, Lake 504
War Spur Overlook 488
War Spur Shelter 488
War Spur Trail 488
Ward Canyon 116
Ward Valley 211
Waring Mountains 54, 63
Warm Springs Indian Reservation 425
Warm Springs Wilderness **134**
Warner Mountains 227
Warren Island Wilderness **72**, 73
Warren, PA 442
Warren Peak 72
Wasatch Range 472, 473
Wasatch-Cache National Forest 469, 470, 471, 473, 477
Wash Branch 463
Wash Branch Trail 463
Washakie, Chief 542
Washakie Wilderness 541, **542**
Washburn, WI 528
Washington 495-520
Washington Island 529
Washington Islands National Wildlife Refuges 518
Washington Islands Wilderness **518**
Washington, Mount (New Hampshire) 367, 368, 369
Washington, Mount (Washington) 509
Wason Park 249
Watauga Lake 453, 458
Watauga River 453
Watauga Scenic Area 458
Watauga Scenic Trail 458
Watch Hill 392
Watch Hill Campground (Fire Island Wilderness) 392
Water Key 273
Water Key Mangroves 273
waterfalls (Alaska) 41, 57, 66, 70; (Arizona) 86, 118, 132, 136; (Arkansas) 140, 146; (California) 156, 181, 198, 218-219, 224, 234, 236; (Colorado) 250; (Georgia) 281-282, 285-289; (Illinois) 302-303; (Kentucky) 309; (Michigan) 322; (Montana) 343; (Nevada) 359, 365-366; (New Hampshire) 370; (New Mexico) 385; (Oklahoma) 409; (Oregon) 412, 414, 419, 424, 433, 436; (Tennessee) 451-452, 458-459; (Utah) 468, 473; (Vermont) 480; (Virginia) 491; (Washington) 517; (Wyoming) 539

Waterman, Mount 215
Watersmeet, MI 327
Watersmeet Visitors Center 327
Watson Lakes 510
Watson Lakes Trail 510
Watson, Mount 510
Wawona 237
Waycross, GA 287
Waynesville, NC 400
Weaver Lake 184
Weaver's Needle 128
Weaverville, CA 232
Welcome Creek Trail 354
Welcome Creek Wilderness **354**
Wellington Lake 251
Wells, NV 361, 365
Wellsville Cone 477
Wellsville Mountains Wilderness 471, **477**
Weminuche Wilderness **264**, 265
Wenaha River (Wild and Scenic River) 438, 518
Wenaha River Trail 438
Wenaha-Tucannon Wilderness (Oregon) **438**, 439, 519
Wenaha-Tucannon Wilderness (Washington) 438, **518**
Wenatchee National Forest 496, 501, 503, 504, 506, 511, 520
Wenatchee, WA 506
Wenden, AZ 94, 95, 119
West Baldy Trail 104
West Big Frog Primitive Area 454
West Branch Trail 260
West Buttress (Mount McKinley) 45
West Chichagof–Yakobi Wilderness **73**, 74
West Clear Creek Wilderness **134**, 135
West Doubtful Canyon 116
West Elk Wilderness **265**, 266
West Fork Trail 383, 385
West Goat Peak 342
West Huron Island 319, 320
West, Lake 502
West Lincoln, VT 480
West Malpais Wilderness 379, **388**
West Plains, MO 336
West Sedona, AZ 119
West Ship Island 332
West Sister Island National Wildlife Refuge 406
West Sister Island Wilderness **406**
West Tensleep Lake 532
West Tensleep Lake Campground (Cloud Peak Wilderness) 533
West Virginia 521-524
West Virginia Highlands Conservancy 524
West Yellowstone, MT 347
Western Oregon Refuge Complex 436
Westfir, OR 437, 438
Weston Lake Loop Trail 445
Weston, OR 429
Westwood, CA 155
Wet Beaver Creek 135
Wet Beaver Wilderness **135**
Wetterhorn Peak 263
Wheeler, Captain George M. 104
Wheeler Geologic Area 249, 250

Wheeler Peak Trail 389
Wheeler Peak Wilderness **389**
Whipple Mountains Wilderness **235**
Whipple Trailhead 476
Whisker Lake Trail 528
Whisker Lake Wilderness **528**
Whiskey Lake 328
Whiskey Lake Trail 328
Whispering Lake 525
Whispering Lake Trailhead 525, 526
Whistler Point Trailhead 423
White Bird, ID 297, 298
White Canyon Wilderness **136**
White Deer Lake 322
White Deer Lake Trail 322
White House Trailhead 115, 474, 475
White Ledge Mountain 124
White Mountain National Forest 313, 314, 367, 368, 369, 370
White Mountain Wilderness **390**
White Mountains (Nevada) 359, 367
White Mountains (New Hampshire) 369
White Mountains (New Mexico) 390
White Oak Mountain 143
White Pass Campground (William O. Douglas Wilderness) 520
White Pine Range 360
White Pine Trailhead 470, 471
White River (Arkansas) 140
White River (Missouri) 335, 336 (North Fork) 335, 336
White River (Vermont) 479
White River National Forest 242, 243, 244, 247, 248, 252, 258, 259
White River Plateau 244
White Rock Campground Trailhead 423
White Rocks 515
White Sister Islands 73
White Sulphur Hot Springs 73
Whiteface, Mount 370
Whitehorse Creek 509
Whitehorse Mountains 497
Whites Creek Cave 337
Whites Creek Trail 337
Whitewater Glacier 425
white-water rafting (see river running)
Whiting, ME 315
Whitley Gap 288
Whitman, Walt 483
Whitney, Mount 184, 221
Wichita Mountains 408
Wichita Mountains National Wildlife Refuge 408, 409
Wickenburg, AZ 94, 95, 131, 133
Wiggins, MS 332, 333
Wilbur Lake 453
Wild and Scenic Rivers 34, 39, 40, 47, 54, 57, 59, 63, 83, 117, 169, 174, 194, 201, 218, 221, 222, 225, 227, 232, 234, 236, 241, 242, 285, 295, 298, 300, 322, 326, 331, 346, 352, 353, 380, 385, 395, 417, 418, 419, 420, 428, 436, 438, 439, 441, 445, 518
Wild Cow Springs Campground (Wabayuma Peak Wilderness) 133

INDEX 589

BOLD PAGE NUMBERS INDICATE MAIN REFERENCES

Wild Rogue Wilderness 421, **439**, 440
Wildcat Campground (Mill Creek Wilderness) 423
Wildcat Campground (Phillip Burton Wilderness) 207
Wildcat Campground Trailhead 423
Wildcat Mountain Trail 433
Wildcat Trail 310
Wilderness Act (1964) 218, 295
Wilderness Preservation System 267
Wilderness Society 343
Wilderness Trail 369
Wilderness Waterway 271, 272
wildflowers (Alaska) 37, 45; (Arizona) 79, 104, 114, 133; (California) 155, 157, 161, 166, 173, 175, 184, 186, 197-199, 215, 217-218, 223, 227, 235; (Colorado) 247, 250, 252, 254; (Georgia) 282; (Idaho) 299-300; (Illinois) 305; (Montana) 344, 348, 350; (Nebraska) 355; (Nevada) 365-366; (New Mexico) 382, 385; (North Carolina) 393; (Oregon) 423-424, 434; (Tennessee) 451, 456, 458; (Utah) 471-473; (Virginia) 493; (Washington) 498, 502, 504, 507-508, 516-517; (Wisconsin) 526; (Wyoming) 530, 535
Wildhorse Peak 263
Wileys Well 205
Willamette National Forest 414, 416, 422, 426, 427, 437, 438
Willamette Pass 416
Willamette Valley 410, 435
Willcox, AZ 84, 85, 125
William O. Douglas Wilderness 511, **519**, 520
Williams, AZ 101, 130
Williams Fork Mountains 258
Williams Fork Rivers (Middle Fork) 258, (South Fork) 258
Williams Lake 389
Williams Mountains 247, 248
Williams River 521, 522 (Middle Fork) 521
Williston, ND 348
Willoughby Cove 62
Willow Creek (Gila Wilderness) 383
Willow Creek (Silver Peak Wilderness) 224
Willow Creek Trail 260, 261
Willow Island 515
Willow Springs, MO 336
Willow Valley 134
Wilson, E. O. 371
Wilson, Mount (Colorado) 250
Wilson, Mount (Vermont) 479
Wilson Mountain 119
Wilson Peak 250
Wilson Ridge 107
Wind River (Arctic Wilderness/Wild and Scenic River) 40, 517, 539
Wind River (Popo Agie Wilderness) 539 (Little South Fork) 539
Wind River (Trapper Creek Wilderness) 517

Wind River Indian Reservation 534, 539, 542
Wind River Mountains 531, 534, 535, 539, 542
Wind River Peak 539
Windham Bay 43
Windigo, MI 320
Windy Saddle 298
Winegar Creek 543
Winegar Hole Wilderness **543**
Winema National Forest 426, 428, 434
Winfield Scott, Lake 282
Winnemucca Lake 197
Winom Creek Trail (National Recreation Trail) 428
Winter Park, CO 264
Winthrop, WA 506, 513
WINWR (see Washington Islands National Wildlife Refuges)
Wire Pass 474
Wisconsin 525-529
Wisconsin Islands Wilderness **529**
Wisdom, MT 343
Wise River, MT 343
Wishbone Lake 527
Withington, Mount 391
Withington Wilderness **391**
Wolf Creek 505
Wolf Creek, OR 440
Wolf Creek Pass 157
Wolf Island National Wildlife Refuge 290
Wolf Island Wilderness **290**
Wolf Lake 432
Wolf Ridge Trail 452, 453
Woman Key 273
Wonder Mountain Wilderness **520**
Wonderland Trail 508, 509
Wood Canyon 109
Wood Krutch, Joseph 392
Wood Lake 171
Woodchute Mountain 136
Woodchute Trail 136, 137
Woodchute Wilderness **136**, 137
Woodenshoe Canyon 468
Woodworth, ND 404
Woolsey Peak Wilderness 126, **137**
Workman Creek 123
Worland, WY 533
Wrangell, AK 49, 67, 68, 73
Wrangell Narrows 61
Wrangell–Saint Elias National Park and Preserve 74
Wrangell–Saint Elias Wilderness **74**
Wrights Trailhead 167
Wrightwood, CA 223
WS Mountain Trail 377
Wupatki National Monument 128
Wymer, WV 523
Wyoming 530-543
Wytheville, VA 484, 486, 487

Y

Yakima Indian Reservation 506
Yakima, WA 520
Yakobi Island 73
Yakutat, AK 62, 74
Yakutat Bay (upper) 62
Yale, Mount 241
Yampa, CO 244, 261

Yampa River 261
Yankee Boy Basin 254, 255
Yankee Paradise 284
Yapashi 375
Yaquina Head Lighthouse 430
Yearling, The (book) 275
Yellow Dog River (Wild and Scenic River) 322
Yellowstone Lake 541
Yellowstone National Park 47, 342, 346, 530, 537, 541, 542, 543
Yellowstone River 541
Yolla Bolly–Middle Eel Wilderness **235**, 236
Yosemite, CA 149, 237
Yosemite Falls 236
Yosemite National Park 149, 170, 179, 236, 237
Yosemite Valley 236, 237
Yosemite Wilderness **236**, 237
Young, AZ 123, 124, 125
Young, Mount 45
Younts Peak 541
Yucca, AZ 78
Yucca Valley 152
Yuha Desert Recreation Area 163
Yukon Delta National Wildlife Area 60
Yukon Delta National Wildlife Refuge 38, 39, 60, 69
Yukon River 39, 50, 60
Yuma, AZ 82, 87, 99, 102, 109, 111, 132, 180, 207
Yuma Military Proving Ground 109, 132
Yunaska Island 38

Z

Zenia, CA 201
Zigzag, OR 425, 433
Zimmerman Lake 256
Zimmerman Trail 242, 243
Zion National Park 475

About the Author

Buck Tilton serves as Executive Director of the Wilderness Medicine Institute in Pitkin, Colorado, and is a contributing editor for *Backpacker* and *Midwest Outdoors* magazines. He has published more than 500 articles, and authored or co-authored 14 books. *Backcountry First Aid & Extended Care* and *Sex in the Outdoors* were bestsellers in 1995, and *Sex in the Outdoors* was selected as a runner-up for the Benjamin Franklin Award for Humor in 1994. He was awarded First Place in the 1989 Writers Digest Writing Competition.

An avid backpacker, canoeist, and sea kayaker, Buck has spent much of his life exploring the wild outdoors by foot and paddle. His journeys include climbing the highest peaks in North and South America, sea kayaking the Alaska Marine Highway, and hiking many of the areas described in this book. Of wilderness and life he says, "Nature's way is perfect. Our job is simply to follow."

FOGHORN PRESS

Founded in 1985, Foghorn Press has quickly become one of the country's premier publishers of outdoor recreation guidebooks. Through its unique Books Building Community program, Foghorn Press supports community environmental issues, such as park, trail, and water ecosystem preservation. Foghorn Press is also committed to printing its books on recycled paper.

Foghorn Press books are sold throughout the United States. Call 1-800-FOGHORN (8:30–5:30 PST) for the location of a bookstore near you that carries Foghorn Press titles. If you prefer, you may place an order directly with Foghorn Press using your Visa or MasterCard. All of the titles listed below are now available, unless otherwise noted.

The Complete Guide Series
California titles include:

- *California Beaches* (640 pp) $19.95
- *California Boating and Water Sports* (608 pp) $19.95
- *California Camping* (848 pp) $19.95
- *California Fishing* (832 pp) $19.95
- *California Golf* (896 pp) $19.95
- *California Hiking* (856 pp) $18.95
- *California In-Line Skating* (480 pp) $19.95
- *Tahoe* (704 pp) $18.95

Other regional titles include:

- *Alaska Fishing* (640 pp) $19.95
- *Baja Camping* (294 pp) $12.95
- *Pacific Northwest Camping* (720 pp) $19.95
- *Pacific Northwest Hiking* (808 pp) $18.95
- *Washington Fishing* (528 pp) $19.95

The National Outdoors Series

- *America's Secret Recreation Areas—Your Recreation Guide to the Bureau of Land Management's Wild Lands of the West* (640 pp) $17.95
- *The Camper's Companion—The Pack-Along Guide for Better Outdoor Trips* (464 pp) $15.95
- *America's Wilderness—The Complete Guide to More Than 600 National Wilderness Areas* (592 pp) $19.95

A book's page length and availability are subject to change.

For more information, call 1-800-FOGHORN or write to:
Foghorn Press
555 DeHaro Street,
The Boiler Room, Suite 220
San Francisco, CA 94107